FOREIGN AND COMMONWEALTH OFFICE

DOCUMENTS ON BRITISH POLICY OVERSEAS

EDITED BY

G. BENNETT, M.A.

AND

K.A. HAMILTON, Ph.D.

SERIES III

Volume I

LONDON: THE STATIONERY OFFICE

First published 1997

ISBN 0 11 591696 2

Published by The Stationery Office and available from:

The Publications Centre
(mail, telephone and fax orders only)
PO Box 276, London SW8 5DT
General enquiries 0171 873 0011
Telephone orders 0171 873 9090
Fax orders 0171 873 8200

The Stationery Office Bookshops
59-60 Holborn Viaduct, London EC1A 2FD
temporary until mid 1998
(counter service and fax orders only)
Fax 0171 831 1326
68-69 Bull Street, Birmingham B4 6AD
0121 236 9696 Fax 0121 236 9699
33 Wine Street, Bristol BS1 2BQ
0117 9264306 Fax 0117 9294515
9-21 Princess Street, Manchester M60 8AS
0161 834 7201 Fax 0161 833 0634
16 Arthur Street, Belfast BT1 4GD
01232 238451 Fax 01232 235401
The Stationery Office Oriel Bookshop
The Friary, Cardiff CF1 4AA
01222 395548 Fax 01222 384347
71 Lothian Road, Edinburgh EH3 9AZ
(counter service only)

Customers in Scotland may
mail, telephone or fax their orders to:
Scottish Publications Sales
South Gyle Crescent, Edinburgh EH12 9EB
0131 622 7050 Fax 0131 622 7017

The Stationery Office's Accredited Agents
(see Yellow Pages)

and through good booksellers

Printed in the UK for The Stationery Office
J18937 C15 11/97 9385 7163

DOCUMENTS ON BRITISH POLICY OVERSEAS

Series III, Volume I

Britain and the Soviet Union, 1968-72

DOCUMENTS ON BRITISH POLICY OVERSEAS

Editorial Team

INTRODUCTION TO SERIES III

The decision to publish a collection of Documents on British Policy Overseas was announced in the House of Commons in 1973 by the Secretary of State for Foreign and Commonwealth Affairs, Sir Alec Douglas-Home, who stated:

'Her Majesty's Government have decided to extend into the post-war period the practice adopted for 1919-1939 of publishing documents on British foreign policy. The new collection of the most important documents in the archives of the Foreign and Commonwealth Office relating to British policy overseas will initially comprise two series to cover foreign policy in the periods 1945-50 and 1950-55 respectively. The preparation of both series will be undertaken simultaneously. So as to keep the work within manageable proportions, at the start the new series will normally include only Foreign Office documents, but, where appropriate, documents from the archives of the Colonial and Commonwealth Relations Offices will also be included' (*Parl Debs., 5th ser., H. of C.*, vol. 859, cols. *45-6*).

Since the launch of *DBPO* in 1984 eleven volumes have been published, seven from Series I and four from Series II. In 1994 it was decided that as part of Open Government initiatives, the FCO's Historians should move forward to cover periods of more contemporary relevance, in line with the original mandate of the series. Series III, which will be published concurrently with Series I and II, will cover the period from 1960 onwards. Most volumes will document events of less than thirty years ago and so will be based on files not yet released to the Public Record Office.

As with the earlier Series, it is the intention of the Editors to concentrate on the most important issues in British foreign policy. The large volume of documents received in the Foreign & Commonwealth Office—711,929 in 1971—and the increasingly multilateral nature of foreign policy during the more recent period, mean that a number of changes in editorial practice have been adopted for the new Series. It is intended that each volume will generally cover a broader time frame than those in earlier Series, which means that a very selective approach must be applied to the archive. Volumes in Series III will not be supplemented by a microfiche collection of related documents nor by calendars summarising them. This has been done to simplify the editorial and declassification process and accelerate the publication of volumes.

In order to allow flexibility of treatment according to subject, there will be two types of volume in the Series: some will cover a wide range of issues and time-span at a high level, and some will focus more narrowly on a specific issue. Volumes of the first, broader type will contain editorial passages to carry the narrative forward and explain the context to the documentation. This device has been adopted in Volume I, *Britain and the Soviet Union*, which covers the complex bilateral relationship within a multilateral context over a period of five years and which has therefore taken a high-level and representative approach to the documentation. Volume II, *The Conference on Security and Cooperation in Europe, 1972-75*, documents in narrower and more detailed focus the negotiations leading to the signature of the Helsinki Final Act in 1975.

The Editors have had the customary freedom, referred to in the Parliamentary announcement, in the selection and arrangement of documents. The principal source for these volumes has been the archives of the Foreign & Commonwealth Office (FCO), formed from the merger of the Foreign Office with the Commonwealth Relations Office (CRO) in October 1968. The merger with the CRO, whose files were opened at three-yearly intervals, and the transition to a common system meant that from mid-1968 papers from the FCO were entered on the same file as papers from 1969. These files are not due for release to the PRO until 1 January 2000, thirty years after the creation of the last paper on the file. From 1970 onwards the FCO operated a system of annual subject files kept by each department. Where a document was entered on more than one file, preference has generally been given to that on which action was taken and relevant correspondence preserved.

Volumes I and II of the new Series comprise documentation taken entirely from the 'closed period', i.e. less than thirty years old. These papers will not be transferred to the Public Record Office in advance of their due date, but documents published or cited in the volumes have been marked for permanent preservation and will be released when they are thirty years old in the usual way. Volumes in Series III will be the first to incorporate material from the files of the FCO's Permanent Under-Secretary's Department (PUSD). Intelligence-related material from these files is withheld from release to the Public Record Office with the approval of the Lord Chancellor under Section 3(4) of the Public Records Act.

FCO documents printed in the volumes, with the exception of PUSD papers, have been given their departmental file reference. Documents quoted or cited in footnotes have only been accorded a file reference where it differs from that of the printed document to which they refer. The Editors have also had access to relevant material from the Cabinet Office and Prime Minister's Office, and are grateful to them for access and for permission to print or cite their documents. The Department of Trade and Industry and the Home Office have also given permission for the publication of documents originating with their department and found on FCO files.

Occasional omissions in the text, usually because of uncertainty in the filed copy, are marked by the insertion of ellipses with an explanatory footnote. All square brackets are editorial unless otherwise stated. Omitted from the headings and formulations at the end of documents are some classifications regarding administration and circulation but the main security classifications (Top Secret etc.) are included where present in such form on the filed copy. The spelling of proper names and places is as in the original text and therefore unstandardized, but minor typing errors have been corrected.

The straightforward Index to main subjects and persons is designed to be used in conjunction with the Chapter Summaries. In this Series, in a departure from previous practice, Index references are to page rather than to document numbers, in order to facilitate the indexing of editorial material.

GILL BENNETT

July 1997

PREFACE

This Volume documents the relationship between the governments of the United Kingdom and the Soviet Union over a five-year period from the beginning of 1968. The focus is bilateral, but just as the skeins of the Anglo-Soviet relationship are inextricable from a more extensive web of European and inter-continental ties and tensions, so the story of how the two governments interacted is firmly rooted in a grander drama on a global scale. Indeed, as the Volume opens in January 1968 against an international backdrop of conflict in Indo-China and the Middle East; the realignment of Western European dynamics through an increasingly strong Federal Republic of Germany; and an emerging challenge to the old Communist order in Czechoslovakia, it is tempting to see *Britain and the Soviet Union 1968-72* as a key episode in a long-running soap opera, *East and West.*

The main theme of this episode is an ongoing policy debate within the British Foreign Office on how best to deal with the Soviet Union in the aftermath of two major crises in relations precipitated by the Soviet invasion of Czechoslovakia in August 1968, and by the British expulsion from the UK of 105 Soviet intelligence officials in September 1971: how to reconcile the desire to leave the Soviet Government in no doubt of HMG's strong disapproval of Soviet behaviour with the need to pursue 'business as usual' on day-to-day bilateral issues; and how to keep British policy on all fours with that of her Western allies and soon-to-be EEC partners, and to avoid exclusion from the US-Soviet axis.

The characters are familiar, each recognisable from their well-known lines: Soviet complaints of West German *revanchisme*, for example, French opposition to NATO, a stubborn British determination to call a spade a spade ('"peaceful coexistence" as used by the Russians is a fraud and should be exposed as such'—Sir John Killick). Members of the cast, in the person of government ministers, may come and go (though in the Soviet Union the *dramatis personae* remains remarkably constant) but the underlying quarrels, passions and dramas are constantly re-enacted. The local setting for a soap opera is traditionally circumscribed, with a suitable meeting place for the cast to interact; in *Britain and the Soviet Union* this meeting place might be Berlin, the subject of the quadripartite negotiations which lay at the heart of *Ostpolitik*, while the characters' homes, in which they gossip and speculate about each others' motives, can well be represented by each country's foreign ministry. The analogy should not be stretched too far: but the continuities of both subject matter and tone between the Anglo-Soviet exchanges documented in Series I of *DBPO*, Volume VI, *Eastern Europe 1945-1946* and those in the current Volume are sufficiently striking to prompt consideration of *1968-72* as a later episode in the same drama.

The British role in the drama, both in the late 1940s and in the late 1960s, appears that of an outsider: with, but not of Europe; bound by close ties and commonality of interest to the United States of America, yet always the gooseberry in the Super Power US-Soviet axis. Foreign Office documents for the period 1968-72 give a superficial impression of Britain as supplicant, seeking approval, agreement, good relations with all. But this impression is misleading. It is true that the British Government would go to considerable lengths to align itself with American policies and wishes; and in the period 1968-72 was a far stronger advocate of European integration than her prospective EEC partners. Underneath, however, the documentation reveals a pragmatic and relentless official realism which underpins the foreign policies of both Harold Wilson's Labour Government (containing some Ministers predisposed to a favourable view of the Soviet Union) and that of Edward Heath, in which Sir Alec Douglas-Home, one of the original members of the *East-West* cast, dealt an astonishingly bold stroke against unacceptable Soviet Intelligence activities and correctly calculated that the Russian bark would be worse than its bite.

The British Government wanted to be on good terms with the Soviet Union, as a Super Power of already formidable and growing military might whose global ambitions were a potential threat to British interests; as the leader of the Communist system which dominated Eastern Europe, a potent counterweight to the Western European grouping with which Britain wished to be allied; as a trading partner; and because the United States Government wished it. They also saw themselves as playing an important make-weight role in the uneasy balance between East and West, though their attempts to fulfil that role, for example by passing on American requests to the Soviet Government to use their influence with Hanoi in seeking a settlement of the Vietnam conflict (see Nos. 7-9), carried little weight; and their determination not to mince words in condemning Soviet threatening behaviour, whether in the Indian Ocean or in Intelligence matters, seemed to gain less in terms of eliciting a positive Soviet response than the less abrasive—not to say pandering—tactics of some other governments (see, for example, Nos. 36, 41, 79, and pp. 417-18).

Although it was the tone rather than the substance which differentiated the British style of dealing with the Soviet Union from that of her Western partners, the Soviet accusation that HMG was 'more outspoken and tougher than other NATO Governments' (No. 16, note 8) was not entirely groundless and provided a useful tool for the Soviet Government's own wedge-driving campaign designed to undermine both a coherent Western European grouping and a close US-European relationship. Throughout the period Foreign Office officials stressed the need to avoid 'running after the Russians', but although countless minutes, memoranda and submissions explored possible methods of doing just that, the policy implemented in London and by the Embassy in Moscow maintained on the whole a consistently hard line.

The continuities in Soviet foreign policy (and personnel) meant that their approach to diplomatic relations and negotiating techniques were familiar to the FCO: the bald polemical style, which might overlay a sophisticated appreciation of the question under discussion but which Russian negotiators found most effective in gaining their desired objective. This predictable and often outrageous Soviet negotiating technique—practised successfully by Litvinov in the 1920s, Molotov in the 1930s and 1940s and thereafter by Gromyko—enabled them to maintain a predetermined line against close reasoning or conclusive evidence, and often led their exhausted opponents to concede far more then they had originally planned in order to avoid the more extravagant Soviet demands. Despite the fact that FCO officials generally recognised these techniques and had developed strategies of dealing with them in day-to-day contacts, in international fora it was still possible for Soviet negotiators successfully to convince their interlocutors that they had secured a bargain rather than made a concession, as Mr. Heath pointed out following the conclusion of the Quadripartite Agreement on Berlin in 1971 (pp. 376-77). Sir Alec Douglas-Home found 'dealing with the Russians' as frustrating and demanding as had his predecessor Ernest Bevin, though both took a robust and no-nonsense line in doing so.

This Volume is divided into five chapters, each representing a year, and the documentation is representative rather than narrative; chosen to provide a snapshot of the Anglo-Soviet relationship, illustrate a point of contention, or summarise a period of uneasy *modus vivendi*. Chapter I opens with the visit to Moscow in January 1968 of Prime Minister Harold Wilson (Nos. 1-3), his talks there dominated by the current international crises in Vietnam and the Middle East, though including some discussion of bilateral issues such as trade and technological cooperation. The Soviet leaders took a somewhat condescending tone, showing sympathy for the decision to devalue the pound in November 1967, expressing approval of the recent Cabinet decision to withdraw from East of Suez by 1971 and dismissing the Prime Minister's attempts to broker a deal with Hanoi at the behest of the Americans. They were willing to cooperate on bilateral issues where they saw benefit for themselves, but Mr. Wilson's interventions on behalf of Gerald Brooke, the British teacher imprisoned in a labour camp for anti-Soviet activities, met a stony response, although eliciting a rare joke from Mr. Gromyko: when the Prime Minister speculated that the British press wished him to 'send a detachment of Marines to break open the prison', the Soviet Foreign Minister replied that 'he doubted whether under the circumstances they would get their visa' (No. 3).

Positive efforts towards closer Anglo-Soviet links on both multilateral and bilateral issues are explored in Nos. 4-12, including the record of a session of the biennial Conference of East European Ambassadors held in London in May 1968 (No. 10). The Ambassadors' remarks make it clear that they generally favoured a more forthcoming and positive British line towards the countries they represented, and felt the Foreign Office in London was insufficiently alive to indications of change in Eastern Europe, not only in Czechoslovakia, and to the potential rewards to be gained from cultivating individual countries, while avoiding any impression of 'wedge-driving tactics'. Their comments were taken into account in drafting the important memorandum of 17 June on *Relations with the Soviet Union and Eastern Europe*, which accepted that 'the desire of East European countries for greater individual independence is also in the interest of the West generally', but the basis for the analysis remained the assumption that the 'Soviet approach to the developed Western countries is still one of hostility' and the paper recommended 'when the Russians talk tough to show that far from yielding to pressures we intend to be just as tough as they are' (No. 11).

This line did not preclude close bilateral cooperation on practical matters, but all efforts in this direction were truncated by the crisis caused by the Soviet invasion of Czechoslovakia in August (Nos. 14-16), which prompted a lengthy re-examination of British policy towards the Soviet Union and towards subsequent Soviet attempts to rehabilitate herself in international fora (Nos. 17-24). The Foreign Office (Foreign & Commonwealth Office, FCO from 17 October 1968) were forthright in their condemnation of the invasion, though their analysis of its causes and consequences was pragmatic. A thoughtful despatch of 30 September from Peter Dalton, Chargé d'Affaires in Moscow, argued that the invasion, with its lack of effective Soviet follow-up, was 'not the action of strong "expansionist" leaders, but of frightened men reacting indecisively to a situation which they judged to be crucially dangerous, but with which they did not know how to deal' (No. 15). The West's reaction to the invasion, however, proved that Soviet fears of increased insecurity in Europe were groundless: as Sir Duncan Wilson, HM Ambassador in Moscow from September 1968, pointed out a year later in a despatch of July 1969, the fact that neither the Hungarian crisis of 1956 nor the Czechoslovak crisis of 1968 provoked any threat or even serious discussion of a NATO response must have made the Soviet leaders feel 'that they have no reason to fear Western military intervention in such difficulties, whatever the West may find it necessary to say publicly on this score' (No. 36).

The British Government, while losing no opportunity of condemning Soviet actions in Czechoslovakia, were quick to rationalise the need to carry on 'business as usual' in terms of day-to-day diplomatic contact and the implementation of existing agreements, even if planned Ministerial visits were cancelled. After all, as Sir Duncan Wilson, pointed out in December 1968 'the Russians themselves give us examples . . . of how to shout indignantly out of one corner of their mouths, so to speak, and to carry on normal business with the other' (No. 22). While officials in London and Moscow Embassy staff continued to chide their interlocutors, routine diplomatic contacts quietly continued. The Russians, however, maintained the line that HMG were pursuing a 'special vendetta against them', citing as evidence the limitation of staff numbers at the Soviet Embassy in London in November 1968, the first move in a long drawn-out campaign to counter the increasingly blatant activities of the Russian Intelligence Services (No. 19).

During 1969 the Soviet Union was determinedly participative in the international sphere, taking a cooperative approach towards efforts to bring peace to the Middle East, entering Strategic Arms Limitation Talks (SALT) negotiations with the United States of America and reacting positively to the opening moves in Herr Willy Brandt's *Ostpolitik* strategy. They remained, however, consistently critical of British policy, asserting that Soviet interests were being ignored and, in effect, that the Soviet Union was being 'excluded' from Europe. The establishment of closer ties between the British and West German Governments, based on technical and defence cooperation and expressed in a joint Anglo-German declaration in February, elicited a strong reaction from the Soviet Government focussed upon the 'bellicose' statements of Defence Secretary Denis Healey (No. 25).

The FCO were well aware of the context of these criticisms of British policy: the Soviet Union's desire to protect her dominant position in the World Communist movement, potentially challenged by Communist China, and difficulties within the Communist Party of the Soviet Union itself (Nos. 25-28). The wide-ranging survey of East-West relations commissioned after the invasion of Czechoslovakia but not circulated until May 1969 (No. 31) provides a detailed insight into the FCO's forward planning and estimation of the basis of Soviet policy, and a clear statement of their view of what Western policy (with the full support of the UK as an important member of NATO) should be—to restore full relations with the Soviet Union while driving a hard bargain and insisting on reciprocal Soviet concessions.

Ministerial visits to Moscow by Tony Benn and Anthony Crosland in May-June 1969 in the context of Anglo-Soviet technological and trade agreements (Nos. 32-33) were instrumental in the normalisation of day-to-day bilateral relations, and the Ambassador's report on his visit to the joint Anglo-Soviet 'Polyspinners' plant at Mogilev (No. 40) shows just how productive those relations could be at ground level. Meanwhile, however, the fate of Gerald Brooke dominated policy discussions in London. The Soviet Government's evident determination to use Brooke as a lever to secure the release of the Soviet spies Peter and Helen Kroger eventually secured a resigned acquiescence from the Cabinet, with the Foreign Secretary, Michael Stewart, convinced by his Permanent Under Secretary, Sir Denis Greenhill, that the exchange was essential to prevent a deterioration in Anglo-Soviet relations (Nos. 30 and 34).

Discussions of Soviet policy from the summer of 1969 onwards focussed on whether the Soviet Union was serious in her sponsorship of proposals for a European Security Conference put forward by the Warsaw Pact in the Budapest Appeal of March (No. 26); the subject was introduced relentlessly by Soviet Ministers or officials on every possible occasion, even when bilateral matters were on the agenda. While not wishing to appear negative, the FCO were both suspicious of Soviet motives and unconvinced that the Soviet Government itself really wanted such a conference (Nos. 36 and 41). Sir Thomas Brimelow's long letter of 14 July to Sir Duncan Wilson is an elegant exposition of the case for and against an enthusiastic British line towards a security conference, while expressing his own wry appreciation of the fact that reasoned and well-founded argument is not always sufficient justification for foreign policy: 'Europe is not a debating society'. Recommending a policy of 'wait and see', his analysis was sober and comprehensive: 'It is true that we may seem to be waiting for something to happen—progress in SALT or in our European policy, the German elections, even the Vietnam talks; and I can understand the feeling that we ought to be taking initiatives in other fields while we wait. On the other side of the balance, I think we must bear in mind that part of the Soviet objective all the time is to hamper the future development of unity in Western Europe, to divide NATO and get the Americans out of Europe, to refurbish their peace-loving image after Czechoslovakia and to play on the German elections' (No. 35).

British Government policy, as expressed by Mr. Stewart at meetings of the NATO Ministerial Council, was that Warsaw Pact proposals for a European security conference and on the related issue of Mutual and Balanced Forced Reductions should not be rejected out of hand, but that NATO should carry out its own study of the relevant issues while encouraging the formulation of concrete proposals by the Eastern *bloc*. The Cabinet endorsed this line: while the US was engaged in SALT talks, the French apparently advocating multilateral preparatory talks and the West German Government engaged in launching *Ostpolitik*, the British Government 'ran the risk of being accused of rigidity and a lack of enthusiasm for a *détente* between East and West' (No. 39).

A positive line for the benefit of NATO partners and public opinion did not negate the essentially gloomy analysis presented by Sir T. Brimelow and others in the FCO. Sir Duncan Wilson, in Moscow, had hoped that once the Brooke/Krogers episode was settled the way would be clear for the improvement of Anglo-Soviet relations at all levels (No. 37). However, the frank assessment of Soviet policy embodied in the Joint Intelligence Committee report of December 1969 printed as No. 40 shows that the gulf between Britain and the Soviet Union remained as fundamental at the end of 1969 as it had been at the beginning.

Prospects for a European security conference remained under discussion in 1970, both before and after the change of Government in June (p. 239). The subject had acquired a momentum of its own in the context of West Germany's *Ostpolitik* negotiations with the Soviet Union, Poland and East Germany, and the Quadripartite negotiations on Berlin (initiated rather surprisingly by Mr. Gromyko in a speech of July 1969, p. 170-1). At their conference in May 1970 HM Ambassadors from the Soviet Union and Eastern Europe were agreed that in view of these ongoing East-West talks NATO must take a more positive line towards the idea of a conference to avoid being perceived as 'dragging their feet'. Sir T. Brimelow again urged caution, emphasizing the danger of 'diplomacy without substance' and the USA's aversion to 'meaningless charades, designed simply to give a false sense of action and movement'. He also stated for the record the difference between the views of Sir D. Wilson and the Secretary of State: 'the latter was still watching for evidence before deciding about multilateral negotiations, whereas the former wished to move forward on the assumption that the other side was also willing to do so' (No. 46). Mr. Stewart continued to maintain this careful stance until Sir Alec Douglas-Home took up the baton with equal caution, concerned by aggressive Soviet attitudes over Egypt, Cuba and Berlin: 'A European Security Conference may be inevitable, but should be approached without haste and with due regard to the possible need for a hardening of Western attitudes' (No. 52). Nevertheless, from mid-1970 onwards the documentation suggests that the combination of Soviet *bloc* pressure, public opinion and the enthusiastic posture adopted by some of Britain's Western European partners was slowly but surely propelling the British Government towards a point where they could not maintain an unrelievedly sceptical attitude without appearing opponents of *détente* (Nos. 48-52, 57, 59).

British progress towards a CSCE, however, was both gradual and grudging. The Government's mistrust of Soviet motives was justified and reinforced by developments which constitute an important theme of the documentation in 1970: the growing official disquiet at increasingly intrusive Soviet Intelligence activities in the UK. The Soviet Trade Delegation in London had provided the Soviet Embassy with means of largely circumventing the restrictions on staffing levels imposed in November 1968, and by early 1970 the Security Service were expressing serious concern about the scale of 'unacceptable' activity in the UK (No. 43). Despite representations at a relatively senior level (Sir Denis Greenhill to Mr. Kozyrev, Soviet Deputy Foreign Minister, No. 45) the situation continued to deteriorate, and with the advent of Mr. Heath's Government a decided stiffening of policy is apparent. Sir Alec Douglas-Home remonstrated with Mr. Gromyko during their important meetings in London in October (Nos. 53 and 54), following this up with a formal letter in December (No. 58). Neither approach received any response.

Chapter IV, covering 1971, is dominated by the Intelligence issue. A Whitehall interdepartmental meeting in May agreed that the time had come to put to Ministers the need for action to curtail the unacceptable activities carried out by 'at least 25%' of Soviet representatives in the UK (No. 66). Documentation on the preparation and implementation of 'Operation FOOT' culminating in the expulsion of 105 Soviet officials in September (Nos. 76-7) includes: a joint memorandum to the Prime Minister from Sir Alec Douglas-Home and the Home Secretary, Reginald Maudling (No. 70); the Secretary of State's last-minute reassurance to the Prime Minister that the impending operation was justified, enclosing lists of possible Soviet reprisals and further measures HMG might take (No. 75); and the text of Sir Denis Greenhill's speaking notes for his fateful interview with the Soviet Chargé on 24 September (Enclosure I in No. 76). The impact of the British Government's unprecedented action (which elicited general admiration from other governments) can be gauged by Sir Alec Douglas-Home's account of his interview in New York with Mr. Gromyko who appeared so overcome with rage and surprise that his (admittedly translated) metaphors became hopelessly mixed: 'Presumably the British Government had taken this step to distract attention from the bottle necks, the rents and tatters of their own policies . . .' (No. 77). The effects of FOOT on both the Soviet Government and on KGB activities are considered in Nos. 84 and 86. Documents relating to Operation FOOT are taken from the files of the Permanent Under-Secretary's Department, to which the FCO's Historians have had full access for the first time.

Although Operation FOOT overshadowed relations with the Soviet Union in 1971, discussions continued on European security and on the implications of the successful conclusion of *Ostpolitik* negotiations (including the signature of the Quadripartite Agreement on Berlin, pp. 376-7), together with ongoing analysis in the FCO of Soviet policies and motives. By early 1971 there had been a perceptible shift in HMG's attitude towards a European Security Conference, based on the conclusion expressed by Mr. Cable, Head of Western Organisations Department, that 'although unlikely to do any good, a Conference is probably inevitable and if properly managed need not be particularly harmful'. HM Ambassadors in Eastern Europe, generally favouring a more positive line on European security, welcomed this change while marvelling somewhat at its magnitude (pp. 315-16).

Other documents of particular interest in 1971 are an FCO memorandum on the implications of the Brezhnev Doctrine for a European Security Conference (No. 62) and an assessment by Sir Duncan Wilson in Moscow of the Soviet naval threat (No. 63); while a quite different tone is struck by the Ambassador's report on the festival *Days of British Music* held in Moscow in April 1971 (No. 65), an illuminating account of the responses of distinguished British and Soviet musicians to the restrictions imposed on them by Soviet bureaucracy (Rostropovich, for example, was unable to attend a lunch given during the Festival by the Minister of Culture, Madame Furtseva, as he had been 'sent on tour among the music-loving Eskimos of Kamchatka').

In the first half of 1972 the attention of both British and Soviet Governments was occupied by developments with potentially far-reaching implications for both bilateral and multilateral relations: British signature of the Treaty of Accession to the EEC in January (see p. 431); and the visits to Peking in February and Moscow in May by US President Richard Nixon (see pp. 446-7 and No. 97). With regard to relations between Britain and the Soviet Union, the documentation for 1972 mirrors in some ways that for late 1968 and early 1969, with both Governments seeking a way back to 'normalised' relations, although the Russians continued their efforts to replace expelled Intelligence officials through a 'visa war' over Embassy staff in which HMG won the first round in May (Nos. 88, 90-91, 96). An important memorandum on policy towards the Soviet Union and East Europe in February noted that although Anglo-Soviet relations were beginning to recover after the shock of the 1971 expulsions, 'by comparison with our continental partners, the British relationship with the Soviet Union and Eastern Europe as a whole seems cool and politically negative'. Its recommendation that better political relations should be sought with Warsaw Pact governments through a programme of Ministerial visits was accepted by the Cabinet's Committee on Oversea Policy (No. 89).

HM Ambassadors from Eastern Europe again expressed, at their Conference in May, their conviction that the régimes to which they were accredited were well-disposed to approaches for the West and their view that HMG should take a more positive approach towards a European Security Conference. In his accustomed role of interjecting the cold voice of reason, Sir Thomas Brimelow was blunter than usual with his colleagues: 'The Conference had shown that the Ambassadors did not seem to be familiar with the difficulty of maintaining an adequate defence for Western Europe. The latter could be aggravated by the CSCE' (No. 95). Nonetheless, by mid-1972 Sir John Killick was discussing the timing and modalities of a conference with Mr. Gromyko (No. 100), in a period of somewhat closer contacts initiated by a wide-ranging conversation between Sir A. Douglas-Home and Mr. Gromyko (No. 98) following the long-awaited ratification of the Quadripartite Agreement on Berlin in June 1972. In September Sir A. Douglas-Home agreed to 22 November for the start of preparatory talks in Helsinki (No. 107), and the balance of the year saw a gradual normalisation of relations in the context of preparations for the Conference on Security and Cooperation in Europe, although Sir John Killick's views on the Soviet concept of co-existence cited at the beginning of this Preface foreshadowed the difficulties attendant upon this ambitious project.

The Volume ends with an Appendix reproducing a report of September 1972 by the Joint Intelligence Committee, assessing the Soviet threat over the next five years. Its statement of Soviet external policy objectives differed little from that of 1970 (No. 40), but now acknowledged that the 'principal Soviet foreign policy preoccupation is the relationship with the United States', a bilateralism which had 'profound implications for United States allies and the rest of the world'; particularly, of course, for the British Government. After analysing the nature of the Soviet threat in global terms, the Report concluded that while the threat of Soviet activity in the Third World should not be underestimated, much the more serious threat was to Western Europe: 'we foresee a period of danger in the immediate future and fear that the Soviet Union may significantly improve its position in Europe in the period under review'.

At the end of 1972 Soviet military strength was at parity, quantitatively if not qualitatively, with that of the US: the Soviet Union retained her strong grip on Eastern Europe; her political system was still founded upon an ideology implacably opposed to that of the West. The British Government had maintained a working relationship of sorts throughout a stormy five-year period, but little 'progress' had been made in terms of influencing Soviet behaviour, policies or negotiating style, or in spreading the Western gospel in Eastern Europe. In these circumstances the CSCE, however gloomy FCO prognostications may have been, offered some chance of breaking the mould, of creating opportunities, of opening up the *status quo*; and in any case opposition to the Conference was a political impossibility. In this spirit—a sort of gloomy realism tinged with optimism—they entered the preparatory talks documented in Volume II of this Series.

In accordance with the Parliamentary announcement, cited in the Introduction to the Series, the Editors have had the customary freedom in the selection and arrangement of documents, including full access to all classes of FCO documentation. In the present volume there have been no exceptional cases, provided for in the parliamentary announcement, where it has been necessary on security grounds to restrict the availability of particular documents, editorially selected in accordance with regular practice.

The main source of documentation for this volume has been the archives of the Foreign and Commonwealth Office held, pending their transfer to the Public Record Office, by the Records Management Services of Library and Records Department, and I should like to thank the RMS staff for their considerable efforts and enduring patience with our exigent requests. I am also grateful to the Records Branches of the Cabinet Office, No. 10 Downing Street, the Department of Trade and Industry and the Home Office for their help and for permission to publish documents within their responsibility.

I should like to thank the former Head of the Library and Records Department of the FCO, Mr. Ian Soutar, and the Head of Records and Historical Services, Mrs Heather Yasamee and their staff for their help and support in the preparation of this Volume. Mr. Tony Bishop of the FCO's Research Analysts, who was present at many of the meetings documented in this Volume, has offered valuable guidance and advice. Above all, I owe thanks to the members of my editorial team, Mr. Richard Bevins, MA and Dr. Liz Kane for their enthusiasm, cooperation and consistently hard work at all stages in the editing process. I would also like to thank other members of FCO Historians, particularly my colleague Dr Keith Hamilton, for their help and advice.

GILL BENNETT

July 1997

LIST OF PLATES

Prime Minister Harold Wilson at the Opera in Moscow during his visit in January 1968, with Madame Furtseva, Soviet Minister of Culture (l.) and Alexsei Kosygin, Chairman of the Soviet Council of Ministers (r.)
Reproduced by permission of Topham

Sir Alec Douglas-Home, Secretary of State for Foreign Affairs, welcomes Soviet Foreign Minister Andrei Gromyko to London in October 1970; Mikhail Smirnovsky, Soviet Ambassador to London, is on Mr. Gromyko's left.
Reproduced by permission of News International

British Ambassadors to Moscow, 1968-72: (*a*) Sir Geoffrey Harrison; (*b*) Sir Duncan Wilson, with Lady Wilson and Mstislav Rostropovich; (*c*) Sir John Killick.
(a) supplied from FCO photographic collection; (b) kindly supplied by Lady Wilson; (c) kindly supplied by Sir J. Killick

Sir Denis (now Lord) Greenhill (b. 1913), Permanent Under-Secretary, FCO 1969-73
Reproduced by permission of the Press Association

Sir Thomas (later Lord) Brimelow (1915-95), HM Ambassador in Warsaw 1966-69, Deputy Under-Secretary, FCO 1969-73
Supplied from FCO photographic collection

(*a*) Mr. (later Sir) Sydney Giffard, Head of FCO Eastern European and Soviet Department 1968-71; (*b*) The Lord Bridges, Counsellor and Head of Chancery in Moscow, 1969-71, Head of FCO Western Organisations Department 1971-72, Private Secretary to the Prime Minister 1972-74; (*c*) Mr. (later Sir) Julian Bullard, Head of EESD 1971-75.
Supplied from FCO photographic collection

CONTENTS

ABBREVIATIONS FOR PRINTED SOURCES

BFSP   *British and Foreign State Papers* (London, 1841-1977)

Cmnd.   Command Paper (London)

Cmnd. 6201   *Selected Documents on Germany and the Question of Berlin 1961-1973 (Miscellaneous No. 16,* HMSO, 1975)

Cmnd. 6932   *Selected Documents Relating to Problems of Security and Cooperation in Europe 1954-77 (Miscellaneous No. 17,* HMSO, 1977)

DBFP   *Documents on British Foreign Policy 1919-1939 (*HMSO, London, 1946-86)

DBPO   *Documents on British Policy Overseas* (HMSO, London, 1984f.)

FRUS   *Foreign Relations of the United States: Diplomatic Papers* (Washington, 1961 f.)

Parl. Debs., 5th ser., H. of C.   *Parliamentary Debates (Hansard), Fifth Series, House of Commons, Official Report (London)*

Parl. Debs., 5th ser., H. of L.   *Parliamentary Debates (Hansard), Fifth Series, House of Lords, Official Report (London)*

Public Papers: Nixon (1969, 1970 1971, 1972)   *Public Papers of the Presidents of the United States: Richard Nixon, Containing the Public Messages, Speeches and Statements of the President* (Washington, 1971-74)

Watt and Mayall (1970, 1971, 1972)   D.C. Watt and James Mayall, eds., *Current British Foreign Policy: Documents, Statements, Speeches* (London, 1971-74)

ABBREVIATED DESIGNATIONS

ABM	Anti-Ballistic Missile	EESD	Eastern European and Soviet Department, FCO
AEC	United States Atomic Energy Commission	EFTA	European Free Trade Area
BIS	British Information Services, New York	ENDC	UN Eighteen Nation Disarmament Committee
BOT	Board of Trade	ESC	European Security Conference (see CSCE)
BW	Biological Weapons	Euratom	European Atomic Energy Commmunity
BST	British Standard Time		
CBI	Confederation of British Industries	FRG	Federal Republic of Germany
CCD	Conference of the Committee on Disarmament	FOB	Free on Board
CIF	Carriage, insurance and freight	GATT	General Agreement on Tariffs and Trade
COCOM	Co-ordinating Committee on Exports to Communist Countries	GDR/DDR	German Democratic Republic
COMECON/ CMEA	Council for Mutual Economic Assistance	GRU	Soviet Military Intelligence Agency
CPSU	Communist Party of the Soviet Union	ICBM	Inter-Continental Ballistic Missile
CSCE/CES/ CESC/ESC	Conference on Security and Co-operation in Europe	IAEA	International Atomic Energy Authority
		KGB	Committee of State Security, USSR
CW	Chemical Weapons	MAFF	Ministry of Agriculture, Fisheries and Food
DRV	Democratic Republic of Vietnam	MBFR	Mutual and Balanced Force Reductions
DTI	Department of Trade and Industry	Mintech	Ministry of Technology
ECGD	Export Credits Guarantee Department	MOD	Ministry of Defence
ECOSOC	UN Economic and Social Council	NATO	North Atlantic Treaty Organisation
EEC	European Economic Communities	NPT	Non-Proliferation Treaty

OECD	Organisation for Economic Cooperation and Development
OGD	Other Government Department (i.e. non-FCO)
PUSD	Permanent Under-Secretary's Department, FCO
QRR	Quadripartite Rights and Responsibilities (in Berlin)
SALT	Strategic Arms Limitation Talks/Treaty
SAM	Surface to Air Missile
SCST	State Committee for Science and Technology, USSR
SPC	NATO Special Political Committee
STD	Soviet Trade Delegation
UAR	United Arab Republic
UKAEA	UK Atomic Energy Authority
UKDEL	UK Delegation to NATO
UKMIS	UK Missions in New York or Brussels
UN	United Nations Organisation
UNESCO	UN Educational, Scientific and Cultural Organisation
UNGA	United Nations General Assembly
WED	Western European Department, FCO
WOD	Western Organisations Department, FCO

CHAPTER SUMMARIES

CHAPTER I

1968

CHAPTER II

1969

CHAPTER III

1970

CHAPTER IV

1971

CHAPTER V

1972

CHAPTER I

1968

This Volume is chiefly concerned with bilateral relations. However, the flavour of the Anglo-Soviet relationship at the turn of 1968 can only be appreciated in the context of each country's internal situation, and of the international backdrop. Although their political systems and international affiliations were quite different, there were a number of similarities between the British and Soviet positions. Both countries were affected by the major conflicts in South East Asia and the Middle East, although their role, for a variety of reasons, was essentially peripheral to and dependent upon United States policy. Both had a strong interest in Europe, East and West (and particularly in Germany, East and West), but again their position was one of association, rather than membership, although of course Soviet control in Eastern Europe far outweighed British influence within the North Atlantic Treaty Organisation (NATO) or the Western European Union. The relationship of the United States to Europe, however, was of close interest to both powers.

The first three documents in this Collection concern Prime Minister Harold Wilson's visit to Moscow from 22-24 January 1968. It was a hastily-arranged visit—the invitation from Mr. Alexsei Kosygin, Chairman of the Soviet Council of Ministers, was conveyed informally in late November 1967 and only confirmed on 11 December. Acceptance meant that Mr. Wilson had to defer a planned trip to Washington for discussions with President Lyndon B. Johnson (also proposed in November) until February 1968. The urgency behind the arrangement of these two visits can be traced to two factors in particular: the British balance of payments crisis, leading to devaluation of the pound on 18 November 1967 and to a series of swingeing spending cuts, especially in the realm of defence; and the Vietnam war, in regard to which a diplomatic stalemate prevailed at the turn of the year. These factors provided the context for Mr. Wilson's visit to Moscow, but the Prime Minister was also hopeful of getting Anglo-Soviet relations off to a good start in 1968 on a whole range of issues, both bilateral and multilateral.

For the United Kingdom, where foreign policy considerations were debated in a climate of global economic recession and industrial unrest on the domestic front, the devaluation of the pound on 18 November proved in some respects a turning-point. It was partly a response to international events: the 6-day Arab-Israeli war in June 1967 and its repercussions, in particular the closure of the Suez Canal, had a damaging effect on British trade, and Britain's continuing exclusion from the European Economic Communities (EEC) made her vulnerable to what Harold Wilson called 'financial manoeuvrings within the Six'.[1] *Rejection of the British application to join the EEC, articulated by the French President Charles de Gaulle on 27 November and confirmed by the EEC Council of Ministers on 18-19 December, was justified on the grounds that the British economy was not strong enough for her to be a member of the Community. Devaluation, and the need to restore the balance of payments, meant deep defence cuts: on 15 January 1968 the Cabinet, though divided—the Secretary of State for Foreign Affairs, George Brown, was amongst those opposing the final decision—accepted a programme which included withdrawal from South East Asia and the Persian Gulf by the end of 1971, with consequent reductions in men and equipment and the cancellation of new defence orders, including that for 50 American F111A aircraft. Although the British Government took a positive approach to the financial situation, regarding devaluation as an opportunity for a new start, the impression given at the turn of the year was one of vulnerability.*

British Ministers knew that the Soviet Government hoped this vulnerability would work to their own advantage. A reduction in British defence commitments could only tip the military scales in favour of Soviet power, and an economically weak Britain might be more inclined to enter agreements to the Soviet advantage, for example on trade or technology, as well as being easier to detach from what the Soviet Government considered an undesirable dependence on the United States. While maintaining the line that the British devaluation was an attack on the working classes, the Soviet Government hoped to foster commercial and technological collaboration with an economically weak UK in order to obtain the goods and expertise they needed if their own economic and social policies were to succeed.

Within the Soviet Union, economic reforms initiated after the fall of Khrushchev in 1964 were starting to run out of steam by 1968. Attempts to give industry greater autonomy were thwarted by tight political control and destabilised by industrial discontent when reform meant job losses. Events in Czechoslovakia, where economic reform was seen to be producing 'undesirable' political developments, contributed to the slowing down of economic change within the Soviet Union. At the same time, the 50th Anniversary of the Bolshevik Revolution celebrated in 1967 had led to a reaffirmation of the central role of the Communist Party of the Soviet Union (CPSU), and its Secretary-General, Leonid Brezhnev. The system of collective leadership established after Khrushchev, which had envisaged a quasi-Cabinet role for the Politburo, had evolved in practice into the exercise of power by a triumvirate of Brezhnev, Kosygin and Nikolai Podgorny, President of the Presidium of the Supreme Soviet. In foreign affairs, while Kosygin and the Soviet Foreign Minister, Andrei Gromyko, professed to pursue a policy based upon the doctrine of 'peaceful co-existence', accepting that states with different social systems could have normal relations, Brezhnev concentrated on promoting Soviet interests through the world communist movement, pressing ahead with plans to convene an international conference of Communist parties.

[1] Harold Wilson, *The Labour Government 1964-70* (Penguin edn, 1974), p. 559.

Soviet concern to maintain the solidarity of the communist bloc also formed the basis of their policy towards East-West relations in general, including British policy in Europe, and the future of Germany. The Soviet Union kept up an unremitting campaign against both NATO and the EEC, both in fear at the prospect of a strong and unified Western Europe, reinforced by American military might, and from whose markets they would be excluded, and in an attempt to discourage their Eastern European fraternal colleagues from straying from the fold, and to assure the more hardline communist parties, such as that of the German Democratic Republic (GDR) of the solidarity and clarity of the socialist vision. For the same reasons, the Soviet Government pursued wedge-driving tactics designed to isolate Western Europe from the United States: in the Foreign Office view, this lay behind Soviet proposals for a European security conference, for mutual force reductions and the withdrawal of foreign troops from European soil.

A brief on European security prepared for Mr. Wilson's visit to Moscow stated that both HMG and the Soviet Government 'share a direct interest in the security of Europe'. Their views on the form this security should take, however, were widely divergent. British policy was founded on the need to strengthen Western European unity, while maintaining that any European settlement must include a solution both of military problems, including arms control and the withdrawal of forces, and of political problems, which included the division of Germany: and HMG believed that 'as long as Germany remains divided, there can be no permanent settlement in Europe'. The Soviet vision was of a Germany unified on East German and Soviet terms: failing that, the division was to be exploited for the good of the communist bloc, and West Germany attacked at every turn. While paying lip-service to the policy of the Vice-Chancellor and Foreign Minister of the Federal Republic of Germany (FRG), Herr Willy Brandt, of pursuing improved relations with Eastern Europe ('Ostpolitik'), the Soviet Union in practice conducted a virulent campaign against the FRG and the supposed resurgence of neo-Nazism and 'revanchism' in West Germany. Denunciation of West German influence in Berlin, and a policy of making access to that city as difficult as possible, was part of the overall policy of disrupting harmonious relations amongst the Western European powers, and weakening US influence in Europe.

At the beginning of 1968 the international scene was dominated by war in Vietnam and continuing tension in the Middle East. The British and Soviet Governments, as co-chairmen of the Geneva Conference of 1954, had a close interest in the conflict in South East Asia, but following the failure of peace negotiations in February 1967 there had been little scope for either power to take the initiative. Though supportive of US policy in general, the British Government and public opinion were growing increasingly uneasy about US operations in Vietnam (in September and October 1967 the Trades Union Congress and Labour Party Conference had both passed resolutions hostile to US policy in Vietnam), and the British military presence in Malaysia reinforced HMG's desire for an end to hostilities. The Soviet Government, though supportive of North Vietnam and exercising some influence in Hanoi, was not in a position to challenge the United States and professed itself in favour of leaving the Vietnamese to sort themselves out. While not in favour of peace at any price—and welcoming the increasing domestic and *international opposition to US policy—the Soviet Government certainly opposed the escalation of hostilities which might begin to draw in other powers, such as China.*

US policy in 1967 had combined an intensification of military pressure with a series of offers to end the bombing of North Vietnam if Hanoi would agree to enter negotiations seriously. At the end of the year President Johnson was awaiting a response to his latest offer, set out in a speech on 29 September to the National Legislative Conference in San Antonio, that he was ready to talk to the North Vietnamese leader Ho Chi Minh and to stop bombing if it would lead to 'productive discussions'. When the President met Harold Wilson at the memorial service for Australian Prime Minister Harold Holt in Melbourne on 22 December 1967, he asked the Prime Minister privately to sound out the Russians during his forthcoming visit to Moscow on reactions to the San Antonio speech, on the basis of Soviet contacts with Hanoi. However, the statement on 30 December by North Vietnamese Foreign Minister Nguyen Duy Trinh to the effect that the Democratic Republic of Vietnam (DRV) would only enter talks if the US stopped bombing unconditionally, with a long gap between the cessation of bombing and the beginning of negotiations (conditions unacceptable to the Americans), indicated, in the view of the British Government, that the DRV were prepared for a long war.

Prospects for lasting peace in the Middle East seemed little better. Despite the resounding Israeli victory of June 1967, the Arab States found it difficult to accept defeat and although acknowledging that some political settlement was essential, at the end of 1967 the situation in the region remained tense. The Soviet Government had lost some standing by their failure to intervene to prevent Arab defeat, and were trying to restore their position in the region by general support of the Arab States at the United Nations and by rapid rearmament of those who looked to them as suppliers. One direct result of this policy was the strengthening of the Soviet naval presence in the Mediterranean—an area of clear strategic importance to the UK. The basic dilemma for Soviet policy, however, remained how to pursue their aims without involving themselves in an unacceptable risk of confrontation.

British interests in the region were both historical and complex. During the Six-Day war the British government announced its neutrality and desire for a 'peaceful solution to the problems of the area', although both government and public opinion were divided on the rights and wrongs of the Arab-Israeli conflict. Since the primary British interest in the area was freedom of navigation in Middle Eastern waters for British trade, and in particular the continued flow of Middle Eastern oil, peace and good relations with the Arab States was certainly the desired option. In a situation of continuing tension, however, in Arab eyes the British were indissolubly linked to US policy and had thus been accused with the US of large-scale intervention in support of Israel and punished accordingly by an oil embargo, later called off. Like the Soviet Union, therefore, the UK wanted containment and control in the Middle East, together with the chance to reestablish good relations with individual countries. Both had a close interest in preventing any renewal of hostilities between Israel and the Arab States and the consequent dangers of confrontation between East and West. Thus the Soviet Government had supported the British draft Security Council Resolution 242 in November 1967 whereby Israel must withdraw from territories conquered in June, while the Arab states must recognise Israel's right to exist. Gunnar Jarring, Swedish Ambassador to the Soviet Union, had been designated UN Special Representative to the region with a mission to promote talks between the parties and try to achieve a peaceful settlement in the Middle East.

Harold Wilson set out for Moscow to talk about Vietnam and the Middle East in particular. He hoped for a useful and productive dialogue on a range of issues, bilateral and multilateral. He was well aware, however, that the two delegations—however pragmatic the politicians involved—came to the negotiating table with diametrically opposed views of the world.

No. 1

Letter from Sir G. Harrison[1] (Moscow) to Mr H.F.T. Smith[2]
(Received 18 January)

[NS 3/3]

Confidential   MOSCOW, *17 January 1968*

Dear Howard,

Press treatment is no sure guide to Soviet policy but, on the eve of the Prime Minister's visit to Moscow a brief analysis of the general pattern of Soviet press coverage of the main relevant items of foreign affairs in recent weeks may be useful.

(*a*) *South East Asia.* The propaganda campaign against American policy and methods of conducting the Viet Nam war continues at full blast, with particular emphasis latterly on American plans to extend the war to Cambodia and Laos. The economic effects on the United States of the war and mounting domestic as well as foreign opposition to the Administration's policy are also prominent themes. Beyond maintaining pressure for an end to the bombing of the DRV, the Soviet press has, however, avoided discussion of the means of bringing about negotiations. Trinh's statement was reported, but its implications and foreign reactions to it have not been examined or commented on.

(*b*) *The Middle East* has been given rather less attention than might have been expected. The main theme of comment has been that the situation remains tense because of Israel's refusal, with the support of the imperialists, to withdraw from the occupied territories. Particular concern has been shown about current Israeli attempts to increase their military strength and apparent Western readiness to supply arms. But apart from factual reporting

---

[1] HM Ambassador in Moscow since August 1965.

[2] Head of the FO Northern Department.

of Jarring's movements and routine assertions that a solution must be dependent on Israel's withdrawal, comment on the prospects of a settlement has, since the Warsaw statement,[3] been sparse and unilluminating.

(*c*) *Disarmament.* Nothing of any significance has been said on this for some time; but Roshchin's return to Geneva has been noted.[4]

(*d*) *Europe.* There are two main themes:

(i) the danger of neo-Nazism, revanchism, and militarism in West Germany and the failure of the Western powers to face up to their responsibilities under the Potsdam Agreements;[5] and
(ii) the need, increasingly recognised in Western Europe, for a weakening of American dominance and the development of wider cooperation on an all-European basis. The latter theme has been given prominence lately in the context of the US Administration's measures to strengthen the dollar. It is alleged that these will cost America's allies dear and show the price of too great dependence on America.

(*e*) *The United Kingdom.* We have had an unrelievedly bad press. A series of background articles has represented Britain as passing through a period of profound malaise and disillusionment. 1967 was a bad year for Britain and 1968 promises to be even worse. The tough price to be paid at home and abroad for the balance of payments crisis and devaluation has been made much of. The pressure on HMG to reduce their foreign commitments and the alleged lack of sympathy from the US have been stressed. Our predicament is said to be the result above all of our consistent policy of following in the wake of the United States: and the solution to be an assertion

[3] A *communiqué* issued on 22 December 1967 after a meeting in Warsaw of East European Foreign Ministers and their deputies stated that Israel's withdrawal 'from all occupied Arab territory . . . is the principal and essential condition for securing the return and consolidation of peace' in the Middle East. The *communiqué* expressed support for Arab endeavours to reach a solution of the crisis and noted that the Ministers had 'pointed to the great importance of carrying out the Security Council's resolution of 22 November' (NS 2 / 17).

[4] Since August 1967 talks had been in progress in Geneva on the draft text of a Non-Proliferation treaty, tabled by the US and Soviet co-chairmen of the UN Eighteen Nation Disarmament Committee (ENDC), respectively Mr. W. Foster and Mr. A. Roshchin. Hopes that early agreement would be reached had not materialised, the crucial problem proving the relationship to be established between the International Atomic Energy Authority (IAEA) and the European Atomic Energy Community (Euratom), since the Soviet Union would not agree to any language which explicitly recognised Euratom or appeared to give it a favoured position under the Treaty. A stalemate on US and Soviet drafts of a paragraph regarding safeguards was reached in November. During the Christmas recess, however, the Russians made a number of important concessions, enabling a full draft text of the treaty to be tabled when the ENDC reconvened on 18 January: it included the article on safeguards, on which the Russians had largely accepted the US wording.

[5] See *DBPO*, Series I, Volume I, No. 603, for the Potsdam Protocol of 2 August 1945.

of independence and the development of relationships outside closed groupings. There was also the Brooke article in *Izvestia*.[6]

2. Against this background I offer, with all the usual reserves, the following brief prognostications for the Prime Minister's visit. The recent Russian reticence on Vietnam and the Middle East may hold out the prospect of useful discussion of various aspects of these two problems. This reticence may reflect genuine uncertainty, together with a desire to maintain full freedom of manoeuvre in both areas. In both cases it can only be useful to probe Russian intentions. On Germany I would expect the Prime Minister to receive strong blasts from any of the Soviet leaders he meets. Europe is likely to be discussed in terms of the need for all Western European countries, including the United Kingdom, to break free from American dominance. I suspect that Mr. Kosygin will consider that the present situation offers an unusually favourable opportunity for wedge-driving and that he will be more interested on this occasion in seeking to place a strain on our relations with the United States and NATO than in using us as a channel of communication with Washington.

3. As regards the internal situation, it is difficult to be precise, but the Leningrad and Ginsberg trials[7] seem indicative that the more reactionary wings of the Party/KGB are at the moment in the ascendant. Some of my colleagues with strong Communist parties at home have received indications through them of increasing stresses and jockeying for position amongst the top leadership. And one can well imagine that the difficulties which are manifestly arising with regard to the calling of a world Communist meeting[8] are sharpening these strains. World reactions, not least in the British press, to the trials

[6] Mr. Gerald Brooke, a British citizen, had been sentenced in July 1965 by a Moscow court to 1 year in prison and 4 years in a labour camp for bringing into the Soviet Union propaganda material destined for the Popular Labour Alliance, an anti-Soviet organisation. The British Government regarded the sentence as 'savage' and had made a number of appeals for clemency, including one from the Prime Minister, Mr. Harold Wilson, on 8 November 1967 in a message to Mr. Kosygin, which also claimed consular access to Mr. Brooke under the Anglo-Soviet Consular Convention signed in December 1965 but not yet ratified. An oral reply, delivered by the Soviet Ambassador, Mr. M. Smirnovsky, on 23 November, maintained that Brooke's sentence was 'extremely lenient' and linked his case to that of Peter and Helen Kroger, US citizens arrested in Britain and sentenced in March 1961 to 20 years' imprisonment for spying for the Soviet Union. An article in *Izvestiya* on 28 December 1967 claimed that Brooke had been fortunate not to be tried as a spy and said that unless 'certain circles' in Britain ceased stirring up public opinion he would be retried and receive a longer sentence.

[7] Four young intellectuals, members of the All-Russian Social Christian Union for the Liberation of the People, had been tried in Leningrad in November 1967 on charges of treason and anti-Soviet agitation, and sentenced to between 8 and 15 years' imprisonment. Mr. Alexander Ginsberg was sentenced by a closed court in Moscow on 12 January 1968 to 5 years' hard labour for compiling a transcript of the trial in February 1966 of the writers Sinyavsky and Daniel on charges of attempting to subvert the Soviet régime.

[8] Mr. Brezhnev's plans for an International Conference of Communist Parties, to which all 81 parties who had attended the Moscow Conference in 1960 would be invited, had not met with enthusiasm, especially in Czechoslovakia and Roumania. A preliminary consultative meeting had been called to take place in Budapest in February 1968.

are likely to make Mr. Kosygin and other Soviet leaders even more sensitive than usual on the subject of Brooke.[9]

Yours ever,
GEOFFREY HARRISON

[9] Mr. D.M. Day, Assistant Private Secretary to the Secretary of State for Foreign Affairs, sent this letter on 19 January to Mr. A.M. Palliser, Private Secretary to the Prime Minister, together with some extracts of Soviet press comment on the UK. He expressed general agreement with Sir G. Harrison, but noted with regard to para. 3 that on the evidence available 'we cannot say with any confidence that there is a struggle which threatens the stability of the top leadership . . . our best guess is that Brezhnev, Kosygin and Podgorny are likely to be together for some time to come unless illness intervenes'.

No. 2

Record of meeting between Mr. Wilson and Mr. Kosygin in the Kremlin at 6 p.m. on Tuesday, 23 January 1968[1]

[*NS 3/47*]

Confidential

Present:

The Prime Minister	Mr. Kosygin
Sir Geoffrey Harrison	Mr. Polyansky
Sir Burke Trend	Mr. Kirillin
Mr. Harold Davies, MP	Mr. Gromyko
Sir Solly Zuckerman	Mr. Patolichev
Mr. A.M. Palliser	Mr. Kozyrev[2]
Mr. T. Lloyd-Hughes	Mr. Smirnovsky
Mr. A.K. Rothnie	and others
Mr. E.E. Orchard (Interpreter)	
Mr. J.H. Symons	
Mr. S.N.P. Hemans[3]	

[1] Mr. Wilson arrived in Moscow on the afternoon of 22 January and was met at the airport by Mr. Kosygin. Over the next three days the Prime Minister was involved in almost non-stop talks, both formal and informal, covering a wide range of topics but dominated by Vietnam, the Middle East and European Security. Only the records of his meeting on bilateral issues, and of a wide-ranging discussion with President Podgorny (No. 3) are printed here.

[2] Mr. Polyansky and Mr. Kirillin were respectively First Deputy Chairman of the Council of Ministers of the USSR, and Deputy Chairman of the Council of Ministers and Chairman of the State Committee for Science and Technology. Mr. Patolichev and Mr. Kozyrev were respectively Soviet Minister of Foreign Trade and Deputy Minister of Foreign Affairs

[3] Sir Burke Trend, Mr. Davies and Sir Solly Zuckerman were respectively Secretary to the Cabinet, Parliamentary Private Secretary to the Prime Minister and HMG's Chief Scientific Adviser. Mr. Lloyd-Hughes, Mr. Rothnie, Mr. Orchard, Mr. Symons and Mr. Hemans were respectively Press Secretary to the Prime Minister, Counsellor (Commercial) in HM Embassy in Moscow, Counsellor in the FO Research Department and Second Secretaries in HM Embassy in Moscow.

Anglo-Soviet Bilateral Affairs

The Prime Minister welcomed the progress made which had resulted in the conclusion of the Claims and Financial Agreement,[4] and the Technological Agreement just signed in London by Mr. Kirillin and Mr. Wedgwood Benn.[5] It was agreed that this should be referred to in the *communiqué*.

The Prime Minister said that good progress had also been made on the Navigation Treaty.[6] The British draft was ready for signature immediately—that night at the Opera, perhaps—if Mr. Kosygin agreed. *Mr. Kosygin* replied that the Soviet side had not had time fully to study the British text; the Opera was not the best place for signing agreements. But he thought that agreement would be reached. The Soviet Union's reply to the British draft would be available in a few days. It could be noted in the *communiqué* that agreement would soon be reached.

The Prime Minister said that considerable progress had been made in the field of Trade since he had last met Mr. Kosygin.[7] The two Trade Ministers had resolved some difficult problems. He also welcomed the fact that the two Planning Departments were working together with some success. He would

---

[4] An Anglo-Soviet Agreement concerning the Settlement of Mutual Financial and Property Claims, signed on 5 January 1968, was published as Cmnd. 3517 of 1968.

[5] An Inter-Governmental Technological Agreement between the UK and USSR was signed in London on 19 January 1968 by Mr. A. Wedgwood Benn, Minister of Technology, Mr. F. Mulley, Minister of State in the Foreign Office, and Mr. Kirillin: see Tony Benn, *Office Without Power: Diaries 1968-72* (Arrow Edition, London, 1989), pp. 17-21 for an account of the final stages of the negotiations. The Agreement provided for the appointment of working groups to recommend specific subjects for co-operation in the fields of technological research, industrial technology and long-term industrial development and production. Co-operation was to be promoted through visits of experts and technicians, provision of facilities for research, and arrangements for the exchange of scientific and technical information and documentation. The Minister of Technology and the Chairman of the State Committee for Science and Technology were to meet regularly, at least once a year.

[6] Agreement on the English text of an Anglo-Soviet Navigation Treaty had been reached in April 1967, but signature had been delayed. In October the Soviet Government re-opened negotiations on the key Article 5, on conditions of competition in the carriage of goods between Britain and the Soviet Union, and between the Soviet Union and third countries (where HMG were concerned to prevent as far as possible the conclusion of agreements which would exclude British ships). The British negotiators had decided to stand firm on this and other points, and were awaiting a Soviet reply.

[7] Since the signature of the Anglo-Soviet Trade Agreement in 1959 (renewed for 5 years in 1964), trade had increased considerably: Soviet exports to the UK rose from £76m cif in 1960 to £123m in 1967, while UK exports to the USSR rose from £37m to £63m fob. HMG, however, took the view that there was ample scope for improvement, and were concerned that the UK should be given opportunities to put forward competitive tenders in areas of special expertise e.g. shipbuilding. During his visit to the UK in February 1967 Mr. Kosygin had suggested the development of longer term trade arrangements, but talks between officials had so far been inconclusive, the Russian attitude being generally to complain that British firms' shortcomings impeded trade, and that the Soviet Union should receive the same favourable trading terms as members of the European Free Trade Area (EFTA), while remaining unwilling to give the requisite undertakings for the UK to liberalise imports from the Soviet Union. The Russian side had suggested that drafts of a new trade agreement might be exchanged in mid-1968.

like urgently to discuss some specific trade issues. He had mentioned to Mr. Kosygin the previous evening the new possibilities opened up by the merger of two of the largest British motor manufacturers, Leylands and British Motor Corporation.[8] As he had also told Mr. Kosygin the day before, the British Government would like to respond to Mr. Kosygin's enquiries the previous year whether trade could not be expanded by a reconsideration of the strategic embargo lists. He would like to know what ideas the Soviet Government had on the areas of trade where strategic embargoes hampered British exports to the Soviet Union. There was also the more delicate issue of easing the strategic embargo on the USSR and tightening it on China; he would welcome Mr. Kosygin's views on this too, but would understand if he preferred not to comment.[9] He assumed that in any case, Mr. Kosygin would not wish this to feature in the *communiqué*. *Mr. Kosygin* replied the Soviet Union welcomed the development of Anglo-Soviet economic relations. An increase in trade had been achieved. Many questions which had been discussed in London had already been solved. The difficult question of claims, which had hindered credit relations, had been solved. A Navigation Treaty would be ready in a few days and the responsible Ministers could meet and sign it.

The Prime Minister asked whether anything could be said in the *communiqué* about aviation. *Mr. Kosygin* replied that the *communiqué* could include a statement that certain progress had been achieved in air communications.[10] *The Prime Minister* said that he thought this was correct but that the next step was for the Soviet Union to take. *Mr. Kosygin* said that if the Prime Minister

[8] The merger of BMC and Leyland had been announced on 17 January. During a conversation after dinner in the Hall of Receptions on the Lenin Hills on the evening of 22 January, Mr. Wilson had 'asked about the prospects for British Leyland to build a factory in the Soviet Union and described the much greater potential the new corporation could deploy since the merger. He also wished to propose an arrangement under which Leyland would deliver 100 or 200 buses to the Soviet Union for a trial period of two years. The Soviet authorities could run them, and only pay for them if they liked them'. Mr. Kosygin had not reacted to these proposals, though he praised the quality of Leyland diesel motors, and would 'only say that the question of Leyland building a factory was still "at the stage of consideration"'.

[9] A Co-ordinating Committee (COCOM) consisting of NATO countries (except for Iceland) and Japan had since 1957 banned the export to communist countries of a uniform list of goods and materials of strategic importance. According to Mr. Benn, the embargo was a 'serious obstacle' to developing closer technical and industrial links with the Soviet Union: cf. Tony Benn, *Diaries 1968-72, op. cit.*, pp. 17-18. On 21 March 1968 the Cabinet Defence and Oversea Policy (OPD) Committee approved decisions taken on 7 March by the Ministerial Committee on Strategic Exports that the next COCOM review, due in October 1968, should, on US initiative, agree a different and more restrictive list for China than for the Soviet bloc; the review should also aim to reduce the embargo list as much as could be justified strategically (OPD(68)6).

[10] At a meeting of officials in Moscow in November-December 1967 agreement had been reached giving Russian permission for British participation in a joint London-Moscow-Tokyo air service, extending the Japanese-Russian service between Moscow and Tokyo which used Russian aircraft. The British side were prepared to offer valuable traffic rights in return for permission to use British aircraft, but the Russians insisted that the route was not open to foreign aircraft.

was referring to flights across Siberia to Japan, the Soviet Union did not grant anyone this right. In the case of Japan, their arrangement was to lease Soviet planes with Soviet crews to the Japanese air line. If such an arrangement would suit Britain, this would be possible. No non-Soviet aircraft were permitted to overfly Siberia. *The Prime Minister* noted this. He asked whether such an arrangement would apply only to flights from Moscow to Tokyo and that up to Moscow passengers would travel by British aircraft and then change. *Mr. Kosygin* confirmed this.

The Prime Minister said that another matter they had discussed in London about which he was often asked, was the proposed Treaty of Friendship.[11] *Mr. Kosygin* said that the Soviet Government now had a draft. The British Government had submitted a draft; now the Soviet Government would submit theirs, immediately if Mr. Wilson wanted.

The Prime Minister said that this would enable the experts to meet soon. *Mr. Kosygin* said that experts were not necessary; the Treaty could be signed right away. *The Prime Minister* said that this was Mr. Kosygin's retaliation for his suggestion that the Navigation Treaty should be signed immediately. *Mr. Kosygin* repeated that the Soviet draft was available immediately; it could now be discussed through the respective Foreign Ministries.

Mr. Kosygin referred to the Prime Minister's question about strategic embargoes. The Soviet Union had no intention of going to war with Britain. Her Majesty's Government need not fear that the Soviet Union would buy any really strategic goods in Britain. The Soviet Union was selling Britain the most strategic goods there were: raw materials. They would like to eliminate these lists and to see a situation where the Soviet Union could buy any goods that Britain had to sell and vice versa. The lists had lost their purpose. If the Soviet Union had any difficulty in buying from Britain, then she bought from Japan or the United States. The United States said that they were not selling strategic goods, but they were; and in any case the Soviet Union could buy them through other countries. Such lists involved discrimination: the Soviet Union and Britain were too serious partners in trade for discrimination of this kind. In practice the situation would not change. If Britain did not wish to sell she would not. She was free to make such decisions, list or no list. The idea of embargoes was out of date.

[11] Mr. Kosygin had proposed a Treaty of Friendship, Peaceful Co-operation and Non-Aggression during his visit in February 1967. The British draft presented to the Russians in April, dealing with various fields for potential Anglo-Soviet co-operation, providing for exchange of information and regular meetings of Ministers and affirming that 'in all matters affecting their mutual relations the two countries will be guided by the principles and purposes of the United Nations Charter', was criticised by the Soviet Government as lacking political content, but they had so far failed to produce a counter-draft. On 12 January 1968 Sir G. Harrison reported in Moscow telegram No. 92 information from the Deputy Head of the Second European Department of the Soviet Foreign Ministry, Mr. Safronchuk, that Mr. Kosygin might table a counter-draft at his meeting with Mr. Wilson: 'He said that opinion on the Soviet side was that many changes would be required to take account of "Developments during the summer and since" and of "The present international situation"' (NS 3/7).

Mr. Kosygin referred to Mr. Wilson's remarks about the motor industry. In the current five-year plan the Soviet Government had no further opportunities for new factories, although they were interested in them. They would like to start such building again in 1971 and would consider the possibilities of collaboration with Britain. This should be discussed. Britain, whether she recognised it or not, was very dependent on the United States; and it was not easy to get rid of this dependence. The Soviet Government were now drawing up their estimates for the next five-year plan (1971-75)[12] and would have completed them within about a year. It would be useful if the British Government could provide some indication of the nature, amounts and prices of the vital imports and exports they envisaged for their trade with the Soviet Union. He was not suggesting a trade agreement, but simply indicative figures. They knew what Britain imported from the United States. If Britain would give an indication of the quantity and nature of the imports she would be interested in receiving from the Soviet Union, a plan could be drawn up in which the Soviet Union could take account of Britain's needs and order equipment to fulfil them. The Soviet Union would in return state what her interests were. This would provide a broad outline for future trade and help to free Britain from dependence on the United States. The Soviet Union would have greater requirements under the next five-year plan, as industrial production would be increased by 50% by the end of the plan period.

The Soviet Government would also be stepping up industrial investment. It might be worth mentioning all these possibilities in the *communiqué*. The Prime Minister said that what Mr. Kosygin had said was very constructive and he welcomed it. The reason why trade had not developed entirely satisfactorily was because it was based on single years. One had to look ahead over the next five years. This was relevant to the Soviet Union's next five year plan; and he saw useful opportunities, for example, for cars buses and lorries. Planning work had now begun between Gosplan and the Department of Economic Affairs during Mr. Kirillin's visit. Mr. Patolichev would be asked to take this further when he came to London. Meanwhile the Planning Departments in both Governments should work out indicators, not as a formal agreement but to establish guide lines. He welcomed a reduction in British dependence on any country. But if Mr. Kosygin made similar offers to France he would face greater difficulties since so much of French industry was American-controlled. Similarly, a study of Soviet trade figures suggested that the Soviet Union was becoming rather too dependent on Japan; but Britain was ready to help. *Mr. Kosygin* replied that he would not refuse such help but accept it, if British terms were better. The Soviet Union was not tied to Japan. The Russians were businessmen; if the terms were all right, they would be accepted. *The Prime Minister* said that they would be. He agreed with Mr. Kosygin about strategic embargoes; many years previously he had arranged

[12] The system of Five-Year Plans for the Soviet economy had been introduced in 1929 by Josef Stalin, then General Secretary of the CPSU, in order to bring about the rapid industrialisation and collectivisation of the Soviet Union. Drawing up the 1971-75 Plan was the responsibility of Gosplan, the State Planning Commission.

for purchases of Soviet furs from Soyuz Pushnina for the Brigade of Guards. This had been the beginning of the end of strategic embargoes. In 1957 he had been discussing the subject with Mr. Mikoyan on the very evening when the House of Commons were debating a tightening of the embargo on certain electronic goods.[13] A month later [*sic*] the Soviet Union had launched Sputnik.[14] *Mr. Kosygin* said that all earlier figures for Anglo-Soviet trade had been exceeded and that there were excellent prospects for the future. *The Prime Minister* agreed. Devaluation had given Britain greater economic freedom and there were now fresh opportunities for more profitable cooperation.[15]

The meeting ended at 6.45 p.m.

[13] At that time, Mr. Anastas Mikoyan was First Deputy Chairman of the Council of Ministers of the USSR and Mr. Wilson Shadow Chancellor of the Exchequer. From 1951-59 Mr. Wilson also acted as economic adviser to Montague L. Meyer Ltd., a firm of timber importers, and regularly visited the Soviet Union on their behalf. He is here apparently referring to a visit he made to Moscow from 26-28 November 1957. The House of Commons debated the need to control the exports of certain electronic goods on 25 November 1957: *Parl. Debs., 5th ser., H. of C.,* vol. 578, cols. 939-45.

[14] The Soviet Union had launched the first earth satellite, named Sputnik I, into orbit on 4 October 1957.

[15] Later that evening, at the Opera, Mr. Kosygin asked the Prime Minister 'whether devaluation of the pound was going to work; and why the British Government had not carried out the American instructions to devalue by 30%'. Mr. Wilson replied that there had been no such instructions, and that the Americans considered the level of devaluation 'about right'. Mr. Kosygin then asked about the American reaction to the decision to cancel the order for F III aircraft, which he said was 'a right decision'. Mr. Wilson said that the Americans were disappointed, but that he too felt the decision right 'once Britain had decided to pull out of East of Suez where the aircraft had a role'. Mr. Kosygin avowed that 'the day of the bomber was over, the Soviet Union could shoot down any bomber in the sky and, as soon as Vietnam was over, a large measure of disarmament could follow'.

Mr. Orchard, in a record of his personal impressions of the visit, also noted an 'interesting exchange over supper at the Opera': when Mr. Kosygin discovered that he had been appointed Prime Minister one day before Mr. Wilson, he remarked: 'This means that they will sack (*snimut*) me one day before.' Mr. Orchard commented that apparently 'Kosygin was conscious of uncertainties in his own position comparable to those which the Russians had evidently estimated to affect Mr. Wilson' (NS 1/10).

No. 3

Record of meeting between Mr. Wilson and President Podgorny[1] in the Kremlin at 10 a.m. on Wednesday, 24 January 1968

[*NS 3/47*]

Confidential

Present:

Prime Minister	Mr. Podgorny
Sir Geoffrey Harrison	Mr. Gromyko
Sir Burke Trend	Mr. Smirnovsky
Mr. Harold Davies, MP	Private Secretary
Mr. Dalton[2]	Interpreter
Mr. Palliser	
Mr. Lloyd-Hughes	
Mr. Symons	

Mr. Podgorny welcomed the Prime Minister and commented on the extent to which Heads of State and of Government had to travel abroad. He referred to his own successful visit to Italy and to Mr. Kosygin's impending departure that day for India. Mr. Kosygin would probably also be visiting Afghanistan briefly, on his return journey. *The Prime Minister* said that a hundred years ago Afghanistan had nearly been the cause of a war between the Soviet Union and Great Britain.

Mr. Podgorny said that a hundred years ago was already deep in history. Since that date there had been no further wars between the two countries; on the contrary, they had fought together as allies. He was happy to welcome the Prime Minister to the Soviet Union on his official visit, which seemed to be going very well.

The Prime Minister said he was grateful for the welcome and was honoured to be received by the Head of State. The visit was short, but a lot of useful work had been done, both at the working meetings and at the agreeable meals and at the opera. The talks had been constructive. There had been nothing spectacular and the British side had not sought to give the press exciting stories. Indeed, they had told the press very little about what was going on and he understood that the Soviet line was similar. It was important that talks of the kind they had been having should be conducted in private without a blaze of publicity. He was due to meet Soviet journalists that

[1] Noting his personal impressions of Soviet leaders (cf. No. 2, note 15) Mr. Orchard described Mr. Podgorny as 'becoming a pleasantly grandfatherly and quite dignified old man. His account of Soviet policies was a bit woolly, and somewhat off the line in some of his phrases. Gromyko displayed a certain amount of nervousness whenever he got under way, and intervened once or twice to keep him on the right line.'

[2] Mr. P.G.F. Dalton was Minister in HM Embassy in Moscow.

afternoon at the Hall of Journalists. He looked forward to this. It was always a pleasant occasion.

Mr. Podgorny said that he had been informed of the course of the discussions between the Prime Minister, Mr. Kosygin and Mr. Brezhnev.[3] He understood that they had been detailed and had covered a number of questions. Although on a number of international political issues in particular the Soviet view was different from that of the British, they nevertheless considered the visit very useful. They also considered it was right not to create sensational results merely for publication by the press. Although there were experienced journalists who could predict the probable positions of the Prime Minister of Great Britain or the Prime Minister of the Soviet Union, they often tried to advise on the questions to be discussed or raised by one side or the other. Journalists usually knew the viewpoints on major issues of the two Governments and they often tried to guess the probable course of the talks and their outcome. For instance, on such international problems as the solution of the Vietnam question and the British and Soviet positions on the question of European security as well as the problem of the Middle East crisis, press speculation was pretty accurate. In particular they were correct in saying that Anglo-Soviet relations and the prospects for their further development were good at present and developing in a normal way.

The Prime Minister said that the press could sometimes be helpful. When they did not know the answers, however, they often tried to guess. They also tried to tell Governments what to do.

The Prime Minister said that the talks had made it clear that there were important differences of view on the three questions Mr. Podgorny had mentioned. Nevertheless, the talks had been useful in helping to identify the position of each Government and in allowing them informally, if not publicly, to achieve some narrowing of their differences. Mr. Brezhnev had summed up the position on Vietnam very well in their discussion the previous day when he had said that neither side should seek to negotiate on the Vietnam question nor indeed had authority from the parties concerned to do so; but that both none the less had the duty, jointly and separately, to do anything they could to get talks started.

The Prime Minister said that the Soviet Union and Britain both had to seek to remove uncertainties about the exact position of the two sides principally concerned.

On the Middle East, while again there were important differences, the Soviet Union and Britain were both in full agreement on the Security

---

[3] A discussion between Mr. Wilson and Mr. Brezhnev at 10 a.m. on 23 January focussed almost exclusively on Vietnam, European security and the Middle East. Mr. Orchard considered Mr. Brezhnev's account of Soviet policy 'very impressive . . . His presentation was consistently hard in spite of a fairly friendly manner . . . He shewed a good deal of interest in what the Prime Minister had to say and also revealed something of an open mind when, after the Prime Minister had repeated several of our points very cogently, he saw the force of our point of view, and said that it was necessary to look again at Soviet policies and to check (*proverit'*) them.'

Council resolution on which their representatives had worked together in New York.

On the issue of European security the Prime Minister said that there were very deep differences, but both Governments desired, if for different reasons, to avoid the mistakes which had led to conflict in the past. He would carefully consider Mr. Brezhnev's suggestion that the two sides should work together to prepare for a conference on European security.[4]

The Prime Minister said that one encouraging development was the progress made by the Soviet and US Governments on the draft non-proliferation treaty.[5] This was a big step forward. But he had been disappointed to hear not only that the French Government had said they would not sign the treaty—as had indeed always been their position[6]—but also, if what he had heard was correct, that Dr. Kiesinger[7] had said that the German Government could not sign the treaty in its present form. If this was so, it was most unfortunate. As a result of all the efforts that had been made, he considered that a generally acceptable draft had in fact now been tabled. The British Government had made their position clear. They thought the treaty should be signed soon by as many countries as possible.

The Prime Minister said that good progress had also been made in Anglo-Soviet relations. Many of the matters which he and Mr. Kosygin had discussed the previous year in London had made good progress. In particular, Anglo-Soviet trade was developing well.[8] Discussions were being arranged between the planning authorities of the two Governments on the possibility of further expanding this trade. The Navigation Agreement was nearly ready for signature. There was very close cooperation in the field of technology and in a number of other fields.

The Prime Minister said that he wished formally to raise with Mr. Podgorny one issue that was still darkening and indeed to some extent poisoning Anglo-Soviet relations. This was the case of Gerald Brooke. He had discussed it informally with Mr. Brezhnev and Mr. Kosygin at lunch the previous day and did not therefore need to go into the detailed arguments of the case. But he felt bound to raise the question with Mr. Podgorny as Head of State, with the right to exercise clemency. The Prime Minister said that it

[4] Mr. Brezhnev had told Mr. Wilson forcefully that 'it was the policies of Federal Germany which were still the great obstacle to the creation of a genuine system of European security', and had asked why the British Government could not 'think in terms of scrapping both NATO and the Warsaw Pact and replacing them by a single genuinely cooperative and comprehensive system of collective security'. The Prime Minister, while maintaining that Soviet fears of a revival of Nazism in Germany were exaggerated, agreed to give 'very careful personal consideration to the suggestion that the British and Soviet Governments should together do preliminary work' for a possible conference on European security: however, 'they could not regard themselves as the co-chairmen for the purposes of Europe, as they were for the purposes of Vietnam'.

[5] See No. 1, note 4. The UN General Assembly had now asked for a full report by 15 March.

[6] France had never taken her seat on the ENDC.

[7] Chancellor of the Federal Republic of Germany (FRG).

[8] See No. 2, note 7.

was not until Mr. Smirnovsky had come to see him in London with the Soviet Government's reply to his message to Mr. Kosygin[9] that he had fully apprised himself of all the facts of the case. Having established the facts about the organisation which had made use of this misguided young man he could more readily understand the indignation and concern of the Soviet Government. Indeed he himself had been indignant and had so expressed himself to Mr. Kosygin and Mr. Brezhnev the previous day. He had also said that he was prepared to consider what could be done about the activities in Britain of this organisation, with which he wished to emphasise that the British Government had no connections whatever. Its activities were to be deplored. He had urged on Mr. Brezhnev and Mr. Kosygin that this whole matter should be thoroughly reviewed by the Soviet Government and he now wished to make the same formal request to Mr. Podgorny. He hoped it would be very carefully considered and the right action taken. The British people could not understand the way Brooke had been treated; indeed he himself had on that very day been attacked in the British press for not being more vigorous about the case. He could not imagine what the press thought he himself should do, unless they expected him to send a detachment of Marines to break open the prison. He thought this would not be very productive. *Mr. Gromyko* interjected to say he doubted whether under the circumstances they would get their visa. *The Prime Minister* said that in addition the prison was in a very cold part of the Soviet Union. He did however wish to make a strong appeal to Mr. Podgorny as Head of State particularly from the point of view of the damaging effect of the case on Anglo/Soviet relations. He asked Mr. Podgorny to consider also the effect that clemency might have in terms of humiliating and putting in the proper setting the activities of this organisation.

Apart from the Brooke case the Prime Minister said that he thought Mr. Gromyko would agree that the hopes expressed the previous year for improvement on the whole bilateral front were being steadily realised. In this connection, he wished to pay tribute to the contribution made by the two Ambassadors, Mr. Smirnovsky and Sir Geoffrey Harrison.

Mr. Podgorny said that before returning to this particular question he wished to say a few words on the other matters raised by the Prime Minister. On Vietnam, he thought that the British Government and people and the Soviet Government and people agreed in their sincere desire for an end to the aggression in Vietnam. On this point the positions of the two Governments were close: the differences arose over the method of solving the problem. He did not wish to dwell at length on the historical aspects of the question. There had been many arguments and statements both by President Johnson and from the Government of North Vietnam, from which the respective positions of both sides were clear. The Government of North Vietnam had stated clearly and unequivocally that as soon as bombing was stopped they would open negotiations. But the US administration, notably President Johnson and Secretary of State Rusk, had made it clear that the US was set on military

---

[9] Cf. No. 1, note 6.

victory in Vietnam, although the whole world knew that this was impossible. There was a steady crescendo of protest against US policy and escalation of the war from world opinion generally as well as within the US and it was no secret that there was loud protest in Britain too. The Prime Minister was shortly to visit the US.[10] If the British Government dissociated themselves clearly and unambiguously from the American policy of aggression, they could exert great influence on President Johnson. Mr. Podgorny said he wished to speak frankly. Britain alone of all the allies of the US really supported the US position. If the British Government withdrew their support from the US this would have a powerful influence not only on the US Government but on world opinion as a whole.

Turning to the Middle East, President Podgorny said that the Soviet Government had supported the British resolution in the Security Council. They considered this an important step forward towards a solution of the Middle East problem. At present, however, it remained simply a resolution and no steps had been taken to implement it. Israel was still occupying Arab territory. The longer this went on the more violence was likely to break out again. Israel was supported mainly by the US, but also to a certain extent by other Western powers. Since the resolution had been sponsored by Britain, the Soviet Government felt that Britain could show far greater firmness in influencing the Government of the US on this question. On European security, Mr. Podgorny agreed there were deep differences of opinion between the two Governments; but it was useful that they had achieved better understanding of each other's point of view. As regards the proposed European Conference, he had discussed this with the Italian Government during his visit to Italy. They had said that they were willing to consult other Governments about the possibility of calling a Conference. The Soviet Government agreed with this position, which had also been so stated in the *communiqué* issued after Mr. Kosygin's visit to London in 1967. Mr. Podgorny said that he had also discussed this with Mr. Brown[11] who had agreed that such a Conference could be important. Unfortunately the suggested consultations had not yet taken place. He was therefore glad to note what Mr. Wilson had just said. This was an urgent problem and should not be pigeon holed.

Mr. Podgorny then said that he had been disturbed by what the Prime Minister had said about the Non-Proliferation Treaty. It was understandable that France was not prepared to sign the Treaty since she was a nuclear power. But it would be deplorable if Dr. Kiesinger was not prepared to sign the Treaty in the form submitted to the Committee of Eighteen in Geneva. Britain and the other allies of West Germany should do everything in their power to ensure that the Federal Republic of Germany signed the Treaty. Otherwise the spirit and purpose of the Treaty would be lost.

[10] Cf. p. 1. Mr. Wilson flew to Washington on 7 February. His talks with President Johnson on 8-9 February were concerned principally with Vietnam: see pp. 31-3 below.

[11] Mr. Brown visited the Soviet Union from 23-26 May 1967.

Mr. Gromyko interjected that in those circumstances there would be no Treaty. *Mr. Podgorny* then turned to the Brooke case. This was a long standing question and there had been much argument about Brooke's innocence or guilt. He was glad to note that the Prime Minister no longer disputed his guilt or considered that the Soviet Government had taken an arbitrary decision. He knew that British public opinion was concerned about this matter but he believed it to be misinformed about the full facts of the case or of Brooke's criminal prosecution. Many still held that he was innocent. The two sides had now, however, agreed that this was not so. The Soviet Government for its part had several times made suggestions which, if only the British Government would accept them would lead to Brooke's release. Much of the agitation and pressure in Britain was in the Soviet view tantamount to an ultimatum; it was said for instance that if Brooke were not released, the British Government would not ratify such and such a Treaty. This had greatly surprised the Soviet Government. If this whole case had been discussed in a calmer and quieter atmosphere without any such pressures, the two sides would he thought have been able to agree quite quickly on a solution and to find some common language. He had read many accounts in Tass of statements by leading British figures and articles in the British press which gave the impression that the purpose of the Prime Minister's visit was not to improve bilateral relations or to discuss questions of international importance or of mutual interest, but solely to bring about the release of Brooke. He appealed to Mr. Wilson to discuss the Brooke question in a quieter atmosphere; if there was a mutual desire to find a solution, a solution could be found.

The Prime Minister said he would like to comment briefly on the issues raised by the President. On Vietnam the British Government had made it clear on many occasions that they considered a military solution to be impossible; there had to be a political solution through talks. But as long as fighting continued, both sides would continue to seek to improve their military position. This underlined the urgent need to get talks started.

Mr. Podgorny said that the Government of North Vietnam had made it quite plain that they were prepared for talks if the bombing were only stopped. *The Prime Minister* replied that the task of the Soviet Union and Britain must be to work on the basis of the statements by Mr. Trinh and by President Johnson at San Antonio and to do what they could respectively to get each of the two sides to understand the full importance of the statements made by the other. The Prime Minister said that he had already expressed the view the previous day that the gap between the two sides was narrower and the bridge needed was now shorter; but a bridge was nevertheless needed. However, he disagreed with Mr. Podgorny's view that the British Government should dissociate from the United States for two reasons. First, the British Government believed that the San Antonio speech, if properly understood, could provide a road to peace in conjunction with Mr. Trinh's statement. He did not therefore propose to dissociate either from Mr. Trinh or from the San Antonio speech. What was essential was to put the two together and get talks started. Secondly, dissociation would in any case make the achievement of peace more difficult. Someone who dissociated himself from what one of his friends was doing did not usually thereby gain greater influence over his friend. More could be achieved by quiet discussions of the kind which had been held in Moscow on his visit than by futile and contra-productive gestures.

On the Middle East, the Prime Minister said that Mr. Podgorny had referred to withdrawal by Israel. This was of course an essential part of the Security Council Resolution to which Mr. Podgorny had referred in such friendly terms. As he himself had said the previous day, the Warsaw declaration in the preparation of which Mr. Gromyko had participated, was fully in accordance with the spirit of the Security Council Resolution. He himself had spoken in the same spirit to the Prime Minister of Israel when Mr. Eshkol was in London the previous week. What was now needed was that all possible support should be given to Mr. Jarring to carry out his mission under the Security Council's Resolution.

On European Security the Prime Minister said that the British Govern-ment agreed with the Soviet Government that a Conference properly prepared and at the right time could be useful. This meant a Conference designed to solve the basic problems and not used simply as a propaganda sounding board and for mutual recrimination and denunciation. He would give careful consideration to what Mr. Brezhnev had said the previous day.

On Non-Proliferation, the Prime Minister said that he wished to make it clear that what he had said about Dr. Kiesinger's position was based entirely on a press report which he had heard over the radio. He personally hoped that the report was incorrect. *Mr. Podgorny* agreed. *The Prime Minister* said that even if it were correct, he hoped that it was not the final position of the West German Government, because he agreed with Mr. Podgorny about the very serious consequences for the Treaty and other related matters if the German Government felt unable to sign it.

The Prime Minister said he wished in conclusion to make a brief further comment on the Brooke case. He had not in any way questioned that Brooke was found guilty by a Soviet court in accordance with Soviet laws, nor suggested that anything arbitrary had been done. But he did not regard Brooke as a serious spy. Brooke had been used—and both sides knew this—by an unscrupulous organisation which lived in a dream world of its own far removed from present politics. Its activities were to be deplored. But his plea to Mr. Podgorny was to take the question of British public opinion seriously.

There were some people who were admittedly more interested in whipping up feeling against the Soviet Union and others who regarded the Brooke case more as a good stick with which to beat the Prime Minister. But Mr. Podgorny should not underrate the strong feeling of many people in Britain whose opinions on other matters Mr. Podgorny would respect. Many Members of the Parliamentary Labour Party had spoken privately to him and bitterly in public about this case. Many of these would share the Soviet view on such matters as Vietnam and Germany, but they were deeply disillusioned by the Soviet attitude on Brooke. He hoped he might be allowed to say that the whole episode gave a false impression of the Soviet Union and the Russians. They both knew that the Soviet Union was strong and self-assured, but, on the Brooke case, the Soviet Union gave an impression of nervousness and uncertainty. Many people in Britain felt that, if the whole weight and power of the Soviet Union had to be used against a foolish young man whose vanity had led to his being used by unscrupulous people, this reflected on the Soviet Government. Brooke had been found guilty and punished. Mr. Podgorny was right in saying that the Brooke case was being presented by some as the sole reason for his visit to Moscow. In fact, he deplored every minute that had to be devoted to this subject and thereby denied to serious discussion of other deeper problems. In conclusion, he urged Mr. Podgorny to consider the matter carefully and, in the meantime to give satisfaction to the British Embassy on the subject of consular access.

Mr. Podgorny said that he would like to say a few words about public opinion generally. There had recently been a case of four young people which had been presented by the press in Britain, Italy and elsewhere as directed against men of letters who represented a group in opposition to the State.[12] He personally had received many petitions protesting against the trial and claiming that the accused were not guilty. But the court had found them guilty, not for their writings but for a normal criminal offence. If one believed and paid attention to what the press wrote, one could get the impression that the laws of the Soviet Union were wrong.

Mr. Podgorny said in conclusion that he had been very glad to meet the Prime Minister and to have such a detailed and useful discussion. He hoped Mr. Wilson would be satisfied with his visit to the Soviet Union and his discussions which had contributed to the improvement of trade relations and scientific/technological co-operation. The talks had clarified the points of view of both sides on a number of problems and had been useful and interesting. Finally, he asked Mr. Wilson to give his best wishes to HM The Queen and to wish her happiness, health and success, and he asked Mr. Wilson to convey the same good wishes to the British people. *The Prime Minister* thanked Mr. Podgorny and said he would certainly pass on his good wishes.

The Meeting ended at 11.35 a.m.[13]

---

[12] See No. 1, note 7.

[13] Mr. Wilson left Moscow on the evening of 24 January: the *communiqué* on his visit was printed in *The Times*, 25 January 1968, p. 3. Reporting to the Cabinet on 25 January, the Prime Minister said that his 'discussions with the Soviet leaders had been conducted in an atmosphere which for the most part had been friendly and co-operative; but the Soviet attitude had considerably hardened when it came to the point of agreeing a form of words on Vietnam for the purposes of the *communiqué* . . . they had maintained their intransigent attitude towards the United States Government and had tried very hard to persuade us to incorporate in the final *communiqué* a form of words which would have clearly implied that the United States should cease bombing North Vietnam but should thereafter be excluded from any part in the settlement of the dispute. We had succeeded in resisting Soviet pressure on this point; and we had also persuaded the Soviet representatives that the *communiqué* should incorporate a reference to the responsibility which the Soviet and United Kingdom Governments shared in the context of Vietnam in their capacities as co-chairmen of the Geneva Conferences of 1954 and 1962. To this

extent our representations must be deemed to have made an impression on the Soviet Government, however careful they might be to conceal this fact.'

With regard to bilateral relations, discussions had generally been 'more relaxed and constructive', with the Soviet leaders showing 'genuine interest in the expansion of trade and technological collaboration between the two countries . . . The one exception to the generally satisfactory outcome of these discussions on bilateral topics had been the case of Mr. Gerald Brooke.'

While the atmosphere of the Prime Minister's discussions in Moscow may have been 'relaxed and constructive', neither Ministers nor officials found it easy to identify any tangible achievement from the visit in terms of bilateral relations. Foreign Office views on its usefulness were summarised in Guidance telegram No. 31 of 26 January, which informed overseas Posts that the visit had been 'short and intensive. Vietnam took up much of the time but the other main international questions were discussed in some detail and there was a useful if necessarily fairly brief review of bilateral questions. The meetings with the three top Russians all provided for substantial discussion and the visit was very useful in thus providing an up to date picture of the views of the leadership.'

The next group of documents is concerned with matters discussed during Mr. Wilson's visit: both on a technical level—the draft Treaty of Friendship, and some unwelcome repercussions of the Anglo-Soviet Technological Agreement—and in the realms of policy formulation. The Secretary of State for Foreign Affairs was not alone in questioning the direction and consistency of British policy towards the Soviet Union, and his desire to air the important issues involved set in train an analytical consideration of future policy which continued throughout 1968. All three documents show how consideration of Anglo-Soviet bilateral relations was inextricably bound up with the wider issues of policy towards Eastern Europe, the future of Germany, the Anglo-American relationship and the role of the US in Europe.

No. 4

Letter from Mr. Day to Mr. Palliser (10 Downing Street)

[NS 3/19]

Confidential   FOREIGN OFFICE, *1 February 1968*

We need to decide what to say to the Russians about the draft which they handed over during the Prime Minister's visit, in response to the ideas which we gave to them last April about a Treaty of Friendship.[1]

The Soviet draft is clearly quite unacceptable. The *Communiqué* of 13 February last year set the proposal in the context of progress, and the prospect of further progress, in bilateral fields. In the House on that day the Prime Minister said that it was to provide a framework for the further development of our bilateral relations.[2] It has always been our position that it must refer to bilateral matters and relationships. We have made this clear to our NATO allies, and it was also, of course, this view which determined the lines of the draft which we gave to the Russians last April.

The Soviet draft does not even pretend to be a Treaty of Friendship. It is entitled 'Treaty on co-operation in European security questions and on foreign policy consultations'. The only article concerned with bilateral relations is article 4. The preamble and the first three articles are standard Communist lines about averting a new war in Europe, recognising the border between East Germany and the Federal Republic (which amounts to recognising the German Democratic Republic as a State); and they are generally informed by anti-German, anti-American and anti-NATO sentiments.

We have long suspected that Mr. Kosygin's idea of a Treaty of Friendship did not meet with the approval of his colleagues in Moscow and the Soviet draft is, in our view, a very strong indication that the Russians wish to kill off the idea altogether by presenting us with something which they know we will not accept. They would thus hope to put on us the onus of abandoning the project.

There is no reason why we should play the Russians' game for them. It is the Foreign Secretary's view that we should tell them that we regard their draft as completely out of line with what we agreed last February; that it is so far out of line that it cannot form a reasonable basis for discussion; but that we hope they will take another look at the draft we gave them nearly a year ago which is consistent with the February undertaking and which does offer a basis for discussion.

[1] See No. 2, note 11. Opening and concluding salutations were omitted from the filed copy of this letter.

[2] *Parl. Debs.*, 5th ser., *H. of C.*, vol. 741, col. 111.

It is also Mr. Brown's view that we should take this action as soon as possible.[3] While we think the Russians must reckon that we are not going to accept their draft, they would not be at all averse to using it as part of their policy of wedge-driving. They might bring it forward in the quite separate context of the bilateral discussions about preparing for a European Security Conference which the Prime Minister and Mr. Kosygin have agreed should take place.[4] They might also, if we delayed our reply, leak the draft in Western Europe and, despite what we have said to our allies in NATO already, try to create embarrassment for us not only with the Germans but also with the Italians and others who have been nervous from the outset that a Treaty of Friendship might contain elements damaging to the alliance and embarrassing to them in dealing with their own internal opinion.[5] It is therefore important, both from the point of view of our dealings with the Russians and from the point of view of our dealings with our allies that we should take action with the Russians very soon.

[3] Mr. Day's letter was based on a submission of 26 January from Mr. Smith to Mr. Hayman, Assistant Under-Secretary of State, approved by the latter and by Viscount Hood, Deputy Under-Secretary of State. Mr. Smith had recommended that 'we should tell the Russians very soon that we regard their Treaty as having nothing to do with the agreement reached last February'. In an undated minute on the submission Mr. Brown commented: 'I agree: but I haven't seen the Moscow records yet. I don't know quite what the P.M. and Mr. K[osygin] agreed about Bilateral talks on European Security. It'll be interesting to see those & also No. 10's comment on the proposed reply. G.A. Brown'. A letter from Mr. Palliser to Mr. Day of 5 February stated that the Prime Minister agreed with Mr. Brown's view 'as recorded in your letter and particularly with the course of action proposed in the fifth paragraph'.

[4] At their meeting at 4.45 p.m. on 23 January the Prime Minister and Mr. Kosygin had agreed that officials should continue consultations about the form such a conference might take: cf. No. 3, note 4.

[5] In a minute to Mr. Hayman of 25 January on the subject of what to say to NATO colleagues, Mr. Smith expressed the view that 'it would be wrong to be evasive about the Soviet draft', and recommended that Sir B. Burrows, UK Representative on the North Atlantic Council, be instructed to tell the Council that the Russians had produced a draft which was, as Mr. Smith said in his submission of 26 January (see note 3), 'clearly unacceptable because it goes beyond our bilateral relations and, in its references to European Security follows familiar Communist lines'. He should, however, refrain from further comment on the grounds that the draft was still under study.

These instructions were sent to Sir B. Burrows in telegram No. 326 of 7 February, adding that once Sir G. Harrison had carried out his instructions (see note 7 below) to tell the Soviet Foreign Ministry that their draft was 'completely out of line' and to express the hope that they would take another look at the British draft of April 1967, Sir B. Burrows should inform the NATO Council and circulate the Soviet draft. The draft was discussed by the Political Committee of NATO on 12 March, and circulated in April, annexed to a report by the Acting Chairman of the Political Committee of NATO on the implications of the Soviet draft treaty.

The draft was handed to us on the Foreign Ministry net, from Mr. Gromyko to Denis Greenhill.[6] The Foreign Secretary suggests that the reply on the lines outlined above should go from Geoffrey Harrison to Gromyko.[7]

D.M. DAY

[6] Sir D. Greenhill was a Deputy Under Secretary of State in the Foreign Office.

[7] Mr. Hayman sent a copy of Mr. Day's letter to Sir G. Harrison on 6 February and instructed him to speak to Mr. Gromyko on the lines of para. 5 above. The Ambassador reported his interview on 9 February the following day in Moscow telegram No. 310: Mr. Gromyko took the line that since the idea of a treaty had only been discussed briefly during Mr. Kosygin's visit to London, the Soviet Government 'had been at liberty to work out their position and develop their views'; however, 'under pressure he admitted that the emphasis of the treaty had changed from friendship and cooperation between our two countries to the broader area of European security'. He maintained that 'the present international situation especially in Europe, did not justify a bilateral agreement of friendship' and 'insisted that it would be possible for the British Government to accept the Soviet draft without damaging their relations with any other power and without formally breaking their obligations to NATO'. Mr. Gromyko said the British draft was 'not a true treaty of friendship. One could have close cultural relations and bad political relations at the same time. One would not wish to sign a bad treaty' (MAS 3/6).

Mr. Smith commented to Mr. Hayman on 14 February that clearly the Russians 'have no intention of signing a Treaty limited to bilateral relations', and recommended that it should be made clear in public 'that the Russians are going too far in their assumptions about what may be said to us . . . It has emerged from the Soviet propaganda before and during the Prime Minister's visit, from some remarks made by the Soviet leadership to the Prime Minister, and from these latest remarks by Mr. Gromyko that the Russians think that this country is faced with such difficulties and is, perhaps, in such a mood, that Soviet pressure may be brought effectively to bear on us. The tone in which they are addressing us nowadays is reminiscent of the tone they have sometimes adopted to small Western countries, e.g. Norway.'

Mr. Day informed Mr. Palliser on 1 March that Mr. Brown considered that there would be advantage in arranging for an inspired parliamentary question 'very soon . . . for the sake of our relations with our friends in Western Europe'. In a written answer to a Parliamentary Question Mr. Brown said on 14 March that the Soviet Government had been told that their draft was unacceptable, and that it did not provide a framework for bilateral relations but was mainly concerned with other matters which 'affect directly the interests of our allies and our obligations to them' (*Parl. Debs., 5th ser., H. of C.,* vol. 760, col. 352).

No. 5

Letter from Mr. Hayman to Sir G. Harrison (Moscow)

[*NS 3/18*]

Secret   FOREIGN OFFICE, *27 February 1968*

Anglo-Soviet Relations[1]

As foreshadowed in my letter of 20 February, we had a talk with the Secretary of State on 23 February about the future of Anglo-Soviet

[1] Opening and concluding salutations were omitted from the filed copy of this letter.

relations.[2] Mr. Roberts, Minister of State, Denis Greenhill, John Peck[3] and Howard Smith were also there. It was a most useful and stimulating discussion.

2. The Secretary of State had called the meeting because he thought there was some inconsistency between the Department's wish to bring home to Parliament and to the general public the iniquities of the KGB (and he particularly mentioned our wish to give publicity to the Drozdov case)[4] and our desire to improve relations with the Russians in many different bilateral fields. He referred to such matters as Ministerial visits, trade relations, the Anglo-Soviet Consultative Committee,[5] etc.

3. During our discussions we said that there seemed to us to be no real inconsistency. We emphasized that we wanted to improve relations with the Soviet Union not only on a bilateral basis, but from the general point of view of East/West relations. In our general policy towards the Soviet Union, however, we must be completely realistic—as realistic in fact as the Russians were themselves. He fully accepted our main thesis that Soviet foreign policy was dictated by her own national interests. A corollary of this policy was a desire to break up all alliances such as NATO which stood in the way of these objectives. In pursuit of this aim the Russians would continue to try and drive wedges between us and our NATO allies.

4. The Secretary of State readily agreed that we should firmly resist these manoeuvres as typified, for example, by their general tactics during the Prime

[2] Mr. Hayman's letter of 20 February is not printed. In a minute of 12 February to the Permanent Under Secretary, Sir Paul Gore-Booth, Mr. Maitland, Private Secretary to the Secretary of State, reported a conversation with Mr. Brown concerning what the latter considered an 'inherent contradiction' in the FO's approach to the Anglo-Soviet relationship. Mr. Brown accepted that the contradiction was 'probably more apparent than real', but was willing to hold an Office meeting 'to discuss this whole problem'. Sir P. Gore-Booth minuted on 13 February that he welcomed this suggestion 'especially as I do not think the conflict is basic'.

[3] Assistant Under-Secretary of State in the Foreign Office.

[4] Mr. V.A. Drozdov, who came to the UK in 1965 as Third Secretary in the Scientific Technical Department in the Soviet Embassy, had been caught in 1968 in the act of collecting sensitive material from a 'dead letter box' and was immediately withdrawn from London at the request of the Foreign Office.

[5] This Committee arose out of a British proposal which the Russians accepted during Mr. Kosygin's visit in February 1967, and was formally set up by an exchange of notes in Moscow on 22 January 1968. Its terms of reference, agreed with the Russians in October 1967, stated that it would 'study opportunities for developing contacts in the spheres of science, industrial development, health, culture, education, art, sport and tourism', but it would not be empowered to control the implementation of existing Anglo-Soviet agreements nor to commit either Government, financially or otherwise. Lord Trevelyan (HM Ambassador to the Soviet Union 1962-65) had been invited to be Chairman of the British Group, whose ten members included the composer Mr. Benjamin Britten, Dr. Alan Bullock (Master of St. Catherine's College, Oxford), Lord Goodman (Chairman of the Arts Council) and Sir Eric Roll (formerly PUS at the Department of Economic Affairs). In January 1968 Dr. Bullock and Lord Goodman threatened to resign from the British Group in protest at the recent writers' trial in Moscow (see No. 1, note 7), but subsequently agreed to carry on. The first meeting of the Committee was planned to take place in the United Kingdom in April 1968.

Minister's visit and by the carefully designed re-draft of the Treaty of Friendship.[6] He also agreed that we should not be over-enthusiastic in running after the Russians; where they considered that it was in their interests to be in touch or make agreements with us they would certainly do so. He thought that if we took the same tough and realistic line with the Russians we should probably be more rather than less able to improve relations with them in the long term.

5. The Secretary of State agreed that in bilateral relations we should be equally firm and realistic. In those fields of trade and technology where it was in our general interest to go on improving relations with the Soviet Union we should continue to do so, and we should encourage the exchange of visits. But as a matter of tactics we should discourage visits, including Ministerial visits, which really did not bring us in any useful dividends.[7] There were certainly one or two visits last year which fell into this latter category.

6. Meanwhile we must continue to take a very firm line in combatting the activities of the KGB in this country. We must also take full propaganda advantage of the embarrassment caused to the Russians by the writers' trials and other incidents in the field in which they were most vulnerable, i.e., their repressive activities at home. This would have the incidental effect of keeping people in this country better informed about the real nature of Soviet policies.

7. I hope that you agree with these various propositions. We are to prepare a paper (for discussion in the Foreign Office and for submission to the Secretary of State) in which these theses will be developed.[8] At a later stage the paper could form the basis of a speech which the Secretary of State might deliver at Chatham House or in some similar forum later in the year, though of course there would be many things in the paper which would not find their place in a speech. There is no thought of a speech which would appear to be an attack on the Soviet Union or a signal that HMG's policies were going into reverse. The purpose of the speech would be to try to show

---

[6] See No. 4.

[7] Summarising the conclusions of the meeting in a minute of 23 February to Northern Department, Mr. Maitland expressed Mr. Brown's view more succinctly: 'The time had come for Ministers who did not have specific business to do with the Russians to lay off visiting the Soviet Union.' Mr. Maitland also reported the following conclusion not reflected in the letter to Sir G. Harrison: 'We might, as a counterpart to reducing the level of our contacts with the Soviet Union, pay more attention to East European countries. There was evidence in these countries of a desire to break free. Moreover the Soviet Union's relationship with these countries was not too easy and the Russians clearly had to consider their own position carefully. In the longer term developing our relations with the smaller countries of Eastern Europe might facilitate a solution of the German problem.'

[8] This paper on Anglo-Soviet relations, the first draft of which was submitted to Sir D. Greenhill on 5 March, went through a number of revisions and is printed in its final form as No. 11 below. In April Mr. Michael Stewart, who had succeeded Mr. Brown as Secretary of State for Foreign Affairs, asked that the paper be enlarged to cover relations with Eastern Europe.

the public here where our own interests lie. I will, of course, keep you fully informed as to how this all develops.[9]

[9] Replying to this letter on 6 March, Sir G. Harrison expressed general agreement but made the following comments: '3. If we divide our relations into ideological, political and bilateral, we find, I think, different degrees of "co-existence" in these various fields. In the ideological field there is no "peaceful co-existence", as Mr. Kosygin made clear in his recent speech at Minsk . . . On the contrary, the struggle in this field is active and continuing. Moreover, the Russians have recently been leaving the world (or, at any rate, those who study *Pravda* and *Izvestiya*) in no doubt that they continue to see relations between the "socialist" and the "capitalist" systems very much through ideological spectacles.

'4. In the political field, the need for restraint in the struggle is recognised and the Soviet leaders are careful not to get themselves into situations where an open conflict could be damaging to the basic interests of the Soviet Union. In this field there is, therefore, some actual practice of co-existence. At the same time, however, the Russians make no secret of where they see the lines drawn and of the difference in treatment to be given to those on the right, or on the wrong, side of the fence . . .

'5. In bilateral relations co-existence becomes positive, with exchanges in many fields and in many practical ways. The over-riding condition, however, is that these shall be of benefit to the Soviet Union, not that they should lead to international understanding for its own sake . . .

'6. In these three fields, I would wholeheartedly agree with you that we should be tough and realistic, standing up for our national interests and exacting a fair return in all our exchanges. We shall not retain the respect of the Russians by doing less. But your paragraph 6 leaves me unsatisfied . . . the second part . . . seems to me to be a *non-sequitur*. Attacking KGB influence and repressive activities within the Soviet Union raises quite different issues and could well have a prejudicial effect on Anglo-Soviet relations both in bilateral and political fields. I am not saying that it is wrong to embarrass the Russians in this way and I accept that it may have the "incidental" effect of educating people at home. But you beg the major question of what the object of the exercise is. I like to believe that we have long outgrown our role as world governess. Is it then retaliation for hurtful attacks by Russian propaganda on our own policies? Or is it part of the battle for the minds of the neutral, uncommitted peoples of the world? In other words, is this a continuation of the "cold war"? . . . I am simply supporting the Foreign Secretary's view that there could be a certain inconsistency here with the pursuit of better relations and that we should therefore be clear what our objective is and that it is a worth while one.'

No. 6

Letter from Sir P. Dean[1] (Washington) to Sir D. Greenhill

[NS 3/18]

Secret and Personal   WASHINGTON, *2 March 1968*

Dear Denis,

American Suspicions about UK/Soviet Relations

I am becoming disturbed by a number of quite separate recent indications of some uneasiness on the part of Americans about where British foreign policy may be going in terms of relations between the United Kingdom and the USSR.

[1] HM Ambassador in Washington.

In the more general sense, this question was raised with me a couple of nights ago at a dinner party I gave for a number of Congressmen who had been at Ditchley.[2] I learned from Paul Gore-Booth that while at Ditchley they had expressed themselves in rather strong terms about our defence cuts, and my main object was to pursue discussion of this with them. They took pretty much the same line at my party, but one of them, Congressman Springer (Republican, Illinois) went rather further. I was particularly impressed because he is a very responsible and sensible man who has been in the Congress since 1950, is a member of the House Republican Policy Committee and Vice Chairman of the Republican Congressional Campaign Committee. He went on from expressing unease about our retraction of overseas commitments to ask whether there was any danger of British policy moving yet further in the direction of neutralism and a separate deal with the Russians. The implication was that the deal would be a bilateral one behind the backs of and at the expense of our allies. I of course did my best to reassure him.

In view of the source, I would in any case have reported the foregoing. By a coincidence, however, at exactly the same time we learned through the British Defence Staffs that searching questions were being asked about the nature and implications of the UK/USSR Technological Agreement.[3] The British representative at Fort Belvoir who deals with cooperative research and development under the ABCA Agreement[4] was asked by an American opposite number how far cooperation was to be pursued under the agreement and whether it might not have undesirable implications for continuing cooperation between Britain and the United States or under ABCA in the military field. The unease lying behind the question was clear, and was underlined in a very similar manner by questions of a very like nature put to a member of the Defence Research and Development Staff by a Pentagon contact.

We are of course briefing both officers to give reassuring replies, drawing on the brief on the agreement prepared for the Prime Minister's visit to Washington.[5] I am not at all sure however how successful they will be in dispelling American worries which probably stem in large part from a feeling that, in dealing with the Soviet Union, it is surely impossible to separate military from civil questions. They are probably struck by this particularly insofar as cooperation may extend into the fields of aviation and atomic energy.[6]

[2] The reference is to Ditchley Park, near Oxford, which since 1962 has hosted regular conferences organised by the Ditchley Foundation to study matters of common interest to the people of Britain and the US.

[3] See No. 2, note 5.

[4] The reference is to an agreement signed by the US, UK, Canada and Australia to further the standardisation of doctrine and equipment in the armed forces.

[5] Cf. No. 3, note 10.

[6] In the brief, 'Concern in the United States about the Anglo-Soviet Technological Agreement', which was sent to Sir P. Dean on 15 May (see note 8 below) US fears regarding

I do not wish to make too much of this at the present stage, but Springer's attitude does worry me a good deal. It could conceivably reflect Administration feelings, hitherto unspoken, and implies a serious worry across the board about our future role as an ally; so I thought it right to warn you of this. I should be very interested in any similar indications you may receive from American visitors in London and so on and I for my part will keep a close eye on further developments and report them. Meanwhile, the two 'technical' enquiries have been reported to London by Littler, the Head of the DRDS who has asked for the full text of the Technological Agreement and any additional guidance it may be possible to give. (I enclose a copy of his telegram).[7]

If you have any comments or guidance to give me I should needless to say be grateful, but you will wish in any case to do what you judge necessary to bring home to those concerned with the further development of practical UK/Soviet cooperation that there does seem to be a real danger of exciting American suspicions with the possible consequence of practical effects on our cooperative arrangements with the Americans in fields where they would see a security angle.

Yours ever,
PAT DEAN[8]

Anglo-Soviet cooperation on aviation and atomic energy were described as 'very wide of the mark'. It was pointed out that the United Kingdom Atomic Energy Authority (UKAEA) had concluded a 5-year agreement with the Soviet State Committee for the Utilisation of Atomic Energy, providing for exchange of information and delegations, as early as May 1961 (renewed in 1966; see *The Times*, 20 May 1966, p. 16), and its implementation had led to no difficulties in Anglo-US collaboration. As far as aviation technology was concerned, when Mr. J. Stonehouse, Minister of State at the Ministry of Technology (Mintech) had visited the Soviet Union in 1967 with representatives of the British aircraft industry, great care had been taken 'to define areas of possible collaboration which could be looked into without this leading to any difficulties in connection with research and development activities on the defence side'.

[7] Not printed.

[8] Sir D. Greenhill replied on 19 March that there was 'no ground for any American fears that the Agreement will lead us to do things which violate COCOM (see No. 2, note 9) or affect adversely in any other way the military or security interests of the alliance' but Sir P. Dean wrote on 28 March that the 'reverberations of the Agreement have continued to grow . . . The Pentagon are worried that we have walked into a quicksand and that, protest as we may, we shall end up by disclosing to the Russians, if not more than incidentally or inadvertently, technical information which the Americans would regard as classified and which is dangerous to Western security. With this goes the clear implication that they will have to be doubly careful what they reveal to us in the future'. He noted that it was the Pentagon, not the State Department, who were worried about the Agreement, but that it was the former, together with the US Atomic Energy Commission, 'from whose attitude we stand to gain or lose the most. We are very far from operating in a buyer's market where technical exchanges are concerned.'

Sir P. Dean suggested that the Secretary of State for Defence, Mr. Denis Healey, should write to Mr. Clark Clifford, US Defence Secretary, but following discussions with Mintech it was decided to prepare a short joint brief for Sir P. Dean, reiterating that the Agreement in no way affected UK security arrangements or obligations under COCOM. Forwarding this on 15 May, Sir D. Greenhill explained to Sir P. Dean that an approach from the Secretary of State for

Defence 'might give the appearance of protesting too much . . . we are inclined to think that this is a question for the patient refutation of each expression of concern as it arises'. He added that the majority of exchanges under the Agreement would be carried out by commercial firms, who 'will be no more inclined to give away information of commercial value to the Russians than to any other foreign industrialist'.

Sir D. Greenhill also commented that 'if the Vietnam war were to come to an end, or even perhaps if it were reduced significantly in scale, pressure might soon develop for greater activity by the large American corporations in what must be regarded as the world's largest untapped market . . . we should beware of the possibility that attempts may be made to extract information from us about the progress of our technological exchanges with the Russians in order to provide our firms' eventual American competitors with useful commercial intelligence'.

In a letter to Sir D. Greenhill of 15 June Mr. E.E. Tomkins, HM Minister at Washington, noted that the policy of 'patient refutation' had not been entirely successful in allaying American suspicions, but expressed doubts whether it would 'be possible to do much about the mentality of those Americans, particularly in the Services, who are doctrinally biased about any "dealings with the Commies". But I think we can be reasonably confident that this will not be allowed to affect the basic criteria governing the exchange of classified military information. The main tests applied will continue to be the need to know and reciprocity . . . I think that our position is still as good as we can hope bearing in mind that we are dealing more and more with a new generation of Americans to whom the precedent of wartime cooperation means less and less.'

The next group of documents concerns the series of high-level bilateral contacts which took place between February and May 1968 between the British and Soviet Governments about the war in Vietnam. When Harold Wilson visited Washington on 7-8 February he had no positive message for President Johnson as a result of his discussions on Vietnam with the Soviet leaders in January, although he assured the President that the terms of the San Antonio offer (see p. 4) were fully understood in Moscow. Despite the apparent intransigence of the Soviet Government, President Johnson, anxious to break a logjam in peace negotiations, alarmed by the escalation in hostilities heralded by the attack on Saigon and other cities in South Vietnam by Viet Cong forces on 30 January (the 'Tet Offensive'), and distracted by a worsening US balance of payments crisis, still sought to engage the offices of the two governments in their role as co-chairmen of the Geneva Conference.

The President asked Mr. Wilson to pass on to the Soviet leaders a detailed account of the discussions in Washington, emphasising that the Americans were determined to fight on till the 'bitter end' in Vietnam unless talks could begin leading to a political settlement. The Prime Minister conveyed this message to Mr. Kosygin on 15 February, emphasising the urgency of continuing the dialogue 'at the top level' between Moscow and London. Mr. Kosygin's reply, delivered to the Prime Minister by the Soviet Ambassador on 1 March, was unhelpful in regard to his acting as an intermediary with Hanoi, but Mr. Smirnovsky added an oral message that the Soviet Government had 'noted what the Prime Minister had said about the need for continuing the dialogue between himself and the Soviet leaders' and 'would keep in mind the possibility of a meeting between the two Prime Ministers at the appropriate time and place'.

31

A wide-ranging review of US policy and commitment in Vietnam, conducted at the President's behest during February and March, had reached the conclusion, as stated in one draft, that current US strategy could 'promise no early end to the conflict, nor any success in attriting the enemy or eroding Hanoi's will to fight. Moreover, it would entail substantial costs in South Viet Nam, in the United States, and in the rest of the world.'[1] The military and civilian authorities were divided as to the best strategy to pursue in this situation, the former favouring an increase in US troop commitments and standing firm on the San Antonio offer, the latter advocating further consideration of alternative negotiating strategies and diplomatic initiatives. Decisions on future policy were made more critical by a gold crisis in mid-March: despite US attempts to maintain the gold value of the dollar, a combination of the effects of the devaluation of sterling in November 1967, the aftermath of the Middle East war and a growing US balance of payments deficit exacerbated by the costs of the Vietnam war led to a run on the gold pool in London and to the closure of the London financial markets on 15 March; a decision taken by the Prime Minister, at President Johnson's request, which led to the resignation of the Secretary of State for Foreign Affairs, Mr. Brown, who was succeeded by Mr. Michael Stewart.[2]

On 30 March President Johnson sent a personal message to the Prime Minister giving details of a major speech to be made the following day. He had decided to send an additional 13,500 troops to Vietnam over the summer, and to call up additional reserves amounting to 48,500 men. At the same time, he would announce that the bombing of North Vietnam would be cut back to the area roughly south of the 20th parallel, thereby excluding all the major populated areas, and that the US hoped for a positive response from Hanoi, with Governor Averill Harriman 'instantly ready' to begin discussions as the President's special representative.[3] The President asked Mr. Wilson's views on a passage in the speech which would 'call upon the United Kingdom and Soviet Union, as co-chairmen of the Geneva Conference and as permanent members of the United Nations Security Council, to exert their influence so that movement toward peace may result from this act of deescalation on our part'. The purpose of this passage was 'to put the pressure on the Soviets—where it rightly belongs in the light of their whole responsibility and particularly their major supply contribution to Hanoi's current offensive'.

Following a meeting with the Foreign Secretary at Chequers on the afternoon of 31 March, the Prime Minister sent two personal messages to President Johnson at 4.30 p.m., the first applauding the latter's 'wise and generous move', though he doubted that Hanoi would respond to it. He agreed that it was 'of great importance to try and get some movement out of the Soviet Government' and proposed 'to make a speedy move towards the Russians'. In his second message Mr. Wilson set out a programme of 'practical steps' to be taken by HMG following the President's speech, which included issuing a

---

[1] Draft of 29 February 1968 by Office of International Security Affairs in the Pentagon, *The Pentagon Papers* (Boston, 1971), vol. iv, pp. 561-68.

[2] Mr. Wilson and Mr. Brown gave their respective accounts of this episode in *The Labour Government 1964-70, op. cit.*, pp. 640-48, and *In My Way* (London, 1971), pp. 169-84.

[3] According to his memoirs Mr. Dean Rusk, US Secretary of State, had suggested the offer of a partial bombing halt to President Johnson: *As I Saw It* (London, 1991), pp. 419-23.

statement of support, sending a preliminary message to Mr. Kosygin, and an announcement by the Secretary of State in the House of Commons that he would be following up this initial contact later in the day with the Soviet Ambassador.

President Johnson's speech was broadcast to the American nation on radio and television on the evening of 31 March.[4] *In addition to the points set out in his message to Mr. Wilson, he stressed the need for the passage of a tax bill or expenditure cuts in order to alleviate the financial crisis and to finance US commitments in Vietnam; he also announced that he would not be seeking nomination for another term as President. At 7 a.m. on 1 April the following statement was issued from 10 Downing Street: 'Her Majesty's Government welcome the statement by the President of the United States about the Viet Nam war, particularly the decision of the United States Government to cut back the bombing of North Viet Nam. They believe that this should offer a further opportunity of achieving a just and honourable peace; and for their part they are examining urgently how best they can respond to President Johnson's invitation to exert their influence to end the conflict'.*

[4] *Department of State Bulletin,* 15 April 1968, pp. 481-86.

No. 7

Mr. Stewart to Sir G. Harrison (Moscow)

No. 885 Telegraphic [DV 10/204]

Immediate. Secret   FOREIGN OFFICE, *1 April 1968*

Repeated for information to Washington, Wellington (for Commonwealth Secretary only).

Vietnam

I summoned the Soviet Ambassador this afternoon, as foreshadowed by my statement in the House about Vietnam.[1]

2. As this was Mr. Smirnovsky's first call on me, I opened with some words of condolence about the death of Yuri Gagarin.[2]

3. I then communicated to Mr. Smirnovsky the texts of:

(*a*) the statement issued by HMG early this morning.
(*b*) the statement I had just made in the House of Commons.

[1] Mr. Stewart told the House on the morning of 1 April that he and his colleagues were examining urgently how they might best give effect to President Johnson's request that HMG and the Soviet Government should help towards peace in South East Asia. He referred to the *communiqué* issued at the end of Mr. Wilson's visit to Moscow (see No. 3, note 13) which expressed the firm intention of the two governments 'to take singly or jointly all actions within their power to achieve the goal of a peaceful settlement of the Vietnam conflict', and announced that he would be seeing the Soviet Ambassador later that afternoon 'to discuss what I and my fellow co-chairman, Mr. Gromyko, can do': *Parl. Debs., 5th ser., H. of C.,* vol. 762, col. 37.

[2] The Soviet cosmonaut, the first man to be propelled into orbit in 1961, was killed during a training flight on 27 March 1968.

(*c*) a copy of the message which the Prime Minister sent to Mr. Kosygin early this morning:[3] the Ambassador said he had not yet been sent the text from Moscow.

4. When I gave the Ambassador (*c*) above I drew his particular attention to the reference in it to the oral message which Mr. Smirnovsky had conveyed to the Prime Minister last month about the possibility of a personal contact.[4]

5. I then gave the Ambassador a letter for Mr. Gromyko and asked him to transmit it urgently to Moscow. The text is in m[y] i[mmediately] f[ollowing] t[elegram].[5] I added that the messages were, I hoped, self-explanatory: I would only emphasise that we considered President Johnson's announcement to be of the first importance and we were therefore examining it both urgently and carefully. We regarded it as opening an opportunity for progress which ought not to be thrown away. I accepted that the Soviet Government would want time to study the situation, and I did not wish to press Mr. Gromyko. Nevertheless I hoped that before long he would give me an idea of how he saw the situation and in particular whether he agreed that we should meet soon. I recalled that I had had a number of talks with Mr. Gromyko,[6] and though there were differences we were agreed on one point: the great danger in the situation if the Vietnam War continued. It was therefore important not to throw any opportunity away, though a good deal of careful thought would be needed on how we got from the present situation to one in which the war was brought to an end.

6. I added that I had been pressed very hard in the House of Commons this afternoon to make a further statement after meeting with the Ambassador, but I did not propose to do so. I felt that the contacts between us at such an important time should be kept strictly confidential.

7. Mr. Smirnovsky agreed on the need for secrecy. He then made a few comments on standard lines. First, the Soviet Government were not and could not be negotiators: this was for the North Vietnamese and the Liberation Front. Second, President Johnson's action did not constitute the complete or unconditional cessation of bombing on which the North Vietnamese had long been insisting. Thirdly, he wondered if there was any time limit to the partial cessation of bombing: if there were a risk of the Americans resuming the bombing it would be quite impossible for North Vietnam to accept (I replied that, as I read President Johnson's statement,

[3] In this message Mr. Wilson referred to President Johnson's speech as 'an important move which our two governments should consider most carefully', and expressed the view that 'the present is the moment for our two governments to keep in close touch'.

[4] See p. 31.

[5] Not printed. Mr. Stewart renewed an invitation extended by Mr. Brown to Mr. Gromyko in September 1967 to visit Britain, adding: 'alternatively I would be glad to come to Moscow.'

[6] Mr. Stewart had been Secretary of State for Foreign Affairs, 1965-66: cf. Michael Stewart, *Life and Labour* (London, 1980), pp. 152-9.

there was no time limit[7]). Fourthly, President Johnson's offer had been made in the context of an increase in troops for Vietnam which would again present a difficulty.

8. I replied that I did not wish to anticipate the longer discussions which I hoped our two Governments would have. I was of course aware that the Soviet Government did not regard itself as a negotiator. But, in the light of the *communiqué* issued after the Prime Minister's visit to Moscow, the Soviet attitude was not one of refusal to play any part at all, but an acknowledgement of responsibility in promoting a solution. As the Soviet Government were not negotiators I assumed that they could not speak with certainty on what Hanoi would accept or refuse. Just as Mr. Gromyko might not be able to say 'yes' for Hanoi, I assumed he could not say 'no.' Finally I stressed the reference in President Johnson's statement to the need for the Americans' unilateral restraint on bombing to be matched by restraint in Hanoi.[8]

[7] In his second message to President Johnson on 31 March (see p. 32), Mr. Wilson had asked for clarification as to what Hanoi would be required to do in order for the US to stop bombing 'unconditionally': 'if we are to go into action with Moscow on your behalf we must have some answer to this question which will be in their minds. In other words what is the real nature of the proposition which we are to try to sell to Moscow?' President Johnson replied in a message to Mr. Wilson of 1 April that he should tell Moscow that the US Government, having made the first move towards peace, considered that 'the next move in trying to bring about peace talks and a reduction in the level of violence is now clearly up to Hanoi, and the world will be watching to see how Hanoi responds'. Mr. Wilson might also 'indicate to Moscow that it is your personal belief that if Hanoi rejects this latest American initiative, the US would be under heavy pressure to take additional military actions'.

[8] At the end of his meeting with Mr. Stewart (and recorded separately), Mr. Smirnovsky raised the question of Anglo-Soviet bilateral relations, which he said were 'developing satisfactorily', mentioning particularly the agreements on technological cooperation and navigation (see No. 2, notes 5 and 6), but suggested that the British Government should 'think again' about its rejection of the Soviet draft of a Treaty of Friendship (see No. 4). Mr. Stewart also raised the question of Mr. Gerald Brooke, stating that 'anything the Soviet Government could do on this case would be very productive in our relations . . . it seemed to him that this question bulked larger with us than with the Soviet Government. Mr. Smirnovsky did not comment. He added however that the British were good at compromises and he hoped we would look again at the various suggestions and counter suggestions that had been made' (NS 3/18).

On 3 April the DRV announced their willingness to meet US representatives to discuss the unconditional cessation of bombing. Sir P. Dean reported from Washington that opinion there was divided as to whether Hanoi's response was prompted by the losses they had suffered during the Tet offensive, or whether it was a tactical manoeuvre to exploit the political situation while gaining time to regroup militarily. In any case, the British and US Governments could only welcome the DRV announcement, and after a period of wrangling over administrative arrangements talks between US and North Vietnamese representatives began in Paris on 10 May.

On 8 May Mr. Smirnovksy called on the Secretary of State and delivered a message inviting him to a 'detailed exchange of views' in Moscow on 12 and 13 May: as these dates did not suit the Secretary of State the visit was arranged for 22-24 May. In the meantime Mr. Stewart was briefed on the negotiations with the North Vietnamese by Mr. Sullivan and Mr. Davidson, members of Governor Harriman's negotiating team in Paris. They conveyed a message from Mr. Rusk, suggesting that Mr. Stewart should urge on Mr. Gromyko the importance of Hanoi's making a response, 'in deed if not in word', to the US cut-back in bombing, for example by agreeing to a joint withdrawal from the demilitarised zone. The Russians should be disabused of 'any idea they might have that political currents in the United States would oblige President Johnson to take a softer line towards Hanoi', and should be asked for their views on an 'ultimate political settlement'. Mr. Stewart told the US Ambassador, Mr. D.K.E. Bruce, on 20 May that the message 'seemed to amount to a suggestion that he should try to find out in Moscow what immediate step Hanoi would take', and doubted that Hanoi would give any reply of the kind desired. His own intention was to 'take the line that it was right for the two co-Chairmen to be talking now about possible measures short of reconvening the Geneva Conference'.

Mr. Stewart flew to Moscow on the evening of 22 May and was met at the airport by Mr. Gromyko, with whom he held two sessions of talks on 23 May, with a dinner that evening. The Soviet Government had made it clear that although Mr. Stewart's visit was arranged in the context of Vietnam they did not want this to be, or to appear to be, the only subject for discussion, and the talks ranged over a number of international questions including the Middle East, Germany and European Security. Little time was devoted to bilateral issues, except Mr. Brooke, where it was clear there was no prospect of clemency but some indication of possible Soviet agreement to the early ratification of the Consular Convention, with its implications for consular visits (cf. No. 1, note 6).

The records of Mr. Stewart's talks in Moscow are lengthy and not reproduced here: Mr. Gromyko was 'personally friendly' but 'had little new to say'. The discussion on Vietnam was largely a restatement of its own position by each side. Documents Nos. 8 and 9 are intended to convey the atmosphere surrounding Mr. Stewart's visit, and to assess its usefulness in the context of Anglo-Soviet relations.

No. 8

Sir G. Harrison (Moscow) to Foreign Office

No. 833 Telegraphic [NS 3/50]

Immediate. Secret   MOSCOW, *23 May 1968*

Please pass following Personal to the Prime Minister from the Foreign Secretary.

Gromyko met me at the Airport last night and on the way in to Moscow he explained to me that Kosygin would not be available since he was 'taking a cure' in Czechoslovakia. He was at pains to impress upon me the 'genuineness' of the cure. Today he told me that Brezhnev was 'out of Moscow'. Nonetheless he clearly made an effort, at some inconvenience, to make himself available all day today. This included the despatch of the President of Austria to Leningrad a day earlier than planned and the Mexican Foreign Minister to Kiev. He also absented himself from the reception for Tun Razak[1] so that he could attend my dinner for him at the Embassy tonight.

2. You will have seen the detailed reports we have sent on my exchanges with Gromyko. You will also have a copy of my personal message to Rusk.[2] All in all I am not dissatisfied with what we have achieved. I stated our position clearly on the major issues and Gromyko can be in no doubt as to where we stand on Vietnam, the Middle East and Germany. Equally he must now realise, if he did not before, how strongly we feel on these issues. He received all I had to say in a perfectly friendly way. On substance however he was uncompromising. He had little new to say on any subject. On Vietnam he seemed not to be privy to what the North Vietnamese were up to in Paris. On the Middle East, however, his suggestion for mutual consultation on a step-by-step approach may afford us an opportunity of making some progress without cutting across Jarring's Mission.[3] On Germany I had to rebuke him for looking too much to the past:[4] I will be giving Willy Brandt a full account of these exchanges tomorrow over lunch.[5]

[1] Deputy Prime Minister of Malaysia.

[2] In this message, transmitted from Moscow to Washington in telegram No. 157 of 23 May, Mr. Stewart said he had made it clear to Mr. Gromyko that he 'thought it perfectly reasonable for the United States to insist on some measure of restraint by the North Vietnamese before the United States could proceed to an unconditional cessation of the bombing of the North', and warned that 'if there were no visible response from Hanoi to the pull-back in the bombing and US soldiers were to be in danger, there would be a serious risk of a movement of US opinion which could make the situation much worse'. Mr. Gromyko's response to this was 'unsympathetic and routine. He drew a distinction between official and public opinion in the United States and professed to doubt whether opinion in America would allow the government to take a tough line again . . . I have no reason to doubt that he will pass on a full account of these exchanges to the North Vietnamese' (DV 10/190).

[3] See p. 5. Mr. Stewart told the Cabinet on 30 May that Mr. Gromyko had suggested 'diplomatic consultation between the United Kingdom and the Soviet Union on the idea advanced by the United Arab Republic of a stage by stage settlement, which the Israelis had so far opposed for fear that it might commit them to immediate concessions with no certainty of an acceptable settlement at the end of the road'. Mr. Stewart had agreed to this suggestion 'on the understanding that it would not interfere with Mr. Jarring's task', and talks were to take place in New York.

[4] Mr. Stewart had expressed concern at Soviet support for recent East German measures limiting access to Berlin, and had urged the Soviet Government to encourage the FRG's desire for better relations with the Soviet Union and Eastern Europe. Mr. Gromyko replied that while he was not against improved relations with West Germany there were 'many aspects of life in West Germany and its foreign policy which gave rise to concern to all those interested in European security', in particular the rise of neo-Nazism.

[5] Mr. Stewart travelled from Moscow to Bonn on the morning of 24 May.

3. I am sure it was right to come.[6] Pegging away at the Russians is, particularly on Vietnam, achieving the double object of keeping them in the act and of giving them an account of our views which they will certainly pass on to the North Vietnamese in Hanoi and Paris.

4. I reminded Gromyko more than once that we expected the next round of talks to be in London.

[6] Mr. Wilson sent a personal message to Mr. Stewart in FO telegram No. 1568 to Bonn on 24 May, saying that the reports of the Secretary of State's talks with Mr. Gromyko 'show how right it was for you to accept the invitation—and particularly how useful it was for you to take the opportunity at this point to leave Gromyko in no doubt of where we stood, especially on Vietnam and the Middle East—and, on the latter, what he said about the step-by-step approach does perhaps afford at least a chink of light'.

No. 9

Letter from Sir G. Harrison (Moscow) to Mr. Hayman

[*NS 3/50*]

Confidential   MOSCOW, *29 May 1968*

Dear Peter,

Secretary of State's Visit

I do not think that we really have much to add by way of comment to the Secretary of State's own 'atmosphere' message to the Prime Minister transmitted in my telegram No. 833,[1] but I might, perhaps, offer some speculative comment on the Russian purpose in arranging the visit (the question put by Rusk as reported in Pat Dean's telegram No. 1669 from Washington[2]) and in amplification of the Secretary of State's own comments on what the visit may have achieved.

2. As regards the Russian purpose, one must, I think, consider the timetable. President Johnson made his statement about a reduction in bombing on 31 March and immediately, on the following day, the Secretary of State invited Gromyko to discuss the situation with him. On 3 April, to everyone's surprise including, it would appear, that of the Russians, Hanoi announced their willingness to talk and on April 5 the Russians made a statement in support of the North Vietnamese. From then until 3 May there was a long wait while the Americans and the North Vietnamese argued over a meeting place. Throughout this period the Russians said nothing and

[1] No. 8.

[2] In this telegram of 24 May Sir P. Dean reported that he had given Mr. Stewart's message about his Moscow talks (see No. 8, note 2) to Mr. Rusk, who was 'most grateful and particularly asked me to thank you for the stout way you had presented your views'. Mr. Rusk had given Sir P. Dean an account of the current state of negotiations in Paris, adding at the end of the interview that he was 'puzzled why Gromyko, after waiting several weeks, should have picked up your invitation to talk about Vietnam when apparently he had nothing new to say or suggest' (DV 10/190).

Gromyko sent no reply to the Secretary of State's invitation. I think it is a fair assumption that while they wanted to see talks take place, they had to be careful not to get out of line with, or out in front of, Hanoi. Hence, whether or not they were in Hanoi's confidence, the care that they took to be 'with but after' Hanoi at all stages and their reluctance to embark on any discussions with us which might appear to be pre-empting the North Vietnamese.

3. On 3 May the North Vietnamese and the Americans announced Paris on 10 May as the place and date for the opening of talks. The way was now clear for the Russians to make a move and on 8 May Gromyko replied at long last to the Secretary of State with an invitation for him to come to Moscow on 12-13 May. These dates were not acceptable to the Secretary of State and the visit was postponed to 22-24 May, by which time a number of meetings in Paris had taken place. One may wonder whether the Russians had a particular purpose in suggesting 12-13 May, i.e., before any substantive talks in Paris, and, if so, whether it was to try to discover whether we knew what line the Americans were going to take, whether there was likely to be any 'give' in their position and whether any influence could be exerted on them through us.[3] If so, this purpose was partly at least frustrated by the postponement of the visit, since, by the time that it took place, it was fairly clear what the American position was and that there was not likely to be a lot of 'give' in it. At any rate, on 23 May, Gromyko was taking the usual line.

4. In any case, the Russian attitude towards the visit had broadened from that of a meeting of the co-Chairmen to discuss Vietnam to one of a more general exchange of views on questions of common interest. There was no attempt on their part to push the co-Chairmanship aspect and, indeed, Gromyko was quick to say that to try to convene a conference in present circumstances would be unrealistic. Personally, I am inclined to think that the Russians may not have seen much mileage in a discussion of Vietnam, even on the dates first proposed by them. They could not, however, postpone much longer a reply to the Secretary of State without gross discourtesy and, now that they were free to take up the suggestion of a meeting, there was some advantage for them in doing so to keep the co-Chairmanship alive (if not for immediate use) and to keep themselves 'in the act' pending developments in Paris. Moreover, there was conceivably still the possibility that they might learn something new from us about American thinking which might be useful at some time. I would guess, therefore, that their motive was a mixed one, but with the object of keeping the dialogue going and themselves in play rather than with the thought of any immediate results.

5. Which brings us to the question of whether, from our point of view, the visit was worthwhile. I think that it was, not because of any immediate results achieved, but because it kept the dialogue going and there is advantage in

[3] Commenting on this letter on 30 May, Mr. Smith noted that 'May 13 was, I believe the first substantive (*sic*) talk in Paris & I think the Russians may not have wanted to miss the chance, however slight, of getting us to join with them in a statement at the very beginning of the talks. The point of this was lost when we said that 12/13 May was not possible.'

keeping the Russians in the act. Moreover, as the Secretary of State said, it is right to keep pegging away in the hope that what is said will be passed on. To put it at its lowest, it would have been wrong, both in fact and for the record, not to have had the meeting when the Russians were ready for it, and the positive, if longer-term benefits can, I would certainly hope, be put higher than that.[4]

6. I am sending a copy of this letter on a personal basis to Pat Dean in Washington, but am not copying elsewhere and leave it to you to do so if you think fit.

Yours ever,

GEOFFREY HARRISON

[4] According to a note drafted by Mr. Smith for Mr. Stewart's use in Cabinet on 30 May (see No. 8, note 3), the Secretary of State's view was that although his discussions produced little that was new from the Soviet side, the visit was useful in enabling him to resume contact with Mr. Gromyko and to form some impressions of Russian attitudes. He had found Mr. Gromyko 'more relaxed than when I last talked with him two years ago, and [he] also looked a good deal older'.

In London, consideration was being given to broader questions of policy towards the Soviet Union and Eastern Europe, and to the practical methods of implementation. The next group of documents concerns policy review and reassessment.

Every two years, HM Ambassadors in Eastern Europe were summoned to a Conference in London to discuss events in the region and HMG's policy. The 1968 Conference was held during the week beginning 6 May, and was attended by HM Ambassadors at Moscow, Belgrade, Bucharest, Budapest, Prague, Sofia and Warsaw, together with HM Minister in Berlin and, for some sessions, HM Minister in Bonn and the Bonn Ambassador designate, Sir R. Jackling. Senior commercial officials from Eastern European posts also attended the Conference, taking the opportunity for trade discussions with officials from interested Whitehall departments, representatives of Chambers of Commerce and the Confederation of British Industries (CBI).

Discussions at the 1968 Conference on political matters were focussed on developments in Czechoslovakia, where the 'Prague Spring', a surging tide of reform, liberalisation and revolt against the constraints of Soviet economic domination seemed set to put the country on a collision course with other communist régimes in the region and, ultimately, with the Soviet Union. A period of unrest in Czechoslovakia in the 1960s, based upon economic recession, discontent with an oppressive régime and pressure from the Slovak minority for greater autonomy, had led to the replacement in January 1968 of Antonín Novotný, First Secretary of the Czechoslovak Communist Party, by Alexander Dubcek. The policies of Mr. Dubcek and his supporters, advocating free socialist development, condemning coercion and permitting dissent—although Mr. Dubcek maintained there would be no change in Czechoslovak external policy—were the cause of increasing consternation amongst other communist régimes, especially in Poland and the GDR, and although the Soviet Union at this stage made no public comment, the question

40

of how far the Soviet leaders could allow the reform process to go had already been raised by HM Ambassador in Prague, Sir W. Barker.

Mr. Dubcek had been summoned to a meeting of the Warsaw Pact countries in Dresden on 22 March, attended by both President Brezhnev and Mr. Kosygin. Although the resulting official communiqué was conventional and uninformative, it was widely assumed that the purpose of the meeting had been to bring Czechoslovakia into line. Mr. Dubcek evidently failed to calm the anxieties of his colleagues, however, and Mr. Brezhnev's speech to the Moscow Party Activ on 29 March and the subsequent Plenum of the Central Committee on 10 April laid down the Soviet line both for internal and external consumption: ideological co-existence was impossible; communism and capitalism would remain irreconcilable forms of society; Western promotion of such activities as bridge-building was intended simply to gain by devious means what the capitalist powers had failed to get by direct assault, i.e. the disintegration of the Socialist camp.

Meanwhile, the progress of reform in Czechoslovakia continued apace. On 10 April the Central Committee adopted Mr. Dubcek's 'Action Programme' which seemed, in its support for the development of democratic institutions (including the secret ballot) and its toleration of dissent to go directly against Soviet control and the supremacy of the Party. Mr. Dubcek was summoned hastily to Moscow from 4-5 May, but again apparently failed to convince the Soviet leadership that he was either willing or able to keep the pace of liberalisation in Czechoslovakia within limits acceptable to them. Following his visit, reports began to come in of Soviet troop movements towards and in the area of the Czechoslovak frontiers.

It was clear that the increasing strain in Czechoslovak-Soviet relations must have important implications for Soviet foreign policy and for the Eastern European region as a whole. Discussion of these developments was, therefore, central to the deliberations of the Conference of Eastern European Ambassadors. At the second meeting of the Conference on 7 May Sir W. Barker commented that the 'Czechoslovak leaders appeared to entertain a naive vision that, by providing the first example of a society in which "Socialism" and democracy were combined, they would so influence the rest of the world that the cause of Communism would be aided by their example. But Dubcek himself had lived in the Soviet Union for 13 years, had then seen the worst of the purges and collectivisation, and could hardly be naive . . .'

No. 10

Record of the Ninth Meeting of the Conference of Her Majesty's Representatives in Eastern Europe, held at 4.15 p.m. on Friday, 10 May, 1968[1]

[*N 2/27*]

Present:
Mr. G.O. Roberts, MP (*in the Chair*)
Sir P. Gore-Booth

Sir G. Harrison and Mr. A.K. Rothnie (Moscow)
Sir D. Wilson and Mr. J.A. Molyneux (Belgrade)
Sir T. Brimelow and Mr. H.T. Kennedy (Warsaw)
Sir W. Barker and Mr. R. de Burlet (Prague)
Sir J. Chadwick and Mr. A. Rendall (Bucharest)
Mr. D.J.C. Crawley (Sofia)
Mr. G.E. Millard and Mr. H.J. Bowe (Budapest)
Mr. R.G.A. Etherington-Smith (Berlin)[2]

Foreign Office

Lord Hood	Mr. J.A.L. Morgan[3]
Mr. P.T. Hayman	Mr. E.E. Orchard
Mr. T.W. Garvey	Mr. J.R. Banks[4]
Mr. H.F.T. Smith	Mr. N.P. Bayne
Mr. W.R. Haydon	Mr. W. St. Clair[5]
Mr. S.C. Giffard	Mr. P.J. Barlow
Mr. T.C. Barker	Mr. D. Beattie[6]

Other Departments

Mr. W. Morris (DEA)	Mr. B. MacTavish (BOT)

[1] The Conference was opened formally by the Secretary of State on 7 May. Discussions that day centred on general political issues, including relations between Eastern European countries and the Soviet Union. 8 May sessions concentrated on information and cultural work, and 9 May was devoted to general economic discussion and UK trade policy (the latter session continuing on the morning of 10 May). The meeting recorded here was the final session: submitting the minutes to Lord Hood on 16 May, Mr. Hayman commented that it provided 'a good summary of the whole Conference'.

[2] The above were respectively Ambassador and (where listed) Commercial Counsellor at the Posts specified: Mr. Etherington-Smith was HM Minister and Deputy Commandant, Berlin.

[3] First Secretary in Moscow 1965-7, now serving in London.

[4] Mr. Garvey and Mr. Banks were respectively Assistant Under-Secretary superintending economic and supply departments, and a Research Assistant in Research Department.

[5] Mr. Haydon was head of News Department, Mr. Bayne and Mr. St. Clair First Secretaries in the Foreign Office.

[6] Mr Giffard was a Counsellor, Mr. Barlow and Mr. Barker First Secretaries, and Mr. Beattie a Second Secretary in the Foreign Office.

Mr. P. Pooley (MAFF) Mr. G.C. Dick (BOT)
Mr. G. Bowen (Mintech) Col. J.M. Pettet (MOD)
Mr. J. Fish (BOT)

Mr. Roberts regretted that the Secretary of State was engaged. He would ask Mr. Hayman to summarise the political conclusions of earlier meetings and Mr. Garvey, the economic conclusions. He would then invite the Permanent Under-Secretary to comment, followed by the Ambassadors, before he summed up.

2. *Mr. Hayman* said that the meetings had considered both the general political trend of events in Eastern Europe, and also what our response should be. Discussion had naturally taken events in Czechoslovakia as their starting point. Czechoslovakia had reached a crucial moment in her history, and might be said to have gone too far in its new policies to be able to turn back. As the Secretary of State had commented, all the countries in Eastern Europe were involved in varying ways and to different degrees, in these developments, with the Bulgarians perhaps being the least affected at present.

3. Sir Geoffrey Harrison had stated that Anglo-Soviet relations might well be relatively unaffected by these developments in the immediate future, but that events in Czechoslovakia would have a major effect on Soviet policy and on relations between the countries in Eastern Europe. There was intense interest in Moscow in the developments in Czechoslovakia, and it was possible that the limit of Soviet tolerance might be reached. He had posed the question how the Soviet Union would handle this problem: they might go on trying to restore rigid unity in Eastern Europe; alternatively they might calculate that the forces working for change were too strong, and decide themselves to initiate a movement towards *détente* in order to ensure Soviet leadership of it.

4. Mr. Hayman observed that the Kremlin still had three reliable prefects left in Europe, Ulbricht, Gomulka and Kadar.[7] The loyalty of Ulbricht in particular had become more important to the Soviet Union as a result of the recent events in Czechoslovakia. It was clear that West Germany and East Germany were growing apart institutionally; moreover local pride in their economic achievements was growing in East Germany. Although there were strong emotional feelings on the subject in both the Federal German Republic and East Germany, there seemed no chance of reunification for a very long time to come, although there could conceivably be slow and gradual progress towards a kind of 'living together'. Turning to the future role of NATO, Mr. Hayman referred to the Secretary of State's remarks at the opening session.[8] As he had said, there was a distinct feeling among many

[7] Herr Walter Ulbricht was First Secretary of the Socialist Unity Party and Chairman of the Council of State in the GDR. M. Wladyslaw Gomulka was First Secretary of the Central Committee of the Polish United Workers' Party and M. Janos Kadar was First Secretary of the Socialist Worker's Party of Hungary.

[8] At the end of the first meeting of the Conference, when he had heard what each Ambassador had to report on conditions in the country to which he was accredited, the Secretary of State had

people in the West, particularly among the young, that NATO should be more concerned with a policy of active *détente*; they needed to be convinced that the alliance's defensive role was not an anachronism. As regards a European Security Conference, the meeting had agreed that the Russians were cold to this idea at present and that it would be wrong for us to pursue it. Any such conference would involve the discussion of proposals for a comprehensive European settlement. This could only result in a hardening of attitudes. The meeting considered, for similar reasons, that there then was no advantage for us in a bloc-to-bloc approach between the Warsaw Pact and NATO.

5. As to the action which might be taken by individual Western countries, including the United Kingdom, Mr. Hayman said the meeting had rightly concluded that we must avoid wedge-driving tactics, which could cause acute embarrassment to Dubcek and perhaps to other like-minded leaders in Eastern Europe. Instead, we should increase the number and variety of bilateral ties between the individual countries of Eastern and Western Europe. Promoting bilateral East-West relations in this way would in time impose considerable strains upon the *bloc*, and increase the Kremlin's difficulties. NATO had a role to play as a clearing house for the exchange of information and plans in this field, and in obtaining a consensus on the way in which individual approaches should be handled and on what were the best subjects for discussion. An example was the talks between Poland and Belgium on force reductions which, although from the Polish side a largely theatrical performance, represented a form of bilateral contact which could have its uses if properly cleared in NATO first.[9] Moreover within NATO itself, we ought to continue studies on force reductions, on East/West relations and so forth, all of which could be of relevance to the future role of NATO. The meeting regarded as of great importance the continued promotion of visits in

concluded that one of his main impressions 'was that events in Eastern Europe were subject to marked national differences. If there was a common feature it was a certain intellectual restlessness, even in Poland and the Soviet Union. Our policy appeared to be broadly on the right lines, and it was evident that the most important field of activity for us was trade, though another aspect to which we ought to devote attention was intellectual and cultural contacts. These might reap considerable political dividends in the long run . . . But there was a similar trend towards intellectual restlessness in the West and we had to consider the effect of this on NATO. A generation was growing up which did not understand the purpose of the Alliance and was not disposed to accept the stock answer that it was not only defensive but was intended to promote *détente*. The problem might be either to construct a new system of collective security in Europe or to persuade a new generation of the validity of the one we now had. Certainly it was no longer possible simply to take NATO for granted.'

[9] In the context of a study being undertaken in NATO on balanced East-West force reductions as a follow-up to the Harmel exercise (a study of the future tasks of the NATO Alliance carried out during 1967 following the adoption in December 1966 of a resolution by the Belgian Foreign Minister: cf. *FRUS 1964-1968*, vol. xiii, pp. 650-52), several models were constructed including a Belgian three-stage plan for a quantitative and qualitative freeze of forces followed by reductions. This plan had been discussed in advance between the Belgians and Poles, causing some annoyance in NATO circles.

both directions not only of Ministers, but also of Parliamentarians, opinion-forming groups, businessmen, and academic and other cultural figures, in contributing to the ferment of change in Eastern Europe. It was necessary to increase our cultural and information work in Eastern Europe, but not at the expense of the Soviet Union.

6. *Sir Paul Gore-Booth* said that he could not improve on Mr. Hayman's summary of the political discussions. The Conference had been arranged a long time previously but it had proved to be ideally timed. What was now happening in Eastern Europe was what many had for long hoped would happen, but had hardly expected to occur in Czechoslovakia. The events in Czechoslovakia had shown that certain things could be done in the name of Communism which had not been done since 1917. The crucial question seemed to be how the Soviet Union and the other East European countries would react to these events, and whether the resulting changes would take place safely or dangerously. Whatever happened, these events would be mostly out of our control; it would not be possible for us to exert much influence over them, though we would do what we could. We should not underestimate the difficulties the Russians faced themselves.

7. *Mr. Garvey* said that in the Soviet Union and Eastern Europe the economic reforms had all begun before the recent upheavals. They had been undertaken for economic, and political reasons, primarily because the old systems were not capable of modernising industrial production. The reforms ought to entail the adoption of many of the features of the market economy, notably that consumer demand should largely determine what should be produced and in what quantities; but many of these features might be thought to be 'bringing in capitalism by the back door' and thus to conflict with official Communist ideology; they might also conflict with the political situation in certain countries, such as Poland, to maintain centralisation. It was therefore wrong to regard the reforms as presaging a rapid transition to a market economy. Some of the countries took a cautious approach to economic reform, but in Hungary and perhaps in Czechoslovakia there was a much greater commitment to change. He forecast that in view of the entrenched resistance of the ideologues and the bureaucrats, the economic changes would proceed in jerks. He cited the example of Yugoslavia, where this long process had already taken 12 years and was still not completed, but experience there suggested that in the long run the economic reforms could not achieve their objectives without eroding something of the essence of the régimes themselves.

8. Mr. Garvey felt that our interests would be served by the success of the economic reforms, although he knew that there was not much that we could do to accelerate it. However, trade was one of our major interests. As the Soviet Union and the East European countries re-equipped and modernised their industries, so their need for our goods was increasing. He regarded technological exchanges as the lubricant to commercial dealings, although he felt that there were certain dangers in them. In general, the purchasing power of the East European countries was not expanding as much as their

desire and need for new purchases, and this was leading to a vicious circle. The Conference had discussed in considerable detail various trade promotion techniques, the granting of credit, and the question of liberalisation; and also the obstacles in the way of increased trade, including COCOM. The Conference had concluded that in the race for exports, while there were certain shortcomings, we were not notably falling behind our main competitors.

9. *Sir G. Harrison* said that the ferment in Czechoslovakia must have serious implications for the Kremlin, both internally and externally. He was sure that the Soviet régime would be able to control internal disturbances, but he wondered what effect the developments in Czechoslovakia would have on the Soviet Union's foreign policy. If the Czechoslovaks succeeded in working out a distinctive road to socialism, this would have important ideological implications for the Soviet leadership, for East Europe as a *bloc*, for the Warsaw Pact in relation to Germany, and for the world Communist movement. These developments were touching very sensitive nerves in the Kremlin. The Russians must now be considering whether the implications were so serious that the Czechoslovak deviation must be crushed, or whether they should live with it and restrict as far as they could the damage which it might do to their own position. As a third alternative, they could perhaps consider putting themselves at the head of a movement for *détente* in Europe. Sir G. Harrison asked what we could do. He felt that we should stimulate cultural, technological and commercial exchanges, not forgetting exchanges of visits at Government level. He considered that in conducting these exchanges we should act as a Western rather than a NATO Power. A neutral or negative response to our overtures would not matter because our overtures would in any case have sowed suspicion among the East European countries.

10. *Sir T. Brimelow* agreed with Sir G. Harrison. Poland feared the development of a movement on the Czech lines. The Government was imposing a brake.[10] It was necessary to carry on with exchanges of all kinds. There was a great fund of goodwill for Britain in Poland, which private as well as officials visits would foster. He remarked that the Polish Government wished to continue to play an international role and therefore favoured conducting dialogues with the Western powers even although those dialogues might not lead to any result. Our policy must be one of patience, understanding and friendliness.

11. *Sir W. Barker* agreed. He considered that it was an ill omen that the Russians were rattling their sabres in Poland. He could not see that the Soviet Union would lead a movement for *détente*. The timing of the pressure

[10] At the first session of the Conference Sir T. Brimelow had described how a growing interest in economic reform, combined with an 'expectation of change' as a result of what was happening in Czechoslovakia, had led to some student riots and attempts to spread unrest in Poland. The Communist leadership had taken a 'moderately tough' line, dismissing some academics and imposing stricter controls on universities. However, 'It was realised that the Soviet Union could not afford to lose its grip on Poland and Gomulka could be expected to persist in his loyalty to the Soviet connexion . . . there was no prospect of a violent uprising in Poland.'

which they were imposing on Czechoslovakia had not been well chosen, since the Czechoslovaks were at present in an elated and determined mood. The Russians ought to have waited for the mood to cool off in the face of the internal difficulties which would inevitably arise in Czechoslovakia. If Mr. Dubcek were to call an extraordinary Party Congress to consolidate his own position, and remove the conservatives from the Central Committee, the Russians might feel obliged to act, but Dubcek's intentions on this point were still unclear. He thought that the immediate result of sabre rattling would be to stiffen Czechoslovak resistance to the Russians. Any active interference in Czechoslovakia would set back Soviet influence in many Communist Parties. He expected further developments in Czechoslovakia to be slow.

12. *Mr. Etherington-Smith* said the Ulbricht regime was very strong. No internal developments on the Czechoslovak model were likely. If the Czechoslovak movement continued, it could influence conditions in Eastern Germany which would lead to a very difficult internal situation and ultimately to stern repression. In view of the presence of Soviet troops in East Germany, repression by the East German leadership of any liberalising movement would be easy. Ulbricht was prepared to consider reunification of Germany only if it were so arranged that the whole country would be subject to a Communist régime. Until that time, Ulbricht would demand recognition as a condition of normal relations with the Federal Republic. Ulbricht would continue a hard line towards the Federal Republic in order to humiliate and weaken it, and to extract concessions. This however could change if the Soviet Union's policy to Eastern Europe changed in the direction of a *détente*. He did not feel that Ulbricht could go so far as to consider a confederal solution.

13. *Sir J. Chadwick* said one must not overlook the quiet development in Rumania.[11] The country was moving internally. Relations were being established with other countries at all levels. He urged that we should encourage a series of visits, preferably at a high political level. *Mr. Roberts* observed that such visits ought to be increased, and they ought to cover a wide spectrum; the emphasis would no doubt vary from country to country.

14. *Mr. Millard* said that Mr. Kadar and his régime were in Communist terms men of the centre. They were pursuing a cautious course. Kadar's main objective was to safeguard his reforms, and therefore he was anxious to avoid offence to the Russians. The Hungarians would accordingly be very cautious in their dialogue with Western countries. In view of the need for foreign trade, the Hungarians had a vested interest in the economic reforms, and this would accelerate the process of liberalisation.

---

[11] At the meeting on 7 May (see note 1) Sir J. Chadwick had identified a number of points of difference between Rumania and the Soviet Union, including Rumania's establishment of diplomatic relations with West Germany and her refusal to join in condemning Israel as the aggressor after the Six Day War. In addition, Rumania had refused to attend the meeting in Dresden on 22 March (p. 41). The Ambassador noted that President Ceausescu repeatedly emphasised the importance of modernisation and innovation and speculated that in the future Rumania might have the same relationship with the Soviet Union as Finland.

15. *Mr. Crawley* said that Bulgaria was very much apart from the rest of Eastern Europe. Mr. Zhivkov[12] was one of the most reliable Soviet prefects, and there was no evidence of internal unrest in Bulgaria, although some anxiety on that score no doubt existed among the leadership. He pointed out that 200,000 Czech tourists visited Bulgaria every year, and this might bring in new ideas.

16. *Sir D. Wilson* said that it was possible to help both the Yugoslavs and ourselves. The struggle between the ideologists and the technocrats had reached an interesting phase at the top level. We could do much to help the technocrats by promoting contacts and exchanges.

17. *Mr. Roberts* said that the meeting had produced a series of valuable ideas. He would single out the following:

(*a*) it was too early to think of a European Security Conference or of consultations between NATO and the Warsaw Pact. We must press on with bilateral contacts and keep NATO informed. We must also widen the range of these contacts.

(*b*) the limit of Soviet tolerance of deviation might vary from country to country, meanwhile, there was little the West could do or say to help the liberals in East Europe;

(*c*) if there were a greater Soviet concentration on developments in Europe, this might modify the Soviet Union's willingness to be involved in the Middle East and the Far East;

(*d*) the economic reforms would progress in a series of fits and starts. The decentralisation of decision-making was a very difficult process. We ought to help the process in any way we could, by extending points of economic contact, especially through technical and scientific agreements.

[12] Mr. Todor Zhivkov was First Secretary of the Central Committee of the Communist Party and Prime Minister of Bulgaria.

No. 11

Memorandum by the Secretary of State for Foreign Affairs on Relations with the Soviet Union and Eastern Europe[1]

OPD(68)45 [N 2/30]

Secret   FOREIGN OFFICE, *17 June 1968*

I have thought it useful to review the state and prospect of our relations with the Soviet Union and Eastern Europe. The attached paper, which I

[1] This memorandum represents the final version of the paper drafted following Mr. Brown's meeting of 23 February on Anglo-Soviet relations (see No. 5), expanded to include relations with Eastern Europe (*ibid.*, note 8) and amended following the Conference of Eastern European Ambassadors (No. 10). The revised text was sent to Mr. Stewart for final approval under cover of a minute by Mr. Roberts, before circulation to members of the OPD Committee.

circulate for the information of my colleagues, has been prepared in the light of a conference recently held in the Foreign Office with HM Ambassadors to the Soviet Union and the Eastern European countries.

M.S.

Enclosure in No. 11

Relations with the Soviet Union and Eastern Europe

I The Soviet Union

As an introduction to a study of our relations with the Soviet Union it is necessary to consider, however briefly, the present state of the Soviet Union. A general comment is that we are in a period when things are happening to the Soviet Union which may in the very long run cause radical changes there. Much is guess work; the Russians do not perceive the process clearly themselves and we cannot predict with any certainty whether, or still less when, the forces that are at work will change the nature of the Soviet Union as we know it now, and produce a régime more liberal in its internal policy and more co-operative in its external relations. It is a common error to exaggerate the changes that have so far taken place and the rate at which they may develop. False assumptions about this are dangerous to our interests and can lead us to behave in a way which would actually impede, rather than foster, an improvement in Soviet attitudes.

The Internal Scene

2. Having abandoned, probably for good, the more brutal features of Stalinism, the Soviet Union has not yet been able to escape wholly from the grip of the old system, and some of the people who operated it are still in positions of power. A conflict of ideas is going on, which will probably continue for a long time, about what sort of society is wanted and can be afforded.

3. The Soviet leaders are seeking to place their economic and military power on a firmer and more diversified base. They also want to demonstrate to their own people and to the world the attractiveness and economic effectiveness of Communism. They realise that new economic attitudes are necessary for the diversified and technological society that is now developing. But they find that measures that would probably be sensible in economic terms run counter to ideological prejudice, vested interests, and the authority of the Party; and they fear for the stability (i.e. submissiveness) of Soviet society. They are thus proceeding slowly, and while they are tackling economic reform they are concerned to control any consequences or other forces leading to social instability or questioning of the régime.

4. This faces the leadership with a contradiction. An essential element of economic reform is some devolution of decision making. As more people are required to exercise initiative and judgement in the economic activities of the country, it is natural that more people should also seek to express their views on other problems of society. Deep changes in Soviet society are likely to depend on the gradual evolution of the attitudes of broad sections of its people. But a lead is already being taken by a still small, but a vocal and

growing minority; and an important point is that they now include scientists and technologists as well as the traditional questioners, the writers. Most of these people say that they are Communists, but they are seeking greater individual freedom and the right to question the policies and practices of the régime. They say that they are not attacking the Constitution, but are only insisting on its proper observance. The influence of these pioneer spirits should not be over-estimated, but neither should it be discounted. These men are pointing the way to the future.

5. In dealing with the critics of the régime the authorities no longer feel able to use the methods of repression used by Stalin. On the other hand they are a very long way from regarding repression of dissenting activity as unnecessary. But they have not yet succeeded in attuning their methods of repression to the different conditions of today. The KGB is an instrument designed to do its job ruthlessly, preferably secretly (or at any rate with complete control over publicity) and without having to explain itself. Stalinist conditions suited it. In the post-Stalin era it remains a very powerful organisation, which is fully integrated with the Soviet government machine.

6. The preoccupation of the Soviet leaders with these problems has its effect on their external policy. In particular they find it necessary to emphasise the continuing struggle with external forces and the alleged hostility to Communist and Soviet interests of the Western world. Unusual play is being made of the alleged attempts by foreign governments and interests to undermine the Soviet Union ideologically. A constant theme in the trials of intellectuals is that they have had dealings with outside organisations, often emigré organisations.

7. There is little doubt that the Soviet leadership is much preoccupied with these problems.

The Soviet Union and the Communist World

8. In this respect too the Soviet Union is going through a period of deeply perplexing change. She is no longer the head of a monolithic Communist movement. Other Communist parties are asserting their individuality. The power and influence of the Soviet Union remain great, notably in Eastern Europe (Czechoslovak and Rumanian behaviour notwithstanding) where economics and geography assist her. But in Eastern Europe the Russians have to have increasing regard for the views and interests of their allies, despite economic, social and even political developments in some of these countries which the Russians regard as dangerous and possible infectious.

9. The Soviet Union is having difficulty in adjusting herself to this changing situation.

External Policy

10. The Soviet leadership not only continue to profess but actually believe that it is their mission to spread Communism. But although this means that Soviet external policy is sometimes distorted by ideology it is mainly determined by a cool estimate of national self-interest which includes, of course, the interest of the Soviet Union in maintaining its influence within the world Communist movement.

11. The basis of the Soviet approach to the developed Western countries is still one of hostility. They seek to disintegrate Western alliances and are particularly concerned to create friction between the United States and other Western countries, and to undermine NATO. Overt propaganda is supported by the formidable machinery of the external services of the KGB which are active in subversion. Between one-third and two-thirds of any Soviet Embassy abroad are members of the KGB and there are over 120 identified Soviet Intelligence Officers in the Embassy and other Soviet offices in London, a number of whom are actively engaged in running agents.

12. The Soviet Union is, however, ready to conclude specific and limited agreements with other countries even while maintaining a broadly hostile front towards them or their governments. Thus Khrushchev concluded a partial nuclear test ban treaty,[2] and the Russians wish to conclude a non-proliferation treaty.[3] Thus the Soviet Union wishes to develop its external trade and to conclude bilateral technological agreements. Bilateral cultural agreements are welcomed, though the Soviet interest in these is predominantly in the advantages they can bring in scientific and technical matters, and many genuine cultural exchanges such as the free flow of ideas, of newspapers, etc. are not allowed.

13. This compartmentalisation of Soviet external policy, under which the Soviet Government assume that certain channels of co-operation can be developed and kept immune from the effects of a policy largely hostile in other respects to their bilateral partner in the exercise, is one which Western countries have thought it worthwhile accepting. The test should be whether a given act of co-operation benefits the Western side as well as the Soviet side. In many cases this calculation of common advantage is made by the Western partner; there is, however, a fascination in the [i]dea of 'getting on with the Russians' which sometimes leads Westerners to bargain less firmly than the Russians. This is dangerous not only in immediate terms of self-interest and because the Russians regard concessions as a sign of weakness unless they result from hard bargaining, but also because it encourages the assumption by the Soviet Union that it is for others to woo them.

[2] In 1963: the treaty was signed by the UK, US and USSR: *BFSP*, vol. 167, pp. 178-182.

[3] Cf. No. 3, note 5. At the 22nd session of the UN General Assembly from 24 April-12 June 1968 the draft text of the Non-Proliferation Treaty was commended by a large majority, and a draft Resolution on Security Assurances (sponsored by the UK, US and Soviet Union to provide security assurances for non-nuclear weapon signatories of the Treaty who were the victim of or threatened by aggression with nuclear weapons) was adopted in the Security Council. Following revision to meet criticism that the provisions for future measures of disarmament and promotion of nuclear energy for civil purposes were inadequate, an amended text of the Treaty and the Resolution on Security Assurances were formally adopted in June. The Non-Proliferation Treaty—according to an FO Background Brief for Ministers, 'without doubt the most important measure of arms control and disarmament that has yet been achieved . . . the first essential step towards the end of the nuclear arms race and general and complete disarmament under strict and effective international control'—was to be opened for signature on 1 July at ceremonies in London, Moscow and Washington (AD 7/1/1).

14. There is an analogy to be made between the internal and the external attitudes of the Soviet Union. Internally, the régime has been obliged to re-examine its policies because of the facts of life, the irresistible demands of an industrially developing society. There is a reasonable hope that in the long run the facts of life will lead to similar modifications in Soviet external attitudes. The nuclear weapon and the determination to avoid confrontation with the United States have already done so, although the emphasis being given by the Soviet leaders to the importance of increasing Soviet military strength generally reveals their feeling that until they have something like parity with the United States they will have to temper their foreign policy more than they would wish. The resolution of the Western alliance in Europe has for twenty years removed one source of temptation to the Russians though they have remained alert to exploit any cracks. In the long run, concern about China, the threat of which undoubtedly looms large in Soviet calculations, may influence for the better Soviet attitudes towards the rest of the world; though there is no evidence that this is at present moving the Soviet Union towards a policy of greater accommodation with the West. The continued loosening of bonds between the Soviet Union and its East European neighbours and the growth of individualism among Communist parties must also have consequences for Soviet international attitudes, and of a kind which are in the long run likely to be helpful rather than the reverse.

15. These processes are, however, certain to be slow and in many fields, including the attitudes to be adopted towards developments in Czecho-slovakia, subject to strong resistance from sections of the Soviet Establishment. For the foreseeable future Soviet policy towards the West will continue to be as described above. The process of improvement would not be encouraged, indeed the reverse, by Western willingness to make unrequited concessions or by Western illusions, leading to the dropping of the Western guard, about any early favourable development in Soviet policies.

Current Soviet attitudes to the United Kingdom

16. Soviet propaganda and the way in which the Russians are conducting themselves towards us reflect their hope that the United Kingdom and Her Majesty's Government may be vulnerable to pressures. This hope rests on an analysis of our economic and political problems including our internal political situation and our difficulties over the Common Market. Since our difficulties are those which Soviet doctrine would lead them to expect, they probably exaggerate them and the possibilities for exploiting them.

17. Examples of Russian attempts to appeal to opinion in this country are to be found in much propaganda about the weakness of our economic position and the measures taken by Her Majesty's Government in the social services, etc., which are alleged to be directed against the working class. The anti-American theme is unremitting, notably on Vietnam but also on our alleged economic dependence on the United States, and NATO is a major target.

18. The anti-American theme was strongly in evidence during the discussions which the Prime Minister held in Moscow in January. There were also occasions when Soviet leaders impertinently criticised Her Majesty's

Government's attitude towards the votes on Vietnam at the Labour Party and TUC Conferences.[4]

19. A further example of the Soviet attitude is their treatment of the Treaty of Friendship, the general nature of which was clearly understood between the Prime Minister and Mr. Kosygin last year.[5] The Soviet draft is an anti-NATO, anti-German and anti-American document. Its purpose may have been to kill the project, and if so this is an example of the present nature of the Soviet approach towards us. But it may have been intended to try us out, and in discussing the draft Mr. Gromyko stated boldly that a Treaty of Friendship would be out of place so long as we continued to play an active part in the military activities of NATO. This sort of language about participation in NATO has in the past been used by the Russians with Norway and Denmark but not with us. The Treaty of Friendship was not mentioned during my visit to Moscow in May.

20. On this occasion Mr. Gromyko and I had a general discussion on all the main international topics. The Russians gave nothing away but the exchanges were reasonably relaxed.

21. The tone of the Soviet approach to our general political relations is at present somewhat worse than usual. This does not affect all our activities. In two fields in particular the position is very encouraging: trade continues to go well[6] and the outlook for technological co-operation is promising. There is no sign that the Russians wish to cut back on the cultural exchange arrangements and although they are being slow about naming their team there is no evidence they are having second thoughts about the Joint Consultative Committee.[7] A minor gesture has been the decision to allow us to sell 100,000 copies of *Anglia* instead of the present 50,000.[8] The Soviet principle of 'compartmentalisation' is operating.

[4] Cf. p. 3.

[5] See No. 4.

[6] During a visit to Moscow from 3-8 June 1968 by the President of the Board of Trade, Mr. Anthony Crosland, agreement was reached on the timetable for discussion of a new long-term Anglo-Soviet trade agreement to supersede the agreement due to expire in mid-1969 (cf. No. 2, note 7). Mr. Kosygin repeated to Mr. Crosland the suggestion made to Mr. Wilson in January that the UK should ensure that Gosplan incorporate British requirements under the trade agreement into the 1971-75 Five Year Plan: *v. ibid.*, note 12. It was subsequently arranged that a Board of Trade delegation would visit Moscow in November for trade and planning talks with Gosplan. Cf. No. 18, note 7 below.

[7] Cf. No. 5, note 5. Delays in the nomination of Soviet members and administrative problems (including the resignation of Mr. Benjamin Britten because of illness) had made it impossible to arrange an early meeting of the Committee, but on 23 April Lord Trevelyan had invited Mr. Kozyrev and other members of the Soviet group to visit the UK for the first meeting of the Committee on 25-28 October 1968.

[8] *Anglia* was a British-produced Russian-language quarterly magazine circulated in the Soviet Union under the terms of an Exchange of Letters signed in Moscow in 1961. A Foreign Office brief on Cultural and Scientific Exchanges with the Soviet Union stated that 'HM Embassy [in Moscow] consider it with the BBC to be the best information activity we can conduct in the Soviet Union' (MAS 3/11).

What should our policy be?

22. We should not allow ourselves to be over-influenced by the propaganda and pressures referred to above. At the same time it is a good principle when the Russians talk tough to show that far from yielding to pressures we intend to be just as tough as they are. This is likely to be far more effective than any attempt to woo them, which they will take as further evidence of weakness. We should, at the same time, use the technique of compartmentalisation, pursuing with all vigour those activities which bring practical benefit to us (notably trade and technology) and keeping open those links which are an investment for the future (the opportunities provided by the cultural exchanges for intellectuals from both sides to meet each other).

23. The policy we should follow towards the Soviet Union might be summarised as follows:

(*a*) we should pursue commercial and technological exchanges, and not allow these to be affected by the general political climate, but we should continue to apply to these exchanges the test of 'balance of advantage' and ensure that we achieve satisfactory reciprocity. The cultural exchanges should also be pursued but we should look carefully at the cost-effectiveness of any major projects, e.g. expensive visits by the Royal Ballet, orchestras, etc.;

(*b*) when the Russians attack Her Majesty's Government and the United Kingdom in their propaganda or when they address themselves to us officially in terms which show less than proper respect we should respond clearly, firmly and seriously; understatement and suavity do not pay when we are trying to make a point clear to the Russians;

(*c*) we should look very carefully before engaging in activities which are largely of a goodwill nature. Ministerial visits should in principle be directed to a specific practical purpose, with the prospect of achieving practical results to our benefit. We should apply a similar test when issuing invitations to Soviet Ministers to visit this country;

(*d*) we should continue to be alert to any opportunities for engaging the Russians in discussion and negotiation on international questions when the moment seems right. But we should also be careful not to appear to be running after them. It does not increase our credibility in their eyes for us to do so, and it provides them with more material for propaganda on the theme that we are American puppets. (It would, incidentally, not improve or increase our power to influence the Russians if we were to dissociate ourselves from the Americans; the French have no influence with them on major international questions.) The Soviet leaders know well enough by now that we wish to play a constructive role and that we are at the service of the international community in this cause. They also know, whatever they may say to the contrary, that we do have an influence, and in particular an influence in Washington. If the Russians themselves have the will, and see the possibility, to find solutions and if, being unable to go direct to the United States, they think we can help, they will not be slow to approach us. They know our address;

(e) opinion in this country is not well informed about the subversive and repressive aspects of the Soviet régime and in particular the activities of the KGB. This ignorance tends to encourage a generally false picture of the Soviet Union and its intentions which provides the Soviet Union with opportunities to attack not only the interests but even the security of the United Kingdom.

There are some inhibitions upon us in publicising the activities of the KGB conducted inside this country, though we should continue to examine on its merits each case as it arises to see whether publicity would be profitable.

We are not under the same inhibitions as regards publicity about the activities of the KGB inside the Soviet Union, directed against their own people. The trials of intellectuals have received much publicity here, and publicity outside the Soviet Union almost certainly leads some people among the Soviet leadership to have doubts about the wisdom of action which offends liberal and even communist opinion abroad. It is also important to the intellectuals, part of whose discontent arises from a longing for contacts with the outside world, to know that the outside world is interested in them, (provided it does not claim credit for what they are doing, or suggest that they are inspired by external links). Publicity about these affairs needs little stimulation in this country but we should not feel inhibited from discreetly stimulating it. Open action by Her Majesty's Government to publicise or condemn the treatment of Soviet intellectuals would, however, be damaging to official relations with the Soviet Union and would not help the victims of the KGB since it would lend colour to the accusations that they are the tools of the West.

II EASTERN EUROPE

Developments in Eastern Europe

24. There is an increasing diversity among the countries of Eastern Europe. In some of them society is changing much more rapidly than in the Soviet Union. In most of them the potential for early change is much greater than in the Soviet Union. The size and shape of their economies call for changes more urgently than in the Soviet Union where the vastly greater economy tends to move more slowly and where a virtual self-sufficiency in natural resources permits the forces of conservatism a greater influence. The countries of Eastern Europe depend to a large degree on external trade. This has until now consisted very largely of trade within the CMEA and with the Soviet Union in particular. Much of this trade has been uneconomic and it has failed to bring to the Eastern European countries the modern equipment and technology which they need. In their search for more efficient economies they see the need to develop their exchanges with the West.

25. Economic pressures are associated with political and social pressures. Western traditions, which exist in most of the East European countries to a

degree far greater than the Soviet Union; the fact that most of these countries had Communism imposed on them from outside; and the memory of many of the more influential people, especially in the fields of trade, technology and science, of the links which existed with the West in their youth, combine to produce an attitude towards internal change and external relations quite different from that to be found in the Soviet Union.

26. At the present time this attitude is to be found only among a minority of the leaders and is therefore reflected in only a limited and uneven way in the policies of the East European countries. But in the field of external relations, including notably foreign trade, the Rumanians have shown a growing and by now a considerable independence. Recent developments in Czechoslovakia are even more important because they are concerned with the nature of the internal régime, with an attempt to introduce liberalism into a Communist state, and with economic reforms which depend essentially upon decentralisation and a great increase in trade with the West. It is possible that the economic reform introduced this year in Hungary will produce important political and social consequences within the next two or three years. In Poland, where the leadership remains highly conservative and unimaginative, where deep alienation exists between a large majority of the population and their rulers, and where the external political factors are particularly sharp (notably relations with Germany and Poland's position on the lines of communication between the Soviet Union and East Germany) the near and middle future may see little progress and some regression but our bilateral relations with Poland nevertheless are, and are likely to continue to be, vigorous and useful.

What should our policy be?

27. In general, Eastern Europe offers the possibility of a faster rate of growth in our relations than we can hope to enjoy with the Soviet Union. In our approach to the countries of Eastern Europe we must be careful not to appear to be driving wedges between them and the Soviet Union. There will continue to be close limitations on what we can hope to achieve with these countries in our discussions of international questions. We must expect that they will in general continue to support Soviet foreign policy either because they consider it to be in their national interest to do so or for tactical reasons. There have been exceptions such as Rumania's decision to establish relations with the Federal German Republic and her attitude towards the Middle East; and there may be some cautious readjustments in Czechoslovak policy. But any changes that come about will result from an estimate of national interest and we should not exaggerate the influence which we can bring to bear. This, however, does not by any means argue against pursuing with all these countries a dialogue on international questions; there is much to be said in favour of the West extending their political contacts with the countries of Eastern Europe on a *bilateral* basis provided that we keep each other fully informed of what we are doing.

28. It is, however, in certain other fields that we can look for earlier and more tangible results. A recent conference held in the Foreign Office with

Her Majesty's Ambassadors from the area identified trade, technology and scientific co-operation, and information and cultural work as fields which offered further scope, with the pattern varying of course as between country and country. Our efforts should be increased in all these fields.

29. Against the background of these opportunities we should substantially increase the number of visits between the United Kingdom and the countries of Eastern Europe—not only visits by Ministers covering a wide range of departmental responsibility, but also by Parliamentarians, intellectuals, administrators, cultural leaders and businessmen. There are also useful opportunities for educational and youth exchanges.

30. There is in this a good argument based on our own direct interest. But the desire of the East European countries for greater individual independence is also in the interest of the West generally. The growth of links with Western countries could make an important contribution not only to the evolution of the Eastern European countries but, in the longer run, may well influence the policies of the Soviet Union itself both in Europe and in the rest of the world.[9]

[9] Mr. Roberts recommended this paper to Mr. Stewart as 'generally admirable' and drew attention to the following 'points of special importance':

'(1) The continuing dependence, militarily and economically of the East European states on the USSR, and their fundamental attachment to communism. The paper makes clear that while the present ferment of thought will undoubtedly liberalise internal policy and external attitudes there is no "Hungarian" revolution in sight.

'(2) It follows that any attempt by us to "drive a wedge" between the USSR and the others would be unsuccessful and even counter-productive. In any case, it is not change by major disturbance that we wish to see but an evolution of effective co-existence.

'(3) The USSR's intense opposition to NATO and indeed to any alliance of the West must be expected to continue. Even if they ceased to respect the strength of such an alliance, they would need some cry of external danger to consolidate their own public opinion and their own alliance.

'(4) The special target of their attack will continue to be the USA, not only because of the latter's military-technological superiority but also because of a genuine apprehension of an impulsive tendency in its diplomacy.

'(5) For this reason, the USSR has a curiously ambivalent attitude to the UK-USA relationship. It seeks to detach us from the USA and it appreciates that in the meantime we have influence in Washington and that that influence is good. In any case, we should firmly repel Soviet attempts to impair or dissolve that relationship.

'(6) And, generally, in our attitude to the USSR we should, as the paper very cogently states, meet toughness with toughness. Utter clarity, bordering on crudity, pays with the Russians. Goronwy Roberts, 13 June 1968.'

No. 12

General observations by the Foreign Office on certain problems associated with the promotion of further co-operation with the Soviet Union[1]

[NS 3/7]

Restricted   FOREIGN OFFICE, *18 June 1968*

The British side of the Anglo-Soviet Consultative Committee has already received a paper describing in general terms the extent of existing contacts with the Soviet Union.[2] The paper did not attempt to assess the more fundamental problems associated with the exchanges. The purpose of the present paper is to remedy this omission. The Soviet side to the Consultative Committee is largely composed of senior officials who will use the Consultative Committee to promote Soviet State objectives though given the nature of the Soviet Union no actions could be taken which did not have the approval of the Government whatever might have been the composition of the Soviet group. This being so, the members of the British Group may wish to be more fully acquainted with British official thinking about Anglo-Soviet co-operation, and about some of the problems and opportunities which may be encountered at meetings of the Consultative Committee.

The Organisational Problem

2. The Soviet Union is highly centralised and *all* contacts abroad, and the funds available for such contacts, are strictly controlled by the Government. But the separation of budgetary control in Moscow leads to bureaucratic divisions which are reflected in the Cultural Agreement.[3] For example, Article II has become the province on the Soviet side of the Soviet Academy. Article V is the province of the Ministry of Primary and Secondary Education. These divisions create serious, but in the overall picture relatively minor, problems of liaison. For example, a British university (regarded by the

[1] This paper was drafted by Mr. R. Brash, head of East-West Contacts Department, as part of the briefing prepared for the British Group of the Anglo-Soviet Consultative Committee in anticipation of their first meeting with the Soviet Group (see No. 11, note 7). In a minute of 13 May Mr. Beattie had suggested to Mr. Smith and Mr. Brash that the briefing was 'likely to be an operation of some magnitude' as the Soviet Group (headed by Deputy Soviet Foreign Minister Kozyrev and including the Deputy Minister of Culture and the Vice-President of the Academy of Sciences of the USSR) consisted of 'highly professional and experienced officials, who will no doubt arrive comprehensively briefed, and having certain well-defined objectives in view', but Mr. Brash argued on 17 May that briefing should be simple and selective, and that it was important to explain as well 'the background problems which we face'.

[2] Not printed.

[3] An Anglo-Soviet Cultural Agreement had been negotiated at two-yearly intervals since 1959. The current agreement, negotiated in London in February 1967 and entitled an 'Agreement on Relations in the Scientific, Technological, Educational and Cultural Fields', covered the period from 1 April 1967 to 31 March 1969, and provided for a limited range of educational, scientific and other specialised exchanges, and more loosely formulated co-operation in the fields of the performing arts, broadcasting, the cinema and tourism (Cmnd. 3279 of 1967).

Russians as falling under the umbrella of Article V, i.e. of the Ministry of Higher Education) seeking to establish direct contact with the Herzen Language Institute (regarded by the Russians as falling under Article VI, i.e. under the Ministry of Secondary and Primary Education) finds it difficult to make any arrangements.

3. On the British side we have a more co-ordinated and flexible system. The British Council acts as general agent for the Government over exchanges of persons under official auspices, using funds granted to it from the Foreign Office vote. The Cultural Agreement is an intergovernmental instrument with the Foreign Office assuming overall responsibility. The British Council has a broad mandate under its Charter of Incorporation to promote a wider knowledge of the English language and to develop closely [*sic*] cultural relations with other countries. Further it has a network of Council offices within the United Kingdom which, coupled with the expertise in the British Council Headquarters, is capable of dealing with exchanges of a very wide variety. The Council deals direct with British universities and other learned institutions, while co-operating with interested Ministries in Whitehall. Generally speaking, the separate Ministries in Whitehall do not dispose of funds for promoting bilateral exchanges of persons with the Communist countries.

4. There is thus a great difference between the two sides in their administrative approach to the bilateral officially sponsored exchanges. We see considerable advantage in *our* system because:

(*a*) it allows flexibility. This is important because the interests of the two sides in exchanges are not the same. Generally the Russians prefer to send scientists and technologists while we send persons interested in the arts and humanities. Our approach allows us some hope of achieving an overall balance in the value of the exchanges despite the differing approaches of the two sides. Since the taxpayer's money is involved and since the Soviet Union is not a 'developing' country, we regard it as necessary to seek a fair balance of advantage in the *subsidised* exchanges. If the separate fields were to be partitioned off and the machinery divided up, the Russians would continue to develop scientific and technological exchanges where for the moment we have the lesser interest, while they might progressively restrict exchanges in the non-scientific academic area, especially at times of strict ideological orthodoxy;

(*b*) our approach allows us greater opportunity to tackle effectively the frustrations described in paragraph 2. This is not unimportant.

(*c*) we regard it as important gradually to enhance the position of the British Council. Ultimately we could hope for recognition by the Russians of the Council as an agent of Her Majesty's Government for the promotion of cultural and academic exchanges, though obviously it would be unrealistic to press for this at the moment.

5. The Russians have never said so openly, but they clearly suspect and dislike the co-ordinated system on the British side. They would like to

undermine the prestige and authority enjoyed by the British Council They would prefer a system whereby their separate Ministries concluded separate deals over exchanges of persons with different official bodies in Britain. They would expect this to bring them more in return for less. There would of course remain a close internal control within the Soviet Union.

Finance

6. The British side has a financial ceiling imposed upon it. There is no likelihood that the funds available for Anglo-Soviet exchanges will substantially increase in the next three years, and indeed the effects of devaluation and rising costs must be borne within the existing budget.[4]

7. It follows from this that our policy, so far as the subsidised exchanges are concerned, must essentially be one of judging where the expenditure of money is most rewarding within the existing pattern of exchanges. This is not a field where one can quickly chop and change about. We are looking for long-term results, and continuity of application over such things as the quotas of our scholarships, lecturers and exchanges of specialists is of great importance. One has to plan months ahead for a postgraduate, for example, to go to the Soviet Union.

8. The Russians do not allow financial considerations to put limits on exchanges in fields which they regard as of importance to their economy, i.e. primarily science and technology, agriculture and medicine. In the face of constant Russian pressure we have taken a cautiously expansionist line, agreeing to expand exchanges in these fields in close relationship to the extent of British interest. Beyond this balance of advantage we regard it as open to the Russians to pay themselves for additional specialist visitors to Britain, subject of course to the convenience of those organisations which receive them.

Accommodation and facilities for families

9. This is a serious underlying problem behind all the exchanges. Generally speaking Russians do not bring their families to England. Their needs of accommodation and other facilities are in consequence relatively modest. In the other direction we face a natural reluctance of married Britons to leave their families behind for any length of time. This has an effect on British interest in exchanges with the Soviet Union which is difficult to quantify but which must be considerable. The result is that longer-term British visitors to the Soviet Union (i.e. for more than three months or so) are usually un-married and therefore on the average on the young side. The more senior people usually prefer a short visit, say, two to three weeks.

10. Exchanges of persons with the Soviet Union unfortunately are not easy and we have a responsibility to British persons, particularly the more youthful, whom we send *under official auspices* to the Soviet Union. It is of importance

---

[4] The 1967-9 Cultural Agreement represented financially about a 10% increase over the level of the previous agreement, the increase being largely devoted to educational exchanges. An earlier Foreign Office brief noted that: 'Given the overall cut in the overseas information budget, this increase represented favourable treatment and was a reflection of the importance we attach to Anglo-Soviet relations' (MAS 3/11).

that they should not find themselves in situations which could expose them to risk or affect their later careers. In their own interest as much as ours therefore we seek to avoid sending persons under official auspices who are likely to get into trouble with the Soviet authorities, for example, because of unstable personality or contact with extremist organisations. We attach particular importance to giving a serious briefing to those who go to the Soviet Union under our official auspices, particularly on the long-term visits and particularly where they are relatively young.

Sources of information

11. Britain is an open society and freely publicises its problems and achievements. It is sometimes not appreciated how very great is the volume of information available. Apart from the newspapers and magazines there are, for example, over four hundred trade journals and magazines covering every facet of the economy. The Russians make full use of this information and their visitors are usually well briefed on where to go and what to see.

12. The same is not true in the other direction. The situation has improved considerably, both as a result of the Cultural Programme and the private contacts established outside it, but there is far from an equal flow of information and very often British specialists are not fully aware (nor are we) of what is available in the Soviet Union and who are the specialists concerned with their fields of interest.

13. This also contributes to the differing character of exchanges in each direction. British specialists outside the fields of linguistics, history and literature, at this stage of our relationship with the Soviet Union, usually prefer a short visit taking in calls at a number of Soviet institutions, to establish initial contact with Soviet colleagues and to assess the chances of further co-operation. The Soviet side on the whole is more interested in longer term visits of two months or more with the acquisition of actual knowhow in mind. They are still generally averse to the penetration (as they regard it) of their system by foreigners and in consequence are interested in cutting down the short-term 'spread' visits which are more difficult to control and in concentrating on the longer term attachments: they do no doubt calculate that there would be relatively less interest in the latter on the British side. This again is an area where we have to maintain a keen eye on our own interest in the intergovernmental exchanges.

Devolution versus Centralisation

14. On the British side we have never regarded the Cultural Agreement as establishing an exclusive machinery for non-political and non-commercial exchanges between the two countries. It was an official attempt on our side to break down the initial barriers, and it also reflected genuine interest in Britain. It was intended as *an introduction* to a free flow of information, persons and ideas. We are not geared to, nor have we the finance to operate more than a small proportion of the whole gamut of exchanges which there could be with so large and in some fields as advanced a country as the Soviet Union *if* the Soviet Union were more liberal in its approach.

15. The Soviet side is of course conditioned to think in terms of state planning and of intergovernmental negotiation. There have been some welcome developments over the establishment of direct contacts with private organisations in Britain, but the Soviet instinct is still to make arrangements through the official channel. Direct contacts are usually made only when the Russians regard it as clearly in their immediate interest as regards knowhow or for commercial reasons, and often when we have said that there is little more that we can do officially. This is illustrated by Russian arrangements with private British impresarios. It is broadly true of relations in the film world. If they cannot get what they want through the private channel, however, they revert to the official and try to put pressure that way.

16. If our exchanges with the Soviet Union are to maintain the rapid rate of development achieved since the early 1960s, the main hope lies in breaking out of the shell of the intergovernmental arrangements, and in expanding contacts which, on the British side, are organised on a private basis. This explains the official support which we give to the Great Britain/USSR Association[5] and lies at the heart of the creation of the Consultative Committee, whose terms of reference include the study of opportunities for developing contacts supplementing those being conducted through the governmental channel.

The areas of possible growth

17. A simple rule of thumb to apply to areas of likely growth in bilateral contacts is that they must either be:

(*a*) areas where one side has sufficient interest to send and pay for individuals to go to the other country; or

(*b*) areas where both sides share a keen interest and where there is a chance of the costs also being shared.

On the whole it is unwise to force exchanges. *An indifferent exchange is often worse than no exchange at all.*

18. The obvious areas for greater co-operation are:

(*a*) language study exchanges. We suspect that a good many British universities and schools would be happy to arrange direct exchanges with suitable opposite numbers in the Soviet Union. These exchanges can be at school pupil, undergraduate, teacher and university teaching assistant levels (not easily above this level—lecturer exchanges in our experience raise great difficulties). Language study exchanges of school children could also breathe life into town twinning arrangements as they often do with town twinnings with France and Germany. Arrangements where school pupils stay with families are often the most suitable for this age group, and staying with families can be arranged either under town twinning arrangements or by inter-school links. We would hope that the organisation of all such links

---

[5] The GB-USSR Association was founded in 1959 to handle the informal and unofficial aspects of cultural relations with the USSR. It was funded to a large extent by the British Council.

would be accompanied by a due sense of responsibility on the British side. It is most unlikely that the Soviet side would agree to an arrangement whereby school children could stay with families in either country, but there would be no harm in floating the idea now, in the hope that it may later become practicable;

(b) other specialist exchanges. This involves lowering the barriers between academic and other learned institutions on both sides. British universities, often particular faculties, like to enter into direct exchange arrangements with other universities, over such matters as visiting professors and lecturers. Similarly independent learned institutions are interested in establishing direct contacts with their opposite numbers abroad. This can be a fruitful field, but it must clearly be closely related to the mutual interest of those learned persons immediately concerned on both sides. The field is potentially enormous, and exceedingly varied. If the British group could discover learned societies interested for their own reasons in promoting direct links, this could provide valuable ammunition to promote expansion in this field;

(c) other non-specialist exchanges. This includes tourism. It also includes the multiplicity of arrangements in this country for youth travel—from Youth Hostels to Agricultural Camps. Work camps are probably a useful idea for Anglo-Soviet relations because travel expense is such an obstacle: students would more easily visit the other country if they had a means of subsistence at the other end. There are a great number of private organisations in this country engaged in this type of activity. The Booklet prepared by the Central Bureau for Educational Visits and Exchanges gives some idea of the potentialities.

(a), (b) and (c) are all fields which in the Foreign Office view afford great opportunities for future expansion of exchanges between our two countries and we believe that the British group could usefully promote this expansion.

Soviet Objectives

19. The overall Soviet outlook is likely to be restrictive. They may be expected to aim to:

(a) reduce co-ordination on our side;

(b) secure greater *quotas* in the fields which they expect to bring them the greatest practical benefit, i.e. science and technology, medicine and agriculture;

(c) secure greater co-operation in their own commercial interest from sectors of the British economy where they have made relatively little progress in the past, e.g. the film world;

(d) stonewall when it comes to the larger issues of freedom of information (press, radio and television, and the flow of specialist information each way) and of greater freedom of exchanges of persons (paragraphs 18 (a), (b) and (c) above).

It would of course be normal tactics for the Soviet Group to concentrate discussion on those areas where they see advantage accruing to themselves. They must surely also accept that their objectives cannot be wholly restricted to the pursuit of their own interests if the work of the Consultative Committee is to be successful, as we are entitled to conclude, from their own repeated statements, that they wish it to be.

The next three documents in this Collection refer to British policy during the crisis caused by the Soviet invasion of Czechoslovakia on the night of 20-21 August 1968, which had an immediate and damaging impact on Anglo-Soviet relations. The documents printed here do not attempt to chart the course of events in detail: instead, they show how the Czechoslovak crisis was viewed in London shortly before and immediately after the invasion, and the reconsideration of British policy towards the Soviet Union which took place as a result.

Czechoslovak-Soviet tension had increased steadily since the Eastern European Ambassadors had discussed the question in May (No. 10). In spite of Mr. Dubcek's frequent protestations of loyalty to the Warsaw Pact, CMEA and the Communist alliance, the Soviet leaders' alarm at internal developments in Czechoslovakia continued to grow throughout the early summer of 1968. They took every opportunity to send delegations to Czechoslovakia or to organise bilateral talks with prominent Czech figures in the Soviet Union, and the Soviet Press constantly emphasised the importance of Soviet-Czechoslovak economic links. There was some relaxation when Mr. Kosygin went to Karlovy Vary in Czechoslovakia from 17-27 May for what was enigmatically described as 'rest and the cure' (cf. No. 8), but whatever he hoped to achieve by a policy of quiet diplomacy, involving perhaps economic incentives as well, he had little success and after his return the pressure built up again and there were direct attacks on Czech public figures. From 20 June Warsaw Pact 'Command-Staff exercises' were held in Czechoslovakia, though no word appeared in the Soviet press about the reluctance of the Czechs to have such exercises on their territory or the dispute about the departure of the troops which followed.

The climax of the campaign came with the meeting of the Soviet, Polish, Bulgarian, East German and Hungarian leaders in Warsaw on 14-15 July, which led to a five-party letter to the Czech leadership setting out a series of demands including the ending of the activity of all anti-Socialist political organisations, the repossession by the Party of the mass information media, and a decisive and bold offensive against Right-wing and anti-Socialist forces. Despite what Sir G. Harrison termed 'this brutal document',[1] however, the Czechoslovak leadership stuck fast to their programme of internal reform, and refused a Soviet invitation to a meeting of East European Communist parties, intended to take Mr. Dubcek to task for the 'Two Thousand Word' appeal for further reform of the Party and increased freedom issued on 27 June by 70 prominent Czechoslovak liberals. Meanwhile, Sir W. Barker reported from Prague that Soviet pressure gave little or no comfort to

---

[1] Moscow despatch of 20 August, N 2/29.

conservative elements in Czechoslovakia, while crude intervention in Czech internal affairs alienated much of the goodwill the Russians had previously enjoyed.

The increasing impetus of reform in Czechoslovakia and the consequent increase in tension both within Eastern Europe and between the Soviet Union and Czechoslovakia had been watched with growing concern by the Western powers, even though the consensus of opinion before 20 August was that the Soviet Union would draw back in the last resort from the use of force to bring Czechoslovakia into line. HMG's policy, as set out on 18 July by Mr. Stewart in the House of Commons[2] was based on the consideration that each country should decide for itself how to conduct its internal affairs. They were also anxious to avoid giving any substance to reports in the Communist press that the West was involved in a campaign to undermine socialism. However, Mr. Stewart and Foreign Office officials had been considering whether there was any action to be taken by Britain or with her allies to deter Soviet intervention in Czechoslovakia. Sir P. Dean's reports from Washington made it clear that although the US Government were also very concerned about the situation they had decided against taking any action: 'there was little disposition on the President's part to send any high-level messages to Moscow unless . . . there was some demonstrable advantage in doing so. A message could well be counter-productive.'[3] In particular, the State Department were firmly opposed to the idea of consultation within NATO, which would be bound to become public knowledge and could do a good deal of harm. Sir G. Harrison expressed his agreement with the American view that Soviet policy would be determined by 'whatever way they think best calculated to achieve their purpose of reinstating a trustworthy leadership in Czechoslovakia' and that they would 'not be deflected by any other considerations'.

Mr. Stewart still felt that some form of 'gentle warning' should be given to the Soviet Union in the hope of achieving a deterrent effect, 'if only to show that no move had been lacking on the Western side to avoid the reversion to a cold war situation'. Mr. Hayman was instructed to speak to the Soviet Ambassador at the Polish National Day Reception on 22 July, pointing out that various 'encouraging signs of an improvement in East/West relations would all be drastically set back if the Russians walked into Czechoslovakia'. Meanwhile, in Washington, Mr. Rusk had taken the Soviet Ambassador, Mr. Dobrynin, to task over continued allegations that the US was interfering in Czechoslovak affairs, warning him that the US Government would not stand for their alleged interference being used as a pretext for Soviet intervention in Czechoslovakia.[4] In this context, Mr. Stewart sought the views of the Ambassadors in Moscow, Prague and Washington on representations to both the Soviet and Czechoslovak Governments.

[2] *Parl. Debs.*, 5th ser., H. of C., vol. 768, col. 1683.
[3] Washington telegram No. 2207 of 19 July, N 2/29.
[4] See *FRUS 1964-1968*, vol. xvii, pp. 212-14.

No. 13

Mr. Stewart to Sir G. Harrison (Moscow)

No. 2005 Telegraphic [N 2/29]

Flash. Secret   FOREIGN OFFICE, *24 July 1968*

Repeated to Prague and Washington, and for information to UKDEL NATO, UKMIS New York.

Czech Crisis

With the growing tension caused by the announcement of large scale manoeuvres in the Western part of the Soviet Union,[1] I am increasingly concerned that we should not fail to bring home to the Russians our appreciation of the very grave consequences for our relations which will follow if they pursue their bullying tactics against Czechoslovakia much further. I appreciate that the Soviet leaders must have taken these consequences into account, and I believe that they still wish to avoid open intervention. Nevertheless, I have it in mind that I should myself put on record with the Soviet Ambassador our view of the very serious consequences of their taking even more extreme action.

2. I would speak to him primarily of the consequences for East/West relations generally, and in particular of the setback to the patient work which has gone into improving the mutual understanding between this and other Western Governments on the one hand and the Soviet Union on the other. These representations would be in parallel with those made by Rusk (Washington telegram No. 7245).[2]

3. The timing of these representations would be most important. I am anxious not to say anything which would hamper the prospects of the Czechoslovak leaders in their impending encounter with the Soviet Politburo.[3] It is however equally important to speak, if we are going to do so, before the Russians have finally determined upon a course of action which goes beyond the limits of toleration.

4. I should be grateful for the immediate views of HM Ambassadors in Moscow and Prague both on the wisdom of the course proposed and on timing; HM Ambassador in Washington should also consult the State Department urgently and telegraph comments.

[1] On receipt on 23 July of a press report announcing military exercises over a large area in the west of the Soviet Union until 10 August, Mr. Giffard commented that the Soviet Union's 'undoubted ability to intervene rapidly with military force will be underlined by these manoeuvres'.

[2] The reference should be to Washington telegram No. 2245 of 23 July, which reported Mr. Rusk's conversation with Mr. Dobrynin: see above.

[3] Following a meeting of the Praesidium of the Czechoslovak Communist Party Central Committee on 22 July a *communiqué* was issued announcing bilateral talks, to be held on Czechoslovak territory, between the full Czech Praesidium and the full Politburo of the Communist Party of the Soviet Union: as Mr. Giffard commented on 23 July, 'a most extraordinary event . . . They want the meeting so that the process of bullying can go on.'

5. I have also been wondering whether there is anything which we could say to the Czechoslovaks. I believe that it would be a mistake to ask their Ambassador or any member of his staff to call at the Foreign Office since any report that we had been speaking to them could well damage their interests. I take the point in para. 3 of Prague telegram No. 396,[4] but if Sir William Barker were able to find a discreet opportunity to make clear to the Czechoslovak authorities what are our views, I believe he should do so.

6. I should of course also be grateful for immediate advice on contributions of the kind mentioned in paragraph 4 of Prague telegram No. 396 of 23 July to Foreign Office.[5]

7. If I do summon the Soviet Ambassador I may be able to avoid publicity altogether; in any event we shall be very circumspect indeed about anything that is said about the interview.[6]

[4] In this telegram of 23 July Sir W. Barker stated that at a time when the Czechoslovaks were being 'warned ad nauseam repeat ad nauseam by their allies that the West is conniving a[t] unhealthy developments in this country, with a view first to undermining "socialism" and then exploiting the situation, and when, moreover, the Czechoslovaks are taking some pride in the unaccustomed feeling that they are paddling their own canoes, any encouraging message from the West would seem to them patronising or naive. Dubcek and his associates well understand the reasons underlying the refusal of Western governments to commit themselves to more than expressions of close interest in developments here, and it accords both with their declared policy and with their own interests.'

[5] Sir W. Barker had suggested that 'the most valuable contributions the West can make at this time are modest but practical ones, such as prompt, definitive and unequivocal cancellation of the *Bundeswehr* "Black Lion" exercise in Bavaria'.

[6] Replies to this telegram from Moscow, Prague and Washington were despatched later on 24 July. Sir G. Harrison commented in telegram No. 1177 that he 'did not think anything said to the Soviet Ambassador will deflect the Soviet leaders from whatever action they consider to be necessary', although he agreed there could be merit in placing British views on record as proposed in para. 2 of Mr. Stewart's telegram. He warned, however, that if the interview with Mr. Smirnovsky were publicised, 'this, taken in conjunction with mounting criticism in Parliament and the British press and from public opinion generally, would almost certainly lead to a strong Soviet reaction'.

Sir P. Dean reported in Washington telegram No. 2256 that Mr. Bohlen, Deputy Under-Secretary of Political Affairs, who was 'in the closest touch all the time with Mr. Rusk' saw no objection to Mr. Stewart's proposed low-key approach to the Soviet Ambassador, although he was 'a little concerned about the danger of any appearance of ganging-up between them and ourselves which might be exploited to our mutual disadvantage by Soviet propaganda'. The Americans had, however, decided against any approach to the Czechs: 'They are greatly encouraged by the skill and steadfastness with which the Czechs are handling the problem. They have had no indications from the Czechs that they would like to hear from the U.S.'

Sir W. Barker, in Prague telegram No. 404, advised that any British initiative 'should be subject to two over-riding considerations: '(A) It should afford no shadow of justification for any suspicion or allegation that we were seeking to play a part in the Czechoslovak-Soviet disagreement and (B) it should leave no slightest loophole for anybody to infer or insinuate that our nerves are less strong than those of the Czechoslovaks, who still look admirably steadfast.' He continued to maintain that an approach to the Czechoslovaks would be a mistake: 'Indeed I find it hard to conceive of any useful result . . . '

In the light of these telegrams Mr. Stewart informed the three Ambassadors on 25 July that he had decided not to summon the Soviet Ambassador, particularly since Mr. Hayman had already informed him of HMG's views (see p. 65). On 30 July, however, the Secretary of State took advantage of a meeting which Mr. Smirnovsky had requested to discuss the uses of outer space to repeat his 'serious concern that events in Eastern Europe should not develop in such a way as to damage the prospects for continued improvement in East/West relations'. Mr. Smirnovsky retorted that 'the Soviet Government would not accept a warning', but Mr. Stewart persisted that he felt it right to speak out, since 'if events went badly over Czechoslovakia, the opportunities for increasing understanding between us would be frozen'.

In Sir W. Barker's words, the 'grand climax . . . of the Soviet Union's ponderous nerve war on the Czechoslovak leaders was unfolded at Cierna nad Tisou' between 29 July and 1 August 'when the final and decisive confrontation between the Soviet Communist Party's Politburo and the Czechoslovak Party's Presidium took place'.[1] The grand climax, however, turned out somewhat anti-climactic: the resulting communiqué spoke blandly of a 'broad comradely exchange of opinion' and merely announced that a conference of the Bulgarian, Czechoslovak, East German, Hungarian, Polish and Soviet Communist Parties would be held at Bratislava on 3 August. It appeared that yet again Mr. Dubcek and his colleagues had stood firm in defence of their programme of reform, and that, faced with a choice between retreat and the use of force the Russians had opted for rationality. This impression was reinforced by the Bratislava Declaration issued after the ensuing conference: again in Sir W. Barker's words, it was 'a hotch-potch of old-fashioned Soviet hate slogans combined with a repledging of Socialist solidarity and co-operation. It was designed to save Soviet face and inhibit Czechoslovak freedom of action'. No further mention was made of the demands in the Warsaw letter (see pp. 65-6).

Although it appeared that a crisis point had been reached and passed, the Czechoslovak-Soviet situation remained unresolved. A Soviet press campaign stressing the importance and achievements of the Cierna and Bratislava meetings gradually gave way to new reports attacking the 'forces of reaction' in Czechoslovakia and accusing the enemies of socialism of plotting the restoration of the old bourgeois order. HM Embassy in Moscow reported an 'intensification of the renewed polemics' in the Soviet press, and indications of Soviet apprehensions that the September Congress of the Czechoslovak Communist Party might lead to radical changes in the membership of the Central Committee. The Soviet military build-up at the Czechoslovak borders continued.

At 1.30 a.m. on 21 August Lord Chalfont, Minister of State in charge of the Foreign Office during Mr. Stewart's absence on holiday, received on the Prime Minister's behalf an oral message and aide-mémoire delivered by the Soviet Ambassador. It stated that in view of the 'threat to the Socialist order in Czechoslovakia' from 'a plot of the external and internal reaction against the social order and the constitutionally established state system', Soviet military units had been instructed to enter Czechoslovak territory 'to comply with the request of the government of the Czechoslovak Socialist Republic to render the fraternal

---

[1] Prague despatch of 8 August, N 2 / 29.

Czechoslovak people all the necessary assistance'. The Prime Minister was assured that Soviet actions were 'not directed against any European state and in no way infringe upon anybody's state interests, including the interests of Great Britain . . . We assume that these developments should not harm the [sic] Soviet-British relations, to the promotion of which the Soviet Government attaches, as before, great importance.'[2]

[2] FO telegram No. 445 to Prague, 21 August, N 10/3.

No. 14

Extract from Conclusions of a Meeting of the Cabinet held at 10 Downing St. on 22 August 1968 at 10 a.m.[1]

CC(68)38 [CAB 128/43]

Secret

Czechoslovakia

(Previous Reference: CC(68)37th Conclusions, minute 2.[2])

1. THE FOREIGN SECRETARY said that we did not know the strength of the Warsaw Pact forces that had invaded Czechoslovakia on the night of 20th-21st August, but it was clear that their grip on the country was complete although some free radio stations were still operating. Ground forces of the Soviet Union, East Germany, Poland and Bulgaria were involved together with Soviet air forces. There were also indications of an increased level of activity in the Soviet long-range air and rocket forces but these did not appear to be in a high state of alert. A remarkable feature of the political situation was that no Czech leader had so far shown himself willing to act as a Soviet puppet. Mr. Dubcek, the Secretary of the Czech Communist Party, and others were in detention, but President Svoboda had issued a statement on the previous evening calling for the withdrawal of the invading troops and for the liberalisation programme in Czechoslovakia to continue; it might be,

[1] Present at this meeting were: Mr. Wilson, Mr. Stewart, Mr. R. Crossman (Lord President of the Council), Mr. J. Callaghan (Secretary of State for the Home Department), Mr. Healey, Mr. F. Peart (Lord Privy Seal), Mr. P. Shore (Secretary of State for Economic Affairs), Mr. W. Ross (Secretary of State for Scotland), Mr. G. Thomson (Secretary of State for Commonwealth Affairs), Mr. E. Short (Secretary of State for Education and Science), Mr. Wedgwood Benn, Mr. C. Hughes (Minister of Agriculture, Fisheries and Food), Lord Shackleton (Paymaster General), Mr. G. Thomas (Secretary of State for Wales), Mr. R. Mason (Minister of Power), Mr. J. Diamond (Chief Secretary, Treasury) and Mr. E. Dell (Minister of State, Board of Trade).

[2] At this meeting on 1 August Mr. Stewart reported to the Cabinet that he had decided that it would be unwise to make a formal approach to the Soviet Ambassador about Czechoslovakia (cf. No. 13), although he had spoken to the Ambassador informally (*ibid.*, note 6). He told the Cabinet that Mr. Smirnovsky's reaction 'had been cautious and defensive and he had laid emphasis on the needs of Soviet military security, with particular reference to Germany. Similar approaches had apparently been made in other capitals; and it was clear that their purpose was to elicit world reaction on the Czechoslovak issue'.

however, that the Soviet authorities hoped that he would be prepared to co-operate with them. The Czech people were behaving with very great restraint and, although there had been some deaths, widespread bloodshed did not seem likely. It was not clear why the Soviet Union had resorted to military action, despite the agreement reached at Bratislava; it might be that they did not consider that censorship was being sufficiently rigidly imposed by the Czech Government as a result of the agreement or that they feared the outcome of the elections for the Presidium of the Czech Communist Party which were due to take place on 9th September.

Our decision to publish a statement on the previous day condemning the Soviet action had been both right in principle and justified in its results.[3] Our objective had been to avoid acting in isolation but to be among the leaders of the reaction of world opinion. Support had been rallied in the United Nations and seven members of the Security Council, including France, had called for a meeting of the Council, at which all but the Soviet Union and Hungary had voted for the matter to be inscribed on the agenda.[4] Those voting in favour had included Algeria and also India and Pakistan, whose High Commissioners had been called to a meeting of Commonwealth representatives in London at the Commonwealth Office on the previous day where they had been briefed on the facts of the situation as we knew them and of our attitude to them. It was possible that there would be a vote on a suitable Resolution in the Security Council by the following day. There would be great advantage if, despite the certainty of a Soviet veto, this happened before a puppet Government had been set up in Czechoslovakia. We should

---

[3] A statement had been issued from No. 10 Downing Street at 12.45 p.m. on 21 August describing 'the action taken by the Soviet Government and certain of her allies in invading Czechoslovakia as a flagrant violation of the United Nations Charter and of all accepted standards of international behaviour . . . It is a serious blow to the efforts which so many countries have been making to improve relations between east and west (*The Times*, 22 August 1968, p. 1). Mr. Stewart had summoned the Soviet Ambassador to the Foreign Office at noon to speak to him in the same vein, pointing out the conflict between the Soviet claim to have been invited into Czechoslovakia and the repeated statements broadcast during the night of 20/21 August by the Czechoslovak Government, the Praesidium of the Czech Communist Party and the Czech National Assembly to the effect that the Russians were not wanted. Mr. Smirnovsky, 'who throughout the interview had been extremely ill at ease', declined to add anything to the oral statement he had delivered to Lord Chalfont: see pp. 68-9; the interview was reported to Moscow in telegram No. 2104 of 21 August (N 10/3).

[4] Foreign Office telegram No. 3106 to UKMIS New York despatched early on 21 August informed Lord Caradon, UK Representative to the United Nations, that Mr. Stewart thought it 'essential that the invasion of Czechoslovakia should be raised urgently in the Security Council' and instructed him to begin 'urgent consultations, especially with other members of the Security Council and notably the US, as to who might take the initiative and in what form the question might best be raised'. Lord Caradon reported later that day that no Communist delegation would raise the issue, but after intensive consultation the UK, US, French, Danish, Canadian and Paraguayan Governments agreed jointly to ask the Brazilian President for an immediate meeting to consider 'the present serious situation' in Czechoslovakia. The Security Council met at 11.30 p.m. BST and sat for five hours, holding a number of sessions in the next few days (NC 2/7).

decide, in the light of events, what further action would be appropriate in the United Nations.[5]

As regards the North Atlantic Treaty Organisation (NATO), he had stressed in an interview on television about our attitude to the Czech crisis that recent events had demonstrated the Organisation's great importance.[6] Nevertheless, it did not appear that we faced the likelihood of general war in Europe but rather a serious setback to a better understanding between East and West. Although some precautionary action had been taken in NATO and some consideration given to the possible refugee problem, no general alert had been instituted.

Looking to the longer term effects of recent events on our relations with the Soviet Union and on East/West relations generally, our objective should remain to obtain world-wide condemnation of the Soviet action but to avoid becoming singled out as particularly hostile. We should need to consider our attitude on trade and on Ministerial and officials' visits to countries which had participated in the aggression and for the present such visits should be avoided. He had himself cancelled his planned visits to Hungary and Bulgaria but was prepared to carry out that to Rumania unless the Rumanian Government preferred him not to do so.

In discussion, there was general agreement with the action which had been taken to issue a Government statement on the previous day and with its terms. There was agreement also that our policy should be on the lines indicated by the Foreign Secretary. It did not appear that there was at present any threat to peace in Europe generally and the Soviet Government had been at pains to impress on NATO Governments the limited nature of the action that was being taken. We had been aware that forces were being concentrated on the borders of Czechoslovakia and were not therefore taken by surprise; but the NATO authorities were being careful to do nothing which might increase tension. So far there were no indications that a similar move was intended against Rumania. There was at present a general understanding that the West would not intervene against the Soviet Union in Soviet bloc countries and that Soviet intervention in Berlin or in a NATO country would involve risk of general war. At the same time, it was clear that the régimes in Eastern Europe, and particularly that in East Germany, only remained in power by the ruthless use of military force and of censorship. If the Soviet Union were to fail in her objectives in Czechoslovakia it was possible that the régimes in the surrounding countries would disintegrate. It was not yet clear, however, that the Soviet Union would be able to find

[5] Soviet use of the veto and filibustering tactics delayed proceedings in the Security Council, and although there was some talk of transferring the debate to the UN General Assembly no decision had been taken by the time the *communiqué* on the Soviet-Czechoslovak talks held in Moscow from 24-27 August was issued (see p. 74 below).

[6] During an interview on *News at Ten* on 21 August Mr. Stewart had said: 'It's because that [North Atlantic] Alliance exists that many countries, members of it, are not subject to what Czechoslovakia is subject now . . . we must maintain the strength of the North Atlantic Alliance.'

Czechoslovak nationals willing to form a puppet government and she might have to withdraw her troops. In that event the Czech people might not totally have lost. We should consider how far it would be in our interest, despite the risks involved, for the Soviet Government to fail and whether we could do anything to encourage the Czechs to insist on the authority of their legal Government and to press for the Russians to withdraw their troops. While we should not seek to stimulate the Czechs to resist, it would be right for us to ensure, in concert with other like-minded countries, that the facts of the situation both inside and outside their country were available to them, particularly in the next few days, before it became clear whether or not a puppet Government would be installed. There would be advantage also in arrangements being made, for example by the Labour Party and the United Nations Association for public demonstrations to be held in this country in support of the Czech people and Government and for the Government to provide speakers for them. It was important that, both in the forthcoming debate in Parliament and in demonstrations, the attitude of the British people as a whole should be made clear to the Soviet Government. We should consider whether our Ambassador in Moscow should be recalled for consultation and whether there would be advantage in using the 'hot line' to Moscow to reiterate our attitude and to ask the Soviet Government, even at this late stage, to withdraw her forces from Czechoslovakia. In general our aim should be to secure the continuance of the existing Czech Government and the withdrawal of Russian troops, though on the understanding that the Czech Government would have to make some concessions to Russian opposition to the programme of liberalisation.

In further discussion, it was agreed that no final decision should be taken at present on whether or not we should recognise any puppet Government that might be installed in Czechoslovakia. This decision would have to be taken in the light of events in concert with our allies. For the present, however, we should continue to recognise the existing legitimate Government. As regards trade, we should adhere to our traditional attitude of not interfering unilaterally with it. Special consideration would, however, be needed of our attitude to the forthcoming Trade Fair at Brno, on which we should seek the views of the Czechs themselves, and of trade concessions which were being considered in relation to the Soviet Union. There were currently 1,000 Czech students in this country on a six weeks' visit as well as other Czech nationals. Arrangements would be made to extend their visas for a month at a time in the hope that the situation would by then have clarified; they would not be sent back against their will.

THE PRIME MINISTER, summing up the discussion, said that there was general agreement in the Cabinet with the action which had been taken so far in relation to events in Czechoslovakia. The likely future course of events was unclear and it might be that another meeting of the Cabinet would be necessary early in the following week to consider the situation further and in particular any question of the recognition of a puppet Government. If in the meantime any urgent action became necessary, he would consider this with the Foreign Secretary. It would be helpful if the transcript of the television interview which the Foreign Secretary had given on the previous evening could be circulated to all members of the Cabinet. Ministers intending to make statements about our policy in relation to Czechoslovakia should consult the Foreign Secretary. An urgent examination should be made of prospective visits by Ministers and officials and other sponsored individuals or parties for cultural and other exchanges to the countries involved in the aggression against Czechoslovakia. In so far as such visits had already been firmly arranged and were to our advantage, they should in general be allowed to take place though they would need to be carefully watched in the light of future developments. But no new arrangements for such visits should be made at present.

As regards trade relations, we should not seek to close the Soviet Exhibition in London prematurely and, subject to the advice of the Czech representatives in London and to no further deterioration in the situation, our participation in the Brno Trade Fair should be allowed to proceed. An examination should be made of the implications of recent events on our trade policy with the Soviet bloc generally, including in particular the relaxation that had been intended of our quota restrictions on Soviet imports into this country when the trade situation permitted this; the implications for our policy on strategic exports and on the strategic embargo should also be examined with a view to Ministerial consideration early in September. Consideration should also be given to the possibility for increased BBC broadcasts of factual material to Czechoslovakia and to the possibility that the 'hot line' to Moscow might be used to reiterate to the Russian Government our attitude to their actions.

The Cabinet:

(1) Took note, with approval, of the Prime Minister's summing up of their discussion.

(2) Invited the Foreign Secretary

(i) to arrange for the transcript of his television interview of the previous evening about Czechoslovakia to be circulated to all members of the Cabinet;

(ii) to arrange for an urgent examination to be made of prospective visits to the countries involved in aggression against Czechoslovakia on the basis indicated by the Prime Minister;[7]

[7] On 23 August Mr. Hayman chaired an inter-departmental meeting to consider the question of visits to and from the Soviet Union and the other East European countries which had participated in the occupation of Czechoslovakia. Ministerial visits were generally cancelled, but it was decided that visits and exchanges in the pursuit of important business should go ahead with a minimum of publicity. MPs were to be advised to cancel all engagements other than business ones, arrangements for sponsored tours were suspended, the proposed visit of two Soviet hydrographic vessels cancelled and the first meeting of the Anglo-Consultative Committee postponed (cf. No. 11, note 7). The Anglo-Soviet Exhibition scheduled to open in Moscow in September (planned under the provisions of the Anglo-Soviet Historical Protocol of 29 June 1966, together with a project for the joint publication of Anglo-Russian documents) was also cancelled.

(iii) to arrange for the possibility of increased factual broadcasts to Czechoslovakia to be considered;

(iv) to consider whether there would be advantage in using the 'hot line' to Moscow to reiterate our attitude on Czechoslovakia.[8]

(3) Invited the President of the Board of Trade to arrange for the Ministerial Committee on Commercial Policy and the Ministerial Committee on Strategic Exports to consider the implications of recent events on our policy in relation to the aggressor countries on trade and strategic exports respectively.[9]

(4) Invited the Lord Privy Seal to draw the attention of the leader of the prospective Parliamentary delegation to Bulgaria to the question whether it was desirable to proceed with the visit at the present juncture.

In his speech during the House of Commons debate on Czechoslovakia on 26 August Mr. Stewart said that while it was 'generally agreed that attempts to break ordinary trade between us and Eastern Europe are not relevant, would not be useful and are not the proper line of policy at the present time', he thought that 'we should avoid contacts which have clear political overtones or are of such a nature that the very fact that one has such a contact should be quoted as evidence that Britain really did not mind what had happened' (*Parl. Debs., 5th ser., H. of C.*, vol. 769, cols. 1417-18).

[8] In a minute to the Prime Minister later on 22 August, Mr. Stewart said he believed 'that the balance of argument comes down against using the hot line on this occasion', explaining that 'I think it is important to keep the hot line for occasions when there is a reasonable expectation that any message you send will receive a reply and not simply a retort . . . I have little doubt that Kosygin would feel obliged to return a totally unhelpful message on Czechoslovakia, if indeed he replied at all . . . a personal message to him at this stage could prejudice him against the hot line as a means of communication with you'. As an alternative, Mr. Stewart proposed to summon Mr. Smirnovsky again to press him on the circumstances in which the invading troops would be withdrawn: 'I doubt whether he will say much but I am sure that he reports to Moscow every detail of our talks. This would seem to be the best way of keeping up pressure on the Soviet Government'. The Prime Minister agreed on 23 August to the Secretary of State's suggestion. Mr. Stewart's unproductive interview on 26 August with Mr. Smirnovsky, who did not appear to have received any recent instructions, was reported to Moscow in telegram No. 2123 (N 10/3).

[9] Cf. No. 2, note 11, and see Tony Benn, *Diaries 1968-72, op. cit.*, pp. 99-100.

President Svoboda flew to Moscow on 23 August where he was reunited with his arrested colleagues (including Mr. Dubcek), who had been taken to Moscow via Poland or Slovakia. According to the US Ambassador in Prague, President Svoboda was 'deeply shocked by the physical and psychological state of his abducted countrymen.'[1] On 27 August a communiqué was issued in the names of the Soviet and Czechoslovak delegations reaffirming the 'mutual decisions adopted in Cierna-nad-Tisou and the provisions and principles formulated by the Bratislava Conference' (see p. 68) and setting out a number of 'practical steps' which amounted to tight Soviet control of

[1] Jacob D. Beam, *Multiple Exposure* (New York, 1978), p. 201.

Czechoslovak affairs and the continued presence, at least 'temporarily' of the occupying forces, although Mr Dubcek retained his position in the government (see The Times, 28 August 1968, p. 1). The Czechoslovak question was removed from the Security Council agenda at the request of the Czechoslovak Government.

Mr. Dalton gave his analysis of the situation in Moscow telegram No. 1408 of 28 August: [2] *'Taking a tally of the pluses and minuses in the communiqué on the Moscow negotiations there is no doubt that the Czechs have suffered a number of reverses. On the other hand, the Russians have failed to unseat Mr. Dubcek and his colleagues and to replace them by more reliable rulers. There can be no clearer sign of their failure to reimpose a Communist system à la russe than the official reacceptance of a man who only a week ago was branded as a "rightist revisionist" and by implication as a traitor. This is, however, still far from being the end of the story. If Mr. Dubcek and his colleagues can control the situation, and particularly the "counter-revolutionary" activities and anti-Soviet tendencies in the press, the Russians would seem to have little option but to tolerate his continued existence with some modified reforms, though they will no doubt try to bind him by economic and other means . . . Other consequences of recent events are likely to be far-reaching. The virus of liberalisation, if temporarily checked, is still there and both actual spread of the infection and fear of it will remain potent factors in the Communist system. The standing of the Soviet Union and of its Communist Party has been gravely damaged not only in the eyes of the "free world" and the uncommitted but not least in those of other Communist parties, with unforeseeable consequences for the Communist movement. And last, but perhaps not least, this affair, and particularly its mishandling, may have consequences in the Soviet Communist Party itself. Its members are not averse to arbitrariness, but they are averse to confusion and bungling and it must be clear to many of the comrades that this matter has been bungled.'*

Sir W. Barker, writing to Mr. Hayman on 3 September, expressed his views on the situation as viewed from the Czechoslovak side: 'the country is occupied by an enormous, hostile military force and . . . the leadership is therefore operating, if I may coin the understatement of the week, with a pistol at its head. In other words, for the foreseeable future the Czechoslovaks have no option but to do the Soviet bidding and, for practical purposes, they have reconciled themselves to this fact.' [3]

[2] N 2/33.   [3] NC 3/11.

No. 15

Mr. Dalton[1] (Moscow) to Mr. Stewart (Received 3 October)
[NS 3/18]

Confidential   MOSCOW, *30 September 1968*

Summary...[2]

Sir,

Czechoslovakia: Soviet Foreign Policy and our Policy Towards the Soviet Union

In my despatches of the 24th and the 27th of September[3] I took up the Czechoslovakia story from the invasion by Soviet and allied forces on the night of the 20th/21st of August and discussed the implications of these events for the international Communist movement, the Socialist camp and the Soviet Union itself. In this despatch I have the honour to consider Soviet foreign policy in the light of these events and the implications for our policy towards the Soviet Union.

2. It has been suggested that the Soviet military intervention was unpredictable and/or that it betokened a more forward or more expansionist policy on the part of the Soviet leaders, in the light of which we should revise our assessment of the Soviet position and, in consequence, our policies towards the Soviet Union.

3. The Soviet action, however, was 'unpredictable' only in the sense of our not being sure how far the Soviet leaders would feel obliged to go to correct the situation in Czechoslovakia. It had already been argued from this post that they would be prepared to go a long way in view of the particular importance which they attach to the strategic situation in Czechoslovakia and the dangers that could arise, both for their 'sphere of influence' in Eastern Europe and the Communist régime in the Soviet Union itself, from any weakening of the 'leading role of the Communist Party'. The case was not comparable with that of Rumania,[4] whose aberrations could be tolerated, since there was no threat to the party and the position of that country is not of such strategic importance to the Soviet Union; nor with that of Yugoslavia, which, again, has no such strategic importance and has, for some time, been outside the Russian Communist family. In the case of Czechoslovakia there were particular reasons for the Soviet leaders wishing to get their way at all costs.[5] One may have doubted whether they would proceed to the ultimate

---

[1] Sir G. Harrison had left Moscow on 25 August and Sir Duncan Wilson, his successor, had not yet taken up his post. Mr. Dalton was acting as Chargé d'Affaires.

[2] Not here printed.

[3] Not printed.

[4] Cf. No. 10, note 11.

[5] On 5 September Mr. Hayman and Mr. Smith had lunch with Mr. Ruzek, the Czechoslovak Ambassador in London, who had just returned from Prague. Later that afternoon Mr. Hayman recorded in a minute that 'When we asked the Ambassador why he thought that the Russians had invaded he replied that the main reason was undoubtedly the strategic dangers which faced the

sanction of invasion. But it should not have been unpredictable that they should consider it and it does not, I suggest, follow that they would strike out 'unpredictably' in other, dissimilar, cases.

4. Nor, I suggest, does the action in Czechoslovakia indicate the embarkation of the Soviet leaders on some new, deliberately planned, expansionist course. The present Soviet collective leadership has long appeared to be uncertain, indecisive and 'compromising' at home and, in foreign affairs, a prisoner, rather than instigator, of events, reacting to them rather than initiating them. As seen from this post, the course of events in Czechoslovakia has been in line with this assessment. At each stage of the affair the Soviet leaders seem to have been reacting on an *ad hoc*, rather than a planned, basis. At each stage, up to the invasion, they appear to have first blustered, then vacillated and finally compromised, and, even after the fateful decision to invade had been taken, they failed to follow up in a decisive way. Faced with Czechoslovak solidarity and the failure to find a quisling government, they compromised again. This is not the action of strong 'expansionist' leaders, but of frightened men reacting indecisively to a situation which they judged to be crucially dangerous, but with which they did not know how to deal.

5. There has been much apprehension, in the light of recent events and of Soviet propaganda, over an increased Soviet threat to West Germany and Berlin. Certainly, the Russians have stepped up considerably their propaganda against the Federal Republic and are accusing it in heightened terms of being the main villain in 'plots' against the Socialist camp, of harbouring designs for the alteration of frontiers in Central Europe and of instigating 'counter-revolution' in, and against, Czechoslovakia. Certainly, also, underlying this propaganda, the Russians have a pathological fear of the Germans, certain aspects of which influenced their attitude towards Czechoslovakia. They no doubt genuinely feared that, if the Communist Party there lost control and Czechoslovakia's position in the Warsaw Pact became prejudiced, the country might become either an 'Imperialist salient' or, at least, a neutral vacuum in which German influence might become predominant. Behind all the propaganda against the German *Ostpolitik* there was also, I suspect, a genuine fear of the spread of German influence and the enhancement of the German position in Eastern Europe. Both in line with these fears and since West Germany is the most convenient whipping boy, the full blast of Soviet propaganda has now been turned on West Germany. It represents both cover for the operation and a scapegoat for the odium incurred. It is likely to be fierce and sustained and to be directed not least

Soviet Union in this sensitive area. He kept on insisting that this was the real reason. When we asked him whether he did not agree that the Russians had been totally unable to find any support in Czechoslovakia he said that the Czechoslovaks had certainly been united and there was no justification for these Russian military measures. On the other hand in many factories there were feelings that the economic reforms were moving too fast and "certain mechanisms" must have made themselves felt in the Soviet Union. All this was very lame and unconvincing . . .' (NC 3/ 11).

against West German activities in West Berlin, against which we may, I think, expect also to see further actual obstruction. It would, however, be quite a different matter for the Russians to embark on actions against Berlin or West Germany itself for which there is no immediate reason and which they know would entail a confrontation with the Western Allies.

6. Nor is there evidence of forward 'expansionist' movement elsewhere. In the Middle East the Russians continue to castigate the Israelis and to support the Arabs. They have, of course, a long-term interest in the expansion of their influence in the Middle East, which they no doubt see as best served by support of the Arabs, and would probably not be averse to a continuation of troubled waters in which they might fish to some purpose. But there is not, I think, any evidence that they wish to see, or to instigate the Arabs towards, a renewal of hostilities which could so easily get out of control. On the contrary, such evidence as we have appears to point in the direction of their favouring some form of political settlement. In Vietnam, to take another trouble spot, the Russians have, for some time now, been taking a back seat and while, for Sino/Soviet and Socialist camp reasons, they could not push the North Vietnamese too much towards a settlement, it seems probable that they would like to see one, At least, so far as I know, there is no evidence that they are working against one.

7. Further, for what it is worth, the Russians appear anxious to continue the East/West dialogue and both in multilateral and bilateral relations appear to be adopting a position of 'business as usual'.[6]

8. I do not, therefore, see any basic change in Soviet foreign policy or in the leaders' attitude towards the world at large. They will still maintain, perhaps, now, to an increased degree, their basic views on the ideological struggle and will be on the look-out for opportunities of improving their position. Conversely, however, and perhaps also in increased degree, they will be anxious to restore the status quo and the balance of *détente* with the West, although in Europe they will, I think, be even more reluctant than before to see any change in the status quo or to contemplate any movement towards a change in the 'two Germanies' situation.

9. To that extent *détente*, with any prospect of force reductions, has been set back.[7] There is, of course, now also increased danger in the presence of

---

[6] In a letter of 30 September to Mr. G.E. Clark, First Secretary and Press attaché in the Embassy in Moscow, entitled 'Soviet "Business as Usual" Activities', Mr. R.D. Clift, a First Secretary in Northern Department, described recent contacts between the Foreign Office and Soviet Embassy staff who 'have been fairly busily trying to keep up the impression that everyday business has not been affected by the invasion of Czechoslovakia . . . Our line in dealing with these Soviet activities has been that of course the Russians are there to do business and that we are not going to obstruct this; but we are not encouraging them to think that their action in Czechoslovakia is in any way forgotten.'

[7] In a minute to the Secretary of State of 11 September Sir P. Gore-Booth expressed the opinion that 'we should avoid as far as possible any use in official, public pronouncements of the stock words used for convenience in describing the state of [East-West] relationships or their development': '*détente*', he said, was 'a very convenient word and indeed basically a desirable one', but was open to misinterpretation, particularly by the press; 'Clearly our policy must be one of

Soviet troops on the Czechoslovak-West German frontier; not, as I have indicated above, because I think that the Russians propose to use those forces to initiate action, but because, by their presence, they have an increased capability and the danger of escalation in the event of trouble is that much higher. There is also the possibility that, if the Russians again felt their own interests to be vitally threatened elsewhere, e.g. in East Germany, as they felt them to be in Czechoslovakia, they might take similar preventive action.

10. It is right, therefore, to look to our defences and deterrents. If, however, it was prudent not to intervene in Czechoslovakia in a way which could have substantiated Soviet fears, real or imagined, I suggest that it will be prudent also to measure our reactions to the present situation and the outpouring of Soviet propaganda. If, as I have suggested, the Soviet leaders are at this juncture frightened and uncertain, it is right that they should be deterred from foolish action, but it could be dangerous to give substance to their fears.

11. By the same token, a return to the 'cold war' could likewise substantiate fears, revive suspicions and put relations back to where they were before all the patient work of recent years.[8] It cannot be denied that relations have been set back and confidence undermined by recent Soviet actions, but, on the basis of the argument in this despatch, this was not a deliberate intention of the Soviet leaders and the East/West situation is no different essentially from what it was before. Nor would anything be gained by encouraging a belief among the Soviet leaders, hard-liners or otherwise, that there is an increased 'aggressive' threat from the West. Moreover, as I have suggested in my despatch of the 27th of September, while a tougher ideological line is now likely to be taken in this country against the intelligentsia and liberals generally, the basic dilemma of balancing this against the need for the talents of the scientists and the technicians will remain, and the slow evolution of more independent thinking will probably continue. In these circumstances, if it was right to work for *détente* before, it should be right again, and, while making it clear to the Russians that we regard, and will continue to regard, their action in Czechoslovakia as disgraceful, and that we are keeping up our guard, we should gradually resume contacts and the interrupted dialogue.[9]

détente with those groups, agencies and individuals with whom a *détente* is possible. It is possible with Czechoslovak intellectuals, Hungarian businessmen etc., but at the moment it would be naive to suppose that it is possible with the leadership of the Soviet Communist Party. It seems therefore better to concentrate on talking about maintenance of contacts where these are fruitful, etc., even if this is a longer way round and less neat than the use of a word which one hopes can be revived but is at the moment inaccurate and susceptible of misunderstanding' (N 2 / 30).

[8] Sir P. Gore-Booth also objected to the use of the term 'cold war': 'The Russians are seeking to pin on us an accusation of a revival of the cold war. It is of course they who by their deeds have revived it. We should clearly not accept the accusation that we are pursuing it but equally we do not need to protest too loudly that we are not doing so since this simply looks feeble in the Czechoslovak context. The best thing is simply to ignore the word altogether.'

[9] On 13 September HM Ambassador designate to Moscow, Sir D. Wilson, called on the Soviet Ambassador, Mr. Smirnovsky (who 'made an extremely good impression, which was assisted by the fact that he served only tea and biscuits and not the usual array of vodka, brandy, etc.'). Discussing Czechoslovakia, Sir D. Wilson said 'it would be idle to pretend that Anglo-Soviet

12. Indeed, although this goes somewhat outside my province, this may, in the long run, be the best hope also for the Czechoslovaks and other East Europeans, who can fulfil their wishes for evolution only under the shadow of the Soviet Union and, therefore, only if the Soviet Union itself evolves.

13. I am sending copies of this despatch to Her Majesty's Representatives in Prague, Belgrade, Bucharest, Budapest, Sofia, Warsaw, Bonn, Paris and Washington, to the G[eneral] O[fficer] C[ommanding] Berlin and to the Head of the United Kingdom Delegation to NATO.[10]

I have, etc.,

P.G.F. DALTON

relations had not been damaged by recent events. I hoped however that, as and when there was some "normalisation" of affairs in Czechoslovakia—in the sense of the Czechs being allowed to pursue their own policies—the previous and on the whole hopeful trend of Anglo-Soviet relations could be resumed. We had never envisaged Czechoslovakia as outside the framework of the Warsaw Pact, or thought that it was going to pursue its own path of development outside a Socialist political framework. There was absolutely no question of any imperialist or capitalist plot to influence events there and direct them outside this framework. Mr. Smirnovsky replied that, as regards Anglo-Soviet relations, as he had said to the Foreign Secretary, it was easier to destroy than to build. On developments in Czechoslovakia, he said that these were now subject to the agreements now reached between the Soviet and Czech Governments. They had good evidence of attempts from outside to influence events in Czechoslovakia in a direction very dangerous to all concerned.'

[10] Submitting this despatch to Mr. Hayman on 4 October (together with Mr. Dalton's despatch of 27 September: see note 3), Mr. Giffard commented that the 'despatch about Soviet foreign policy . . . does not mention the distinction between Soviet policy towards Western Europe and Soviet policy towards the United States which has, I think, become clearer over the period of the Czechoslovak crisis . . . In general, however, I think that the conservative judgement which Mr. Dalton makes about Soviet policy is the only one possible in present uncertain circumstances.' Mr. Hayman submitted the despatches to Lord Hood, who commented on 7 October: 'These are two interesting despatches: reassuring in their belief that the USSR has not gone over to an expansionist policy; depressing in bringing out how difficult it is going to be to reach any real understanding between West and Eastern Europe. Hood 7/x.'

The next group of documents shows the British Government seeking a modus vivendi with the Soviet Union in the aftermath of the invasion of Czechoslovakia. Although, as stated in a brief prepared for Mr. Stewart's visit to the United Nations and Washington 7-15 October, it was impossible for the invasion not to affect East-West relations, it was accepted that a 'healthy realism is essential'. While losing no opportunity to condemn the Soviet action, therefore, Ministers and Foreign Office officials were well aware of the need to maintain a certain level of 'business as usual', and not to relinquish their efforts in the field of global security, disarmament and détente in general.

Sir Duncan Wilson, as foreshadowed by his talk with Mr. Smirnovsky (see No. 15, note 9), arrived in Moscow determined to take a positive view of Anglo-Soviet relations if he could. The briefing notes prepared for the Secretary of State's conversation with Sir D. Wilson on 25 September prior to the latter's departure for Moscow the following week expressed the Foreign Office view that 'while we must maintain our position on the

Czechoslovak invasion, we must also be ready to take advantage promptly of any changes in Soviet attitudes, if there should be signs of changes for the better; or take account of any indications of changes for the worse.' With this message in mind, Sir D. Wilson prepared for a round of introductory calls.

No. 16

Sir D. Wilson (Moscow) to Mr. Stewart[1]

No. 1690 Telegraphic [ENS 3/2]

Priority. Restricted   MOSCOW, *22 October 1968*

Repeated for information to UKMIS New York, Washington and Saving to Belgrade, Bonn, Bucharest, Budapest, Paris, Prague, Sofia, UKDEL NATO and Warsaw.

I presented my credentials yesterday to President Podgorny. In answer to my speech he made a short and conventional reply (full text follows by bag[2]), emphasising that cooperation between our countries should continue 'without pause' and enumerating a standard list of international issues to be solved—Vietnam, the Middle East, disarmament and the 'remnants of colonialism'.

2. In his private interview with me, a good deal of time was devoted to the normal courtesies and small talk. The President then gave a brief and rosy-coloured view of the development of Anglo/Soviet relations until recent months, dwelling particularly on the exchange of visits between the Prime Minister and yourself on the one side and Mr. Kosygin and other high Soviet personalities on the other.[3] He said that things had been changed unnecessarily by the Czechoslovak affair. It was plain now to all that Soviet aims in Czechoslovakia were limited and did not harm our interests. Nevertheless he had the impression that HMG, unlike the Soviet Government, was pursuing an 'opportunist policy' in this connection: ours for example, was the only government which continued to put restrictions on high-level visits. We should, in his view, look carefully at the long-term interests of the United Kingdom. It was important not to check the positive development of Anglo/Soviet relations, and to make uninterrupted progress towards the solution of various major international problems. President

[1] On 17 October 1968 the Foreign and Commonwealth Offices combined to form the Foreign and Commonwealth Office (FCO), responsible to one Secretary of State. Mr. Stewart was henceforth known as Secretary of State for Foreign and Commonwealth Affairs. Some departmental changes were made at the time of the merger, including the creation of Eastern European and Soviet Department (EESD) to replace Northern Department, dealing with political and bilateral economic relations with Bulgaria, Czechoslovakia, Hungary, Poland, Rumania, the Soviet Union and Yugoslavia. Mr. Sydney Giffard was the first Head of EESD: Mr. Smith, formerly Head of Northern Department, succeeded Sir W. Barker as HM Ambassador at Prague in December 1968.

[2] Not printed.

[3] Cf. Nos. 2-3 and 8-9.

Podgorny developed these themes at considerable length and in very correct diplomatic language.

3. In reply I dwelt on the severe shock caused not only to HMG and the British people, but to other governments and peoples throughout the world and indeed to many communist parties, by the events in Czechoslovakia. We could agree that our immediate interests might not be immediately threatened. But we had other important long-term interests which were affected. In particular it was important for us that the terms of the United Nations charter should be observed and that there should be no interference in the internal affairs of independent states, under whatever excuse. The signature of the Soviet-Czech Treaty[4] clearly marked a new stage, and HMG would have to consider their attitude carefully in the light of events following its signature: I could not, however, conceal our impression that it was a Treaty signed under unequal conditions. As regards the 'cut off' in Anglo/Soviet relations I emphasised that in fact a great deal of contact was still taking place on the cultural and commercial sides. HMG was moreover always ready and indeed anxious to discuss major international issues, particularly the Middle East and disarmament. I said in conclusion that personally I was very much interested in 'bridge-building', and that in this respect perhaps my best credential was the fact that one of my daughters had been studying already for four years in the Soviet Union.

4. Before concluding the interview President Podgorny took up one or two points that I had made. He said that at the start of the Czechoslovak episode many governments and even communist parties had certainly misunderstood Soviet aims, but these were now clear and widely accepted. As regards the Treaty, there were many governments which did not share HMG's view that this was negotiated under unequal conditions—in particular the Czech government. It would be a waste of time for HMG to 'consider the Treaty', which had been signed and represented an unalterable fact (we had short and unprofitable further exchange about what I had said on this subject). President Podgorny concluded our conversation by asking me to transmit messages of goodwill to the Prime Minister, yourself and Mr. Brown. As we rejoined the rest of the party, he told me in a joking way that we should be busier in pressing our allies to solve the burning problems of Vietnam and the Middle East. I said that the President probably underestimated how busy we

---

[4] Following discussions in Moscow on 3-4 October during a visit by the Central Committee of the Czechoslovak Communist Party, a *communiqué* announced agreement on a Soviet-Czechoslovak Treaty (signed on 16 October) providing that an undisclosed number of the Soviet troops in Czechoslovakia would 'temporarily' remain there, while the rest of the Warsaw Pact troops would withdraw within two months. The treaty was described by Sir W. Barker as a 'bitter humiliation' for Czechoslovakia, with a considerable psychological impact on the population who appeared 'noticeably more depressed, pessimistic and fearful' even though there had never been any real hope that the Soviet troops would withdraw (ENC 3/303/1).

already were, and that I would like to talk about these problems further, especially the Middle East, with Mr. Kozyrev (on whom I hope to call soon).[5]

5. The President's private talk with me lasted nearly an hour. He showed minor signs of impatience at my not very long exposition of HMG's attitude, but replied and concluded our interview in the friendly and courteous tone with which he had begun it. This contrasts sharply with the very bitter terms used by the Soviet press to describe HMG's attitude to the Czech crisis, and even (my telegram No. 1688[6]) HMG's long-term policy towards Eastern Europe. There is however nothing surprising in the alternate hot-and-cold treatment.

6. While I was talking with President Podgorny the acting head of Second European Dep[artmen]t, commented to the Minister that my speech was 'unusual' for such an occasion and asked whether it had your approval. Minister said that it had.[7] It is also worth noting that my interview with the President was of quite unusual length. A full report about it has been printed in the Soviet press, which refers to a 'frank conversation touching certain international problems of common interest' (this treatment also is unusual but not unprecedented). What stands out is that HMG's attitude on the Czech

[5] Sir D. Wilson saw Mr. Kozyrev at the latter's request on 25 October and reported their conversation in Moscow telegram No. 23 Saving of 28 October. In response to Mr. Kozyrev's advice to let the subject of Czechoslovakia 'completely alone' and 'concentrate on other international questions and on Anglo-Soviet relations', Sir D. Wilson said that he 'had not noticed any inhibition on the part of the Soviet Government from raising questions that concern HMG's relations with other countries in, for example, the United Nations'—evidently a reference to Soviet criticism of British policy on Southern Rhodesia. Mr. Kozyrev then said that the Soviet Government did not regard differences on Rhodesia or similar questions 'as a reason for any "pause" or interruption in their bi-lateral relations with us. He concluded by repeating that "if I wanted to" I could help in the satisfactory development of Anglo-Soviet relations, and that he wished me well in my task. Kozyrev's remarks, even when concerned with normal courtesies, were at best tepid in tone and punctuated by incidental observations that were clearly intended to sting. The whole tone of the interview corresponded much more nearly (and intentionally) to the present state of Anglo-Soviet relations than did the tone of my exchanges with President Podgorny. There is, however, one interesting implication . . . that the Soviet Government would swallow continued public criticism by HMG of their policy in Czechoslovakia, provided that we got "back to normal" in the development of bi-lateral relations.'

[6] This telegram of 21 October reported that a lengthy article in that day's *Pravda* had attacked British bridge-building with Eastern Europe as 'designed to further subversive activity'. Sir D. Wilson commented that following the Secretary of State's speech to the UN, 'which is frequently referred to and clearly rankles, we have been accorded increasingly hostile treatment in the central Soviet press. [This] article is the harshest attack so far, and casts new doubt on the whole basis of our policy' (ENS 3/1). Mr. Stewart's speech to the UN on 14 October, in which he stated that the conscience of the world had been affronted by the invasion of Czechoslovakia, was reported in *The Times* of 15 October 1968, p. 4.

[7] In a submission to Mr. Hayman of 23 October, Mr. Giffard commented that he did not think that the remark about Sir D. Wilson's speech was of any significance: 'The speech, in the drafting of which Sir D. Wilson himself had a large hand, was more plainspoken than is customary, but the circumstances in which it was delivered were themselves much more unusual than the speech. I regard this simply as another example of Russian sensitiveness to our insistence that what they have done in Czechoslovakia must profoundly affect our relations with them.'

crisis has caused concern to the Soviet Government and that they are anxious by all means at their disposal to normalise relations. I shall make recommendations on this when I have had a few more occasions to feel the temperature here.[8]

[8] Telegram No. 2324 to Moscow of 29 October informed Sir D. Wilson that he had spoken well: 'We should be glad to receive your further recommendations for policy towards the Soviet Union in good time to consider them before the NATO Ministerial meeting which opens on 12 [*sic*] November. Meanwhile, our intention in brief is to continue to show willing to do business of every kind with the Russians and their allies where we see advantage in it, but without any manifestations of goodwill such as might seem to condone their conduct in Czechoslovakia. We see the hot and cold treatment at least partly as a continuation of the old game of attempting to split us from our allies.'

In his submission (see note 7) Mr. Giffard recommended that while awaiting Sir D. Wilson's further comments on the normalisation of Anglo-Soviet relations, a guidance telegram should be issued to Posts 'in order that there should be no misunderstanding about HMG's position' (see No. 17). He argued that while it was 'satisfactory that HMG's attitude on the Czech crisis should have caused concern to the Soviet Government . . . my impression is that what they are trying to do by suggesting that we have been more outspoken and tougher than other NATO Governments is to induce us to become more compliant than our allies and thus to continue their normal process of driving wedges between us where they can'. He concluded that the Soviet Union would like to 'tempt' the UK back into their position before the invasion of Czechoslovakia, when they 'had achieved a greater degree of relaxation in East-West relations, and over a wider field, than any other member of the Alliance'; but HMG must 'be chary of being so tempted. The important thing at the moment is the unity of the NATO Alliance. In the pre-Czech days it made sense for us to be some way in advance of our NATO allies because the possibilities of *détente* were then very real and we were effectively exploiting them. This is not likely to be the case in the months immediately ahead.' Mr. Hayman, Lord Hood, Sir P. Gore-Booth and Mr. Goronwy Roberts expressed agreement with Mr. Giffard.

In a minute of 24 October, however, Mr. Brash took issue with Mr. Giffard's point regarding East-West relations over 'a wider field': 'It was clear at the meeting of the NATO ad hoc Working Group on East West Contacts last May that we are fourth in the league, when it came to subsidised exchanges, coming after the French, who are way ahead, the Germans and the Italians . . . This suggests to me that the Soviet attacks are particularly directed towards the collapse of exchanges at the political level, and from this point of view I agree with your conclusions. The question of temptation to revert however hardly applies to the more general field. The Russians may indeed feel that we have been tougher than some NATO partners over cultural exchanges, but I would judge that they would regard this as marginal. We have certainly been tougher than the French, who, for example, allowed the Red Army Ensemble to continue its tour, where we denied it entry. Even the West Germans allowed a music tour of the Soviet Union to continue at the time of the invasion. All NATO, as far as I am aware, has continued with professional and academic exchanges'.

No. 17

Mr. Stewart to Certain Missions and Dependent Territories
Guidance Telegram No. 264[1] *[EN 2/8]*

Confidential   FCO, *29 October 1968*

Guidance telegram No. 216: Czechoslovakia: East-West Contacts.[2]

The purpose of this Guidance is to explain the thinking on which our policy towards the Soviet Union and the other invading countries will be based in the next few weeks. Separate instructions have been sent to you about representation at the Soviet National Day Celebration on 7 November.[3]

Instructions for use

2. You may draw on the material in this Guidance at discretion for use with reliable contacts.

Detailed operation of contacts

3. The outline in Guidance No. 216 remains generally valid. The only modification is that we are adopting a somewhat less restrictive attitude when asked for advice about privately organised visits and functions involving the aggressor countries. We are now leaving it primarily to the organisers to make up their own minds against the background of the strong public condemnation of events in Czechoslovakia. If they are disposed to be more flexible towards the East European countries than to the Soviet Union, we will not discourage this.

General philosophy

4. We recognise that our policy, with that of our allies, must continue to be based on both defence and *détente*. The need to break down the present barriers in Europe remains and the desire in Eastern Europe for contacts with the outside world has not diminished. We recognise that in the longer term contact with Eastern Europe is the principal means by which we can hope to encourage the liberal forces in these countries. On the other hand, we have to be wary of a level of contacts which might cast doubt on the

[1] Sent to Ankara, Bonn, Brussels, UKDEL NATO Brussels, Copenhagen, The Hague, Lisbon, Oslo, Paris, Rome, Belgrade, Berne, Helsinki, Stockholm, Vienna, Bucharest, Budapest, Moscow, Prague, Sofia, Warsaw, UKMIS New York, New York (BIS), Washington, Bangkok, Ottawa and Canberra.

[2] This telegram of 30 August informed Posts that visits by Ministers and MPs to Warsaw Pact countries which took part in the invasion of Czechoslovakia were being cancelled, but that official contacts with the countries concerned were to continue, particularly in such fields as trade and technology and at multilateral conferences. Cultural visits and manifestations under official auspices were, by and large, to be cancelled. Student exchanges were to continue and organisers of privately arranged visits and functions were to be left to make their own decisions: 'where these . . . fall into the social or entertainment category . . . and when our advice is sought, we are speaking in favour of a restrictive attitude' (N 2/30).

[3] Circular telegram No. 63 of 23 October informed Heads of Mission that they should decline invitations to Soviet functions on 7 November, 'though there would be no objection to a few junior members of your staff attending'.

sincerity of our condemnation of Soviet actions. We do not want to accept the Russian claim that we can already revert to 'business as usual' with its accompanying suggestion that nothing important has happened.

5. There may thus well have to be a considerable period during which we avoid actions which could give an impression of a goodwill inappropriate to a time of invasion [and] continued occupation of one member of the United Nations by the Armed Forces of another. The length of this period will depend on Soviet actions including the occupation of Czechoslovakia by Soviet troops and on the assessments which we and our allies make of them. In particular suggestions that the Treaty with Czechoslovakia on partial troop withdrawals makes a resumption of normal contacts possible should be firmly resisted. It will be necessary to see the practical effect of the Treaty on Czechoslovakia's position: to assess when to expect the complete withdrawal of Soviet troops and to watch developments in Eastern Europe generally. It may be possible to treat the Soviet Union's allies somewhat less rigidly as their troops leave Czechoslovakia but this is still premature for the moment.

6. We intend to pursue only those contacts where there is a clear balance of advantage in our favour. In this category come professional and academic exchanges and some other cultural contacts; normal business meetings, even between Ministers (e.g. the Secretary of State's meeting with Mr. Gromyko in New York);[4] trade; and disarmament and arms control.

7. Your own contacts with Soviet and other aggressor countries' representatives should be governed by these considerations. While showing willing to do official business with them, you should avoid public expression of goodwill. This would not exclude the acceptance, or even the giving of informal hospitality where there is business to be done. In this, you should as far as possible keep in step with the representatives of other NATO countries. For the present at least, you should continue to treat Czechoslovak colleagues as the representatives of a country with which HMG has normal relations, while avoiding such public expressions of warmth as might embarrass them.[5]

[4] During his visit to New York to attend the UN General Assembly (cf. p. 80), Mr. Stewart had a wide-ranging conversation on 7 October with Mr. Gromyko, covering UN matters, the Middle East, East-West relations, disarmament and Germany, with only a brief reference to bilateral relations. A record of this conversation is filed with Moscow telegram No. 1690 (No. 16).

[5] In a submission to Mr. Hayman of 31 October Mr. Giffard recommended that there was no need for the Secretary of State, who had approved Guidance telegram No. 264, to seek the views of his Cabinet colleagues on the broad lines of policy towards the Soviet Union before the NATO Ministerial meeting. He argued that the conclusions of the OPD Memorandum of 17 June (No. 11) remained generally valid, and that minor modifications made in the light of the invasion of Czechoslovakia were unlikely to be contested by other Ministers. Mr. Giffard also drew attention to 'continuing evidence in correspondence from Moscow of Russian readiness, even eagerness, to pursue commercial and industrial relations with us'. He cited recent cases of valuable export contracts won by British firms, and commented that 'so far, we are not up against serious problems in reconciling our desire to maximise exports with our inability to show political goodwill. There may be difficulties ahead' (EN 2/2).

No. 18

Sir D. Wilson (Moscow) to Mr. Stewart
No. 1733 Telegraphic [ENS 3/2]

Priority. Confidential   MOSCOW, *4 November 1968*

Repeated for information to Washington, UKDEL NATO and Saving to Bonn, Paris, UKMIS New York, Prague, Belgrade, Budapest, Sofia and Warsaw.

Your telegram No. 2324 of 29 October,[1] paragraph 3: policy towards the Soviet Union.

My recommendations are based on the following assumptions:

(1) There are no more invasions by Warsaw Pact troops of independent countries in Eastern Europe or elsewhere.
(2) Before end of the year there are substantial withdrawals of Soviet troops, even if large numbers remain in Czechoslovakia.
(3) The Czechoslovak government continues nominally to manage its own affairs without being subject to greater obvious pressure than at the moment: I assume further that any wholesale purges in Czechoslovakia could be taken as a clear sign of greater Soviet pressure.

2. If by the end of this year, such conditions still obtain, and if Anglo-Soviet relations have not been further embittered by events outside the framework of Eastern Europe, I hope that we can extract ourselves from the period of what the Soviet authorities call a 'pause', and gradually resume the full range of contacts, including Ministerial and representative visits, though still for some time on a basis of decreased frequency and a strictly business-like atmosphere.

3. The arguments in favour of my recommendations can be summarised as follows:

(1) One of our principal long-term objects remains to familiarise the younger generation and the technocrats of the USSR with our ways of thinking and thus to wean them very gradually from Marxist dogmatism. Our principal means towards this end must remain increased commercial, technical, cultural and individual contacts with the USSR in order gradually to affect the way of thought, particularly of the younger generation here.
(2) The emergence of a more restrictive Soviet policy at home *vis-à-vis* Eastern Europe makes the pursuit of our long-term policy more necessary, not less.
(3) The most effective way in which we could help the Czechs and others in Eastern Europe would be to hasten any helpful process of change in the USSR by any means, however small, available to us.
(4) After our initial reaction of outrage at the invasion of Czechoslovakia, consistency and dignity demanded that Ministerial contact and goodwill

[1] See No. 16, note 8.

manifestations should be cut off for some time. But I doubt whether this sort of boycott has in itself been a deterrent to further armed action by the Russians in Eastern Europe. Nor will reversion to a rather more normal policy of contacts, including Ministerial contacts, give them a green light for further action. If they want to act, they will probably do so in any case, unless convinced that there will be a military response from NATO, or conceivably that they will be subject to commercial sanctions. Hard words and purely political gestures will not suffice, if they think that the 'vital interests of socialism' are at stake.

(5) Aloofness along present lines if sustained for too long, will certainly be interpreted by Soviet official propaganda, and perhaps will be genuinely misunderstood in certain quarters, as sulks at the collapse of 'imperialist-revanchist' hopes of 'subverting' Czechoslovakia.

(6) The pursuit of business and cultural exchanges with the Russians wherever we see advantage in it for ourselves cannot be carried beyond a certain stage without involving HMG in manifestations, and Ministers in visits.

(7) 'Business exchanges' between Ministers can be combined with continued public statements against Soviet policy in Czechoslovakia. I do not think that the Russians would regard this as intolerable hypocrisy: cf. my telegram No. 23 Saving of 28 October para. 5, where I recorded that Vice-Minister Kozyrev seemed to be obliquely suggesting such a policy.[2] It should be borne in mind, when these arguments are considered, that we are thought here, rightly or wrongly, to have set an example by reacting very sharply to Soviet action in Czechoslovakia. This is not merely suggested to me orally (I recognise that similar suggestions may be made to my NATO colleagues about their own governments' policies): it is also noticeable in the special attention devoted by the Soviet press to British policy. This is in part a tribute to your own very effective speech at the UN[3] and may thus be regarded as a point of pride. It makes undesirable however at this stage any further steps by HMG which can reasonably be interpreted by the Soviet Government as evidence that HMG want to subject them to a special vendetta, started on the Czechoslovak issue. For example the imposition of a numerical limit on Soviet Embassy staff[4] will probably be regarded here precisely in this light: such action, while no doubt justified and desirable in itself, will cause more resentment now than it would have done if taken at some time nearer to 21 August last. In other words I hope very much that, pending any major change of policy, the climate of Anglo-Soviet political relations need not be reduced below the present freezing point.

5[*sic*]. If my recommendations are accepted, the 'de-freezing' of our relations will need careful handling if it is not to be exploited here as

---

[2] *Ibid.*, note 5.   [3] *V. ibid.*, note 6.   [4] See No. 19 below.

admission of defeat and to cause us loss of face. I shall make suggestions about this aspect later on. My present thought is that the process could best be started by the visit of a Minister of State from the FCO to discuss some actual problem of foreign affairs, e.g. disarmament (see New York tel[egram] No. 2689 of 1 November).[5]

6. Another point to consider is how far I and members of this Embassy should go in attending Soviet functions or in inviting Soviet guests. It will ease our position for the future, and show that we are not pursuing a restrictive policy with positive gusto, if you approve of us exercising in a positive spirit the discretion already given to us (Giffard's letter of 30 September to Millard[6])[.] I am confident that most of my NATO colleagues will be more rather than less forward than ourselves in this respect. (See my letter of 2 November to Giffard about the receptions for Beregovri.)[6] I would for instance propose, after the holiday to put in for calls on the Soviet Ministers with whom we have most current business to do, and also to ask appropriate Soviet officials, including Ministers, to a reception to meet the BOT/DEA Official delegation[7] in mid-November.[8]

[5] In this telegram Lord Caradon reported a conversation with Mr. Semenov (Soviet representative at the UN), who requested British cooperation in a lobbying operation to speed up ratification of the Non-Proliferation Treaty (see No. 11, note 3) and in reconciling differences between nuclear and non-nuclear states.

[6] Not printed.

[7] Cf. No. 11, note 6. A summary record of the exploratory trade talks with Gosplan on 12-15 November was sent to Mr. Giffard on 18 November by Mr. MacMahon of the Board of Trade. He reported that the talks had been conducted 'in a very friendly atmosphere', although Gosplan had shown no willingness to discuss their plans for 1969-70 or the outline of the next Five Year Plan. Gosplan made a number of suggestions for Anglo-Soviet cooperation, and it was agreed that further meetings would be held in London in a few months' time. The record concluded that 'Gosplan's objectives are, without doubt, (*a*) to organise their external trade so far as possible in a manner (e.g. by long-term contracts) which will enable them to include it as a predictable element in their plans, and (*b*) to find ways of widening the range and increasing the volume of Soviet exports. They confirmed to us that so far as western countries are concerned the import content of the plans is limited by their exchange resources, not by their needs. If they earned more convertible currency they would buy more.' In his covering note to Mr. Giffard Mr. MacMahon noted that 'It seems that Gosplan may be trying to develop their trade with us so as to obtain for the Soviet Union some of the benefits attributed to the COMECON system' (ENS 6/1).

[8] Mr. Giffard submitted this telegram to Lord Hood on 7 November, commenting that it conformed generally with FCO views. He questioned, however, Sir D. Wilson's tentative proposal 'that we might make a start on the unfreezing process by a Ministerial visit to Moscow to discuss disarmament. No matter how we were to explain it in advance to our allies, there might be uneasy feelings that we were getting out ahead again . . . If we *need* to approach the Russians about a particular piece of business, then—subject for the time being to NATO requirements—let us do so. But it is very difficult to say now whether the particular need for contact will make itself felt first on the disarmament, UN . . . technological, or any other front. We can be wholly pragmatic about this.' Mr. Giffard also considered Sir D. Wilson's premise about the likely course of events in Czechoslovakia 'too optimistic', and disagreed with his argument regarding the 'timing of our operation to limit the size of the Soviet Embassy in London [see No. 19 below]. Obviously we shall not want to go out of our way deliberately to make relations between us and the Soviet Union colder, just for the sake of doing so. But when

there is a job to be done . . . then we should do it and we should not be deterred by Soviet resentment.'

In minutes of 7 and 8 November Lord Hood and Sir P. Gore-Booth concurred that Mr. Giffard's comments were 'most pertinent' and his judgement 'rightly balanced', and agreed to the despatch of telegram No. 2377 to Moscow on 11 November, thanking Sir D. Wilson for his 'very valuable analysis of our future relations with the Russians', and expressing broad agreement with the Ambassador's recommendations, qualified on the lines of Mr. Giffard's comments. The telegram agreed with the recommendation 'that our contacts with the Russians should for the time being be held in a strictly business-like atmosphere', and with Sir D. Wilson's proposed action regarding calls and attendance at Soviet functions.

During November the focus of British policy towards the Soviet Union was the NATO Ministerial meeting held in Brussels from 15-16 November. This meeting, which had been brought forward from its usual mid-December date so that NATO members could consider the implications for the Alliance of the Soviet invasion of Czechoslovakia, presented the opportunity for much public and well-publicised criticism of the Soviet Union. It was attended by NATO Foreign, Finance and Defence Ministers, and considerable prominence was given in the press to the dinner held by Mr. Healey for Defence Ministers on 13 November, at which it was agreed to exchange views informally with the aim of forming a coherent European view of NATO problems which might be discussed with the new US Administration in due course (the Republican candidate, Richard Nixon, had been elected President on 5 November).[1]

The communiqué issued at the end of the NAC meeting (and read out to the House of Commons by Mr. Stewart on 18 November)[2] emphasised the serious view taken by NATO of the Soviet action against Czechoslovakia, and the 'grave anxieties' the invasion had aroused. A number of countries, including Britain, announced increases in their defence contribution to NATO in the light of the changed situation.[3] The communiqué urged the Soviet Union to 'refrain from using force and interfering in the affairs of other States. Determined to safeguard the freedom and independence of their countries they [i.e. NATO members] could not remain indifferent to any development which endangers their security. Clearly any Soviet intervention directly or indirectly affecting the situation in Europe or in the Mediterranean would create an international crisis with grave consequences.'

[1] Mr. Healey gives an account of the setting up of this 'Eurogroup' in his memoirs, *The Time of My Life* (London, 1989), p. 316.

[2] *Parl. Debs.*, 5th ser., *H. of C.*, vol. 773, cols. 858-61. Extracts from the *Communiqué* are printed in Cmnd. 6932, No. 10. Documents relating to the NATO Ministerial meeting are also printed in *FRUS 1964-1968*, vol. xiii, pp. 781-94.

[3] *V. ibid.*, cols. 146-7 for the announcement on 14 November of an increased UK naval presence in the Mediterranean, extra aircraft for Germany, the secondment of personnel to the Allied Combined Europe Mobile Force and plans for a military exercise on the Northern Flank in 1969.

Document No. 20 shows that the tone of this warning, combined with the repeated admonitions delivered by British Ministers and officials at every opportunity, was not well received in Moscow. Meanwhile, as far as the Soviet Government were concerned, the situation was exacerbated by action taken by HMG on 11 November to restrict the size of the Soviet Embassy in London. As document No. 19 shows, the activities of the Russian Intelligence Services in Britain, exercised through the Soviet Embassy and through other Soviet organisations such as the Soviet Trade Delegation (STD), had become increasingly obtrusive and worrying. Hitherto the Government had hesitated to take any action because of the possibility of reprisals against HM Embassy in Moscow. Following the trial in 1968 of the spy Douglas Britten, however,[4] it was decided that the situation could not be allowed to continue.

[4] See Christopher Andrew and Oleg Gordievsky, *KGB: The Inside Story* (London, 1990), p. 431.

No. 19

Mr. Stewart to Sir. D. Wilson (Moscow)

No. 2380 Telegraphic [PUSD]

Immediate. Confidential   FCO, *11 November 1968*

Soviet Ambassador called on 11 November on Permanent Under-Secretary who spoke substantially as follows. He was speaking to Mr. Smirnovsky on instructions. HM Government had been considering seriously the increase in recent years in the staff of the Soviet Embassy and in particular the increase in the numbers of those engaged in work which was not the normal work of diplomatic officers. Sir Paul Gore-Booth recalled that he had talked to the Ambassador in 1966 about the misdemeanours of Mr. Danilov but we had made no public fuss about this. Again about a year ago we had spoken about Mr. Drozhdov, who had been caught in practices improper to a Diplomatic Officer.[1] Again we had avoided publicity.

2. Now public opinion had been much disturbed by the part played by Mr. Borisenko who announced himself as a First Secretary dealing with cultural affairs, in the matter of obtaining secret information by illegitimate means in the Britten case.

3. These continued incidents, whether they took place with the Ambassador's knowledge or not, were a great hindrance to any efforts that might be made by the Ambassador or by the Permanent Under-Secretary or by their political authorities to improve Anglo-Soviet relations.

4. In view of the continuance of these practices and the very serious nature of the latest one, HM Government must now ask the Soviet Government to limit the numbers at the Soviet Embassy in London to the present strength of 80 diplomatic staff, 60 non-diplomatic staff and 8 service staff. HM

[1] See No. 5, note 4.

Government would not insist on rigidity as between diplomatic and non-diplomatic staff so long as the present pattern was generally maintained.[2]

5. Sir Paul Gore-Booth also mentioned to Mr. Smirnovsky that there had been complaints about two officials of the Soviet Embassy, I.A. Kulikov and A.A. Benyaminov, who had been seeking to collect confidential information by illegitimate means. It was not intended to ask for their removal but the Permanent Under-Secretary requested the Ambassador to take steps to warn them against continuing these practices. He also mentioned that we were making no difficulty about Mr. Filatov, the newly arrived Counsellor, but would like him to be briefed also. The Soviet Ambassador mentioned on a point of detail that Filatov was a Counsellor and it was proposed to appoint a Minister-Counsellor above him to succeed Vasev and Rogov or Popov. Would there be any difficulty about this? PUS said that if the Soviet Government appointed a professional diplomatic officer there would be no difficulty at all provided that the total numbers at the Embassy were not thereby increased.

6. Sir Paul Gore-Booth said that the Soviet Government might contemplate action in respect of the British Embassy in Moscow. He must make it clear that this would be considered quite inappropriate. Apart from not indulging in the practices of which we were complaining, the British Embassy was half the diplomatic strength (40) of the Soviet Embassy in London.

7. Finally, the Permanent Under-Secretary said that it was known that the Soviet Ambassador was calling at the Foreign and Commonwealth Office. The News Department would say that the Permanent Under-Secretary had informed him on instructions that HM Government had decided that in the context of the Britten case they must ask the Soviet Government to limit the numbers of the Soviet Embassy. The exact nature of the limitation would not repeat not be published.

8. The Soviet Ambassador received this oral communication with half a minute's gloomy silence. He said that he regarded this decision as an unfriendly gesture connected with the general hostility in Britain towards the Soviet Union and recalling the worst of the Cold War days. (Permanent Under-Secretary interrupted to say that the measure had been taken as a practical step and that the whole situation could be cleared up if members of the Soviet Embassy staff would desist from improper practices. At his request Mr. Smirnovsky promised to report that this was our view, whatever his own different view might be.)

9. Ambassador appeared then to say (but his English is imperfect) that the Soviet Government could do more harm to our Embassy in Moscow than we could to them, but on repetition he only said that we would not like what they could do in demonstrating hostility to us. He referred to recent cartoons, hostile articles, etc., which the Soviet Embassy in London had deeply

---

[2] It was subsequently agreed that 86 should be the ceiling figure for diplomatic staff at the Soviet Embassy.

resented[.] Permanent Under-Secretary replied that we were accustomed to this kind of thing, but it was worse for us because while the British press did not represent the Government, the Soviet press did.

10. Smirnovsky then insisted several times that the Soviet Government had never thought in terms of limiting the numbers of the British Embassy in Moscow. One reason why the Soviet Embassy had greater numbers was that, rightly or wrongly, they did not employ local staff. He insisted also that the Soviet Government made no difficulties about the granting of visas to people posted to the British Embassy in Moscow. Permanent Under-Secretary reminded him that the Soviet Government had refused a visa to Mr. Michael Duncan, a member of our Diplomatic Service. Mr. Smirnovsky replied that of course, like the British Government, the Soviet Government was bound to apply certain criteria in individual cases.

11. Ambassador reiterated that he was much grieved that this decision should have been taken at this time. He felt that Anglo-Soviet relations had got on to a very wrong course and he feared that they might deteriorate further. Sir Paul Gore-Booth repeated that this particular decision was not symptomatic of any political deterioration in relations. The case was simply that things continued to happen which neither the British public nor HM Government could tolerate indefinitely. He added that if within their numbers the Soviet Embassy could diminish the number of people engaged in the activities complained of, increases which the Ambassador had justified by growing scientific and cultural work could then be taken up by people genuinely engaged in the legitimate pursuit of such work.

12. Ambassador undertook to report accurately what had been said to him, but insisted again that this was a negative development which could lead to further difficulties between the two countries.

No. 20

Sir D. Wilson (Moscow) to Mr. Stewart

No. 1828 Telegraphic [ENS 3/2]

Immediate. Confidential   MOSCOW, *2 December 1968*

Repeated for information routine to Washington, Paris, Bonn, UKDEL NATO, UKMIS New York, Prague, Warsaw, Belgrade, Berlin, Bucharest, Budapest, Sofia.

I was summoned to the Ministry of Foreign Affairs today to receive from Gromyko a statement on Anglo-Soviet relations.[1]

[1] In a letter to Mr. Hayman of 3 December Sir D. Wilson commented that there were 'one or two curious points' about his interview with Mr. Gromyko: 'It was laid on at short notice, which is not normal here in the case of subjects which are not the centre of a crisis. It looks also as if Gromyko had taken his own staff by surprise. There was no English translation ready to hand to me . . . although the interpreter was reading the English translation from a written version. It was also noticeable that the Head of Second European Department, Makeev, who was also

2. The main points were:

(a) HMG had altered their policy, 'using events in Czechoslovakia as a pretext', and now intended to nullify much of the positive achievements in Anglo-Soviet relations in recent years.

(b) Various unfriendly acts are listed, including the 'discriminatory and unjustified decision to limit the staff of the Soviet Embassy in London'.[2]

(c) An anti-Soviet propaganda campaign had been officially inspired.

(d) In international forums British spokesmen had attacked the Soviet Government and had made inflammatory calls to 'limit and reduce relations with the USSR to the minimum['].[3]

(e) At the NATO Council meeting, Britain was among those who irresponsibly adopted a 'position of direct confrontation with the Soviet Union and the Warsaw Pact powers.[']4 This cast new light on the British share in the development of NATO's militaristic plans.[5]

(f) The Soviet Union 'does not wish our countries to embark on a course leading back to the time of the cold war'.

(g) The present course of HMG's policy suggested that 'the normalisation and development of Anglo-Soviet relations possibly do not form part of their plans. This forces the Soviet Government to examine from a new point of view not only the present state but also the future prospects of Anglo-Soviet relations in their various forms.'

3. Full text follows by bag.[6]

4. I said that you would no doubt consider an official reply after study of the text but that I must at once point out that there was no question of using events in Czechoslovakia as a pretext for a previously planned policy. HMG were seriously disturbed by what appeared to be a new and dangerous development of Soviet policy. So also was public opinion, whose reaction had been entirely spontaneous. I added that the decisions taken at the NATO meeting were of a purely defensive character, and that *détente* remained an important element in NATO and British policy.

present was taking down some of Gromyko's remarks with great diligence, as if he was not well acquainted with them.'

[2] See No. 19.

[3] The English text of the Note distributed by the Soviet Embassy in London continued at this point: 'Some people in Britain are apparently so naive as to believe that their wish is sufficient to "exclude the USSR" from the sphere of international relations.'

[4] See p. 90.

[5] The Soviet note (cf. note 3) continued at this point: 'The choice of Britain's foreign policy is, naturally, the business of the British government. But, in the Soviet government's opinion, the British government should realise that the road of hostility and aggravation of relations with the Soviet Union—a road leading to the intensification of tension in Europe—will not bring Britain any advantage or benefit in the world, European or any other aspect.'

[6] Not printed. The Soviet note was released to the British press on 3 December, before a copy of the full text had been received in the FCO: see *The Times*, 4 December 1968, p. 5. Lord Caradon reported in UKMIS telegram No. 3070 of 4 December that the text of the note had also been issued that day as a Soviet press release to the UN press corps.

5. Gromyko's reply was that Britain had no right to interfere in the internal affairs of the socialist community. He scoffed at the idea of 'British Statesmen, or rather *some* British Statesmen' lecturing the socialist powers on the conduct of their mutual relations. There had of course been no change in Soviet policy—he did not believe that HMG had thought otherwise—British statements had been 'dictated by other considerations'. He stressed that the future of Anglo-Soviet relations depended on our attitude.[7]

6. I replied briefly, pointing out:

(*a*) That the events in Czechoslovakia were of direct concern to HMG, since the talk of a 'NATO plot', which we had known to be untrue, had forced us to draw our own conclusions:

(*b*) We were not alone in giving public expression to our concern and:

(*c*) The development of our mutual relations depended on the actions of the Soviet Government as well as on HMG.

7. Gromyko did not insist on having the last word, and the atmosphere was no cooler than recently. I shall send my comments by a subsequent telegram.[8]

[7] In his letter to Mr. Hayman (see note 1) Sir D. Wilson commented that this was the only point in the interview 'at which Gromyko rather let himself go . . . I might add that this was not provoked by any remarks of mine. Otherwise he was not bad-tempered, and indeed, before we started off, "a joke was in order".'

[8] In Moscow telegram No. 1829 of 3 December Sir D. Wilson expressed the view that the Soviet note 'is, I think, intended in something like a conciliatory sense and gives us a chance, which I hope will be taken, to explain our policy towards the Soviet Union frankly, privately, and at the highest level'. The FCO reaction, however, expressed later that day in telegram No. 2475 to Moscow, was that the Soviet publication of the note 'without warning, and before we had seen it [see note 6] . . . suggests that their object, to some extent, is to make some sort of impact on public opinion here in the hope that this will embarrass Her Majesty's Government: and that it may be intended in a less conciliatory sense than at first seemed likely.'

A speaking note prepared by Mr. Giffard for Mr. Mulley to use in Cabinet on 5 December (Mr. Stewart was on a visit to India and Pakistan) discussed possible Soviet motives in publishing the note so quickly: in addition to 'a belief that they could appeal successfully to sections of British opinion to bring pressure on HMG to adopt a more accommodating policy towards the Soviet Union' (a belief not borne out by the generally hostile press reception to the note), Mr. Giffard considered it possible 'that the Russians do in fact believe that there *has* been a change in our policy towards them', and acknowledged that HMG had 'taken a lead in NATO [in] determining the Alliance's reactions' to the invasion of Czechoslovakia, though 'We certainly have no reason to be ashamed or concerned about our attitude . . .

'I do not think we should exaggerate the implications of seemingly being the only country in the West to be singled ou[t] for this treatment by the Soviet Union. We are an obvious target. The range of our contacts with the Soviet Union prior to Czechoslovakia was perhaps wider than those of other NATO countries. Clearly the Russians did not regard it as being in their interests to make a similar attack on the United States at present if only because they want to create as favourable an atmosphere as they can in that quarter for serious discussions with the new American administration next year. It is perhaps, therefore somewhat in the nature of a second best that the attack has been made on us. The Soviets probably regard their relations with us as very much more expendable. They recognise that they can afford to attack us; and they might even hope that, quite apart from any possible changes they might achieve in our own policies, they might even have some scope for frightening other Western countries and inducing them to take a fresh look at their policies towards the Soviet Union.'

Mr. Mulley spoke briefly on these lines in Cabinet on 5 December, and said that the Soviet note 'would have to receive a reasoned reply', which was being drafted for the Secretary of State's comments. In discussion, the Cabinet agreed that despite the strong feelings the invasion of Czechoslovakia had aroused 'we should not over-react, and should maintain correct relations without indulging in petty pinpricks. Any other course would only give Soviet propaganda opportunities which would be exploited. It was noted that the Russians themselves appeared to wish to keep relations on an even keel. In particular, they had not referred to any of the contentious issues raised in the note during the course of the current trade discussions.'

The drafting of a reply to the Soviet note proved more complex than expected, with the Secretary of State expressing firm views amid a stream of comment from Sir D. Wilson in Moscow urging a positive line, and a tendency within Eastern European and Soviet Department towards a more minatory tone. The initial FCO draft, telegraphed to Mr. Stewart in New Delhi on 5 December and copied to Sir D. Wilson, began by expressing surprise at the terms of the note and the manner of its publication, and proceeded to a detailed explanation of HMG's position on the points raised in the Soviet statement, refuting the charge that a hostile propaganda campaign had been mounted in Britain and denying that the British Government had taken a 'different road': 'We remain loyal to the United Nations Charter. It is that loyalty which caused the people of many countries in the world to be shocked by what happened in Czechoslovakia.' An accompanying telegram to New Delhi (No. 2353) analysed the Soviet note on the lines of No. 20, note 8, and concluded that 'we should send a firm and reasoned reply, wording it as constructively as possible . . . in the form of a personal message from yourself to Mr. Gromyko'. Commenting on the draft in Moscow telegram No. 1843 of 6 December, Sir D. Wilson agreed with the above conclusion, but was 'not convinced that Soviet motives are as exclusively malicious as suggested', and thought that 'the Soviet Government may genuinely be puzzled by certain points of our policy, which they misunderstand and which they are giving us an occasion to explain fully'.

In Madras telegrams No. 137 and 138 of 6 December, however, Sir P. Gore-Booth was informed that the Secretary of State favoured a reply in the third person, and felt that it 'should be as concise as possible and end with a firm and positive statement of our policy'. Mr. Stewart's redraft on these lines was confined to a brief but robust defence of HMG's line on Czechoslovakia, rebutting the Soviet suggestion that the invasion had been used as a pretext for a change of policy. This text was used as the basis for a revised draft submitted by Mr. Giffard on 8 December, which also took into account comments from Mr. Roberts and from Sir D. Wilson, and was sent to Moscow on 9 December, and to Mr. Palliser for the Prime Minister's comments.

No. 21

Mr. Stewart to Sir D. Wilson (Moscow)

No. 2489 Telegraphic [ENS 3/2]

Immediate. Confidential   FCO, *9 December 1968*

Repeated for information to Washington, Bonn, Paris, UKMIS New York, UKDEL NATO, Prague, Warsaw, Belgrade, Berlin, Bucharest, Sofia and Budapest.

Your telegram 1843: Statement on Anglo/Soviet Relations.[1]

I am grateful for these views, with which I generally agree.

2. My immediate following telegram contains the text of a reply[2] which, subject to consultation with the Prime Minister and to any further comments from you (which I should be grateful to receive flash), I propose to give to the Soviet Ambassador here as soon as possible. We intend to publish it immediately thereafter, and will keep you informed on timing.

3. The text, as you will see, has taken account of certain of your comments. However, as you will know from Madras telegram 137,[1] I want to keep our reply as short as possible: and I have therefore not been able to take in all your points on the text. However, I shall make these to Smirnovsky orally, together with the points in paragraph 6 of your telegram under reference,[3] the oral presentation of the powerful argument at paragraph 5(ii) of your telegram under reference[4] will enable us to avoid referring specifically to cold war points in our reply.

[1] See p. 96.

[2] The text contained in telegram No. 2490 to Moscow is printed as an Enclosure to the present document.

[3] In this paragraph Sir D. Wilson recommended that Mr. Stewart should hand the reply to Mr. Smirnovsky personally: 'This will lend it more weight, and it might be useful for you to make certain extra points in the informal and unpublished conversation which may develop afterwards, e.g. about the propaganda in the Soviet press, and the frequent attacks on us by official Soviet representatives in the UN, or on the other side of the account about e.g. forthcoming cultural negotiations.'

[4] This sub-paragraph read: 'So far as the Soviet audiences are concerned, they will be less impressed by references to the UN Charter, important as this is, than by stress on other points bearing on our more immediate interests . . . A. The doctrine of 'socialist sovereignty' might easily imply threats to other independent countries. B. The Soviet justification of their action in Czechoslovakia by reference to a 'NATO plot' might easily imply a threat to NATO countries. C. The attacks on our alleged 'bridge-building' implied that it was the Soviet leaders who wanted to limit contacts.

'What we want to convey is that A. and B. forced us to take out a new insurance policy, and C.—the doctrine of Brezhnev himself—to examine the whole basis of our Eastern policy very seriously. Something to this effect might perhaps be inserted . . . leading to the point that there is no special vendetta by HMG against the Soviet Government and nothing which has not been forced on us by the need either to look to our defences, or to accord with public opinion.'

4. Your telegram 1847 has just been received.[5] I am most grateful for your further comments. I have considered them very carefully. I would still prefer to keep my reply as short as possible and to make the points in paragraph 5(ii) and paragraph 6 of your earlier telegram orally. I shall also deal orally with the question of the size of the Embassy.

5. I think that the draft as now amended meets the substance of your preoccupations in paragraph 4 of your telegram 1847.

6. I fully recognise that this is a document which is of great importance for Anglo/Soviet relations. While I do not think I need discuss it with you personally I should be glad of your final comments before I send for Smirnovsky.[6] I want to do this well in advance of the foreign affairs debate on 12 December.[7]

[5] In this telegram Sir D. Wilson referred to the Secretary of State's draft reply in Madras telegram No. 138 (see p. 96) and advocated a 'rather fuller statement of our policy and the considerations involved in forming it', suggesting the inclusion of points raised in his telegram No. 1843, including para. 5.ii (see note 4). He added: 'So far as relations with the Soviet Government is [*sic*] concerned, there is no hurry for a reply. I hope that I may be given the chance of comment on a final draft [of] a document which I regard as of great importance for Anglo-Soviet relations, and can come to London at short notice if you think desirable.'

[6] In Moscow telegram No. 1852 of 10 December Sir D. Wilson suggested only one amendment to the text printed in the Enclosure below, relating to the last sentence: cf. note 10 below.

[7] Mr. Stewart handed HMG's reply (printed in *The Times*, 11 December 1968, p. 1) to Mr. Smirnovsky at 4 p.m. on 10 December: the interview was reported to Moscow in telegram No. 2498 of that date. The Soviet Ambassador expressed regret that the reply used 'unfounded terminology' and disappointment that 'in giving examples of helpful action which the Soviet Government could take, in order to improve our relations [Mr. Stewart mentioned in particular consular visits to Mr. Brooke (cf. p. 36), help with marriage and personal cases and an end to the jamming of Russian language broadcasts by the BBC], I had not mentioned "really important questions" . . . In conclusion, the Ambassador said that he was unable to accept the main point in our reply, regarding the responsibility for the deterioration in Anglo-Soviet relations, but he would convey it to the Soviet Government . . . I said that I would take up the Ambassador on two points only. He was very wrong if he thought that the bilateral issues to which I had referred were unimportant, in particular if he applied this to personal cases such as that of Mr. Brooke. I assured him that action by the Soviet authorities in cases of this kind would have an important effect on our relations generally. Secondly, I took him up on his remarks about the relations between the Soviet Union and Czechoslovakia being, in effect, nothing to do with us. I said that if the word relations meant what it normally meant, I would accept this. But the invasion of an independent country was of concern to all.'

Telegram No. 2497 to Moscow reported Mr. Stewart's supplementary oral statement to Mr. Smirnovsky, in which he made the points referred to in notes 3 and 4 above, and stated that HMG's recent decision to limit the size of the Soviet Embassy staff 'had no connection with our concern about events in Czechoslovakia'. The Secretary of State concluded by emphasising that 'so far from wishing to take the road back to cold war times (as the Soviet note had alleged) we were ready to respond to any move by the Soviet Government which might lead our two countries back towards the enjoyment of good relations with each other. It all depended on them. There were a number of bilateral issues on which they could show by their actions that they wished to see an improvement in our relations. We were always ready to discuss international problems on which there might be real prospects for progress.' For Mr. Stewart's statement regarding the exchange of notes with the Soviet Government during the Foreign Affairs debate on 12 December see *Parl. Debs.*, 5th ser., H. of C., vol. 775, cols. 604-605.

ENCLOSURE IN NO. 21

Text of the British reply to the Soviet Note of 2 December, as transmitted in FCO telegram No. 2490 to Moscow of 9 December

Her Majesty's Government have considered the Soviet Government's statement on Anglo/Soviet relations which was made to Sir Duncan Wilson on 2 December. This statement affirms that the past few years have seen the beginning of the establishment between the Soviet Union and Britain of favourable conditions for the fruitful development of our relations. This is true and Her Majesty's Government have played an active part in promoting this relationship.

Her Majesty's Government must entirely reject the suggestion that they have used the invasion of Czechoslovakia as a pretext for a change of policy. On the contrary, Her Majesty's Government desires [*sic*] to pursue the policy of better understanding and deplore the fact that the progress so far made should have been halted by the Soviet Union's invasion of Czechoslovakia —a sovereign independent member of the United Nations.

Before the invasion it was clearly explained to the Soviet Government through their Ambassador in London that action of this kind against Czechoslovakia would inevitably affect our relations. There is no truth in the Soviet Government's statement that Her Majesty's Government have sought to 'end contacts and exchanges' between our two governments and peoples. Her Majesty's Government firmly believe that we must continue to do business together where there is business to be done, in the political, commercial and cultural fields. But the goodwill that existed before does not exist at present.[8]

The Soviet statement claims that a propaganda campaign hostile to the Soviet Union has been started on a wide scale in Britain with the encouragement of official agencies. Her Majesty's Government must state, not for the first time, that British citizens are free to express their opinion on the invasion of Czechoslovakia, as on all other matters. British citizens have exercised this right. Condemnation of the invasion of Czechoslovakia has accordingly been expressed by people of all shades of political opinion in this country, inside and outside Parliament as well as by Her Majesty's Government.

The Soviet statement also refers to the policies of NATO. The North Atlantic Council at their meeting in June at Reykjavik showed their desire for better relations by suggesting mutual force reductions.[9] If the Soviet Union

---

[8] In a letter of 9 December to Mr. N.J. Barrington, Assistant Private Secretary to the Secretary of State, transmitting the Prime Minister's comments on the draft reply, Mr. Palliser said that the preceding sentence struck Mr. Wilson 'as one which could be damaging if taken out of context'. On his suggestion it was deleted and a sentence substituted on the following lines: '"But the Soviet Government's action against Czechoslovakia inevitably caused a set back to the mutual confidence between the two Governments".'

[9] Papers relating to the NAC meeting in Reykjavik 24-28 June 1968 are printed in *FRUS 1964-1968*, vol. xiii, pp. 712-25. NATO Ministers referred to the study of mutual East-West force reductions undertaken in the follow-up to the Harmel Exercise (cf. No. 10, note 9), and adopted a

had responded constructively to this initiative much progress could have been made. In fact the Soviet Government's response was to invade Czechoslovakia. This use of armed forces against a European country could not fail to be of concern to all members of NATO when they met at Brussels, and indeed to other States.

Her Majesty's Government and, they believe, the whole British people want the best possible relations with the Government and people of the Soviet Union. If the future policy of the Soviet Union shows respect for the Charter of the United Nations and in particular for the Sovereign rights of independent countries, the search for these good relations can go forward.[10]

Declaration on Balanced Force Reductions reaffirming that NATO's overall military capacity should not be reduced except by balanced reductions, and expressing the hope that the Soviet Union and Eastern European states would enter discussions with a view to East-West agreement on mutual force reductions. The Declaration and extracts from the *Communiqué* issued after the Ministerial meeting are printed in Cmnd. 6932, Nos. 8 and 9.

[10] Mr. Palliser (cf. note 8) said that the Prime Minister objected to the last sentence of the draft as 'a shade "governessy". He would prefer to substitute a sentence on the following lines: "This is still their aim. But to achieve it is not the sole responsibility of the British Government and people. It depends also on the policies and actions of the Government and people of the Soviet Union".'

No. 22

Sir D. Wilson (Moscow) to Mr. Stewart (Received 12 December)

No. 2/46 [ENS 2/2]

Confidential   MOSCOW, *9 December 1968*

Summary ...[1]

Sir,

Soviet Foreign Policy

I have the honour to present some reflections on Soviet foreign policy, in the light of the first major public pronouncement made by prominent Soviet leaders since the invasion of Czechoslovakia at the end of August, and of subsequent events. For an abnormally long time the defence of Soviet action in Czechoslovakia was left to newspaper commentators or routine official spokesmen (up to and including Mr. Gromyko). It took the Soviet leaders two and a half months to evolve an authoritative version of the party line and to prepare it for the most authoritative form of presentation. This is a measure of their embarrassment on the subject of Czechoslovakia.

[1] Not here printed. In his telegram No. 1829 (see No. 20, note 8) Sir D. Wilson had announced his intention to send the following week 'a despatch on Soviet foreign policy, giving wider background to the Gromyko memorandum. I can telegraph conclusions in advance, if this will be useful.' In telegram No. 1834 of 5 December he accordingly telegraphed the summary of his despatch, which was taken into account when drafting the reply to the Soviet note (cf. p. 96).

2. Mr. Mazurov spoke at a meeting in Moscow on the eve (November 6) of the celebrations of the October Revolution; and Mr. Brezhnev made his contribution on November 12 at the Fifth Congress of the Polish United Workers Party in Warsaw.[2] The main effort of both speakers was to present the theme of Czechoslovakia within a broader historical-mythological framework as follows:

(i) The inexorable struggle between Imperialism and 'Socialism' continues.
(ii) The Czechoslovak case marked a new phase, in which the Imperialists, having failed by direct confrontation to shake the 'Socialist camp' were trying to exploit differences within it by more subtle means.
(iii) In Czechoslovakia they relied on 'anti-socialist' elements in responsible positions to help them in subverting the power of the Communist Party, in creating economic links with the West, and finally, they hoped, in inducing Czechoslovakia to leave the Warsaw Pact.
(iv) The intervention of Soviet and other Warsaw Pact troops was justified in order to restore the political integrity and strengthen the frontiers of a member of the 'Socialist Commonwealth'. It did not essentially infringe Czech national sovereignty, which must within the 'Socialist Commonwealth' take second place to 'Socialist solidarity'.
(v) Similar developments elsewhere in the 'Socialist Commonwealth' would produce similar reactions from the Soviet and other 'Socialist' Governments.

3. It is my first task in this despatch to examine the main points and implications of this new re-stated Soviet doctrine. First there are the concepts of the *Socialist Commonwealth*, with its much debated geographical implications, and of *Socialist Sovereignty*. The phrase 'Socialist Commonwealth', goes back, if memory serves me, at least to the end of October 1956, when Khrushchev's Government wished to justify intervention in Hungary by reference to wider

[2] Mr. Brezhnev's speech in Warsaw was regarded as the definitive statement of the so-called 'Brezhnev Doctrine', claiming 'the right to intervene, by force if necessary, to protect socialism'. He said: 'when the internal and external forces hostile to socialism seek to revert the development of any socialist country towards the restoration of the capitalist order, when a threat to the cause of socialism in that country, a threat to the security of the socialist commonwealth as a whole emerges, this is no longer only a problem of the people of that country but also a common problem, the concern of all socialist countries. It goes without saying that such an action as military aid to a fraternal country to cut short the threat to the socialist order is an extraordinary, enforced step, it can be sparked off only by direct actions of the enemies of socialism inside the country and beyond its boundaries, actions creating a threat to the common interests of the camp of socialism. Experience shows that in present conditions the victory of the socialist order in this or that country can be regarded as final and the restoration of capitalism can be regarded as excluded only if the Communist Party, as the guiding force of society, firmly carries through a Marxist/Leninist policy in the development of all spheres of public life; only if the Party indefatigably strengthens the defence of the country, the defence of its revolutionary gains, if it maintains itself and propagates amidst the people vigilance with regard to the class enemy, irreconcilability to bourgeois ideology; only if the principle of socialist internationalism is being sacredly observed, the unity and fraternal solidarity with other socialist countries is being strengthened' (quotation taken from WDW 1/1 of 1971, cf. No. 62 below).

regional and political interests. What is new, if anything, is the world-wide application which at times seems to be given to the concept (here it would be interesting to know if it was ever invoked in relation to Soviet support of Cuba 1961-2 or of North Vietnam from 1964 onwards). A number of texts can be cited for the widest possible interpretation of the phrase 'Socialist Commonwealth', and the principal ones which have come to my attention are cited in the Annexe to this despatch.[3] These passages, however, have to be seen against a great many statements, mainly in press comment but not confined to it, which state or clearly imply that the 'single links' not to be broken from the 'Socialist Commonwealth', and the frontiers not to be violated, are those of the contiguous bloc of East European countries. It is here above all that national independence must give way to the class interest of 'socialism', if the latter is thought by the Soviet Government or by a consensus of truly 'Socialist' Governments (i.e. those of Poland and East Germany) to be in danger. This is the doctrine of *Socialist Sovereignty*, probably not new (there may well be precedents among the texts of 1956), but certainly much refurbished to meet and justify the events in Czechoslovakia.

4. Against this background I do not think that the doctrine of the 'Socialist Commonwealth' should be seen as a charter for expansionism. No doubt some of Mr. Gromyko's phrases have been left deliberately vague. He would not wish (and you, Sir, have no doubt suffered from the mirror-image of this dilemma), by defining too precisely the sphere of the Soviet Union's most vital interests, to encourage 'Imperialist' intervention elsewhere. Albania could for example be regarded as a sheep strayed not too far from the fold —perhaps even Yugoslavia. Both are contiguous with orthodox 'Socialist' states; orthodox elements might be supposed by the Russians to be active in each country and worthy of at least some verbal encouragement. But these are, I think (and the great majority of my colleagues agree with me), only incidental purposes. It is not the way of the Soviet Government to explain its moves a long way ahead by laying down a doctrinal basis in Hitler's manner. They are much more inclined to justify by theoretical statements action already taken. I therefore think that the doctrines of the 'Socialist Commonwealth' and 'Socialist sovereignty' have been evolved or revived primarily to defend the invasion of Czechoslovakia, secondarily to ease the way for any similar action that might be thought necessary within the present bounds of the Soviet bloc, and only very incidentally as a possible justification for action further afield.

5. I believe that a doctrine quite as dangerous for East-West relations, and ultimately for world peace, is that of the *New Threat of Imperialism*. This doctrine involves the attribution to HMG, among other Governments, of considerable subtlety. The main theme of Soviet commentators on the international scene, from Mr. Brezhnev down, is that the 'Imperialists', foiled in their attempt to roll back the frontiers of socialism, or in their hope that the 'Socialist' system would be eroded by economic weakness, have evolved a

[3] Not printed.

policy of peaceful penetration, masked under the slogan of co-existence. Economic and cultural 'bridge-building' is used to encourage 'anti-socialist' or insufficiently 'socialist' forces in Eastern Europe. The 'Imperialists' hope that political results will follow. Mr. Brezhnev himself outlined (in a speech at a Warsaw factory) the rake's progress which might have taken place in Czechoslovakia, in the following stages:

(i) Establishment of diplomatic relations between Bonn and Prague.

(ii) The growth of Bonn's influence on Prague with the help of credits and other means.

(iii) The weakening of the influence of the Czech Communist Party, and the establishment in Czechoslovakia of 'social democracy with capitalist hues'.

(iv) The change of régimes in Poland and East Germany, the assimilation of East to West Germany and the denunciation of the Warsaw Pact.

To judge by the Soviet press, something very like this process was publicly envisaged recently by Mr. Herman Kahn in an address to the Hudson Institute.

6. Mr. Brezhnev has, of course, been painting a deliberately horrific picture, but its main lines probably correspond to the shape of genuine and deep-seated Soviet fears. Moreover much of the more routine Soviet propaganda about Western 'bridge-building' is a reasonably fair distortion, so to speak, of our own hopes about the possible course of events in Eastern Europe and the Soviet Union itself—increased contact in the economic and technical fields particularly, leading to a gradual 'occidentation' of outlook and an increasing readiness to look for converging interests. The Russians have, of course, never accepted this concept and have attacked it when events demanded. But Soviet attacks on the whole idea of gradual 'convergence' have never been so bitter, continuous and authoritative as at present (a particular target has been Professor Brzezinski, a former special adviser to President Johnson). I cannot help remembering the Chinese warnings to Khrushchev (which I regarded at the time as the best justification of our policy) to the effect that he who supped with Western devils would need a much longer spoon than Khrushchev possessed, and that by his policy of co-existence he was leading the Soviet Union into a bog of revisionism. It is sad to see Mr. Brezhnev coming near to the adoption of Chinese doctrine, and (if he would prefer a Russian precedent) to the view on foreign affairs of one of the stupid princes in Pushkin's 'Golden Cockerel'. This may be roughly translated:

> *The source of all our woes is clear,*
> *Our neighbour is a lot too near.*
> *Our troops should found, beyond our borders,*
> *New capitals to take our orders.*

7. The actions and doctrine of the Soviet Government can best be explained, and can be sufficiently explained, by a desire to maintain the

existing order, and to prevent the spread of new forms of 'socialism' within the Warsaw Bloc and within the Soviet Union itself, thereby safeguarding the dictatorship of the CPSU and the personal position of the Soviet leaders. The attitude of the Soviet leadership thus appears, as Mr. Dalton remarked in his despatches Nos. 3/43 S of the 27th and 30th of September,[4] to be profoundly defensive and conservative. This is shown even more clearly in measures taken to seal off the home front in the USSR against ideological infection (I shall be commenting on these in a later despatch).

8. Conservatism normally implies caution, and the Soviet leaders' practical conduct of international relations over the last three months has been cautious and pragmatic, whatever the uninstructed reader or listener might deduce from Soviet routine propaganda. I need not rehearse the signs at length, but should say that the Soviet Government has, off the record, shown genuine interest in a Middle East settlement; on the Vietnam talks it has not been unhelpful by its own standards (admittedly not a high compliment); on Berlin there has been some huffing and puffing, but so far no action; and on disarmament Mr. Kosygin in particular has gone out of his way to indicate to recent distinguished visitors from the USA (Mr. Macnamara and Senators Gore and Pell)[5] that his Government is ready to pursue talks on the reciprocal reduction of missile strength. No less important is the caution which the Soviet Government has displayed towards Mr. Nixon, both before and after the American Presidential elections. The impression which they have tried to give to the Western powers, and at least to the reasonably well-instructed Soviet reader, is that, while they guard their own immediate sphere of influence as jealously as ever against any form of Western intervention, on major international questions business can go on as usual with the West (on the commercial front it is certainly doing so).

9. The conclusions which the Soviet Government thus want us to draw is [*sic*] that the Czech episode is over and done with; they have made their position clear about the ideological integrity of the Warsaw bloc. The NATO powers have issued a reasonably plain warning about further movements of Warsaw Pact troops.[6] Now there is no reason why the policy of 'peaceful co-existence' (*à la russe*) should not be resumed and be seen to be resumed, after this salutary warning to the Warsaw Pact countries and to the Western powers about its scope. I think that for the present at least the Soviet leaders sincerely mean to stick within the sort of limits now achieved. I say 'the sort of limits' because they themselves have given plain indication (see paragraph 4 above) that developments elsewhere in the Warsaw Treaty area similar to those in Czechoslovakia would produce similar Soviet reactions. Moreover I think that, having gone so far in Czechoslovakia, they are bound to satisfy

[4] See No. 15, and *ibid.*, note 3.

[5] Mr. Robert McNamara, President of the World Bank and a former US Secretary of Defense, called on Mr. Kosygin at his request on 11 November. US Senators Albert Gore and Clairborne Pell (Democrat, Tennessee and Rhode Island respectively) met Mr. Kosygin on 19 November.

[6] Cf. p. 90.

themselves that there is no further threat there to the Soviet ideas of 'Socialism'; if absolutely necessary I fear that they will try to impose some kind of colonial government until they can train Czechoslovak nationals to work for them. But they do not want this to happen.

10. The Soviet leaders are in fact subject to two sets of constraints which constitute a fair guarantee of their sincerity, when they claim that the Czech 'episode' is for them a short story, now nearly completed, and not the first chapter of a new adventure tale. Within what they consider their own sphere of influence—the Warsaw bloc—they are restrained from further action against the Czechs, the Rumanians or anyone else, not so much by any warnings on the part of the NATO powers, as by the possible repercussions on world communist opinion. They evidently set very great store on holding the Conference of Communist Parties, now planned for next May, in the first place no doubt in order to rally opinion (particularly in the French and Italian parties), which was profoundly disturbed by their reaction in Czechoslovakia. But the Conference is more to them than a convenient means of soothing world communist opinion on this one subject, and their anxiety to hold it dates from well before the invasion of Czechoslovakia. The Soviet leaders must, I think, long have wanted to assert the effective, if not formal, primacy of the CPSU, in a world where other Communist parties have been showing increasing independence. They want above all to make themselves secure against 'revisionism' (the Czech crisis can be seen as one phase of this continuing effort); but they also want to ensure that 'anti-revisionists' remain within bounds and do not follow the Chinese example or lead.

11. The other major set of constraints operating on the Soviet leaders —and this is why they have long been so hostile to the 'adventurist' style of the Chinese—is strategic and economic, and acts as a check on their foreign policy outside the Warsaw Pact area. The Soviet leaders remain well aware of the nature of nuclear war, of American nuclear strength, and of the cost of a further arms race. Given the strength of the warning signals already issued in the NATO *communiqué* (and the very virulence of Soviet propaganda suggested that the message has been read here and understood), the danger of provoking the incoming US Administration, and the present Soviet need to devote more economic resources to their home front, I think it unlikely that the Soviet leaders will risk more than they are forced to in the Middle East, Mediterranean or in Germany. The Soviet presence in the Mediterranean is the most difficult piece to fit into this jigsaw; but it is not necessarily a sign that the Soviet leaders want immediately to pursue a forward policy. The increase in the Soviet naval presence took shape in the context of the Arab-Israeli war of summer 1967, and of what immediately followed. The Soviet Government had to do a good deal for the Arabs after the event, having let them down badly on the spot. At the same time they were provided with an irresistible opportunity of achieving a long-standing Russian strategic aim by moving warships into the Mediterranean. They may have had an additional reason for doing so if, as seems possible, they have been engaged in restructuring

their navy (hitherto a mainly defensive arm) in accord with the maritime role of a great power ready to intervene anywhere in defence of its world-wide interests. This of course means an increase in Soviet offensive capability in the long run, and capability might in this case give rise to intention.[7] But the Soviet Government is for the present anxious at least to play down the significance of their Mediterranean fleet (as witness the Tass denial of intention to use bases in Algiers) and such signs as can be read in Moscow suggest that they want to take no immediate risks in using it. Politically their Mediterranean fleet has indeed caused the Soviet Government some embarrassment. Last spring they did not get very far in an attempt to use it as a lever to secure the withdrawal of the US Sixth Fleet. More recently the reinforcement of the Soviet presence has induced NATO to strengthen its southern flank, alerted the Yugoslavs and made life even more difficult for French and Italian communists.

12. I would conclude that the Soviet Government is not anxious to take any further military-political action inside the area covered by the Warsaw Pact, but would do so, if they thought necessary, undeterred by fear of reprisals from the West; and that outside the Warsaw Pact area they will be constrained by economic pressures and fear of nuclear war to display considerable caution.

13. I have spoken throughout of the 'Soviet Government'. This is not because I think that the Soviet leaders are likely to have been unanimous in their discussions of whether and how to intervene in Czechoslovakia, or that they are likely to be unanimous when other critical issues of foreign policy arise in future. It is all too easy to foresee cases where it is even more difficult than at present to reconcile the four imperatives of Soviet foreign policy —guard against ideological infection, rally the 'Socialist Camp', take no risks *vis-à-vis* the West, and profit to the maximum from technical and commercial exchanges with the West. One can easily envisage sharp debates among the Soviet leaders on how to balance these demands. There may be temptations to quick action or miscalculations about its consequences (e.g. over Berlin). There might be fire-eating Generals and hopeful political analysts in the Kremlin who think that a military move on Yugoslavia is desirable and would find political backing on the spot. But at present, the risks in further action are clearly very large, and the political leaders are likely to use against the Generals the argument that Khrushchev used against the Chinese in 1959—a

[7] The Soviet Union had been building up their naval forces in the Mediterranean since 1964, and the process was accelerated by the Arab-Israeli War of 1967. This build-up was being analysed during 1968 by the Chiefs of Staff as part of their input to a NATO study. A guidance telegram sent to various missions on 6 June 1968, based on ongoing military assessments, stated that: 'The Russians apparently regard their Mediterranean force primarily as an instrument for political influence in the area This matches a wider trend in Soviet strategic thinking towards the development of an overseas military capability. There is, however, no sign that the Russians intend to build up their strength at an early date to a point at which they could match the capability of the United States Sixth Fleet, although it obviously complicates the task of defending NATO's southern flank' (MAS 2 / 2).

policy of 'adventurism' argues a lack of faith in the political prospects of Socialism, or in other words 'wait a little and the fruit may fall from the branch'. There may later be doves and hawks in the Kremlin, but at present they are all crows.

14. It remains to make some recommendations on how we should deal with the Soviet Government under present conditions. Here I must repeat what has been made very plain in the Soviet Memorandum of the 2nd of December. We seem to have acquired a quite special position in the context of Western reactions to the events in Czechoslovakia. I have the honour to represent in Moscow a Government which is said by the Soviet leaders to have taken an important lead in stimulating a very tough reaction, both before and during the recent meeting of NATO Ministers; we have, they say, exploited these events to further an anti-Soviet policy already adopted for quite different reasons, and are interested in fostering a 'cold war' atmosphere in order to increase our influence in Western Europe. For some time we have been treated in a more hostile manner than other NATO powers, though in the second half of November there had been a relaxation of Soviet propaganda against us. How much does such propaganda represent the real thoughts of the Soviet leaders? And how much do their real thoughts matter, if these are that we are reverting to a Cold War atmosphere!

15. Some light is thrown on the first of these questions in the Soviet Memorandum of the 2nd of December. It contains some absurdly exaggerated charges, e.g. that 'someone in England hopes to exclude the USSR from the sphere of international relations'. It also contains, I believe, some genuine misinterpretation, as when you, Sir, are virtually charged with having said that relations with the USSR should be reduced to the minimum. The Soviet Government also include among their accusations at least one on a subject (limitation of Soviet Embassy staff) which has nothing to do with Czechoslovakia; but though they may know this at one mental level, at another and perhaps deeper level, good Marxists will always see subtle connections between unconnected subjects (the whole East-West tension is contained in the contrasting phrases 'it so happens that' and 'it is not by chance'). The immediate publicity given to the memorandum by the Soviet Embassy in London certainly suggests that it is at least in part designed, however clumsily, to appeal over HMG's head to British public opinion, on the assumption that this can be mobilised against HMG's 'anti Soviet' line of policy. This very probable hypothesis does not however exclude the further possibility that the Soviet Government genuinely misunderstands HMG's attitude on certain points.

16. I think that there is nothing to be lost, and something to be gained, from trying to clear these up, and from an attempt to move forward a little from our present state of minimum routine contact and mutual newspaper abuse. The alternative is (and I recognise that it may happen anyhow) to lapse into a sort of private Anglo-Soviet cold war, which would tend to spread into a more general East-West Cold War. The first stage would leave us at some disadvantage *vis-à-vis* our NATO allies; and I find it hard to believe

that the Soviet Government, hard-headed as they are on trade and commercial questions and well as Anglo-Soviet trade has been doing in recent months, cannot find some means of discriminating against our trade in some degree, if they wish. The second stage—a more general Cold War is obviously undesirable. Even the very partial pursuit of our objectives in Eastern Europe which is now possible would be further hampered. More important is the probability that the Soviet leaders would withdraw even further from contact with the outside world into the recesses of their own mythology. They would convince themselves even more deeply of the 'imperialist-revanchist threat', and this state of mind, in spite of the inhibitions listed in paragraph 5 above, could involve dangers for the world as a whole, for instance in miscalculation about the need to prevent some action in Western Germany—at a certain point the risks of inaction may seem greater than the risks of action to minds oppressed by imaginary threats. It is, I believe, with these possible dangers of a lesser and greater Cold War in view that we should try to frame our own policy now towards the Soviet Government though I recognise that, if there is to be any hopeful change in our relations, they have a very important part to play.

17. I have little doubt that the main lines of our policy in the last three months have been both inevitable and right. It has clearly been right to insure, by strengthening NATO, against any further possibilities of Soviet aggression. It remains right to make plain our dislike of the Soviet doctrine of 'Socialist sovereignty'. The *communiqué* of the NATO Ministerial meeting at Brussels marked an important stage in making clear to the Soviet Government the collective attitude of the Western powers, and in laying down the new limits of East-West relations. The necessary deterrence has in fact been provided as far as possible by NATO action.

18. At this stage, however, having publicly taken out a new insurance policy, so to speak, against the Soviet Government, I think that (even apart from their recent memorandum) we should examine very carefully other aspects of our policy towards it, with a view to dispelling any idea that we want to impose further restrictions on our dealings with the USSR, beyond the minimum imposed by our security needs and public opinion. In particular, I hope that we can start working back to something like the previous range of contacts, with the proviso that these are, and are seen to be, directly or indirectly designed for business purposes and do not look like expressions of official or public goodwill, at a time when such goodwill can exist only in a very limited degree. There is, outside the NATO field, little that we can do by way of deterrence (I assume that we do not contemplate economic sanctions which would affect our own trade). The only effect, I believe, of what now look to the Russians like pin-pricks in the political and cultural fields will be to induce the feeling that we are reverting with gusto to cold war, and to strengthen the sense of contrast which, in Russian eyes, exists between our trade policy and our policy in other fields. On the other side of the account, we may *not* under present conditions, and given Russian fears of ideological infection, gain a great deal from continuing bilateral contacts elsewhere than

the commercial field. But, as Mr. Dalton said in his despatch already cited, if the policy of 'peaceful penetration' was worth pursuing before, it is worth pursuing now—in fact the deeper frozen is the condition of Eastern Europe, the greater is the need. And it is, I think, worth hanging on to what footholds we have here, against the possibility of brighter days and social changes in the USSR, remote as these possibilities may now appear.

19. I do not think that there is any danger of getting too far ahead of our allies if we take or refrain from taking certain small actions in order to achieve a partial restoration of bilateral contacts to their former level. It is more likely that we are already falling behind the other NATO powers. Even the USA, though technically in step with us, is in fact well ahead so far as gestures of courtesy and general interest are concerned—I would cite President Nixon's message to President Podgorny,[8] and the recent interviews of Mr. Macnamara and Senators Gore and Pell with Mr. Kosygin. There are also, as already pointed out, certain commercial issues involved in falling behind our NATO colleagues.

20. I do not of course recommend any action, in the resumption of Anglo-Soviet contacts, which would expose HMG to legitimate charges of callousness or inconsistency. Obviously we cannot behave or speak as if the events of August 1968 and onwards had never happened. It is clearly right to voice on occasions explicit public condemnations of direct violation of the UN Charter and interference in the internal affairs of other states. And I think that, given exaggerated Soviet suspicions mentioned in paragraph 15 above, there will be positive advantage in having given to the Gromyko memo-randum a reply which, amongst other things, sets out firmly the basis of our policy hitherto. But the Russians themselves give us examples (not of course always edifying) of how to shout indignantly out of one corner of their mouths, so to speak, and to carry on normal business with the other. Indeed both I and my Belgian colleague have been given hints by Foreign Ministry officials that this would be a policy which they would accept and understand; and chary as I am of advice from this quarter, in this case I regard it as good.

21. It may be helpful if at this stage I give more concrete examples of the way in which I hope that Anglo-Soviet relations can be conducted on a working level at this stage. The first requirement is, I think, to refrain from small gestures of discourtesy—e.g. failure to send conventional messages of congratulation or to attend routine receptions. The second point is that bread and butter decisions about Anglo-Soviet relations should be taken in full consideration of the fact (and it is by now a fact) that HMG is thought in Moscow to be pursuing a special vendetta against the Soviet Government. I am glad for example that it has been decided not to put off negotiations for a new Cultural Agreement early next year,[9] on the grounds that a further agreement is unnecessary.

[8] Apparently a reference to a message from the newly-elected President to Mr. Podgorny on the anniversary of the Soviet revolution.

[9] Cf. No. 12, note 3. On 28 November Sir D. Wilson had been instructed to ask Mr. J.C.C. Bennett, Cultural Attaché to HM Embassy in Moscow, to suggest to the Russians that a British

22. I would add three further considerations. I do not think that it makes sense in the Moscow context to classify all Ministerial visits as 'goodwill' and all official ones as 'business'. It would, for example, be normal procedure here, and not necessarily carry 'goodwill' implications, for a junior minister to visit Moscow for the signature of a new cultural agreement (it would on the contrary be regarded as a sign of bad will if he did not do so). The second and third points are more personal and affect my own usefulness as Ambassador. I can say to Soviet officials, as I have said, that there is plenty of business to be done within the new and limited framework set for Anglo-Soviet relations by events in Czechoslovakia, and that I am always ready to do it. The fact remains that it will not be at all easy for me to exchange informal views on any subject with the Ministry of Foreign Affairs until Anglo-Soviet relations are put back on to a more normal level. I do not want to dwell too much on this point, since I am aware that Soviet diplomats are much readier at any time for frank and informal discussion outside Moscow (and especially at the UN); moreover the particular Vice-Minister with whom I normally deal, Mr. Kozyrev, is never likely to be very helpful. Finally, there is the question of entertainment. So far I and members of my staff have confined ourselves since 21 August to entertaining Soviet officials only when the presence of a visiting delegation or the departure or arrival of one of my staff has given us a normal excuse for doing so at a fairly low level. It is possible that only in such circumstances and at such a level would any Soviet officials at present attend any social function at this Embassy. I regard it, however, as important for the conduct of official business to be on reasonable social terms at least with the main functionaries who might have to do business with us. Entertainment of such people on something like a 'goodwill' basis is in fact business in itself. I hope therefore to have discretion to feel my way gradually forward on this front.

23. I am sending copies of this despatch to HM Representatives in Washington, Paris, Bonn, Belgrade, Berlin, Bucharest, Budapest, Peking, Prague, Sofia and Warsaw, and to the Heads of the United Kingdom Delegation to NATO and of the United Kingdom Mission in New York.[10]

I have, etc.,

DUNCAN WILSON

delegation come to Moscow to negotiate a new Cultural Agreement in the week beginning 17 February 1969. In telegram No. 7484 to Washington of 11 December, responding to a question from the State Department (Washington telegram No. 3537 of 6 December) as to what plans HMG had for 'high visibility cultural exchanges with the Soviet Union in 1969', Sir P. Dean was informed that apart from a visit by the Bolshoi Ballet planned for July 1969 'the only major event in the cultural field is that we intend to carry out a regular renegotiation of the Anglo-Soviet Cultural Agreement . . . we have no wish to let it lapse'. HMG did 'not intend to be put off course' by the Soviet note of 2 December (No. 20).

[10] Mr. Hayman minuted on this despatch: 'We are preparing a commentary on this in the form of a draft despatch. This will have two purposes (a) to comment on Sir D. Wilson's views on Soviet foreign policy. We accept some, but by no means all and (b) to comment on his recommendations about future British policy towards the Soviet Union. Again we accept some but not all of the Ambassador's ideas. P. Hayman 17.12.68.'

CHAPTER II

1969

Britain's relations with the Soviet Union at the turn of the year seemed at a low ebb, and when Mr. Smirnovsky was unexpectedly recalled to Moscow in late December Sir D. Wilson thought it 'very possible that he may have been summoned to Moscow for serious consultations about the present state of Anglo-Soviet relations', which may be 'in for a long deep freeze'. Bilateral relations with the UK, however, were evidently not at the top of the Soviet agenda at this point. The Soviet Ambassador's recall coincided with a hastily arranged visit to Cairo by Mr. Gromyko which, it soon became clear to the FCO, was made in order to clear the lines for a new Soviet initiative for a peace settlement in the Middle East, communicated to Mr. Stewart by Mr. Smirnovsky on 2 January: see No. 23, note 4 below. The next group of documents shows that the FCO's views on the state of Anglo-Soviet relations were less optimistic but also more pragmatic than those of HM Ambassador in Moscow; and that the Soviet initiative in the Middle East seemed to be part of a broader effort to play a full part in multilateral fora, in an attempt both to overcome the stigma of the invasion of Czechoslovakia and to prevent the emergence of a strong Europe dominated by a resurgent West Germany.

No. 23

Mr. Stewart to Sir D. Wilson (Moscow)

[ENS 3/2]

Confidential   FCO, 7 January 1969

Sir,

Soviet Foreign Policy and Anglo-Soviet Relations

Let me begin this despatch by saying how grateful I am for the forthright manner in which Your Excellency has represented Her Majesty's Government's views since your arrival in Moscow. It is seldom that such an important Mission opens in such wholly unfavourable circumstances. Please convey to your staff also my appreciation of the valuable work which they are doing under your direction. I am fully aware of the trying conditions in which you are all now serving and I recognise that the action which we have taken, in the national interest, to limit the size of the Soviet Embassy in London[1] may have repercussions on you all in Moscow.

[1] See No. 19.

2. I have studied with great interest the lucid analysis in your despatch of the 9th of December on Soviet foreign policy.[2] I hope it may be helpful if I set down in reply some of my own thoughts on Soviet foreign policy, as it looks to us from here, and my comments on your proposals about handling our relations in the immediate future.

3. I accept broadly the analysis in your despatch. In particular, I agree with what you say about the caution and conservatism which underlies [*sic*] Soviet foreign policy. On the other hand, I believe that there is a real danger that Russian capability may give rise to intention. This phrase which you use in the context of the Mediterranean is one which could have a more general application. While, for example, the revived doctrine of the 'socialist commonwealth' may have been meant primarily to apply to the countries of Eastern Europe, it has been left deliberately vague and certainly could be used as a charter for intervention elsewhere. If the invasion of Czechoslovakia was in itself primarily a defensive measure in the broadest sense in what the Soviet Union regard as their own back garden, we cannot ignore the possibility that the Soviet leaders will grasp anything elsewhere that they think they can safely obtain. In Czechoslovakia, despite the strength of world reaction and their continuing difficulties in Prague, they may consider that they have achieved at least their main purpose so that, when opportunities offer, they can consider other 'back garden ventures' which could have more serious international consequences.

4. For example, there may well be Warsaw Pact manoeuvres in Rumania next year. Even if these manoeuvres start and finish on the advertised dates, with no troops left behind, and even if they are held well away from the Yugoslav border, they will constitute a threat to Rumanian independence and sovereignty—and the Russians may well act more boldly than this.

5. The Yugoslavs too may fear that the Russian appetite will grow with feeding. Chance events, including even the retirement or the death of Tito,[3] might provide the Russians with opportunities not merely to strengthen but to extend their grip on Eastern Europe. They will only move forward if circumstances are favourable and if risks can be minimised, and they will not necessarily do so by direct military intervention. But there is a real possibility that circumstances may favour a patient forward policy.

6. The dangers which may be expected from some of these half-defensive, half-aggressive moves may be increased by Russian fears of what you well describe as their concept of the 'new threat of imperialism'. In general, I agree that the main purpose of Soviet policy in Europe remains to maintain the existing order and prevent the spread of new forms of socialism within the Warsaw bloc. But this is certainly combined with the vigorous pursuit of a traditional policy of driving wedges between the various countries of NATO so as to try to cause the Alliance to disintegrate (and here do not let us be deceived by Russian humbug about a private British vendetta); this in turn

[2] No. 22.

[3] Marshal J.B. Tito had been President of the Republic of Yugoslavia since 1953.

might achieve one of their basic aims—which is to reduce the United States' commitment to Europe.

7. In the wider international field, I find your assessment of Soviet foreign policy a little optimistic. It is too soon for example fully to assess the implications of recent Soviet initiatives in the Middle East.[4] This must take account of the Gromyko visit to Cairo, Dr. Jarring's discussions in Moscow, and the recent moves by Moscow in Washington, London and Paris. I am inclined to think that if, as seems to be the case, the Russians are now working for some form of political agreement (as opposed to a solution of the problems involved) this is essentially because the dangers of a conflagration seem to them to outweigh the advantages of keeping the pot near the boil.

8. I agree generally with your assessment of the three major limitations on Moscow foreign policy; the Russians certainly want if possible to preserve a dialogue with the Americans; they need to pay regard to world communist opinion; they must take account of hard economic facts. Of these three major limitations, I suspect that the need to respect world communist opinion is for the time being the weakest. There are already signs that those parties which disapproved most strongly of the invasion of Czechoslovakia are beginning to come to heel. As has been well said, they have nowhere else to go. Recent speeches in Warsaw emphasised that the non-ruling communist parties are a lesser breed. The Russians may have to pay rather more attention to this factor between now and the date of the World Conference.[5] But, once the Conference is over, this element of restraint may count for no more than it did in August.

Anglo-Soviet relations

9. Here our aim must certainly be to re-establish a good, clear-sighted and workmanlike relationship which is consistent both with our wider international interests and our national security. It must also take full account of the strength of British feelings over the invasion of Czechoslovakia. We certainly

---

[4] Cf. p. 111. Soviet proposals for a settlement in the Middle East, first communicated to the US Government on 30 December 1968 (also communicated to the French Government) were considered a significant advance on previous Russian peace plans. They embodied the concept of a 'package' settlement, encompassing the problems of refugees and freedom of navigation, and spoke of an agreement which would embody the settlement, as opposed to the parallel declarations previously suggested. This agreement, the proposals suggested, might be a signed 'multilateral document' which the British Government believed could be made binding in international law. The proposals were accompanied by an oral statement stressing the peaceful intentions of the Arab States, criticising the negative attitude of the Israeli Government and calling on all states with an interest in stabilising the Middle East to take decisive measures, though the medium of Dr. Jarring (who had now returned to Moscow) to bring about a peace settlement based on UN Resolution 242 of 1967 (see pp. 4-5). The British reply, communicated to Mr. Piadshyev of the Soviet Embassy on 23 January, welcomed the emphasis on finding a settlement through the Jarring Mission but asked for clarification on points of detail. The American reply emphasised the importance of negotiations between the parties, and agreed to the French suggestion for four power talks as a means of providing a new basis for Dr. Jarring's mission and at the same time to embark on further bilateral discussions with the Russians.

[5] Planned for May 1969: see No. 22, para. 10.

do not want to relapse into a private Anglo-Soviet cold war, nor do we want the Russians to make more difficulties for us in the trade and technological fields than for our NATO allies.

10. On this basis I endorse the main proposals in your despatch, with some differences in emphasis:

(*a*) Certainly we should be ready to discuss international problems with the Russians whenever there are opportunities. I made this clear when I had my long talk with Gromyko in New York.[6] I quite agree that you should be ready to discuss current international problems with Kozyrev whenever opportunity arises, although I can understand that this may be difficult. In handling all these problems in the aftermath of Czechoslovakia, it is more important than ever to act in the closest consultation with our NATO allies.

(*b*) We should also continue our commercial and technological exchanges as fully as possible. This will undoubtedly mean Ministerial visits from time to time. But I am not ready to restore the full range of visits that had been organised before the invasion of Czechoslovakia. These were more important than those arranged by our other NATO allies. Inevitably many of them carried implications of goodwill which I consider to be inappropriate, and indeed inexpedient, at the present time. But if we carry out only those visits which have real commercial advantages, we shall not be falling behind our NATO partners. It is true, as you point out, that the Russians could try to harm us by giving, perhaps to the French, contracts which our own industrialists might have hoped to win. But I doubt whether they will push things very far in this direction because they see advantages to themselves in trade and technological exchanges with us.

(*c*) On cultural exchanges, I have, as you know, agreed that we should re-negotiate the Cultural Agreement.[7] I hope that these cultural exchanges will let some light and air into the Soviet Union.

(*d*) I agree that small discourtesies will get us nowhere. We have full diplomatic relations with the Soviet Union and in our day-to-day exchanges we should take full account of this. I am content to leave it entirely to your discretion how you entertain the Soviet Ministers and officials.

11. I would like to conclude with some general observations. I have sometimes noticed in the past few years a note of contempt in the manner in which the Russians deal with and speak of this country. I believe that there are definite advantages now in letting them see that we cannot easily be pushed off a position of principle once we have adopted it. But above all the Russians respect power. On the basis of co-equal power they would deal exclusively with the United States. While we need to be realistic about the limitations on the influence which we can bring to bear upon them, our own power is, I believe, raised many times in their estimate when we speak firmly

[6] See No. 17, note 4.　　　　　　　　　　　　[7] Cf. No. 22, note 9.

and honestly to them and when they know that we are acting in concert with our allies. I also believe that they value our diplomatic experience and resourcefulness. We can perhaps claim that our patient logic has helped to move them on one or two questions in recent years. Finally, they value their technological and commercial exchanges with us, for what they gain, including the foreign exchange, and because of the inconvenience of upsetting traditional patterns.

12. Against this background, and also because of the valid security considerations which are involved, we do not intend to make concessions over the limitation of the Russian Embassy staff, although this is clearly going to cause us difficulty for some time. Provided that we are always willing to talk business with the Russians when there is business to be done, a firm but reasonable tone is the one which I would like to sustain. We should seek to dispel genuine misunderstandings, but I see advantages in a period of plain speaking, provided that we avoid the vocabulary and tone of the cold war. This was the basis of my reply to Mr. Gromyko's memorandum,[8] which has been notably well received in this country.

13. I look forward to discussing all these matters with you when you come to London later in the month.[9]

14. I am sending copies of this despatch to Her Majesty's Representatives in Washington, Paris, Bonn, Belgrade, Berlin, Bucharest, Budapest, Peking, Prague, Sofia and Warsaw and to the United Kingdom Permanent Representatives on the North Atlantic Council and at New York.

I am, etc.,
MICHAEL STEWART

[8] See Nos. 20 and 21.

[9] Sir D. Wilson was returning to the UK for consultations on 28-30 January.

No. 24

Letter from Sir D. Wilson (Moscow) to Mr. Hayman

[ENS 3/2]

Confidential   MOSCOW, *11 February 1969*

Dear Peter,

We gave a small lunch yesterday for Smirnovsky and his wife, attended also by the Daltons and Bridges[1] on our side, and by Vasev and Loginov from Second European Department (the latter had served in the Soviet Embassy in London during my time as Under-Secretary). It was a peace-loving and pleasant occasion. Most of the awkward subjects were mentioned and we had

[1] The Hon T.E. Bridges became Counsellor and Head of Chancery in Moscow in January 1969.

quite a long discussion after lunch about the gas centrifuge plans and the non-proliferation treaty,[2] but there was no heat and the atmosphere was good.

The following are the main points which emerged:

(i) *Anglo-Soviet relations.* Smirnovsky was reasonably cheerful about general developments, and before lunch we went over the subject[s] on which concrete discussions were now proceeding or would soon proceed— technological collaboration (Mr. Benn's visit)[3], trade (he mentioned the visits of Messrs. Davies and Ross),[4] Middle East and possibly disarmament. Smirnovsky delicately conveyed the impression that, if relations were on the mend, this was only after long discussions in Moscow, in which he himself had argued for a more positive line. He said that this had not always been an easy task (cf. (iii) below), and that he could have wished to have had stronger arguments at his disposal. I did not fail to draw his attention to my recent visit to London, which I claimed to have been very useful in the same context.[5]

(ii) *Cultural Negotiations.* I explained to Smirnovsky the difficulty which was being caused to us by the delay in the Soviet reply,[6] not least because of

---

[2] Mr. Benn announced in the House of Commons on 22 November 1968 that he and Mr. Mulley would be attending a meeting in The Hague on 25 November with Ministers from the Netherlands and the Federal Republic of Germany 'to discuss the implications of recent developments in relation to the technology of the gas centrifuge method of uranium enrichment', and to 'consider the possibility of establishing collaborative arrangements for the exploitation of this method of uranium enrichment' (*Parl Debs., 5th Ser., H of C,* vol. 773, col 352). It was agreed that any cooperation would have to be consistent with the UK's international obligations under the Non-Proliferation Treaty (NPT: see No. 11, note 3).

The Soviet Union had not yet ratified the Non-Proliferation Treaty: in conversation with Sir Solly Zuckerman on 22 November 1968 Mr. Smirnovsky had 'reaffirmed the fact that the present position of the USSR is not to ratify until West Germany had signed'. Sir Solly 'used this statement as an opportunity to say we hoped that collaboration on the gas centrifuge would provide us with some leverage in encouraging the Germans to this step' (DS 5/303/1). On 10 December 1968 the Cabinet decided not to make collaboration conditional upon the FRG's signature of the NPT, but agreed that 'we should press the German Government to sign the NPT and in this context use could be made of the proposed gas centrifuge collaboration' (CC(68)50).

[3] On 1 January 1969 Mr. Stewart had agreed that Sir D. Wilson should approach the Soviet Government about a visit to Moscow by Mr. Benn to meet 'something very nearly approaching an obligation' to review the Anglo-Soviet Technological Agreement (cf. No. 2, note 5), Mr. Benn's planned visit in September 1968 having been cancelled after the invasion of Czechoslovakia. Mr. Kirillin sent a message to Mr. Benn on 7 February agreeing to the visit, which was subsequently fixed for 13-20 May.

[4] Mr. John Davies, Director-General of the Confederation of British Industry (CBI), visited the Soviet Union from 16-27 January. Mr. Alex Ross was Chairman of the East European Trade Council.

[5] Cf. No. 23, note 9.

[6] Cf. No. 22, note 9. Mr. Dalton wrote to Mr. Brash on 5 February that the Soviet side were taking the line that they were 'not yet ready to exchange drafts and, until they were, could not discuss dates.' In a minute of 7 February to Mr. Giffard and Mr. Peck Mr. Brash expressed unease about the present position: 'In effect we are allowing ourselves to be cold-shouldered by the Russians over the Exchange [Cultural] Agreement, while on the other hand all seems

the long list of other engagements which had to be fulfilled by the people concerned in London. Smirnovsky said that we could expect an early reply. The Soviet side also had many engagements to fit in. He said that he thought this was the prime cause of delay, but hinted that decisions on this sort of thing had not been made easier by 'other events'; in answer to my question, he said that he was referring to the decision about Soviet Embassy staff in London (cf. (iii)).[7] Vasev, to whom Peter Dalton spoke separately, expressed surprise that we had not already heard from the Cultural Relations Department, saying that he understood that we should have done so by the end of last week and that he would enquire on return to his office. We have still heard nothing and the senior members of the Cultural Relations Department have been unobtainable. We will keep trying.[8]

(iii) *Soviet Embassy Staff.* Smirnovsky mentioned the London decisions twice in passing (cf. (i) and (ii)) and also said that sometimes it was not only the matter but the manner of certain decisions that caused difficulties. I said that he knew why we had felt bound to take these decisions, but he showed no inclination to discuss the subject further. It would be unwise to build too much upon this, but there was no suggestion of counter-action and the normal inference from what Smirnovsky said and the way in which he said it would be that he considered the subject closed.

(iv) *Gas Centrifuge, Non-Proliferation, etc.* After lunch, we settled down as a team to discuss this complex of themes, starting from the recent Soviet press articles, the tone of which (and the references to the Munich agreement in this connection)[9] had, we said, surprised us. We explained that the centrifuge development had arisen on purely technological grounds, and that neither Britain nor Germany could be excluded from a

sweetness and light in the context of the Technological Agreement [see note 3]. . .'. Mr. Giffard, however, minuted on 10 February that he doubted 'whether the Russians are calculating that they can get out of the Technological Agreement all the substantial advantages which they have hitherto obtained from the Exchange Agreement . . . I think that our own tactics should be to maintain our willingness to negotiate and certainly not to seem to go cold ourselves; but equally not to run after the Russians. To some extent, I think that they are trying to make our flesh creep at the prospect of no negotiations at all' (PWS 1/2).

[7] See No. 19.

[8] Mr. Brash minuted on 27 February that the Russians had now agreed that negotiations should open in Moscow on 20 March. They had also sent a copy of their proposed text of the new Cultural Agreement, which kept broadly to the pattern of the existing text but contained 'a number of Russian try-ons'; Mr. Brash's impression was 'that we are in for a tough negotiation, where the atmosphere will be cold throughout' (PWS 1/2).

[9] Sir D. Wilson had reported on 10 February that recent Soviet press comment 'had sought to show the danger of the regrowth of German militarism and there has been some attempt to draw parallels between Britain's agreement at the time of Munich and current signs of British enthusiasm for a Bonn/London axis . . . Readiness to co-operate over the centrifuge has been attacked as contrary to our expressed policy of support for the non-proliferation treaty and as further evidence of willingness to help Bonn to acquire nuclear weapons in return for German help to achieve British entry to the Common Market' (Moscow telegram No. 101, SMN 2/1).

new process giving access to cheap energy. West European states, unlike the super powers, could not afford to go it alone. Equally, as a signatory of the non-proliferation treaty, we would not be a party to anything inconsistent with our obligations: we attached great importance to the strict observation of the treaty, which affected our own security as well as that of the Soviet Union and we were anxious that the Federal German Government should also sign the treaty. They had genuine difficulties, which were reflected in their anxiety about the 'enemy states clauses' in the United Nations Charter,[10] but we hoped that the Soviet Government would help them to overcome these. Smirnovsky expressed the suspicion that these difficulties were just an excuse for not signing, and we had a short exchange on the wisdom of the extremely suspicious nature of Soviet policy towards the Federal Republic. Reverting to the centrifuge, the Soviet team seemed in general surprised by our emphasis on the subject, and Vasev even said that we should not take everything which appeared in the Soviet newspapers as an exact reflection of official Soviet policy. They then made the point that Germany was not yet a party to the non-proliferation treaty and that it would seem to take too much on trust if Britain were to sign an agreement of the kind proposed on the gas centrifuge before Germany had formally acceded to it. We countered with the argument that the Germans had already gone some way in developing centrifuge technology, and that it was in the common interest that their technology should be tied up with ours as soon as possible, so that there was less danger of separate and undesirable development later.

I don't suppose that we got very far towards convincing our Soviet colleagues, but I think there is some significance in the fact that they did not counter-attack with more zest. I would conclude that the press references to the centrifuge and Anglo-German collaboration in general are not intended as a signal to slow up the process of working towards 're-normalisation' of Anglo-Soviet relations.[11]

Yours ever,

DUNCAN WILSON

[10] A brief of 4 February prepared for the Prime Minister's visit to Bonn and Berlin (see pp. 119-20 below) stated that the FRG's chief concern with the NPT arose from the Soviet interpretation of Articles 53 and 107 of the UN Charter (cf. *BFSP*, vol. 145, pp. 805-32) that the wartime Allies had a right to take coercive action against the FRG, notably in case of any 'renewal of aggressive policy'. The UK, US and France had made it clear publicly that they did not regard the Articles as giving the Soviet Union a unilateral right of intervention by force (cf. *Selected Documents on Germany and the Question of Berlin 1961-1973*, Cmnd. 6201, No. 96).

[11] Sir D. Wilson noted on the bottom of this letter that he was sending a copy to Sir R. Jackling in Bonn. The letter was also submitted to Mr. Stewart's Private Secretary in preparation for an interview on 18 February with Mr. Smirnovsky.

Two important visits took place in the second half of February 1969: the Prime Minister visited Bonn and Berlin, 11-14 February, and the new US President, Richard Nixon, visited London 24-26 February as the second leg of a European tour which began with a visit to the North Atlantic Council in Brussels. The objectives of British policy during both sets of discussions were similar: to express concern about progress in (and French obstruction to) European unity and reaffirm British commitment to it; and to stress the fundamental importance of the Atlantic Alliance for European security. In a minute of 7 February setting out his ideas on European policy for the Prime Minister in the light of the forthcoming talks, Mr. Stewart stated that 'a main purpose of British policy in Europe must be, not merely to maintain the Atlantic Alliance and to hold on to such cohesion as has been achieved since 1948, but to use the new administration in the United States and eventually new governments in France and Germany to make substantial steps forward . . . there can be no dispute about the vital role that Germany is going to play in our own future and in the calculations of the American President. We ourselves must get our relations with Germany on to a basis of genuine confidence'.[1]

Discussions between Dr. Kiesinger and Mr. Wilson focussed on: European integration, where Dr. Kiesinger was much disturbed by the Prime Minister's account of conversations between the British Ambassador in Paris, Christopher Soames, and General de Gaulle, who criticised his European partners as pro-American and anticipated the disappearance of NATO and the replacement of the EEC by a looser form of free trade area;[2] East-West relations, where the Prime Minister reaffirmed his support for—though not his agreement with—the Federal Government's decision to hold their Presidential election (Bundesversammlung) in Berlin on 5 March (a decision which provoked condemnation and threats by the Soviet and East German Governments); and technological collaboration, including the European Airbus and the gas centrifuge project (see No. 24, note 2). On 13 February a joint Anglo-German declaration was issued affirming the two countries' determination to 'go forward in partnership', challenging the Gaullist position on Europe, reaffirming that the security of Europe depended on the Atlantic Alliance and pledging both governments to further the aim of Britain's joining the European Economic Communities.

In a press statement released on 6 February President Nixon announced that his intention in visiting Brussels, London, Bonn, Berlin, Rome and Paris was 'to underline my commitment to the closest relationship between our friends in Western Europe and the US . . . to discuss, not to propose, for work, not for ceremony'. FCO officials considered that a desire to reverse the decline in the international prestige of the US also lay behind the tour, a view confirmed in part by Mr. Nixon's own statement in his Memoirs that he wanted 'to establish the principle that we would consult with our allies before negotiating with our potential adversaries. I also wanted to show the world that the new American President was not completely obsessed with Vietnam, and to dramatize for Americans at

---

[1] PM/69/13, ANU 2/11.

[2] For Mr. Wilson's account of 'l'affaire Soames', as it became known, see *The Labour Government 1964-70, op. cit.,* pp. 768-70; cf. *Life and Labour, op. cit.,* pp. 225-26 for Mr. Stewart's view on what he described as 'the only occasion on which Harold and I seriously disagreed on foreign policy'.

home that, despite opposition to the war, their President could still be received abroad with respect and even enthusiasm.'[3] In any case, Mr. Wilson appreciated the fact that London was first on the list after NATO, and was glad to have the opportunity to set out his government's views on international questions, to build a close and friendly relationship with the President and to stress the importance of full US commitment to the defence of Europe. He told the Cabinet on 27 February that the visit had gone well: he had been 'agreeably impressed by the President's pragmatic attitude and his evident desire for close consultation with Britain and his other allies' (CC(69)10).

Reports from Moscow make it clear that both these sets of talks were closely watched by the Soviet Government. Evidence of a closer Anglo-German relationship, and re-affirmation of US commitment to Europe, were unwelcome to the Soviet leadership. The next group of documents can be read in the context of Mr. Nixon's verdict, recorded in his Memoirs, that his trip 'served warning on the Soviets that they could no longer take for granted—nor take advantage of—Western disunity'.[4]

[3] *The Memoirs of Richard Nixon* (London, 1978), p. 370.

[4] *Ibid.*, p. 375.

No. 25

Sir D. Wilson (Moscow) to Mr. Stewart

No. 219 Telegraphic [ENS 3/2]

Priority. Confidential   MOSCOW, *6 March 1969*

Repeated for information to Bonn, UKDEL NATO, Washington and Saving to Paris, Belgrade, Bucharest, Budapest, Prague, Sofia and Warsaw.

Your telegrams Nos. 179 and 180: call on Kosygin.[1]

[1] Sir D. Wilson had reported in Moscow telegram No. 214 of 5 March that he had been asked to call on Mr. Kosygin the following morning for 'my much delayed courtesy call', and asked for 'urgent guidance on any themes which you particularly wish me to raise or avoid'. FCO telegram No. 179 of even date contained points for Sir D. Wilson to make on the Middle East, Vietnam, President Nixon's visit to London and Berlin (see No. 23, note 4 and pp. 119-20); telegram No. 180 instructed him to take the general line on Anglo-Soviet relations 'that we are glad to note that these are now beginning to develop again on a businesslike basis', mentioning forthcoming negotiations on the cultural and trade agreements, and Mr. Benn's forthcoming visit to Moscow to discuss progress under the Technological Agreement (see Nos. 29 and 32-3 below).

The Ambassador was also instructed in telegram No. 180 to stress 'the very great importance which we attach to personal cases as influencing the climate of our relations' and to renew the request for consular access to Mr. Gerald Brooke (who had not been allowed a consular visit since 20 June 1968). In the light of recent suggestions by Soviet officials that Mr. Brooke might face trial on further charges, and of renewed attempts to equate his case with that of the Krogers (cf. No. 1, note 6), Sir D. Wilson was told that the matter was under further consideration in London and that meanwhile he should reaffirm that there was no comparison between the two cases.

I saw Kosygin for half an hour this morning. Makeev (Head of Second European Department) was present.

2. After a short exchange on bilateral relations (see my immediately following telegram),[2] Kosygin said that although he did not wish to introduce anything unpleasant into our first meeting he must ask me to convey the following to the Prime Minister and to HMG. The Soviet Government were disturbed by the policy of HMG and in particular by the 'bellicose' statements of Mr. Healey. The latter's pronouncements on nuclear war and on the fact that the Soviet Union constitutes the principal threat to European security were matters of grave concern to the Soviet Government.[3] In this context the Soviet Government noted that the United Kingdom's military expenditure was increasing[4] and that we were strengthening our ties with West Germany.[5] Mr. Healey's statements and HMG's policy did not accord with our expressed desire to improve and develop our relations with the

[2] Telegram No. 220 stated that in response to Mr. Kosygin's question whether there was any particular point he wished to raise, Sir D. Wilson had spoken in the sense of FCO telegram No. 180 (see note 1). Mr. Kosygin had expressed agreement with Sir D. Wilson's remarks on the general state of Anglo-Soviet relations, but said that he was 'not *au fait* with the details of the Brooke case', although he was aware that the matter was 'frozen' for the time being. Sir D. Wilson had no opportunity to revert to this subject during the interview.

[3] In speeches at the NATO Defence Planning Committee on 16 January and at a defence symposium in Munich on 5 February Mr. Healey had stated that the early use of nuclear weapons by NATO would be the only alternative to surrender in the event of a major Soviet attack; in an interview published by *Der Spiegel* on 11 February he stated that the entire Soviet fleet in the Mediterranean would be sunk within minutes in the event of war, and announced that the British fleet in the Mediterranean was to be enlarged; and on 4 March in the course of the debate on the Defence White Paper (see note 4 below) he announced that joint Anglo-German proposals for guidelines on the use of nuclear weapons in Europe to deter a Soviet advance would shortly be put to NATO's Nuclear Planning Group (see *The Times*, 17 January, 3 and 11 February, 5 and 6 March). Mr. Bridges reported in a letter of 12 March to Mr. M.R.H. Jenkins of EESD that the '"warlike" content of these speeches has been a recurrent theme in recent Soviet press treatment of Great Britain', indicating genuine Russian concern and surprise 'at this British "bellicose" attitude' (ENS 3/1).

[4] The Defence White Paper (Cmnd. 3927 of 1969) published on 20 February announced increases in Britain's contribution to NATO and in the strength of British forces in Germany and the Mediterranean, although overall defence expenditure was £11m less than in the preceding year. Mr. Healey told the House of Commons on 4 March that the increased contribution to NATO had been made possible only by the reductions in Britain's role outside Europe made in 1968 (see pp. 1-2). He stressed that the strength and solidarity of NATO were 'a precondition of achieving our wider aims. The purpose of NATO is not to produce heaven on earth. It is to prevent hell on earth', and defended the nuclear component of NATO's deterrent strategy: 'When the use of strategic nuclear weapons is likely to involve the deaths of hundreds of millions of human beings, NATO must aim to bring the conflict to a close before either side is tempted or compelled to initiate an all-out nuclear exchange.' NATO's conventional forces must demonstrate a determination to resist and to use nuclear weapons if necessary, 'to win sufficient time to enable diplomatic action to bring the aggressor to his senses, or failing that, to enable the awesome decision to cross the nuclear threshold to be taken in full knowledge of the facts' (*Parl. Debs.*, 5th ser., H. of C., vol. 779, cols. 230-47).

[5] See pp. 119-20, and cf. note 3 above.

Soviet Union and to see a *détente* in Europe; indeed they boded ill for our future bilateral relations. Although defence ministers were expected to do their job, no minister on the Soviet side had gone as far as making the kind of statements which Mr. Healey had uttered. Contrary to what Mr. Healey had said, the Soviet Government's sole aim was to see a *détente* in Europe and to develop our bilateral relations, for which there were good possibilities.

3. After replying to the last point I said that I would transmit Mr. Kosygin's message to the Prime Minister, who would no doubt want to consider it carefully. In the meantime I felt bound to say a few words on this subject, treated by Mr. Kosygin. The NATO powers had last summer put forward a proposal for the mutual reduction of troop levels in Europe.[6] We had never received a reply. As far as our present military policy towards Europe was concerned HMG had been gravely disturbed by the movement of Russian troops in Europe in August of last year and our new dispositions represented a sort of insurance policy. Our military relations with West Germany were governed by the normal requirement to cooperate with our allies within the NATO framework. We had no desire to stimulate any alleged German 'revanchism'. I did not wish to go into the question of Mr. Healey's statements which had been to a considerable extent misinterpreted.

4. Kosygin made no further comment than that his understanding of Mr. Healey's statements was based on what he had been reading in the British press. He then brought our conversation to an end with the usual courtesies. His manner throughout was firm, but not hostile.

5. There was no time to discuss any further international themes, but in answer to Kosygin's remarks about the possibilities of cooperation between our two countries, I was able to mention that you had found bilateral talks on the Middle East valuable[7] and hoped that they would continue fruitfully.[8]

[6] See No. 21, note 9.

[7] In response to the British request for clarification of some points in the Soviet note on the Middle East (see No. 23, note 4), the Soviet Embassy had suggested bilateral discussion of the Soviet proposals in parallel with the proposed four-power conversations in New York (now postponed until 3 April). Mr. Stewart described this suggestion to the Cabinet on 20 February as an 'encouraging development', although a 'four-power initiative was needed to break the deadlock created by the fact that the opposing sides, and to some extent Dr. Jarring, had all taken up rigid positions' (CC(69)9th Conclusions, CAB 128/44). Bilateral talks between Lord Caradon and the Soviet Ambassador to the UN, Mr. Malik, began on 15 February, but as Lord Caradon reported: 'Malik and I are on very good jovial terms personally but he shows no signs of being ready to negotiate' (UKMIS telegram No. 262 of 22 February, NE 2/25).

[8] In telegram No. 230 of 7 March Sir D. Wilson commented that Mr. Kosygin's message to Mr. Wilson should be viewed against a background of intense Soviet press propaganda against HMG's defence policy, and of 'longer-term and less publicised fears that the FRG may assume the leading role in Western Europe, and that HMG are in effect, if not in intention, helping them to do so'. Sir D. Wilson referred in this context to his Annual Review of the Soviet Union for 1968, dated 2 January 1969 (ENS 1/7), in which he stated that according to the Soviet thesis HMG was 'adopting a strong anti-Soviet line to please the Germans, and in the hope of securing their support against the French for entry in the Common Market. This . . . would result in the substitution of a comparatively closely-knit political alliance, dominated by "revanchist" Germany, for the "Europe des Patries" dominated by Gaullist France, with its anti-American

and pro-Soviet tendencies.' In Moscow telegram No. 230 Sir D. Wilson submitted that it would be useful if the Prime Minister could find an opportunity to explain to Mr. Smirnovsky the aims of HMG's defence policy and HMG's views on Anglo-German and Anglo-Soviet relations: 'Such a statement would for the present at the least form a very useful text for use in conversations at official level.'

FCO officials did not think that there was any need to hurry in preparing a reply to Mr. Kosygin's message. As Mr. Cambridge of EESD minuted on 7 March, the attacks on Mr. Healey, and on strengthening British ties with West Germany, were 'standard features of Soviet propaganda' and merely provided fresh evidence 'that the Russians really do not care about a serious dialogue with us (as distinct from the Americans); and that they intend to pursue their divisive tactics among the members of NATO, with the UK continuing to be singled out for rough treatment'. Nor did officials agree with Sir D. Wilson's suggestion of an interview between the Prime Minister and Mr. Smirnovsky: as Mr. Barrington remarked on 12 March, sending a short draft reply for Mr. Wilson's consideration, 'it would be dignifying Mr. Kosygin's remarks much more than they deserve were the Prime Minister himself to intervene'.

Mr. Wilson, however, found the FCO draft 'excessively negative at a time when the Americans are making no secret of their willingness to have practical talks with the Russians and when we ourselves are doing so in regard, for example, to the Middle East'. He favoured a fuller, firmer and more positive reply, 'refuting the misconceptions and criticisms' in Mr. Kosygin's message but expressing willingness to enter 'a constructive dialogue with the Soviet Union'. The revised draft, sent to Sir D. Wilson on 25 March, took the line that Mr. Kosygin's remarks had been based on a 'misconception' which would be removed following HMG's explanation of why 'British policies accord very well with our desire to improve Anglo-Soviet relations', as shown in their reply of 10 December 1968 to the Soviet note of 2 December (Nos. 20 and 21): Mr. Healey had 'simply been restating the clear policy of the Atlantic Alliance on its response if an attack was ever made against it'; it was 'natural and inevitable' that we should seek to strengthen ties with our allies; HMG's declared policy was 'to limit defence expenditure as much as circumstances allow'. The reply concluded that HMG welcomed discussion on a range of topics with the Soviet Government, and did not consider differences of view a 'bar to useful discussion'.

No. 26

Sir D. Wilson (Moscow) to Mr. Stewart

No. 299 Telegraphic [*ENS 3/2*]

Priority. Confidential   MOSCOW, *28 March 1969*

Repeated for information to UKDEL NATO, Bonn, Washington, UKMIS New York, Paris, Belgrade, Bucharest, Budapest, Prague, Sofia, Warsaw.

My telegram No. 297 (not to all): reply to Kosygin's message.[1]

After I had read out the reply which he undertook to pass on to Kosygin, Gromyko opened by saying that he wished to make some preliminary comments on HMG's communication. Both sides naturally had different points of view on international problems but it was important that such differences did not lead to fruitless polemics between HMG and the Soviet Government. HMG must realise that the purpose of Kosygin's remarks was to find a way of bringing about a 'favourable turn' in Anglo-Soviet relations. HMG would mistake the spirit of such remarks if it considered that their purpose was to emphasise Anglo-Soviet differences.

2. Gromyko then moved on to a description of those international problems, not necessarily (he said) in order of priority, towards a solution of which Britain and the Soviet Union might jointly contribute.

3. *Middle East.* If HMG considered objectively the question of settlement of the Middle East crisis it should be clear that in this context Britain and the Soviet Union should be moving in the same direction. The Middle East situation was fraught with danger. The closure of the Suez Canal was both economically and financially damaging not only to the Soviet Union and to Britain but to many other countries. The Soviet Government's position was well known to HMG. It believed in a just settlement for both sides, which would guarantee the security of both Israel (Gromyko particularly emphasised this) and the Arab States. HMG would gain positive capital in the world by pursuing a similarly constructive policy. Britain and the Soviet Union should be more active in seeking together a settlement.

4. *Europe.* Gromyko continued by saying that European questions were many and complicated and that he only wished to touch on two of them. HMG was familiar with the address of the powers of the Warsaw Pact.[2] The

---

[1] In this telegram of 27 March Sir D. Wilson reported that he had seen Mr. Gromyko that day and read out HMG's reply as instructed: see p. 123.

[2] At the closing session on 17 March of the meeting of the Political Consultative Committee of the Warsaw Treaty Organisation held in Budapest, an 'address' was issued to all European countries calling for an early conference on European security and cooperation (cf. Nos. 3, note 4, and 4, note 4), to be attended by all interested European States, with a preliminary meeting of officials. The Address stated that preconditions for firm European security would include recognition of the inviolability of all European frontiers, including the Oder-Neisse line (i.e. the Polish Western frontier) and the GDR/FRG frontier, and the abandonment of Bonn's claim to represent the whole of the German people. Sir D. Wilson had commented in Moscow telegram No. 268 of 18 March that 'all in all the wording of the address looks noticeably mild and

British Government should understand that the countries of the Warsaw Pact were not following their own narrow interests. Some kind of big conference at which all European governments were present would provide the best forum in which to discuss the problems dividing Europe. Not all states would agree on a solution to all problems but agreement on one or two points would be better than nothing. It was the Soviet Government's positive hope that such a conference could be convened.

5. Gromyko's second point concerned Berlin. Every now and again Bonn aggravated European tension by its policy towards West Berlin. There seemed to be groups in West Germany whose existence in a fantasy world led them to damage relations between the states of Europe. It only needed this kind of irresponsibility to undermine European security. HMG might look at this question from a higher plane and exercise its influence on the Federal German Government to prove that it was in no one's interest to resort to such provocative measures as the holding of the presidential elections in West Berlin.[3]

6. Gromyko concluded by making some observations in English. The second half of last year and the first few months of 1969 had seen an unfortunate 'explosion' of hostile propaganda against the Soviet Union in Britain. Certain statesmen had helped to inspire this. Why did HMG countenance such 'phenomena' when they were contrary to the long term interests of both countries and of Europe? Each side had its position. But a certain correctness was demanded in relations and if this was to be maintained then there were limits beyond which no side should go. When such 'phenomena' occurred, the Soviet Union 'did not like to remain in debt to anyone'. This was a situation which the Soviet Government wished to see changed.

7. I replied that I would not answer his points in detail but would make a few comments on what had been said. HMG both recognised and favoured Kosygin's positive remarks on Anglo-Soviet relations. The Soviet Government would see from a study of the text of HMG's communication that we had taken up these positive comments. (At this point I once again passed on the Prime Minister's personal good wishes to Kosygin.) As far as hostile propaganda was concerned the Soviet Government had to face the fact that its action in Europe last year had evoked strong disapproval from both HMG and the British people. We had several times made the point that this disapproval needed no stimulation on the part of HMG. As regards hostile comment, we certainly did not think the Soviet Government was in debt to us, and it was to be hoped that this was a chapter in our relations which was now drawing to a close.

reasonable, although that is perhaps the only novelty in a fairly well-worn proposal. The inability of the Western powers to respond collectively to the earlier versions, and their evident differences in approach, have presumably led the Soviet authorities to conclude, with some justification, that this is a promising public line. We will hear a lot more about it in the coming months' (WDW 1/2).

[3] Cf. p. 119.

8. I went on to say that I thought that the Soviet Government had under-estimated HMG's attempts to achieve a settlement in the Middle East. We might not have identical points of view on this question, but our interests in a settlement were the same. I said that I hoped that the bilateral and quadri-lateral talks in New York would prove fruitful.

9. I concluded by saying that the Warsaw Pact address would be carefully considered by the coming meeting of the NATO Ministerial Council.[4] We of course wanted to further European cooperation. As far as Berlin was concerned, I said that your talk with Smirnovsky[5] would have made it clear to the Soviet Government that HMG wished to ease tension between East and West Germany.

10. Comment follows by telegram.[6]

[4] The North Atlantic Council was to meet in Washington on 10 and 11 April: see pp. 129-30 below.

[5] Mr. Smirnovsky had called on Mr. Stewart on 17 March to deliver an oral statement critical of the West German Government's handling of the *Bundesversammlung*. Mr. Stewart had asked 'whether anything was achieved by keeping alive the argument about the Presidential election' and added that both he and Mr. Smirnovsky 'could agree that they had no desire to increase tension between the two parts of Germany'.

[6] In telegram No. 303 of 28 March Sir D. Wilson expressed the view that 'the crucial phrase in Gromyko's remarks, and one which he repeated more than once, was "to bring about a turn in Anglo-Soviet relations". In effect, I think that the Soviet Government are now ready to make the best of what we can do to co-operate with them in various spheres on a business-like basis, without paying too much attention to a normal rate of criticism from our side of their policies, and of course without hesitating to criticize our policies themselves in a routine way.' He added that the volume of anti-British propaganda had diminished over the last fort-night, and that the cultural negotiations (see No. 29 below) had been conducted in a 'good and business-like atmosphere', and concluded: 'I think that the sort of modus vivendi which the Soviet Government now seem ready to accept continues to be in our interest and compatible with our principles.'

Mr. Gromyko's reception of HMG's reply indicated to the FCO that he was more preoccupied with international than with bilateral problems, though harmonious Anglo-Soviet relations were desirable both in terms of day-to-day business and within a wider East-West context. The Soviet Government was clearly keen to cooperate in both bilateral and multilateral efforts to secure peace in the Middle East, and the Budapest Address (also referred to as an Appeal or Declaration) could be seen as a positive initiative towards European cooperation. However, the FCO were aware that this keenness to play a constructive role in solving international problems had to be seen against a background of tension within the communist world. The next document shows the Soviet Government under pressure in their relations with their client states in Eastern Europe, particularly Czechoslovakia and Rumania, and with China. They also faced division and indecision within the ranks of the CPSU itself. Sir D. Wilson was in no doubt about the interconnection between unrest in the communist camp and a policy of Soviet cooperation with the West: 'the USSR cannot afford a tough policy all round.'

No. 27

Sir D. Wilson (Moscow) to Mr. Stewart

No. 341 Telegraphic [ENS 2/2]

Immediate. Confidential   MOSCOW, 9 *April 1969*

Repeated for information Immediate to Washington, Routine to UKDEL NATO, Peking, Prague, UKMIS New York and Saving to Bucharest, Tokyo and UKDIS Geneva.

East-West Relations

I send you the following assessment of Soviet policy in the aftermath of the Ussuri incidents[1] in the hope that it may be of use at the NATO meeting.[2]

2. There can be little doubt that the troubles on the Chinese border, although not of recent origin, have by reaching the level of regimental battles presented the Soviet leadership with a new current issue of serious concern to them. To this must be added the latest difficulties in Czechoslovakia.[3] The question is what effects these problems will have within the leadership and on the conduct of Soviet external policy in general.

3. Within the leadership the alignment on these matters is quite uncertain, but it can be expected that continuance of the Chinese crisis at a high level would lead the military to ask for a larger share of resources, especially on the Eastern border. This would make it all the more necessary to reach

---

[1] A frontier clash between Soviet and Chinese troops at Damasky Island on the Ussuri River on 2 March had been followed by further incidents on 14 and 15 March. On 17 March Mr. Smirnovsky had raised the matter with Mr. Roberts, describing the 2 March clash as 'a very serious matter' with 31 Soviet troops killed and 14 wounded, and emphasising that the Soviet Government would not hesitate to 'take the right measures'. Sir D. Wilson commented in Moscow telegram No. 265 of 17 March that 'the main motive for Soviet publicizing of these incidents still appears to be a desire to establish the rectitude of their own position within the world Communist movement and to discredit the Chinese . . . It is moreover a logical continuation of earlier Russian criticism of Mao's [Mao Tse-tung, Chairman of the Communist Party of China, CPC] anti-Soviet policies, and their attempt to relate Chinese attacks to the internal needs of the CPC and that party's impending congress.' Mr. Smirnovsky had raised the matter again at an interview on 1 April with Mr. Stewart, with whom he left a statement on the dispute by the Soviet Government (ENS 3/301/3).

[2] See No. 26, note 4.

[3] Czechoslovak victory over the Soviet Union in an ice hockey match in Stockholm on 28 March had led to rioting in Prague and other towns where Soviet troops were lodged: Mr. Smith had reported in Prague telegram No. 3 Saving of 1 April that the 'overwhelming majority' of Czechoslovak people 'saw in this something more than a victory in a game . . . so deep and wide does the hatred of the Russians run that in the heat of passion generated by the win in Stockholm many a normally solid citizen may well have taken pleasure in this sadly impotent outburst' (ENC 3/303/1). The incidents provoked a strong Soviet response and increased pressure on the Czechoslovak leadership culminating in the displacement on 17 April of Mr. Dubcek as First Secretary of the Czechoslovak Communist Party by Dr. G. Husak, to preside over a period of 'normalisation'.

agreement with the US on limiting the arms race.[4] In military logic the Soviet leaders should be readier to accept reductions of forces in Eastern Europe: but this could have dangerous political effects in Poland, Czechoslovakia and Eastern Germany. The Politburo will experience new strains in reaching collective decisions on these essential matters.

4. A further subject of debate will be the role of the international communist movement, with the impending conference requiring action in the next few weeks.[5] Those who believe in the importance of the movement will be seeking to avoid its further disruption, and to win support for the Soviet position on China and against the Czech revisionists. The logical conclusion, given the importance of the Chinese question on the one hand, and the increased trouble with the Czechs and self-assertiveness of the Rumanians on the other,[6] would be that the USSR cannot afford a tough policy all round, and should make at least some concessions to the trend to national communism in Eastern Europe. But these might affect the Soviet stand on China, and there may well be fierce discussions in the Kremlin on this question.

5. Towards Western Europe, Soviet efforts to appear respectable will, I think, continue. We have recent examples of this in the Budapest Appeal and in Soviet conduct of our own bilateral relations. This line is formulated to distract the attention of the European members of NATO from their efforts to strengthen their defences in the post-Czechoslovakia situation, and with an eye on the communist parties in Western Europe. But it is very doubtful if the Russians are yet ready for measures such as troop reductions in Central Europe which might have political effects in Eastern Europe, or for any political manoeuvres (e.g. for *rapprochement* with Western Germany) which could produce the same unsettling result.

6. As regards the United States, I have already noted the Soviet interest in arms limitation. The Soviet leaders probably take more seriously than we do

[4] US-Soviet exchanges on the limitation of nuclear armaments had begun in 1962, but little progress was made until President Johnson announced in January 1967 that there would be talks on the limitation of anti-ballistic missile (ABM) deployment. After much delay the Russians agreed in principle to talks on nuclear disarmament as a whole, and on 1 July 1968, in connection with the signing of the Non-Proliferation Treaty (see No. 11, note 3) President Johnson announced that agreement had been reached 'to enter in the nearest future into discussions on the limitation and reduction of both offensive strategic nuclear weapons, delivery systems and systems of defence against ballistic missiles'. The invasion of Czechoslovakia put negotiations into abeyance, but the Russians continued to express interest, President Nixon had declared himself in favour of strategic arms limitation talks (SALT) with the Soviet Union and discussions had been proceeding within NATO about the basis for such talks.

[5] The Conference of Communist Parties was now due to open on 5 June: cf. No. 22, para. 10, and No. 23, note 5.

[6] The Rumanian Government, and President Ceausescu personally, had denounced the invasion of Czechoslovakia and subsequently maintained a public opposition to Soviet claims that in certain circumstances interference in the internal affairs of another country was justified, indicating that their participation in the Conference of Communist Parties depended on agreement that the Conference would not formally condemn China. Cf. also No. 10, note 11.

the possibility of a *rapprochement* between the US and China, and are consequently that much readier to be moderate in their conduct of relations with America. But any radical steps in this direction would lead to great difficulties within the leadership, as well as causing recrimination by the Chinese and some other parties, and further strains in Eastern Europe where it would encourage liberal and revisionist tendencies.

7. In other areas, the mounting difficulties now confronting the USSR mean that they have an increased interest in promoting a settlement in the Middle East: Soviet officials here in talking to US Embassy have recently gone out of their way to stress the urgent need for progress in the Four Power talks.[7] And in the longer term the new stage in the Chinese quarrel gives an increased importance to Soviet relations with Japan.

[7] Four Power talks on the Middle East had begun in New York on 3 April, but the unwillingness of the US and Soviet Governments to moderate their support of the Israeli and Arab positions inhibited progress and threatened stalemate. The situation was exacerbated by a statement on 6 April by the Israeli Government rejecting the Four Power talks on the grounds that a settlement could only emerge from the nations directly involved. Meanwhile, the security situation along the Suez Canal had deteriorated sharply, with daily artillery exchanges between Israeli and UAR forces. On 29 April Mr. Stewart summoned the Israeli and UAR Ambassadors to express his concern at the recurrent breaches of the cease-fire and warn that they could damage the Four Power talks.

While there were signs that the Soviet Union's preoccupation with the need to consolidate its position in Eastern Europe and in the world communist movement led it to seek a period of calm with the West, there were also indications that some NATO countries favoured an early move towards the resumption of East-West contacts at the level obtaining before the invasion of Czechoslovakia. An FCO background brief prepared for the NATO Council meeting held in Washington from 10-11 April drew attention to plans for the Belgian Foreign Minister to visit Moscow, to the French Government's agreement to hold bilateral talks with the Russians on European questions, and to signs that the West German Government were 'ready and willing to take up the dialogue with the Russians as soon as possible'; on the British side, following a successful re-negotiation of the Cultural Agreement (No. 29), preparations were in hand for the visit to Moscow in May of a Minister, Mr. Benn (see No. 24, note 3, and No. 32 below).

In Washington on 10 and 11 April the NATO Council considered a long paper prepared by the Permanent Representatives on 'The State of East-West Relations and its Implications for the Alliance', and subsequently approved a set of policy guidelines which included the removal, on a 'deliberate, differentiated and gradual basis' of restrictions imposed on East-West contacts after Czechoslovakia, though the pursuit of such contacts should be conducted 'so as not to validate the concept of Soviet domination of Eastern Europe', and in their bilateral contacts with the Soviet Union and the invading Warsaw Pact members NATO members would 'continue to exercise restraint on political contacts at the highest level'.

There was, however, no weakening of the *NATO* position on defence. The Communiqué issued after the *NATO* meeting[1] stressed the political solidarity of the Alliance and reaffirmed Members' determination to maintain a strategy based on forward defence and a 'credible conventional and nuclear deterrent'. At a 'private and restricted' meeting with *NATO* Foreign Ministers on *11* April President *Nixon* explained the US decision to proceed with the SAFEGUARD programme for an anti-ballistic missile system, pointing out that the Soviet Union had widened its advantage in conventional weapons and substantially closed the gap in ICBMs; though the US was still ahead in submarine weapons and aircraft, it was 'important to maintain defensive capability at a level sufficient to make United States diplomacy credible . . . so that the United States should not fall into a position of inferiority compared to the Soviet Union', particularly during a period of arms limitation talks. Ministers did not argue with the President: as Mr. Healey, who attended the meeting with Mr. Stewart, stated: 'The United States' deterrent capacity was the most important single defence interest of the Allies.'

In the Communiqué the *NATO* powers also welcomed the prospect of US-Soviet arms limitations talks, and stated that 'secure, peaceful and mutually beneficial relations between East and West' remained their political goal. The Budapest Declaration, discussed in Washington, was not mentioned by name, but the communiqué stated that the Allies proposed 'to explore with the Soviet Union and the other countries of Eastern Europe which concrete issues best lend themselves to fruitful negotiation and an early resolution'. The *NAC* was instructed to draft a list of these issues and to study how a useful process of negotiation—in which 'all governments whose participation would be necessary to achieve a political settlement in Europe should take part'—could best be initiated.

Discussions in the *NATO* Council reflected the preoccupations of the *FCO*: how to reconcile the need to 'do business' with the Soviet Union while remaining alert and cautious on the political and strategic front. The next group of documents shows how this dual policy worked out in practice: in No. 28, Sir T. Brimelow muses on the implications of Soviet internal difficulties for East-West relations, in the light of the results of the *NATO* Ministerial meeting; No. 29 reports on the negotiation of a new Anglo-Soviet Cultural Agreement (cf. No. 24, notes 6 and 8); and in No. 31, the Secretary of State sets out for the benefit of HM Representatives Overseas, in a wide-ranging study begun after the invasion of Czechoslovakia, the official view on East-West relations during the next 5-10 years. Interspersed with these is a reminder that policy considerations were, in April and May, overshadowed by the crisis in Anglo-Soviet relations over Gerald Brooke (No. 30).

[1] Extracts from the *Communiqué* are printed in Cmnd. 6932, No. 12.

No. 28

Minute by Sir T. Brimelow on the Soviet Leadership[1]

[*ENS 1/9*]

Confidential   FCO, *15 April 1969*

Sir Duncan Wilson's despatch of 17 March about strains in the Soviet leadership and the possibility of changes at the top is honest.[2] It does not go beyond the evidence. It comes to the common-sense conclusion that the present leaders will stick together if they possibly can and that this task may be made easier by a period of calm, even of stagnation in the internal life of the USSR. The despatch is tentative in its assessment of the ambitions and prospects of the men from whom the next leaders are likely to be chosen.

2. The Soviet leaders may find it easier to agree on a successor to Mr. Kosygin than on a successor to Mr. Brezhnev. They may also find it easier to hide their differences than to solve them. These considerations make it difficult to draw firm conclusions from Sir Duncan Wilson's analysis. If the present leaders are in difficulties behind the facade of unity, is this the moment to put to them ideas which might help to solve at least some of their problems?[3] If Mr. Brezhnev's successor proves to be deficient in authority, and if he feels that the arrangements for the leadership are unstable, will he be in favour of *détente* with the West, as Mr. Malenkov seemed to be in 1953 and Mr. Khrushchev in parts of 1960? Or is there likely to be a reaction against the present collective and pragmatic leadership and a return to harsh, dogmatic, one-man rule? If the latter, would it be a mistake to delay negotiation in the hope of better prospects later? The evidence does not

---

[1] This minute was addressed to Sir Denis Greenhill, Permanent Under-Secretary of State in the FCO since 1 February 1969, to Mr. Roberts and to the Private Secretary to the Secretary of State. Sir T. Brimelow was appointed Deputy Under Secretary in April 1969, superintending EESD, Disarmament Department and Southern European Department.

[2] In this despatch Sir D. Wilson referred to recent speculation in the world press about possible changes in the Soviet leadership. After reviewing the present position of Mr. Brezhnev, Mr. Kosygin and Mr. Podgorny, and identifying likely contenders for power in the Politburo, he expressed the view that collective leadership appeared to have weathered the crisis over Czechoslovakia. He doubted that criticisms of the 'soggy and ineffective nature of the present Soviet leadership' applied to Soviet foreign policy, 'which seems to be entering a phase of considerable activity, even if there are frequent traces of confusion', and concluded that 'a period of calm, even of stagnation, in Soviet life is more acceptable to the men who run and live in this country than might appear to observers abroad'.

[3] On 11 April Mr. Orchard sent to Sir T. Brimelow a copy of a minute he had written on Sir D. Wilson's despatch at the request of the PUS, in which he expressed the view that the current state of the Soviet leadership 'should encourage us to attempt to commit the Soviet Union to policies and arrangeme[n]ts, especially in Europe, which are to our advantage *now*, while the leadership is weak, pragmatic, and possibly receptive to new ideas which might diminish some of their current problems'. He also attached a copy of a memorandum, 'Suggestion for an initiative by HMG on European Security', in which he argued that the time was ripe 'for some fundamental rethinking on the future of Europe'.

warrant any firm predictions regarding the best timing for Western initiatives. The present leaders seem inhibited by the requirements of maintaining their own unity and the unity of the international communist movement. Any *détente* with the West might bring them new troubles in Eastern Europe and in their struggle with China. They seem to be imprisoned by their agreed doctrines and to be in no mood to respond imaginatively to Western initiatives. We do not know who will succeed them, nor what policies their successors will follow. But the NATO governments committed themselves at Washington to examine which questions might lend themselves to early and fruitful negotiation. It is only by such negotiation, conducted with caution because of the risk of weakening NATO, that we can hope to establish to what extent the problems of the present Soviet leaders may hold out prospects for some improvement in East-West relations. The consensus of opinion in NATO was in favour of exploring Soviet willingness to come to specific agreements. Nothing in Sir D. Wilson's despatch suggests that that consensus was mistaken. Rather the contrary.[4]

THOMAS BRIMELOW

[4] Sir D. Greenhill minuted on 15 April on this paper: 'I agree. I think the P.M. would like to see Sir T. Brimelow's comment' and a copy was sent by Mr. Barrington to Mr. E. Youde, Private Secretary to Mr. Wilson, on 25 April.

No. 29

Letter from Sir D. Wilson (Moscow) to Mr. Peck

[PWS 1/4]

Confidential   MOSCOW, *15 April 1969*

Dear John,

Anglo-Soviet Cultural Agreement of 28 March, 1969[1]

I understand that Bob Brash is himself writing a report on the negotiations[2] and I therefore do not propose to send a blow-by-blow account from here. However, you may like to have a few general impressions.

2. It seemed clear from the outset that the Russians were ready to conclude an agreement comparatively quickly and to conduct the negotiations in a non-polemical, business-like fashion. At the opening meeting, Moshetov, deputising for the sick Lunkov, referred to the various cancellations of last autumn, but briefly and non-polemically. I replied accordingly and that

[1] Published as Cmnd. 4063 of 1969, *Agreement between the Government of the United Kingdom of Great Britain and Northern Ireland and the Government of the Union of Soviet Socialist Republics on Relations in the Scientific, Educational and Cultural Fields for 1969-71.*

[2] Not printed. Mr. Brash commented that the negotiation had been 'the most speedy . . . we have yet had with the Russians', and explained that the British approach, post-Czecho-slovakia, had been 'in effect to limit the primarily goodwill features, while continuing with practical arrangements which we regarded as much in our interest as that of the Russians'.

was the last we heard of them (it did, however, emerge during the negotiations that the Russians would raise the question of compensation, if we tried to revive the Anglo-Soviet Historical Exhibition).[3] In the event, the actual negotiations took only four days, compared with the forty taken last year by the US/Soviet negotiations. The atmosphere throughout was good and, unlike our previous negotiations, these were concluded without a final plenary meeting involving Heads of Delegations. This result was no doubt largely due to the extraneous factors mentioned in paragraph 6 below; but I think that much credit also goes to Bob Brash, who, if I may say so, handled the tactical side of the negotiations very well.[4] We found ourselves in the end with a bizarre but acceptable horse-trade, under which we did not insist on a mention of freedom of thought and a provision for exchanges of specialists in fisheries, while the Russians did not insist on a mention of Lenin's centenary and the question of equivalence of degrees.

3. The resulting Agreement is, I think, quite satisfactory, given the general political climate and our own financial limitations. It is, of course, very much the same as the preceding one; but I am glad that we have obtained a modest increase in the number of teaching assistants and in the quota of post-graduates in the performing arts. We shall have to see how the latter works out in practice: I suspect that some of our promising musicians and ballet dancers will be offered places of study outside Moscow and Leningrad.

4. As far as one can judge these things, the Russians also appear to be pleased with the Agreement. Kozyrev (Deputy Foreign Minister), Lunkov and Makeev (Head of the Department dealing with our affairs) all expressed satisfaction to me and members of my staff. Looking back, it appears that the one thing which the Russians were determined to preserve was the previous quota for post-graduate exchanges. This may have been partly due to the simple fact that, as we have since discovered, they had, before the start of the negotiations, completed the process of selecting next year's group under the old quota. But it is also a sign of the value which they place on the work done by their post-graduates, nearly all scientists, in Britain. In order not to reduce their number, the Foreign Ministry, in the person of Sofinsky, were clearly putting pressure on the Ministry of Culture and on the Ministry of Primary and Secondary Education to make the necessary corresponding adjustments in our favour.[5] We had the general impression that, after a year's existence, the Cultural Relations Department of the Foreign Ministry is gradually acquiring more authority as a coordinating body.

5. Both the social arrangements made for our delegation and the publicity accorded to the Agreement here were on predictable lines, with perhaps an

[3] Cf. No. 14, note 7.

[4] Mr. Peck sent Sir D. Wilson's letter to Sir T. Brimelow, who minuted on 23 April: 'Many thanks. I agree that Mr. Brash's tactics were good.'

[5] In his report on the negotiations Mr. Brash commented that the allocation of post-graduate places had led to 'perhaps the most difficult argument during the negotiation . . . After a good deal of to-ing and fro-ing, some of it rather comical, the Soviet side eventually accepted an amalgamation of all our post-graduate long term study proposals into a general quota . . .'

extra touch of attention. Lunkov gave a luncheon and the delegation were taken to the Puppet Theatre, to a private showing of the unreleased film 'Andrei Rublev' (about which we have written separately to the Department) and to the restricted exhibition of the state jewels in the Kremlin. There was a very good Soviet attendance, including the Minister of Higher Education, at a reception which I gave for the delegation. As I have already reported, Kozyrev turned up at the signing ceremony, as had Kuznetsov[6] at the signing of the US/Soviet Cultural Agreement last year. Owing to a delay in preparing the signature copies, we had twenty minutes of private talk in Lunkov's office, when Kozyrev was certainly trying a lot harder than usual to make himself agreeable. Lunkov was uniformly urbane and affable on his reappearance half-way through the talks after a brief illness (for which I was jokingly held responsible—he had attended a very late night session at my house after one of John Ogdon's concerts). A very brief announcement of the signature of the Agreement appeared in the press on the following day. I would not have expected more. However, the Soviet television gave the signing ceremony rather more than usual attention and *Moscow News* (in English) reproduced a truncated version of an interview which I gave to a correspondent of Moscow Radio.

6. All in all, the whole proceeding confirmed that the Russians regarded this Agreement as something worth continuing in its own right, and the negotiations for it as an occasion for demonstrating their wish to exhibit themselves as respectable negotiating partners for a Western European country, to let last year's byegones be byegones [*sic*] and to conduct without fuss practical business with us in this and, by implication, other fields, whatever arguments might be going on between us on wider issues. For my own part, I am very grateful to all the members of the delegation from London for their rapid and efficient work.

7. I am sending a copy of this letter to John Henniker at the British Council and to the Chanceries at posts in Eastern Europe.[7]

Yours ever,

DUNCAN WILSON

---

[6] Presumably Mr. Vasily Kuznetsov, then Deputy Soviet Foreign Minister.

[7] Mr. Peck replied to Sir D. Wilson's letter on 24 April, stating that Mr. Brash's blow-by-blow account of the cultural negotiations tallied very closely with the Ambassador's: 'I thought, however, that as he was involved in the previous negotiations in London two years ago you might be interested in his comparison of the atmosphere during the two sets of meetings. He says that on this occasion he found it was considerably cooler than our last negotiation in London two years ago and there were times, for example when he criticised Soviet jamming of BBC broadcasts, when it was very definitely cold. The social arrangements made for the delegation by the Soviet side were also on a significantly less extensive scale than those which we made in London . . . However, the main point is that the negotiation was businesslike and the end result satisfactory and we are very grateful to you.'

The next document concerns the case of Gerald Brooke, whose fate dominated Anglo-Soviet relations during the spring and early summer of 1969. In response to Soviet hints that Mr. Brooke might face further charges and an extended period of imprisonment (see No. 25, notes 1 and 2), the possibility of trying to avoid this by agreeing to the premature release of Peter and Helen Kroger (cf. No. 1, note 6) had been reconsidered by the FCO and appropriate authorities. Their verdict remained, however, that such an arrangement was unacceptable: 'The evidence which the KGB would have to show that they could get professional agents back in exchange for comparatively harmless individuals, who can always be framed, would be used to damage our national security.'[1] Sir D. Greenhill rejected the idea of an exchange on 20 March in an interview with Mr. Smirnovsky, who replied that HMG was being 'totally uncooperative'. However, continued warnings from Sir D. Wilson that there was a strong possibility that Brooke might be retried meant that the question was kept under review in London. The US Government, when consulted, replied that they would very much prefer the Krogers not to be released, but that it was a matter for HMG to decide.

Discussions continued during April, as it became increasingly clear that the Soviet authorities were determined to use Gerald Brooke as a tool to secure the early release of the Krogers. Despite the strong arguments against an exchange, Sir D. Greenhill had now formed the firm view that the idea of releasing the Krogers before the end of their sentence (1974) in return for Brooke's release at the end of his current term (in 1970) should be pursued, both on humanitarian grounds and to avert the damage which might be done to Anglo-Soviet relations if Brooke were re-tried; as he submitted to Mr. Stewart on 25 April, 'other Western Governments are trying to get [rid] of similar obstacles to the improvement of their relations with the Soviet Government, and there is some risk that we may lag behind' (PUSD records). He recommended this course of action to the Secretary of State, suggesting that an offer should be made to the Soviet Ambassador that if Brooke were released on his due date the Krogers would be released 3 months later. A decision on the matter became urgent when on 28 April the British Embassy in Moscow was informed that Brooke was to be charged with the 'preparation of and attempts at crime', and with espionage. If convicted he faced a further long term of imprisonment. Sir D. Wilson stated in Moscow telegram No. 433 that the only chance of stopping a further trial was to 'come forward very soon with some version of the exchange desired by the Russians'; he did not think that any threats of retaliation (such as expelling known Soviet intelligence agents, or severing trade contacts) would have any effect.

On 29 April Sir D. Greenhill spoke to Mr. Smirnovsky on lines agreed that morning at a meeting between the Secretary of State, the Home Secretary and the Prime Minister: if Brooke were tried and sentenced, the Soviet authorities could dismiss any thought that the Krogers would be released prematurely; if Brooke were not tried or sentenced, the release of the Krogers could be discussed after Brooke's sentence ended in 1970. If a trial were proceeded with, HMG would be 'fully justified in taking immediate counter-action against the personnel in this country of those authorities responsible for the treatment to

[1] Telegram No. 198 to Moscow of 12 March, ENS 14/1.

which it is proposed to subject Mr. Brooke in an effort to secure the premature release of the Krogers'. Ministers had agreed that there was 'no suggestion of an early direct exchange', but as Mr. Bridges' minute printed below shows, the tide of official opinion in favour of settling the matter sooner, rather than later, was gaining momentum.

No. 30

Minute from Mr. Bridges to Mr. Giffard

[*PUSD*]

Secret and Personal   FCO, *1 May 1969*

The Brooke case: retaliation

Before leaving for Moscow tomorrow[1] I would like to set down a few points about the next stage. I start from the position of one who has from the beginning opposed an exchange, but believes that the best course open to us now is to make an arrangement on the most favourable terms we can.

2. As I understand it, the starting point of the current phase was the feeling that we should not allow the Brooke case to become a festering sore in our relations with the USSR; that we should if possible dispose of the affair so as to allow Anglo-Soviet relations to develop creatively and progressively, in step with the general trend in relations between East and West Europe. This should remain a constant objective. Although we have to make an unambiguous response to a decision to press further charges against Mr. Brooke, we should not allow our anger at the monstrous behaviour of the Russians in the Brooke case to destroy the whole prospect of a useful political and commercial relationship with the Soviet Union. Our task is to select the response which will both express our indignation, and damage the Soviet organisations responsible for the act. It is not in our interest to be carried away by an anti-Soviet frenzy, which might lead to the rupture of relations and the destruction of so much productive work in recent years. The history of Anglo-Soviet relations in the 1920s and 1930s shows how long it takes to get things going again after emotive reactions of this kind.

3. Yet it is difficult to see exactly where a process of retaliation would stop. Could we ignore a Soviet decision to declare eight or more members of our Embassy p.n.g.?[2] We would presumably have to cancel the two forthcoming Ministerial visits to the USSR:[3] what would be the effect on the programme of cultural and technological exchanges, and how could we expect to conclude a new and larger Trade Agreement if Mr. Crosland does not visit

---

[1] Mr. Bridges had returned to London on 27 April for consultations on the Brooke case.

[2] i.e. *persona non grata*.

[3] For Mr. Benn's forthcoming visit see No. 24, note 3. It was intended that Mr. Crosland would also visit Moscow to sign the new Anglo-Soviet trade agreement currently under negotiation (cf. No. 18, note 7: talks had been held in London in February and resumed in Moscow in May), although a final decision on his visit was not made until 20 May.

Moscow in June? These considerations, and others of the same kind, argue strongly in favour of reaching an exchange agreement if we can: once the decision is taken to expel a substantial number of the Soviet Embassy, it is hard to see where the process would stop.

4. The strongest argument against an exchange is that the future safety of British nationals in the USSR would be placed in hazard whenever we have custody of a convicted Soviet spy. This is undeniably so, but the case can be overstated. We should realise that we are not the first nation to exchange a Soviet spy for a student detained in the USSR: the Germans have recently done so in the Felfe case. We must recognise that, if we do hold a Soviet spy, pressures will always be brought on us, however we react in the Brooke case: and although an exchange for him may endanger others in future, this effect will only be marginal. What is more, we have yet to catch another Soviet spy.

5. Conversely, I believe that a refusal to come to an arrangement now would have serious effects on British nationals now in the Soviet Union. The position would be that Brooke would be serving his extended term (unless, of course, the blackmail is increased by threatening him with the death penalty. It should be noted that one of the Articles of the RSFSR[4] under which he is charged, No. 65, can carry the death penalty). It is still open to the KGB to tighten the screw further by framing other British subjects in the USSR—this would not be difficult. We should be clear in our own minds that, if we refuse to be blackmailed at present, we have not stopped the process. It is more likely that the blackmail will continue, for higher stakes.

6. In short, unpalatable though it may be, I fear that the wisest course for us is to agree to the exchange, even if the Russians should insist on it taking place now.

T.E. BRIDGES[5]

[4] i.e. the Soviet penal code.

[5] Mr. Giffard submitted this minute to Sir T. Brimelow on 1 May, commenting that 'we may want to ask Ministers to consider at least something nearer a direct exchange than we have in mind at present, before we embark on retaliation of the kind which we have threatened'. Sir T. Brimelow commented, also on 1 May: 'The reason we have not been able in the past to accept the idea of an exchange is that, for various reasons, Ministers were not willing to contemplate it; and the Home Secretary is still opposed to an early exchange. The reason we have threatened action against KGB personnel in this country is that unless we give them cause to think that they may be hurt, they have no incentive to abstain from bringing further charges against Brooke. The outcome may well be retaliation, and Ministers will certainly want to control the scale and pace of escalating retaliation. For the time being we can only await the Soviet Ambassador's reply to the communication made to him by Sir D. Greenhill or, alternatively, news from Moscow that Brooke is to be subjected to a new trial.'

Mr. Smirnovsky informed Sir D. Greenhill on 9 May of his Government's reply to the British offer, rejecting 'categorically' its tone and content; only a pardon from the Praesidium could remove the charges against Brooke. A pardon would only be considered in the light of British replies to two questions: when would the Krogers be released and would they be free to go to Poland on release? (the Krogers claimed they were Polish, rather than US citizens); and would the Krogers be allowed a visit by the Polish Consul and improvements in their prison régime? Mr. Smirnovsky stated that Gerald Brooke could be released 'in the nearest future' if these questions were answered satisfactorily: 'Gerald Brooke and the Krogers could be released prematurely, not on the basis of an exchange, but arising from a mutual desire by both governments to remove from the sphere of their relations these two difficult matters.'

Reporting this interview in a minute of 12 May for the Home Secretary, Sir D. Greenhill put forward the 'special considerations' which in his view justified early release of the Krogers: 'First, and most importantly, the political situation. I believe it is necessary to get the threat to Anglo-Soviet relations which the Brooke case represents out of the way as soon as we can. I foresee the strong possibility of a period ahead of East/West negotiations with the Americans in the lead. I regard it as essential that we are not disqualified from taking an appropriate part in these negotiations by having this quarrel with the Russians, legitimate as it is, as an albatross around our necks' (PUSD records).

No. 31

Mr. Stewart to Sir D. Wilson (Moscow)

[*RS 3/2*]

Confidential   FCO, *15 May 1969*

Sir,

I have been considering the implications of the Soviet invasion of Czechoslovakia for East-West relations in the next five to ten years. My conclusions are contained in the enclosed Memorandum which has received general interdepartmental agreement in Whitehall.[1] This will provide the underlying guidelines for our relations with the Soviet Union and other members of the Warsaw Pact and for discussing with our allies what should be the policies of the West as a whole. The complete text of the Memorandum should be treated as if it were marked 'United Kingdom eyes only', but you and other recipients of this despatch should of course draw on it as appropriate in discussion with Governments and reliable contacts.

[1] This memorandum was commissioned on 22 August 1968 following the Soviet invasion of Czechoslovakia: see Nos. 14-16. A first draft, prepared by Planning Staff in conjunction with EESD, was submitted by the PUS to the Secretary of State on 13 November in advance of the NATO Ministerial Meeting (cf. p. 90). A revised draft prepared after extensive consultation with other Whitehall departments was sent to the Prime Minister on 19 December as part of the briefing for the meeting of Commonwealth Prime Ministers to be held in London from 7-15 January 1969. Mr. Roberts commented on 31 December that the memorandum 'consolidates effectively UK policy as it has emerged since the invasion of Czechoslovakia' but asked 'Do we sufficiently emphasise the US guarantee to ourselves, Europe, and the US itself? . . . It is the American attachment to the European cause that counts . . . The USSR hardly notices our attempt to join Europe; it constantly tries to separate us from the USA. This is what we should be most concerned about. On *détente* . . . the balance is right, except that I do not see why "goodwill" contacts should be indefinitely postponed. The objective of influencing Soviet thinking is as important in this area as in the fields of commerce and technology.'

These points were incorporated into a draft submitted for the OPD(O) Committee by Sir P. Gore-Booth and considered on 29 January 1969. After further amendment Mr. Stewart submitted the Memorandum (OPD(69)8) to the Committee who 'took note' of it on 18 March (OPD(69) 4th meeting), and Planning Staff subsequently recommended and arranged its printing and wide circulation under cover of the present despatch.

2. This despatch and its enclosure are being printed for distribution in Whitehall and to Heads of Missions in all overseas posts.

I am, &c.,

MICHAEL STEWART

ENCLOSURE IN No. 31

The longer term prospects for East-West relations after the Czechoslovak crisis

Summary . . .[2]

INTRODUCTION

Aim

The purpose of this paper is to examine the implications for Western policies in the next five to ten years of the underlying trends in relations between the Soviet bloc and the Western Alliance: in short to consider how in the future we should interpret or modify the policy of *détente*.

2. The paper considers briefly likely Soviet bloc policies in the Third World and their implications for the West, but concentrates on the issues likely to affect direct relations between the Soviet bloc and the West in the longer term. The Czechoslovak crisis is the starting point rather than the theme of the paper.

3. The following are the paper's main headings:

(i) Soviet objectives.
(ii) Developments likely to affect Soviet policies: in the Soviet Union and Eastern Europe; in the West; and in the Third World.
(iii) General trends in East-West relations.
(iv) Western objectives and policies.

Assumptions

4. Any study which looks ahead as far as ten years must inevitably be speculative, particularly at a time of rapid and large-scale technological change. Western society itself does not stand still. In this paper we assume that Western standards and ways of life will continue to develop along broadly their present lines.

5. We also assume that within the next ten years there will be no fundamental change in the pattern or attitudes of the Soviet leadership. The indications are that any conceivable alternative collective leadership will be as conservative, as lacking in self-confidence and as burdened with the Stalinist past as the present leaders. To a large extent this is likely to apply also to the next generation of Party leaders, though their attitude may possibly be affected by the spread of new ideas in Soviet society. A return from a system of collective leadership—which deliberately maintains a balance between Government and Party—to one man rule might well alter this state of affairs. Even though the basic interests and aims of Soviet policy

[2] Not here printed.

might not alter, the nature of the leadership would be bound to affect the speed and boldness and emphasis of its execution. The checks and balances of a collective leadership make for a comparatively slow moving and cautious régime. The structure of the power mechanism in the Soviet system allows one man in power to exercise a remarkable degree of influence. We assume that no such leader will emerge but we cannot be sure.

6. Even given these assumptions, an assessment of Soviet intentions and policies must leave room for considerable uncertainty. Soviet policy is empirical, opportunistic, and often short-sighted. The Russians have long-term objectives but are content to move towards them *ad hoc*. Soviet opportunism is complemented by the highly secretive nature of Soviet policy-making. This makes it particularly difficult to put ourselves imaginatively in Russian shoes. The judgment in this paper must be seen against the background of these uncertainties.

Soviet Objectives

7. We believe that for the next ten years the objectives of Soviet foreign policy will continue to be:

(i) *Political, military and economic consolidation and strengthening of the Soviet Union and the Soviet bloc.* The defence of the Soviet heartland and the preservation of the Soviet Union's contiguous sphere of influence are intertwined in an inextricable amalgam of political, economic, strategic and ideological interests. The purpose will be to ensure that the satellite countries of Eastern Europe remain oriented economically as well as politically towards the Soviet Union. This will be equated with the maintenance in each country of a Soviet model of Communism.

(ii) *The undermining and disruption of the Western Alliance and other forms of co-operation between the United States and Europe.* Deep-rooted Soviet fear and distrust of Germany will continue to play a central part in Soviet policy.

(iii) *The expansion of Soviet influence to the detriment of the West, in particular in the Third World.* Soviet ambition is to assume all the political, commercial and military trappings of a Super Power, to strengthen the World Communist Movement, and to maintain Soviet control of it.

(iv) *The containment of China.* The Soviet Union will be increasingly preoccupied with the threat from China both in direct territorial and military terms and in terms of ideological and political competition throughout the world.

(v) *The avoidance of a nuclear confrontation with the United States.* For the Soviet Union this is a condition of all the above objectives. The Soviet Government will continue to seek limited accommodations with the United States on major issues, e.g., offensive and defensive strategic weapons (including ABMs), the Non-Proliferation Treaty and some other disarmament and arms control issues, and at the least to maintain a dialogue on major questions.

Developments Likely To Affect Soviet Policies

Soviet Union

8. Soviet foreign policies will be affected by a number of conflicting pulls within the Soviet Union. These include the tensions between Soviet political, economic and military requirements.

9. One lesson of the Czechoslovak crisis has been to emphasise the extent to which ideological prejudices and preconceptions play a part in the formation of Soviet foreign policy. The present generation of Soviet leaders and their likely successors are entirely committed to a rigid, bureaucratic and centralised brand of Communism. They remain wedded to this form of Communism out of conviction and because it has become increasingly identified with the pursuit of Soviet national interests. The Party will continue to pervade Soviet life. Within the Soviet Union this will mean a continuing emphasis on Communist doctrine, limitations on the type of economic reforms which the Soviet Government will accept, and continuing attempts to stimulate support for the régime among younger disaffected Russians. Anything more than minimal variations from Communist orthodoxy as currently understood will be suppressed.

10. As a result we can expect to see exacerbation of the conflict between economic efficiency and centralised political control by the Communist Party. The Soviet economy will continue to grow and become more complex. Soviet income per head has now risen to about $1,900, which is broadly comparable to the EEC's though distributed in a way much less favourable to the consumer. As a result of this growing complexity there are likely to be difficulties in maintaining an acceptable rate of growth in the future without increasing devolution in decision-making at the executive level. The Soviet leaders will resist any significant step in this direction. This will make it more difficult for them to take account of consumer demand and allocate economic resources efficiently.

11. The growing number of intelligent and educated managers in industry, of scientists in universities and intellectuals throughout Soviet society, all dealing with involved problems and looking for solutions outside the range provided by Communist dogma, are another problem. Inevitably they become sceptical about the dogma itself and question the efficiency of the political structure and the management of the economy. There is likely to be a growing wish for greater freedom and opportunity to get on with one's own business. As the standard of living improves the pressures for building a consumer society for its own sake increase.

12. Economic efficiency and growth require some Soviet involvement in international trade. The Soviet leadership feels bound to maintain the same rate of growth as the West, and if possible to exceed it. The West's rate is defined by the capabilities of the combined economies of North America and Europe, which are very closely linked at the technical level. For the Soviet Union even to keep up on its own with the West would be a difficult and probably impossible task. It cannot cut off its commercial links with the West without serious economic and social costs. The Soviet Union is conducting an

increasingly aggressive trade policy, developing international air routes and building a larger merchant fleet. The contacts so developed may contribute to the trend towards greater freedom of thought. But the Soviet leaders are determined to control the risks to Soviet society of the emergence of the Soviet Union as a world Power in the commercial as well as the strategic sense. In the longer term—say over a period of 20 years or more—this may become less easy.

13. A further factor is the pressure of military needs on economic resources. So far at any rate the Soviet leaders have seemed relatively unconcerned with the problem of finding sufficient manpower for its fighting services. They devote a higher proportion of Soviet GNP to defence than any Western country. They have deployed a substantial missile force, re-equipped their services with modern weapons and are in the process of acquiring a significant capacity to give military support overseas with conventional forces. However, in the next five to ten years the Soviet leaders' determination to maintain sufficient military strength to ensure the security of the Soviet Union and the expansion of Soviet power will limit the other uses to which Soviet economic resources could have been devoted. This will slow down the Soviet Union's rate of economic growth and reduce Soviet capacity to compete in economic terms with the West. Failure to reach an agreement with the Americans about limiting new generations of weapons, e.g., ABMs, could add a new dimension to defence costs.

14. The Soviet leaders continue to have a deep-rooted and dogmatic belief in the eventual universal triumph of their model of Marxism-Leninism. Time will prove them wrong. Over the next half-century the spread of freedom of thought and the growth of new aspirations in Soviet society will be incompatible with the maintenance of the present Soviet model of Communism. Moreover, within the next few years the present Soviet Government cannot completely prevent these ideas beginning to spread, since a return to absolute repression would jeopardise the Soviet Union's internal and external image as well as economic growth. However the Soviet Union will do what it can to slow down the spreading of these ideas and will continue to subordinate economic to political and military needs. A policy of this sort will create tensions in the Soviet Union but it need not lead to explosions at any rate within the next ten years.

15. The process of change will be slowed down by the dead weight of traditional Russian bureaucratic methods and organisation. By following a pragmatic policy, e.g., limited economic reforms, the Soviet leaders will be able to retain much of the central control on which their power rests. They can make use of the profound Russian sense of identity and patriotism and of the still ingrained reluctance of ordinary Russians to take responsibility. Moreover, despite increasing economic pressures, the Soviet leaders will retain a far wider control of the allocation of resources than their Western counterparts.

16. In brief, well beyond the time-scale of this paper, there are likely to be far-reaching changes in Soviet society. In the next ten years there may be

some loosening-up. It is difficult to say whether this loosening-up will be enough to have a major effect on Soviet foreign policies. We should not under-estimate the vested interest of the Soviet leadership and the Soviet Communist Party in the existing system, their capacity to preserve it, and the fact that even in younger age groups recruitment to the Party tends to perpetuate existing attitudes.

Eastern Europe

17. Such loyalty as there is in Eastern Europe to the Soviet Union and the Soviet form of Communism is mainly from established members and leaders of the several Communist parties who look to the Soviet Union to maintain them in power. Among most other East Europeans their countries' enforced links with the Soviet Union in the past 20 years have not eradicated their desire for independence. They have different cultural and historical traditions to the Soviet Union.

18. In the first ten months of 1967, 336,000 Czechoslovaks visited the West (mainly West Germany, France and Austria). The Soviet action in Czechoslovakia and subsequent restrictions will inhibit this flow. The Soviet Union will probably now make an attempt to improve and tighten relations within the bloc. Whatever they do, disillusion with the Soviet Union will stimulate the interest of Eastern Europeans in the West.

19. On the economic side, awareness of the higher standard of living available in the West will be a constant source of pressure. There is likely to be increasing dissatisfaction in Eastern European countries with the way in which COMECON obligations, including a non-convertible rouble, prevent them increasing their trade with the West and securing access to Western technology and capital equipment. However, these dissatisfactions will be tempered for as long as Eastern European economies are run by people who believe dogmatically in planning and distrust the market mechanism.

20. For the Soviet Union COMECON is a useful instrument for binding together the economies, trading relations and monetary systems of the member countries and for keeping a critical eye on the development of the Eastern European countries' trading links with the West. The Soviet Union meets its partners' complaints of the working of the COMECON system by pointing to the fact that Eastern European countries import Soviet primary products at prices which the Soviet Union claim to be very favourable and that the Eastern European countries are able to export to the Soviet Union manufactures which could not command a market in the West. In economic terms it would be more efficient to liberalise COMECON arrangements to allow greater Eastern European contact with the West. The Soviet Union has an interest in an efficient Eastern European economy. However, for political reasons the Soviet Government will continue to do all it can to maintain an economic stranglehold on their recalcitrant satellites. The present level of Eastern European trade with countries outside the bloc—in broad terms a third, of which half is with developing countries and half with the West—is compatible with this objective.

21. Like the Soviet Union the Eastern European Governments seem relatively unconcerned with problems of finding manpower for their fighting services. They can buy Soviet arms out of balances earned by their trade with the Soviet Union. Although it is possible that economic pressure to reduce the demands of defence may begin to build up in bloc countries over the coming years, there is no reason to expect that force reductions will become economically essential to the Warsaw Pact allies of the Soviet Union. The Eastern European Governments do not need to respond to economic pressure to reduce their defence expenditure. For political reasons the bloc countries will be more concerned than the Soviet Union to achieve a negotiated security system in Europe. However even if the structure of the Warsaw Pact were formally dismantled the Soviet Union would probably still be able, through economic and military power, to bend the other countries of the Warsaw Pact to its will.

22. Taking all these factors into account it seems likely that in the short run Soviet policies in Eastern Europe will succeed in holding up the rate of change for some time. The threat of the use of Soviet force without any prospect of Western assistance will for the time being inhibit any other attempts to achieve greater independence. The Soviet Union can play on some Eastern European countries' fears of Germany. It can also attempt to play one Eastern European country off against another. However, aspirations for independence and faster economic growth, the pressure of Western economic competition and the attractions of more liberal Western society are bound to have an increasing effect in the long run, provided the West remains strong and prosperous. The Soviet Union cannot isolate the people of Eastern Europe from these influences as it can, to a large extent, the Soviet people. In short, change will come faster in Eastern Europe than in the Soviet Union; and, within the next ten years, may well begin to create far-reaching tensions and instabilities within the Soviet bloc.

The United States

23. The United States attitude to East-West relations will be affected by developments in Vietnam, and by domestic political problems (race, law and order, etc.). Certain longer-term trends are discernible. The deliberate moderation of United States policy during the Czechoslovak crisis resulted in part from their wish not to make Czechoslovakia's task harder, in part from the fact that there was nothing that the West or the United States could do. It was also an indication of the overriding importance which the United States attach to preserving world peace in a nuclear age. This is why they put their relations with the Soviet Union in a special category. The United States inclination to stress their relationship with the Soviet Union will be strengthened. They will share the Soviet wish for agreements on important strategic issues.

24. In NATO United States policies have reflected their genuine belief in the need for a more effective Western defence effort. The crisis has also been useful to the United States in their efforts to persuade the Europeans to do

more in their own defence on the argument that this will help the United States Administration to maintain United States troops in Europe.

25. In general, however, the Czech crisis has had somewhat less impact on United States public opinion than Hungary did in 1956. It is unlikely to delay for more than a few months the popular and Congressional pressures for withdrawing more United States troops from Europe. Substantial troop withdrawals could affect the credibility of the United States commitment even if this was not the United States intention. In due course a combination of neo-isolationist sentiment in the United States, European reluctance to do sufficient in their own defence, and concern about the uncertainty of Soviet policies, might persuade the United States that their interest no longer lay in maintaining an absolutely firm 'frontline' in Europe. In these circumstances they might come to fear that European instability could trigger a conflict between the United States and the Soviet Union. Despite the powerful United States interests to the contrary, they might conclude that it would be better for the United States to be less committed to Europe. If a crisis in Europe developed which seemed to threaten a strategic nuclear exchange between the Super Powers the United States and the USSR might effect a hasty ad hoc *rapprochement* to safeguard their own interests. On balance, the fact that the United States could not avoid being embroiled in a European conflict, together with the size of the United States economic stake in Europe, make it unlikely that the formal United States commitment to defend Europe will be modified. Nevertheless, even a small doubt about the United States commitment to, e.g., Berlin could offer the Soviet Union a substantial opportunity. Alternatively it could tempt the Soviet Union to take some risk justified by the appearance, but not by the realities of the situation.

26. In Europe and throughout the world the United States will continue to expect their friends and allies to bear more of the common burden. So far as possible they will wish to limit the areas where they might become involved in confrontation with the Soviet Union. They will seek to limit their commitments in Africa and, once they have disengaged from Vietnam, on the mainland of Asia. But they will continue to be prepared to run major risks to prevent an expansion of Communist influence in Latin America, Australasia, Japan and Western Europe. For domestic reasons the United States will continue to have an unwritten commitment to Israel. China will be an increasing preoccupation.

Western Europe

27. In Western Europe the Czechoslovak crisis has reduced, at any rate temporarily, the tendencies to unravel NATO, but without any change in fundamental trends. In the longer term there are several possible fates for Western Europe in the 1970s. The Western European countries may begin to cohere into one or more communities including Britain and so lay the foundations of a European federal state. Alternatively, something like the present situation may last throughout the period with no break-up of NATO and continuing but ineffective efforts to create a more united Europe on a wider basis. A third possibility is that Western Europe may begin to fragment,

with the EEC losing all its drive, the Mediterranean and the Scandinavian countries becoming gradually more neutral, France remaining aloof, and two or three countries still trying to preserve the fragments of the NATO system round Germany. In this last scenario a United States commitment, however expressed, might well lose its credibility. Which of these possibilities occur will depend to a large extent on developments in France and Germany, as well as on our own economic recovery.

28. The credibility of French policy towards East-West relations has been seriously undermined by the Czechoslovak crisis. This is not to say that de Gaulle and French Governments after him[3] may not continue to attempt to develop special relations between France and the Soviet Union and France and Eastern Europe. But the claim that France could be *interlocuteur valable* in an East-West reconciliation in Europe has been shown to be empty, and French assessments of Soviet attitudes over-optimistic. Any developments in France's relations with the Soviet bloc depend on the political interpretation that the Soviet Union chooses to put upon them. Increasing economic difficulties and the fact that no successor to de Gaulle can inherit his authority will prevent France re-establishing a dominant position in Western Europe. This might encourage the French Government to re-establish closer co-operation with the United States and with her European partners in defence, politics and economics. However, such moves are likely to be a change of tactics rather than a change of objectives. For de Gaulle, and for a number of his possible successors, independence of French action will continue to be the basic aim of French policy. Arrangements tending to derogate from French sovereignty will be resisted as long as possible. Because of France's geographical position, her natural and industrial resources, and her technical competence, French policies on these lines will continue to have a serious effect on the West's strength. Persistent domestic disturbances, on the pattern of the events of May 1968, would be equally damaging.

29. Even before de Gaulle leaves office, and certainly afterwards, German influence in Western Europe will increase. This will not affect the Germans' aim of maintaining good relations with France but it will give them greater freedom of action. Greater strength will not affect their policy of dependence on the United States guarantee. The Czech crisis and its aftermath is unlikely to put a stop to their 'Ostpolitik' but it may contribute to the continuing change in its nature. There is a growing feeling in Germany that the Federal Republic must at the least come to *de facto* terms with the existence of East Germany. After the September 1969 elections there are likely to be an increasing number of attempts to improve relations with East Germany. Reunification will become an even more distant objective. In taking these steps the Germans are likely to rely on the allies to preserve the position of West Berlin. The Germans will continue to use economic inducements in an

[3] General de Gaulle resigned on 28 April 1969 following the rejection in a referendum of proposals he had put forward for constitutional reform. He was succeeded as President of the French Republic on 20 June by M. Georges Pompidou, leader of the Gaullist Party.

attempt to improve their political relations with the Soviet Union and Eastern Europe.

30. In the worst case political disarray in Europe may offer the Soviet Union a tempting target. The Soviet Union attaches great importance to wedge-driving and disrupting the Alliance. It will exploit energetically any openings that occur. Yet so long as the American commitment to Europe remains firm Europe may seem much less badly disarrayed to the Soviet Union than it does to us. Despite present monetary difficulties[4] most of the economies of the Western Alliance seem likely to grow at a substantial rate. There are threats to democracy in the West but on balance free institutions are likely to survive. If so the attractions of the West for the peoples of the Soviet bloc will grow. These attractions and in particular the increasing strength of the Federal Republic of Germany will be more significant to the Soviet leaders than any apparent failure of Western Europe to unite more closely.

31. The Soviet Union uses 'German Revanchism' as a convenient stick to beat the West. But this propaganda reflects deep-rooted and persistent fears. These fears are compounded by uneasy admiration for German economic and industrial achievements. In due course this could make the Soviet leaders as suspicious of good relations between the two Germanys as they are now determined to prevent reunification. It might limit Soviet efforts to drive the United States out of Europe because of the Soviet Union's wish to retain an agreed framework for the restraint of Germany. On balance, however, the Soviet Union is more likely to maintain its efforts to reduce United States influence and to attempt to deal with the problem of restraining Germany on its own.

China and Japan

32. The Chinese will continue to use the Czechoslovak situation as an anti-Soviet talking point. So long as Mao survives a Sino-Soviet rapprochement is unlikely. Even afterwards differences of national and ideological interest are unlikely to permit more than limited accommodations. In the next five to ten years the Chinese will acquire a limited but significant number of inter-continental ballistic missiles. It is conceivable that after Mao China will be faced by unmanageable internal tensions, but it is more likely that political unity will survive and economic development continue even if slowly. If so, the Soviet Union will be increasingly concerned with the security of its borders with China. In South-East and South Asia Chinese ambitions are to establish a Chinese sphere of influence. At present China has only a limited military and political capacity to attempt this. As it grows, Soviet preoccupation with pre-empting and containing China in these areas will increase. The Soviet Union will do what it can to eliminate the foothold which Chinese political

[4] In the first half of 1969 the fixed exchange rate system established at Bretton Woods in 1944 came under increasing pressure, which was only temporarily eased by the devaluation of the French franc in August 1969, the revaluation of the German mark in October and international agreement to increase world reserves by the creation of a new financial instrument, Special Drawing Rights.

influence now has in Eastern Europe[,] in Albania and Rumania; and to undermine China's ideological challenge to the Soviet brand of Communism throughout the Third World.

33. The Czech crisis will make the Japanese more cautious but will not fundamentally affect Japan's policy of attempting to regularise relations with the Soviet Union before tackling relations with China. The Japanese recognise that this will take a long time. Japan is interested in the return of the Japanese islands held by the Soviet Union since the Second World War,[5] in acquiring a share of Siberian resources and in expanding her exports of manufactured goods to the Soviet market. The Soviet Union are interested in using Japanese finance for developing Eastern Siberia, in securing Japanese help in containing China and in detaching Japan from the United States. Both sides are likely to move cautiously. The Soviet Union is conscious of the dangers of Japan becoming a nuclear power, the Japanese of the risks to their relations with the United States of arrangements with the Soviet Union. By the end of ten years Japanese gross national product will be approaching the Soviet Union's, but throughout most of the period Japanese-Soviet relations are likely to be a function of relations between the United States and the Soviet Union.

The Third World

34. In the Third World in general the Czech crisis has had little lasting impact. It may induce greater realism and suspicion of Soviet motives. In the last few years while the image of the West and in particular the United States was tarnished by the Vietnam war, the Civil Rights Movement and Black Power, the Soviet Union was the gainer. This advantage, which it acquired by default, has temporarily disappeared. To a number of more developed countries in the Third World the Soviet approach to economic and industrial problems can be attractive but on the whole these countries equate Soviet and American power politics and base their policies towards the Soviet Union not on any particular illusions about Soviet motives but on the usefulness of the Soviet Union to them in pursuing their own national objectives. Their aim is to extract what they can from both the West and the Soviet bloc, e.g., in aid, capital investment, etc.

GENERAL TRENDS IN EAST-WEST RELATIONS

35. Both the United States and the Soviet Union have and recognise a common interest, transcending current ideological and power differences, in maintaining a good understanding on certain vital questions including nuclear problems and dangerous regional issues like the Middle East. Much depends on their maintaining these understandings. East-West relations will be particularly affected by their success in reaching agreement on limiting offensive and defensive strategic weapons. One possible danger for the United States' allies is that the Super Powers will reach agreement over our

[5] Cf. Series I, Volume II, No. 337.

heads. Another is that the Super Powers themselves may miscalculate their real interests. Both these risks are greater in Europe than elsewhere.

36. In Eastern Europe the Soviet leaders see trends of the sort underlying the Czech reforms as a fundamental threat to the whole Soviet system. Whenever they believe there is a risk of any of their East European satellites escaping from their ideological and military control, they will judge that they have no choice but to meet the risk head-on as in Czechoslovakia. Short of this they will tolerate some failure to meet Soviet requirements but will work hard for their fulfilment. Despite the advantages of meeting pressures in Eastern Europe with more flexible policies the Soviet leaders will screw down the safety valve rather than risk developments which would in their eyes jeopardise the Soviet system, threaten the break-up of the bloc and in the longer term even endanger their own hold of the Soviet Union. The Soviet Union may face dilemmas on a number of occasions in the next ten years—a change of leaders in Poland, the death of Ulbricht and, outside their own bloc, the death of Tito.

37. On these and other occasions the Soviet Government will continue to attribute its problems to Western machinations. It will not react violently against the West provided on the one hand the West does not provoke it by open interference in Eastern Europe and on the other that the West remains and is seen to remain strong and united. The visible continuation of a credible United States commitment to Europe, the strengthening of NATO, and the development of a more cohesive Western Europe will not prevent repressive Soviet policies in Eastern Europe but it will help to prevent them spilling over outside the bloc. Otherwise there is a risk that the Soviet Union may miscalculate Western reactions to high-risk policies in places more sensitive to us than Czechoslovakia, e.g., Yugoslavia or Berlin.

38. One effect of the Czechoslovak crisis on Soviet policies might be to increase Soviet preoccupation with Eastern Europe and to reduce Soviet interest elsewhere. However both in the shorter and longer term it is more likely that a continuing desire to assert its position as a Great Power will incline the Soviet Union to be active on a world-wide scale. The present Soviet posture is to emphasise world-wide Soviet interests and to deny that Czechoslovakia is the business of anyone but the Socialist countries. In the next ten years we may expect an intensification of the already significant Soviet interest in the Mediterranean, the Middle East and the Indian Ocean. In the Middle East the Soviet Union may see some advantage in a short-term understanding on some of the issues while profiting from Western embarrassment at the failure to reach a comprehensive settlement. In particular the Soviet leaders will attach a high value to the Soviet Union's special relationship with the revolutionary Arab States. If they press these relationships too far and too fast, they risk local defeats to which they could react in a manner dangerous to Western interests and to peace. The present Soviet leaders are aware of the need for caution and of the fact that no vital Soviet interests are involved. The next generation of leaders may have more nationalist and expansionist ideas. Increased Soviet involvement in the Middle

East and elsewhere might persuade these leaders that there were important Soviet interests at stake in these areas, which had to be defended at any cost.

39. Throughout the world, the increasing Soviet merchant fleet and the growing Soviet ability to give military support and to intervene overseas with conventional forces will continue to be signs of the Soviet leaders' objective of extending the influence of the Soviet Union as a Super Power, reducing the influence of the United States and the United States' allies, and containing China. In general the Soviet Union will continue to work within the bounds of the present international system, including the United Nations, while making full use of it for Soviet political and propaganda purposes. The Soviet Government will aim to increase the Soviet Union's economic links with countries such as Iran. It will take such opportunities as arise—e.g., Nigeria—for getting a foot in where it had little influence before.[6] In certain situations the Soviet Union may use its conventional capability to pre-empt the West by establishing a presence, however small, in advance of Western reactions. If it does so, this will be an important signpost of Soviet policy.

40. In general the Soviet Union's world-wise [*sic*] policies and its assertion of its status as a global Power are likely to be inhibited by a number of factors including the desire to avoid nuclear war, the cost of an unlimited arms race and the wish to maintain some understandings with the United States. Economic factors will be particularly important. Since 1954 the Soviet Union have committed between $6,000 million and $7,000 million in civil aid and disbursed about $2,500 million—to be matched against United States expenditure well in excess of $100,000 million. The lion's share of Soviet aid has gone to India, UAR, Indonesia and Afghanistan. In India in particular the Soviet Union will continue to be aware that Soviet resources are insufficient to meet India's needs, that chaos in India could only be to China's advantage, and hence that continuing United States aid to India is a Soviet as well as an Indian interest.

41. Soviet policies will also be coloured and at times inhibited by the Soviet leaders' attitude to World Communism. In many parts of the world, including Latin America and the Middle East, the Soviet leaders will continue to subordinate the interests of local Communist parties to Soviet national interests and inter-governmental relations. At the same time, as their continuing efforts to hold a World Communist Conference show[7], they are

[6] Civil war in Nigeria followed the declaration on 30 May 1967 of a separate 'Republic of Biafra' in the eastern region of the country. The Soviet Union was supplying aircraft and artillery to Nigeria's Federal Government, which also received arms from the UK. Biafran forces surrendered on 15 January 1970.

[7] Cf. No. 27, note 5. The Conference was eventually held in Moscow from 5-17 June 1969. China, Yugoslavia, Albania, North Korea and North Vietnam were not represented. Reporting on the Conference in a despatch of 24 June Sir D. Wilson said the CPSU's main objectives had included holding a well attended Conference, burying the Czechoslovak issue and the 'Brezhnev doctrine' as deep as they could, mobilising the maximum of support against China, securing a free hand for dealings with the US Administration and emphasising their own leading role in practice in the Communist movement. He concluded: 'Given the difficult background and unambitious objective, I think one might describe the Conference as a modest success which

concerned with orthodoxy and with the need to have Soviet views and actions accepted as gospel by other Communist parties. The Soviet action in Czechoslovakia has damaged the Soviet Union's ability to use non-governmental Communist parties, in particular in the West, as an instrument of Soviet policy. Because of the Soviet leaders' inflexibility and conservatism, the Soviet Union will find it difficult to strengthen the Communist parties in either developing or developed countries. However it will go on trying and this may put something of a brake on Soviet policies towards Eastern Europe.

42. In short, while outside Europe the Czechoslovak crisis implies little change in the general nature and trend of East-West relations, in Europe the present uncertainties, tensions, and instability will persist. The fundamental cause of this instability will be the Soviet Union's reactions to the continuing internal evolution in Eastern Europe. How great risks the Soviet Union will be prepared to take to maintain its position in Eastern Europe will depend on the strength and cohesion of the West, United States policies, and the attitudes and position of Germany. Weakness and disunity in the West will compound the instability and encourage the Soviet Union to assert its influence in Western as well as Eastern Europe.

WESTERN OBJECTIVES AND POLICIES

Détente

43. The policy of *détente* has been defined by the West as 'the search for secure and peaceful East-West relations leading in time to a European security settlement'. This search has been going on for a long time and clearly must continue. Equally clearly, however, the aims of the search are not likely to be achieved within the time scale of this paper. From the Western point of view the aims postulate an end to Soviet attempts to subvert the West and to Soviet policies hostile to the West throughout the world. The previous analysis of Soviet policies shows that the Russians have an entirely different view: in so far as they use the concept of *détente*, it means no more than the status quo in Europe, limited understandings with the United States and the continued attempt to extend their influence world-wide, often by employing subversive techniques. The West looks forward to the day when relations with the Soviet Union are the same mixture of competitive rivalry and respect for national independence under the United Nations Charter as those of any two members of the free world: the Soviet Union to the universal establishment of Soviet models of Communism and the subordination of other countries' interests to the interests of the Soviet Union.

justified the decision of the Soviet leadership to hold it, as well as being a success for Brezhnev personally', although the Basic Document signed on 17 June did not contain a formal condemnation of China and bore little relation to international realities. Mr. Giffard submitted this despatch to Sir T. Brimelow with the comment that 'There is no doubt that as regards the short term issues the Russians chalked up a number of successes . . . we would, however, be inclined to shade the longer-term implications for the Soviet Union a little darker than the Ambassador does' (EN 2/10).

44. A consequence of Soviet doctrines of Communism is that, just as we see Soviet aims as focused on the subversion of our society, so the Soviet leaders recognise that if we achieve our aims *vis-à-vis* Eastern Europe it will mean a change in what to them is the fundamental basis of Soviet society. The Soviet leaders have been giving added emphasis to their doctrine that in the course of the class struggle the Imperialists will attack the more fiercely as the Capitalist world declines and the Socialist world develops. In the upside down way of Communist doctrine this leads the Russians to believe that the West is intensifying its attack and that bridge-building is part of this. For the Soviet Union peaceful co-existence is only a framework for the struggle between two ideologies.

45. One condition, therefore, for the successful conclusion of a policy of *détente* in the Western sense is a fundamental change in the attitudes and outlook of the Soviet leadership. Our belief is that existing pressures within Eastern Europe and the Soviet Union will, beyond the time-scale of this paper, begin to reduce ideological preoccupations in Soviet policy. This may result finally in a greater inclination on the part of the Soviet leaders to see Soviet interests in more national terms, which may make it easier to do business with them. In the meantime over-vigorous attempts to speed the process up might well increase the dangers of Soviet initiatives against the West and further Soviet repression in Eastern Europe. At the same time the pressures for change in the Soviet Union will be reduced if the West does not present a solid front.

Overall Objectives

46. In short the overall objectives of Western policy must be:

(i) to unify and strengthen the West, and to deter and resist Soviet attempts to disrupt it;

(ii) to do what is possible to encourage change in the attitudes of the Soviet and Eastern European leadership, without provoking retrograde reactions in Soviet policy.

Western unity and strength

47. The first of these objectives is fundamental. It is the key to achieving the second. In the field of defence it includes the need to strengthen NATO and to maintain the United States guarantee to Europe. The pressures for some United States troop withdrawals in the next few years make it essential for the Europeans to strengthen their defence posture and to collaborate more closely. It is important that the United States-Soviet dialogue on strategic issues should continue but equally important that the United States should keep its Western allies fully informed about it. In the political, military, and economic field we have to continue our efforts to create a more united and cohesive Europe and to enlarge the EEC. We also have to do all we can to make real progress in solving the West's economic and social problems and so demonstrating to the non-committed and the Communist bloc the superiority of the Western system. The United Kingdom is already working in a number of fields to convince its allies of the need for policies on these lines. We do not

need to say more about them here except to repeat that they are fundamental to the improvement of relations with the Soviet Union and that it will be a very long time before we can relax our efforts.

Outside the NATO area

48. As noted above, in certain areas, e.g., India and Pakistan, the Soviet Union and the West, in particular the United States, have some common interests. In some other places, e.g., Latin America, the Soviet Union recognises tacitly an American sphere of influence at any rate so far as any overt military intervention is concerned, and within the timescale of this paper is likely to continue to do so. United States membership in SEATO and association with CENTO,[8] as well as bilateral United States obligations to other countries, e.g., Japan, are a continuing check on Soviet activities. However throughout the world the West has to deal with increasing political, economic, commercial and military competition from the Soviet Union. Given the United Kingdom's decision to withdraw military forces from East of Suez and the United States reluctance to increase American commitments the West will have to rely to a greater extent than hitherto on its political, economic and commercial policies to meet the Soviet challenge in this area. In the Persian Gulf, the Indian sub-continent, South-East Asia and other areas where the West has essential interests our aim will have to be to fortify the indigenous strength and independence of the countries of each area. In this competition the West starts with the advantage of having greater material resources than the Soviet Union. Its advantage will be more marked if Western policies become more closely co-ordinated. The West will also have to keep under review whether policies on these lines will suffice.[9]

Direct relations with Eastern Europe and the Soviet Union

49. In the past few years most Western European countries have devoted a lot of effort to improving their political, economic and cultural relations with Eastern Europe. It is now evident that these policies will take many years to bring about significant progress. There are arguments for being somewhat more cautious in future. Our policy is not actively and publicly to seek the break-up of the Soviet empire but unobtrusively to encourage the process of gradual change in Eastern Europe and the Soviet Union. We have to strike

---

[8] The South East Asia Treaty Organisation and Central Treaty Organisation. In 1969 the members of SEATO were Australia, France, New Zealand, Pakistan, the Philippines, Thailand, the UK and the USA; CENTO consisted of Iran, Pakistan, Turkey and the UK.

[9] On 28 May, in a widely-publicised article in *Izvestiya*, the foreign affairs commentator V. Matveyev stated that the 'dismantling of the network of foreign military bases . . . would pave the way for the laying of the foundations of collective security' in Asia, to which the Soviet Union would contribute 'every effort'; and a reference by Mr. Brezhnev in a speech on 7 June at the World Communist Conference (see note 7) to the need to create a system of collective security in Asia was followed by the recall to Moscow for consultations of Soviet Ambassadors in Asian countries. In a minute of 10 June Mr. Orchard commented that if the Russians were to proceed with the idea of an Asian collective security system 'there could be consequences which would be prejudicial to our interests . . . we should need to see first how they follow it up'. Mr. Gromyko referred to the idea in his speech of 10 July (see p. 170-1 below), but no firm proposals appeared to have been formulated (FA 3/303/1).

a balance between on the one hand allowing the Eastern European countries to think that we condone Soviet policies or have given them up and on the other provoking the Soviet Union to dangerous counter reactions. There is a risk that too energetic attempts by the West to establish closer relations with Eastern Europe may seem to the Soviet Union to threaten its vital interests. We should therefore put at least as much emphasis on our relations and contacts with the Soviet Union as on our relations and contacts with Eastern Europe, and pursue the latter with prudence.[10]

50. Given that in the longest run the Soviet system is likely to change because of internal pressures, one policy might be to cut down our contacts with the Soviet Union to a bare minimum and leave it to 'stew in its own juice'. The general arguments to the contrary are that reducing our contacts with the Soviet Union will increase the possibility of serious if not fatal misunderstandings; and that the damage to Soviet interests of reduced contacts, though significant to the Soviet Government (as its recent outburst shows) is outweighed in the longer term by the advantages to the West (in terms of encouraging change) of maintaining them. The following paragraphs briefly set out the particular arguments for maintaining contacts in a number of particular fields.

Trade

51. Trade with the Soviet Union, often involving the extension of substantial credits, adds to Soviet total resources and speeds technological progress in the Soviet Union. Any Western dependence on Soviet resources may well add to the Soviet Union's bargaining power. On the other hand, quite apart from the direct commercial benefit to the West of trade with the bloc, the more closely tied the Soviet Union and Eastern Europe become to the world trading system the less likely they are to act dangerously or irresponsibly. In addition the personal contacts resulting from trading relations are a good way of injecting Western ideas into the Soviet system. Western European trade with Eastern Europe is probably less worrying to the Soviet Union than any other form of contact though this might not be so true of proposals for financial loans.

52. These general considerations are in line with the United Kingdom's particular interests. United Kingdom trade with the Soviet Union has expanded rapidly in recent years. In 1968 our exports are likely to be of the order of £100 million f.o.b. (double the 1966 figure) and our imports about £150 million c.i.f. (20 per cent up on 1966). Our trade with other Eastern European countries is also growing. Exports to these countries will be nearly £120 million this year and imports from them nearly £150 million. In total, our trade with the USSR and Eastern Europe represents little more than 3½ per cent of our total overseas trade. By far the greater proportion of our imports represent raw materials and foodstuffs which it is in our interest to buy

[10] Mr. Youde told Mr. Barrington on 29 May that 'The Prime Minister welcomes the thought in . . . paragraph 49 of the paper that we should put at least as much emphasis on our relations with the Soviet Union as on our relations with Eastern Europe' (EN 2 / 6).

in the best markets. Many of them are subsequently re-exported to the benefit of our balance of payments.

53. All these countries are anxious to increase their exports to us of manufactured goods, especially the products of their newly-developed engineering industries, but so far their progress has been slow. In so far as they can supply goods more cheaply than other overseas suppliers, or their competition drives down the prices we pay to other suppliers, it is, as a general proposition, in our interest to allow them to compete in our market (subject always to our retaining powers to prevent disruptive competition). Equally, it is in our interest to develop sales to these expanding markets, in order to pay for what we buy and if possible, over and above this, to receive payment in gold or in sterling earned elsewhere by the East Europeans.

Technology

54. A risk of technological collaboration with the Soviet Union and with Eastern Europe as a whole is that having acquired a given technology the Soviet Union will exploit it to strengthen its self-sufficiency. In fact there is little reason to suppose that a refusal of collaboration on general technological matters achieves anything more than a short delay in Soviet acquisition of the technology involved though we must clearly continue to safeguard the details of certain technologies, processes and equipments used for or associated with defence purposes. Moreover as explained earlier in the paper the Soviet Union, like the countries of Western Europe, is now too advanced a society to be able to achieve adequate progress relying only on self-sufficiency. As with trade, while technological collaboration undoubtedly increases the Soviet Union's resources, it also increases its inter-dependence with the West. It brings us into contact with a new managerial and technological class. Moreover it is only by trying to get in on Soviet development planning that we can hope to take a good share of what may become a very large market; it is too early to say that the prospects are bright, but we must, if possible, be in a position to exploit them.

Cultural relations

55. One difficulty with cultural contacts is the contrast between the freedom of access allowed in the West and the close control exercised by the Soviet Union. Nevertheless increasing contacts of all sorts with Soviet scientists, intellectuals, technologists, etc., even allowing for the fact that they have little immediate effect, are an essential part of our long-term effort to change attitudes in the Soviet Union. Official policy in the last few years has favoured a trend towards greater cultural contacts with Eastern Europe. For the reasons outlined above this should not be taken too far. There will be advantage in maintaining our effort with the Soviet Union. This will not be difficult since there is more interest in the West in contacts with Soviet society than with the societies of Eastern Europe. The Soviet Union has always attracted the largest injection of official British funds and this should continue.

Political contacts

56. We have to bear it in mind that their ideological convictions preclude any genuine goodwill towards Western societies on the part of the Soviet

leaders. We should have no illusions about the efficacy of unrequited concessions or mere expressions of goodwill on our part. However there are strong reasons for maintaining political contacts with the Soviet Union wherever the West has specified business to transact, seems likely to derive concrete benefits or has an opportunity through informed discussion to influence Soviet thinking. Because of the secretive nature of Soviet policy-making and the relative lack of Soviet contacts with the outside world, political contacts are an important way of reducing the risk of misunderstanding on both sides. They also provide some insights into Soviet thinking. It would have to be clearly understood that such contacts should be invariably conducted on a serious and frank basis with a clear eye to the defence of Western interests and the maintenance of Western points of view and not on the basis of a deferential attitude of a medium Power towards a bigger one. We should also maintain political contacts with Eastern European countries wherever we have business to do. In the immediate future, we shall need to make, though not to overdo, some distinction between the aggressors against Czechoslovakia on the one hand, and Czechoslovakia and Rumania on the other.

European security

57. One question on which the West will have to reach a co-ordinated view is the ultimate shape of a security settlement in Europe. Our long-term objectives in this respect will inevitably affect our shorter-term policies. In NATO the United Kingdom has been taking the line that the West should continue to prepare for the day when fruitful East-West negotiations will be possible, even if this is a distant prospect. We are trying to persuade our NATO allies to continue discussions of European security so as to reach agreed NATO positions as far as we can.[11] There is no reason to discourage individual initiatives or discussions with Eastern European countries, provided they are co-ordinated in the Alliance and neither likely to provoke the Soviet Union nor to generate pressures of unrealistic expectation in Western public opinion. We should keep under examination our own assumptions about the conditions in which it might be possible in the long term to begin to improve prospects for European security, bearing in mind that the Germans have come to accept that reunification can only be the outcome of a long period of *détente*.

Summing-up

58. In sum Western policy in the longer term should be to restore full relations with the Soviet Union provided that they are and are seen to be directly or indirectly designed to further concrete Western interests. The West need not cut back its contacts with Eastern Europe but should be prudent about increasing them too energetically.

59. In dealing with the Soviet Union the West must drive hard bargains and insist on tangible Soviet concessions in return for any Western concessions to the Soviet Union. To prevent the Soviet Union picking off Western

---

[11] Cf. pp. 129-30. NATO's Senior Political Committee was working to produce a list of issues for East-West negotiations, for submission to NATO Ministers in December.

countries one by one the West must co-ordinate its policies as closely as possible. In assessing the balance of advantage between the Soviet Union and the West on any issue we have to recognise that Soviet policies in every sphere will always be strongly conditioned by political considerations. On the other hand, however much the Soviet leaders aspire to autarky, the Soviet Union will become more dependent on its links with the West, if it is to maintain the desired rate of growth. While increasing Western contacts with the Soviet Union, the West has to avoid becoming too dependent in any particular respect on the Soviet Union, and to be prepared to reduce these contacts whenever we think that such reductions will bring effective pressure to bear. Given the skill of Soviet propaganda this will not always be so easy as it has been after the Czechoslovak crisis; and will demand a considerable inform-ation effort by the Western Powers in their own countries.

60. The role of the United Kingdom, as an important member of the Alliance, will be to follow the policies outlined in the previous paragraphs, to co-ordinate them closely with our allies and to contribute and be seen to contribute our full share to the Alliance. On the basis of carefully considered views of our own, we may be able to influence our allies towards a fruitful collective policy.

61. The Soviet Union is and will remain an extremely powerful military Power. Throughout the next ten years and beyond Soviet influence will expand. Given the fundamentally hostile attitudes of the Soviet leaders a successful policy of *détente* on the lines described in this paper means a very long haul. In the longer as in the shorter run it will depend above all on maintaining the United States links with Europe and on increasing the strength and unity of the West.[12]

[12] Sir D. Wilson commented to Mr. Giffard on 9 June that he 'would not dissent from the general line of its argument and conclusions . . . Naturally if the paper were to be written now one might have drafted some passages rather differently. I am thinking in particular about the effects of the Sino/Soviet dispute on the whole appearance of Soviet foreign policy' (EN 2/2).

Further comments were received from Mr. J.N. Henderson (HM Ambassador in Warsaw since March 1969), Mr. Millard, Mr. Smith, Sir T. Garvey (HM Ambassador in Belgrade since September 1968), Mr. Crawley and Sir D. Wilson and considered at a meeting held by the Secretary of State on 21 July, attended by Sir D. Wilson. Summarising its conclusions in a letter to the latter on 28 July, Sir T. Brimelow wrote that 'our impression is that the importance which we attach to consultation in NATO (for reasons which have as much to do with Western as with Eastern Europe) is perhaps underrated in the correspondence. On the whole the Alliance has kept together well; and it is obviously in our interest that it should continue to do so.' He referred to Mr. Henderson's view that 'we should worry less, in our contacts with the East Europeans, about provoking the Russians into taking counter-measures. We have not, I think, held so exaggerated a view of our own or of the collective Western influence in Eastern Europe as to believe that this influence in itself could provoke developments calling for Soviet intervention . . . [But] it is right for us to be careful.' In the Secretary of State's view 'it was now in our interests to try to return gradually and discreetly to the kind of bilateral relations with the Soviet Union and other East European Governments which we maintained before the invasion of Czechoslovakia', and the 'best form of initial contact' would be a discussion with Mr. Gromyko in New York in September when both attended the UNGA (EN 2/6).

The next two documents record the visits to Moscow of two British Ministers, Mr. Benn and Mr. Crosland. FCO records make it clear that while Mr. Stewart and FCO officials considered that the Ministers should confine their discussions strictly to the purpose of their visits—technology and trade respectively—both Mr. Benn and Mr. Crosland intended to take the opportunity to discuss other matters of interest to them. In these circumstances the FCO provided what briefing they could, hoping that neither Minister was drawn into any contentious discussion either of political matters in general, or in particular of the case of Gerald Brooke (cf. No. 30).

Mr. Benn's visit to Moscow, recorded in No. 32, included a conversation with Mr. Kosygin.[1] The Secretary of State had only a brief word with Mr. Crosland before the latter's departure for Moscow, but speaking notes prepared for their planned meeting show that he intended to ask the Minister not to allow himself to be drawn into political discussions by the Russians, and in particular to decline to make any comment about the Brooke case. Mr. Crosland, however, had told FCO officials that he 'wanted to make a minimum mention of the strength of feeling about Brooke' in Britain, and felt that he could not 'return to this country and admit that he made no reference to the case'. The record of Mr. Crosland's visit in No. 33 does not mention his talk with Mr. Kozyrev on 3 June, though Sir D. Wilson reported separately on it. When the Minister said that 'as a member of HMG he felt bound to leave the Soviet authorities in no doubt of the grave concern which the case was still causing to HMG', Mr. Kozyrev replied that he 'did not think that the Brooke case should be a really important problem in Anglo-Soviet relations, unfortunately there were certain elements even within Her Majesty's Government, not least the Defence Secretary [cf. No. 25, notes 3 and 4], who did not seem to be interested in the improvement of these relations'.[2]

[1] See Tony Benn, *Diaries 1968-72, op. cit.,* pp. 166-71 for the origins of this meeting, recorded in No. 32, note 6 below, and for the apparently conflicting advice given to him by Mr. Stewart and the Prime Minister.

[2] Moscow telegram No. 541 of 3 June, ENS 14/1.

No. 32

Sir D. Wilson (Moscow) to Mr. Stewart

No. ECO 6/5 [ENS 17/4]

Confidential   MOSCOW, *27 May 1969*
Summary . . .[1]

Sir,

    Visit of the Rt. Hon. Anthony Wedgwood Benn, MP, to the Soviet Union

I have the honour to send you the following report on the visit paid to the Soviet Union by the Right Hon. Anthony Wedgwood Benn, MP, Minister of Technology, between the 13th and the 20th of May, 1969.[2] I enclose a list of

[1] Not here printed.

[2] See above and Tony Benn, *loc. cit.,* pp. 169-79 for his account of the visit.

the main items in his programme, and a text of the agreed protocol of his discussions with the Soviet authorities.[3] The Minister will himself be reporting on the results of his visit in the technological field, and I shall confine myself in this despatch to its political aspects.

2. From this point of view, the most important things about the visit were that it took place at all, and that it took place at this particular time. Article 5 of the Anglo-Soviet Agreement of the 19th of January 1968 on technological cooperation[4] provides that a regular review should be held annually, to examine progress made and to consider the further development of technological exchanges. The first such review was due to be held in October, 1968, in Moscow, but Her Majesty's Government decided that it would be inappropriate for a British Minister to visit the USSR so shortly after the Soviet invasion of Czechoslovakia, and while the strong public reaction to that event was at its height in Britain. The review was therefore postponed until the spring of 1969, by which time a number of other visits by members of NATO Governments were in prospect (the French Minister of Science in fact arrived in Moscow on a similar mission during Mr. Wedgwood Benn's visit). This was in fact the first visit to the USSR by a Minister from any NATO country since Czechoslovakia, and it therefore represented something of a landmark in Anglo-Soviet relations, and in East-West relations generally. I am all the more glad that it did not have to be postponed again as the result of recent difficulties in Anglo-Soviet relations caused by Soviet threats to Mr. Gerald Brooke.[5]

3. These difficulties, as well as the general state of East-West relations, made it important for us that Mr. Benn's visit should be, and should be seen to be, on a business basis. As is clear from the Minister's programme the Soviet authorities evidently shared this view. The main objects—to conduct the review called for under the Agreement, to evaluate the work done by the various working parties, and to produce plans for future collaboration—were achieved without undue difficulty. The protocol signed on the 19th of May records the decisions reached. Both delegations agreed to encourage the Chairmen of the working groups to produce within a few months estimates of the practical results which they expect to achieve; this should help to concentrate effort on the potentially most rewarding groups. It was further agreed that some further groups could usefully be established on subjects newly identified as promising lines of enquiry.

4. While the Soviet authorities made no attempt either to engage Mr. Benn in political discussion outside the proper field of the joint talks, or to make capital out of his presence by undue publicity, they took certain steps to mark their own sense of the importance of a return to business at Ministerial level. The most considerable of these was to arrange at short notice a visit to

[3] Not printed.   [4] See No. 2, note 7.   [5] Cf. No. 30.

Mr. Kosygin,[6] at which the latter was able to display his great personal interest in the success of the Agreement and his impressively detailed knowledge of modern technical developments. The meeting was reported as having taken place in a 'friendly atmosphere' (the first use of this adjective in any Anglo-Soviet context since I arrived at this post); and apart from this Mr. Benn's visit received good, but not excessive, publicity in the Soviet Press.

5. The programme arranged by the Soviet authorities allowed Mr. Benn, apart from visiting a number of factories and research institutions both in Moscow and Leningrad, to have informal talks with his host, Academician Kirillin, Chairman of the State Committee for Science and Technology, and with one of Mr. Kirillin's deputies, Mr. Gvishiani (Mr. Kosygin's son-in-law), among others. These were, I am sure, useful in re-establishing and confirming the excellent personal relationships which had previously existed. It was also, if I may say so, very useful as well as pleasant for me and other members of the Embassy staff to have the advantage of meeting, under Mr. Benn's patronage so to speak, some of the most important Soviet technocrats. These are the men in whom lie perhaps our best hopes of the gradual evolution of Soviet policies away from the more primitive forms of Communism and towards some kinds of understanding and cooperation in the political as well as the technical field. In this context I was grateful to Mr. Benn for taking the chance on a social occasion, of explaining to 'my' Vice-Minister of Foreign Affairs[,] the redoubtable Mr. Kozyrev, the scope and limits of our technical collaboration with the Germans and Dutch over the gas centrifuge. In answer to a parting question, Mr. Kozyrev said that he was 'almost convinced' by the case put to him by Mr. Benn (but I do not count too much on this!).

6. It was also useful that in the course of the visit Sir Solly Zuckerman was given the chance to resume his contacts with Soviet Academicians Millionshikov, Reutov and Kapitsa. These contacts may be of great value most immediately in the context of the Geneva disarmament talks,[7] and again I was grateful myself to have the chance of meeting the people concerned under Sir Solly's auspices. I am sure also that, for the development of Anglo-

[6] At their meeting on 14 May Mr. Benn and Mr. Kosygin discussed progress made in the Anglo/Soviet Technical agreement and the general situation in Europe, including international monetary problems and the increasing strength of the FRG. In the course of the conversation Mr. Kosygin extended an invitation to Mr. Wilson to visit Moscow 'for a day or two in June or July' to talk about 'political questions of interest to the two Governments'. Mr. Benn said that 'he would convey this message to Mr. Wilson, and added that the Prime Minister had asked him to say that Anglo-Soviet relations had been through a difficult year for reasons that were understood but that he hoped relations would improve'. Mr. Kosygin replied that 'the reasons why our relations had been difficult over this period were not understood'.

[7] When the Conference of the ENDC (cf. No. 1, note 4) had reconvened on 18 March 1969 the Soviet Union had tabled a draft treaty prohibiting the use of the sea bed for military purposes, which was rejected by the USA on 25 March. The Conference went into recess on 23 May, after the Soviet and American delegations had announced that its membership was to be expanded. On 26 August the enlarged Conference, now consisting of 26 states, decided to change its name to the Conference of the Committee on Disarmament (CCD). On 7 October the US and USSR delegations tabled a joint draft treaty prohibiting the use of nuclear weapons on the sea bed.

Soviet relations and of long-term Soviet policies, Sir Solly's contacts with Mr. Gvishiani to arrange further discussion on 'problems of Advanced Societies' are potentially of great importance.

7. It must of course be recognised that in the economic sphere, the Soviet Government have ends of their own to pursue through the Technological Agreement, and that these are not identical with our own. On the economic side, it has always been recognised on the British side that the purposes of the two partners are basically different. The Russians are primarily interested in access to modern technology, while we wish to see the technical talks ending in important export contracts. These aims are, I believe, not inconsistent, partly because the Soviet authorities have in general shown no lack of readiness to conclude major contracts with foreign firms where this was necessary to enlarge the productive capacity of their industry on modern lines, and also because some of the work done in Soviet research establishments is of real interest to their counterparts in Britain.

8. Similarly on the political side the Russians have an interest in resuming contact, particularly Ministerial contact, with the NATO powers, in order to show that they are once again respectable political partners and that the case of Czechoslovakia has been duly forgotten. Our own political interest is of a longer term nature; it lies in the importance of dealing directly at the appropriate level with technocrats of the calibre of Academician Kirillin, in gaining access through them to other key scientists and technicians in the USSR, and in influencing them gradually towards our own views of the possibilities of cooperation. I am very glad to note from the memorandum enclosed in your own despatch to me of the 15th of May[8] that the importance of these long-term objectives is fully recognised by Her Majesty's Government.

9. In the present case it must, I fear, be admitted that the Soviet authorities may be rather too ready to conclude that the hostility in Western Europe to their invasion of Czechoslovakia is now receding. The fact that the visit of the President of the Board of Trade will follow so soon will give them some further encouragement.[9] But, as we have explained to our allies in NATO, both these visits had specific purposes, and arose from earlier undertakings, and they could not be indefinitely postponed without repercussions over a wide field. Moreover, as there are a number of visits to Moscow by Ministers in other NATO Governments pending this summer, it now seems likely that some relaxation of the Alliance's policy of restricting Ministerial visits to the USSR will in practice occur.

10. This development is, I think, inevitable and generally welcome. Although a period of restraint and coolness in relations with the USSR was necessary after the Czechoslovak crisis last August, it remains in our long-term interest to encourage the habit of consultation on the part of the Soviet authorities. The visit by the Minister of Technology will, I am sure, have contributed to this process. I am grateful to him for coming and for

[8] No. 31.   [9] See No. 33 below.

undertaking a very strenuous programme. His energy and enthusiasm were clearly much appreciated by his Soviet hosts, and were, I believe, particularly valuable at a time when a rather dismal picture of British affairs is emerging from the press, and when Her Majesty's Government and the British people may be too easily pictured as engaged mainly in the licking of wounds.

11. I would also like to thank Mr. Benn for undertaking two 'extra-curricular' tasks. His visit to the impressive British pavilion at the Automation Exhibition currently being held in Sokolniki Park was much appreciated by our own exhibitors. It was also particularly good of Mr. Benn to find time for giving an informal talk to the staff of this Embassy on the work of his Ministry. I hope that the questions put to him afterwards did something to indicate how stimulating we found his talk.

12. I am sending copies of this despatch to the Minister of Technology, the President of the Board of Trade and to UKDEL NATO.

I have, etc.,

A.D. WILSON

No. 33

Sir D. Wilson (Moscow) to Mr. Stewart

[*ENS 6/10*]

Restricted   MOSCOW, *10 June 1969*

Sir,

I have the honour to report that a new Long-Term Trade Agreement between the United Kingdom and the Union of Soviet Socialist Republics was signed in Moscow on the 3rd of June, 1969.[1] Mr. Anthony Crosland, MP, President of the Board of Trade, who visited Moscow from the 1st to the 3rd of June, signed on behalf of the United Kingdom, and Mr. N.S. Patolichev, Soviet Minister of Foreign Trade, on behalf of the Soviet Union. The text of the Agreement, in the English and Russian languages, together with the Full Powers authorising Mr. Patolichev to sign, is enclosed.[2] Another text, in the Russian and English languages, together with the Full Powers authorising Mr. Crosland's signature, remains in the custody of the Soviet Government. In accordance with instructions, I have to report that Mr. Patolichev's signature, when transliterated from the Cyrillic into the Latin script, reads 'N. Patolichev'.

2. The new Agreement, which replaces the Anglo-Soviet Trade Agreement signed in Moscow on the 24th of May, 1959, and renewed in London on the 23rd of April, 1964,[3] comes into force on the 1st of July, 1969, and is valid until the 31st of December, 1975. It follows broadly the lines of the previous

[1] Published as Cmnd. 4132 of 1969.   [2] Not printed.

[3] See No. 2, note 9.

Agreement and provides for a continuing increase in trade between the two countries. The long-term objective of the Soviet Union remains that the conditions applicable to Soviet exports to the United Kingdom should be no less favourable than those applicable to exports from the United Kingdom's EFTA partners. In the absence of any meaningful guarantees of comparable freedom of access for United Kingdom exporters to the Soviet market, such a perspective still seems remote.

3. The present Agreement was reached following two rounds of negotiations, one in London in February of this year and another in Moscow in May. These were conducted in a friendly atmosphere and revealed no major difficulties. A further measure of liberalisation, affecting the régime governing the importation of Soviet goods into the United Kingdom, was announced in April, 1969,[4] and reflected a substantial increase in United Kingdom exports to the Soviet Union in 1968; while not entirely meeting Soviet aspirations, this undoubtedly facilitated the conclusion of the Agreement and no substantial points were left for discussion between the Ministers concerned.

4. Mr. Crosland received a warm welcome from Mr. Patolichev and the Soviet officials concerned with the negotiations. In a general review of Anglo-Soviet trade which took place on the 2nd of June, Mr. Patolichev assured Mr. Crosland that it remained the Soviet intention that the volume of United Kingdom exports to the Soviet Union in 1969 should show an increase over the 1968 figures, and that the somewhat disappointing results for the first four months of the year should not be taken as revealing any change of trend. Such a general assurance of course does not constitute a commitment on the Soviet side, but has some value as proving that they recognise our legitimate concern about reciprocity of trade.

5. Mr. Crosland also received categorical assurances from Mr. Patolichev on two points. Firstly, that requests for permanent representation in Moscow by United Kingdom firms transacting substantial business with the Soviet Union would receive favourable consideration. Secondly, that the Ministry of Foreign Trade would be willing to help this Embassy over any problems relating to the living conditions of the increasing number of United Kingdom technicians temporarily working in the Soviet Union, in connexion with the erection of plant and equipment at various sites. Both these assurances, which

---

[4] FCO telegram No. 242 to Moscow of 31 March had stated that the President of the Board of Trade would announce in Parliament on 2 April 'the extension to the Soviet Union and Rumania of the liberalisation which was negotiated with Czechoslovakia, Poland and Hungary in 1964 and with Bulgaria in 1965. This will remove quota restrictions and substitute open individual licensing arrangements on a wide range of goods including machinery, furniture, paper, chemicals, plastics, leather footwear, foodstuffs of various kinds, carpets, books and periodicals and tyres and tubes. The announcement will explain that the decision to place all these countries on the same footing is taken in the context of the substantial increase in our exports to USSR and Rumania in 1968 and our confidence of further expansion' (EN 6/7). The new arrangements would be extended to East Germany 'only when we are satisfied with the current and future level of our exports there'. For Mr. Crosland's announcement, given in a written answer of 2 April, see *Parl. Debs., H. of C., 5th ser.*, vol. 781, cols. *110-111*.

depend for their implementation on the cooperation of Soviet Ministries other than Mr. Patolichev's own, may turn out to be not fully effective, but it is useful to have obtained them.

6. While the present Agreement provides a convenient framework within which Anglo-Soviet trade can conveniently take place, it contains little in the way of firmly binding provisions, and the further development of this trade will depend, as hitherto, on the continuing exertions of both United Kingdom firms and of Her Majesty's Government in the exacting Soviet market. The rapid industrialisation of this very large country, and its substantial earnings of foreign exchange, not least of sterling, undoubtedly offer plenty of scope for British enterprise.

7. The annual review stipulated in Article 6 of the Agreement will provide a useful opportunity to check performance against expectation.

8. Outside the framework of the Trade Agreement, Mr. Crosland had a useful talk with the Soviet Minister of Civil Aviation, Marshal Loginov, in the course of which they agreed that discussions should begin in July at expert level about the possibility of BOAC using the Trans-Siberian air-route to Japan.[5]

9. I am most grateful to Mr. Crosland for making time for his quick trip to Moscow. Even if there was no major point of substance for him to discuss with Mr. Patolichev, a number of interesting points were raised incidentally in their talks, and it is important particularly at this stage of our political relations to keep high-level 'business' contacts with the Soviet authorities in good repair.

10. I am sending copies of this Despatch to HM Representatives at Washington, Paris, Bonn, Tokyo, Belgrade, Bucharest, Budapest, Prague, Sofia, Ulan Bator, Warsaw and to the United Kingdom Delegation, NATO.

I have, etc.,

DUNCAN WILSON

[5] Cf. No. 2, note 10. Following the announcement in February 1969 of a Soviet-Japanese agreement opening the trans-Siberian route to Japan Airline's services with Japanese aircraft from March 1970, it had been agreed with BOAC and the Board of Trade to approach the Soviet Government with a view to obtaining rights for BOAC to fly 'pretty well the last major undeveloped trunk route in the world of aviation, and several hours shorter in journey time than the existing trunk route to Japan via Alaska'. Following a preliminary approach by Sir D. Wilson, Mr. Crosland told Marshal Loginov on 2 June that HMG realised 'that the Soviet authorities were "sitting on a gold mine" now that the trans-Siberian route had been opened up to international traffic. We were prepared to offer attractive transatlantic rights to Aeroflot in return for concessions to BOAC.' Discussions on a trans-Siberian route for BOAC opened on 21 July but adjourned on 25 July as the 'large set of USSR demands made it impossible to reach agreement'; the demands included 'full traffic rights out of London to two points in North America not only from us, which we had offered, but also from the US and/or Canada', and British negotiators suspected that the USSR 'may have Havana in mind as one of these points' (MUA 4/303/1). Negotiations did not resume until December.

Negotiations on the release of Gerald Brooke and the Krogers (cf. No. 30) proceeded throughout May and June. Despite the continuing reservations expressed by Mr. Callaghan and others, Mr. Stewart was convinced by Sir D. Greenhill's argument that an arrangement for early release should be made, both on humanitarian grounds and because a retrial of Mr. Brooke would cause a disproportionate deterioration in Anglo-Soviet relations. On 10 June the Secretary of State minuted to the Home Secretary that in his view HMG should 'bring this situation to an end as quickly as we can' (PUSD records). On the advice of the Prime Minister, Mr. Stewart put his views to the Cabinet orally.

No. 34

Extract from Conclusions of a Meeting of the Cabinet held at 10 Downing St. on 26 June 1969 at 10 a.m.[1]

CC(69)30 [CAB 128/44]

Secret

Oversea Affairs: Mr. Gerald Brooke

(Previous Reference: CC(69)29th Conclusions, minute 4.)[2]

2.[3] THE FOREIGN AND COMMONWEALTH SECRETARY informed his colleagues of recent developments in regard to Mr. Gerald Brooke.

The Foreign and Commonwealth Secretary said that, as he had already informed his colleagues, the Soviet Government had been contemplating bringing further charges against Mr. Gerald Brooke, the British lecturer arrested in April 1965, and sentenced to one year's imprisonment and four years' detention in a labour colony. When he had learnt of this he had caused the Soviet Ambassador in London to be informed that, should Mr. Brooke be subjected to a further trial and sentence, there would be no possibility of the release before 1974 of Mr. and Mrs Kroger, the two Soviet agents sentenced to 20 years' imprisonment in 1961 for their part in the

---

[1] Present at this meeting were: Mr. Wilson, Mr. Stewart, Mr. Roy Jenkins (Chancellor of the Exchequer), Lord Gardner (Lord Chancellor), Mr. Crossman (now Secretary of State for Social Services), Mrs Barbara Castle (Secretary of State for Employment and Productivity), Mr. Callaghan, Mr. Peart (now Lord President of the Council), Mr. Shore, Mr. Crosland, Mr. Ross, Mr. G. Thomson (now Minister without Portfolio), Mr. Short, Mr. Wedgwood Benn, Mr. Richard Marsh (Minister of Transport), Mr. Anthony Greenwood (Minister of Housing and Local Government), Mr. Hughes, Lord Shackleton (now Lord Privy Seal), Mr. Thomas, Mrs Judith Hart (Paymaster General), Mr. Diamond, Mr. Robert Mellish (Parliamentary Secretary, Treasury) and Sir Elwyn Jones (Attorney General).

[2] At this meeting on 18 June Mr. Stewart had commented briefly on the preliminary discussions which had taken place with the Soviet Ambassador about the possibility of the release of Mr. Brooke by the Soviet authorities in exchange for the release of Mr. and Mrs Kroger (cf. pp. 135-6 and No. 30, note 5). He had undertaken to make a fuller report in due course.

[3] *Note in the original:* 'Previously recorded in a Confidential Annex.'

Portland spy case. If, however, it were agreed that Mr. Brooke would be released at the end of his current sentence, we would be prepared to discuss the matter of the Krogers further. The way had thus at any rate by implication been opened to discussion of an exchange of Mr. Brooke for the Krogers. Subsequently, the Russians had taken this up and had asked for clarification in terms of dates.[4] Mr. Brooke's current sentence would expire in April 1970, by which time the Krogers would have served nine years of their sentences, and might be considered for a remission of the remainder. We had accordingly proposed to the Soviet authorities that if they would release Mr. Brooke on or about 1st September, 1969, we should release the Krogers on or about 1st April, 1970. The Soviets had refused this on the grounds that the release date for the Krogers was too late and the gap between the two proposed releases too long. They had then proposed the release of Mr. Brooke on 1st July, 1969, and that of the Krogers on 1st October, 1969.

In his view there was a convincing case for accepting the Soviet offer. Humanitarian considerations, on which a decision to accept it would have primarily to be based, argued strongly in favour of acceptance: Mr. Brooke's health was bad. The Soviets seemed fully determined to bring him to trial again if we did not accept, and acceptance of the Soviet proposal offered in his judgement the only practical means of securing the release of Mr. Brooke and avoiding the genuine hardship—and the public outcry—which would result if Mr. Brooke were to receive a further sentence, as he almost certainly would if he were tried again. In view of the Press leakages which had occurred, it would be easy for the Soviets if we refused their offer to attribute the prolongation of Mr. Brooke's ordeal to British obduracy. Account had also to be taken of possible repercussions on Anglo-Soviet relations, though it would be inadvisable to make too much of them in our public presentation of the case. If the Soviet authorities retried Mr. Brooke for alleged violation of prison regulations and sentenced him to a further term of imprisonment or detention, we could not let this pass, and we might be forced to take retaliatory measures. These would have an adverse effect on Anglo-Soviet relations at a juncture when it was important for us to be able to play a full and effective part in the dialogue between East and West, for example in the context of the forthcoming discussions between the United States and the Soviet Union on strategic arms limitation;[5] of the North Atlantic Treaty Organisation's consideration of the Budapest Declaration by the Warsaw Pact Powers on European Security;[6] and of the Four-Power talks between the United States, the United Kingdom, France and the Soviet Union on the Arab-Israel problem.[7] In making his recommendation, he had taken full

[4] See No. 30, note 5.

[5] See No. 35, note 6 below.

[6] *Ibid.*, note 1.

[7] Cf. No. 27, note 7. Despite an exchange of American and Soviet proposals for a Middle East settlement between May and July the gap between the two sides was still wide, and the Four Power talks had gone into recess. Bilateral US-Soviet talks continued, however, and a paper submitted to Sir D. Greenhill on 3 July by Mr. G.G. Arthur, Assistant Under Secretary

account of the Home Secretary's earlier view that it would be difficult to explain to public opinion why the Krogers should be released before they had served a reasonable proportion of their sentence. He had also given careful consideration to the argument that in accepting the Soviet offer we might be held to be yielding to blackmail and presenting the Soviets with the opportunity of securing the release of any of their agents whom we might arrest in future, since they would in that event only have to arrest some innocuous British visitor to the Soviet Union, charge him with some trivial offence, and offer to trade the innocent against the genuinely guilty. But the 'hostage' technique was a well-established Soviet practice, and it was unlikely that the Soviets would abandon it, even if we held out over Mr. Brooke. Repugnant though it was to yield to pressures of this nature, both we and others—for example the United States in the case of the USS *Pueblo*[8] —had been forced for humanitarian reasons to do so. We had indeed kept the United States informed of developments in the present case, and they had indicated that they were content to leave us to judge how best to proceed.

The Foreign and Commonwealth Secretary added that if it were agreed in principle that he should seek an arrangement on the basis of the Soviet offer, he would attempt, as a makeweight, to secure agreement also on a number of subsidiary matters, for example, the detention of two British subjects on charges of drug smuggling and the grant of visas to two British subjects who wished to marry Soviet girls.

In conclusion, the Foreign and Commonwealth Secretary pointed out that if the decision to release Mr. Brooke and the Krogers on the lines proposed were taken and publicly announced, this might well lead to renewed pressure for the release of Mr. Anthony Grey, the British journalist at present held under house arrest by the Chinese authorities in Peking.[9] Here too, there was an element of exchange, in that it was now probable that Mr. Grey would be freed as soon as the Chinese journalists under detention in Hong Kong were released. The sentences imposed on the latter had been reduced so far as legal procedures permitted. The Chinese journalists would all be released in

superintending Arabian and Near Eastern Departments, concluded that the Two Power talks, with the US and Soviet Union acting in effect as lawyers on behalf of their clients, represented 'the best hope of progress towards a Middle East settlement'; although it was planned to resume the Four Power talks later in the year, HMG should 'not make proposals in the Four Power talks on the major issues in dispute until the probable outcome of the Two Power talks become clearer' (NE 3/548/1).

[8] On 22 January 1968 the US naval intelligence ship *Pueblo* had been seized by North Korean maritime forces: one crew member was killed, and the others mistreated during their captivity. Despite the sending of a nuclear-powered aircraft carrier and other warships to the area and a series of warnings by the US Government, the *Pueblo*'s surviving crew were not freed until 23 December when US General Woodward signed a document admitting that the ship had violated North Korean territorial waters, although he also made a public statement declaring the document was at variance with the facts. The *Pueblo* remained in North Korean hands.

[9] Mr. Grey, the Reuter's correspondent in Peking, had been held under house arrest since July 1967 in retaliation for the imprisonment of Communist Chinese journalists involved in riots in Hong Kong in that year.

September, with the exception of one who would be released early in October. The Governor, whose judgement in this matter had proved to be sound and should be accepted, was anxious, both for legal reasons and for reasons of security, not to bring the release date further forward, and it would be unfortunate if he were subjected to pressure which he would be bound to resist.

In discussion, it was pointed out that while full weight had to be given to humanitarian considerations and to Mr. Brooke's state of health, we should by agreeing to the Soviet proposal, be yielding to blackmail. If the Soviets could recover two valuable agents in exchange for a British subject who had committed no real offence they would score, and would be seen to have scored, a notable success. Moreover, an exchange of this kind would lay British visitors open to the sort of dangers to which the Foreign and Commonwealth Secretary had alluded. Another time, it might not be possible to justify an exchange on the ground that, as in the present case, the Soviet agents had already served a substantial part of their sentence. It was conceivable that the Soviet authorities, who must realise that the usefulness of the Krogers as agents was at an end, might, if we adopted a firmer attitude, be less adamant in insisting on the early return of the Krogers. With regard to the misgivings expressed by the Foreign and Commonwealth Secretary in the context of Anglo-Soviet relations, it was pointed out that in other instances, for example that of the Spanish campaign of harassment of Gibraltar, we had considered taking counter-action, but had been restrained from doing so by the danger of damaging broader political relations and worsening the position of those we were trying to help. Similar considerations might apply in this case. If the Krogers (who were Polish nationals)[10] were released after serving only part of their sentence, it might become necessary to consider the position of British subjects, for example Vassall and Miss Gee, who had been sentenced to long terms of imprisonment for similar offences. In this connection, it was pointed out that in recent years sentences in the British courts for offences involving espionage had tended to become heavier. It might also become necessary to review the position of those who had been given very long sentences for other offences, for instance those involved in the mail train robbery of 1963.[11]

On the other hand, support was expressed for the Foreign and Commonwealth Secretary's view that the 'hostage' technique was a well-established

[10] Mr. and Mrs Kroger had both been born in the US of immigrant, nationalised parents from Poland and the Ukraine. After a stay in Poland from 1950-54 the Krogers claimed that had adopted Polish nationality, a claim rejected by the US Government. While HMG agreed with the US Government that the Krogers' dominant nationality was American, the FCO considered that as nationality was not a key issue in the case it should not be allowed to stand in the way of arrangements for an exchange with Gerald Brooke which included allowing the Polish Consul to visit the Krogers; once the latter had been released, they would be free to go where they pleased.

[11] i.e. the 'Great Mail Robbery' of 8 August 1963, when the Glasgow-London mail train was ambushed by a gang who stole £2.5m.

Soviet device. It was unlikely that by standing out against it in this particular instance we should succeed in inducing the Soviets to abandon it. While there was force in the argument that the danger of the arrest of British visitors to the Soviet Union who were innocent or had committed offences which were trivial by Western standards might be increased, this could be met by warnings to intending visitors to the Soviet Union or by imposing restrictions on such visits. Though the Soviet insistence on the early release of the Krogers might be a bluff, such evidence as we had indicated the contrary, and that the Soviet authorities genuinely intended to bring Mr. Brooke to a fresh trial. If we had to engage in reprisals we should get the worst of both worlds, in that damage would be done to Anglo-Soviet relations at a crucial juncture without in any way advancing our prospects of securing Mr. Brooke's release. In view of what had become publicly known about our discussions with the Soviets it would be difficult to withdraw from the discussions or to counter the charges of British obduracy which might be made on the lines referred to by the Foreign and Commonwealth Secretary.

Further discussion turned on the means by which the Krogers should be released. It appeared, from recent reports of their state of health, that there was no basis for releasing them on medical grounds. Release on parole would not be appropriate since they would leave the country; and a free pardon would not be appropriate, nor, with its implications that they were not guilty of the offences of which they were convicted, would it be acceptable to public opinion. A recommendation that the remainder of the sentence be remitted by the exercise of the Royal prerogative might be the most suitable course.

THE PRIME MINISTER, summing up the discussion, said that, although there was clearly a division of opinion, the majority appeared to be in favour of proceeding on the lines advocated by the Foreign and Commonwealth Secretary and accepting the Soviet proposal. As regards the form of the Krogers' release, it was clearly desirable to avoid any implication that they had been wrongfully imprisoned. The Foreign and Commonwealth Secretary and the Home Secretary should agree on an appropriate procedure, and should also concert the terms of a statement in the House of Commons, which should not be made until Mr. Brooke had returned to this country.

The Cabinet:

(1) Took note with approval of the Prime Minister's summing up of their discussion.

(2) Invited the Foreign and Commonwealth Secretary and the Home Secretary to take the action indicated in the Prime Minister's summing up.[12]

[12] After further negotiations conducted through the Soviet Ambassador Mr. Brooke was released and returned to the UK on 24 July. For Mr. Stewart's statement in the House of Commons that afternoon, and the ensuing discussion, see *Parl. Debs., H. of C., 5th ser.*, vol. 787, cols. 2146-56. Mr. and Mrs. Kroger were released on 24 October and flew immediately to Poland.

Once a decision had been taken on Gerald Brooke and the issue ceased to cloud Anglo-Soviet relations, the focus of British policy turned towards a range of important East-West issues on which the Soviet Union seemed to be taking a more positive and cooperative stance, and on which HMG needed to formulate their response. These issues were indicated by Mr. Gromyko in an important speech to the Supreme Soviet on 10 July, which Sir D. Wilson described as a 'carefully constructed exposition of Soviet policy, building up to a very clear statement of Soviet preparedness for negotiations with the United States'.

In the first section of the speech, described as 'strikingly short', Mr. Gromyko restated the inalienable right of members of the Socialist community to ask for and provide mutual assistance in times of crisis (with 'special and favourable' mention of Soviet relations with Cuba and Czechoslovakia); the second section, dealing with areas of tension such as Vietnam and the Middle East, was 'remarkable for mildness of the accusations against the United States', and the third section, dealing with European questions, was again restrained. Soviet willingness to improve relations with West Germany was clearly expressed, with the rise of neo-Nazism accorded less attention than usual, and Mr. Gromyko put forward a proposal on Berlin: 'if his country's former war allies, who bear their share of responsibility for the position in West Berlin, were to approach the question of the city taking into account the interests of European security, they would discover on the part of the Soviet Union a readiness to exchange opinions with the object of eliminating now and forever complications around West Berlin', with the proviso that the Soviet Union would of course take no steps to infringe the interests of East Germany or the special status of West Berlin. On European security, Mr. Gromyko laid down no explicit pre-conditions for a conference, agreed on the need for careful preparation and commended the Finnish initiative (see No. 35, note 7 below) in proposing Helsinki as the site of the conference.

The fourth section of the speech was a strongly worded attack on China, and the fifth a 'lengthy and deliberately reasonable' section on disarmament which suggested possibilities for progress on SALT, nuclear testing and chemical warfare. This was followed by a short discussion on Asian security, leading to 'important and explicit remarks on bilateral US/Soviet relations', stating that 'a common language could be found, and the United States Government would find a willingness on the Soviet part to agree both bilateral questions and on as-yet-unsolved world problems'. In the concluding section, on Soviet bilateral relations with other countries, the development of Franco-Soviet relations was given a particularly warm welcome, while on Anglo-Soviet relations Sir D. Wilson commented that 'it was notable that Gromyko made no anti-British accusations. Against the background of bitter exchanges last winter, his declaration that the Soviet Union hoped to see our relations develop not only in the economic but also in other fields, and that the Soviet Union were ready for an appropriate exchange of opinions with the British Government, was not unhelpful.'

Sir T. Brimelow's reaction to Mr. Gromyko's speech was less optimistic than Sir D. Wilson's: he pointed out that 'one of Mr. Gromyko's functions is to make Soviet foreign policy seem more accommodating than it in fact is'. As the next group of documents shows, he favoured a cautious approach while giving the Soviet Union the opportunity to show how ready they were in practice to make progress on important East-West issues such as Berlin, European security and disarmament. At the same time, practical considerations, and the need to do business with the Russians on major political issues such as the Middle East and South East Asia, indicated a gradual and discreet return to the kind of bilateral relations maintained before the invasion of Czechoslovakia. In this context Sir D. Wilson's views on Soviet policy towards Western Europe (No. 36) were timely.

No. 35

Letter from Sir T. Brimelow to Sir D. Wilson (Moscow)

[WDW 1/2]

Confidential   FCO, *14 July 1969*

Dear Duncan,

European Security

In his letter to Bernard Burrows of 1 July, John Waterfield said that I would be replying in due course to your letter of 24 June with which you enclosed an interesting memorandum on European security.[1]

[1] In his memorandum Sir D. Wilson had argued that while he appreciated the difficulties inherent in the proposal for a European security conference, he thought that 'by restricting ourselves to an extremely logical, but rather formal, response we may run the risk of losing an opportunity for at least laying the foundation for some genuine future progress . . . give the impression to elements in Eastern Europe that are comparatively friendly to us that we are rigid and disinterested, and incidentally miss the chance (for what it is worth) of causing some genuine embarrassment to the Soviet Government'. He suggested a 'rather more active line' including encouraging the discussion of European security problems in both official and non-governmental fora, and a Ministerial statement re-endorsing the NATO *communiqué* (see pp. 129-30). In his covering letter to Sir T. Brimelow he expressed the view that 'by taking such limited measures as we can over the next few months, and adopting a position of greater sympathy towards the objects of the Budapest appeal, we would be able to prevent domestic criticism from gaining ground, and at the same time to serve some of our general foreign policy objectives.'

In his long letter to Sir B. Burrows, Mr. Waterfield, Head of Western Organisations Department, referred to the work undertaken by NATO's Senior Political Committee (see No. 31, note 11) and expressed the view that the Committee's report should cover the 'process of negotiation' just as much as the list of issues: 'Although Warsaw Pact propaganda for a security conference has so far exercised little influence on public opinion in Western Europe, we must be careful to ensure that our own position remains acceptable to British public opinion and to Parliament. For this we should not adopt too defensive an attitude. Indeed, we can point out that European security is essentially about the safeguarding of national liberties and independence of all countries in Europe and the creation of a peaceful climate in which these can thrive. This means that any eventual security settlement should include the necessary safeguards for all the nations of Europe, whether West or East, against external threats, invasion or occupation. There

2. We are quite willing to look at this whole question in depth and to consider whether we have been paying as much attention as we ought to the case for taking a more activist line on European security than we have so far regarded as likely to be in our interests. Your memorandum has done its job in stimulating us to thought and I should like to comment in this letter on the various pertinent points you raise. Others have commented in the same general sense, including Nicko Henderson during a recent visit to London.[2] I think it is true that some of HM Representatives in Eastern Europe feel generally that we are being a bit negative.[3]

3. I will not attempt to deal here with the timetable in NATO on which our present views are set out in Waterfield's letter to Burrows, except to add that there now seems a possibility that the Americans may aim for a discussion in NATO on the subject in September, to which they may send Mr. Richardson, Deputy Secretary of State. As you will see from Waterfield's letter, it is not we who have been hanging back in the NATO studies. Indeed we have been one of the most active contributors to the work which has been going forward in the senior Political Committee. Most delegations in NATO have seemed to want to handle this subject in slow tempo and pre-vacation inertia has now set in. Bernard Burrows has commented that although he will try to persuade his colleagues to focus their attention before the summer break on the programme for NATO studies on this subject between now and the end of the year, he is by no means confident that he will have much success in this. I think we must accept therefore that a further response from NATO is going to be a slow business, whether we like it or not, particularly because of the German attitude.

4. As regards the substance of the problem, I am sure you are right to distinguish between the real possibilities for progress (if any) and the need to show public opinion all over Europe that we are taking this subject seriously. Inevitably this is a field for a propaganda battle and it will not be enough for our policy to be right. It must look right as well. I am not sure though that I

should be opportunities for some propaganda advantage here. But, at the same time, we must not be mesmerised by the requirements of propaganda to the extent of putting forward half-baked proposals which we could live to regret if, contrary to present expectation, they were taken up by the other side' (WDW 1/7).

[2] At a meeting with Mr. Stewart on 2 July, Mr. Henderson said that the Polish Government found that 'when it came to discussion of the Budapest appeal for a conference on European security, we were not ready with any ideas'. He considered that a greater willingness to discuss political problems with Poland could improve trading relations: 'At present, we were losing ground in Poland by imposing a sort of intangible political ostracism on the Poles . . . we should not allow communications with Warsaw to be cut because of Soviet policy in Prague' (EN 2/6).

[3] In a minute of 27 June to Mr. Giffard Sir T. Brimelow commented: 'I am not sure that the Heads of Mission in Eastern European countries realise how little steam there is behind the idea of a European Security Conference on our side of the Iron Curtain. Things might change, but until things do change I think we can afford to let NATO continue its work on its present assumptions. What we need to do is simply to clear our ideas as to the line to take if public opinion in Western Europe does begin to change' (WDW 1/7).

accept the argument inherent in your memorandum and in some of the other comments we have been receiving from posts in Eastern Europe that our position is all that negative or difficult to defend. We have some pretty strong counter-arguments to deploy. We can point out that the East has never replied to the invitation given by NATO at Reykjavik in June, 1968, to discuss ways of achieving a system of mutual and balanced force reductions.[4] Indeed, the only Soviet response was to invade Czechoslovakia two months later. We can point to the work now going on in NATO and we can also emphasize the point, made clear in the last NATO Ministerial *Communiqué* at Washington, that NATO Governments will explore all appropriate openings for negotiations. The Warsaw Pact Governments have produced singularly few ideas about the subjects that might be discussed or the channels through which discussion could best be started. With the exception of Marko's talks with Harmel in May,[5] all our contacts with the other side have failed to elicit a single positive issue, even in the economic fields mentioned in the Budapest Declaration, on which the *bloc* countries have been brought to say positively that any practical agreements can be worked out. This should help to dispose of any suggestion that a conference on European Security is being delayed simply because NATO has not finished its home-work. Then, as you cogently argue in paragraph 11 of your memorandum, we could, if we so wished, carry the war into the opposite camp by stressing other problems bearing on European security and connected with limited sovereignty, non-interference and non-use of force. This means that European security should be regarded as essentially to do with the safeguarding of national liberties and independence of all countries in Europe against external threats, invasion, occupation or subversion. All these arguments are available to us here and now. Are they really so feeble?

5. But this is not enough, you may say. Of course the West has good arguments. It has had them for twenty years and they are stronger than ever since Czechoslovakia. But Europe is not a debating society. The main requirement is to show public opinion in both Western and Eastern Europe that we in the West really do want to achieve a European security settlement as a means of diminishing our enormous expenditure on armaments and of achieving a lasting climate in which we can confidently look forward to a peaceful future. It is not a question of showing that we have good arguments but of proving by positive action that the good intentions which we profess are meaningful. From this premise you may argue that our response so far, correct and rational though it has been, has not really convinced anybody that we treat the subject with the necessary sincerity and urgency.

6. I can see these arguments. But you must recognise that our Ministers are in something of a dilemma here. There are two tricky relationships

[4] See No. 21, note 9.

[5] The Czechoslovak Foreign Minister visited Belgium 27-29 May for talks with M. Harmel, in the course of which Mr. Marko set out a detailed list of issues for discussion at a security conference.

involved; the standing of the Government *vis-à-vis* public opinion here and our relationship with other Western European Governments and with the Americans. If we were to adopt the more forthcoming public posture suggested by the requirements of successful propaganda, is there not some danger that we should risk deceiving our own side? The more Ministers emphasize the importance we attach to reaching a European security settlement, the more difficult it becomes to establish the equally important point that a conference *now* would probably not be in our interests in that it could not hope to deal successfully with the major issues of European security, especially those relating to Germany. A conference that failed would lead to disillusion. It might also have the effect of weakening our own security. If we allow ourselves to become involved in competition with other NATO Governments in promoting *détente* policies, we could find ourselves, as no doubt the Soviet Union desires, eroding our own position piecemeal in advance, without obtaining any improvement in the Soviet position at all.

7. The truth is surely that a conference on European security is not a serious possibility in present circumstances and it would be irresponsible of us to pretend that it is. There is absolutely no sign of any compromise in the attitude adopted by the Soviet Union and East Germany towards the Federal Republic. It would be absurd to embark on a conference or even a pre-conference which we knew in advance would be bound to fail on this issue alone. There are of course certain points on which the West might eventually be prepared to compromise. One such is Germany's frontier with Poland, but the United Kingdom would be rash indeed to offer sacrifices on behalf of Germany until the Federal Government themselves were prepared to accept them; and we must surely have some understanding of the German argument that it would be foolish to offer concessions so long as the other side shows no signs of doing so.

8. More generally also it seems to me that there is a total lack of similarity between the Western and Eastern concept of European security. For the Russians, European security means upholding and guaranteeing the status quo in that part of Europe which they control. Our concept of security is that no state in Europe should be exposed to the risk of pressure or armed intervention from any other. The invasion of Czechoslovakia last August and the reactions to it in Western Europe showed how wide a gap remains between these two concepts of security.

9. Then again the arms control elements of a European security settlement would surely require a far greater degree of mutual confidence than exists at present in Europe. The Super Powers may well have a great deal in common and their similarity of interests, which has already helped to promote the signature of the Non-Proliferation Treaty, may have a helpful effect on, and be carried further by, the forthcoming Soviet-American SALT talks.[6] But

[6] Cf. No. 27, note 4. The start of the SALT talks continued to be deferred, and although both sides continued preparations for the talks, HMG had received little information about the US Government's detailed thinking on possible forms of agreement with the Russians.

the prospects for those talks cannot yet be assessed and it is too early to speculate on their probable effects on the climate of confidence in Europe. It is in Europe that the most intractable political differences lie and I should have thought that arms control measures in Europe were in present circumstances among the less promising measures under consideration in the disarmament field.

10. I deduce from all this that until there is a radical change in national attitudes, an early conference on European security is not something which we should really want. But even if a settlement did seem to be in sight, it would still be a very moot point, as you yourself point out, whether a large assembly of all the countries concerned, even if labelled a preliminary conference, was the most helpful and appropriate forum in which to achieve real progress. This is perhaps where the Finns have been unrealistic in their offer which seems to carry with it the connotation of a great conference of the old-fashioned sort.[7] If, during President Kekkonen's visit, we are given to understand that the Finns have something different in mind, we shall let you know.[8]

11. The best way of making progress both now and in the future is no doubt, as you yourself suggest, to think in less ambitious terms of quiet, patient bilateral contacts with the Soviet Union and the countries of Eastern Europe. As you point out, this is where the Eastern European states may have a particular part to play since many of them are anxious for a European security settlement which would reduce the political and military pressure to which they are now subjected by the Soviet Union. Such bilateral contacts can be useful and I have nothing against them provided that we do not expect too much from them or lead others to do so; and provided also that we do not give the impression of seeking to drive a wedge between the Soviet Union and her Warsaw Pact Allies which could have the very opposite of a stabilising effect on Europe generally. These bilateral contacts surely need no push from us. Monsieur Harmel will carry them as far as he can in Moscow[9] and President Nixon's visit to Rumania is bound to have some

[7] On 5 May President Kekkonen had offered Helsinki as a site for the European security conference. The offer was extended to all governments concerned with European security, including the US and Canada. After some inconclusive discussion in NATO it was left to individual governments to reply as they thought best in the light of the Washington *communiqué* (see pp. 129-30): HMG had told the Finnish Government that they had noted the offer and would bear it in mind.

[8] President Kekkonen visited the UK from 15-18 July. At a meeting with the Prime Minister on 17 July, the President explained that he believed preparatory talks should be held to see if there were any subjects on which agreement might be reached at a conference. Mr. Wilson replied that 'our strongly held views were the same' (WRM 3/548/5).

[9] M. Harmel paid an official visit to the Soviet Union from 23 to 26 July, and had talks with Mr. Kosygin and Mr. Gromyko. A joint *communiqué* issued at the end of the visit stated that the Soviet and Belgian Governments 'advocate the increase in contacts on a bilateral and multilateral basis for the purpose of bringing views closer together, of revealing possible questions for discussion and for actively promoting the preparations for [the] conference'.

effect.[10] We too have our bilateral contacts and we shall when appropriate take opportunities to probe the position of the other side. It may be that we should be rather more active here, particularly in our dealings with the Eastern Europeans. In the immediate aftermath of Czechoslovakia it was obviously right that we should be especially wary of provoking the Soviet Union into taking counter-measures which might only make the last state worse than the first. I think the time has now come to take a fresh look at the risks involved here, and this we shall now do.

12. The Soviet Union is in a different category; and here HMG are perhaps in rather a special position. I think the Soviet Embassy here may be telling the truth when they tell us, as they have done, that the Soviet leadership believed as a result of visits to Moscow by the Prime Minister and the then Secretary of State in 1967 and early 1968,[11] that HMG were prepared to join with them in an attempt to begin preparing for a conference. Now, the Embassy say, their Government is disappointed in our negative attitude. We can retort with justice that the change in our position, if indeed there is a change, has been caused by the invasion of Czechoslovakia. But we would certainly not want to rule out the possibility of probing the Soviet position further, provided, as I have said above, that this did not look like preparations for an imminent conference or preparatory meeting. After all, the Soviet line is still ambiguous even on the modalities. They say that it is for the European countries to decide on participation of other countries at a conference. This is far from accepting North American participation as of right from the very beginning. It may be that the Finnish invitations to the USA and Canada are intended to get round this problem without loss of face by the Russians; but the latter have not seized the opportunity of implying that they accept this. As regards the general Russian attitude, the Swedes told us during the Prime Minister's recent visit to Stockholm,[12] that they thought the Russians might now have little genuine interest in a conference, since they have succeeded in bringing their allies into line behind the Warsaw Pact declaration. The Swedish view is that after the dissensions caused by the invasion of Czechoslovakia, the primary concern of the Soviet Government was to find a theme on which unity could be re-established. This has been achieved in the form of the Budapest Appeal. The actual holding of a Conference may, the Swedes suspect, be secondary.

13. You will see from the foregoing that I accept a good deal, though not all, of the basic argument in your memorandum. I agree that we really want to divert attention away from the idea of a conference or any other form of huge collective meeting. We should concentrate, as you suggest, on fruitful

[10] President Nixon visited Rumania from 2-3 August at the end of a round-the-world tour beginning with his flight to the South Pacific on 23 July for the splashdown of Apollo XI, whose astronauts had been the first men to set foot upon the moon on 20 July. The President stopped off briefly in Britain on his way from Rumania to the US on 3 August, and had an informal but wide-ranging conversation with the Prime Minister at Mildenhall airfield.

[11] See Nos. 2 and 3.

[12] Mr. Wilson visited Sweden from 4-8 July for talks with European Socialist leaders.

contacts in all relevant fields including the appropriate technical and economic international bodies and the various possible forms of non-governmental activity. But in all this I think we had better proceed empirically and I am not sure whether in present circumstances Ministers would in fact want to come out openly with a statement of the objections to the conference type of procedure as suggested in your draft. This might stir up unnecessary controversy. At present there seems to be relatively little interest in this whole subject in Western Europe.

14. Indeed I doubt whether it would be right for us to ask Ministers here to review the policy until we see the outcome of the German elections and are beginning the detailed preparations for the NATO Ministerial Meeting in December. So much inevitably depends on the German attitude and we ourselves so badly need German support for our European policy that I am doubtful whether we should try to take positive decisions in the European security field until we know the complexion of the new German Government.

15. Meanwhile, I agree with what you say about non-Governmental seminars. The recent one in Bucharest seems to have done little if any harm, and it may have done a little good. We are certainly ready to consider positive action here. I also agree that we need not be too negative about the Group of Ten. I think we sometimes exaggerate the dangers of unwelcome initiatives coming out of the forum.[13]

16. It is true that we may seem to be waiting for something to happen—progress in SALT or in our European policy, the German elections, even the Vietnam talks; and I can understand the feeling that we ought to be taking initiatives in other fields while we wait. On the other side of the balance, I think we must bear in mind that part of the Soviet objective all the time is to hamper the future development of unity in Western Europe, to divide NATO and get the Americans out of Europe; to refurbish their peace-loving image after Czechoslovakia and to play on the German elections. I take your point that Soviet preoccupations with China may produce a moment of opportunity which could pass. But if we cannot move now, as I believe we cannot, I fully accept that we must seek to avoid giving a wholly negative impression to the Russians, as to opinion in the West, and in the United Nations, where we may be in for a debate this autumn on the Rumanian initiative, whether we like it or not. We should also be alert to the possibility that pressures for accommodation with the West arising from the Sino-Soviet dispute, may at any time lead the Russians to be genuinely more forthcoming on their side; but hitherto the Soviet leaders have given the impression that they can cope with the threat from China and that they are in no pressing need to reach an accommodation with the West.

[13] The Group of Ten was a sub-group of the UN, consisting of small European countries, including members of NATO, the Warsaw Pact and neutrals. The Rumanian Government wished the Group of Ten to co-sponsor an initiative at the UN General Assembly designed to produce a resolution suggesting that 1970 be proclaimed as a 'year of peace, action, security and co-operation in Europe', but their suggestion was received unenthusiastically in Europe.

17. Since the foregoing paragraphs were drafted, I have seen Helsinki telegram No. 215 of 11 July which suggests that, as a matter of tactics, it might be preferable to consider possible Western reactions to European security proposals in the context of the Finnish rather than the Warsaw Pact initiative.[14] Sir David Scott Fox suggests that the vagueness of the Finnish proposals gives us the opportunity of interpreting them in conformity with our own views. This is a good suggestion, but the need to carry it into effect will only arise when we reach the conclusion that the time has come to work for a Conference. In discussion with Koivisto[15] at Harpsund on 6 July, the Prime Minister said that it was for further consideration whether preparations for the Conference should be done multilaterally with Finland playing a leading role, or by further bilateral discussion. Until there was agreement on who should participate and a prospect of progress in Europe, there was probably not much point in seeking to hold a Conference. Koivisto spoke of Finland's willingness to undertake some preparations.

18. I am sending copies of this letter to HM Representatives at UKDEL, NATO, Bucharest, Sofia, Prague, Budapest, Warsaw, Belgrade, Helsinki, UK Mission to the United Nations, Geneva, UKDIS Geneva, Bonn, Washington, Paris, Brussels, The Hague and Rome.

Yours ever,

THOMAS BRIMELOW[16]

[14] See note 7. In telegram No. 215 HM Ambassador at Helsinki, Sir D. Scott Fox, expressed the view that if HMG 'were to respond specifically to the Budapest appeal and ignore the Finnish move, it would put the Finns' noses out of joint. More substantially, when the Communist countries themselves seem prepared to treat the Finnish *pour-mémoire* as the effective starting point for further consideration of this matter, it would surely be a step backwards from our point of view to do anything which might bring the discussions back to the original Warsaw Pact proposals, which are obviously more objectionable to us' (WDW 1/2).

[15] Mr. M.H. Koivisto was Prime Minister of Finland: cf. note 12.

[16] The various proposals for a conference on European security were discussed, together with policy towards Eastern Europe, at the Office meeting held by the Secretary of State on 21 July at which Sir D. Wilson was also present (see No. 31, note 12). In a letter of 28 July to Sir B. Burrows Sir T. Brimelow recorded the conclusions of the meeting, which included endorsement of active participation in the NATO study, although HMG should 'continue to do our own thinking on this subject and make sure that we were not missing any opportunities for making progress, in spite of the major procedural and substantive difficulties about holding a conference on European security at the present time. It was agreed that we should watch our own public presentation of our position on European security and try to make it as convincing and constructive as possible.' Meanwhile HMG would examine all proposals to 'try to work out whether we see any practical possibilities for progress'; the Secretary of State's view was that possible elements of a settlement might be a modus vivendi between the two Germanies, a settlement of frontiers in central Europe, some form of force reductions, stabilisation of the Berlin situation and some form of declaration of rights against infringements of national independence. Following the meeting Planning Staff were asked to prepare a paper answering two questions: to ascertain the premises on which progress on European security was possible; and whether HMG should take the lead in pursuing a more adventurous line on the issue. A draft of this long memorandum was sent to Moscow and other East European posts on 26 September. It concluded that 'given the rigid situation produced by Soviet intransigence, any new modus vivendi

between East and West is likely to be on the basis of implied, if not explicit, acceptance of the present Soviet sphere of influence', and that 'a situation substantially better than the present fluctuating modus vivendi between East and West may not be attainable on acceptable terms' (RS 11/10).

No. 36

Sir D. Wilson (Moscow) to Mr. Stewart (Received 18 July)
No. 2/46S [ENS 2/10]

Confidential   MOSCOW, *14 July 1969*

Summary... [1]

Sir,
The Soviet attitude to Western Europe
The departure of General de Gaulle from the Presidency of the French Republic[2] has created a new fluidity in the political relationships between the states of Western Europe, and this seems an appropriate moment to set down some reflections about the Soviet view of West European affairs, and the likely course of Soviet policy in coming months.

The importance of Europe
2. Perhaps the most helpful point of departure in a survey of this kind is to establish the priority of Western Europe in the minds of the Soviet leaders. I think there can be no doubt that this has changed considerably in recent years, and that Western Europe now figures less prominently amongst their preoccupations. In the early years of the Soviet state the industrialised countries of Europe constituted Lenin's main hope as a target of revolutionary expansion; in the 1930s these same states were intimately connected with the security of the Soviet Union; in the post-war years, Europe was the principal scene of confrontation with the United States. But the Soviet Government now has a number of quite different preoccupations, which arise from the Sino-Soviet quarrel[3] and a new phase of the super-power relationship with the United States. These involve the main subjects of Soviet anxiety: the national safety of the Soviet state and the integrity of its frontiers; the quantity of economic resources needed for defence, and thus by subtraction the volume of resources available for economic advance; and the future leadership of the communist movement. The last consideration also involves the Russians in the need for action in a further non-European area, in order to counter Chinese influence by party and diplomatic activity in Asia, Africa and Latin America.

[1] Not here printed.   [2] See No. 31, note 3.
[3] Cf. Nos. 27, note 1, and 31, notes 7 and 9.

3. An additional general factor which is important to the USSR is the differential time-scale operating between European developments and those arising from the new relationships with China and the USA. To us the economic and political integration of Western Europe may appear a very slow process at best. To the Russians it may look different. They evidently reckon that their troubles with China are likely to continue for many years, and the ultimate possibilities of the super-power relationship with America can probably not be gauged for some time to come. By contrast the movement towards greater unity in Western Europe could acquire a sudden momentum, and produce important results, within a relatively short period—the consequence of like talking to like, confident of agreement, urgently wishing it. The process could have important results for the Soviet Union, but is likely to be seen against the background of their more lasting preoccupations with China and the USA.

4. It can I think be accepted from the foregoing that Europe is less the centre of attraction to the USSR than before. The addition of new dimensions of the Soviet view of the world has brought about many important consequential changes—some transfer of Soviet military strength to the East, a redirection of Soviet political effort toward East and South East Asia designed to contain China and deny her a sphere of influence, and special interest in the Middle East as a potential area of confrontation with the USA. The European scenery, while still an integral part of the Soviet view of the world, is thus a smaller portion of the whole. Nevertheless, in this new context, European questions retain much interest and importance for the Soviet Government.

General aims in Europe

5. The most important Soviet interests in Europe might be tabulated as follows:

(*a*) To protect the vulnerable East European states from potentially disruptive cultural and other influences emanating from Western Europe and the United States. This is a defensive process against hostile external ideology, and involves discouraging the East Europeans from building up any close connexions with the West.

(*b*) To defuse political relations with the West and to avoid any deliberate cold war confrontation (e.g. by East Germany over Berlin), so as to avoid involving the USSR in crisis on two fronts, or increasing the likelihood that Western Europe would be actively hostile in the event of major Soviet trouble with China.

(*c*) To carry on commercial and other exchanges with a strict eye to their benefit to the USSR, both in economic terms and as a source of technology to the USSR (this does not mean that both sides will not benefit).

(*d*) To prepare the way for the ultimate advance of communism amongst the industrialised countries. This involves continuing to undermine the institutions of the West, including NATO, and to discredit the capitalist way of life in Europe.

Particular aims of Soviet policy

6. The current line being followed by the USSR on *European security* is a useful method of carrying out the first two general objectives above. By establishing more definitely the existing line of division in Europe, the Soviet Union would generally stabilise its European position. This would contribute to military security, since any agreed or unilateral military reductions which followed would allow the USSR to diminish the number of its forces stationed in Europe, thus saving money and manpower now needed further East. In strictly military terms the USSR has in fact no particular reason for feeling insecure in Europe at the present time. The strengthening of NATO forces which occurred after the Czechoslovak crisis was unwelcome but still leaves a preponderance of Soviet military power in central Europe. Moreover, the successive crises in central Europe in 1956 and 1968 have occurred without any threat of NATO intervention, or even serious discussion of that possibility: the cumulative effect of this experience must be to make the Soviet leaders feel that they have no reason to fear Western military intervention in such difficulties, whatever the West may find it necessary to say publicly on this score. Probably, the Soviet leaders calculate that if they felt bound to undertake military intervention in Rumania, there would not be any military counter-move by NATO, though they may well feel less confident of the result if Yugoslavia were also involved. The case which appears most likely to involve actual danger of a military confrontation would be a major crisis over Berlin (the Russians might not be able in all circumstances to restrain the East Germans).

7. But it is not, I suggest, the possible military dangers which have led the Soviet Government to put forward the proposals for European security contained in the Budapest Appeal. The main point for the Soviet Union is political. There would be something like formal recognition by the Western countries of Soviet rights to exclusivity within their own sphere of influence. Western recognition of the limits of the existing communist advance would be a useful political gain. The Appeal policy has incidental advantages, in providing a pacific dress for post-Czech policies, and holding out to the East European states the possibility of direct conversations with the Western countries in which they could play a real part in discussing their own destiny. Moreover, if the Chinese problem were to become suddenly more acute, the Appeal could be handled more flexibly and urgently so as to give the USSR more chance of benefiting from a settled situation at the western end of her sphere of influence.

8. A further more specific objective of Soviet European policy will be to protect any of its own interests which may be threatened by the movement for a *united Europe*. An enlarged and successful Community would present numerous real disadvantages to the Soviet Union. There is the purely tactical consideration that the Community's larger unity of view in political and commercial affairs would make it more difficult to play off countries against each other. The emergence of supra-national institutions might perhaps jeopardise the political possibilities of individual communist parties. The

Russians must also fear that the orthodox autarkic line followed by the EEC in economic affairs will be continued by an enlarged body; the detrimental effect on Soviet economic interests would be enhanced if the creation of a larger homogeneous unit were to exercise a magnetic attraction on countries like Sweden and Finland. Moreover, the greater prosperity of a successfully united Europe would make it still more difficult for the Soviet Union to achieve its historical ambition of surpassing the levels of production and prosperity in Western Europe. The possibility that all this may happen within a relatively short period of time must give the Russians some food for thought.

9. The European development which causes the Soviet Government even more concern is the possibility that a separate *European nuclear force* may emerge. Any tendency towards an independent European nuclear force is likely to be vigorously opposed by the USSR as definitely inimical to Soviet security interests. The prime reason for Soviet opposition to such a development is the deeply felt suspicion about the role which Germany would play.[4] The more Germany can be kept out of nuclear matters, the safer the Soviet Union will feel. The Russian view is that, on the basis of historical experience, a situation must be avoided in which Germany has any voice in the control over nuclear weapons, or could reach independent control merely by tearing up international agreements. Whatever the formal position of the Federal German Government in relation to a European nuclear force, the Russians think that it must be stronger than the present position of the Federal Republic in connexion with the mainly American NATO force. Since a number of nations are known to share the Soviet views about German participation in nuclear weaponry and strategy, this is also a good point to be stressed by the Soviet propagandists.

10. It is of course possible that in the longer term the Soviet Union might take a different view on the whole European question. It would in theory be possible for the USSR to welcome the creation of a genuinely independent Europe, since this could pave the way for the ultimate separation of North America from the European states, for so long the goal of Soviet Governments. But this separation would be dearly bought from the Soviet angle if it involved the creation of a new Western European unit, at the very least strongly influenced by the Federal Republic, and with nuclear weapons at its disposal. Nor would the Russians overlook the powerful position of US capital and business within the community.

11. These nightmares about possible future trends in European politics must make the current threat posed by the 'aggressive designs' of NATO[5] almost innocuous by comparison. Even Soviet strategists themselves may conclude that it does not represent any serious menace to the communist states. These

[4] In conversation with Lord Chalfont on 18 June Mr. Smirnovsky said it was 'very disturbing' to the Soviet Union that HMG were prepared 'even to discuss with the Federal Republic contingencies in which nuclear weapons might be used'. Lord Chalfont assured him that 'we had no interest in lowering the nuclear threshold but that we had a perfect right within NATO to coordinate our security effectively' (ENS 3/2).

[5] Cf. No. 25, notes 3 and 4.

strategists would naturally feel even safer if it did not exist at all, provided it was not replaced by a smaller tighter and German-led European group. But NATO is to some extent a ritual target. Any fragmentation which might occur within the Alliance, for example by the withdrawal of individual members, would be a useful bonus, but only if they did not lead towards the much-feared alternative. Attacks on the organisation are thus probably either the result of habit, or designed to serve a strictly limited purpose.

12. If the Soviet Government have some nightmares about developments in Western Europe, some of their other dreams may be very rosy. The picture represented to the Russian reader by Soviet propaganda is of Western European countries in which anti-American and pro-Soviet feeling is growing; where the organised workers are striking more and more often and with more and more effect against the capitalist system and NATO war policies; and where 'student power' creates an atmosphere of anarchic protest from which the Communist Parties of the West could profit. This is, of course, propaganda, and known by responsible Soviet leaders to be such. But they may believe it to some extent, and to the same extent be encouraged to play a waiting game, in the hope that 'social forces' (duly encouraged by Soviet help) will shake some ripe fruit into their ready hands.

Soviet attitude to individual countries

13. It is within this policy framework that the Soviet attitude to the individual countries of Western Europe should be considered. As I suggested in paragraph 7 of my despatch of the 2nd of January,[6] the *Federal Republic of Germany* is becoming increasingly the most important state in Western Europe for the USSR. There is little doubt that the Soviet authorities are concerned about the industrial and financial power now at the disposal of the Federal Republic. Moscow also probably realises that Germany could make a more relevant contribution to Soviet industrial development than any other European state. Theoretically, one way of harnessing West German industrial and financial power to Soviet economic needs would be a Rapallo-type bilateral pact between the USSR and the FRG.[7] But in practice, it is hard to see such a pact being concluded in the foreseeable future, even with the 30th anniversary of the Ribbentrop-Molotov pact approaching. From the Soviet point of view alone, there are many obstacles. Perhaps the most superable of them is current Soviet propaganda, which represents the Federal Republic as the apotheosis of the anti-state, and Herr Strauss[8] as the archetypal German gorilla. There are greater difficulties than this. It is hard to see how any genuine reconciliation could take place without some further Soviet undertaking over Berlin, which would be most unwelcome to the DDR.[9] No doubt

[6] See No. 25, note 8.

[7] On the Treaty of Rapallo signed by Germany and Russia in 1922 see *DBFP*, Series I, Volume XIX, No. 75.

[8] Herr F.J. Strauss, Minister of Finance in the FRG.

[9] Discussions had been proceeding for some months within the Bonn Group (representing the FRG and the three Occupying Powers) on a possible approach to the Soviet Government on Berlin and intra-German traffic and communications. In a minute of 17 July, Mr. Mallaby

other Eastern European Governments would toe the line, but they would surely be deeply outraged, particularly the Poles. Nor should one under-estimate the depth of popular feeling in the USSR. Khrushchev's attempt to mend fences with Bonn was widely regarded as premature, as well as being one of the more immediate causes of his fall from power. The present Soviet attitude towards Bonn is very cautious, and this is reflected in the leisurely tempo of their exchanges with Bonn about a declaration prohibiting the use of force.[10]

14. I would not say that there are no circumstances in which the USSR would contemplate a political bargain with the Federal Republic: they might be tempted to consider such an arrangement if, for example, the United States were to leave Europe, and no enlarged Western European unit had at that time been formed. But even in such an eventuality, which for the present there seems no reason to expect, they might prefer a waiting game; and for the time being current Soviet attitudes to the Federal Republic are likely to continue.

15. The policies of the new Government of *France* will no doubt be watched with much interest in Moscow. The disappearance of General de Gaulle, who played such a considerable role as an *enfant terrible* in the Alliance, is regrettable from the Soviet point of view; they may hope that France still has possibilities in this respect. The greatest bonus of de Gaulle was his disruptive influence within the Alliance. The Kremlin must be rather disappointed that

commented that Mr. Gromyko's remarks on Berlin in his speech of 10 July (see pp. 170-1) seemed 'designed to encourage the western powers to approach the Soviet Union about Berlin'. The British, French and US Governments made separate *démarches* on similar lines to the Soviet Government on 6 (French) and 7 (British and US) August, calling attention to the FRG's desire to remove points of friction with the GDR, and to discuss problems concerning railroad matters, inland waterways, post and telecommunications. With reference to Mr. Gromyko's remarks, the Allied Powers and the FRG would welcome Soviet moves to improve access to Berlin and contribute to the prevention of crises. The FRG might also be willing to make 'certain compromises' with respect to federal activities in Berlin 'if the Soviets and the East Germans were to show a constructive attitude towards problems arising from the division of the city and from the discriminatory treatment of the economy of the Western sectors of Berlin'.

The Soviet reply to the British *démarche* was given to Sir D. Wilson on 12 September, and similar replies were made to the French and US Governments. The replies reaffirmed the Soviet Government's readiness to exchange opinions on West Berlin, taking into consideration the 'sovereign rights and legal interests' of the GDR, and stated that the 'constructive position' of the Soviet Union, GDR and their allies on relations between the GDR and FRG was widely known. The questions raised by the Allies should be the subject of 'continuing exchanges conducted through normal diplomatic channels'. The Soviet replies were studied by the Allies, who agreed that no follow-up could be considered until after the West German elections on 28 September.

[10] Discussions between the West German and Soviet Governments on a declaration renouncing the use of force had begun in 1966, and after a breakdown in 1968 following a Soviet *aide-mémoire* reaffirming that Articles 53 and 107 of the UN Charter (the 'Enemy States' clauses: cf. No. 24, note 10) gave the Soviet Union the unilateral right to intervene in the affairs of the FRG, had resumed in April 1969. On 3 July the FRG's Ambassador in Moscow, Herr Allardt, had presented draft texts of a declaration, and the Soviet reply proposing discussions in Moscow led to the opening of talks on 8 December 1969.

the commercial awards doled out to France during the de Gaulle epoch did not produce more anti-American gestures by other members of NATO; these might still come, but not in the wake of the Gaullist wave. The drawback to the Franco-Soviet bilateral arrangements is that France cannot provide the necessary access to modern technology to develop a really striking bilateral commercial relationship. Perhaps the most productive moment of the Franco-Soviet dual alliance has passed.

16. The mirage of a communist *Italy*, which has for so long tantalised the watchers from the Kremlin, is again looking more substantial with the possibility that after its years in the wilderness the P[*artito*] C[*ommunista*] I[*taliano*] may at last be nearing its ultimate goal of participation in the Italian Government. If this goal should be achieved some further policy problems will arise, notably the choice between a respectable parliamentary role for the party in the immediate future, or an early *coup d'état* on the model of Czechoslovakia 1948. This and other choices would be much complicated in Soviet eyes by the current independence of the leaders of the Italian party. Participation in the Government by the PCI would be a major landmark for communism in Western Europe, but it is a prospect which the Soviet leaders must face with mixed feelings, bearing in mind the examples of Yugoslavia and Rumania, and in the knowledge that the performance of the other communist parties in Western Europe would be greatly influenced by the Italian example.

17. It remains to consider how *Britain* fits in the Soviet picture. The British are, I think, of continuing interest in Moscow because of our strategic position on the Atlantic/European hinge. If Britain were to become primarily a European power, she would be less interesting to the Soviet Union (her entry to the European Community, as a solid contributor to a real European unit, would probably be unwelcome to the Soviet Government for reasons already given). Britain should perhaps in logic no longer occupy a central place in Soviet political calculations; but it seems to me that our position may well be more important than the strength of our economic base and military power currently justifies. This is in part a relic of earlier historical attitudes (as in the case of Germany): since the British Empire was the main imperialist enemy of the USSR in the 1920s and 1930s, we probably still appear rather larger than life. It is also possible that the imperial British past may have some points of contact with the emerging Soviet policy in Asia: they may attach some importance to our residual role in South East Asia, as a possible help in containment of China, on which the USSR seems about to embark. Moreover, there is some hope for the Soviet Government, as well as for others, in the traditional independence of British political attitudes (the effect of Mr. Macmillan's visit to Moscow on other European countries is still remembered).[11] There may be a feeling that the possibilities of using Britain as a rogue elephant within the Western alliance are not yet exhausted; and, if

[11] An account of Prime Minister Harold Macmillan's visit to Moscow in February 1959 is given in Alistair Horne, *Macmillan 1957-1986* (London, 1989), pp. 120-33.

need arose, there may be hopes of working through British influence to restrain a resurgent Western Germany (the two possibilities may of course merge into one). Meanwhile in the bilateral field, there is no doubt that the Soviet authorities see much that is useful and profitable in our commercial and technological exchanges, as we do ourselves.

18. We shall learn more of the Soviet attitude to individual political problems as 1969, which has been such an eventful year in Europe, draws to a close, after the elections in Germany.[12] For the present, I would summarise my conclusions about the Soviet attitude as follows:

(*a*) The Soviet leaders are probably not too unhappy with the present state of Western Europe, including European links with the United States, which may, in their view, serve to lessen the role of the Federal Republic and to control the course of its future development.

(*b*) They attach real importance to their economic relations with the Western European countries, which are growing and proving useful in the development of the USSR.

(*c*) Their main fear is the possible emergence of a Europe united in economics, politics and defence, in which the Federal Republic is closely associated with nuclear developments, and the United States less in control.

(*d*) But it is doubtful if this appears an immediate danger at present. It is more probable that the political analysts in the Kremlin, just as we are forecasting the ideological problems of the USSR (my despatch of the 8th of July),[13] are prophesying the decay of western society, as exemplified in student unrest and industrial strikes. These same analyses may be portraying hopeful pictures of the possibilities open to Soviet political activity in Western Europe, and pointing to Italy.

(*e*) Meanwhile their main political interests are defensive: to prevent the infection of Eastern Europe; and to avoid crises in Europe which would distract their attention and resources from other parts of the world scene, where they are confronted by the Chinese, or want to counter Chinese influence.

(*f*) Their main effort is thus to consolidate the status quo.

(*g*) The prospect of a diplomatic rapprochement with the Federal Republic on Rapallo lines is remote for the time being, but could not be excluded in certain apparently remote circumstances.

19. Since the above was drafted, my conclusions have been (I think) broadly confirmed by a major speech by Mr. Gromyko, of the 10th of July, to the Supreme Soviet in Moscow.[14] I hope to write elsewhere more fully about

---

[12] In the federal election on 28 September the Christian Democratic Union (CDU) polled 46.1% of the votes, followed by the Social Democratic Party (SPD) with 42.7%, but the Free Democratic Party (FDP, 5.8%) joined the SPD to form a coalition government. Herr Willy Brandt was elected Chancellor by a majority of 3 votes in the *Bundestag* on 21 October: Herr Walter Scheel (FDP) was appointed Vice Chancellor and Foreign Minister.

[13] Not printed.

[14] See pp. 170-1.

the lessons for British policy which can be deduced from the general picture thus presented. There is certainly nothing here to discourage us from continuing our efforts to build up a solid community in Western Europe, while continuing the attempt to calm any legitimate Soviet fears (for example, about the centrifuge)[15] about the extent to which Western European policies will be determined by the 'revanchists'. So far as concerns bilateral relations, now that the effects of the Czechoslovak crisis are beginning to wear off, most of our allies are re-establishing their bilateral relations in much the same way as the British Government. This suits the Soviet Government in pursuit of the general objectives which I have outlined, and it is not, for that reason, against our own common interests.

20. I am sending copies of this despatch to Her Majesty's Representatives at Paris, Bonn, Washington, Berlin, Prague, Warsaw, Bucharest, Budapest, Belgrade, Sofia, Brussels, The Hague, Helsinki, to the United Kingdom Delegation to NATO, to the United Kingdom Delegation to the European Communities, and to the United Kingdom Disarmament Delegation, Geneva.[16]

I have, etc.,

DUNCAN WILSON

[15] Cf. No. 24, note 2.

[16] Mr. Giffard submitted this 'important and timely' despatch to Sir T. Brimelow on 6 August, commenting that its 'penetrating and comprehensive, but concise, analysis . . . will be of the greatest value in our study of matters connected with European security'. Sir T. Brimelow commented on 19 August: 'I agree with Mr. Giffard's comments. As regards the containment of China in South East Asia, my impression is that the Russians regard the North Vietnamese as the nation best qualified for this task. 2. As regards Western Europe, the Russians have hitherto proved inept at exercising influence. But as their power & experience grows, they may improve their performance.'

During the next three months the matters discussed at the Secretary of State's meeting on 21 July—European security and general policy towards the Soviet Union and Eastern Europe—remained under consideration within the FCO. There were, however, no significant developments on either front in relation to contacts with the Soviet Union. During his visit to New York and Canada Mr. Stewart assured Mr. Gromyko at their meeting on 20 September that HMG were not negative towards the idea of a European security conference, but re-emphasised the need for adequate preparation and reaffirmed that the US and Canada must attend. During his trip Mr. Stewart also emphasised to his NATO colleagues the importance of producing at the December Ministerial meeting practical proposals which would 'give some reality to the proposed conference'.

On a bilateral level Anglo-Soviet relations during this period were businesslike if not warm. By the end of October Sir D. Wilson felt that it was time to make a renewed effort towards a 'more active kind of political dialogue with the Russians' if there were to be any hope of producing a 'fresh relationship' (No. 37). The Ambassador's visit to the joint Anglo-Soviet 'Polyspinners' plant at Mogilev, recounted in No. 38, provides an insight into the difficulties—and advantages—of bilateral cooperation at ground level.

No. 37

Letter from Sir D. Wilson (Moscow) to Sir D. Greenhill
[*ENS 3/2*]

Personal. Confidential   MOSCOW, *29 October 1969*

Dear Denis,

The return of the Krogers[1] marks the end of a difficult chapter in Anglo-Soviet relations. By removing the largest bilateral restraint on the development of these relations, it enables us to concentrate our efforts on carrying out the Secretary of State's directive that we should restore them to the position which existed before Czechoslovakia (paragraph 2 (a) of the record of the Secretary of State's office meeting of 21 July).[2]

2. In the special situation of the past twelve months or so we have avoided cultivating the Soviet Government except on essential business. If we are now to evolve what will in effect be a fresh relationship between the United Kingdom and the Soviet Union, we must begin the more active kind of political dialogue with the Soviet Government that it is logical for a Mission to a Super Power (rather than an outpost of Kremlinological studies) to conduct. There is also the important point that, if the Prime Minister's visit[3] is to be successful, it will need careful preparation by the resumption of more active dialogue at official level.

3. I don't of course mean that we should talk for the sake of talking, or that we should start talking to the Russians here on all fronts of policy at once. I would however welcome your thoughts on the best subjects for discussion in the light of the Prime Minister's projected visit. When Robin Edmonds[4] talked to Teddy Youde early in September, Youde said that two subjects which were in the forefront of the Prime Minister's mind were European security and SALT. They are also in mine, although I doubt if there is much that I could usefully say to the Soviet Government about the latter at present.[5] The Middle East (on which telegrams from Washington, New York and the Department keep us well briefed) seems a good candidate, at least as soon as talks move from the bipartite to the quadripartite stage;[6] but we don't

---

[1] See No. 34, note 11.

[2] See No. 31, note 12.

[3] Following Mr. Kosygin's invitation to Mr. Wilson extended during his talk with Mr. Benn on 14 May (see No. 32, note 6), discussion had taken place in the FCO on possible dates and an agenda for such a visit. However, the proposal did not come to fruition before the General Election in 1970.

[4] Mr. Edmonds had succeeded Mr. Dalton as HM Minister in Moscow in September 1969.

[5] Cf. No. 35, note 6. The British and US Governments had been engaged in bilateral talks on technical and political issues relating to the SALT talks, which were now due to begin in Helsinki on 17 November.

[6] Cf. No. 34, note 7. The US and Soviet Governments had continued their dialogue, although the intensification of hostilities around the Suez Canal and the burning of the Al Aqsa mosque

want to cross wires with New York. What about Vietnam?[7] On this, I should find it hard to begin any kind of dialogue without knowing a good deal more about the situation on the spot and—perhaps more important—in Washington than I do at present. So far as the Washington end is concerned, we depend largely on the *New York Times*, supplemented by close contact with the United States Embassy. Other possibilities are UN affairs (the Soviet initiative, etc.) and disarmament.[8]

4. I also wonder whether you might think it advisable to summon me to London for a brief visit before the Prime Minister comes here. As you know, I have found my trips to England extremely useful; and as power becomes more and more polarised between Washington and Moscow, I believe that it will become increasingly important for the Ambassador here to be kept informed as closely as possible of what is going on behind the scenes both in London and in Washington. If it were possible for me to time one of my visits to coincide with a visit by John Freeman, I should welcome this warmly.

Yours ever,
A.D. WILSON[9]

in Jerusalem by a Christian fanatic on 21 August (leading to Islamic and Arab summit meetings in Rabat in September and December) complicated the task of peacemaking. New American proposals made on 28 October, which were substantially more attractive to the Arab states, were nevertheless rejected by both the UAR and Israel, and the Soviet reply in December made it clear that they were not willing to regard the US proposal as a joint working paper. This reply effectively ended the bilateral dialogue and transferred negotiations to the Four Power talks which resumed in December 1969.

[7] HMG had had little involvement with matters relating to the Vietnam conflict during 1969. As an FCO brief pointed out, although the US continued to value HMG's public support, once they had established direct contact with the North Vietnamese in Paris (see No. 9), and had established better working relations with the Russians, other allies, particularly co-belligerents, were considered to have a greater direct interest than the UK in the negotiations.

During the autumn of 1969 the US Government exerted diplomatic pressure on both the North Vietnamese and Soviet Governments to reach a settlement, imposing a deadline of 1 November for a 'serious breakthrough', otherwise 'measures of great consequence and force' would follow (see *The Memoirs of Richard Nixon, op. cit.*, pp. 392-400). As part of this pressure the US Government asked HMG, following President Nixon's speech of 3 November on 'Vietnamization' (*ibid.*, pp. 406-12), to approach the Soviet Government asking them to urge the North Vietnamese to enter serious negotiations. Sir D. Wilson delivered a message to this effect on 14 November from the Prime Minister to Mr. Kosygin, who replied that 'the Russians were doing all they could, but that an end to the war depended not on them but on the Americans' (FAV 2/1/11).

[8] In a letter and in a speech to the UN General Assembly on 19 September Mr. Gromyko requested the inclusion in the UNGA agenda of a declaration on strengthening international security, whereby UN members would affirm their adherence to the principles of the Charter. Attached to the letter was a draft 'Appeal to all States of the World' on the strengthening of international security, which was considered together with draft resolutions by the First Committee. The UNGA adopted a resolution on 16 December 1969 inviting the views of member states and placing the item on the agenda for the 25th Session in 1970; a 'Declaration on the Strengthening of International Security' was adopted by the UNGA on 16 December 1970.

[9] Mr. Freeman was HM Ambassador in Washington. Replying to Sir D. Wilson on 4 November, Sir D. Greenhill said that the FCO had the idea of opening up a more active political dialogue with the Russians 'very much in mind', but made no concrete suggestions: 'there

is quite a lot cooking, even if we cannot yet give you much to get your teeth into'. On 19 November, Lord Bridges (the Hon. T.E. Bridges succeeded his father as Baron Bridges in August 1969) wrote in similar vein to Mr. Giffard, including a list of subjects on which a useful dialogue with the Soviet Foreign Ministry might be opened: Nigeria, Asian security, disarmament and the Mediterranean were on the list. In his reply of 25 November Mr. Giffard admitted that he was sceptical of the prospect of a useful dialogue: ' . . . these are all areas of policy where the Soviet Union is or has been the outsider and where she is now aspiring to be an insider . . . It may only assist hostile Soviet designs if, by taking the initiative ourselves to raise these questions with the Russians, we encourage the latter to press harder for a greater standing in them.'

No. 38

Sir D. Wilson (Moscow) to Mr. Stewart

No. 22/6 ES [ENS 6/17]

Confidential   MOSCOW, *2 December 1969*

Summary . . .[1]

Sir,

Visit to joint Anglo-Soviet 'Polyspinners' plant at Mogilev

From 17 to 19 November I paid a brief visit to the plant for the production of artificial fibres which is being erected at Mogilev by the British 'Polyspinners' combine. It may be worth recording some impressions derived from this visit, first of the problems of Soviet industrial construction in what is virtually a new town; and secondly of the more particular problems of cooperation between British and Soviet technicians on the Mogilev project. Both sets of problems are typical, the latter of a pattern which may be of great importance in the future of Anglo-Soviet commercial and technical relations.

2. First, some words about the setting. Mogilev, the seat of Tsar Nicholas II's headquarters during the First World War (and apart from that a name of ill omen, too reminiscent of the world 'mogila' or grave), lies west of Moscow, on the stripling Dnieper, three-quarters of the way towards Minsk. It was occupied by the Germans for some two and a half years during World War II, and emerged heavily scarred, with a much reduced population of about 100,000 (a large number of the inhabitants had been Jews). During this time Mogilev gained a metalled road to the nearest railway junction, Orsha, built under German supervision. This remains the city's principal means of communication. Now it has been largely reconstructed (though a surprising number of 19th and early 20th century buildings remain in the citadel district above the Dnieper), and there is a large new district on the other side of the river. There are over 200,000 inhabitants. Communal services are badly overstretched; there are frequent water shortages and power cuts. Accommodation in the new town takes the form of large barrack-like blocks of flats. Roads are apt to dissolve in a quagmire of mud. There is only one large

[1] Not here printed.

universal store for the whole town, though not only the Russians, who took us on a tour of the town, but also some of the British technicians, who had been in the Soviet Union before, say that it is far better stocked with consumer goods (textiles etc.) than they would have thought possible ten years ago. Virtually the only entertainment in the town, even for Russians, is the cinema; but, typically of this country, there is a fine secondary school of music (which I was allowed to visit). Mogilev in fact is a typical new boom town, with perhaps rather more ancient foundation than usual in the USSR as a whole.

3. The artificial fibre factory, on the construction of which Polyspinners are collaborating with the Russians, is a huge complex about three kilometres outside the new town of Mogilev. The site of the finished buildings will occupy some 700 acres. The largest of the workshops under construction (to house the production of filament yarn) is in itself not much under half a mile in length. Perhaps the most impressive indication of size is the store shed, which at present houses over 2,000 crates of machinery, many of them of enormous size. The shed (of Russian design) took far too long to complete, but it is most impressive as it stands, with a system of overhead cranes to move the heavy cases. The total labour force now employed is about seven thousand; in the completed factory it will be between eleven and thirteen thousand (the latter is the present estimate of the Russian director, Mr. Beliavski). He also told me that it would supply some 12 per cent of the Soviet Union's needs for artificial fibres (British estimates are that the figure will probably be nearer 25 per cent). These random data are included as a rough indication of the scale of the enterprise.

4. Something should also be said of general working conditions at the site. At present only the pilot plant (put into operation just over a year ago) is in production. The main work is on construction of workshops and installation of machinery. Much of the building is done by local prison labour (particularly the construction of the enormous shed for filament yarn production, which is protected by a double barbed-wire fence). Incidentally the Polyspinners team, though not at all shocked by the use of prisoners (who appear cheerful enough), are understandably frightened by the possibility of suggestions in British newspapers that they are relying on and helping to maintain a system of slave labour. Communication between the various parts of the site are complicated, particularly in spring and autumn (as we found by personal experience) by the universal mud. 'This looks like my idea of Passchendaele', the British administrative manager remarked, as we made our way, with many skids and false starts up impassable lanes, from the office block to the store shed. His Russian counterpart comforted him by suggesting that soon 'Russia's best civil engineer', the winter (the 'Russian Macadam' was Pushkin's term), would have got to work. Luckily the soil is sandy; it dries out quickly, and also allows the Russians to undertake enormous excavations without the shoring operations which would be necessary in a heavier soil.

5. British and Russian managers alike are faced with certain problems deriving from the habits, innate and induced, of Soviet workmen. A large proportion of those whom I saw on the site were doing nothing in particular,

usually with cigarettes in their mouths. But clearly a lot of work gets done, very quickly if absolutely necessary; and this includes the crash building operations in winter conditions which elsewhere would be considered a sufficient bar to any building work. The influence of Soviet Trade Unions is strongly felt, in some directions for the good. In one case the effect is not intentional. Their safety regulations are so inadequate that workers are forced to look after themselves, and do so quite effectively. More positively, the Trade Unions organise effective 'voluntary' work drives by their control of facilities for workers' holidays. At other points their influence is not so healthy. The setting of norms (and special wage-rates), with which they are largely concerned, produces some odd results. The norms are usually low and general overtime rates not specially attractive (this is partly because the Trade Unions prefer to get results by 'voluntary' work which provides some index of political reliability). But particularly towards the end of each month there is a widespread and unnatural urge to move heavy packing cases about; this is part of the usual 'storming' campaign to fulfil the monthly plan target, and the bonus rate for 'heavy work' is high. Again welding (paid by piece-rate) is such a well-paid occupation that the standard length of pipe sections is unusually short.

6. Further differences are caused all round by the independence of the construction works from the Russian director of the Polyspinners' *Kombinat*. He employs them on contract from another *Kombinat* to which they are responsible (as a result, any dispute might in theory have to go [to] the responsible Ministries in Moscow). He can at most make suggestions and cannot give orders to them. The same applies *a fortiori* to the British advisers on the spot, who are often sorely tempted to say 'No—not that way, this—, and sometimes find means of doing so without creating difficulties all round.

7. Labour supply, apart from labour habits, is another difficulty for Soviet and British managers alike. The Russian director is as much concerned with quantity as quality. 'What we need here', he said to me, 'is just live people'. The labour shortage at Mogilev may be in part the result of inadequate housing facilities; it is also typical of the general labour shortage in European Russia today. The British advisers are more concerned with the number of potential foremen and skilled workers, and are helping to operate a crash training programme which illustrates neatly both the defects and the advantages of the Soviet labour system. Batches of forty or so are sent on short training courses in England at the ICI works in Wilton. They then return to skilled work at Mogilev, and the instruction of their fellow-workers, for four months only. After this they return to the ranks, so to speak, to let others train on the few machines already in operation. No difficulty arises, it seems, in keeping the trained workers on at the plant on unskilled work until new machines start to operate and another skilled job is available. At this point at least in the Soviet Union it looks as if labour can afford to be mobile.

8. Of more particular significance are the long-term difficulties between Russian management and the British advisers. One may assume that the Russian director is subject to two main pressures from above (and it is clear

that they come from the Moscow Ministry and purchasing organisations concerned rather than from the authorities of the Belorussian Republic). The first will be to produce results quickly, the second to keep within a fairly strict budget, or to cut down on current expenses. There is thus a double temptation to cut corners and apply constructional and operational standards which cannot be approved by the British technical advisers. The temptation is reinforced by the calculation that, if anything goes wrong, it may be possible to recover money from the British supplying firms under the guarantees applying to the machinery imported from them. In spite of literally tons of detailed specifications in the various contracts signed, it is extremely hard to prove that the Russians have infringed them. And they have no hesitation (as was proved in the case of the pilot plant) about first appealing to the spirit of comradeship in order to cut corners and get a move on, and then insisting that any defects in operation are entirely the fault of the British. There is also some pressure building up from the Russian side to cut down on the number of British advisers. This would directly save them money on salaries and accommodation, it would spare them some administrative bother (see below), and it might make it harder for the remaining British to insist on the technical standards which they know should be applied.

9. These are long-term factors in what may be a long drawn-out industrial-diplomatic battle. I hope to have the opportunity later to talk over these aspects with Mr. Connor, the principal British director, who unfortunately had to be away at the time of my visit. I had the impression that some of the British on the spot thought that it might be necessary before too long to re-negotiate the original contract, to lessen the British suppliers' responsibility for a situation which (whatever the letter of the present contract) they could not effectively control, and to work towards an advisory status, thus escaping the risk of being caught under the guarantee clauses (which involve a sum of about £1,500,000 on a total contract of some £30,000,000). But these are only half-formed thoughts. There are certainly men on the spot at Mogilev who feel that by this time the prestige of the British firms concerned is irrevocably committed to the success of the project. Whatever the formal nature of their association, their reputation is bound to suffer if the Russians make a mess of the operation.

10. The problems of the British team do not of course start on the factory site. They are at least equally concerned for much of the time with maintaining a tolerable way of life for themselves and their families in what are essentially Russian conditions. We are not always content with our living conditions at HM Embassy in Moscow, but an eye-full of Mogilev is a good corrective to self-pity. The British team live in a large 'korpus' or block of three-storey flats, one of a series in the new town of Mogilev, inhabited otherwise by Soviet citizens. The immediate surroundings are not inspiring. The blocks border at one end on the communal graveyard of the concentration camp maintained by the Germans at Mogilev during the last war. On the other side is a primitive grass airfield, still in use, and inhabited mainly by what look like prehistoric biplanes. The approach to the blocks from the main

Orsha-Mogilev road is often and rapidly transformed into a quagmire. A general purpose shop has just been opened on the spot, but till now any local purchase has required twenty minutes walk. There is the minimum of local entertainment (the cinema at Mogilev) and a full share of the local shortages (particularly of power, water and fresh vegetables). Only the potato flourishes, and the local cookery book—Belorussian specialities—is said to list over eighty ways of serving it.

11. The immediate prospect for the British newcomers and their families is in fact daunting. My wife and I were very deeply impressed by the way in which they have tackled their difficulties. Many of the two or three room flats have been turned with much ingenuity and pride into neat and attractive houses. There is a canteen for the 'bachelors' (mostly acting temporary) which produces plenty of hot food, though the variety is clearly not great. There is a bar, opened last year by my wife, which flourished (but not I believe too greatly). Most impressive of all is the children's school, run by a young Welshman, who clearly has something of a genius for his job. One or two of the children go to the local Russian school, and the schoolmaster's own daughters study at the local elementary music school (there is a special 'music stream' in the Soviet Union from the age of seven on). But apart from these exceptions, the British children are very well looked after on the spot. The chief Russian administrative officer, who took us on a tour of the town, told me—obviously from the heart—how much he was impressed by the discipline as well as the cheerfulness of the British children, who gave, he said, a much-needed example to the Russian contemporaries.

12. Of course, there is a constant supply of material and morale problems for the British administrative officer, who has to solve them as best he can from a tiny office with one telephone, one full-time and one part-time secretary (her main job is that of nursing sister to the British community) for the whole block, and a succession of doubtfully efficient interpreters (one or two of the more experienced British specialists understand some Russian, but there is only one ex-student of Russian attached to the team who speaks the language with any fluency). The administrative officer's main chores are the minimum maintenance of accommodation, the organisation of travel and leave arrangements, and also of supplies of food and drink from outside the USSR. He has to cope with the minor or even major tensions which are likely to arise between the representatives of different types of British firms working together at such close quarters (the immediate prospect of sixteen 'long-haired professors' from ICI arriving to join the construction engineers was already causing some concern). Above all he has the difficult task of dealing with the Russian administration of the works.

13. Here there are inevitable tensions. At first sight the British find it quite unreasonable—even intolerable—that, for instance, they cannot get house repairs done quicker, that the Russians cannot agree in advance to the arrival of regular extra supplies by lorry from Helsinki at a fixed customs rate, that the owning and driving of cars is prohibited, that they cannot in summer use boats with an outboard motor, that the British who want to experience

the bright lights of Minsk at a weekend cannot be sure of getting passes to do so—all this in spite of detailed written guarantees and oral promises of most favoured treatment. The first really difficult task in such cases is to determine how much of each problem results from inertia and inefficiency, how much from malicious and avoidable bureaucracy, and how much from real and intelligible difficulties on the Russian side. Undoubtedly the presence of a large foreign community right in their midst sets genuine problems of popular morale for the Russian authorities. The British find their accommodation inadequate, but it is much the same as that enjoyed by their Russian opposite numbers—except that the latter will probably have to fit two or three more of their relations into a three room flat. The British want to import more supplies from abroad—but so do the Russians, and I suppose that too obvious a disparity between the visitors' standard of living and that of the Russians in the next block of flats could create problems of popular morale for the Soviet authorities. The British want regular passes to Minsk and elsewhere. But, the Soviet authorities say to themselves, can they be trusted not to get into trouble there, and can they be left without interpreters? If the answer is 'no' (and this is undoubtedly the answer that the Soviet authorities, not entirely without reason, will give to themselves), how often can they spare the necessary interpreters, and won't it be essential to organise group outings? And so on. My point is of course not that the Soviet authorities are right in such cases, but that they often have some rational grounds for apparently arbitrary behaviour, and that much patience and understanding is needed to move them from apparently stick-in-the-mud attitudes.

14. If, in spite of all these problems and troubles on and off the job, the morale of the British team is reasonably high, as I think it is, there are various reasons for this. First of all they are, to judge by the cross-section which my wife and I saw, a thoroughly admirable lot of people, carefully picked for character as well as for technical qualifications. Secondly, they are doing a big job, where progress is visible over weeks, and not months or years, in spite of all frustrations. Thirdly (and I believe this is a point of real advantage to them, as well as of interest to us) they live in far closer contact with the Russians than we can imagine for ourselves at this Embassy. Obviously this applies to the men on the factory site. Naturally it applies to the children, who play easily and happily enough with Russian children from the neighbouring blocks (Dr. Desmond Morris would be happy to learn that as the British group grows, they become more exclusive, and the boys in particular have developed an almost entirely combative relationship with the counterpart gangs of young Russians). What is more unexpected and cheering to the visitor from Moscow is that there appears to be free contact, so far as language allows, between the British and Russian communities as a whole. There are for example regular sporting fixtures between them, including football matches, which the British have little trouble in losing by a comfortable margin, thus improving international relations. I also have the impression that far the greater number of the British specialists also have their own private contacts and have been welcomed as guests in Russian houses. In

fact at present the main inhibiting factor is likely to be lack of time and interest on the British side, rather than suspicion on the part of the Russians. With all the working problems described above, there is a pleasant general atmosphere of un-suspicion (rather than mutual trust) which contrasts happily with the atmosphere of Moscow. There are incidental pleasures in talking to the walls here, and one rapidly acquires a technique of total silence or minimum allusion among friends. But it is refreshing to find at Mogilev that no one worries about such things. Perhaps they worry too little, but at least their condition is one which gives them confidence in the value of their own job and in the possibility of comparatively decent Anglo-Soviet relations. My wife and I returned from Mogilev more confident on this point and prouder than before of our countrymen.

15. I am sending copies of this Despatch to the Minister of Technology,[2] the President of the Board of Trade, and to Her Majesty's Representatives at Warsaw, Prague, Bucharest, Budapest, Sofia, Belgrade, Berlin, UKDEL NATO and UKMIS Geneva.

I have, etc.,
DUNCAN WILSON

[2] Mr. Benn wrote to Sir D. Wilson on 19 December: 'Your Mogilev despatch was, if I may say so, both fascinating reading and a classic for this type of reporting. It manages to bring out in comparatively short compass all the manifold troubles that can beset a major British undertaking in Eastern Europe, and should be required reading for all our contractors.'

On 11 December Mr. Stewart reported to his Cabinet colleagues on progress—or lack of it—regarding proposals for a European security conference. Following the meeting of Warsaw Pact Foreign Ministers in Prague on 30-31 October, the Pact had issued a public declaration calling for an all-European conference in the first half of 1970 on two subjects—renunciation of the use of force and expansion of trade—and issued two draft documents expanding these agenda items, including a demand for the respect of the 'territorial integrity of all European states within their existing borders', a demand interpreted in the FCO as an 'attempt to obtain recognition of the division of Germany and of the Oder-Neisse frontier'. These documents were discussed at a reinforced meeting of the North Atlantic Council on 5 November, at which Mr. George Thomson, Chancellor of the Duchy of Lancaster, made a speech critical of the Prague Declaration, and which issued a statement commenting on the 'absence of a concrete approach to the problems of European security and the vague formulation of subjects for discussion' in the Prague statement.

The proposed European security conference was discussed again at the NATO Ministerial meeting held in Brussels from 4-5 December. A Declaration attached to the final Communiqué stated that NATO members remained 'receptive to signs of willingness on the part of the Soviet Union and other Eastern European countries to discuss measures to reduce tension and promote cooperation in Europe', but that 'careful advance preparation and prospects of concrete results' would be essential to any conference: 'The Ministers affirmed that, in considering all constructive possibilities, including a general conference or conferences, they will wish to assure that any such meeting should not serve to ratify the present division of Europe and should be the result of a common effort among all interested countries to tackle the problems which separate them.' A Warsaw Pact meeting in Moscow held on 3-4 December, which discussed principally the implications of the election of a new West German Government and the forthcoming FRG-Soviet talks on the renunciation of force (see No. 36, notes 10 and 12), expressed satisfaction at the international support being given to the idea of a security conference, called for the international recognition of East Germany and welcomed in particular the signature on 28 November by the FRG of the Non-Proliferation Treaty.[1]

These deliberations did little to convince the British Government that the Soviet Union was ready for serious discussions on European security. The Joint Intelligence Committee report summarised in No. 40 below encapsulates this view succinctly: 'The Soviet-inspired campaign for a European Security Conference is an instrument of propaganda and of pressure for acceptance of the status quo, in particular the division of Germany.'

[1] Extracts from the Prague Declaration and the *communiqués* issued at the end of the NAC and Warsaw Pact meetings in December 1969, and the text of the Declaration of the North Atlantic Council are printed in Cmnd. 6932, Nos. 14-17.

No. 39

Extract from Conclusions of a Meeting of the Cabinet held at 10 Downing St. on 11 December 1969 at 10 a.m.[1]

CC(69)60 [CAB 128/44]

Secret

Oversea Affairs: East-West Relations

3. The Foreign and Commonwealth Secretary said that there had been no significant response from the Soviet bloc to the North Atlantic Council's offer in the declaration issued at their meeting at Reykjavik in June, 1968, to join with the Soviet Union and other Eastern European countries in discussing mutual force reductions.[2] The invasion of Czechoslovakia which had followed in August of that year had soured the atmosphere and brought about a major setback.[3] The Warsaw Pact Powers, at a meeting in Prague in October, 1969,

[1] Present at this meeting were: Mr. Wilson, Mr. Stewart, Lord Gardner, Mrs Castle, Mr. Callaghan, Mr. Healey, Mr. Peart, Mr. Crosland (now Secretary of State for Local Government and Regional Planning), Mr. Wedgwood Benn, Mr. Ross, Mr. Shore, Mr. Short, Mr. Roy Mason (now President of the Board of Trade), Mr. Hughes, Lord Shackleton, Mr. Thomas, Mr. Diamond, Mr. Harold Lever (now Paymaster General), Mr. Mellish and Sir Elwyn Jones.

[2] See No. 21, note 9.

[3] See Nos. 14-16.

had put forward their own proposal for a European Security Conference.[4] They had agreed, albeit with some reluctance, that the United States and Canada could take part in such a conference, provided that the 'German Democratic Republic' was allowed to attend the conference on the same footing as other participants. The Prague conference had produced documents proposing the discussion of economic relations between East and West and the conclusion of an agreement on the renunciation of the use of force. The latter document had included the proviso that any arrangement which might be reached as a result of the proposed conference should not prejudice the existing obligations of the participating states, i.e., the continuing existence of the North Atlantic Treaty Organisation (NATO) and the Warsaw Pact, and—by implication—the 'Brezhnev doctrine',[5] under which the Soviet Union and her allies claimed the right of intervention in the internal affairs of other 'socialist' states. In general, the reaction in the North Atlantic Council to the Warsaw Pact proposals had been reserved. Misgivings had been expressed about the restriction of the agenda of the proposed conference to only two items, one of which (economic co-operation) was being discussed through other channels. It had been pointed out that the participation of the 'German Democratic Republic' would, in fact if not in form, constitute a step towards recognition of the East German régime. Attention had also been drawn to the danger of recognising, even by implication, the rights of intervention claimed under the 'Brezhnev doctrine'. The United States, who no doubt had their current discussions with the Soviet Union on strategic arms limitation in view, had been cautious. The Germans were evidently chiefly interested in the outcome of the bilateral discussions in which they were at present engaged with the Soviet Union, with other Eastern European governments, and with the East German régime. The Dutch had been more forthcoming, but the unwillingness of the French to co-operate with the rest of the North Atlantic Alliance in military matters seemed now to extend to political matters also. They appeared to prefer that any discussions between East and West should be on bilateral rather than on a collective basis. Progress on such lines was likely to be very slow.[6]

Despite these reactions, he had felt that the North Atlantic Council should not reject the Warsaw Pact proposals out of hand, unsatisfactory though they were. He had therefore urged that the Alliance should maintain its interest in balanced force reductions and should in particular produce 'models'

[4] See pp. 196-7.

[5] See No. 22, note 2.

[6] The declaration issued by the North Atlantic Council (see pp. 196-7) also stated that 'peace and security in Europe must rest upon universal respect for the principles of sovereign equality, political independence and the territorial integrity of each European state; the right of its peoples to shape their own destinies; the peaceful settlement of disputes; non-intervention in the internal affairs of any State by any other State, whatever their political or social system; and the renunciation of the use of the threat of force against any State. Past experience has shown us that there is, as yet, no common interpretation of these principles' (Cmnd. 6932, No. 17).

illustrative of various possible situations.⁷ The approach should be that we wanted to deal with concrete matters and were prepared to put forward concrete proposals to the other side. The documents which had emerged from the Prague conference were admittedly inadequate; and there were divergent views in the Alliance as to how they should be handled. The members of the Alliance should discuss their differences with a view to agreeing at the next Ministerial meeting on a common line of approach to the Warsaw Pact powers, In doing so, they should not underestimate the importance of the contacts which had already been initiated. A number of approaches were possible. It was unlikely that all the problems outstanding between East and West could be settled in one conference; and there might have to be a series of conferences. Another possibility might be to set up some kind of standing commission on East-West relations.⁸

In a short discussion it was pointed out that the United States had initiated talks on strategic arms limitation with the Soviet Union; the Federal Republic of Germany was having bilateral discussions with that country and other Warsaw Pact members; and the French had declared themselves in favour of a system of bilateral contacts. We did not appear to have taken any comparable initiative; and we therefore ran the risk of being accused of rigidity and a lack of enthusiasm for a *détente* between East and West. If this impression were allowed to gain ground, the consequences, both internally and externally, might be damaging. On the other hand, it was argued that so far as the United States was concerned, strategic arms limitation was a subject which only that country and the Soviet Union could profitably discuss. It was we who had kept alive in NATO the concept of balanced mutual force reductions. We had played a leading part in negotiating the Non-Proliferation Treaty and in urging others to sign and ratify it. We were playing a major part in the talks between the Soviet Union and the three Western powers with special responsibilities for Berlin.⁹ While there had been

⁷ In the *Communiqué* and Declaration of 5 December NATO Ministers stated that East-West mutual force reductions should be balanced in scope and timing so as to maintain the present degree of security, and that any agreement should contain provisions for adequate verification and control. The Council was to submit a report on the preparation of MBFR models as soon as possible.

⁸ The idea of a standing committee on East-West relations, composed of representatives of NATO and the Warsaw Pact, had been suggested to Sir T. Brimelow by Sir B. Burrows in UKDEL NATO telegram No. 597 of 19 October. Sir T. Brimelow's reaction was that since constant contact was 'the only way to make sure of not missing any fleeting opportunity of real negotiation' it was important to examine this further. Sir D. Greenhill was also attracted to the idea and an FCO working party was set up (WDW 1/2). In the House of Commons on 9 December Mr. Stewart referred to the proposal as one 'which NATO should most carefully consider' (Cmnd. 6932, No. 18).

⁹ Cf. No. 36, note 9. Further discussion between the British, French and US Governments on the best way to take forward FRG/GDR issues led to the delivery on 16 December of separate *aides-mémoire* by Sir D. Wilson and his French and US colleagues in Moscow, proposing Four Power talks in Berlin at an early date with a view to improving the internal situation in Berlin and its link to the outside world, and to reducing tension in the area. The *aides-mémoire* also

some misunderstanding of our attitude in the early stages of the NATO Ministerial meeting, the attitude we had taken during it and the ideas we had put forward, many of which were reflected in the Declaration and *Communiqué* issued at the end of the meeting, had done much to dispel misconceptions.

The Cabinet:

(1) Took note of the statement by the Foreign and Commonwealth Secretary and of the points made in discussion.

noted that discussions about an exchange of declarations between the FRG and Soviet Governments on the non-use of force had begun in Moscow (see No. 36, note D) and stated that HMG considered that 'both these topics have relevance to efforts to improve the situation as regards European security' (WRL 2 / 1).

No. 40

Report by Joint Intelligence Committee(A)[1] *on Soviet Foreign Policy*

JIC(A)(69)41 Final

Confidential   CABINET OFFICE, *15 December 1969*

The paper at Annex[2] first considers the fundamental factors influencing the formulation of Soviet foreign policy and the principles which now appear to underlie it. It then examines likely Soviet policy objectives in different parts of the world, paying particular attention to those oriented towards the United States and West Germany. It also reviews briefly Soviet attitudes towards the international Communist movement and disarmament. Soviet defence and foreign policies are very closely co-ordinated, but military issues are dealt with only cursorily in this paper: they will be examined in a further study of Soviet defence policy now in preparation. Intelligence has access to no comprehensive secret source documents on Soviet foreign policy: the findings of this paper proceed from analysis of Soviet interests, actions and other data.

2. The following is a summary of our findings.

Summary

PART I THE BASIS OF SOVIET FOREIGN POLICY

3. Soviet foreign policy is primarily influenced by two powerful and often contradictory factors: State interest (i.e., the pursuit of national security, influence and wellbeing) and ideology. To a large extent these are mutually supporting since the transformation of the present 'Socialist' State into a far more powerful 'Communist' society is seen as the key to the ultimate spread of Soviet-type Communism. When they conflict the issue is habitually resolved

---

[1] At this time the Joint Intelligence Committee was divided: JIC(A) dealt with military and political matters, while JIC(B) dealt with economic and industrial issues.

[2] Not printed: see, however, notes 3-10 below.

in favour of national interest and security.[3] Nevertheless the pursuit of State interest has not eclipsed Soviet commitment to the ideological goal.[4]

4. More specifically Soviet foreign policy decision will, at the present juncture, be influenced by the following considerations:

(a) the present form of collective leadership, the character of the present rulers, and the increasingly bureaucratised decision-making process;

(b) the now urgent need to revitalise the economy on whose performance the régime's internal position and their long-term hopes for spreading Communism largely rest. This requires time, development of links with the West (above all, technological), and, if possible, a reduction in the share of national resources devoted to defence;

(c) Soviet recognition that their State interests could be put at risk by attempts to pursue their aims through direct political or military intervention.

5. These factors will make for a continuation over the next several years of the present relatively cautious and pragmatic foreign policy whose broad objectives are:

(a) to safeguard and strengthen Soviet society, and to secure acknowledgement of the Soviet Union as a Super Power and leader of the world Communist movement;

(b) to weaken the West (its military alliances, political groupings and economic strength[]);

(c) to isolate China, while trying to win her back to the fold; and

(d) to further the general expansion of Soviet influence.

6. As a base for pursuing these three objectives Soviet foreign policy will seek to create a comparatively stable international environment which will facilitate the consolidation of the Soviet system and the development of an image of the Soviet Union as a respectable and responsible Power. Acknowledged leadership of world Communism will be sought by combating the ideological challenge of China and other 'Communisms'. Expansion of Soviet influence will be attempted through propaganda, diplomacy, economic and technical activity. Military deployments, assistance and training will also be important instruments of this policy in many areas, particularly those where Western influence is weakening. Moscow will not neglect to exploit any

[3] The full Report stated: 'Russia's past subjection to invasion from East and West and the openness of many of her land frontiers have instilled a "fortress" mentality. Russia's position as a "heartland" power gives rise to permanent fears of encirclement and of two-front wars. However, this "heartland" position also facilitated the slow but steady territorial expansion of the Russian State over a long historical period.'

[4] The full Report stated: 'The ideology legitimises the absolute rule of the Party and conditions the outlook on the world of Soviet policy makers. Soviet foreign policy is formulated in the Politburo . . . Neither the Foreign or Defence Minister is a member of this and final decisions on foreign policy will be taken by leaders whose background lies in the Party and who may overrule, on Party grounds, professional advice from the Foreign Ministry.'

opportunity that might arise for making gains or exclude the application of limited pressures. But Soviet moves will be subject to the following basic principles:

(*a*) avoidance of conflict with the United States;

(*b*) retention of control, if necessary by military means, of areas vital to the defence of the Soviet Union and to its political power and influence, e.g. in Eastern Europe and along its borders with China;

(*c*) avoidance of initiatives or commitments beyond the reasonable ability of the Soviet armed forces to back them up in the last resort.[5]

PART II SOVIET FOREIGN POLICY BY GEOGRAPHICAL AREAS

The industrialised ('capitalised') world

7. In the industrialised ('capitalist') world the Russians can only hope to make headway by the gradualist approach implicit in peaceful co-existence. They will seek to widen 'contradictions' within and between Western societies (including Japan) by propaganda and diplomacy and, by posing as a 'peace-loving' Power, to expunge the image of Communism as a 'military threat'. They have recently stressed the crucial importance of science and technology as an area of 'competition between the two social systems'.[6]

The United States

8. Themselves constrained from actions which might lead to armed conflict with the United States, the Russians believe the United States to be operating under similar limitations. They allow, however, for the risk of miscalculation. Soviet policy towards the United States is aimed, broadly, at countering American military, economic and political power which the Russians regard as the mainspring of world anti-Communism. The Soviet Union therefore seeks to be acknowledged as the equal of the United States in Super Power and as a 'peace-loving, progressive' Power restraining an 'aggressive, reactionary' adversary. This policy is designed to persuade third parties that alignment with the Russians brings greater benefits (and Soviet hostility greater disadvantages) than alignment with the United States. The Russians' position is that the realities of the world Power balance should induce the United States to enter a 'consultative working arrangement' with the USSR, in order to regulate the risk of conflict and define the limits of competition between them. They will regard the SALT talks and the bilateral contacts on the Arab-Israel conflict as steps in this direction. This would further benefit the Russians by establishing the two Powers as equals, preventing a United States-Chinese line-up, and possibly lightening the

[5] The full Report stated that providing the above rules were not infringed, the Soviet Union would be ready to 'seek ways of extending its influence by political, economic and military means . . . Successes are likely to be reinforced, and failures abandoned, but the effort to find Western and Third world weak spots will go on.'

[6] The full Report commented: 'When the Russians speak of "relaxing tensions" they mean tensions that could result in fighting, not the abatement of other forms of competition between the two social systems.'

economic burden of armaments. However, the Russians will not negotiate with the United States if the latter attempt to do so from a position of strength. They do not see themselves as suppliants and are prepared to wait until the United States are prepared to negotiate as equals. They also evidently hope that the passage of time will strengthen the hand of those in the United States who favour a modus vivendi with the USSR. Should such a relationship be established, however, political competition would continue at the maximum permissible level.

Western Europe

9. The Russians' chief concern in Western Europe, which they term a critical area for their security, is to control the evolution of Western Germany (see paragraph 11). Apart from this their chief interests in the area are to prevent cultural and other influences from undermining Communist rule in Eastern Europe, to avoid political crisis (e.g. Berlin) which might precipitate a military clash, to undermine Western institutions (including NATO) and diminish United States influence, and to carry on commercial, scientific and other exchanges so as to benefit the USSR economically and technologically.[7]

10. The Soviet-inspired campaign for a European Security Conference is an instrument of propaganda and of pressure for acceptance of the status quo, in particular the division of Germany. There is no evidence at the present stage that the Russians expect early negotiations on the overall political and military situation in Europe, and no firm evidence of interest in arms control or balanced force reductions. The campaign is also designed to obstruct development of the EEC and a more united Western Europe, possibly with an integrated nuclear force.

Germany[8]

11. Soviet policy towards Germany is to keep it divided and out of reach of nuclear weapons. Ultimately the Russians hope to draw West Germany into their orbit or establish its neutrality. But for the moment too forthcoming a policy towards Bonn would involve considerable political risks for the Russians in East Europe. A cautious dialogue will therefore be conducted and the normalisation of relations encouraged. This will promote acceptance of the status quo and allow freer play to the natural complementariness [*sic*] of the West German and East European economies.[9]

[7] The full Report stated: 'The Russians' and their allies' need to redress their technological backwardness in some fields relevant to economic advance is likely to be a major and restraining factor in their relations with West European countries, which are potentially the chief sources of the desired plant and expertise.'

[8] The full Report stated: 'The key to Soviet policies in West Europe is the German Federal Republic. Although their propaganda about German revanchism is partly designed to promote solidarity in the Soviet Union and Eastern Europe, there is no doubt that the Soviet old guard is hag-ridden by the spectre of a strong Germany, dominant in Europe, backed by American strength and with its own nuclear weapons.'

[9] The full Report noted that West Germany was now the USSR's chief Western supplier.

Eastern Europe

12. As regards Eastern Europe the Russians face the task of maintaining their grip, for which purpose Comecon and the Warsaw Pact will be strengthened, while allowing the countries concerned the benefit of increased economic contacts with Western Europe and perhaps a semblance of independent political manoeuvre where a European Security Conference might help. Nevertheless, anti-Russian sentiment and desire for political relaxation may again erupt overtly; and the Russians would again use force to repress it.

Third World

13. Towards the Third World the Russian approach will be selective and gradualist. They must pre-empt Maoist influence and will therefore profess support for revolutionary movements. In practice, however, while they would give practical support to any such movement where this carried no military or political risk to themselves and promised assured and durable success, their general policy will be to work for long-term change through undermining Western influence, substituting and expanding their own, and trying to manipulate social change in the countries concerned. To this end they will employ the instruments of propaganda, diplomacy, aid and trade, and, where appropriate, subversion. Military aid and professional (especially scientific) contacts will be of particular importance, as will also their widespread naval activity which contributes markedly to the Super-Power image, gives confidence to revolutionary activists, and deters the West from military intervention. Of recent years the Russians have given priority to countries on their southern border to promote stability there and undercut the Chinese.[10]

14. The Russians' immediate aim towards China is to achieve a limited modus vivendi against a background of ideological and political rivalry, but they are hoping to see Mao replaced by more co-operative rulers. Meanwhile they try to undermine Chinese influence everywhere and to deter Chinese military action against their borders. If this deterrence fails they will answer in kind, while attempting to keep their response at a level low enough to avoid uniting the Chinese people and army behind Mao. They will also seek to appear not to be dealing with Mao from a position of weakness. The Russians must allow for the worst case prospect that they will one day have a strong, nuclear and hostile China to the East, and a unified, anti-Communist and possibly nuclear Europe to the West. If there is no reconciliation, therefore, the Russians will continue to work for China's isolation (and possibly disintegration), while weighing the pros and cons of forming an anti-Chinese alliance with the United States (for which they would have to pay a price) or

[10] The full Report stated: 'Though a considerable effort is still maintained towards Africa and Latin America in the fields of diplomacy, propaganda, arms and commerce, these appear now to be regarded as "go-slow" areas, perhaps because Soviet Great-Power interests are less in evidence there, and because, generally speaking, conditions there are judged as unripe for effecting durable social change . . . The main effort has gone to the Middle East, to Asian countries on Russia's southern periphery and in the sub-continent, and latterly to South-East Asia.'

of allowing a triangular Super-Power relationship to emerge that would be fraught with difficulty. Much would depend on United States policies.

Certain Other Issues

World Communist Movement

15. Consolidation of the world Communist movement has high priority, but the Russians will not expect it to play a major part in promoting their ultimate ideological goals. This will depend primarily on the actions and example of countries already ruled by Communist Parties, outstandingly by the Soviet Union itself. In the meantime the movement could be an embarrassment to the Russians.

Disarmament and arms control

16. The Russians stress their association with disarmament and arms control as a means of undermining Western Governments. While they hope that in certain circumstances agreements could increase their military security and relieve their economic burden, they put their main trust in their military posture and will not lower their guard other than against reciprocal measures whose implementation can be unconditionally guaranteed and verified according to their understanding of the term.[11]

Likelihood of change

17. The character of Soviet foreign policy is determined by the impact of today's complex pattern of international relations on Soviet institutions. Neither of these is likely to change fast and we therefore expect the present policy of cautious expansion of Soviet political influence by the means we have described to continue. Since the position of the present régime is upheld by the Marxist-Leninist ideology, and since this also determines their assessment of the forces at work in the world, we do not expect them to change their objective, albeit a long-term one, of substituting Communism for the way the West now lives nor abate their fundamental hostility to our system. If they seek agreements with the West it is to promote their own national interests, particularly in the security field and to create conditions which, as they see it, enables them the better to advance economically at home and ideologically abroad.

HAROLD MAGUIRE[12]

---

[11] A report of 23 December 1968 by JIC(A), *Soviet Policy on Disarmament and Arms Control* (JIC(68)55 (Final)) had argued that Soviet policy was a 'component of their broader defence and foreign policies, whose purpose it serves': enlightened self-interest might prompt the Russians to seek agreements which might reduce the economic burden of the arms race, help stabilise the balance of deterrence and reduce the risk of Soviet involvement in war, but 'any measure of arms control or limitation negotiated by the Russians will in no circumstances be allowed to prejudice the Soviet defence posture. It must show a clear advantage to the Soviet Union, though not necessarily in the sense of putting her adversaries at a disadvantage . . . the Russians will seek to conserve the political advantages which flow from a military posture which, though predominantly deployed in Eurasia, has elements gradually extending further afield.'

[12] Air Marshal Sir H.J. Maguire, Director of Intelligence in the Ministry of Defence and Chairman of JIC(A).

CHAPTER III

1970

Although it had seemed in the summer of 1969 that Soviet policy towards the West was going through a static period—the Russians preoccupied with developments in the World Communist movement, Czechoslovakia and the Sino-Soviet dispute—events in the last quarter of 1969 had indicated some progress: the Prague Declaration, the start of Sino-Soviet talks in Peking, the opening of SALT talks and of talks with the FRG seemed to signal a change of presentation; for example, no pre-conditions were set to the opening of the Soviet Union's and Poland's talks with the FRG. In no field, however, did the FCO see any concrete change in Soviet policy. Indeed, the Russians were extremely tough in their talks with the Germans. Their aim in European security seemed to be to obtain Western ratification of the status quo, especially enhancement of the status of East Germany and Western acceptance of a Soviet zone of influence, and their aim in calling for a Conference was becoming more apparent: they evidently hoped, by propaganda tactics and demands for all-European economic cooperation, to discredit the EEC and distract attention from the work of consolidating the unity of Western Europe which was the prime concern of British policy.

While HMG welcomed a more reasonable Soviet style, they still looked for the kind of change which might make real steps towards détente easier. It was important not to lose sight of the successes of Soviet foreign policy: not only had they largely succeeded in overcoming the effects on their international position of the invasion of Czechoslovakia, but they had also continued to extend their presence and influence, especially in the Mediterranean, the Middle East and the Indian Ocean. The FCO view was that the Russians might come to realise that they could not achieve their short-term objectives in East-West relations without genuine negotiations involving give and take. HMG's role should be to probe Soviet positions and to demonstrate in public and in private their readiness to do serious business if the Russians would reciprocate.

While not dissenting from this analysis, Sir D. Wilson remained concerned about the state of Anglo-Soviet relations. In his Annual Review of the Soviet Union in 1969, despatched on 1 January 1970, he described the linkage in Soviet policy towards Europe of the issues of EEC enlargement, NATO's continuing political development and the European Security Conference and said that on this complex of issues HMG was for Soviet purposes 'the main European villain, or simply the main villain, of the drama "Will Europe be saved?"'. He cautioned that 'so long as the present special factors [favouring France and Germany] continue to operate, we shall have to follow our chosen course with some care and deliberation if we are to avoid further trouble in both our economic and political relations with the Soviet Union'. Negotiations for Britain's entry to the EEC were due to open on 30 June. Sir D. Wilson feared that in the interim period before membership of the Community was achieved, 'we shall find ourselves increasingly the odd man out' unless steps were taken to develop a more active political dialogue with the Soviet Union, of the kind already embarked on by the USA, Germany and France. In paragraph 13 of his review Sir D. Wilson argued that such a dialogue should be based on the assumption that as a member of the EEC Britain would have more to offer the Russians as a compact European power in the 1970s than as a declining world power in the 1960s and would be ready for discussions and negotiations on any concrete issue where there was hope of some coincidence of interest, in or beyond Europe. The Ambassador saw potential gains from steps towards such a dialogue in the encouragement they would offer the more technocratic and sober elements among the Soviet leadership and looked forward to the possibility of discussions between the Prime Minister and Mr. Kosygin in Moscow in 1970, which could play a valuable role in setting the tone for the next stage of Anglo-Soviet political relations.

No. 41

Extract from a minute by Mr. Giffard[1]

[ENS 1/1]

Confidential   FCO, *6 January 1970*

The Soviet Union

. . . 4. I wish to offer the following preliminary comments on the despatch, about which I have not consulted other Departments. Sir D. Wilson's main thesis for British policy is that we cannot afford to sit tight. There will, I think, be little argument with his recommendation that we should develop still further our existing bilateral relationship in the field of trade, technology and culture. We have told the Russians that we agree to the establishment of a Joint Commission which will review trade and technology,[2] and they have

---

[1] This minute submitting Sir D. Wilson's Annual Review of the Soviet Union (see above) was addressed to Sir T. Brimelow and the Private Secretary to the Secretary of State. Paras. 1-3, not printed here, concerned the printing and distribution of the Review.

[2] The possibility of establishing a joint commission to undertake annual reviews of the Anglo-Soviet Trade and Technological Agreements and promote cooperation in those areas had been raised during Mr. Benn's discussions with Mr. Kirillin in Moscow in May 1969 (cf. No. 32). Following interdepartmental discussions Mr. Crosland had submitted the proposal to the Prime Minister on 17 September, advising that 'it would be to our advantage if there were in existence a body which brought together on the Soviet side the State Committee, Gosplan and the Ministry of Foreign Trade'. It was proposed that Mr. Crosland would alternate with Mr. Benn as Chairman of the British side. When Sir D. Wilson spoke to Mr. Kirillin on 8 December about HMG's agreement to the proposal, he 'went out of his way to show that the Soviet Government is extremely pleased by HMG's decision,' and they agreed that the first meeting of the Commission would be held in London, at a date to be arranged in 1970 (ENS 6/23, 1969).

agreed that the first meeting of the Anglo-Soviet Consultative Committee, which will supplement our efforts in the cultural field, should take place.[3]

5. The position is rather less clear as regards the Ambassador's recommendation that we should also maintain an active political dialogue. There is no difficulty as regards the non-governmental part of this, which I take it would refer to parliamentary groups, and activities of that kind. But I submit that we need to think very carefully about the governmental dialogue in this field. There will be an opportunity to discuss this with Sir D. Wilson himself next week.[4]

6. Before making this recommendation, Sir D. Wilson notes, in paragraph 12 of his despatch, that we must expect determined efforts from the Soviet side designed to deter us from pursuing our aim of entry into the EEC. He goes on to say that he thinks the Soviet Government will make the best of the situation once the EEC has been enlarged, and that *at this stage* 'new forms of East-West discussions . . . could be really useful'.

7. The point to beware of is that the interim period before our entry into the EEC, because it is the period when Soviet attempts to prevent it will be strongest, is the period when governmental discussions in the political field will hold some dangers for us. This is an obvious point. One has only to recall the skill with which Mr. Kosygin presented us publicly with the proposal for a Treaty of Friendship during his visit to London in early 1967.[5] The almost inevitable effect was to arouse the suspicions of our allies.

8. I have recommended separately, in connection with the Joint Commission, that we should be careful not to get into competition with the French as to who can inject the greater political content into trade and technological exchanges with the Russians.[6] Separate political exchanges will bring equal pressures for political *danegeld*.

9. The Ambassador draws attention to the dangers that we shall face because of discrimination in the commercial field in favour of France, Germany, and perhaps others (e.g. Japan and Italy). The following are the

---

[3] Cf. No. 14, note 7. Lord Trevelyan had renewed the invitation to hold the first meeting of the Committee in the UK in a message of 2 September 1969 to Mr. Kozyrev, who accepted the proposed dates of 3-6 April on 8 January 1970. Mr. Kozyrev was to head the Soviet delegation and it was later agreed that he would remain in London after the Committee's meeting for talks on 7 and 8 April with Lord Chalfont, Sir D. Greenhill and Mr. Benn (ENS 3/5, 1969; ENS 3/548/2, ENS 3/548/14).

[4] Sir D. Wilson was to return to London for consultations from 14-21 January.

[5] See No. 2, note 11, and No. 4.

[6] In a submission of 19 December 1969 Mr. Giffard had argued that the political advantages arising out of the Commission's activities 'will be long-term and indirect and will indeed depend mainly upon our success in keeping the actual work of the Commission based firmly on practical economic, technological and commercial matters . . . It is partly because the French Prime Minister and Foreign Minister have got involved [in the *Grande Commission* established after General de Gaulle's visit to Moscow in 1966] that I believe we should stick firmly to practical matters if we can'. Sir D. Greenhill subsequently expressed concern that the FCO should 'keep a close watch on the situation. The Russians are apt to tempt the economic departments with all sorts of seductive visions in order to isolate this office' (ENS 6/548/6).

figures in £millions for British, French and German exports to the Soviet Union in 1967, 1968 and the first 10 months of 1969:

	1967	**1968**	**1969** (Jan-Oct)
UK	63.250	102.105	78.902
France	55.3	106.6	76.6
Germany	73.6	113.0	135.0

The French did marginally better than ourselves in 1968, while the Germans made a rapid advance in the first ten months of 1969. I must add that the Board of Trade expect some recent large contracts with the French to show up in the figures in 1969, and stress that I am not attempting to cast doubt on the Ambassador's thesis. On the contrary, I believe it to be absolutely correct.

10. It does not, however, follow that we could gain substantial commercial favours simply by maintaining a political dialogue. We should have to say things which would please the Russians if we were going to profit in this way. I am not sure whether there are things to say at present which would please the Russians without embarrassing us in Europe.

11. This is not to say that I am against maintaining a political dialogue with the Russians. I believe that it is right to go on explaining our own policies to them. This is most effective at ministerial level where it has [?had], over the years, some effect on the thinking of the Soviet leaders. But it would be inevitable that ministerial discussions in the near future would centre on Europe, and it seems to me that what we would have to say, even though it might have a beneficial long term effect, would not be anything which the Russians could admit to being pleased to hear.

12. While, therefore, I would see advantage in trying to explain to the Russians at a high level what kind of Europe we are trying to create, I do not believe that this advantage would be reflected on the commercial side. Indeed, it seems to me that the contrary could be the result. Nevertheless, an effort may have to be made, for political reasons, fairly soon. It may be worth adding, in case the Prime Minister should decide that he cannot accept Mr. Kosygin's invitation to visit Moscow at an early date,[7] that the Russians are in our debt over political visits. Since Mr. Kosygin was last here, not only has the Prime Minister himself been to Moscow, but both Mr. Brown and Mr. Stewart have been as Secretary of State.[8] We invited Mr. Gromyko to visit this country some time ago[9] (before the invasion of Czechoslovakia) and we could consider pressing him to come here, say, on his way to New York this autumn, if there is no other opportunity for political discussions at ministerial level.

[7] Cf. No. 37, note 3.   [8] See Nos. 2-3 and 8-9.   [9] Cf. Nos. 7-9.

13. It is also perhaps worth noting that the five NATO Foreign Ministers who visited Moscow in 1969 were those of France, Turkey, Belgium, Denmark and Luxembourg. In this respect, we are not yet the odd man out.

14. If one looks at our policy towards the Soviet Union as part of a western strategy (and although there are difficulties in so doing, there is also at least a possibility that a better coordinated strategy may be evolving) our role would seem to be satisfied for the present by our participating in the allied approach over Berlin, which the despatch does not mention.[10]

15. Finally, it is easier to speak to the Russians when there are one or two clearly defined subjects in which there is some hope of finding that coincidence of interest to which the Ambassador refers. I am sure that we should pursue any such subjects or points as and when they arise or can be found. I do not wish to subscribe to the simple thesis which was perhaps an epigram by Mr. Kennan that only those can get on with the Russians who have shown that they can get on without them; but I do not at present see obvious subjects of this kind which are not already being pursued satisfactorily.

16. I apologise for the length of this minute. Sir D. Wilson's despatch gives much food for thought, and raises many other points which should be discussed.[11]

C.S.R. GIFFARD

[10] See No. 39, note 9. The Soviet reply delivered to Sir D. Wilson on 10 February agreed to talks in Berlin, and suggested they be held in the building formerly used by the Allied Control Council, to which the Western Allies agreed. The representatives in Berlin of the four Occupying governments later agreed that talks between the UK, US and French Ambassadors in Bonn and Mr. P.A. Abrasimov, Soviet Ambassador in East Berlin, would begin on 26 March (WRL 2/4, WRL 2/10).

[11] Sir T. Brimelow agreed on 7 January that 'At present the scope for Anglo-Soviet political agreements is small. This is not an argument against talking to the Russians. But we should not expect political discussion to yield concrete results. The Soviet leaders would try to exploit any such discussions for their own purposes—principally, at present, the furtherance of their campaign for the acceptance by NATO of a Security Conference which would consolidate the status quo in Eastern Europe'. Sir D. Greenhill thought (8 January) that Sir D. Wilson 'belittles what we are now doing' for example in the Four Power talks in New York on the Middle East or in the approach over Berlin: 'It is true that these discussions are not bilateral, but the last thing we want to do is to create an artificial dialogue with the Russians which has no purpose of value. The fact that the UK is the most unpopular boy in the NATO school does not worry me too much. It is an indication that we are an obstacle to the Russian purpose which is inimical to our interests . . . I think we must stick to our present line which gives priority to our entry to Europe and "damn the torpedoes" of the Russians.'

While the debate on the overall stance to adopt in relation to the Soviet Union remained open, day-to-day business continued—and continued to prove problematic. The next three documents illustrate the difficulties involved in managing the Anglo-Soviet relationship in three contrasting areas: cultural, intelligence and commercial relations.

No. 42

Letter from Sir D. Wilson (Moscow) to Mr. Brash

CU 9/43 [PWS 1/1]

Confidential   MOSCOW, *13 January 1970*

Dear Bob,

Thank you very much for your letter PWE 1/13 of 10 December enclosing a memorandum about our cultural contacts with Eastern Europe.[1] I was greatly interested to read this memorandum, and respond to your invitation by sending you the following comments.

2. I think that the first subject which requires comment is whether, in general terms, we are still justified in pursuing an expensive policy of this nature *vis-à-vis* the USSR. My answer to this is that, while it may be necessary to raise the question at regular intervals, at present the answer must be emphatically yes. Indeed I think that the motives which led us to a deliberate policy of contacts with the USSR have become even stronger in recent years. As you will have noticed from recent political reports from this Embassy, it is now our opinion that the Soviet leaders will be obliged to seek an increasing degree of contact with the civilised West if they are to maintain the necessary technological progress at home. An increasingly widely diffused knowledge of what the West has to offer has been propagated in Russia thanks to a variety of official policies pursued by the British Government and her allies. Such knowledge does, I believe, lead to better understanding, a gradual approximation to Western standards, and thus to some diminution of international tension. The best confirmation of this theory is the strong official Soviet propaganda against what is called the 'convergence theory'. I am sure that it is worth our while to continue on the lines already laid down. Although governments and ministries of finance may consider the sums involved to be large, and it is clearly difficult to quantify the effects of the policies pursued,

[1] In this memorandum Mr. Brash reviewed the background to exchanges of persons and of cultural manifestations with the Soviet Union and Eastern Europe. He referred to the continuing problem of 'judging a balance of advantage' in these exchanges, when the Warsaw Pact countries sought scientific and technological knowhow and cultural prestige while resisting any impact of Western policies on their people; the FCO and other British authorities sought knowledge and experience, and to project Britain abroad. He recommended that in the long term there should be a levelling off in exchanges of persons, and that more effort should be applied to other aspects of the British Council's work, such as the provision of library facilities and greater assistance for English language teaching. The pattern of 'one major outgoing manifestation per year in alternate years to the Soviet Union and to the rest of Eastern Europe', disrupted after the invasion of Czechoslovakia, should be resumed. He concluded that while arguments against concluding cultural conventions with Warsaw Pact Powers had weakened, there was no pressing reason to pursue them: the attitude of the Soviet Union was the key, and they showed 'no signs of interest in moving away from the present rigid system' (PWE 1/13). HM Representatives in Moscow, Bucharest, Budapest, Prague, Sofia and Warsaw were asked for their comments on the memorandum.

there is at least a chance that this money may turn out to be amongst the best investments in the future ever made by the western democracy. I should also say that there is always room for some marginal expansion in these programmes, and I hope that, as soon as the background of financial stringencies begins to ease somewhat, the planned expansions recommended in the Beeley report can be allowed to proceed.[2] I would also steadily oppose any attempt to economise on our expenditure in this area, for the same broad reasons.

3. Apart from this general comment, there are one or two interesting matters of detail covered in your memorandum on which I think I should comment.

4. First, there is the difficult question touched on in paragraph [36] concerning the relative merit of theatrical and musical productions.[3] I think that we may be at fault here in not having commented earlier on your letter of 12 August 1969[4] which put this point very directly. I should say that personally I regard this generalization as rather misleading. I am not sure that I would agree with the thesis that the theatre is more effective than music as a means of conveying ideas, or at least those ideas which we wish to convey. We cannot hope in this very tightly controlled society to present plays with overtly desirable political messages. What we mainly want to convey, I take it, is that our society is intellectually and artistically lively (the Soviet audience will draw any necessary contrasts for themselves). Whether a production of Shakespeare or a performance of a new musical work produces such a train of ideas in the beholder or listener is, I think you will agree, difficult to foretell. I would not wish to draw the opposite conclusion, but merely to state that adequate representation of both forms of art are in my opinion necessary. Perhaps rather too much has been drawn out of Sir Geoffrey Harrison's letter of 16 January, 1968:[4] I think that he was discussing the particular difficulty of the expense of bringing the Royal Ballet to Moscow and the comparatively better value for money obtained from theatrical visits; but not all musical events are as expensive as the Royal Ballet.

5. Another difficult question is the composition of our element in a programme of student exchanges. As we all realise, and as you correctly stress in the memorandum, the Soviet students are chosen deliberately with State interests in mind, and this results in a preponderance of scientific students visiting Britain. On our side, it seems that the resources tend to be used up by those sectors where there is the greatest demand, and that for this reason the

[2] In a report of 1967 Sir Harold Beeley, HM Ambassador in Cairo 1961-4 and 1967-9, had recommended increased expenditure in the cultural sphere in order to promote East-West relations, but financial retrenchment meant that not all his recommendations had been accepted.

[3] Discussing the question of value for money, Mr. Brash wrote that 'On the whole it seems to us in the FCO that priority should be given to good theatrical productions and second priority to musical events. The theatre is (or should be) a means of conveying ideas, and the British theatre enjoys the highest of reputations.'

[4] Not printed.

largest proportion of our students are in artistic and linguistic subjects. Nearly all these students are of a high calibre, and their presence here is undoubtedly helpful in a general sense. It is also undeniably useful that the number of professional linguists in British universities with recent experience of this country is steadily increasing. Nevertheless, I think that those critics who point to the unnecessarily large preponderance of art students in these exchanges have a fair point: and while I realise that the nature of our own society prevents us from correcting the ratio in the way that the Russians themselves would, I hope that we may be able to give rather more encouragement to scientific students, particularly post-graduates, to come here under the agreement.

6. A further general subject which one needs to consider in examining the memorandum is the relative importance which should be played [*sic*] by English language teaching and the promotion of strictly cultural events. It is of course most undesirable that we should ever be thrust into the position of choosing between one and the other, since both are an important aspect of our cultural programme in the USSR. In any case, the encouragement of English language teaching has been on an extremely modest scale, and has produced good results for the sums spent. There is probably more we can do which would also produce a handsome return for very little expenditure. But we should take care to ensure that we do not allow our spending on English teaching to have any effect on our major cultural events in this country. In this Embassy we fully subscribe to the remarks contained in the relevant section of the Duncan Report (Chapter 8, paragraphs 37 and 48) on the need for occasional major cultural events.[5] I think that the pattern recommended in the memorandum of one such event in alternate years is about right, and I would certainly not be content with any policy which envisaged less than this.

7. There is one subject not directly mentioned in the memorandum but which we should keep in our minds as an important objective as soon as it can be realised: namely the provision of a good British Council library in Moscow and, later, in Leningrad. I do not think that we are likely to succeed in establishing a library here yet, and believe it would be pointless to make the attempt for the time being. I hope that we may be able to introduce a library eventually, perhaps initially as part of the universities in the two major cities, and if a moment occurs when I think that the atmosphere has changed sufficiently, I will let the Department know. But I do not think that this will happen in my time here.

[5] The *Report of the Review Committee on Overseas Representation* 1968-1969, commissioned in August 1968 under the chairmanship of Sir Val Duncan, was published as Cmnd. 4107 of 1969. Chapter VIII, entitled 'Information and Culture', noted that a comparatively low proportion of the British Council's budget was devoted to cultural manifestations in comparison to English language and related activities, and suggested a change in the balance in favour of the former. Cultural manifestations were described as 'highly important parts of the Council's work', where 'the value of the whole activity is greater than the sum of its parts'.

8. Finally, I should comment briefly on the administrative structure of the British Council referred to in paragraph 48 of the paper.[6] I believe that the arrangement for staffing the small cultural establishment in Moscow is satisfactory, and I do not think that any change is needed at present.

Yours ever,

DUNCAN WILSON

I hope to see you when in London shortly,[7] and we cd. perhaps discuss any of the above points, if you wish.

[6] This para. referred to the Duncan Committee's recommendation that Embassies should provide the administrative infrastructure for British Council activities abroad, and noted that there was in any case justification for 'maintaining an exceptionally close link between Council and Embassy in Eastern Europe because of the security and political overlays'.

[7] See No. 41, note 4.

No. 43

Note by Mr. A.M. Simons[1] on the Scale of Soviet Intelligence Activity in the UK

[*PUSD*]

Secret   FCO, *19 January 1970*

Sir Denis Greenhill held a meeting in his room at 4 p.m. on Thursday, 15 January, with HM Ambassador in Moscow. Sir Edward Peck,[2] Sir Thomas Brimelow and Mr. Simons were also present.

2. The meeting considered Sir Duncan Wilson's concern at the effect which certain British intelligence or counter-intelligence operations against the Russians might have on the level of Anglo-Soviet trade, or on Anglo-Soviet relations in general. Discussion also took place about the level of intelligence activity of members of the Soviet Embassy in London, and of the Soviet Trade Delegation.[3]

3. Sir Denis Greenhill noted that we had slipped into a position where we appeared to regard the present (high) level of Soviet intelligence activity here as reasonable. This was not good enough. We should seek opportunities

[1] Deputy Head of the Permanent Under-Secretary's Department (PUSD).

[2] Deputy Under-Secretary of State in the FCO, superintending PUSD.

[3] The possibility of action against the Soviet Trade Delegation (STD) to counter its increasing exploitation by the Russians for intelligence activities against the UK had been under consideration since limitations were imposed on the size of the Soviet Embassy in November 1968 (see No. 19). Between January and March 1969 the size of the STD had risen by 15%, and although its growth had slowed in the latter half of the year the Security Service had expressed their concern and provided evidence of the increasing exploitation of the STD for the reconnaissance of defence, industrial and commercial targets and for the recruiting of spies. At an inter-departmental meeting in October 1969 it had been decided that further examination of several aspects of the question was necessary before proposals for action were submitted to Ministers.

for Ministers to inform Soviet representatives that improvement in Anglo-Soviet relations was unlikely while the Russians conducted intelligence operations here at the present level.

4. Sir Denis Greenhill noted that Members of Parliament would take considerable exception to the present position if they were aware of the scale of Soviet intelligence activity. We should seek opportunities to make our point of view known to the Russians, and should be quite firm in expelling members of the Soviet Embassy (or cancelling the residence permits of members of the Soviet Trade Delegation) caught engaging in intelligence activity.

5. It might be especially effective if the Prime Minister and the Foreign and Commonwealth Secretary could agree to represent to Soviet representatives our concern at the scale of Soviet intelligence activity.[4]

A.M. Simons

[4] Sir D. Greenhill raised the subject of unacceptable Soviet intelligence activities during his conversation with Mr. Kozyrev on 7 April: see No. 45 below.

No. 44

Letter from Mr. D.E.T. Luard to Mr. Roberts (Board of Trade)[1]

[MUA 4/303/1]

Confidential   FCO, *18 February 1970*

UK/USSR Air Services Negotiations

As you know, following negotiations undertaken in Moscow in December last year by a delegation from your Department,[2] a document was initialled which was, subject to revision by legal and treaty experts and approval by Governments, intended as the basis of an agreement supplementary to the UK/USSR Air Services Agreement concluded in 1957.[3] The new agreement will give BOAC the right to operate across the USSR to Tokyo in exchange for certain traffic rights for Aeroflot.

[1] Mr. Evan Luard and Mr. Goronwy Roberts had been appointed respectively Parliamentary Under Secretary in the FCO and Minister of State at the Board of Trade in October 1969. Opening and concluding salutations were omitted from the filed copy of this letter.

[2] Cf. No. 33, note 5. A delegation led by Mr. Le Goy of the Board of Trade with representatives of BOAC and BEA had held talks with officials from the Soviet Ministry of Civil Aviation in Moscow from 10-18 December 1969. The present letter arose from a submission of 17 February by Mr. T.L. Crosthwait, Head of FCO Aviation and Telecommunications Department, recommending that Ministers resolve a difference of view between FCO and BOT officials preventing Sir D. Wilson from receiving instructions to agree the final text of an Agreement with the Russians.

[3] This agreement, published as Cmnd. 798 of 1957, did not come into force until 25 March 1959.

In consultation with officials in the Board of Trade, our treaty and legal advisers have recast the original document and it is now in the form of a final draft which could be handed to the Russians. I enclose a copy.[4] There is, however, one point in connection with this draft which causes us considerable difficulty and which has been the subject of anxious discussion between our officials. This is the reference to Hong Kong in Article 5 of the draft.[5]

Both the Governor of Hong Kong and our Chargé d'Affaires in Peking have represented strongly to us that any mention of Hong Kong in a published document which will undoubtedly attract considerable attention would be deeply resented by the Chinese—if they did not indeed regard it as a provocative act. As you know, the Chinese regard Hong Kong as Chinese territory and, in the present state of Sino-Soviet relations, they are particularly sensitive to any expansion of Soviet influence along their borders. The Chinese mood is unpredictable and it is possible that they might express their concern and suspicion in a way which might hamper our efforts to secure the release of detained British subjects in China[6] and better treatment of our Mission in Peking. In addition it could have serious consequences for Hong Kong.

Secondly, it is our belief that the Russians may intend to make use of any reference to Hong Kong in the agreement to bring pressure to bear on us to permit the establishment of a permanent quasi-official Soviet presence in Hong Kong in the form of an Aeroflot office or similar agency. I realise that the reference to Hong Kong does not specify what form of collaboration might be involved, and that there are forms which would not involve any physical Soviet presence even in the long run; but the text as it stands leaves this issue open and can therefore be represented by the Russians—and the Chinese—in a variety of ways going beyond what we are able to accept.

I am advised that, from a purely legal point of view, we would be safeguarded under the terms of the agreement against any Soviet claim that they had an automatic right to a presence in Hong Kong. But this would certainly not inhibit the Russians from invoking Article 5 in support of their case: nor, upon our rejection of it, would it prevent them from claiming that we had misled them as to the intentions and scope of the agreement.

In recent years the Russians have made repeated attempts to establish a foothold in Hong Kong, e.g. a Trade Mission and a Tass agency. It has been our policy to resist these attempts to the best of our ability. The Chinese are well aware of what has been happening; they have not failed in their propaganda to express strong disapproval of these Russian designs and we

---

[4] Not printed.

[5] Article 5 provided that 'Aeroflot and BOAC will do everything necessary to determine by agreement methods of commercial collaboration and by agreement will take steps towards organising—from summer 1971—the carriage of passengers and freight on the circular line London-Moscow-Tashkent-intermediate points in Asia-Singapore-Hong Kong-Tokyo-Moscow-London . . . Any agreement between the airlines under the provisions of this Article shall be subject to approval by the aeronautical authorities of both parties.'

[6] Cf. No. 34, note 9.

must recognise such statements as an indication of their official attitude. Regardless of the strict legal interpretation of Article 5 of the draft agreement, it seems to us that there is a real danger that the Chinese may interpret the mention of Hong Kong in the agreement as a deliberate move on our part to give the Russians what they are seeking. We doubt whether any adverse Chinese reaction could be made less severe by any assurance we might subsequently give them about our attitude towards a Soviet presence in Hong Kong.

It is unfortunate that owing to the omission of some key words in a telegram,[7] this point was not picked up when the text of the agreement initialled with the Russians was sent to London after the agreement was initialled. Officials of our two departments have, however, discussed how we can now recover the position in order to take account of the considerations I refer to above. They have agreed that our Ambassador in Moscow should be instructed to approach the Soviet Government at the political level and should make the following alternative suggestions to them:

(*a*) In Article 5 of the published agreement the reference to Hong Kong and Singapore should be omitted from the 'circular line' which would be defined as follows: 'London-Moscow-Tashkent-intermediate points in South and South East Asia and the Far East-Tokyo-Moscow-London, and also between the points London-Moscow-Tashkent . . . etc., etc.'

(*b*) If the Russians do not accept this approach, then our Ambassador should be empowered to suggest that the whole of Article 5 should be extracted from the published agreement, the substance being incorporated in a confidential document which would be signed either by the aeronautical authorities of our two countries, or would take the form of a confidential exchange of letters between the Chairman of Aeroflot and BOAC.

The Ambassador would stress that an open reference to Hong Kong in the agreement would be in neither of our interests, and would be able to assure the Soviet Government that neither of these courses would represent any weakening of the Aeroflot position as compared with what was agreed in Moscow in December: the change was being suggested solely for political reasons which would be well known to them. He would also explain frankly why he would continue to oppose a Soviet presence in Hong Kong and would make it clear that we do not construe any confidential document as permitting this.

The suggestions in paragraph 7 accord with the advice received from our Ambassador on how we should handle this question.[8] The only difference

---

[7] BOT telegram Allot 31 from Moscow of 16 December was evidently corrupted in transmission.

[8] In Moscow telegram No. 165 of 13 February Sir D. Wilson had warned that he 'would not rule out the possibility that in the end the whole Agreement might founder' and suggested placing the reference to Hong Kong and Singapore in a confidential exchange of letters: 'I feel strongly

between our Departments is what we should do if the Russians insist that Article 5 should be included as it stands in the Agreement with the reference to Hong Kong. I understand that your officials consider that, in that event, the Ambassador should be instructed not to insist upon these alterations but should tell the Soviet authorities that we agree to conclude the Agreement as it stands. I appreciate the urgency of this question. I feel, nevertheless, that it would be wiser to postpone a decision on what we should do in the event of a Russian refusal to accept an amendment to the agreement in the sense above, until we have had the Ambassador's report of his discussion and have considered any alternative suggestions that the Russians themselves may have to make. The political considerations to which I refer in the earlier part of this letter, the force of which you will be the first to appreciate, are, I feel, such that we must leave ourselves open to explore any alternatives which the Russians may put forward. We would of course undertake to treat the matter as one of the utmost urgency at that time.

I hope you are able to agree to this. If you do, we will despatch the necessary instructions to the Ambassador in consultation with your Department as soon as possible. I think we are all agreed that we should make progress on the Agreement as rapidly as possible.[9]

D.E.T LUARD

that something should be done on these or other lines to rescue an agreement of major importance.'

[9] In his reply of 19 February Mr. Roberts agreed that if 'the Russians will not take seriously amiss an approach to remove explicit reference to Hong Kong from the documents for publication' then Sir D. Wilson could be authorised to put alternatives (*a*) and (*b*) above to the Russians, adding that 'it would surely be folly not to arm HM Ambassador with a mandate to use his discretion to settle by retaining Article 5 . . . if he judges from Soviet reactions that otherwise significant delay, or a move to re-open the air services negotiations, or a crystallisation of adverse Soviet attitudes is probable'.

Mr. Luard accepted this point, but in a letter of 23 February to Mr. Roberts Lord Shepherd, Minister of State in the FCO with responsibility for Hong Kong, objected that 'the dangers of a very serious Chinese reaction to the inclusion of "Hong Kong" in Article 5 is [*sic*] such that I could not agree to giving the Ambassador the discretion you have suggested'. After further discussion instructions were sent to Sir D. Wilson in telegrams Nos. 153-156 of 24 February, explaining that HMG accepted the Agreement subject to the resolution of difficulties over Article 5. Sir D. Wilson handed over on 27 February a draft Agreement omitting Article 5, whose text was instead contained on a separate piece of paper, and on 1 April Mr. Besedin of the Soviet Ministry of Civil Aviation gave the Embassy a revised Soviet text of the Agreement, which referred to 'intermediate points in South and South East Asia and in the Far East' in Article 5, and proposed that the question of Hong Kong be dealt with in a separate confidential letter. After a further exchange of drafts, Marshal Loginov, Soviet Minister of Civil Aviation, visited London to sign the Agreement on 13 April, when he received a letter from the Board of Trade recording the position with respect to Hong Kong. BOAC's services to Tokyo via Moscow began on 2 June.

The visit of the Soviet Deputy Foreign Minister Mr. Kozyrev to London for the first meeting of the Anglo-Soviet Consultative Committee (see No. 41, note 3) provided an opportunity for an intensive programme of discussions with Ministers and senior officials on matters of pressing interest to both countries, including events in South East Asia and the Middle East (which had also been discussed during the Prime Minister's visit to Canada and the United States from 25-28 January, and by Mr. Stewart in Washington 26-28 January). Both regions were currently in a state of heightened tension.

No. 45

Record of talks between Sir D. Greenhill and Mr. Kozyrev at the Foreign & Commonwealth Office on 7 April 1970

[ENS 3/548/1]

Confidential

Present:

Sir Denis Greenhill	Mr. S.P. Kozyrev
Mr. C.S.R. Giffard	Mr. M.N. Smirnovsky
Mr. R.Q. Braithwaite	Mr. I. Ippolitov
Mr. G.G.H. Walden[1]	Mr. V. Vasev[2]
Mr. M.B. Nicholson (Interpreter)	Mr. B. Piadyshev
	Mr. V. Sukhodrev (Interpreter)

Sir Denis Greenhill began by welcoming Mr. Kozyrev, and expressing his satisfaction that he had found time to stay on after the meeting of the Consultative Committee.[3] He was also glad to see that Mr. Kozyrev was

[1] Mr. Braithwaite and Mr. Walden were respectively Assistant Head of WOD and Head of Section in EESD.

[2] Mr. Ippolitov and Mr. Vasev were respectively Counsellor in the Soviet Embassy in London and Deputy Head of the Second European Department of the Soviet MFA.

[3] Cf. No. 41, note 3. Following a dinner on the evening of 3 April attended by Mr. Smirnovsky, Sir T. Brimelow and Mr. Giffard, the Committee held a plenary meeting on 4 April then divided into groups which reported back to a second plenary meeting on 5 April. A number of general recommendations relating to aspects of Anglo-Soviet relations were agreed: those regarded as unacceptable, such as Soviet attempts to by-pass the British Council, and to enlist British support for pro-Communist British organisations; or British proposals regarding the treatment of the BBC's Russian programmes, were omitted from the final Report (not printed). The FCO's overall verdict was that the first meeting of the Committee had gone 'rather better than expected' though as Mr. Walden pointed out on 20 May it was 'not an easy exercise. The British Group was composed of personalities eminent in their own fields, but not all well versed in dealing with the Russians. By comparison, the Russian team was composed of professionals. The recommendations to some extent reflect this difference in composition: the more general propositions are often British, and the more specific proposals Russian'. Mr. Walden considered it 'still too early to forecast the effect of the Committee's recommendations in expanding bilateral contacts. The problem is that the implementation of the recommendations, which are intended as supplementary to our officially sponsored exchanges, will largely depend on the decision of other organisations which are not subordinate to the FCO.' Mr. Stewart

accompanied by advisers who were so well known to us, and whose knowledge of the United Kingdom and of United Kingdom policies we had learned to respect. It was some time since Mr. Kozyrev had been in this country; at least since 1947. He was sure that Mr. Kozyrev had seen during his short stay the great changes in the streets of London, and that the people were enjoying a high and rising standard of living. This was true not only of the capital, but also in all parts of the country, industrial and agricultural. The Soviet Ambassador, who did a considerable amount of travelling, had probably already reported this.

2. In the last two decades our own approach to international relations had of course changed. The strategic interests that once arose from the existence of the British Empire, and the political consequences of these strategic interests, had been reduced in importance. More and more the interests of this country had come to be associated with policies of cooperation with those countries which were prepared to cooperate with us. It was for this reason that we had taken the decision to join the European Community. Our place, we believed, was with countries which had similar political philosophies and which were at similar stages of economic development. Together we could constitute an important and useful element in world affairs.

3. The Soviet Ambassador had once asked Lord Chalfont whether our increased interest in Western Europe meant that we were losing interest in relations with the Soviet Union. The answer was emphatically no. We sought active cooperation, not just peaceful co-existence, with the Soviet Union. We had no wish to pursue an exclusive policy against the Soviet Union either economically or politically. Economically a larger West European unit might be the best way of developing resources needed for large scale economic cooperation with the Soviet Union. Mr. Thomson would be explaining our approach to the European Economic Community in more detail, and about the developments we expect to flow therefrom.[4]

4. So far as this country was concerned the Soviet Union, with its enormous potential in many fields, was of great interest not only to Her Majesty's Government but, as Mr. Kozyrev would have heard in the meetings of the Consultative Committee, to many people in many walks of life. These people

wrote to Lord Trevelyan on 21 May: 'I think we can agree with Mr. Kozyrev (despite our different motivations) that the work of the Committee has made a contribution to the improvement of the atmosphere in which our relations are conducted' (ENS 3/548/2).

[4] During a conversation with Mr. Kozyrev on 8 April Mr. Thomson explained that an 'integrated Western European economy with a population of almost 3 hundred million should give us an opportunity to compete on equal terms with countries such as the USSR and the USA. It would be a mistake to regard the enlargement of the Communities as in any way harmful to the interests of the Soviet Union. There was no reason to think that it would adversely affect East/West trade; it was significant that Eastern Europe's trade with the EEC had grown significantly more rapidly than its trade with the world generally.' Mr. Kozyrev replied that the Soviet Union regarded the EEC as a 'restrictive economic grouping' and 'did not conceal their view that the economic integration of Western Europe would lead to an intensification of the divisions within the continent, and build new barriers. But he repeated that what Mr. Thomson had said would help him to understand the British position' (MWE 5/303/1).

and the organisations and professions they represented, were free to develop relations with the Soviet Union to the extent they wished. Her Majesty's Government would encourage them to do so.

5. Turning to current relations between the British and Soviet Governments, Sir Denis Greenhill said that we recognised that there were limits imposed by a difference of ideologies, but that these limitations did not preclude mutually beneficial trading arrangements, far in excess of those currently undertaken. Given good will on both sides, the possibilities for the expansion of our commercial relations and for the fruitful exploitation of our commercial and technological agreements were great. We attached importance to the work of the new Joint Commission,[5] of which, he was happy to know, Mr. Kozyrev was a member, and would exploit these opportunities to the full. The nature of Anglo-Soviet trade was such that it should be able to continue at a high level in any foreseeable future.

6. In the international field, he wished to refer to only three matters, as examples of situations in which Soviet and British interests coincided to a large measure.

7. First, he wished to discuss European security. Mr. Kozyrev had already spoken to Mr. Stewart on this subject,[6] but he would like to repeat across this table some of the points made on Thursday evening. The interest of the British Government in satisfactory arrangements for the security of Europe was no less than that of the Soviet Government. It was wrong to suggest that Her Majesty's Government were taking a negative attitude in this matter. However, we were not prepared to tinker with the subject. We were ready to discuss issues of substance. We considered that the proposals put forward in the Prague Declaration[7] had not gone to the heart of the matter and were not sufficiently substantial to form the basis of a worthwhile conference. There were already talks in progress between the Soviet Union and the United States of America,[8] between the Federal German Government and the

[5] Cf. No. 41, note 2.

[6] At a reception on the evening of 2 April Mr. Stewart and Mr. Kozyrev had discussed European security, Berlin and West German foreign policy. The record of their conversation reveals a somewhat bad-tempered tone: for example, Mr. Stewart told Mr. Kozyrev that 'a cocktail party was no place to rehearse the full arguments on the Berlin question', and protested that HMG were not negative towards European security: 'For goodness' sake could the Soviet Government not give us a chance. It was wrong of any of us to claim to be infallible. The Russians should not think that simply because they had put forward proposals these could be the only possible proposals' (ENS 3/548/24).

[7] See pp. 196-7.

[8] See No. 37, note 5. The preliminary session of SALT on limitation of missile and missile defence systems was adjourned on 22 December 1969, with an agreed US-Soviet programme of work for the second round of talks which were due to begin in Vienna on 16 April. No fundamental points of difference arose in the preliminary talks, although the Russians raised a number of 'third party' issues, such as a suggested ban on the transfer of strategic armaments, which the FCO's Defence Policy Department felt might affect UK and other NATO interests. It was agreed to try and raise such points in bilateral discussions with the Americans before the next

Soviet Union[9] and between the three Western Powers and the Soviet Union on the subject of Berlin,[10] which in our opinion were dealing with concrete issues which were relevant to European security.

8. But we were not opposed to a conference as such. There was much work to do in the discussions which were already taking place, and there was plenty of scope for an advance in these matters. We considered that one of the most useful and important subjects which should be discussed was that of mutual and balanced force reductions.[11] We would consider agreement on this an essential element of any satisfactory European security arrangements. The agreement would of course have to be implemented by a process which throughout would maintain satisfactorily the assurance of equal defensive security for all parties involved. As Mr. Kozyrev knew very well, NATO was carrying out intensive studies on these matters. Was the Soviet Union willing to discuss them? Mr. Stewart had explained to Mr. Kozyrev that we were studying with our Allies, as alternatives to a conference, procedures for organising further East-West exchanges of European security.

9. The second international subject Sir Denis Greenhill wished to mention was the Middle East. Here he believed that our objectives were similar. We wished to see a just and lasting political settlement based on the United

round of talks began, and SALT had been discussed during Mr. Wilson's and Mr. Stewart's visit to Washington (see p. 219).

[9] Cf. No. 36, note 10. Three sessions of talks were held in December 1969, during which, according to Mr. D.A.S. Gladstone of WED, there was 'no evidence that Gromyko had listened seriously to a word Allardt has said' (minute of 31 December, WRG 3/303/1). Herr Egon Bahr, Special Adviser to the FRG's Ministry of Foreign Affairs, flew to Moscow on 27 January for a new round of talks which lasted until 17 February; a further round was held from 3-21 March. Little progress was made in view of Mr. Gromyko's insistence that any agreement must embody the FRG's recognition of all European frontiers including that between the FRG and Poland and the FRG and the GDR, and Herr Bahr's insistence on referring to a possible reunification of Germany. However, a modicum of agreement was reached on fringe issues, and Herr Allardt remained convinced that the Soviet Government were genuinely interested in finding a political *modus vivendi*. The talks had adjourned for a 'pause for reflection' and for a decision by both governments on whether to proceed to serious negotiation of an agreement.

[10] See No. 41, note 10. At the first meeting of the Four Power talks on Berlin on 26 March the Ambassadors had made formal statements of their position. Preparatory work was now under way for the second quadripartite meeting to be held on 28 April.

[11] Cf. No. 39, note 7. A working group had been set up from NATO's Senior Political Committee and Military Committee to prepare two models for force reductions in time for the May Ministerial meeting: the first model was for equal proportionate reductions (EPR), and the second for asymmetrical reductions (the 'equal security', ES model). In a minute of 16 January on the future course of work on MBFR, Mr. C.C. Wilcock of Disarmament Department noted that the EPR model was likely to be rejected by the military authorities as being 'unsafe' under present NATO strategy, whereas the ES model would be unacceptable to the Warsaw Pact as it required larger reductions from them than from NATO: 'Ministers will be confronted with one model which may be negotiable but is militarily unacceptable and another which is militarily acceptable but seems most unlikely to be negotiable. There still seems to be a political necessity for the continuation of work on MBFR. Ministers, particularly UK ministers, have made a great deal of use of it since June 1968 as a propaganda point showing NATO's readiness for *détente*. It is also the only genuinely NATO initiative in this field' (DS 12/2).

Nations Resolution No. 242. He was sure that Mr. Kozyrev could assure him that the Soviet Union had the same objective.[12] But the Soviet Union had been critical of our tactics in the Four Power talks and critical of the part we had played.[13] He asked Mr. Kozyrev to consider what we had done against the background of our interests in the area and of public opinion in this country. The United Kingdom had legitimate and substantial material interests in the Arab world; we also had interests in Israel (currently our exports to Israel exceeded in value those to the Soviet Union). Public opinion in this country was well informed on the Middle East and traditionally this country had felt sympathy for the Jews which translated itself today into an active desire for the survi[v]al of Israel. We were ready to work with the Soviet Union in seeking a solution to the present situation. But he was sure that Mr. Kozyrev would agree that neither of the parties—Arab or Israeli—had the monopoly of right or of wisdom. In these circumstances and in an area where great power confrontation might arise by miscalculation or by accident we saw dangers to us and to the Soviet Union in allowing the present struggle to continue and to escalate both in violence and in the sophistication of the arms supplied. Mr. Hayman would discuss this further that afternoon.[14]

[12] On 5 March Mr. Malik had presented in New York Soviet peace proposals based on Resolution 242 and an irrevocable agreement signed by the parties, and deposited with the UN.

[13] The Four Power talks had resumed on 3 December 1969: cf. No. 37, note 6. They focussed on the development of guidelines for Mr. Jarring with regard to the Israel-Jordan dispute, while broader Arab-Israeli issues were left to bilateral US-Soviet talks; the Prime Minister noted on 3 December that 'we should not get at cross purposes with the Americans on their efforts to promote a Middle East settlement' (NE 2/25/5). The Four Power Talks polarised into two camps, with the Soviet Union and France pressing for the detailed drafting of guidelines for Jarring, while the US and UK disagreed. On 8 January 1970 Mr. Stewart informed Lord Caradon that the UK should hold back from presenting detailed proposals so as to 'avoid being forced to choose between accepting or rejecting language which the Americans could not accept, that is to choose between isolating the Americans or appearing to agree with them on subjects where our real position does not coincide with theirs' (FCO telegram No. 21 to UKMIS New York, NEM 2/3). To break the deadlock in the Four Power talks, the Deputies were instructed on 31 March to prepare a memorandum on the extent of the accord on key issues of a Middle East settlement. They began their work on 14 April.

[14] The start of Israeli deep penetration raids into Egypt in early January had prompted President Nasser to ask the Soviet Union for increased arms supplies: between 31 January and 2 February the Soviet Union delivered messages in Washington, Paris and London warning that 'if Israel continues with its adventurism and keeps bombing the territory of the UAR and other Arab states, the Soviet Union will be obliged to see to it that the Arab states have at their disposal such means which would help them to give a proper rebuff to the arrogant aggressor'. The Prime Minister had replied on 6 February expressing concern at the Soviet statement, but Israeli and Egyptian military activity continued to increase and on 20 March General Moshe Dayan, Israeli Defence Minister, announced on Israeli radio that Soviet missiles and planes had been deployed in Egypt. Mr. Rabin, Israeli Ambassador in Washington, had been told that the US Government would ensure that the military balance was maintained in Israel's favour.

In their conversation later on 7 April Mr. Hayman asked for Mr. Kozyrev's views on the Jarring mission, the deputies' discussions in New York, Soviet-American bilateral discussions and arms limitation. Mr. Kozyrev replied that 'the Russians felt that what was needed was resolute

10. The third area was South East Asia. Sir Stanley Tomlinson would speak to Mr. Kozyrev in detail that afternoon.[15] In the British view, there was much that we could do together. The Soviet Union, he believed, shared our view that it was essential for the stability and development of the whole region that there should be a settlement in Indo-China. We should both lose no opportunity of bringing a settlement nearer. Equally, we should both use our influence to discourage anything that might exacerbate the position.

11. He had not mentioned disarmament, which Mr. Kozyrev would be discussing with Lord Chalfont,[16] but this was manifestly an area where our practical interests coincided and where we could both contribute to further progress in arms control and in disarmament. Our delegates both in Geneva and in New York worked together well in this field, and we felt that this was an area where we could make joint efforts.

11. Lastly, Sir Denis Greenhill said that there was one subject which he introduced into the discussion with some reluctance. He did so because he believed that it was directly related to the development of our relations which he thought both countries desired. Her Majesty's Government in no way welcomed the troubles which arose from security issues, which deflected the attention of public opinion in both countries from major issues of political and

action by all those interested in bringing about peace', and said that Britain could have influence in prompting Israel to take a 'more realistic position about a settlement'. Mr. Hayman welcomed the statement of Soviet views but said that 'it took two to make a bargain. In the end, only the United States could deliver Israel. We would, however, do what we could to contribute to progress' (NEM 3/303/1).

[15] In South East Asia, the strategic emphasis had moved towards Cambodia and Laos, with the US Air Force in action in February responding to an appeal for help from the Laotian Premier, Prince Souvanna Phouma against a Pathet Lao/North Vietnamese offensive in Laos on the Plain of Jars. On 6 March President Nixon sent letters to both Mr. Wilson and Mr. Kosygin asking them, as co-Chairmen of the Geneva Conference, to help restore the 1962 agreements on Laotian neutrality, but an approach by Sir D. Wilson had been met by the Soviet reply that it was US bombing which presented the 'major obstacle' to an improvement in the Laotian situation. On 27 March Laotian forces had recaptured the Plain of Jars. Meanwhile, Prince Sihanouk had been deposed as leader of Cambodia on 18 March by General Lon Nol: the Prince fled to China where he declared war on the Lon Nol government and was supporting the Khmer Rouge, assisted by North Vietnamese troops, in their attempt to take Cambodia.

During their conversation Sir S. Tomlinson (Deputy Under Secretary superintending South East Asia Department) and Mr. Kozyrev set out their respective Governments' positions, the latter insisting that 'it was the Americans who were blocking progress towards a solution in Indo-China. When Tomlinson said in the Cambodian context, that he hoped the Russians would us[e] their influence with Hanoi in favour of moderation and restraint, Kozyrev responded somewhat tartly that it was for the British to try to influence their American friends' (telegram No. 304 to Moscow, 8 April, ENS 3/548/14).

[16] On 8 April Lord Chalfont discussed with Mr. Kozyrev differences between the Soviet Union and UK on how to tackle the control of chemical and biological weapons, an issue currently under discussion in the CCD. The Soviet Union wanted to ban both types of weapon in a single treaty whereas the UK preferred to start with a 'ban on BW and go on to CW'. Lord Chalfont also welcomed the Soviet Union's willingness to accept a treaty banning the emplacement of nuclear weapons and other weapons of mass destruction on the seabed (cf. No. 32, note 7), and expressed the hope that a treaty would be signed later that year.

economic importance which required all our energies on both sides. But, because of intelligence activities against British citizens both in the Soviet Union and the United Kingdom, security issues had become a major pre-occupation of British public opinion as well as of Her Majesty's Government.[17] We did not encourage publicity in these matters. But we had not only to safeguard national security, but to be seen to be doing so. It was our earnest wish to develop bilateral relations in a positive way and without repetitions of the difficulties which had arisen over the last year on these issues. Any indication that the Soviet Government shared this desire would be welcome. Sir Denis Greenhill added that he could not over-emphasise how important Soviet attitudes on these matters were to the assessment of Soviet motives by British opinion.

13. He said that he had spoken to Mr. Kozyrev with frankness and with sincerity, and he hoped that he had persuaded him that there was an earnest wish on the British side to do constructive business both on the political, economic and cultural fronts.

14. *Mr. Kozyrev* said he would first like to thank Sir Denis Greenhill and all others concerned for the invitation he had received to stay on for an exchange of views on the problems that had been mentioned. He would like to say that, as a member of the Consultative Committee, he had gained the impression that the meeting of the Committee had been useful for developing our relations in the various spheres it was competent to deal with. All the members of the Soviet Group had proceeded from the general line of the Soviet Government towards the United Kingdom: this was the line of the all-round development of our relations on the basis of our mutual interest. The Soviet Union had always considered, and continued to consider, that the United Kingdom could play as important a role as before in international affairs. In relations between the United Kingdom and the USSR, the Soviet Union thought that the United Kingdom could play a beneficial role in strengthening peace and security, not only in Europe. The Soviet Union had a high regard for all the actions of the United Kingdom which were directed to this aim. He had noted with gratification Sir Denis Greenhill's remarks about a desire in the United Kingdom to develop cooperation with the Soviet Union. The Soviet Union was ready for such cooperation. This had been stated on more than one occasion to Sir Duncan Wilson in Moscow and by the Soviet Ambassador in London. The Soviet Union placed particular importance on the possibilities for cooperation in the field of European security. When they said they were ready to bring about such cooperation, and that they advocated an all-European security conference, they did not want to harm in any way the existing Economic Community, which the United Kingdom wished to join. It did not follow at all from the second item in the Prague proposals[18] that the Soviet Union wished to tread on the corns of the European Economic Community. Mr. Kozyrev would like to make

---

[17] Cf. No. 43.

[18] i.e. the expansion of trade.

more detailed remarks about this later on. In the meantime, he wished to turn to our bilateral relations.

15. Both sides knew that our relations had developed unevenly. On the one ha[n]d relations had developed in trade, science, technology, culture, education and sport. The Soviet Union attached considerable importance to scientific and technological cooperation, and work was already proceeding in the 16 Working Groups.[19] The new Joint Commission would give this a new impetus. He approved of Sir Denis Greenhill's remark that Her Majesty's Government would encourage the development of contacts in these various fields. In so far as economic, technological and cultural contacts were concerned, he thought that these were developing satisfactorily.

16. On the other hand, however, it was important to note that political contacts were limited and that political relations left much to be desired. But, as the Italians said, it took two to make a love-match. When we said that we were ready to develop contacts and ties we naturally proceeded from the existing social and political systems of our two countries. But this should not impede the development of these relations. There had also been periods when they had been by no means good, and these periods had done nobody any good. In brief, Mr. Kozyrev agreed that there was undoubtedly unused potential for the development of economic, scientific and technological cooperation, as well as in other fields, but there was also room for broader and more fruitful political contacts. The Soviet Union had emphasised many times that it attached great importance to personal contacts at the highest levels, for example between our respective Ministers, and also between officials of the Foreign Ministries of the two countries. This was why he had been glad to accept the invitation to remain in London, and to have a useful, frank and sincere exchange of views. This would enable us to understand better each other's point of view, and help us to solve some if not all of our problems. The Soviet Union thought that topics for such consultations could include, apart from bilateral relations, European security, the Middle East, and disarmament. There were also questions affecting the activities of the United Nations, such as the strengthening of international security, peace-keeping operations, the peaceful use of the sea bed, the United Nations Budget and other matters.

17. He did not need to emphasise what he had already said on the Soviet Union's readiness for such contacts. He wished to finish his remarks on bilateral relations with an expression of surprise at what he believed Sir Denis Greenhill had referred to as activities affecting security, or some such phrase. He had not quite understood this. But he wished to reject emphatically and categorically the unfounded charges against the Soviet Union and its authorities. (*Note:* Mr. Kozyrev used the word 'Services'—*Sluzhby*—which was interpreted by Mr. Sukhodrev as 'authorities'.) Unfortunately he felt bound to state that the Soviet side was firmly convinced, and had facts to prove it, that

[19] Set up under the terms of the Anglo-Soviet Technological Agreement: cf. No. 2, note 5, and No. 32.

the 'Special Services' of the United Kingdom conducted constant, hostile and provocative activities against Soviet nationals. Every such act by the 'Special Services' of the United Kingdom caused indignation in the Soviet Union. Mr. Kozyrev said that he wished to say this in all frankness and to give it some emphasis. He did not want anybody to introduce such elements into our relations, which aroused hatred or hostility instead of sympathy between our peoples.

18. He had already said that the question of developing relations was always a two-sided matter. We should believe that he was serious when he had affirmed that the United Kingdom could play an important role in world affairs. This was why they were willing to talk with us about convening a European Security Conference. He had spoken to Mr. Stewart about this question, and had asked him why the United Kingdom took a negative attitude to the Conference. He found this hard to understand. It seemed that we agreed about the need to ensure European security. In proposing a Conference, the Soviet Union had proceeded from the need to take concrete measures to ensure European security, which was the pivotal problem in Europe. The Soviet position was based on the desire to avoid a new military confrontation in Europe. This was in the interests of all European countries, and of others beyond Europe. It was not fortuitous that the proposal had been welcomed by an overwhelming majority of European countries. Everyone agreed that a Conference was expedient and necessary, and had an important role to play in bringing about *détente* and cooperation on an all-European basis. The Soviet Union considered that European countries could solve these problems and undertake this noble task. He wished to add that in the bilateral and multilateral talks which the Soviet Union had held, concrete preparations for a Conference had been discussed. The principle was already accepted by all. It was the time, place, and agenda that were being discussed now. The Soviet Union's choice for the agenda was not accidental, but a product of consultation with other countries. The proposal paid due regard to the opinions of many European countries, the majority of whom said that the questions to be taken up were those on which a broad degree of agreement was possible, thus assuring the success of the Conference.

[19.] All European countries agreed on the need to preserve European security. The first item in the Prague list met this need. The signing of a solemn pledge on the non-use of force, that is the renunciation of war to resolve quarrels, would be very important, particularly in Europe, where there was a direct political and military confrontation. The strengthening of security and improvement of the atmosphere would also be promoted by acceptance of the second Prague document. The development of economic cooperation without discrimination would be in the interests of all European countries. It would raise employment levels and the well-being of all peoples. The Soviet Union thought that the Conference should not be overloaded. Some people said that one Conference would be insufficient. They suggested that some permanent organ should be set up. There had been other considerations voiced. The Soviet proposal was for one Conference, but other proposals could be discussed most attentively at the Conference. Some countries had suggested discussing the human environment at the Conference. The Soviet Union thought this an important topic, and much had been done in the USSR. It could be discussed under the second item. There were also other suggestions. But the Conference must not be overloaded, otherwise it would not be able to conclude its work successfully.

19. [*sic*] As for balanced force reductions, the Soviet Union did not think that this could be discussed at the first Conference. This question involved many other problems; for example, disarmament, especially nuclear disarmament, which was being discussed at Geneva. It seemed that such proposals would lead to bloc-to-bloc discussions, since not all European countries were concerned. The Soviet Union had the impression that the suggestion of this item for the European Security Conference, like the proposals that Germany or West Berlin be discussed, was intended for propaganda purposes or with the concealed aim of impeding the convening of the Conference. He must add that this impression was strengthened by Sir Denis Greenhill's remarks on NATO's deliberations about an alternative to the European Security Conference. Some people said that it would be best to see the outcome of SALT, or of the talks between Germany and the USSR, or those between Germany and other socialist countries, before a Conference. He thought that this was a wrong approach. One could reverse the argument: the Conference might help the talks. He accepted Sir Denis Greenhill's assurance that the United Kingdom was not opposed to a Conference. But he hoped that the United Kingdom would adopt a more positive approach. He would like Sir Denis Greenhill to reconsider the British attitude.

20. [*sic*] *Sir Denis Greenhill* thanked Mr. Kozyrev for his extremely helpful exposition of the Soviet point of view. He suggested that the discussion be continued over a working lunch.[20]

---

[20] In a letter of 14 April to Sir D. Wilson, Sir D. Greenhill commented that the FCO had found Mr. Kozyrev 'pretty sticky, and his main subject of conversation throughout . . . was the desirability of an all-European Conference as proposed by the Soviet Union, and the inflexibility of our own reaction to this proposal. But I think it was very useful to expose him both to London itself, which must make quite an impression on a man who last saw it in 1947, and to our own thinking on international affairs generally . . . I hope we succeeded in convincing him that our interest in developing all the positive aspects is very keen.' Sir D. Greenhill explained that he had 'decided to raise the matter of the KGB's activities across the table rather than, as you had recommended, taking Mr. Kozyrev aside about it separately . . . In my view, it is a good thing to have this on record, so that we can refer back to it as necessary . . . I do not think Mr. Kozyrev could possibly be justified in interpreting what we said to him as showing a lack of interest in the development of what is valuable in our relations. Equally, for reasons of which you are aware, I wished to avoid leaving him with the impression that we were happy to put up with any amount of nonsense from the KGB' (ENS 3/ 548/ 14).

No. 46

Record of the Seventh Meeting of the Conference of HM Representatives in Eastern Europe, held at 11.00 a.m. on Friday, 8 May, 1970[1]

[*EN 2/21*]

Confidential

Present:
Sir T. Brimelow (*in the Chair*)
Sir D. Greenhill

HM Representatives[2]	*Foreign and Commonwealth Office*[3]
Sir D. Wilson (Moscow)	Mr. C.S.R. Giffard
Sir T. Garvey (Belgrade)	Mr. C.L.G. Mallaby
Mr. D.S. Laskey (Bucharest)	Mr. P. J. Weston
Mr. D.S.L. Dodson (Budapest)	Mr. J.R. Paterson
Mr. H.F.T. Smith (Prague)	Mr. R. Brash
Mr. D. A. Logan (Sofia)	Mr. J.P. Waterfield
Mr. J.N. Henderson (Warsaw)	Mr. E.E. Orchard
Mr. J.C.W. Bushell (Berlin)	Mr. J. Maslen
Mr. L. Fielding (Paris)	Mr. M. Jones
Mr. W.B.J. Ledwidge (Helsinki)	*Other Departments*
	Mr. Thomson (Assessment Staff)

Sir T. Brimelow said that the subject for the meeting had to some extent been anticipated on the previous day, when conclusions for presentation to the Secretary of State had been formulated.[4] He then read out a summary

[1] The biennial conference of Ambassadors in Eastern Europe (cf. No. 10) began on 4 May 1970. Senior commercial officers also attended. The first meeting on the morning of 4 May discussed political developments in individual countries of Eastern Europe and attitudes towards the West, a discussion continued that afternoon when Mr. Thomson (Chancellor of the Duchy of Lancaster) was also present. 5 May was free for individual discussions with EESD and other Whitehall departments. The 3rd and 4th meetings on 6 May considered commercial prospects in Eastern Europe and UK trade policy, and the 5th and 6th meetings on 7 May information and cultural work. The 7th meeting was followed by a final session on personnel and administrative matters.

[2] Ambassadors at their respective Posts, except for Mr. Logan (Ambassador designate), Mr. Bushell (HM Minister and Deputy Commandant, Berlin) and Mr. Fielding (First Secretary, Paris). Although Sir R. Jackling was not listed as present at this meeting, his views as expressed in an earlier session are summarised below by Sir T. Brimelow.

[3] Mr. Weston and Mr. Paterson were members of EESD, Mr. Maslen and Mr. Jones of Research Department and Information Research Department (IRD) respectively.

[4] The Ambassadors had held a separate meeting the previous afternoon, chaired by Sir T. Brimelow and attended by Mr. Giffard, Mr. Mallaby, Mr. Bache (EESD) and Mr. Marshall (IRD). They discussed East-West relations, the desirability of political exchanges with Eastern European countries and the prospects for a European security conference. A note of the agreed conclusions formed the basis for a discussion with Mr. Stewart immediately after the 7th meeting of the Conference: see note 15 below.

of the views presented by each Ambassador during earlier sessions of the Conference. (This summary is incorporated in paras 2-13 below.)

2. *Sir D. Wilson* thought that Soviet attitudes towards the West may be becoming more accommodating. He put this forward only as a hypothesis. He thought that political and economic pressures must at least be causing an internal debate on the desirability of having a better relationship with the West. The last few months have shown how deeply the Soviet leaders are now concerned with technological backwardness. They need scientific and technical co-operation. It may be that by agreeing to the political talks now in progress with the Americans, the West Germans, the French and ourselves they are trying to create a stable political foundation for long-term scientific technical co-operation. This is at least, in Sir Duncan Wilson's opinion, a reasonable hypothesis. If correct, it implies readiness on the part of at least some of the Soviet leaders to have with the West some more lasting arrangement than a temporary and tactical *détente*. They may be willing to pay no higher price for this than the mere maintenance of negotiations, with no progress on substance. But this would risk creating disappointment in the West. It would not improve the prospects for their European Security Conference and it might provoke a backlash in Germany. They must therefore have in mind the possibility of moves by them which would be capable of producing a more stable relationship with the West. If this assumption can be made, the West should have a flexible policy and should be prepared to respond with more than the development of technical and commercial and cultural relations. Sir D. Wilson asked for more visits—by Ministers, officials, parliamentary groups, in order to keep a dialogue going from which something might emerge. He pointed out that many other NATO Governments are already doing this, and that by pursuing such a policy we should only be catching up with them. He thought that if we do not try to embark on a meaningful dialogue with the Soviet Government, we may be missing a chance. Our attitude of aloofness may not affect East-West relations generally, but it might have an adverse effect on our own position in Soviet eyes. The French gained economic advantages from their policy of talking to the Russians. The UK could have got more if our attitude had been different. Sir D. Wilson thinks that recent developments in Cambodia[5] have not so far invalidated this analysis.

[5] Cf. No. 45, note 15. On the evening of 30 April President Nixon announced in a televised speech that US ground and air forces, with South Vietnamese forces, were undertaking operations in Cambodia against North Vietnamese and Viet Cong bases. He denied that the purpose of these operations was to occupy Cambodia, and made clear his readiness to negotiate a peace settlement 'whenever Hanoi is ready to negotiate seriously' (*Public Papers: Nixon, 1970*, pp. 405-10). On 1 May Mr. Stewart announced in the House of Commons that he was going to approach the Russians to urge the use of the Geneva machinery to help in the problem of Cambodia (*Parl. Debs., H. of C., 5th ser.*, vol. 800, col. 1613), and later that day spoke to Mr. Smirnovsky on these lines, handing him a message to Mr. Gromyko expressing his belief that the co-Chairmen of the Geneva Conference had an 'obligation to take urgent action'. Mr. Smirnovsky delivered Mr. Gromyko's reply on 20 May, stating that the 'present situation in Indo-China created by the US aggression makes the convening of a new Geneva Conference under the

3. *Mr. Henderson*, whose views were close to those of Sir D. Wilson discussed the independence of the Governments of Eastern Europe and its relevance to the value of developing a political dialogue with them. He admitted that the Polish leaders were subservient, but thought that they none the less had interests which were different from those of Moscow, and they had room for manoeuvre. Their main wish (more important for Poland than for other East European Governments) is to have their frontiers finally settled.

4. The economic malaise in Poland is deep. Neither Moscow nor Comecon can solve the problems. The Poles fear a deal between the West Germans and the Russians over their heads. To avert this, they are talking to the West Germans themselves, in the hope that they can settle their own future.[6] Yet they find that it is Moscow that is really playing the hand. We should encourage them in their talks with the West Germans, since it has been fear of Germany which has kept the Poles clamped to Moscow. We ourselves can help to lessen their subservience to Moscow by talking to them. The possibility that we ourselves may derive no benefit from talking to the Poles need not deter us. Other NATO Governments are talking to them. The Poles regard us as the most censorious, the most rigid and the least understanding of all NATO Governments. The Polish Foreign Minister is in Paris. The French Prime Minister will go to Poland this autumn. Mr. Henderson would like us to resume political talks with the Poles and to show greater interest in their views on European security.

5. *Mr. Smith* had said that in Czechoslovakia there was no great demand for a European Security Conference. There have been no visits to Prague by United Kingdom Ministers since the 1968 invasion, yet Czechoslovakia is far from having returned to Stalinism. We should not be too dejected about the present state of affairs in Czechoslovakia. On the other hand, Mr. Smith questioned what would be achieved by talks of the kind suggested by Sir D. Wilson and Mr. Henderson. On European security the Czechoslovak Government said what the Russians wanted them to say. Yet they were happy to talk. Indeed they would like to talk and talk and talk—if not about the kind of European Security Conference proposed by the Warsaw Pact, at least about European security. Mr. Smith doubted whether the holding of a

---

prevailing conditions unreal', and calling for the US to withdraw its troops immediately. Mr. Smirnovsky declined to be drawn when the PUS said that the Soviet suggestion was 'not realistic' and that 'the important thing was to try to take some practical measures to improve the situation', and Sir D. Wilson was told that nothing further would be said formally to the Russians, although he should 'take any appropriate opportunity to urge them informally to modify their attitude' (telegrams Nos. 467, 468, 496 to Moscow, 21 and 29 May, FA 3/303/2).

[6] Political discussions between the FRG and Poland had begun with talks in Warsaw between Herr Duckwitz, Deputy Foreign Minister of the FRG, and Mr. Winiewicz, Polish Vice Foreign Minister, on 5 and 6 February. The Poles pressed for a demarcation treaty recognising the Western frontier (Oder-Neisse Line) as agreed at Potsdam, while the FRG maintained that recognition would have to be embodied in a peace treaty. Further rounds of talks were held in Warsaw on 9-11 March and 22-24 April, after which the Polish Government asked for time to study the FRG proposal for a two-part agreement encompassing an agreement on the border question and a declaration on the renunciation of the use of force (ENP 3/309/1, WRE 4/1).

European Security Conference of the kind proposed by the Warsaw Pact would in fact be in the interests of the countries of Eastern Europe. It would serve neither them nor NATO. Moreover if we were to have political talks with the Governments of Eastern Europe, and if in these talks we were to remain faithful to the NATO line, such talks could in themselves be counter-productive. So far as Czechoslovakia was concerned, Mr. Smith did not think that the French are reaping commercial advantages from their independent policy. He thought that the level of trade depended on the efforts of businessmen.

6. *Mr. Dodson* examined, on the basis of experience in Hungary, where the process of economic reform is fairly advanced, the theory that economic reform may impose political liberalisation. He pointed out that the Party leaders oppose political liberalisation, and thought that if political liberalisation does eventually come about, the process will be a lengthy one.

7. As regards European Security, Mr. Dodson suspects that the Hungarian Government hope that the holding of a Conference (which has economic and technological co-operation as the second item on its agenda) might help to diminish Soviet pressures on Hungary to buy more from the USSR. Mr. Dodson would welcome more Ministerial visits. The Hungarians would like to develop their relations with the West.

8. *Mr. Laskey* said that although the Rumanians were not subservient to the Russians, they were conscious of the degree of their economic dependence on the USSR, and were realistic in their relations with the Soviet Government. They studied and would like to strengthen the restraints which limit Soviet intervention in Eastern Europe. They would like to see *détente* in Europe. They argued that if, in 1968, preparations for a European Security Conference had been under way, it would have been more difficult for the Russians to invade Czechoslovakia. They thought that today it would be more difficult for the Russians to invade a Warsaw Pact country. Although they realised that Rumanian resistance to a Soviet invasion would be ineffective, they said publicly that Rumania would be defended against attack from any quarter, believing that if a Soviet invasion were to be resisted by force, this would have such a shattering effect within the World Communist movement that the Russians would not attempt it. As regards a European Security Conference, they wanted not a date but preparations. They wanted a new declaration about sovereignty, in the belief that this would implicitly condemn the Brezhnev doctrine. They held that even a paper declaration would be better than nothing. They wanted a preparatory meeting of officials. They were pleased to have bilateral talks, but they wanted multilateral talks as well. They wanted such multilateral talks to be open-ended. Let all who wished take part.

9. *Sir Roger Jackling* said that the Federal German Government was disappointed with the results so far achieved in its talks with the Soviet, Polish

and East German Governments.[7] The opposition had become more strident, and there was trouble in the Bundestag, which would have to ratify any formal agreement. But Brandt was going to push ahead at all costs. Only thus could he hope to maintain a momentum capable of producing results. But if he could make no progress at the Kassel meeting, he might change the emphasis to technical agreements. Brandt believed that progress in relations with the Governments of Eastern Europe depended on progress in the Berlin talks. The Germans think that the Russians have not made up their minds whether to reach a genuine *détente* with the West. Meanwhile the East Germans are trying to gain unqualified international recognition, and it is an open question whether the process of creeping recognition can be kept under control. If the East Germans are prepared to make some concessions in the humanitarian field, Sir R. Jackling believes that Brandt will be prepared to go a long way on the issue of recognition. Sir R. Jackling believes that the British interest is to encourage the Federal German Government in every way, though he conceded that we could do with more, better and earlier information from the Federal Government about the moves it intends to make. The right line is for the United Kingdom to point out what difficulties we may foresee, but not to seek to hold the Federal Government back from the improvement of its relations with the East.

10. Commenting on the views expressed by Sir D. Wilson, Sir R. Jackling said that, as seen from Bonn, it looked more likely that the normal ambivalence of Soviet policy would be resolved in favour of rigidity. The dangers to the Russian position in East Germany and Eastern Europe from a marked improvement in East-West relations seemed to outweigh the advantages.

11. *Mr. Ledwidge* summarised the views of the Finnish Government on European Security. They thought that the Soviet Union was militarily strong, but that the Soviet Government was confronted by grave problems. They believe that Finland could best preserve her neutrality if the Soviet Government were on not too bad terms with the Western powers. On European security, the Finns would not put forward any proposals which the Russians might reject, but their aim would always be to protect Finnish neutrality. Kekkonen thinks we are at a point where there are more hopes of finding a way to European security. He thinks that the old bloc to bloc confrontation is breaking up. He fears that the Russians may make greater use of their military strength if the West is tough: but if the West is flexible, the chance

---

[7] Cf. No. 45, note 9, and note 6 above. Preliminary talks between the FRG and GDR had been in progress since 2 March, and on 19 March Herr Brandt met Herr Willi Stoph, Prime Minister of the GDR, at Erfurt to exchange views on inner-German relations—the first time that two German Heads of Government had met. On 21 May they met again at Kassel in West Germany, when Herr Brandt put forward twenty points for an inner-German agreement, including the maintenance of Four Power rights with respect to Berlin. Herr Stoph, however, insisted that the recognition of the GDR in international law must precede all other arrangements, and the talks adjourned for a 'pause for thought'. Documents relating to these talks are printed in Cmnd. 6201, Nos. 110-19.

that the Russians may make counter-concessions is greater than it was five years ago. But the Finns see value in talks *per se*. They themselves avoid taking sides on questions of substance. They wish their own proposals to be differentiated from those of the Warsaw Pact. Their assumption is that talking may produce results, whereas a refusal to talk may incur danger. The United States have discouraged the publication of an interim report on Mr. Enckell's letter.[8]

The Finns would welcome a more positive NATO approach next May.

Mr. Ledwidge said that his French colleague was freer to discuss European security with the Finns than he himself was.

The Finns also believe that if a discussion on European security is in progress at the time of our accession to the Common Market, this will to some extent protect the smaller neutrals against heavy Soviet pressure designed to prevent their coming to terms with an enlarged EEC. For the Finns, the break-up of EFTA presents economic problems. They fear they may be forced into greater dependence on the USSR.

They have found from their own experience that the Russians are easiest to deal with when they are not worried about their own security. The Finns are simply extending this experience of theirs to the European theatre. They want a dialogue that will go on for a long time.

12. *Sir T. Garvey* said that Yugoslavia, whose non-aligned policy was based firmly upon the balance of strength between the two blocs, had not been keen to see a Conference take place which might undermine the existing basis of East-West relations and replace it with something even less satisfactory. The Yugoslavs however now reckoned that a European Security Conference of some sort was in the end likely to come about and would wish, if it did, to turn it to their own purposes. They saw a Conference as an opportunity for putting the Brezhnev doctrine in the dock. Though perhaps less hopeful than the Rumanians, they believed that it could, by providing opportunities for semi-independent action by the East European countries, become an instrument for the 'emancipation' of the latter, which was one of Yugoslavia's aims. They also insisted that a European Security Conference should discuss the problem of balanced force reductions, although they probably had only a hazy idea of the difficulties involved. It was, for them, axiomatic that the Conference should be open to all, including countries not members of blocs.

[8] On 23 February Mr. A. Karjalainen, Finnish Foreign Minister, had issued a statement announcing that 'in order to give its own contribution to advancing the process of European security' the Finnish Government had appointed Ralph Enckell, representative of Finland at the OECD in Paris, as roving ambassador to report on progress with regard to the possible establishment of a European Security Conference. He had already visited Budapest, Berne, Vienna, Belgrade, Paris, Brussels, Moscow, Warsaw, Helsinki and Ottawa, and had just returned from Washington. It is not clear which 'letter' is under reference here, but accounts of Mr. Enckell's visits are filed in WDW 1/138/1. He was due to visit London on 14-15 May.

13. There was no serious difficulty about maintaining a dialogue with the Yugoslav Government, who were ready to talk, and from a point of view which was quite distinct from that of the Warsaw Pact Governments.

14. *Mr. Thomson*,[9] after discussing the East-West talks now in progress, said so much was now going on that it might be held that a European Security Conference had become superfluous. It was not very likely that we should find a basis for multi-lateral talks with a serious agenda. But it was vitally important to show to public opinion that if real progress cannot be made, it is not NATO's fault. The Heads of Mission seemed to feel that they were not getting enough ammunition, that they were frustrated by our adherence to what had been agreed in NATO. Yet we could only hope to make progress on the basis of the Alliance. A balance had to be struck between the wish to talk, and faithfulness to NATO. There was no truth in Soviet charges that we were dragging our feet. The opposite was true. He could not pre-judge what would emerge from the next NATO meeting.[10]

15. On the question of Ministerial visits to Eastern Europe, Mr. Thomson pointed out how busy Ministers were with other things; how deep the effect of the invasion of Czechoslovakia had been; and how important it was to deal at this stage with our accession to the Communities; but he said he would consider the possibility of more Ministerial visits to Eastern Europe.

16. He also said that if the May NATO Ministerial visit [*sic*] proved to be a dead loss, Ministers would have to consider what line they should take.

17. The *Permanent Under Secretary* emphasized the danger of our taking part in any diplomacy without substance. He mentioned the United States aversion to diplomacy by meaningless charades, designed simply to give a false sense of action and movement. He drew attention to the much greater burden on United Kingdom Ministers than on some of the NATO Ministers who were engaging in East-West diplomacy. He questioned whether a conference that failed would be a good thing.

18. The *general conclusion* was that there is a real demand in Eastern Europe for political talks with this country; that after the May NATO Ministerial meeting it may be disadvantageous for us to persist in the reticence we have shown hitherto; that this will be so no matter what reservations we may have about the motives and intentions of the Warsaw Pact Governments; that there will be no point in being reserved with the Finns once we have spent two days talking to Mr. Enckell in London on 14-15 May;[11] and that there is a

---

[9] It is not clear whether Mr. Thomson was present at the 7th meeting of the Conference, or if Sir T. Brimelow was here reporting his views as expounded at the 2nd meeting (see note 1).

[10] The NATO Ministerial meeting was to be held in Rome from 26-27 May.

[11] See note 8 above. During his visit Mr. Enckell called on Mr. Luard, Sir D. Greenhill, Sir T. Brimelow and Mr. D.V. Bendall, Assistant Under-Secretary superintending SED, WED and WOD. Sir T. Brimelow told Mr. Enckell on 14 May that the Secretary of State's approach was 'not negative on issues of European security. We had explained this to Mr. Kozyrev when he had been here recently [No. 45]. The conclusion Mr. Kozyrev drew was that we were genuinely interested in European security if not in their proposals for an ESC.' Mr. Enckell said 'In the Finnish view the conference should not only have a reasonable assurance of some progress, there

case for developing a cautious political dialogue with the Warsaw Pact Governments after the next NATO Ministerial meeting, partly through Ambassadors, partly by visits of officials, and at Ministerial level where appropriate. These conclusions are consistent with the line taken in the Anglo-Belgian draft *Communiqué*,[12] for which we shall try to gain acceptance at the NATO May Ministerial Meeting.

19. After Sir T. Brimelow had finished reading his summary of earlier comments, (which were agreed by individual Ambassadors) *Sir D. Greenhill* asked the Ambassadors for a collective judgement of the rightness of the line we intended to take at the forthcoming NATO Ministerial Meeting. What did they think of the idea of a Standing Commission on East-West relations?[13] *Sir D. Wilson* said that a Standing Commission stood no chance of Soviet acceptance if it was to be a substitute for a Conference, but it could provide a vehicle for multilateral discussions following a Conference. *Mr. Henderson* said that he did not believe we would attain our objectives at the NATO Meeting, but that we should not be too inhibited by discussions in NATO. Other NATO countries pursued policies with regard to Eastern European countries which went beyond general policies accepted in NATO. He did not think the idea of a Standing Commission was likely to succeed in NATO. The main aim, from the British angle, was to give the impression of taking the East European countries seriously. *Mr. Ledwidge* supported the Dutch idea that whatever conclusions were reached in NATO should be put in a form that could be communicated to individual East European countries. This would give an impression of progress. *Mr. Laskey* thought that Mr. Thomson's formula of multilateral exploratory conversations was preferable to a Standing Commission.

20. *Sir D. Greenhill* said that the idea of a Standing Commission was to see if we could produce sufficient topics to discuss to make a Security Conference sound a sensible proposition. The agenda so far proposed for a Security Conference was not enough. A Standing Commission would have the definite purpose of producing real things to talk about. *Sir D. Wilson* said he believed that multilateral exploratory talks were a good way of putting it, and one which did not suggest that we were proposing an alternative to a Conference.

should also be a certainty that it would not disturb or complicate progress in talks elsewhere', and described his task as 'explaining their own position, exploring others and examining what ought to be done'. Sir T. Brimelow concluded that it was 'accidental that talks on substantial questions of European security should have started within a few months of the Budapest Declaration . . . He wondered to what extent the Russians were sincere in seeking a conference. Were they really after the security of Europe or after private ends which had nothing in common with European security but only Warsaw Pact security[?]' (WDW 1/ 138/ 1, WDW 1/ 2).

[12] Agreed Anglo-Belgian texts of a draft *communiqué* for the forthcoming NATO meeting and a draft declaration on MBFR advocated a positive if cautious move forward to exploratory multilateral discussions. The drafts were discussed when Mr. Stewart visited Washington for the CENTO Ministerial meeting 13-15 May; the US draft presented to NATO was much less positive in tone.

[13] Cf. No. 39, note 8.

Mr. Smith asked what was really meant by multilateral exploratory talks. *Mr. Dodson* said that the Hungarians were in favour of a Conference followed by some kind of permanent machinery. *Sir. D. Wilson* said that in the exploratory talks one could put forward certain ideas of one's own and hope to exclude certain ideas put forward by the other side. *Sir D. Greenhill* said that we had never excluded the idea of a Conference, but questioned whether the other side wanted to discuss matters which really had a bearing on European security. This could be done in multilateral exploratory talks or a Standing Commission, but there must be a businesslike approach.

21. *Sir T. Brimelow* said that the Secretary of State believed that in the talks now going on we had a means of ascertaining whether the other side were prepared to engage in productive negotiations. The difference between Sir D. Wilson's view and the Secretary of State's was that the latter was still watching for evidence before deciding about multilateral negotiations, whereas the former wished to move forward on the assumption that the other side was also willing to do so. *Sir D. Wilson* and *Mr. Henderson* said that they were under the impression that London had suggested that a Standing Commission was an alternative to a Conference. *Sir D. Greenhill* said that this was true if they meant the Conference as proposed at present by the other side. The Russians had proposed a Conference with two items on the agenda, but we did not think that this was a worthwhile proposition. We preferred the idea of a Standing Commission to discuss real and important matters which could then form the agenda of an acceptable Conference. *Mr. Dodson* said that the first item of the Conference agenda proposed by the Russians, non-use of force, was superfluous since the Germans were already discussing it. The second agenda item about economic co-operation was one we might be prepared to discuss if the agenda was to be enlarged. *Sir D. Greenhill* said it had never been clear to him what the Russians were after in their second item. They proposed increases in trade and technological contacts, but these exchanges were already covered in various bilateral Agreements. It was suggested by several speakers that Soviet aims might be to undermine COCOM, to weaken the EEC, and to get more export credits.

22. *Sir. T. Brimelow* read out the key passages of the Anglo-Belgian draft *Communiqué* at present before NATO. He said that the American attitude was much more reserved than the one expressed in the Anglo-Belgian draft. *Mr. Smith* asked if it was proposed that any declaration on force reductions should be communicated to Governments. *Sir T. Brimelow* replied that this was so. *Mr. Waterfield* said that the *Communiqué* might be communicated by each NATO country to every non-NATO country in Europe with which it had relations. *Sir D. Wilson* asked what should be his answer to Mr. Kozyrev when he handed over the *Communiqué* and Mr. Kozyrev asked for our views on the scope of the exploratory talks, and participation in them? *Mr. Waterfield* said that the idea was to explore the subject matter for any eventual multilateral negotiations, taking into account the subjects proposed for negotiation by all parties. *Sir D. Greenhill* said he agreed with *Sir D. Wilson* that we should supply posts with material for dealing with questions about

aspects of our proposals for the exploratory talks. *Mr. Laskey* asked whether it would be practical to have bilateral discussions before multilateral ones. *Mr. Waterfield* said that, since Heads of Mission would be handing over *Communiqués* to Governments, a limited amount of preliminary bilateral discussion would take place. *Mr. Henderson* requested confirmation that failure to get our ideas accepted in NATO would not preclude us from taking our own line with East European Governments afterwards. *Sir. D. Greenhill* said that Heads of Mission should await the outcome of the NATO Meeting: if NATO's decisions went against us, the situation would be considered by Ministers, and Ambassadors would receive instructions.[14]

[14] At the meeting with Mr. Stewart held at 12 p.m. (see note 1) Sir T. Brimelow reported the views expressed by HM Representatives and said that 'there was a consensus that it might be disadvantageous to us if we remained reticent after the NATO meeting in May. There was a case for developing a cautious political dialogue, and for ministerial visits.' Mr. Stewart concluded that 'we must wait for the outcome of the NATO Ministerial meeting before making any major new move. If we got the *communiqué* we wanted, well and good. If we did not, we should have to consider making it clear that we would have liked a more forthcoming attitude . . . We could not put ourselves entirely in the hands of those members of the alliance who would not work for a constructive political position and who were less reliable than ourselves on the military side' (EN 2/21).

The Ministerial Session of the North Atlantic Council held in Rome on 26-27 May was, in the FCO's opinion, 'decidedly successful'. NATO Ministers issued a communiqué and a declaration on mutual and balanced force reductions which, as Mr. Stewart informed Sir D. Wilson, embodied 'in every essential the proposals which I put to the meeting'.[1] The Communiqué envisaged a three stage approach to East-West negotiations beginning with bilateral exploratory contacts: then, dependent upon progress in these exchanges and in other related negotiations (such as SALT and the Berlin talks), 'multiple exploratory contacts' would ensue to discuss the subjects for eventual negotiations and the methods of such negotiations (including the creation of a permanent body such as the Standing Commission suggested by the UK). The third stage would be actual negotiations. The separate Declaration on Mutual and Balanced Force Reductions (signed by all the Allies except the French) proposed exploratory talks in order to see whether and how negotiations could take place. It also set out certain considerations which, in the view of NATO Ministers, would be relevant in any negotiations, including problems arising from the Warsaw Pact's geographical advantages, and the need for adequate verification.

[1] Telegram No. 491 to Moscow, 28 May (WDW 1/2).

Caption 1a: Prime Minister Harold Wilson at the Opera in Moscow during his visit in January 1968, with Madame Furtseva, Soviet Minister of Culture (l.) and Alexsei Kosygin, Chairman of the Soviet Council of Ministers (r.)

Caption 1b: Sir Alec Douglas-Home, Secretary of State for Foreign Affairs, welcomes Soviet Foreign Minister Andrei Gromyko to London in October 1970; Mikhail Smirnovsky, Soviet Ambassador to London, is on Mr. Gromyko's left.

Caption 2
British Ambassadors to Moscow, 1968-72: (*a*) Sir Geoffrey Harrison; (*b*) Sir Duncan Wilson, with Lady Wilson and Mstislav Rostropovich; (*c*) Sir John Killick.

Caption 3a: Sir Denis (now Lord) Greenhill (b. 1913), Permanent Under Secretary at the FCO 1969-73

Caption 3b: Sir Thomas (later Lord) Brimelow (1915-1995), HM Ambassador in Warsaw 1966-69, Deputy Under Secretary at the FCO 1969-73

Caption 4

(*a*) Mr (later Sir) Sydney Giffard, Head of FCO Eastern European and Soviet Department 1968-71; (*b*) The Lord Bridges, Counsellor and Head of Chancery in Moscow, 1969-71, Head of FCO Western Organisations Department 1971-72, Private Secretary to the Prime Minister 1972-74. (*c*) Mr. (later Sir) Julian Bullard, Head of EESD 1971-75;

The Italian Government, as hosts to the meeting, transmitted these documents formally to all interested countries. Meanwhile, HM Representatives in Warsaw Pact countries were instructed to seek interviews 'at a very senior level', preferably on 1 June, drawing the attention of the Foreign Ministeries to the NATO documents and expressing the hope that the Warsaw Pact would respond 'in the same constructive spirit as NATO has shown'. Mr. Stewart spoke on these lines to Mr. Smirnovsky on 1 June, adding that NATO countries wished to widen the scope of any agreement on the renunciation of the use of force to cover the principles governing <u>all</u> relations between all states, including cultural exchanges and the free movement of people. Mr. Smirnovsky's reaction to the NATO documents was non-committal, though he remarked that the Communiqué seemed 'to mark an attempt to go back to square one', proposing 'talks about talks about talks'.

The Warsaw Pact's response to the NATO documents was transmitted in three documents delivered to the FCO by the Hungarian Ambassador on 26 June, following a meeting in Budapest on 21-22 June of Warsaw Pact Foreign Ministers. The most important of these was a memorandum admitting the right of the US and Canada to participate on an equal basis in an all-European conference, apparently taking up NATO's suggestion of 'multilateral exploratory contacts', and proposing that the conference should discuss the creation of an 'organ' similar to the standing commission suggested by the UK. It also contained for the first time a public statement (though ambiguous and highly qualified) of the Warsaw Pact's willingness to discuss force reductions. NATO embarked on an analysis of these documents, while bilateral exploratory contacts proceeded.[2]

Mr. Stewart's part in the continuing round of planning and discussion relating to a possible European security conference came to an abrupt end on 18 June with what the Annual Register called 'the most dramatic and unexpected electoral turn-round of the century'. The Conservative Party gained 74 seats in the General Election and won with 330 seats to Labour's 287. Mr. Edward Heath was appointed Prime Minister on 19 June, and announced his Cabinet the following day, including the appointment of Sir Alec Douglas-Home as Foreign Secretary. Sir Alec had served as Parliamentary Under Secretary for a time in 1945, as Secretary for Commonwealth Affairs 1955-60 and as Foreign Secretary from 1960-63, and Sir D. Greenhill described his return in 1970 as 'most welcome', noting his determination to get on better terms with the Soviet Union, encouraged 'by his long experience of dealing with Gromyko'.[3] The new Secretary of State's first meeting with the Soviet Ambassador was on 29 June.

[2] Extracts from the Rome *Communiqué*, the Budapest *Communiqué* and Memorandum, and the text of the Declaration on MBFR are printed in Cmnd. 6932, Nos. 20-23.

[3] Denis Greenhill, *More by Accident* (1995), pp. 144 and 157.

No. 47

Record of Conversation between Sir A. Douglas-Home and Mr. Smirnovsky in the Foreign and Commonwealth Office at 3.45 p.m. on Monday, 29 June, 1970

[*ENS 3/548/8*]

Confidential

Present:
The Rt. Hon. Sir Alec Douglas-Home, MP   HE Mr. M. Smirnovsky
Mr. N.J. Barrington   Mr. Y. Pavlov

Sir Alec Douglas-Home said that he had already sent a message of greetings to Mr. Gromyko.[1] He hoped Mr. Smirnovsky would convey his best wishes and he hoped that it might be possible to repeat some of the previous successes they had had together: the Test Ban Treaty, Laos etc.[2] He looked forward to seeing Mr. Gromyko at the UN in September. He also thanked Mr. Smirnovsky for what he had done to clear up the problem of visas for BOAC crews.[3]

2. Sir Alec Douglas-Home asked Mr. Smirnovsky about the results of the latest Warsaw Pact meeting.[4] *Mr. Smirnovsky* said that he felt they were important. The Warsaw Pact countries had moved half way to meet the NATO countries on East-West problems and if one examined what they had agreed it included most of the points put forward in the NATO *Communiqué*. They believed that the agenda for a conference should include their previous two points about renunciation of force and co-operation on the technical and trade fields (and also in the cultural field), together with a third point which

[1] In telegram No. 587 to Moscow of 25 June Sir A. Douglas-Home asked Sir D. Wilson to tell the Soviet Foreign Ministry that 'the Prime Minister and I are in favour of maintaining an Anglo-Soviet dialogue on established lines on matters of bilateral and international concern . . . If asked about high-level exchanges, you should say that I much look forward to taking advantage of any opportunities for meeting Mr. Gromyko' (ENS 3/548/7).

[2] In August 1963, Lord Home (as he then was) had visited Moscow to sign with Mr. Gromyko the Partial Test Ban Treaty prohibiting the testing of nuclear weapons in the atmosphere, sea or space (*BFSP*, vol. 167, pp. 178-81). Lord Home and Mr. Gromyko had also been co-chairmen of the International Conference for the Settlement of the Laotian Question held in Geneva from 12 May 1961 to 23 July 1962, which agreed a Declaration and Protocol on the Neutrality of Laos (*op. cit.*, vol. 166, pp. 702-31).

[3] The inauguration of BOAC's new service to Tokyo (cf. No. 44, note 9) had been threatened by the Russian refusal to grant a sufficient number of visa exemptions for BOAC pilots and crew. Strong representations in Moscow had achieved little, but following the intervention of Mr. Ippolitov BOAC had been told that their list of required visa exemptions had been granted in full. Mr. R. Hanbury-Tenison of Aviation & Telecommunications Department noted on 29 June that 'Without the Embassy's help it is likely that the Tokyo service would have had to be discontinued at the end of this month, with most unfortunate results for this new and promising venture in Anglo/Soviet cooperation' (MUA 4/303/1).

[4] See p. 239.

would be the creation of a permanent body to discuss further problems of European Security, so that one could move step by step to resolve them.

3. When *Sir Alec Douglas-Home* asked whether the idea of a permanent body was a useful one, and whether it might duplicate the work of the Disarmament Committee in Geneva, *Mr. Smirnovsky* defended the idea of a permanent body. He explained that it would be concentrated on European issues and not affect the work being done in Geneva on world problems such as the sea bed.[5] The time was right to make practical arrangements for increasing security in Europe. Mr. Smirnovsky confirmed that the Warsaw Pact countries were prepared to discuss withdrawal of foreign troops from the territories of European states including not only withdrawal of American troops, but withdrawal of Soviet troops from Eastern Europe. *Sir Alec Douglas-Home* said that it was a good thing that the points of view of both sides were coming closer together.

4. He then asked about other world problems which were preoccupying the Russians. *Mr. Smirnovsky* mentioned the Middle East. He said that his Government were studying the American proposals.[6] His personal view was that more precision was needed in the instructions for Dr. Jarring. His Government had recently made a constructive step by putting forward proposals for 'peace' in the four power talks. This had been recognised as constructive. They thought it would be useful for the four powers to be involved and to give instructions to Dr. Jarring.

5. In answer to a question Mr. Smirnovsky explained that the Soviet plan for the Middle East included a guarantee of frontiers which would be in effect a guarantee by the Security Council itself.

6. *Sir Alec Douglas-Home* pointed out that from his experience he knew that Israel would need very special guarantees. It would be important to have cast iron security for both sides. *Mr. Smirnovsky* agreed it would be difficult to do this but said that one still had to continue to search for an agreement. The situation was dangerous and people were being killed.

7. Turning to Vietnam and Cambodia *Sir Alec Douglas-Home* said that he thought that the more the Americans were involved in South East Asia the

[5] Cf. No. 45, note 16.

[6] US proposals for a three-month ceasefire and the resumption of indirect talks under the auspices of the Jarring mission were presented first to the Israeli Government, to HMG on 19 June and to the Egyptian, French, Jordanian and Soviet Governments on 22 June. HM Minister in Washington, Mr. G. Millard, was informed by Mr. J. Sisco, US Assistant Secretary of State, that the US Government expected a positive response from Israel, to whom it had been made clear that further arms shipments 'would be influenced both by the effectiveness of the ceasefire and by the success of the negotiations' (Washington telegram No. 1892, 19 June, NEM 3/304/2). An undated minute by Sir A. Douglas-Home on this telegram stated: 'I think it is long odds against this succeeding but it is worth a try. Certainly we agree to try it.' President Nasser, who flew to Moscow on 29 June, accepted the US proposals on 23 July, on the same day that the Soviet Union, who had themselves tabled further peace proposals on 24 June, informed the US Government that they were prepared to agree to the resumption of the Jarring mission on the basis of the American proposals. The Israeli Government accepted the proposals on 31 July and the cease-fire started on 7-8 August.

greater the need for reconvening the Geneva Conference.[7] It had worked in Laos. *Mr. Smirnovsky* explained the Soviet position. The situation was complicated, but fighting must stop and troops must be removed before looking for a settlement. The American operations in Cambodia had made it more difficult. And even with their withdrawal they were not going to stop bombing over Cambodian territory. Cambodia had been neutral until the American intervention. *Sir Alec Douglas-Home* pointed out that there had been many North Vietnamese and Viet Cong in Cambodia. He thought that Mr. Smirnovsky's arguments were all arguments for a conference.

8. Sir Alec Douglas-Home concluded by saying that he would like to keep in touch with the Soviet Government on all these issues. *Mr. Smirnovsky* then touched on the subject of bilateral relations: there were one or two problems on trade and there was the Anglo-Soviet Joint Commission,[8] but he would not bother Sir Alec Douglas-Home with these minor problems now. (He did not in any way suggest that Anglo-Soviet relations were bad.)

[7] Cf. No. 46, note 5.

[8] Cf. No. 41, note 2. Difficulties had arisen in agreeing terms of reference for the Joint Commission because of Soviet attempts to extend the competence of the Commission to cover all cooperation in the fields of science, education, culture, atomic energy and agriculture instead of restricting it to matters dealt with under the Trade and Technological agreements as originally discussed. In addition, the Soviet Ministry of Foreign Trade did not believe that the Joint Commission should incorporate the work of the Annual Trade Review, which should continue to be held separately. The FCO did not agree with these proposals, and interdepartmental discussions were under way on how to respond to them.

An intensive study of Soviet policy was undertaken in the FCO in the summer of 1970 in connection with a long despatch from Bonn on Herr Brandt's Ostpolitik, which led to voluminous correspondence on the implications for British policy and for Europe as a whole of a change of dynamic in inner-German and Soviet-German relations. Speculation was increased by the progress of the Soviet-FRG talks (see No. 45, note 9), which had resumed on 13 May and adjourned on 23 May with the production of a 'non-paper' for submission to the two governments, a document considered by the FCO to be remarkable more for the fact that it was agreed at all than for its content, four 'theses' which included recognition by the FRG of existing European frontiers, though falling short of recognition of the GDR itself. The FRG decided on 5 June that it was willing to enter substantive negotiations for an agreement with the Soviet Union on the renunciation of the use of force. The FCO were surprised by the degree of agreement reached in the talks, and by the apparent and uncharacteristic willingness of the Soviet Union to accept less than their full demands, though as Mr. Mallaby pointed out, they were not giving anything up: 'What the Russians are doing is to <u>lower their sights for the time being</u>'.[1] The FCO were also concerned that Allied rights and responsibilities in regard to Germany were not sufficiently acknowledged in the 'non-paper', Sir D. Greenhill commenting on 13 July: 'I have an uneasy feeling that we are being conned by the Germans into accepting a situation in which our rights may be fundamentally affected.'

[1] Minute of 2 June (WRG 3/303/1).

Documents Nos. 48 and 50 below, on Ostpolitik and on East-West relations, encapsulate the debate on what were, at this stage, essentially hypothetical problems. No. 49 shows that the bilateral relationship, from the Soviet viewpoint at least, remained rooted in traditional polemics while functioning relatively smoothly on a practical level.

No. 48

Letter from Sir D. Wilson (Moscow) to Mr. Bendall

[*EN 2/18*]

Confidential   MOSCOW, *3 July 1970*

Dear Bendall,

I have read with very great interest Roger Jackling's despatch of 25 June on the implications of Herr Brandt's *Ostpolitik*,[1] and would like to offer a few comments on Soviet/West German relations, and more broadly on the Kremlin's *Westpolitik*, as seen from Moscow. I think that much of what I have to say is implicit in Tom Brimelow's letter to me of 13 February (quoted by Roger Jackling in his paragraph 7) and in my reply of 23 February.[2] None the less, a lot has happened in the last four months, and it is worth while to look at our analyses again in the new context.

[1] In this despatch Sir R. Jackling summarised the 'package' of agreements with the Soviet Union, Poland, Czechoslovakia and the GDR envisaged by the Federal German Government and identified the Soviet Union as the key to further progress. He foresaw (in paragraphs 9(*a*) and (*b*)) two possible scenarios developing from Herr Brandt's *Ostpolitik*: either the emergence and acceptance by all concerned of a package of agreements between the Federal Republic and her Eastern neighbours, coupled with a quadripartite agreement on Berlin; or the gradual recognition that such a package was not at present acceptable to one or other of the parties. Sir R. Jackling predicted that neither the Germans nor the Russians would see the package of agreements as a definitive European settlement and described in paragraphs 12 and 13 the possible changes to the situation in Europe which each side would hope for. He recommended that HMG continue to offer firm support for *Ostpolitik* 'because it appears to coincide with our own aim of reducing tensions in Europe, and because we need close bilateral relations with the Federal Republic' (WRG 3/513/1).

[2] In his letter to Sir D. Wilson, Sir T. Brimelow had analysed Soviet objectives and intentions with regard to the Federal Republic and the German question generally against a background concern that the 'Eastern policy of the new Federal German Government may put at risk at some time in the future both our interests in the German question and also our position in Berlin'. In concluding his reply, Sir D. Wilson said 'I am impressed both by the real difficulties which the Russians are up against in these negotiations [with the FRG] and by the conspicuous effort that they have put into them so far . . . The fact is that although it is the Russians who have been probing the German position, they are in effect exposing themselves to a test of the whole range of their European policies, particularly their intentions in the field of European security . . . they may in the end find themselves obliged to sacrifice some of Ulbricht's interests in order to secure for themselves a goal towards which other pressures—China, SALT and the technological gap, in shorthand—are already working.'

2. In particular I think it worth while to look at the present tactics of the Soviet *Westpolitik* in the light of what we conceive to be their long-term strategy; or, more concretely, to consider their policy on talks with the Federal Government, and with the Western allies over Berlin, together with their policy on European Security in general. That these policies are linked in the Russian mind is, I think, becoming increasingly clear. It looks increasingly as if the Soviet leaders have decided to work actively not only for a *de facto* accommodation in Central Europe, but also to provide a framework for the future development of Europe as a whole. One can only speculate about the motives of an otherwise rigid and unimaginative Soviet administration for taking such a major foreign policy decision. There are a number of possibilities, not mutually exclusive: the need to be free to concentrate on China in the new decade; the knowledge that Brandt is the best West German Chancellor that the Soviet Union can expect for a long time to come; the fact that Ulbricht is drawing near to the end of his time; and—probably most important of all—De Gaulle's departure from the European scene and the subsequent opening of negotiations for the enlargement of the European Economic Community.

3. I believe that the Soviet leaders are genuinely alarmed at the possibilities, which may seem to us uncomfortably remote, of an enlarged EEC which will pursue an exclusive economic policy and more integrated political and defence policies. The former would hamper their own economic development, which has reached a crucial stage and relies increasingly on technical co-operation with the West. The latter is and remains obviously a principal bogey for the Soviet leaders.

4. I believe that the long-term perspective of possible developments in EEC is one of the main factors behind the Soviet desire for a European Security Conference, and for some permanent European consultative machinery. The immediate Soviet objective in holding such a Conference is to set a general seal on the agreements separately reached by the Federal Government with the Soviet Union and Poland[3] and on whatever may be agreed by the Four Powers on Berlin[4]—i.e. to achieve a sort of substitute Peace Treaty. Thereafter, I foresee one short-term and one long-term objective. The former is to use the subsequent series of Conferences, or the standing machinery established at the first Conference, or both, as a platform from which the Soviet Union may be able to sow doubt about the wisdom of

[3] Cf. p. 242 for FRG-Soviet negotiations. The fourth round of FRG-Polish talks (see No. 46, note 6) was held in Bonn from 8-11 June, when the Polish Government, while critical of the FRG position on the Oder-Neisse Line, indicated some readiness to compromise. It was agreed that the preliminary stage of talks had ended and that the next meeting in Warsaw from 22-25 July would be devoted to formulating the texts of a treaty (ENP 3/309/1).

[4] See No. 45, note 10. Further rounds of the Four Power talks had been held on 28 April, 14 May, 9 and 30 June. Mr. Abrasimov had shown himself accommodating at some meetings, obdurate and inflexible at others. Little concrete progress had been made because of the Soviet insistence that West Berlin was a separate political entity and their rejection of any quadripartite status in East Berlin. The next meeting was due to be held on 21 July.

enlarging the EEC, e.g. by drawing attention to the huge possibilities of East-West trade that are being 'sacrificed' to the idea of West European econ-omic integration, and, should the negotiations for enlargement run into troubled waters, to fish in them as effectively as they can. I do not suppose that the Soviet Ministry of Foreign Affairs are under any illusions about their chances of securing this objective for any length of time, unless, of course, the EEC negotiations fail for a third time. Sooner or later they will face the fact that a new politico-economic entity is about to be brought into being in Western Europe. Once this stage is reached, the second Soviet objective will be paramount: in broad terms, to provide an all-European framework within which the Soviet Union will seek to contain the danger to their interests posed by the new Western European grouping. If I am right in thinking that this is their final objective, we must expect them to use the Conference from the outset, and any standing machinery that it may establish, in order to promote the idea of an 'All-European co-operation' as against any exclusive Western policy. There is, of course, an obvious inconsistency here: having used the Conference to endorse the consolidation of Eastern Europe, they will then be trying to use it to prevent the crystallisation of Western Europe. But I am sure that they will not be put off by this difficulty of logic.

5. If this is the general outline of the Soviet *Westpolitik,* the Soviet leaders will probably try to manage their dealings with the Federal Government and with us over Berlin in order to keep open the wider options indicated above. This would suggest scenario (*a*) in Roger Jackling's paragraph 9, rather than scenario (*b*).[5] It would also explain why the Soviet Government should be willing to see some change in a situation which has been basically quite satisfactory to them (his paragraph 10) and to run the risks to themselves which are the obverse of the advantages seen by Bonn in their own *Ostpolitik* (his paragraph 12). There is the further implication that, just as the NATO Governments have established a kind of linkage between ESC[6] and the on-going talks, so the Soviet Government may establish a reverse linkage. They might follow our example in denying that they were imposing conditions, but simply point to the fact that, from their point of view, Western reluctance to take part in a European Security Conference would increase Soviet reluct-ance to reach the kind of agreements with Bonn and over Berlin which would be acceptable to ourselves.

6. The argument sketched in summary form above does lead to one very large policy question: If the Soviet Government have such an interest in an ESC and a Standing Committee as I have supposed, can this be in our interest too? This is too big a theme for HM Embassy in Moscow and for this letter. I personally believe that the answer is largely implicit in Roger Jackling's paragraph 12. Provided that our negotiations with the Six do not run into the sand, the situation likely to result immediately from the sort of ESC which could be accepted by both sides may be of advantage to both

---

[5] Cf. note 1.   [6] i.e. European Security Conference.

sides; on longer-term results, each will have its own probably very disparate calculation of where the advantage will lie.

7. I should perhaps add that I have discussed some of the more general themes of this letter recently with my French colleague, Seydoux, who is always stimulating on such subjects. He is particularly impressed with the Soviet long-term fears about a more integrated EEC (no doubt he had heard plenty about the need for France to prevent this); also with the present head of steam behind the Soviet push for an ESC. I am sure this is right, whatever impression Gromyko may have given the French in Paris (paragraph 8 of Marshall's letter to Giffard 312 of 22 June).[7] Incidentally, you may like to glance at the enclosed summary of a recent article by Yuri Zhukov in *Pravda*.[8] This seems to be a good indication of the present Soviet line.

Yours ever,

A.D. WILSON

I look forward to seeing you soon in London, when we might discuss this further.[9]

[7] In this letter, which dealt principally with President Ceausescu's official visit to France 15-19 June, Mr. P.H.R. Marshall, Counsellor and Head of Chancery in HM Embassy in Paris, contrasted the Rumanian approach to the idea of a European Security Conference to that of Mr. Gromyko, who had paid a five-day visit to France at the beginning of June. Mr. Marshall said that 'Gromyko's order of preference in discussing issues was (i) the Middle East; (ii) Indo-China; and (iii) German questions; with the Security Conference idea being mentioned only "in the last quarter of an hour". For Gromyko the idea seemed to be only an iron to be kept hot in the fire, for use in case the discussions with the Germans did not yield the desired results' (ENR 3/312/1).

[8] Not printed.

[9] Sir D. Wilson was to return to London on 8 July for consultations before going on leave. Submitting the Ambassador's letter to Mr. Bendall on 9 July, Mr. Mallaby commented that the *de facto* accommodation in Central Europe for which the Russians appeared to be working would involve the maximum attainable degree of Western ratification of the *status quo* and the creation of a situation in which it may be safer and easier for the Russians to adopt in due course a forward policy in Western Europe: 'if the Russians have a real interest in negotiations on European Security, they may be prepared to pay a price which would be of value to us. The West should therefore probe Soviet willingness to pay a price and should insist on the discussion of issues which really matter. Until Soviet intentions in these respects become clear—and I suggest that they are not fully clear yet—we should not allow ourselves to become committed to a conference and should not make any advance concessions.'

Sir A. Douglas-Home's comment, passed on to Mr. Giffard by Mr. P. Langmead, Assistant Private Secretary, on 15 July, was: 'Sir Duncan's letter is very interesting. Probably the Russians are thinking as he indicates on an enlarged EEC. But is there not a possible alternative that if the Europeans get together and America begins to withdraw her military presence the Soviet Union might have a better chance to manipulate the European scene and penetrate by showing herself co-operative and friendly?'

No. 49

Minute from Mr. Walden to Mr. Giffard

[*ENS 3/548/8*]

Confidential   FCO, *22 July 1970*

Anglo-Soviet relations

Mr. Pavel Filatov, First Secretary at the Soviet Embassy, invited me to lunch today specifically to discuss Anglo-Soviet relations. His brief was clearly:

(i) to sound me out on the likely attitude of the new Government to Anglo-Soviet relations;

(ii) to emphasise that the Soviet Union was in favour of maintaining the trend towards improvement in our relations, and of expanding further our political contacts;

(iii) to deny that the Soviet attitude towards this country had hardened as a result of the change of Government;

(iv) to elicit information and views about the prospects for Anglo-Soviet relations, particularly in the commercial sphere, should we succeed in our attempt to join the Common Market.[1]

2. Filatov began by asking for my views on the attitude of the Conservative Government towards our relations. I stressed our continuing interest in developing our contacts with the Soviet Union in practical fields. When he pressed me to forecast the likely evolution of Conservative policy towards the Soviet Union, I said it was too early to speculate, as the new Government had been in office only a short time and was faced with a series of pressing and vital decisions, concerning in particular our attempt to join the Common Market.

3. Filatov agreed that we should continue to develop businesslike contacts. However, he seemed anxious for reassurance that the new Government would not go back on the decision to establish the Joint Commission.[2] He

---

[1] Preparations for the opening of negotiations for British entry into the EEC had continued over the change of government, and on 30 June Sir A. Douglas-Home and Mr. Anthony Barber, Chancellor of the Duchy of Lancaster charged with leading the entry negotiations, travelled to Luxembourg for the first formal British meetings with the Six. Mr. Barber's opening statement confirmed HMG's desire to negotiate entry on the basis of the Treaties establishing the three Communities and the decisions resulting from them, subject to satisfaction on a number of points mainly concerned with transitional periods, Community finance and Commonwealth questions (Cmnd. 4401 of 1971). The first working session of the negotiations was a bilateral Ministerial meeting between Mr. Barber and the Communities' Council of Ministers on 21 July, when agreement was reached on future procedure. Five Deputies' meetings (at which Britain was represented by Sir Con O'Neill, Deputy Under Secretary of State) took place before the second bilateral Ministerial meeting on 27 October attended by Mr. G. Rippon, who had succeeded Mr. Barber when the latter became Chancellor of the Exchequer on 25 July after the sudden death of Mr. Iain Macleod.

[2] Cf. No. 47, note 8. On 20 July Mr. Andrews, a Private Secretary to Mr. Heath, told Mr. Barrington that the Prime Minister, who had earlier asked for a note on the functions on the

then went on to emphasise very strongly the Russians' desire to expand our political exchanges. He made it clear that the Soviet Government wished to see more frequent political contacts at a high level. He referred in particular to Mr. Kozyrev's invitation to the Permanent Under Secretary to visit the Soviet Union,[3] and asked what Sir Denis Greenhill's reaction would be if such an invitation were issued now that there had been a change of Government? He also mentioned the proposal that there should be an exchange of visits between yourself and Mr. Makeev, but said that he understood that this was a complex question since you were both extremely busy. Finally, he pronounced himself in favour of more regular contacts between the Soviet Embassy and the FCO at our own working level.

4. Filatov drew an unfavourable contrast between our own relations with the Soviet Union, which he implied were 'stagnant', and the progress made in developing Franco-Soviet and West German-Soviet relations. He said that we were in danger of becoming the odd man out. I contested his implication that our relations were stagnant, and said that the parallel with France and Germany was not really applicable, since there were special factors involved in the recent improvement of their relations with the Soviet Union. Nevertheless, I made it clear that we were always willing to develop our own links with the Russians, particularly in the fields of commercial, technological and cultural exchanges.

5. When I remarked that the new Conservative Government was no doubt as interested in the Soviet attitude towards itself as the Russians were in the new Government's policies, and that they were bound to take notice of any negative sentiments expressed on the Russian side, Filatov launched into a defensive justification of Soviet reporting on Northern Ireland.[4] He got very close to admitting that Dunayev's pieces were somewhat irresponsible, suggesting that they were merely 'journalism'. He strongly resisted the suggestion that they reflected a more hostile attitude on the part of the Soviet Government. He also played down the significance of the recent

Joint Commission and the Anglo-Soviet Consultative Committee, considered that these bodies were 'further examples of the spawning of organisations . . . it is time that they were all rationalised in order to save taxpayers' money as well as the time of Ministers and senior officials'. In the light of this and of the difficulties in agreeing on the Joint Commission's terms of reference, Mr. Walden informed Lord Bridges on 24 July that in discussion with the Russians 'While we do not wish to suggest that we are reconsidering our decision to establish the Joint Commission or to discontinue the Consultative Committee, we should avoid implying that progress in setting up the Joint Commission will be swift, or that the Consultative Committee has completely fulfilled our expectations'. Mr. P.J.S. Moon (Private Secretary to Mr. Heath) later informed Mr. Barrington on 7 August that Mr. Heath now accepted that the decision to establish the Joint Commission was based on 'careful consideration of our own best interests', but wished to see its terms of reference 'before finality is reached' (ENS 3/548/6).

[3] The invitation was extended during Mr. Kozyrev's visit to London in April: see No. 45.

[4] The security situation in Northern Ireland had deteriorated in the early summer of 1970 with fresh rioting leading to the sending of extra British troops. The Soviet press were consistently critical of HMG's Ulster policy, and the new riots sparked off by the arrest of Miss Bernadette Devlin, MP for mid-Ulster, in June had led to an intensification of hostile reporting.

Izvestiya article criticising British foreign policy in rather sharp language, and claimed that *Izvestiya* had complete freedom to comment as it thought appropriate. I voiced my doubts on this score, and said we had little choice but to regard the tone of such articles and broadcasts as a reflection of official policy. There was an exchange, in standard terms, about the BBC. The only noteworthy point to emerge from this was a fairly clear proposal from Filatov that if the BBC would agree to tone down its broadcasts to the Soviet Union, the Russians would discontinue their jamming. (You will recall that the representative of Soviet radio at the Anglo-Soviet Consultative Committee made a similar proposal to his BBC counterpart.[5])

6. Filatov again expressed, more in sorrow than in anger, his Government's surprise at what he considered to be hostile references to the Soviet Union in the Secretary of State's speeches. He also confessed himself completely unable to understand our motives in resuming sales of arms to South Africa.[6] I sought to defend this on the appropriate lines, but Filatov's puzzlement seemed to be genuine.

7. There was no mention of our recent expulsions of STD personnel, or of our visa refusals.[7] At one point I sought to convey to Mr. Filatov in general terms our attitude towards such questions by regretting that we were sometimes obliged to react against Soviet actions which were not conducive to good relations. However, he did not seem to hoist this aboard, and I did not attempt to be more specific.

8. Filatov expressed concern about the impact on Anglo-Soviet trade should we succeed in joining the Common Market. He displayed strong interest in our own assessment of the likely economic effects of our entry on relations with the Soviet Union, and asked whether I could provide him with any detailed study of this question. He strongly implied that his Embassy were having difficulty in securing considered papers on which to base their assessments. I undertook to draw his attention to any work on this topic by British institutions involved. I then went on to contest his suggestion that Anglo-Soviet trade would suffer if we joined the EEC, and pointed to French

[5] Cf. No. 45, note 3.

[6] On 20 July Sir A. Douglas-Home had announced in the House of Commons that the Government intended to resume a limited supply of arms to South Africa. He referred to the 'overriding duty to take account of present and future strategic needs of the United Kingdom' and stated that in view of evidence of the growth of the Soviet naval presence in the Indian Ocean it was intended to supply arms in certain categories 'so long as they are for maritime defence directly related to the security of the sea routes' (*Parl. Debs.*, 5th ser., H. of C., vol. 804, col. 49).

[7] Cf. No. 43, note 3. Despite Sir D. Greenhill's representations to Mr. Kozyrev (see No. 45), the Soviet Trade Delegation continued to play an increasing role as a cover for Soviet intelligence activities in the UK. The Home Office had already expelled four members of the STD in 1970 and several prospective members had been refused visas. A submission of 3 August from Mr. Walden to Sir T. Brimelow recommended that the FCO seek the agreement of other Departments concerned to a contingency plan involving strong representations to the Soviet Ambassador and a limitation on the size of the STD; Sir D. Wilson, however, was concerned at the possible implications for Anglo-Soviet relations and favoured instead the negotiation of a new trade representation agreement.

and German experience. Somewhat curiously, he countered this by claiming that Anglo-Soviet commerce was 'traditional', and could not therefore be compared with the French and Germans. I got the impression that the Soviet Embassy had been asked for a detailed assessment on this subject.[8]

9. At one point in our conversation Filatov said that there were different views on Anglo-Soviet relations in the Soviet Union. I would be inclined to interpret this merely as a rather feeble attempt to imply the existence of a democratic process of debate within the Soviet MFA.

10. Filatov was demonstratively affable throughout. He expressed the wish that the fruitless back-biting which had characterised our relations all too often in the past could now be dispensed with. He also asked permission to call me by my Christian name, and gave me two tickets for the first night of the Kirov Ballet on Thursday. This seemed to me the most fruitful aspect of our meeting.

G.G.H. WALDEN

[8] This paragraph was drawn to the attention of Economic Integration Department and Mr. M. Pakenham, a Second Secretary in EID, drew up a table comparing trade figures for UK/French/FRG-Soviet dealings in 1967-8, commenting: 'From these figures it will be clear that the export pattern for all 3 countries to the USSR is remarkably similar, while there are certain differences in the import pattern. Presumably Mr. Filatov's reference was not to the Muscovy Company, or fur-trading in the Baltic. In which case, what did he mean by traditional[?] It does seem rather specious.' Mr. W.J. Adams, Assistant in EID, agreed, minuting to Mr. Walden on 30 July: 'We hope you will find Mr. Pakenham's material useful when you next see Mr. Filatov. We think it is worth answering Soviet allegations of this kind.'

No. 50

Letter from Sir T. Brimelow to Mr. Edmonds (Moscow)

[*WDW 1/2*]

Confidential   FCO, *14 August 1970*

East-West Relations[1]

The Ambassador's letter 2/23 of 3 July to David Bendall[2] commenting from the Soviet point of view on Sir R. Jackling's despatch of 25 June on the implications of Herr Brandt's *Ostpolitik* led to a certain amount of correspondence between posts and to considerable discussion in London. We thought it better to await the outcome of the Treaty negotiations between the Government of the Soviet Union and the Government of the Federal Republic of Germany before replying.[3] You and the other posts to which this

[1] Opening and concluding salutations were omitted from the filed copy of this letter.

[2] No. 48.

[3] Cf. p. 242. The final round of negotiations between the Soviet Union and the FRG took place in Moscow from 27 July to 7 August, when the text of a treaty was initialled (signed on 12 August). The two Governments agreed to refrain from the threat or use of force in any matters affecting security in Europe or international security, as well as in their mutual relations, and

letter is copied may find it useful to have our preliminary views on the tactics which we expect the Warsaw Pact Governments to follow in the situation created by the signature of the Soviet-Federal German Treaty.

2. The Treaty goes a long way towards meeting Soviet wishes as regards the acceptance of frontiers in Europe, including the frontiers of Poland and East Germany. Its provisions regarding non-recourse to force fill, from the Soviet point of view, the gap resulting from the fact that the Federal Republic of Germany is not yet a member of the United Nations. That Soviet wishes have in large measure been met on the two issues of frontiers and non-recourse to force must be regarded as a success for Soviet diplomacy. The Federal German Government, conscious of criticism from the CDU and CSU opposition that they have made too many concessions and obtained too little in return, have said that they will only ratify the Treaty when the Four-Power talks on Berlin have been carried to a satisfactory conclusion.[4] The Soviet Government know that the Federal German Government expects an appreciable improvement in the situation in and around Berlin; but we do not know what concessions, if any, the Soviet and East German Governments may be prepared to make. At the last Ambassadorial meeting, Abrasimov took a fairly hard line. If, for internal political reasons, the Federal German Government wish to proceed to ratification of the Soviet-German Treaty, they may urge the Americans, the French and ourselves to accept as satisfactory an outcome of the Berlin talks which in reality might be less than satisfactory. Herr Scheel's comments on the textual modification negotiated by him in Moscow may encourage the Soviet Government to think that it may not be difficult to create such a situation. But apprehensions on this score may be unwarranted. We shall have to see how the Berlin talks develop.

undertook to respect the territorial integrity of all States in Europe within their present frontiers, including the Oder-Neisse Line. On 7 August the FRG's Embassy in Moscow also sent notes to the British, French and US Embassies concerning the rights of the Four Powers with regard to Germany as a whole and Berlin: Herr Scheel, FRG Foreign Minister, had in the course of the negotiations 'set forth the position of the Federal Government as regards the rights and responsibilities of the Four Powers with regard to Germany as a whole and Berlin', as a result of which Mr. Gromyko had agreed to make a declaration, transmitted separately to the French, UK and US Governments, that the question of the rights of the Four Powers was not affected by the Soviet-German treaty.

[4] Cf. No. 48, note 4. At the Four Power meeting on 21 July the Western Ambassadors put forward a paper listing their views on the essential elements in a Berlin agreement, including provision for specific measures of improvement as regards access to Berlin, communications between Western sectors and the Soviet sector and Zone, and the relationship between the Western sectors and the Soviet Union and its allies. There must be no attempt to redefine the legal status of Berlin. Mr. Abrasimov replied with a tough statement reiterating the Soviet position and complaints about Federal activities in Berlin. Sir R. Jackling commented in Berlin telegram No. 213 of 21 July that although 'the bones of a bargain' were visible 'it is still to my mind a completely open question whether the Russians are prepared to move far enough towards the Allied position to enable such a bargain to be struck' (WRL 2/10). The talks had now adjourned for the summer: the next round was later arranged for 30 September.

3. As regards future negotiations between the Federal German Government and the Polish Government,[5] the Germans seem to believe (and we regard the belief as reasonable) that Warsaw is now likely to accept an agreement embodying the Bahr formula on the Oder-Neisse line, i.e. that the Polish frontiers will be respected, rather than explicitly recognised, and that no attempt will be made to alter existing frontiers. It seems to be the intention of the Federal Foreign Ministry that priority should now be given to their negotiations with Poland.

4. As regards inner German relations and negotiations between the Federal and East German Governments, speeches by Ulbricht and Winzer have suggested that some progress may be possible.[6] But the Federal German Foreign Ministry do not seem to expect quick or important progress on this front. Nor do we.

5. In the SALT talks a limited agreement now seems likely.[7]

6. Because there has been some progress under these various headings, and because there may be more progress under some of them before the end of the year, the Warsaw Pact Governments may urge that there should now be progress towards a European Security Conference. The provisional answer to this is that we for our part are still waiting to see whether satisfactory progress can be made in the Berlin talks.

7. Turning to the less immediate future, we must consider the comment in paragraph 2 of the Ambassador's letter that it now looks as if the Soviet leaders have decided to work actively not only for a *de facto* accommodation in Central Europe, but also to provide a framework for the future development of Europe as a whole. I have some reservations about the phrase 'a *de facto* accommodation in Central Europe'. It is true that the Soviet Government have negotiated with the Federal Government on a basis which omitted one of their traditional demands, namely explicit and unqualified Federal recognition of the Government of the German Democratic Republic. It is also true that they have accepted with regard to the question of frontiers wording different from that used in earlier Soviet demands. It is therefore correct to say that the Soviet Government have for the present

---

[5] Cf. No. 48, note 3.

[6] Cf. No. 46, note 7. During Baltic Sea Week Dr. Otto Winzer, Foreign Minister of the GDR, implied at a press conference at Rostock on 13 July that inner-German talks might soon be resumed if the Soviet-FRG talks reached a successful conclusion. Herr Ulbricht made a major speech on 16 July at Rostock praising Herr Brandt's government for showing a 'certain recognition of realities', and said that the conclusion of a Soviet-FRG agreement should make it possible to conclude a treaty between the GDR and FRG 'with equal rights based on international law' (WRE 3/309/1).

[7] Cf. No. 45, note 8. At the second round of SALT which opened in Vienna on 16 April the US delegation had presented ambitious proposals for either a freeze or planned reduction in missiles, but these were rejected by the Soviet Union. A less sweeping American proposal for a limited agreement setting a ceiling on offensive strategic weapons was presented on 24 July to the Soviet delegation, who appeared 'seriously interested' but had received no instructions prior to adjournment on 14 August (DS 10/6). The next round of SALT was due to open in Helsinki on 2 November.

lowered some of their sights *vis-à-vis* the Federal Republic of Germany, and to this extent one might speak of a *de facto* accommodation. But in substance, they have secured the acceptance of their basic requirements, whereas we do not know what concessions they may be prepared to make on Berlin. Herr Brandt has argued that since nobody was proposing to change the *status quo* in Central Europe, the Soviet-German Treaty does not in itself constitute a concession to the Soviet Union. Presumably the Warsaw Pact Governments could argue that in this case it is not incumbent on them to make counter-concessions. But the fact remains that the signature of this Treaty has changed the political situation in Europe in accordance with some of the long-standing aims of Soviet diplomacy, whereas neither the Soviet Government nor the Warsaw Pact Governments have yet committed themselves to any changes favourable to the West. This is not necessarily a criticism of the Soviet-Federal German Treaty. Herr Brandt's long term calculation has been that only by recognizing realities can the Federal German Government create a situation in which the future reunification of Germany may become possible. The long term 'accommodation' which Herr Brandt envisages assumes a re-united Germany. But whether the long term advantages for which Herr Brandt hopes will ever be achieved is an open question.

8. In paragraph 2 of his letter, the Ambassador says that the Soviet leaders would like to provide a 'framework' for the future development of Europe as a whole. We agree that the CPSU and the Soviet Government would like to influence the future development of Europe as a whole. But we are not sure that they would prefer to exercise their influence in Western Europe through any specific 'framework'. There exists a formidable 'framework' for the exercise of Soviet influence in Eastern Europe; but as regards Western Europe, my present impression is that the CPSU and the Soviet Government would still prefer to see us with no 'framework' at all. They would like to see the countries of Western Europe disunited and bereft of any 'framework' for collective action.

9. We regard as insufficiently precise the statement in paragraph 4 of the Ambassador's letter that 'the long term perspective of possible developments in EEC is one of the main factors behind the Soviet desire for a European Security Conference'. It may have recently become such a factor, but I doubt whether it was a dominant factor when the current phase of the Warsaw Pact campaign for a European Security Conference was launched with the Budapest Appeal of March, 1969.[8] At that time there seemed to be no likelihood that de Gaulle would soon disappear from the scene, and advances in European integration did not seem imminent. It follows, I believe, that the campaign for a European Security Conference was not launched primarily to block European economic integration or the political and defence cooperation that might accompany or develop from economic integration. The Americans are inclined to question whether it was launched with any serious intent, on the simple grounds that the Soviet Government

[8] See No. 26, note 2.

had not mentioned it to them beforehand. At the time, we assumed that the main motives underlying the Budapest Appeal of March, 1969 were to overcome the adverse consequences for the Warsaw Pact of the invasion of Czechoslovakia, to regain lost respectability, to get back into active diplomacy, to enhance the status of the DDR and to obtain recognition of frontiers and the *status quo* in an Eastern Europe dominated by the Soviet Union. Many of these considerations still in our opinion hold good; but, as the Ambassador points out in paragraph 2 of his letter, the situation in Western Europe has undergone striking changes in the past year, and we would agree that this must have affected the thinking of the Warsaw Pact Governments. The Soviet Government, and no doubt the other Warsaw Pact Governments, must already be giving serious consideration to the implications for them of the probable enlargement of the Europe Economic Communities. We know that the Soviet Government does not like economic or other groupings from which they are excluded, and which may harm Soviet interests. The place occupied by Western European integration in their thinking must have increased greatly during the past year and there is both truth and weight in what the Ambassador wrote in paragraph 4 of his letter. Yet what strikes me at present is that the Soviet Government are not in fact taking any determined or large-scale action to frustrate integration in Western Europe. Apart from some propaganda directed at the Scandinavians and Austrians, together with some weak and unconvincing criticism of the EEC as an exclusive grouping less desirable than 'all-European cooperation' they are doing very little. There has been no campaign against Western European integration comparable to the campaign in favour of a European Security Conference. No serious attempt has been made to mobilize opinion in the United Nations against the enlargement of the European Communities. Mr. Gromyko's remarks to Herr Scheel about the EEC were fairly relaxed.[9] The Soviet Government is showing a certain amount of understanding as regards Finland's relations with an enlarged EEC.

10. We have pointed out to the Russians that in the first ten years of the EEC, the Soviet Union and its allies increased their trade with the members of the Community one and a half times as fast as with the members of EFTA. The enlargement of the EEC admittedly will create problems for all the Warsaw Pact countries; but it need not necessarily prevent the expansion of East-West trade.

11. The Prague documents on the agenda of a European Security Conference[10] gave more prominence than the earlier Budapest Appeal had done to the subject of economic cooperation. This no doubt reflected the changed situation in Western Europe and the traditional Soviet policy of dangling

[9] Herr Scheel had told Sir R. Jackling that 'in the private part' of his talks in Moscow there had been some discussion of European integration which had prompted Mr. Gromyko to comment that 'the EEC was a dinosaurus which had been born in a zoo: it had a strongly civilized character and was not regarded as a threat . . . he saw no reason to fear even an enlarged Community' (Bonn telegram No. 949 of 10 August, MWE 5/303/1).

[10] See pp. 196-7 and No. 39.

bright prospects of economic cooperation before the Governments of Western Europe. But by now the Governments of Western Europe are sober in their assessment of the probable growth rates of trade with the various Warsaw Pact countries, and the Warsaw Pact Governments are aware of this. The probability is that the Soviet Government and the other Warsaw Pact Governments are less worried about economic integration in Western Europe than about the possibility that one day integration, however difficult, may spread to the fields of politics and defence.

12. We would agree with the contention in paragraph 4 of the Ambassador's letter that the Soviet Government would now like a European Security Conference to set a general seal on the agreements separately reached by the Federal Government with the Soviet Union and Poland and on whatever may be agreed by the Four Powers on Berlin. We would also agree that if there are subsequent conferences, or if some standing machinery or 'organ' is established at the first conference, these conferences, or the standing machinery, or both, might be used as a platform from which the Soviet Union might be able to continue its propaganda against the enlargement of the EEC. We would agree that as the Communities are enlarged, the Soviet Government would see danger to their interests if tendencies towards political or defence integration within the new Western European grouping emerged. To this end they might advocate all-European cooperation. But they would not wish the countries of Western Europe to exercise influence within the Warsaw Pact area. The Soviet concept of the proper exercise of influence is one-way. The question is to what extent the CPSU and the Soviet Government are likely to be able to develop their influence in Western Europe. In the short term, defined as the period of the Brussels negotiations, we doubt whether the Soviet policies as outlined above are likely to affect the negotiations for the enlargement of the Communities. The present EEC Governments have decided to work for the enlargement of the European Communities, and although the negotiations may conceivably fail, we do not think that Soviet propaganda or Soviet diplomacy can substantially influence the outcome one way or the other. We can accept your analysis of Soviet hopes without assuming that Soviet policies are likely to exert any important influence in the short term on progress towards the enlargement of the Communities.

13. In the medium and longer term, however, we admit the possibility that Soviet propaganda may be able to complicate the intrinsically difficult policy of developing political and military cooperation in Western Europe (it is still much too early for us to speak of integration in these fields). A series of conferences on European Security, or continuing Soviet propaganda in some standing machinery or 'organ' of the kind now contemplated by the Warsaw Pact, could conceivably influence the thinking of a number of West European Governments on the problems of political and defence cooperation. In Western Europe there is a fairly widespread propensity to indulge in wishful thinking about *détente* in relations with the USSR, while few European Ministries of Finance are willing to authorise adequate defence expenditure.

Our difficulties are chiefly of our own making, but it should not be hard for skilful Warsaw Pact diplomacy and propaganda to increase them. This suggests that our approach to the idea of a series of Conferences or to a Soviet-style 'organ' (which is very different from our concept of a Standing Commission on European Security) should be cautious.

14. Although Mr. Gromyko spoke to Herr Scheel about the prospects for *détente* and cooperation, the Soviet Government have been careful of late to avoid any suggestion of a new Rapallo,[11] and given Herr Brandt's insistence that his 'Ostpolitik' is only a part of his general European policy, we ourselves doubt whether the Soviet Government entertain any hopes of detaching the Federal Government from the West in the short or medium term. There is plenty of evidence that over the years the Soviet Government have kept toying with the idea of a new Rapallo, and they seem to have enjoyed, on occasion, trying to make our flesh creep. They may still entertain hopes that one day they may be able to impose a radical change on the balance of power in Europe by playing the card of German reunification. Pending that day, they may try to encourage the Federal German Government to show greater independence *vis-à-vis* the West, just as they will continue to try to exploit the French advocacy of independence in the conduct of foreign policy. But in the short and medium term we do not think that this is going to be a major problem.

15. In the medium and long term, it cannot be assumed that the aims of Soviet policy with regard to Western Europe will be limited to the purely defensive obstruction of any evolution towards Western European integration. The Soviet Union, conscious of its status as a super power, will no doubt try to exercise an active and growing influence on world affairs in general and on Western Europe in particular. The only status quo they wish to see respected is that established by them in their part of a divided Europe. They no doubt calculate that their control over Eastern Europe, stabilised by the acceptance of their status quo, will one day be supplemented by an opportunistic and more vigorous exercise of pressure on the Governments and publics of Western Europe. This policy will not be conducted in its entirety through the channels of the Soviet state. The Soviet state is controlled by the CPSU, which has channels of its own for the exercise of influence abroad. The potential Soviet threat to Western Europe is complex, and Soviet probing for weak points in Western Europe is likely to be pursued through many channels. It is hardly to be assumed that the CPSU, which for over 50 years has been trying to change the world balance of power in its favour, is going to renounce this strategy in Europe now that it has obtained in relations between the Soviet Government and the Federal Republic of Germany a tactical diplomatic success for which it has worked and waited throughout so many years.

16. We believe that our priorities in Europe should continue to be the collective security of Western Europe and Western European integration. It

[11] Cf. No. 36, note 7.

would be dangerous for the Governments of Western Europe to adopt as the central aim of their policy an undefined '*détente*'. The Soviet concept of '*détente*' in Europe and of the ending of the cold war still seems to involve the abandonment by the Governments of Western Europe of all the collective measures they have taken since the end of the Second World War to ensure or at least to improve to some extent their own security. But this does not mean that the Soviet German Treaty and its accompanying talk of *détente* is in any sense unwelcome. Herr Brandt's policies are making it harder for the Soviet Government to make plausible propaganda about German *revanchisme*. In the medium term, they may make possible an easing and an increase in the scale of East-West relations. If this were to happen, it might contribute to some extent to the internal evolution of the Communist systems in Eastern Europe, though the nature and pace of any such evolution is likely to be determined primarily by indigenous factors, and we must expect the present leaders in the Soviet Union and the countries of Eastern Europe to seek to limit both the pace and the extent of change. Moreover, if the tendency towards cooperation in Western Europe should flourish, we may find that the reaction of the Soviet leaders is to tighten their control over their Allies and to prevent that gradual process of *rapprochement* on which Herr Brandt seems to be pinning his hopes.

17. It can be argued that if *détente*, as understood by the Warsaw Pact Governments, is something to be exploited to our disadvantage, we ourselves should not pursue it until we are satisfied with the arrangements which will be needed in Western Europe in the coming decade for collective security and for economic, political and defence cooperation. The political difficulties of such a course are manifest. They point to the need for precision in the definition of *détente*.

18. There is a good case for seeking to minimize the cost and danger that accompany tension in East-West relations. There is also a good case for seeking to get at the root of the difficulty by minimising that tension. But the experience of the post-war years has shown that the causes of this tension are numerous and intractable. In the last decade the difficulty of dealing with them has been increased by the development of the Sino-Soviet dispute, in that the Soviet Government may now consider itself compelled, for reasons in no way connected with Europe, to maintain armed forces of a size which will constitute a permanent potential threat to Europe.

19. To sum up, I think that the Warsaw Pact pressure for a European Security Conference will continue and may increase. I do not think however that any Soviet or Warsaw Pact manoeuvres which might be launched against Western European economic integration will seriously affect the course of the Brussels negotiations. If however the enlargement of the Communities is followed by attempts to develop political and defence cooperation, I think that in this period Soviet propaganda and diplomacy could seriously complicate our task. If Western Europe eventually achieves a significant degree of political and defence cooperation, at that point a genuine *détente* in East-West relations could be valuable; but for the time

being, we must expect that Warsaw Pact propaganda regarding European security and *détente* will be designed to change the balance of power in Europe to our disadvantage. So long as this remains the case, the need for wariness and caution is not likely to diminish.

20. I am sending copies of this letter to the Chanceries at Berlin, Washington, Paris, Bonn, Warsaw, Prague, Budapest, Bucharest, Sofia, Belgrade, Rome, The Hague, Brussels, Luxembourg, Ottawa, Copenhagen, Athens, Reykjavik, Oslo, Lisbon, Ankara, Stockholm, Helsinki, Vienna, UK Delegation to NATO, UK Mission New York and UK Mission Geneva.[12]

THOMAS BRIMELOW

[12] Mr. Edmonds thanked Sir T. Brimelow for his 'long and important' letter on 21 August. Sir D. Wilson replied to it on 21 September, agreeing that 'the European scene is changing very rapidly . . . on the whole the signs point by now towards a major change of Soviet tactics towards Western Europe as a whole'. He considered that this change included a Russian decision that 'new talks with the West on European security are desirable despite the risks involved on their side; conversely, there are advantages to be gained by the West from such talks which could outweigh the dangers involved (dangers which might in any case exist and even increase if we back away from an ESC)'. He recommended that at the NATO Ministerial meeting in December 'it would be desirable and may be possible at that time to achieve NATO agreement to proceed to multilateral exploratory contacts' with the objective of arriving 'if possible at agreement on an ESC from which a Standing Committee would emerge and at which we would be at liberty to raise such other items as we wish, even if only for the record; we should not be unduly inhibited by the desire to avoid controversy, or by excessive caution about the long-term risks, from taking a lead in this matter in NATO'.

No. 51

Record of a meeting between Sir Alec Douglas-Home and Mr. Smirnovsky at 12.15 p.m. on Wednesday, 9 September 1970[1]

[ENS 3/548/8]

Confidential
Present:

Rt Hon Sir Alec Douglas-Home, MP	HE Mr. M. Smirnovsky
Mr. N.J. Barrington	Mr. Filatov
Mrs M.B. Chitty[2]	

Mr. Gromyko's Movements

Mr. Smirnovsky gave the Secretary of State Mr. Gromyko's reply to the invitation to visit London.[3] Mr. Gromyko was glad to accept, and would stop

[1] The Soviet Ambassador had called at his own request to discuss UN matters in advance of the opening of the 25th session of the United Nations General Assembly (UNGA) on 15 September.

[2] Assistant in UN (Political) Department.

[3] On 21 August Sir D. Wilson had delivered a message from Sir A. Douglas-Home inviting Mr. Gromyko to London on his way back from the UNGA in New York. The message said that

in London in the second half of October on his way back from the Commemorative Session in New York.[4] *Sir A. Douglas-Home* welcomed this news and agreed to keep in touch to fix a precise date for his meeting with Mr. Gromyko.[5] Mr. Smirnovsky said he did not know if Mr. Gromyko would also attend the General Assembly in September.

The Agenda for the General Assembly

2. *Mr. Smirnovsky* listed the main items on the Agenda for the 25th Session which his Government thought of importance as follows:

(a) *International Peace and Security*

The Soviet Government thought it important that active efforts should be made to enable the United Nations to fulfil its essential task of maintaining international peace and security; this would lead to an easing of social and economic problems also. The Soviet Government hoped that the resolution to be adopted under this item by the General Assembly would contain the following elements: the inadmissibility of acquiring foreign territory through aggression; the withdrawal of foreign troops from occupied territory; the fulfilment by States of the terms of Security Council resolutions; the observance of the principles of the UN Charter; the need for general and complete disarmament; the establishment of regional systems of collective security; the strengthening of international security as a means of promoting world-wide economic and social development, including the environment.

3. In discussion, *Sir Alec Douglas-Home* said that we would be willing to examine every proposition which furthered the cause of international peace and security. Was the Soviet Government aiming primarily at disarmament to achieve this end, or to an improvement in the organisation of the United Nations? *Mr. Smirnovsky* replied that both methods should be used; he referred to Mr. Gromyko's speech to the 24th Session of the General Assembly and the Soviet Government's reply to the Secretary General's note on the subject which revealed Soviet thinking.[6] *Sir A. Douglas-Home* expressed the view that the peacekeeping role of the United Nations should be strengthened through the Security Council and the Secretary General;

the 'signature of the Treaty between the Governments of the USSR and the Federal Republic of Germany [see No. 50, note 3] . . . which may be of great importance for the future of Europe, suggests that there might be advantages in our having rather fuller talks than might be possible in New York. My hope is of course that the Soviet-German Treaty will be followed by the negotiation of satisfactory arrangements in and around Berlin and by progress towards a general reduction of tension in Europe. But there are of course many other questions not limited to Europe which I should be glad to discuss' (ENS 3/548/33).

[4] A Commemorative session of the UNGA was to be held from 14-24 October to mark the 25th anniversary of the signing of the UN Charter on 26 June 1945.

[5] On 1 October Sir D. Wilson reported that Mr. Gromyko agreed to the dates of 26-29 October for his visit.

[6] Cf. No. 37, note 8. At its closing session on 24 October the UNGA adopted a *Declaration on Principles of International Law concerning Friendly Relations and Cooperation among States in Accordance with the Charter of the United Nations,* and a *Declaration reaffirming the Dedication of States to the Charter.*

was there any change in the Soviet view that there was only a limited role for the UN in peacekeeping? *Mr. Smirnovsky* seemed to agree that there should be more peacekeeping activity but emphasised that all peacekeeping activities must be under the authority of the Security Council, working unanimously, and strictly in accordance with the Charter. He made a hedging reply when asked directly whether the USSR would subscribe military forces.

(*b*) *25th Anniversary Declaration*

4. Mr. Smirnovsky said that the Soviet Government's view was that the Declaration should contain an appraisal of the activities of the United Nations and of its main future tasks. The Declaration, which should be brief, should reaffirm the principles of the United Nations; it should contain references to the end of the arms race, the fulfilment of the UN Declaration on the inadmissibility of intervention in the domestic affairs of States (i.e. Resolution 2131 (XX); the working out of a definition of aggression and of more effective measures to prevent aggression; the fulfilment of the Declaration on decolonisation (i.e. Resolution 1514 (XV)), and to economic, social, cultural and human rights objectives.[7]

5. *Sir A. Douglas-Home* said that we would have liked to reach agreement with the Soviet Mission in New York on the draft of such a Declaration but unfortunately this had not been possible. If there were to be agreement on a text for adoption by the General Assembly, it was essential that the Soviet Union should not insist on certain reference which they knew were unacceptable to us, for example, the demand for independence for *all* colonies. The fact was that some colonies simply did not want independence and we could not therefore accept such language. They should also omit references to 'shameful colonial régimes'.

(*c*) *Disarmament*

6. *Mr. Smirnovsky* acknowledged that the UK and the USSR had different positions on the subject of chemical and biological warfare.[8] The Soviet Union's view was that the General Assembly should ban both chemical and biological weapons simultaneously; otherwise the ban on chemical weapons would be postponed indefinitely. The Soviet delegation would be putting forward specific proposals during the Assembly for the banning of production and storage of weapons and for an appeal to the Security Council if a State transgressed. Mr. Smirnovsky hoped that at the forthcoming Session there would be approval for the Sea Bed Convention which could then be opened for signature.[9]

[7] Resolutions 2131 and 1514 had been adopted in 1965 and 1960 respectively. The *UN Declaration on the Occasion of the Twenty-Fifth Anniversary of the United Nations* was adopted on 24 October 1970 as Resolution 2627/XXV.

[8] See No. 45, note 16.

[9] *V. ibid.* The US-Soviet draft of a Treaty on the Prohibition of the Emplacement of Nuclear and Other Weapons of Mass Destruction on the Sea Bed and the Ocean Floor had been tabled on 1 September at the CCD, which transmitted it to the UNGA. The Treaty was signed on 11 February 1971.

7. *Sir A. Douglas-Home* said he noted what Mr. Smirnovsky had said about disarmament; he thought that verification was a difficult problem and was sceptical about the role of the Security Council in this.

(*d*) *The Breadth of the Territorial Sea*

8. *Mr. Smirnovsky* thought that the thinking of the United Kingdom and the Soviet Union was close on this subject and he hoped for early agreement on the item proposed by Bulgaria and Syria.[10] *Sir A. Douglas-Home* took note.

(*e*) *The Second Development Decade*[11]

9. *Mr. Smirnovsky* said that the Soviet Government were critical of the results of ECOSOC 49; they would take part in some aspects of the Decade but proper consideration had not been given to the matter by the Economic and Social Council.

European Security Conference

10. Mr. Smirnovsky said that he had no instructions but he wished to draw attention to the Soviet Government's treaty with the Federal Republic of Germany; they hoped that this would prepare the way for a European Security Conference. They looked forward to an early answer from the NATO countries to their proposal for a Conference.[12] He confirmed that the Soviet Government remained keenly interested in the proposal. *Sir A Douglas-Home* assured Mr. Smirnovsky that this matter would be given close study and that a constructive response would be made.

The Middle East

11. Again speaking without instructions *Mr. Smirnovsky* said he felt bound to mention that Israel was continuing to behave irresponsibly with the object of obstructing the Jarring talks. The Soviet Union were convinced that the UAR had not violated the cease fire and he was sorry that the FCO had accepted this allegation against them.[13] *Sir A. Douglas-Home* said that the interest of the United Kingdom was that the talks should start; we would certainly do all we could to achieve this end, but it must be recognised that the USA and the USSR were the countries with power in this issue. The trouble was that neither side in the dispute now believed the other and without trust it was difficult to make any progress. A start must be made somewhere. For

[10] On 17 December 1970 the UNGA adopted Resolution 2750 convening a conference on the Law of the Sea for 1973 which would consider, *inter alia*, this question.

[11] As part of a UN initiative to coordinate and promote an international development strategy, a document proclaiming the Second Development Decade as beginning on 1 January 1971 was adopted by the UNGA at the close of the commemorative session on 24 October 1970. Proposed changes to the UN development programme, including guidelines for the reorganisation of the UN development aid system, had been submitted to the Economic and Social Council (ECOSOC) for endorsement before submission to the UNGA.

[12] Cf. pp. 238-9.

[13] Cf. No. 47, note 6. Israeli claims that Egypt had violated the cease-fire by moving SAMs into the Suez Canal Zone had been confirmed by the US State Department on 3 September. Israel had participated in talks with Mr. Jarring in New York at the end of August, but withdrew on 7 September and stated that she would not return until ceasefire violations had been rectified.

example, would both sides agree to admit a third party to check dispositions in the ceasefire area? There was strong circumstantial evidence that the UAR had added to their missiles since the ceasefire began; if this were so Israel would be at a disadvantage. *Mr. Smirnovsky* said that the UAR were acting only in self-defence and in response to occupation by Israel.

Ballerina Makarova

12. Mr. Smirnovsky said that he was making a strong appeal to the UK to accede to their 'legitimate and only' request that they should be allowed to see Miss Makarova.[14] She was a Soviet citizen and they had an obligation to protect her interests; the Director of the Kirov Ballet who had known her from childhood was waiting in London in the hope of being able to see her. Mr. Smirnovsky apologised for raising what he called an unpleasant subject but he felt bound to say that the situation affected the state of USSR/UK relations. *Sir A. Douglas-Home* said that in many ways it would be convenient if Makarova would agree to see a member of his Embassy. He understood the Soviet Ambassador's wish. At the moment, however, Miss Makarova did not want to see anyone from the Soviet Embassy. She was not in detention and we could not put pressure on her; she was free to decide whom she wished to meet. *Mr. Smirnovsky* continued to press his appeal and asked that the United Kingdom authorities should tell her of the Soviet wish to see her. He said that they wished to hear directly from her; they were suspicious because on a previous occasion, in similar circumstances, a Soviet citizen had been instructed to say that he did not wish to see anyone from the Soviet Embassy. Until they saw Miss Makarova they could not be sure that it was her own decision. *Sir A. Douglas-Home* again explained Miss Makarova's freedom of decision in this matter.

[14] Miss Natalia Makarova, a leading ballerina with the Kirov Ballet, applied successfully to the Home Office for permission to prolong her stay in the UK on 4 September, the day before the company was due to leave after its visit to London. The Soviet Embassy had lodged a 'standing request' to see Miss Makarova, who maintained a consistent refusal. On 12 September parallel Soviet representations were made in Moscow and London claiming that the refusal of the British authorities to allow meetings with Miss Makarova 'could not be considered but as an action inflicting serious damage on Anglo-Soviet relations'; on 13 September Miss Makarova emphasised publicly the independence of her decision to apply to stay in the UK. Further representations to Sir A. Douglas-Home by Mr. Smirnovsky on 18 September resulted in a message from the Secretary of State to Mr. Gromyko, stating that it was Miss Makarova and not the British authorities who refused a meeting with the Soviet Embassy, and expressing the hope that the incident would not affect Anglo-Soviet relations: 'Artists are notoriously temperamental. We are always losing them to go and live in other countries. We take it lightly as it makes room for the young' (ENS 3/548/34).

During September Planning Staff and Western Organisations Department prepared a group of papers on the general situation with regard to European security, mutual and balanced force reductions and on possible tactics at a European security conference, submitted to Sir Alec Douglas-Home by Mr. Bendall on 16 September: their broad conclusions were that many East-West tensions sprang from too deep a source to be removed by negotiation, other than MBFR which was 'almost certainly unnegotiable with the Soviet Union'; and that the kind of conference likely to emerge was not likely to do substantial business and would probably do no great harm to the West; it was 'not in UK interests to take up a prominent position either way since this might involve damage to relations with our major allies'.[1] The Secretary of State, however, continued to maintain the measured and cautious line on European security that he had taken in conversation with Mr. Smirnovsky in No. 51. While not in disagreement with the analyses presented to him, he made it clear that progress on all these issues was dependent on Soviet behaviour elsewhere. This, he considered, seemed distinctly unsatisfactory, with continued Soviet military build-up in the UAR and violations of the cease-fire (cf. No. 51, note 13) compounded by reports of nuclear submarine facilities being built in Cuba. Even closer to home, the Soviet announcement of the closure of the Northern and Central air corridors to Berlin for two hours early on 30 September had provoked a tripartite protest to the Russians and 'probing flights' by US and UK air forces during the hours of closure. Reports from HM Embassy in Washington indicated that Sir Alec's misgivings were shared by Secretary of State Rogers and by Dr. Kissinger, who told a press briefing on 16 September that 'if we ever put ourselves in the position where our survival depends on (Soviet) goodwill or on their good faith, or even if our security is dependent on it, we are in bad shape'.[2]

Soviet policy was also discussed when President Nixon visited Mr. Heath at Chequers on 3 October for a brief meeting on his way back from a visit to the US Sixth Fleet. Reporting their conversation to the Cabinet on 5 October, the Prime Minister said that the President 'clearly wished to establish a close relationship with the new British Government' and had reviewed United States objectives in different areas of the world, indicating that the US Government 'intended to continue to resist the probing of the Sino-Soviet bloc wherever it was necessary to do so'; he advised the British Government, in dealing with the problem of safeguarding trade routes across the Indian Ocean and round the Cape, to 'consult our own interests and our own security, in the assurance that the United States Government would do nothing to embarrass us'.

The potential threat posed by the Soviet Union's clear intention to achieve a global naval capability was already under close consideration by HMG. At his meeting with Mr. Nixon Mr. Heath agreed to cooperate with the US in a project to build a new US naval communications centre at Diego Garcia atoll, part of the British Indian Ocean Territory, supplying specialised personnel as required. On 28 October a Supplementary Statement on Defence Policy was published as Cmnd. 4521, containing details of new Five Power defence arrangements related to the external defence of Malaysia and Singapore, and involving increased British expenditure of £5-10m. These arrangements replaced the former bilateral Anglo-Malaysian defence arrangements, which seemed out of date in the face of the perceived Soviet threat, underlined by Mr. Lee Kwan Yew's

---

[1] Minute by Mr. Bendall covering three papers, together with a summary, WDW 1/2.

[2] Letter from Mr. B.L. Crowe (First Secretary, Washington) to Mr. P.W. Unwin (Assistant in WED), 28 September, WRL 2/10.

refusal to put off the visit of a Soviet team to investigate possible repair and other facilities at Singapore for Soviet naval and merchant ships.

Increased defence expenditure East of Suez was, however, not to be matched by any decrease in the British defence contribution to NATO. In this context the Secretary of State was not anxious to hasten the progress of force reductions or preparations for a European security conference: 'I rather prefer the line that only real security has any interest for the Allies . . . the Soviet performances in Egypt and Cuba may help us to stall and insist that much more than a "token" reduction is needed if confidence is to be built between East and West . . . I think that the Conference will probably happen. But we can play it slow and if Russian moves elsewhere reveal a hardening of policy we can harden too. I think that education in the difficulty of avoiding disadvantage to the West should be begun'.[3] A NATO Council meeting on 14 October offered a good opportunity for this 'education' to begin, and the telegram of instruction to UKDEL NATO printed as No. 52 sets out the agreed British view on European security problems and the possibility of negotiations with the Soviet Union. In submitting the draft on 12 October Sir T. Brimelow warned, however, that in view of public statements by Herr Brandt and by President Pompidou during a visit to Moscow, welcoming the idea of a European security conference, the US and UK might be accused of obstructing progress: 'The question will need delicate handling.'

[3] Minute from Mr. Graham to Mr. Bendall, quoting Sir A. Douglas-Home (WDW 1/2).

No. 52

Sir A. Douglas-Home to Sir E. Peck[1] (UKDEL NATO)

No. 344 Telegraphic [WDW 1/2]

Confidential   FCO, *12 October 1970, 5.20 p.m.*

Repeated for information Saving to Brussels, Ottawa, Copenhagen, Paris, Bonn, Athens, Reykjavik, Rome, Luxembourg, The Hague, Oslo, Lisbon, Ankara, Washington, Moscow, Budapest, UKMIS New York, Bucharest, Prague, Sofia, Warsaw, Berlin, Helsinki, Berne, Stockholm, Vienna, Dublin, Holy See, Nicosia, Valletta, Belgrade, Madrid, UKDIS Geneva and UKMIS Geneva.

To be on desks at 08.30Z on 13 October.

European security problems
My telegram number 236 [*sic*] to UKDEL NATO.[2]

[1] Sir E. Peck had succeeded Sir B. Burrows as Permanent UK Representative to NATO in September 1970.

[2] The reference should evidently be to FCO telegram No. 276 of 24 July, which set out Sir A. Douglas-Home's views on the problems of East-West relations, and his distrust of Soviet motives in promoting a European security conference. He went on to list the main considerations which would underlie his approach to East-West relations during the next few months, including diplomatic pressure from the Warsaw Pact and pressure from public opinion, the possibility that

Recent Soviet attitudes, notably over Egypt, Cuba and the Berlin corridors, have reinforced the arguments for a carefully measured approach in Western dealings with the Soviet Union and its allies on the complex of subjects coming under the general heading of European security. I have been looking again at the attitude which HMG should adopt in the discussions which are likely to take place during the next few weeks among the Western allies[3] concerning:

(A) reducing East-West tensions in Europe;
(B) seeking mutual and balanced force reductions;
(C) responding to proposals for a European Security Conference.

2. These are all issues which appeal to public opinion, particularly to that of some of our allies, and which public pronouncements have committed NATO to regarding with sympathy. But negotiations with the Soviet Union on any of these issues are unlikely to bring us substantial advantage: and there are grounds for viewing Soviet motives with scepticism.

3. East-West tensions, for instance, mostly spring from sources (e.g. the fundamental imbalance caused by the Soviet Union's geographical position and political control of Eastern Europe) too deep to be removed by any negotiations now foreseeable. It is true that the Germans have made some progress in their *Ostpolitik* negotiations with the Russians[4] and the Poles[5] and hope for progress with the East Germans.[6] There is also a possibility that we shall be able to make progress in the current Four Power talks over Berlin, although we still do not know whether the Russians mean business there.[7] But

---

the Warsaw Pact's proposals (see pp. 238-9) reflected a genuine desire to negotiate, a highly sceptical American attitude and the need to preserve unity in NATO (WDN 21/3).

[3] It had been agreed that British and American officials would exchange views on European security in Washington in preparation for the NATO Ministerial meeting in December; informal discussions were being held between the UK and West German delegations to NATO, and the NAC was considering papers prepared by the Secretariat on European security.

[4] See No. 50, note 3.

[5] See No. 48, note 3. At the fifth round of talks held in Warsaw on 23-24 July agreement was reached on four articles to form the basis of a treaty, but further negotiations were postponed until after the signature of the FRG-Soviet Treaty. Talks resumed in Bonn on 5-8 October and after a final round in Warsaw from 3-9 and 11-14 November the Polish and FRG Foreign Ministers initialled a treaty on 18 November in which the FRG accepted the Oder-Neisse as Poland's Western frontier, but maintained that its final delimitation must await a peace treaty and that the FRG could not speak for an all-German Government. It also included a declaration on the renunciation of force. Herr Brandt and Mr. Cyrankiewicz, Premier of Poland, signed the treaty in Warsaw on 7 December, but the FRG announced that it would not be ratified until a solution had been found to the problems of Berlin.

[6] See No. 50, note 6. No further inner-German talks had taken place.

[7] Cf. No. 50, note 4. A Russian paper of 23 September setting out general principles and procedures for implementation of a Berlin settlement had been considered at the 7th Quadripartite Ambassadors' meeting on 30 September. Although Sir R. Jackling, in the Chair, had opened the meeting with a strong protest at the attempted closure of the air corridors earlier that morning (see p. 263), the Ambassadors' decision to meet in a more informal and restricted session encouraged a trend to more practical negotiating procedures, and the Soviet side 'showed

we must be careful not to encourage Soviet expectations of unrequited Western concessions by appearing over-eager. We believe that the government or governments which show the greater impatience will come off second best in dealings with the Russians.

4. Mutual and balanced force reductions, if they are not to be detrimental to NATO's military security, will require considerably greater reductions on the part of the Warsaw Pact than of NATO. Such reductions are unlikely, and so therefore is the prospect of meaningful negotiations. We should accordingly emphasise to our allies that we must keep our eyes firmly on the realities of our security and recognise that 'token' reductions, which we believe is the most the Soviet Union now contemplates, would amount to dealing with the symptoms rather than disease and would not suffice to create a solid basis of confidence between East and West. This is a point to bear in mind in preparing for the December meeting at which NATO ministers may decide to propose multilateral exploratory talks in order to deepen the probing of Warsaw Pact intentions on MBFR.

5. A European Security Conference may be inevitable, but should be approached without haste and with due regard to the possible need for a hardening of Western attitudes if Russian moves elsewhere make this necessary. I am myself thinking of making a gentle start at the December meeting of the NATO Council in pointing out the difficulty, inherent in the idea of a European Security Conference, of avoiding disadvantage to the West.

6. We are considering how we might best enlist support for these ideas during the coming weeks. President Pompidou has probably made this task more difficult by his statement in Moscow that the preparation of the European Security Conference could now enter into an active phase.[8] We expect the Warsaw Pact governments to exploit these words while ignoring what President Pompidou had to say about independence and freedom. We shall be letting Posts concerned have a fuller analysis of the problems as we see them, together with some suggestions on possible tactics.[9] At present,

a clear desire to accelerate the negotiations' (Bonn telegram No. 1157 of 3 October). In telegram No. 661 to Bonn of even date, Sir A. Douglas-Home cautioned against any move towards intensive negotiations 'unless the three Western Allies and, above all, the Federal German Government, are prepared to settle for much less than what they have hitherto regarded as the essential elements of a satisfactory agreement'.

At the next Quadripartite meeting on 9 October Mr. Abrasimov adopted a markedly harder line: Sir R. Jackling and his colleagues thought that the 'most plausible reason for the obvious toughening of the Soviet position . . . is that it was conceived as a softening-up negotiating tactic . . . The general situation is that the negotiations have moved into a more specific phase with both differences and points of potential agreement more clearly posed' (Bonn telegram No. 1203 of 14 October, WRL 2/10).

[8] Cf. p. 264. President Pompidou's speech of 6 October was reported in *The Times*, 7 October 1970, p. 6.

[9] Telegram No. 374 to UKDEL NATO of 7 November stated that there had not yet been enough progress in the Berlin or inner-German talks to justify a Western initiative towards a European security conference, and that the Warsaw Pact countries had failed to clarify their agenda for a conference: 'Short of a major change in the situation before the December meeting,

however, there is no need to make detailed proposals to our allies. In general you (and Posts in NATO capitals) should be guided by the foregoing and by the more detailed considerations set out in paragraphs 1-9 of my telegram under reference (except where these have been overtaken by events, e.g. paragraph 6 (iii)).[10] You should, therefore, take any suitable opportunity to indicate to our allies that our attitude to the choices which face the Alliance will be one of caution, and of maintaining unity in the Alliance.

7. Posts in Warsaw Pact and neutral countries should continue to follow the line in paragraphs 10 and 11 of my telegram under reference.[11]

therefore, we doubt if it will be appropriate for the Alliance to move forward . . . If the majority wish to make a further commitment to moving forward, however, it will still be necessary for the Alliance to agree on a reasonably precise tactical timetable, with built-in guarantees to ensure that we did not end up with a conference on Russian terms and nothing in return . . . It is still our aim to avoid becoming associated with proposals which our major allies find objectionable.'

[10] See note 2. Para. 6(iii) of telegram No. 276 had referred to the possibility that NATO Ministers might need to meet in advance of their scheduled December meeting.

[11] This line instructed Posts to emphasise Sir A. Douglas-Home's desire 'to see a real improvement in East-West relations generally . . . and—if there is business to be done—at a properly prepared conference'. Posts in neutral countries were further authorised to refer to Sir Alec's views on the problem of East-West relations in Europe as quoted in note 2 above.

On 26 October Mr. Gromyko arrived in London from New York, as planned (see No. 51, note 5) and was met at the airport by Sir A. Douglas-Home. Over the next two days the Soviet Foreign Minister had a series of discussions with the Secretary of State and with the Prime Minister, before leaving on the morning of 29 October for a visit to West and East Germany.[1] The records of Mr. Gromyko's talks with Sir A. Douglas-Home on 27 October, covering German questions and European security in the morning, and trade and bilateral questions in the afternoon, are printed as Nos. 53 and 54 below. The latter part of the afternoon meeting, dealing with Middle Eastern matters, is summarised in footnote 13 to No. 54. On the morning of 28 October Mr. Gromyko discussed Berlin, European security and the Middle East with Mr. Heath, on the same lines as with Sir A. Douglas-Home. A further conversation with the Secretary of State on Middle Eastern and South-East Asian questions was followed by a lunch at 10 Downing Street.

After a dinner at the Soviet Embassy on the evening of 28 October, Sir Alec spoke privately to Mr. Gromyko regarding the unacceptable activities of the Soviet Trade Delegation: cf. No. 49, note 7. In a minute to Mr. Heath of 27 October the Secretary of State had informed the Prime Minister that yet another member of the STD had been detected in intelligence activities, and recommended that the Prime Minister should speak to Mr. Gromyko the following day 'in order that he should understand that you are personally familiar with and concerned about these activities . . . In my view, there are at the present time no general political considerations of a bilateral or international nature

[1] The *communiqué* issued at the conclusion of Mr. Gromyko's visit is printed in Watt and Mayall, 1970, pp. 584-6.

which should inhibit us from speaking plainly to Gromyko on this subject . . . you might ask Gromyko to ensure that the Soviet Government were fully aware of your own concern about this. Previous representations had apparently been disregarded. You wished him to ensure that appropriate conclusions were drawn from what you had said.' However, it was evidently agreed subsequently with No. 10 that Sir A. Douglas-Home rather than Mr. Heath should speak on this matter to Mr. Gromyko, who said that he knew nothing of the particular case complained of but thought it 'only too likely' that the person concerned was a victim of the practice of 'planting faked cases against Soviet officials'; he asked the Secretary of State to write to him about the case.

No. 53

Record of conversation between Sir A. Douglas-Home and Mr. Gromyko at the Foreign & Commonwealth Office at 11 a.m. on Tuesday, 27 October 1970

[ENS 3/548/37]

Confidential

Present:

The Rt Hon Sir Alec Douglas-Home, MP	Mr. A.A. Gromyko
Mr. Anthony Royle, MP	Mr. M.N. Smirnovsky
Sir Denis Greenhill	Mr. P.A. Abrasimov
Sir Duncan Wilson	Mr. L.E. Mendelivich
Sir Roger Jackling	Mr. I.I. Ippolitov
Sir Thomas Brimelow	Mr. V.M. Vasev
Mr. D.V. Bendall	Mr. V.G. Makarov
Mr. J.A.N. Graham	Mr. V.G. Filatov
Mr. C.S.R. Giffard	Mr. Y.E. Fotin
Mr. W.R. Haydon	Mr. A.M. Vavilov
Mr. C.L.G. Mallaby	Mr. Sukhodrev[1]
Mr. K.A. Bishop[2]	

Sir Alec Douglas-Home welcomed Mr. Gromyko to London after too long an absence. He had no doubt that there would be some differences between the two sides. But, when last he and Mr. Gromyko had been colleagues, the Test Ban Treaty had been concluded and there had been successful talks on Laos.[3] The results might not be so important this time, but the two parties should look for common points of view. He strongly desired closer Anglo-

[1] Messrs. Mendelevich, Fotin and Vavilov were respectively Soviet Deputy Representative at the UN, a member of the Soviet Ministry for Foreign Affairs and a Second Secretary in the Soviet Embassy in London.

[2] Mr. Royle (later Lord Fanshawe of Richmond) was a Parliamentary Under Secretary of State in the FCO, and Mr. Bishop of Research Department acted as Interpreter.

[3] See No. 47, note 2.

Soviet relations, to which Mr. Gromyko's visit would contribute. *Mr. Gromyko* expressed thanks and agreed that past contacts between himself and Sir Alec Douglas-Home had been useful to Anglo-Soviet relations. The Soviet Government viewed the present visit in this light and expected the exchanges to contribute to the development of relations. *Sir Alec Douglas-Home* suggested that the discussion might begin with European matters. For his part, he was interested in the Federal German Government's *Ostpolitik* and particularly in making progress over Berlin. Mr. Gromyko, he believed, was interested in a European security conference. *Mr. Gromyko* agreed.

Berlin

2. *Sir Alec Douglas-Home* said that the British Government took a favourable view of the Federal Government's *Ostpolitik*. The Soviet Government were keen to see the ratification of the Soviet/German Treaty. The future of Berlin came into this context. The British Government were interested in a more tolerable life for the West Berliners, and especially in access questions. The Soviet Government, he believed, were interested in certain Federal activities. He would be glad to know Mr. Gromyko's views about possible steps. The three Western Allies governed the city, and not the Federal Government. Each exercised responsibility in its own sector, as did the Soviet Union in the Eastern sector.

3. *Mr. Gromyko* said he thought the British Government might not fully understand the Soviet position. He wished to stress that the Soviet Union had no interest whatever in undermining the status of West Berlin, which must be governed by the three 'Western Powers and not the Federal German Republic. The three Western Governments had more than once declared that West Berlin had not, did not, and could not belong to the Federal Republic. This was quite right. The Soviet Union had no intention of undermining or weakening the past Allied Agreements which determined the status of West Berlin. The British Government should be aware of this from the outset, so as to remove all misunderstanding.

4. *Sir Alec Douglas-Home* thanked Mr. Gromyko for these helpful statements. *Mr. Gromyko* said he was not surprised to receive this expression of thanks: when he had made the same clarification in Washington and to the French Government, the reaction had been similar.[4] All this should ease the situation and eliminate misunderstanding. The Western Allies should not need to

---

[4] During his visit to the USA Mr. Gromyko had discussed Berlin with Mr. Nixon and Mr. Rogers in Washington, and with M. Schumann, French Foreign Minister, in New York. He told the US Secretary of State on 19 October that the Western objective of securing practical improvements in the conditions for access to Berlin and the Soviet objective of loosening the Federal Republic's ties with West Berlin could be dealt with concurrently. On 22 October Mr. Gromyko assured President Nixon that the Soviet Union 'had no intention of weakening the status of the Allied powers in West Berlin', described the FRG's political presence in the city as the 'principal question there' and suggested the Four Powers should list those political activities which could and could not be permitted in Berlin. Submitting a note on Mr. Gromyko's conversation with the President to Mr. Bendall and Sir D. Greenhill on 10 November, Mr. Giffard commented that 'Gromyko seems to have taken the same line on all the subjects raised as he did in London.' (FA 3/304/2).

discuss what should form the subject of the negotiations. There might perhaps be differences about formulations, but not about the substance. The foundation for any possible understanding was that no party intended to undermine past agreements. As for the practical matters on which agreement was needed, some of them had political as well as practical significance. The first he would name was the political, repeat political, presence of the Federal Government in West Berlin. No-one could assert that the present Federal activities could be considered normal. They were a violation of the status of West Berlin and of Allied Agreements. This violation must be eliminated. It was therefore necessary to eliminate or curtail the Federal political presence in West Berlin. The Soviet proposals contained certain concrete points which needed to be resolved, including the questions of the *Bundestag* and its committees and commissions and other parliamentary bodies; the activities of the Federal Government, the Chancellor and the President; and the activities of Federal agencies. In proposing the elimination of violations of the special status of West Berlin, the Soviet Union was defending that status to a greater degree than the Western Powers. The British Government should be grateful for this. The Federal Government knew the Soviet position on Federal activities. But they had developed the political activities and this fact had to be taken into account. Agreement was only possible, however, on the basis of the elimination of all violations of the status of West Berlin. There should be no great difficulty in reaching agreement. The Soviet Union called on the Western Powers to be consistent. The Soviet Union proposed the following practical approach: we should together consider what precise activities should be forbidden, by discussing a list.

5. Mr. Gromyko said that, as regards the other side of the matter, which concerned the GDR and its rights, there should be discussion about transit between the Federal Republic and West Berlin, and of access, which basically was a humanitarian question. Here it was a matter of meeting certain desires of the Federal Republic and the West Berlin *Senat*. Here too, however, the Four Powers should first reach an understanding. All the three questions Mr. Gromyko had mentioned should be taken as a single package. What was the British reaction to this? In Washington and in talking with the French, the reactions received by the Russians had been positive. After a Four Power understanding in principle, there should be practical agreements based upon it, in order to formulate practical measures. These agreements, Mr. Gromyko wished to stress, should be between the Federal Republic and the GDR, and the West Berlin *Senat* and the GDR. At the end of Mr. Gromyko's discussion of this question in Washington, President Nixon had said that the United States representative in the Quadripartite Talks would be given the requisite instructions. After the meeting with the President, Mr. Rogers too had said that the United States favoured an understanding as soon as possible. Mr. Gromyko had expressed satisfaction.

6. Mr. Gromyko said he would also like to express satisfaction at Sir Alec Douglas-Home's earlier statement of the favourable British attitude towards the Soviet-German Treaty. The Soviet Government had also noted the

favourable British reaction which had been given immediately after the signature of the Treaty.[5] The Soviet Government valued the British reaction.

7. *Sir Alec Douglas-Home* pointed out that Mr. Gromyko, in talking of Federal activities in Berlin, had used the expressions 'eliminate' and 'curtail'. These meant two very different things. We understood Soviet concern about certain Federal activities. We hoped therefore that, in the context of possible curtailment, Mr. Gromyko could give clarification about the activities which the Soviet Union had in mind. It would be more profitable, as Mr. Gromyko had said, to talk of practical steps, rather than complaining about general matters, which we also could do in respect of violations of Allied Agreements in East Berlin.

8. *Mr. Gromyko* said that, when this matter had been discussed in Washington, the same question had also arisen, but in another form. President Nixon had referred to low profile activities. Mr. Gromyko had said to the President that perhaps there were activities which could not be seen without a microscope and perhaps there were some activities of which the Soviet Union knew nothing. It was easy to resolve this difficulty. The Soviet Union proposed that certain precisely defined categories of activity should be banned. We should together go over a list of activities. This should contain first of all the activities of the *Bundestag,* then the activities of the President, and the Chancellor, of Federal political bodies and so forth.

9. As regards West Berlin's economic ties with the outside world, Mr. Gromyko said the Soviet approach was somewhat different. The Soviet Government had explained that they had no perfidious plans to strangle West Berlin's economy. Everything must be done to rule out political concepts which violated the status of West Berlin under the guise of economic ties. That was what concerned the Soviet Union. He said this to dispel any doubts in British minds.

10. *Sir Alec Douglas-Home* said he did not doubt what Mr. Gromyko said and thanked him for his assurances. It would not however be reasonable to look at all Federal activities in Berlin. We should look at a list and decide which activities were to be affected. Our representatives in the Quadripartite Talks should proceed in this sensible way. As regards access, we wanted individuals to have a more comfortable life; train delays, for instance, should be prevented. We therefore wanted Four Power agreement on practical arrangements. What had been done in Berlin was perfectly consistent with the Four Power Agreements. It was for those who were sovereign to decide what should be allowed to happen in West Berlin. He wished to point this out, since, perhaps at his own request, Mr. Gromyko had stated what the Soviet Union wanted, but not what it was prepared to give. *Mr. Gromyko* said he had stated quite specifically that steps should be taken towards meeting the desires of the West Berlin *Senat* and of the Federal Republic, and therefore of course

---

[5] A statement issued by the FCO on 7 August welcomed the initialling of the Soviet-West German Treaty (see No. 50, note 3) as a 'most important development in the context of improving East/West relations': see Watt and Mayall, 1970, p. 447.

of the three Powers, on transit and access. These matters should be resolved in specific agreements. He doubted whether detailed discussion of this was necessary at the present meeting. The Soviet Union was suggesting a package. He believed this approach coincided with the British approach.

11. *Sir Alec Douglas-Home* thanked Mr. Gromyko for his definite statement that transit and access should be covered. The details should be left to the negotiations. He agreed with the package approach. Our representatives in the Quadripartite Talks should be instructed accordingly.[6]

12. *Mr. Gromyko* asked whether he could report to the Soviet Government that the British Government favoured reaching agreement on questions concerning West Berlin and that agreement should be reached as soon as possible. This would be similar to the United States and French attitudes, as conveyed to the Russians.

13. *Sir Alec Douglas-Home* said the British Government were very anxious for an agreement as soon as possible, although much would depend on more detailed formulation of the contents.

European Security

14. *Sir Alec Douglas-Home* said he was familiar with the Soviet proposals concerning a European security conference. There was no need to examine the origins of this at the present meeting. But it would be useful to know what Mr. Gromyko thought a conference should do.

15. *Mr. Gromyko* said he would explain briefly and then ask for more information about British views. All Governments, including he believed the British Government, agreed that there were problems needing resolution in Europe. Equally, the British Government could not deny that the European States had not met together in order to discuss common problems. Why should this be ruled out, when States met on a world-wide basis and in other regions of the world? As for the questions to be discussed, the Warsaw Pact States had made proposals.[7] Understanding and agreement on the non-use of force and on the obligation to resolve difficulties in a peaceful way would be a positive step. An understanding on the preservation of the territorial *status quo* in Europe would also be of positive importance. Surely the United Kingdom did not want to alter European frontiers and did not favour *revanche*? Indeed the British Government were on record as favouring the *status quo* in Europe. They had welcomed the Soviet-German Treaty and therefore should be favourable towards a similar arrangement on an all-

---

[6] Sir A. Douglas-Home and Mr. Gromyko's conversation about Berlin was reported in telegram No. 905 to Moscow of 27 October, repeated for information to Bonn (ENS 3/ 548/ 37). At the next round of Quadripartite talks on 4 November Sir R. Jackling noted that 'Abrasimov went out of his way to be affable and to avoid confrontation' (Bonn telegram No. 1328, 6 November). The FCO assessment after this meeting was that 'we have now moved into a phase of real negotiation where there is an apparent willingness on all sides for give and take . . . We see some grounds for optimism about the possibility of an agreement on Berlin from which the Allies and the Federal Germans also get real benefits' (telegram No. 748 to Bonn, 6 November, WRL 2/ 10).

[7] See p. 239.

European basis. Why would it be bad if the conference expressed itself in favour of consolidating economic relations in Europe? All countries would stand to gain. This would not be prejudicial to various economic ties which had come into being in Europe. The Soviet Union had made similar proposals on cultural ties. The questions of disarmament and the reduction of armed forces in Europe had sometimes been named as questions for a conference. The Soviet Government were not in principle against their discussion, but they were too complicated for resolution at a relatively brief conference. The conference could, however, establish a special body, as the United Kingdom had earlier suggested, to discuss these questions and perhaps others. Or disarmament could be discussed in some other forum outside the conference. The Soviet Government did not understand the apparent British reservations about the conference proposal.

16. *Sir Alec Douglas-Home* said that the British, as practical people, would like to know, before endorsing the idea of a conference, what the conference would do. One meeting might not be of value. But a permanent organ would certainly be worth considering. Such an organ might do useful things over the years. NATO would be looking at these questions again in December. He could not say what would be the response of the Alliance. But he thought we should be prepared to consider any effective lasting machinery. Rather than suggesting just one or two conferences, the Soviet Union now seemed to be suggesting a permanent organ which could discuss many problems. *Mr. Gromyko* said that the Soviet Government sympathised with the idea of holding not just one conference but several, and with the establishment of a permanently functioning organ. The word 'organ' was the Russian translation of the word 'body', used formerly by the British. The Russians considered the British to be the authors of the idea. *Sir Alec Douglas-Home* said it was useful for us to know that the Soviet Government were considering permanent machinery. We certainly would not deny our authorship of the idea of a permanent body.[8]

---

[8] Reporting this conversation to the Cabinet on 29 October, Sir A. Douglas-Home commented that 'On Berlin Mr. Gromyko had shown some interest in easing the restrictions on access from the West; but it was clear that the Soviet Government would expect any concessions in this respect to be matched by reductions in the scale of the activities, especially in the political sphere, undertaken by the Federal Republic of Germany in West Berlin. Apart from this there had been few signs of flexibility in the Soviet position. It had not proved possible to make any mention of Berlin in the *communiqué* (see p. 267) . . . since Mr. Gromyko would not accept any wording implying the continuance of Four-Power responsibility for the city as a whole. It was clear, therefore, that it remained the long-term aim of the Soviet Government to make the position of West Berlin still more anomalous and to weaken still further the position of the Western Powers in the city.

'As regards the possibility of a European Security Conference Mr. Gromyko had expressed the hope that we would give favourable consideration to the proposal . . . for a standing body to deal with questions of this nature. The Soviet Government perhaps hoped to include some of the non-aligned countries of Europe in the membership of such an organisation and so to secure additional support for their policies. We should therefore need to proceed with caution' (CM(70)34).

No. 54

Record of conversation between Sir A. Douglas-Home and Mr. Gromyko at the Foreign & Commonwealth Office at 3 p.m. on Tuesday, 27 October 1970

[ENS 3/548/37]

Confidential

Present:

The Rt Hon Sir Alec Douglas-Home, MP	Mr. A.A. Gromyko
Mr. Michael Noble, MP	HE Mr. Smirnovsky
Sir Denis Greenhill	Mr. P.A. Abrasimov
Sir Duncan Wilson	Mr. L.E. Mendelevich
Sir Thomas Brimelow	Mr. I.I. Ippolitov
Sir Philip Adams	Mr. B.S. Gordeev[1]
Mr. B.E. Bellamy[2]	Mr. V.G. Makarov
Mr. C.S.R. Giffard	Mr. V.M. Vasev
Mr. W.R. Haydon	Mr. V.A. Kopteltsev
Mr. N.J. Barrington	Mr. V.M. Sukhodrev
Mr. G.G.H. Walden	
Mr. K.A. Bishop	

After an exchange of pleasantries, *Sir Alec Douglas-Home* said that, following the discussion of international matters that morning, he now wished to turn to bilateral relations, and to trade in particular. It was our main concern to balance our trading accounts, though trade was increasing and this was all to the good. He then invited Mr. Noble to speak.

2. *Mr. Noble* explained that he was now the Minister responsible for trade. Mr. Gromyko would no doubt remember that it was the present Prime Minister who had begun the relaxation of discriminatory restrictions on our trade with Eastern Europe,[3] which now applied to only 10 per cent of our trade. Mr. Noble said that he had taken a personal interest in these matters when he was last in the Government.[4] He was glad they had developed well. But one point caused us concern. The balance of Anglo-Soviet trade tended to be in the favour of the Soviet Union. This would not matter if it continued for only a year or so. However, while our trade with the rest of the world was

<hr>

[1] Head of the Soviet Trade Delegation.

[2] Mr. Noble was Minister of Trade in the new Department of Trade and Industry (DTI) formed on 15 October by the merger of the Board of Trade and Mintech. Sir P. Adams was Assistant Under Secretary superintending Arabian, Near Eastern and UN departments, and Mr. Bellamy was an Under Secretary in the Commercial Relations and Exports division of the DTI.

[3] Mr. Heath had been Secretary of State for Industry, Trade and Regional Development and President of the Board of Trade when the list of embargoed goods for export to the Soviet *bloc* and China was reduced on 29 January 1963.

[4] Mr. Noble had been Secretary of State for Scotland 1962-64.

increasing, our exports to the Soviet Union were at best stagnant, although Soviet imports from other Western countries were constantly rising. The fact that our exports were expanding in the rest of the world showed that we were competitive in price, quality and delivery dates. We hoped to regain the growth which we appeared to have lost for the moment.

3. Mr. Noble then referred to the immediate prospects of Soviet purchases of major capital goods from this country. Many of these projects had been in discussion for some time, and could help to rectify the balance of trade. The visit of Mr. Misnik had provided a useful opportunity to discuss major questions of industrial and technological cooperation in exploiting Soviet resources for the benefit of both countries.[5] The British government would do all it could to help British firms involved in these discussions.

4. The Soviet Government had suggested the establishment of a Joint Commission on trade and technology.[6] We were interested in this, and if it materialised, Mr. Noble looked forward to renewing his acquaintance with Mr. Patolichev. The Soviet Minister of Foreign Trade had visited him in Scotland in 1964, and he had held discussions with Mr. Patolichev when he himself had visited Moscow for the Agricultural Exhibition in that year. In the past his main aim had been the expansion of agricultural relations with the Soviet Union. His objective was now wider: to expand trade in general. He saw prospects of success if the right decisions were made. If the Russians wished to import sheep, he would compete with Sir A. Douglas-Home to supply them.

5. *Mr. Gromyko* invited Mr. Gordeev of the Soviet Trade Delegation to speak. *Mr. Gordeev* said that in July this year, representatives of the Board of Trade and of the Soviet Ministry of Foreign Trade had had detailed discussions on our bilateral trade.[7] He was sure Mr. Noble would agree that, as a result of these discussions, both sides had confirmed that trade was developing satisfactorily, and both had expressed their confidence that this should continue in the future. At the same time, these representatives had put forward certain considerations about additional measures to expand bilateral trade. As Mr. Noble had said, the British side had emphasised the need to increase Soviet purchases in the United Kingdom in order to bring trade into balance. The Soviet side had raised a number of considerations which they considered to be obstacles to the increase of trade, for example, certain restrictions which were still in force on our side, and unfair tariffs, amongst other questions. But both sides had agreed that the main factor to be emphasised was the growth which had taken place and the favourable prospects for the future. They had agreed that attention should be mainly

[5] Mr. Misnik, Vice Chairman of Gosplan, visited the UK from 22 September-2 October as guest of the CBI.

[6] Cf. Nos. 41, note 2 and 49, note 2.

[7] Mr. A.N. Manzhulo, Head of the Western World Department at the Soviet Ministry of Foreign Trade, came to London for the annual review of Anglo-Soviet trade and held discussions at the Board of Trade from 27-29 July.

devoted to the question of increasing trade and to ensuring that nothing should impede this.

6. On the imbalance of Anglo-Soviet trade, Mr. Gordeev said that this was not so much a physical as a moral impediment. Detailed discussions on this subject had already been held. He would elucidate the Soviet view in arithmetical terms. If the monetary value of British imports from the Soviet Union which were subsequently re-exported at a profit were taken into account, the question of an imbalance was practically eliminated. Examples of such imports were diamonds and precious metals. More than 80 per cent of the former were re-exported by the United Kingdom. In addition, virtually 100 per cent of our imports of Soviet furs and carpets were also re-exported. These alone were sufficient to account for an apparent imbalance. However, if differences in f.o.b. and c.i.f. were also taken into account, together with credit repayments, the picture was quite different, and an imbalance could be said to exist in favour of the United Kingdom. This problem was a moral impediment to the expansion of trade because there was too much talk about it. If the time and energy spent in these discussions were devoted to the question of increasing our trade, this would yield positive results. However, the Soviet side had never refused to discuss this question as long as the British side wished. As to the possibility of increased Soviet purchases of British industrial goods, and in particular of machinery, this depended on many factors: for example, cost, quality and delivery dates. There was also the question of the conditions of credit, namely, the terms offered by the ECGD.[8] On 1 October, there had been an important change in the British credit rate. This was bound to inhibit the expansion of Soviet purchases in this country. The increase from 5½ per cent to 7 per cent made the British less competitive than the Italians, Japanese, French and others. Lastly, he wished to mention that the list of embargoed items, particularly machine tools, also obstructed Soviet purchase of British goods.

7. *Mr. Noble* congratulated Mr. Gordeev on his recent promotion, and on his skill in presenting the trade figures. He himself had been careful to emphasise not so much the imbalance of trade but the need to put this right by increasing trade. The figures over the last three years showed that Soviet exports to this country were £123 million, £154 million and £195 million. British exports to the Soviet Union, on the other hand, had been £64 million, £104 million and £95 million in the same period. They were expected to reach about £100 million this year. Thus for three years our exports had been stagnant. He fully appreciated Mr. Gordeev's point about diamonds, furs and precious metals, and had taken this into account. On credits, Mr. Noble said that we had always been able to match other countries in this field. There was a level rate, but in the case of particular projects we were always ready to match other countries. He did not believe that this would be a serious impediment to our exports. On embargoed goods, consecutive Governments had greatly reduced the number of items involved. He

[8] Export Credits Guarantee Department.

appreciated that this caused problems: but these were small and the field affected was narrow. With goodwill on both sides trade could be increased, and he looked forward to discussing any problems freely and openly.

8. *Mr. Gromyko* asked whether the British Government had any plans to reduce the embargo list to zero. *Mr. Noble* said that he had not consulted Sir Alec Douglas-Home on this question.

9. *Mr. Gromyko* then said that, according to his information, there had been satisfactory growth in trade during the first eight months of this year. British exports had also been growing as compared with Soviet exports. He wished to emphasise the importance of the existence of the Long Term Trade Agreement as a basis for trade.[9] He trusted that his attitude was shared by the British side. He wished to state on behalf of the Soviet Government that he did not think that the possibilities of Anglo-Soviet trade had been exhausted. The Soviet side would do its best to achieve further development, and would look into any possibility of securing this. He hoped that the British side would do the same.

10. Mr. Gromyko then turned to the Anglo-Soviet Joint Commission. He said that an agreement had been reached in principle for the establishment of such a Commission, which would facilitate the conduct of trade and economic relations between the two countries. He had heard that the British side was reluctant to place scientific and technological cooperation under the Commission.[10] In Soviet exchanges with other countries, they had found that it was sometimes difficult to divide economic cooperation from scientific and technological cooperation. In practice, the Commission would deal primarily with economic relations because this was the most extensive field. But the Soviet feeling was that the two fields should be taken together. The *communiqué* after his visit could say that the Joint Commission could start functioning in the near future.

11. *Sir Alec Douglas-Home* said that he would consider the Soviet proposal. He wished to include a reference to trade in the title of the Commission, and this had been agreed. But we were under some difficulty over the inclusion of scientific exchanges. The Royal Society was not a part of the government. However, this could be overcome. When listening to Mr. Gordeev, he had thought of the saying about turning black into white. Mr. Gordeev had presented the figures skilfully, but he could not deny that British exports to the USSR were only £95 million as opposed to £196 million for Soviet exports to Britain. But he agreed that we should concentrate on increasing our trade. He asked if there were any other bilateral matters.

13. *Mr. Noble* referred to the British Petroleum protein project, which he said was going forward very well. This was a good example of the spreading of technological know-how.

13. *Mr. Gromyko* said that it was agreed that both sides would take measures to secure a growth in bilateral trade. But our bilateral relations were not

---

[9] See No. 33.   [10] Cf. Nos. 47, note 8 and 49, note 2.

confined to trade. Speaking in the name of the Soviet Government, he said that he wished to develop political relations with the United Kingdom in such a way as to ensure their expansion. At the moment, it was impossible to say that our relations were bad. But nor could it be said without reserve that they were good and that political contacts were intensive and fruitful. The Soviet Government were ready to make further efforts in this field, but the result would depend on both sides.

14. Mr. Gromyko said that the long term trade agreement, the consular convention,[11] and the air agreement[12] were all useful. But there was also a need to strengthen cooperation in the political sphere. It was naturally difficult to isolate our political relations from the position each side occupied on acute international issues, especially those which remained unresolved. When the Soviet side spoke of an improvement in political relations, they were therefore conscious that this was connected with our positions on international problems, which could not fail to influence our bilateral relations.

15. *Sir Alec Douglas-Home* said that he echoed Mr. Gromyko's desire for improved relations across the board. It would be a good thing if the two countries' Ambassadors, who were both such distinguished men, were to explain their governments' respective policies to Ministers in each other's country more frequently. His own door was always open, and he would always be happy to explain the British government's policies in order that they should be understood in the Soviet Union. He hoped that the Russians would do the same. This would help each side to see where they agreed and where they differed.

16. He wished to give one example. When we were attempting to find a solution to the Rhodesia problem which would be consistent with democratic principles, or to the problems of territories still dependent on us, the Soviet Union sometimes denounced our actions as naked imperialism. This was out of date. We were no longer an imperialist power. Some territories remained under our control because they were small. Where possible, we had conferred independence. Soviet press criticism in these cases was not well received by British opinion. Increased contacts would therefore be advantageous. Differences must not be exaggerated through a lack of understanding. One illustration of this was the treatment by Soviet news agencies of events in Northern Ireland, where we were attempting the difficult task of reconciling opposing religious points of view. He was sure Mr. Gromyko understood this. But Soviet news agencies had excelled themselves in their references to the situation in Northern Ireland.

17. *Mr. Gromyko* said that differences of view, particularly about foreign policy, were bound to exist. This was the result of a fundamental difference of principle. But we must identify areas where our positions were close and seek to expand them. We would not find a common language on the international

---

[11] See No. 1, note 6.   [12] See No. 44

aspects of the problems of colonialism and race. But this should not impede cooperation in fields where our positions coincided or were close. Mr. Gromyko said that this was his reply to Sir Alec Douglas-Home's reference to Rhodesia and Northern Ireland. However, an objective analysis of the British press on the USSR would show, he thought, that, in volume, there was a great imbalance in favour of the United Kingdom. But all this should not be an obstacle to the identification of common interests on political questions, for example European security. This would help to improve relations in other spheres, and the Soviet side was ready to attempt to solve other problems.

18. Mr. Gromyko said that he would welcome more systematic and regular contacts on matters of international concern, particularly through our respective Ambassadors. They could visit their respective Foreign Ministries more often for an exchange of opinion and for consultations. Ministers themselves should also display initiative on this.

19. Before terminating the discussion on bilateral relations, Mr. Gromyko wished to extend an invitation to Sir Alec Douglas-Home to visit the Soviet Union at a time convenient to him. He was sure that agreement could be reached on precise dates. *Sir Alec Douglas-Home* replied that he would be happy to go to the Soviet Union, and that dates could be considered.

20. As for Mr. Gromyko's remarks on the British press, Sir Alec Douglas-Home said that he was sure that the Soviet Foreign Minister had noticed that the British press criticised the Conservative Government as much as the Soviet Union. *Mr. Gromyko* pointed out that this was domestic criticism, which was distinct from foreign policy. *Sir Alec Douglas-Home* asked for Mr. Gromyko's advice on how to avoid press criticism. He emphasised that discussions should cover not only areas where our positions were close, but where we disagreed. *Mr. Gromyko* agreed.

21. It was then agreed that the discussion should turn to the Middle East.[13]

[13] The remainder of the discussion, relating to Middle Eastern affairs, is not printed. Mr. Gromyko pressed Sir A. Douglas-Home to agree to a date being set for the resumption of the Jarring talks, and to the extension of the 90-day cease-fire which was due to end on 5 November. The Secretary of State, while reaffirming British support for Mr. Jarring and the cease-fire, said that only the US could persuade the Israelis: it was 'not practicable' for the UK to do so. He agreed that Resolution 242 was still the basis of British policy. Israeli forces should be withdrawn from the occupied territories, but minor rectifications should be made to the pre-1967 boundaries and the demilitarisation of some areas should be agreed. The conversation was continued the next morning, when Mr. Gromyko reiterated that the Israelis were obstructing the Jarring talks because of US support. Sir A. Douglas-Home reminded him that Israel had withdrawn from the talks because of the movement of missiles by Egypt into the cease-fire zone (see No. 51, note 13).

The Secretary of State set out more fully his views on the Middle East—'the oldest battlefield in the world'—in a speech to the Yorkshire Area Conservative Party in Harrogate on 31 October: see his memoirs, *The Way the Wind Blows* (London, 1976), Appendix B, pp. 296-301.

No. 55

Letter from Sir D. Wilson (Moscow) to Mr. Bendall
[*WRL 2/10*]

Confidential   MOSCOW, *9 November 1970*

Dear David,

Berlin Talks

I have been following with close interest the reports on the latest discussions on Berlin[1] and am grateful to the missions concerned for keeping us so fully informed on these important developments. I have not offered any comments from here on the detailed points under discussion since, although these are of course vital, I am not sure that there is much which I can usefully contribute: an interview with a leading Soviet official would lead to a repetition of the kind of discussion I had with Falin on 14 October (my telegram No. 1199).[2] But it may be helpful if I make one or two general points about the Soviet attitude to these talks as it appears from here, in the light of Gromyko's recent talks with the Secretary of State[3] and his other Western colleagues[4] and the latest Ambassadorial meeting in Berlin on 4 November.

2. I do not think there can now be any doubt that the Russians want a Berlin agreement, that they want it fairly soon and that they are prepared to pay something to get it. This is not, I believe, because they think the West has so lowered its guard and the Germans are so keen to show that *Ostpolitik* brings results that they have a golden opportunity to hack another slice off the salami; but primarily because they themselves are anxious to be able to demonstrate to the 24th Party Congress[5] the success of their *Westpolitik*. This is for them an important consideration. The Congress looms larger in the minds of the Soviet leadership than any other predictable forthcoming event, and it is necessary for them on that occasion to show that their policies are bringing results. They are not doing too well on the domestic economic front, and do not seem to have got anywhere near solving the formidable problems of allocation of resources; they cannot yet promise any mitigation in the ever-growing burden of defence costs, although they may well hope by the time of the Congress to be able to show some results from SALT: they have made

---

[1] See Nos. 52, note 7 and 53, note 6.

[2] In this telegram of 15 October Sir D. Wilson reported a conversation the previous day with the Head of the German Department of the Soviet Foreign Ministry, which 'did not seem to me to throw any fresh light on the substance of the Soviet position'.

[3] See Nos. 53 and 54. In Moscow telegram No. 1287, also of 9 November, Sir D. Wilson reported that in conversation on 7 November Mr. Gromyko, 'after referring to his useful talks with you in London, said that it appeared that there had now been some movement in the right direction in the Four-Power talks on Berlin'.

[4] See No. 53, note 4.

[5] The 24th Congress of the CPSU was due to be held in March 1971.

some progress, but not a great deal, in mending fences with the Chinese[6] and can claim no successes for Soviet diplomacy in Indo-China;[7] and they remain very worried about the future course of events in the Middle East.[8] But they can claim some progress towards *détente* in Europe and this is the area in which it is in their power, to a much greater extent than in other areas of tension, to bring about a substantial degree of improvement in the atmosphere on their own initiative, without having to take too much account of intransigent or unpredictable allies (they have their problems with the East Germans, to which I shall refer later, but these are much more under control than in the case of, say the North Vietnamese or the Egyptians). And whereas it is arguable that continued tension in the Middle East and South-East Asia is in their interests (though I would not accept the validity of this argument in either case, or at least not without major qualifications), they plainly want to reduce tension in Europe where nothing likely to be attainable in the foreseeable future (except the weakening of NATO which they may hope will result from a *détente*) suits them better than the *status quo*.

3. There are increasingly clear signs that, even though the new Five-Year Plan is still unpublished, the 24th Party Congress will be convened in March as planned. The Russians have clearly given up any hopes they may have entertained of being able to set up a European Security Conference even in time for a tentative date to be announced before the Congress, although there may be increasing pressure on the West to move by then to the stage of Multilateral Exploratory Contacts; they are now beginning to talk of the summer or autumn of 1971 as a desirable target date for the conference itself. So I am sure the Germans are right in thinking (see my letter of 5 November about my talk with Allardt)[9] that the one major achievement in European policy which they hope to be able to claim at the time of the

---

[6] Sino-Soviet border talks, begun in Peking in October 1969 (cf. No. 27, note 1) continued throughout 1970 but had made little progress. A new Soviet Ambassador, Mr. Tolstikov, had arrived in Peking in October 1970 and a new Chinese Ambassador to Moscow had been nominated. Sino-Soviet trade talks in Peking in August led to the signature of a protocol on 22 November. A brief on Chinese policy prepared before Mr. Heath's visit to the UN in October concluded that 'Although there could be some improvement in State relations, the underlying differences and competition will continue into the foreseeable future'.

[7] In discussion with Sir A. Douglas-Home on 28 October (see pp. 267-8) Mr. Gromyko had again rejected the proposal that the British and Soviet Governments, as co-Chairmen of the Geneva Conference, should use their influence to put some peace-making machinery into operation: ' . . . what could the co-Chairmen do without the other countries? Nothing useful could come of any initiative. If the Americans withdrew, however, the situation would be quite different' (ENS 3/548/37).

[8] Anwar Sadat, who had become President of Egypt following President Nasser's death on 28 September, had renewed the cease-fire for a further 90-day period from 5 November, but had warned that it would not be extended after this date and Egyptian forces would be ready for war in February 1971.

[9] Not printed. Herr Allardt had stated 'emphatically' that 'the Russians really wanted to have an arrangement on Berlin and to see the Moscow treaty ratified in time for their Party Congress in March 1971' (WRG 3/303/1).

Congress is ratification of the Soviet-German treaty. It would be interesting to know whether the Russians realise, or have been told by the Germans that the process of ratification in the Federal Republic will take about three months (Bonn telegram No. 1233).[10] If so, this might well increase their anxiety to get the process started and they may be prepared for this reason to move quite a long way to meet Western requirements on a four-power agreement containing directives for the inner-German talks.[11] (If on the other hand the Russians have not taken aboard the fact that ratification in Germany will take three months, perhaps it should be suggested to the Germans that they should be so informed.)

4. As regards the substance of the agreement, I think we must recognise that it will be necessary for the Russians, both for internal reasons and in order to be able to 'deliver' the GDR, to be in a position to present the agreement as having 'confirmed' the status of West Berlin as an independent political entity. As I see it, the Russians have given some pretty clear indications that they are prepared to be flexible about the substance of most aspects of the Federal presence in Berlin and Berlin representation abroad provided that the facade of West Berlin's 'independent status' is preserved. (I was particularly struck by the Russian remark quoted in Bonn telegram No. 1311 that the 'optical content of this issue was very high'.)[12] It looks to me as if the Russians would be prepared to stomach a considerable range of existing Federal activities in West Berlin provided that these are dressed up in such a way as to be compatible with their contention of West Berlin's independent international status. Even *Bundestag* Committees meeting in Berlin could perhaps be dressed up as sub-committees of a *Bundestag* Committee on Relations with Berlin, or some such title, if the *Bundestag* can be persuaded to wear this. I mention this because it seems to me important that the Germans and the three Allies should soon make up their minds on how far they can accept the appearance of an independent status for Berlin in order to pre-

[10] This telegram of 22 October reported Herr van Well of the West German Foreign Ministry as saying that the 'actual ratification process, even with goodwill, would take three months and nothing had yet been done to put it in hand'.

[11] According to telegram No. 748 to Bonn (see No. 53, note 6), HMG supported a French-West German plan for 'a precise Four Power agreement followed by inner-German implementing agreements, to be endorsed in a final Four-Power agreement . . . it would tie the Russians down and prevent their later denying responsibility for details on matters such as access on the grounds that this kind of thing had been left to the two Germanies to settle. In our view it is important not to let the Russians nudge us into a position where all we get on a Four Power basis is a vague statement of principles while negotiations on practical matters, which will make or break a Berlin agreement, are entrusted to the GDR and the FRG and *Senat*.' There had been no resumption of inner-German talks (cf. No. 50, note 6), but on 29 October, following a visit by an East German emissary, the FRG announced they were to exchange views with the GDR on questions 'whose settlement would serve *détente* in the centre of Europe'.

[12] According to this telegram of 5 November this remark was made during a lunchtime conversation on 4 November between Messrs Audland and Jackson (respectively Counsellor in Bonn and Political Adviser in Berlin) and Messrs Kvitsinsky and Khotulev (Soviet MFA, and Soviet Embassy in Bonn).

serve as much as possible of the substance of existing links (I see this point is made in FCO telegram No. 748 to Bonn). If the Federal Government feels that it can be safely (from the point of view of internal politics) be flexible about outward forms, I suspect that they will get most of what they want. But we should have no doubt in our own minds that however we regard the agreements reached, arrangements of the kind under discussion would be presented by the Russians in due course as recognition of the independent status of West Berlin: and in strict logic, this is certainly one way of looking at it.

5. The same considerations apply to some extent to the question of access and communications. Here again I hope I am not being unduly optimistic in thinking that the Russians are prepared to lean fairly heavily on the East Germans to meet Western requirements, provided that the form in which the agreement is reached does not call in question either the sovereignty of the GDR or the independent status of West Berlin.[13] I agree that form is of great importance to the Western powers too, in that their own rights and responsibilities in Berlin as a whole must not be directly called in question; but if I am right in thinking that the form of the agreement is pretty well all that matters to the Russians, it should not be impossible to reconcile the conflicting requirements. It may, for example, be significant that the *Neues Deutschland* article of 5 November (Berlin telegram No. 329),[14] which stated that agreements on access to and from Berlin could only be reached between the GDR and the *Senat*, has so far had no echo in the Soviet press (which has throughout preserved a most encouraging reticence about the whole process of the Berlin talks) and that on the same day Abrasimov had a meeting with four top East German leaders responsible for these questions.

6. To sum up, I am encouraged by recent developments to think that, provided the three Western powers and the Germans are prepared to show understanding of Soviet cosmetic requirements, and provided in particular the Germans feel able to sell to the *Bundestag* a number of major changes in the *appearance* of the Federal relationship with Berlin, the pressure of time will bring the Russians quite soon to agree, and to persuade the East Germans to agree, to a settlement which will in substance meet our minimum requirements. But the importance of the 'optical content' to the Russians of course makes it essential that the Western powers should stick very firmly to their guns on at least these minimum requirements,[15] and I very much agree with

[13] Mr. J. Cable, Head of WOD since October 1970, here minuted 'Difficult' in the margin.

[14] Not printed.

[15] Mr. Abrasimov's conduct at the 10th Four Power meeting held on 16 November strengthened Sir R. Jackling's impression that 'the Russians are in something of a dilemma. They seem anxious for an early agreement and prepared to do their best to improve access procedures, in order to obtain one. But they cannot meet the Allied requirements for the inclusion of agreed specific additional improvements in a Four Power agreement without weakening their traditional position that there are no quadripartite responsibilities over access and GDR claims to sovereignty over the access routes. It also looks as though they may be having genuine difficulty with the GDR in finding formulae to resolve the dilemma' (Bonn telegram

the point made in FCO telegram No. 748 to Bonn that the four-power agreement should be as clear and precise as possible in order to give the DDR the minimum opportunity to pull a fast one in the inner-German talks.[16]

Yours ever,
DUNCAN WILSON

No. 1391 of 17 November). Sir A. Douglas-Home commented that 'It might be worth telling the Russians that if they can't do better we shall lose interest' (minute from Mr. Barrington to Mr. J.K. Drinkall, Head of Western European Department, 18 November).

At the next meeting on 23 November the Russians 'were plainly marking time . . . the best Allied tactic seems to be to stand fast and insist that Soviet concessions are inadequate' (Bonn telegram No. 1452 of 25 November).

[16] Sir D. Wilson copied this letter, which Mr. Cable considered was 'just the sort of periodic advice that we want from Moscow', to Bonn, Berlin, Paris and Washington.

No. 56

Sir A. Douglas-Home to Sir D. Wilson (Moscow)

No. 955 Telegraphic [*ENS 10/16*]

Confidential   FCO, *12 November 1970, 10 a.m.*

Repeated for information to Washington, UKDEL NATO.

My telegram No. 947: collision at sea.[1]

We see advantage, subject to your views, in lodging a protest about this incident immediately. Dangerously close surveillance, of which this was an example, has been causing us growing concern. Unless you see objection, therefore, please deliver a note at whatever level you judge appropriate in the terms of my immediately following telegram.[2]

2. You might point out orally that the essence of our complaint is that the Soviet vessel disregarded international regulations for preventing collisions at sea, in failing to pay due regard to the lights which *Ark Royal* was showing, which indicated that she was operating aircraft and was consequently a hampered vessel. You could add that the circumstances leading up to this incident are not unusual in that Soviet vessels are often in dangerously close attendance on exercising R[oyal] N[avy] vessels. We should be grateful for

[1] This telegram of 10 November referred to the collision on the evening of 9 November between the aircraft carrier HMS *Ark Royal*, currently participating in an exercise in the Mediterranean, and a Soviet Kotlin class destroyer. Further details of the incident are given in the Enclosure to this document: a Ministry of Defence press statement issued on 10 November stated that the *Ark Royal* would continue with her exercise programme as soon as the search for missing Russian crew members had been completed, and that a naval board of enquiry would be convened. Telegram No. 947 informed Sir D. Wilson that HMG were considering a protest to the Soviet Government.

[2] See Enclosure below.

an assurance that international regulations for the prevention of collisions at sea will be scrupulously observed in future by Soviet vessels in the proximity of HM Ships. In particular, we should like to draw attention to the dangers inherent in sailing close to carriers which are operating aircraft.

3. You may care to repeat our expression of regret that Soviet sailors are believed to be missing as a result of this incident.

4. Should the Russians express surprise that you should be making a protest before the holding of the naval board of enquiry which has been announced, you should say that boards are mandatory in such circumstances, but that sufficient facts are now available to show that the protest is appropriate.

5. If the Russians raise the question of their representations about *Nubian* and *Lincoln*,[3] you should say that a reply to these representations on an entirely unrelated matter is in preparation, and will be made as soon as possible. For your own information, we have in the past contested both the Soviet territorial waters claim and the Soviet regulation in question, which purports to prohibit innocent passage through territorial waters without prior permission. We hope that you can avoid being drawn into discussion on this subject.

6. Please report by telegram when you have taken action.[4]

[3] In September 1970 the Soviet Government had protested to HMG about the alleged infringement of Soviet territorial waters by HMS *Lincoln* and *Nubian*. HMG's reply of 30 December, that no prior notification was required for the innocent passage of warships through a coastal state's territorial waters, was not accepted by the Soviet Government.

[4] Moscow telegram No. 1308 of 13 November reported that the Head of Chancery had carried out the instructions in FCO telegram No. 955 that morning, leaving the note with Mr. Vasev, who rejected the British representations, maintaining that the Soviet ship had been on a 'routine training trip', and attributed the collision to 'an abrupt change of course' by the *Ark Royal*. A note on these lines was communicated to HM Embassy on 14 November. On 26 November Lord Bridges reported to Mr. Giffard a conversation at a lunch on 25 November attended by himself, Mr. Edmonds and Sir D. Wilson, with Mr. Makeev, Mr. Vasev and Mr. Rogov from the Second European Department of the Soviet MFA. When Lord Bridges brought up the subject of the collision and suggested that 'if Soviet vessels engaged in this kind of activity kept their distance, the incident would not be repeated', the Soviet officials had made a 'strong counter-argument', protesting that the incident had been inflated in press coverage by information made available from British official quarters. Lord Bridges concluded that the discussion 'confirmed that senior officials of the Ministry of Foreign Affairs remain extremely suspicious, and are very far from behaving as if a new era had dawned with Gromyko's visit to London [Nos. 53-4]. In particular it showed us clearly that the Soviet Government resent the public remarks made in Ministerial speeches in Britain about their naval activities as a whole—in the Indian Ocean as well as in the Mediterranean—and I feel that what was said should be reported for that reason.'

ENCLOSURE IN No. 56

Note of protest to Soviet Government:[5]

Begins:

During the evening of Monday, 9 November 1970, the aircraft carrier HMS *Ark Royal* was engaged in night flying exercises in open waters in the Eastern Mediterranean to the south of Greece. She had commenced the launching of her aircraft, and, in accordance with the 'International Regulations for Preventing Collisions at Sea' (Rule 4), was displaying three lights in a vertical line one over the other, the highest and lowest being red and the middle being white, these indicating that she was a hampered vessel and could not therefore get out of the way.

2. At 18.40, after the launch of *Ark Royal's* first aircraft, the Soviet destroyer Kotlin 365 approached from her starboard bow on a collision course. The carrier took what avoiding action she could and put her engines at full astern but she was unable to miss the Soviet vessel, whose port quarter struck the *Ark Royal's* port bow.

3. The *Ark Royal* immediately stopped her night flying exercise and diverted the aircraft already airborne so that she and her accompanying frigate could undertake a search for Russian crew members who were understood to be in the water. Although some were picked up by the *Ark Royal* and her escort and returned to their ship, it is regretted that two are still believed to be missing.

4. Her Majesty's Government wish to lodge a protest against the action of the captain of the Soviet vessel who disregarded international regulations for preventing collisions at sea, in that he failed to keep clear of a hampered vessel, thereby creating a dangerous situation and causing his ship to collide with the *Ark Royal*. Her Majesty's Government reserve the right to make a claim in respect of the incident.

[5] Cf. note 2 above: the text was transmitted in telegram No. 956 to Moscow, also despatched at 10 a.m. on 12 November.

No. 57

Sir A. Douglas-Home to Sir D. Wilson (Moscow)
[*ENS 2/4*]

Confidential   FCO, *1 December 1970*

Sir,

I found your despatch of the 16th of November on Soviet foreign policy[1] helpful and timely. If in this reply I set out certain reservations with regard to your analysis and your conclusions, it is not in any carping or disputatious spirit but in the belief that the discussion of the assumptions underlying differences of opinion is essential to the formulation of policy.

2. In your despatch you concentrated on the foreign policy of the Soviet Government. Yet in the USSR power rests not with the Soviet Government, but with the Communist Party of the Soviet Union, whose present leaders still seem to regard the foreign policy of the Soviet Government as only one part, and neither the major nor the determining part, of a world-wide historical and political process which follows the laws of the class struggle as formulated by Marxism-Leninism (whatever that may be—views on this differ widely these days). I was interested to note that according to *Pravda* of 25 November, Mr. Brezhnev, speaking at the Congress of the Hungarian Communist Party, said that 'In the international arena an acute class struggle is in progress, without remission . . . The front of this struggle is exceptionally broad. It (i.e. the struggle) is conducted in various forms, peaceful and not peaceful, but our workdays of intense toil, the struggle of the workers of the capitalist countries for their social emancipation, the offensive

[1] In this despatch Sir D. Wilson identified changes in the context in which Soviet foreign policy operated, which had led to a major shift in Soviet tactics in Europe. He argued that conflicting policy aims posed difficult choices for the Soviet leadership, and thought the opportunity existed for the West to influence the outcome of the debate between advocates of rival policies. In the Ambassador's assessment the 'need for economic development now seems to be dominant and to justify in the minds of the leadership the taking of certain political risks'. He developed in paras. 11 and 12 the argument that a refusal of technological collaboration 'would be not only self-defeating but also politically counter-productive, in that it would drive the Soviet leadership back to isolationism or cold war hostility'. In paras. 13 and 14 Sir D. Wilson put forward the view that 'a reasonably flexible response to current Soviet tactics, including the European Security issue, does not involve serious risks for the West and could bring important dividends not only in trade, but in the longer term also in encouraging political and social change in Eastern Europe and the Soviet Union itself'.

Sir A. Douglas-Home minuted that the despatch was 'very helpful', but Mr. Giffard submitted that it 'necessarily omits, in the interests of brevity, much of the background against which Soviet foreign policy is considered. As a result of this compression, the despatch in my view gives an overall impression which is rather too optimistic. For this reason, I recommend that the despatch should receive a reply from the Secretary of State, which puts some of its points into a wider perspective.' Sir D. Greenhill minuted on the draft of the outgoing despatch, prepared by Mr. Giffard and Sir T. Brimelow: 'The tone of this rejoinder is sharp but it is useful to remind the Embassy in Moscow of some of the unpleasant realities.'

of the peoples against colonialism and neo-colonialism, all these are links in a single chain of great class battles, in which a better tomorrow for the whole of mankind is being born.' I will not labour this aspect of the communist understanding of the historical and political process; and I will not contest that there is much force in a remark you once made that the sum of successive stages in the execution of a policy rarely if ever leads to the fulfilment of a preconceived political strategy. But a Russian proverb of which Solzhenitsyn has made telling use warns against omitting some of the words from the song. I have just had occasion to ask for your comments on a message to Mr. Gromyko about the scale of Soviet espionage in this country.[2] Against this background I feel that the analysis in paragraphs 11 to 14 of your despatch[3] is perhaps too selective and too optimistic.

3. I also feel that in paragraph 11 of your despatch you are to some extent tilting against windmills. No one in this country is at present thinking in terms of a 'really tough approach to the whole problem of technological aid to the Soviet Union' or of 'letting them stew in their own juice'. The problem for this country, with its current high rates of inflation and interest, is that the Soviet Government, who dislike paying high rates of interest, are likely to place their orders elsewhere. No responsible person in the United Kingdom is thinking of enforcing an economic blockade against the Soviet Union, but many are worrying whether the Soviet Government will in the event substantially increase its purchases from this country. And we doubt whether decisions concerning the placing of orders in this country, as opposed to placing the same orders in France, Italy or the Federal Republic of Germany are going to be decisive in any power struggle between the 'toughest and most hostile Soviet leaders' and the 'less implacable men among their numbers'. The attitude of the West as a whole might conceivably be important at times when there are turning points in Soviet policy. But I do not think that our current policies are of critical importance at present in the determination of how and by whom the Soviet Union shall be ruled.

4. Turning now to the analysis in paragraph 12 of your despatch, it seems to me that it is an incomplete and possibly misleading definition of current Soviet policy to say that 'the Soviet leaders seem to have decided to take certain political risks in order to pursue, mainly for economic reasons, a new policy of intensified contact with Western Europe'. It seems to me that the current French ideas about the need for a broad development of such contacts have met with a cool reception amongst the Soviet leaders who, to quote the *Pravda* leader of the 23rd of November, are determined not to permit 'even a shade of liberalism' in their conduct of the ideological struggle. What they are after is technical advice, know-how, and long-term loans at lower rates of interest than the average now prevailing in Western money markets. You argue that the Soviet leaders require a new political

[2] See No. 58 below.   [3] See note 1.

framework to make intensified contacts with Western Europe acceptable. There may be something in this argument, speculative though it is. But I do not think that the point you make is by any means the whole story. From the Soviet-German Treaty, the proposed Berlin Agreement and the European Security Conference, the Soviet leaders wish to extract specific political benefits for themselves and the GDR. It may be that these benefits will help them internally against potential opponents of a policy of *détente* and such help would no doubt be augmented if, in the atmosphere of euphoria in the West following a number of political agreements, the Soviet Government were to be able to acquire Western aid and Western technology on the cheap. But I am sure that the Soviet Government intends to exercise the tightest control on the extent and the possible political implications of the increased contacts with Western Europe (or the USA) which might have to be accepted as inevitable concomitants of more trade with and help from the West. They have done quite well in the task of minimizing the political impact of such contacts as already exist.

5. You say, in paragraph 12 of your despatch, that 'if we, out of distrust or sheer caution, appear to be hampering the development of this framework, we may be faced with a Soviet swing towards isolation or cold war . . .'. I agree with your underlying thought in this sentence, though I think the term 'we' should be interpreted as 'the West in general' and not just the United Kingdom. Whenever the Soviet Government is in a mood to walk a mile in the direction of *détente*, we (in the same broad sense) should be willing to go with them twain. But we should walk warily. You rightly point to the element of ambivalence in their attitudes.

6. As you know, we agree that the European Security Conference is not in itself likely to prove important either for better or for worse. It is chiefly the Federal German Government who, in their wish to see progress in the Berlin negotiations and in the inner German talks,[4] are pressing their allies to go slow on the question of the Conference.

7. You express the opinion, in paragraph 17 [13], that 'there will be some economic rewards for a rather more forthcoming line by HMG on political questions'. The difficulty here is that we have politically less to offer than the Federal German Government, as regards the acceptance of the status quo in Europe, and less than the French Government as regards dissociation from '*blocs*' while the United Kingdom constitutes a less promising field for Soviet political influence than Italy. It is questionable whether the economic rewards to this country of any forthcoming line by us in our political relations with the USSR would be great. I think we should be better advised to treat business propositions on their merits, while making clear our interest in developing worthwhile commercial relations for their own sake.

[4] Cf. No. 55. Following the announcement of 29 October (*ibid.*, note 11) a meeting was arranged between Dr. Kohl and Herr Bahr in Berlin on 27 November. Further discussions were planned for 23 December.

8. I do not dissent from the argument in your paragraph 15 [14].[5] The arguments you deploy have underlain much of our work in the development of scientific and technological activity in the last 15 years. But I am reminded of a remark of Bertram Wolfe's[6] thirteen years ago, that the CPSU will keep its technicians on tap, not on top. Experience teaches us not to expect too much.

9. I also think it right to point out that the Soviet Government have never acknowledged or expressed appreciation of the fact that over the years this country has had a steady and good record of developing contacts with the Soviet Union and the countries of Eastern Europe in trade, culture, science, technology and so on; and that in NATO and COCOM our role, apart from periods such as 1956, 1958 and 1961 and 1968 (when we were reacting to outrageous behaviour by the Soviet and East German Governments) has been liberal and constructive. The Soviet Government has tended to bestow its favours where it has sensed opportunities for wedge-driving. We have no intention of letting ourselves be exploited for such purposes, and experience suggests that if we remain loyal members of NATO, not much in the way of political and economic lollipops will come our way. I make no mention of the fact that for many years we were the chief source of freely disposable foreign exchange for the USSR. They show us no gratitude for this, on the grounds that we were only doing what suited us. This was indeed so, and I see no reason to complain about this Soviet attitude. But they could have been more gracious had they so wished.

10. The plain fact is that in the near future, our national interest is to develop our relations with Western rather than Eastern Europe. This is not to say that our policies will be anti-Soviet or anti-Warsaw Pact. But our priorities lie elsewhere. In the current negotiations on Berlin, we shall expect improved conditions for the West Berliners. When the Federal German Government are ready for a Conference on European Security, we shall not oppose it. In the field of trade and contacts, we shall treat each opening on its merits. It is in this spirit that we shall approach the first meeting of the Anglo-Soviet Joint Commission.[7]

[5] In para. 14 Sir D. Wilson said that 'the technocrats and scientists are the only class in the Soviet Union which can bring pressure to bear on the Party for social changes. They are in present circumstances fairly accessible. And it would in my view be quite wrong not to encourage contacts with them directly and indirectly (by agreeing to some kind of political "umbrella" which will make such contacts respectable to the Soviet Party leaders).'

[6] Author of a large number of books on the Russian Revolution and Soviet system, including *Khrushchev and Stalin's Ghost* (London, 1957), *Communist Totalitarianism: Keys to the Soviet System* (Boston, 1961) and *Marxism: one hundred years in the life of a doctrine* (London, 1967).

[7] Terms of reference for the Joint Commission had been agreed in November and approved by the Secretary of State and Prime Minister (cf. No. 49, note 2). The Commission was formally established by an Exchange of Notes on 4 January 1971, and its first meeting arranged for 12-15 January (ENS 6/548/6, 1970; PW 1/303/1, 1971).

11. At the forthcoming Ministerial meeting in Brussels of the North Atlantic Treaty Organisation,[8] I expect a consensus to emerge in favour of a re-affirmation of the willingness of the Alliance to pursue the negotiation of questions relevant to European Security without, however, entering into any new or specific commitment to prepare for a Conference. I am not opposed to such a Conference. I believe that it will eventually take place. But it is essential that the timing and the agenda should be right. On all matters relating to such a conference I attach importance to our moving in consult-ation and agreement with our NATO allies. Within NATO we have at times been criticized by some for being too forthcoming; by no one for being too negative.

12. I am sending copies of this despatch to HM Representatives in Washington, Paris, Bonn, Warsaw, Prague. Budapest, Bucharest, Sofia, Belgrade, Berlin, the UK Delegation to NATO and the UK Mission to the United Nations in New York.[9]

I am, etc.,
ALEC DOUGLAS-HOME

[8] See pp. 294-5 below.

[9] In a letter to Sir D. Greenhill of 31 December Sir D. Wilson stated: 'Where I think that I part company with the Department is over the view expressed or implied in the Secretary of State's despatch of 1 December, of the present state of the Soviet Union and the prospects for the future development of Soviet society. If I understand this rightly, I find it out of date, and so, I am sure, would many observers on the spot. The despatch leaves readers here with the impression that in the Soviet Union we are confronted with essentially the mixture as before in a "stable state"—the past projected into the future; whereas the basic element in my view and in that of all my senior political and economic staff is that, in spite of all too much continuity in some aspects of policy, the Soviet Union is undergoing changes which may in the long or even medium term produce a different mixture—and different in some potentially very important respects.

'Either way, there is no need for any basic change of policy, but I believe that there is much need for some change of style in our relationship with the Soviet Union. It still seems to me that your personal intervention in winding up the Brooke case [cf. pp. 135-8] cleared the way for this. I hope we can take a hard look together at the pros and cons of such a change . . . I really am convinced that, in the general style of our dealings with the Soviet Union, there are concrete British interests involved: trade, the closer co-ordination of East-West policy with our West European allies, and the realistic protection of important British positions outside Europe' (ENS 3/548/12).

No. 58

Letter from Sir A. Douglas-Home to Mr. Gromyko[1]

[*PUSD*]

FCO, *3 December 1970*[2]

Dear Mr. Gromyko,

You will remember that on 28 October, at the Soviet Embassy in London, I mentioned to you the case of F.D. Kudashkin.[3] As you requested I have gone carefully into this case. F.D. Kudashkin's activities in the United States were referred to in court proceedings which were reported at length in the *New York Times* of 9 March, 1965. I enclose a copy of that report.[4] If you will read it, you will certainly understand why my colleagues and I regard F.D. Kudashkin as unacceptable for any appointment in this country. I hope you will agree that we should both regard the visa application made on his behalf as having lapsed.

[1] This letter was the follow-up to Sir A. Douglas-Home's conversation with Mr. Gromyko on 28 October concerning Soviet intelligence activities: see pp. 267-8. The copy of the letter preserved in the file and printed here differs slightly from the draft, and, it appears, from the text as handed over in Moscow: see note 7 below. On 28 November a draft had been sent to Sir D. Wilson for comment, the covering telegram pointing out that account had been taken of a letter from the Ambassador of 12 November, in which he expressed the opinion that the unacceptable activities of the Russian Intelligence Services in the UK should be dealt with 'from first principles' rather than by a piecemeal approach. Sir D. Wilson did not like the draft, stating in telegram No. 1365 of 30 November: 'This is not the kind of letter which I had in mind. The object of the letter, as I see it, is to make Gromyko aware that we have a substantial problem on our hands which is an obstacle to better relations, and to invite his cooperation in settling it. The letter is not likely to induce this frame of mind in Gromyko if it makes detailed charges about individuals which are bound to be resisted, and which would probably be in Gromyko's view inappropriate for inclusion in a letter from one Foreign Minister to another . . . It would I submit be a mistake to raise this matter at such a high level without having first decided how far we are prepared to go. The letter as drafted contains no suggestion that the British Government has any policy on the question, beyond being irritated by what the Russians are doing.'

The Ambassador submitted an alternative draft, but was informed by Sir T. Brimelow in a personal telegram from Brussels (where he had accompanied the Secretary of State to the NATO Ministerial meeting) that Sir A. Douglas-Home, while accepting that Mr. Gromyko would not like the message, 'regards the present situation as pretty intolerable' and wished to adhere to the FCO draft: 'Our assessment of Soviet motives and of the prospects for the development of Anglo-Soviet relations is to some extent affected by the scale and nature of Soviet intelligence activities in the United Kingdom. The purpose of the message to Mr. Gromyko is partly to make this clear and partly to prepare the way for any unilateral measures which may be necessary for the protection of our security. This in no way diminishes our interest in the conduct of a political dialogue with the Soviet Government on all matters of mutual concern' (Brussels telegram No. 2 to Moscow, 3 December).

[2] Sir D. Wilson did not have the opportunity to deliver this letter until 9 December, when he gave it to Mr. Kuznetsov.

[3] Mr. Kudashkin had been nominated for the post of Third Secretary at the Soviet Embassy.

[4] Not printed.

The case of F.D. Kudashkin is by no means isolated, and it is with regret that, after the enjoyable and constructive discussions I had with you in London, I find myself constrained to write to you about the scale and nature of the intelligence activities conducted by Soviet officials in this country and about the frequency of the attempts which have been made in recent months to introduce into this country officials who, in the past, have been engaged in such activities.

In 1970 alone we have refused visas to more than half a dozen Soviet officials assigned to this country because we had every reason to suspect, on the basis of what we know about their previous activities, that if they were admitted to this country they would not restrict themselves to work which we regard as legitimate and conducive to the maintenance and development of good relations.[5]

Most of the men to whom we have refused visas had been appointed to the Soviet Trade Delegation. I know that the Soviet Trade Delegation is not directly subordinated to your Ministry, but since you, as Minister for Foreign Affairs of the USSR, are concerned with all matters which affect the foreign relations of your country, I wish to invite your attention to the number of cases which have come to light of late in which members of the Soviet Trade Delegation have been found to have engaged in totally inadmissible activities. This year alone, permission to stay in this country has had to be withdrawn from four members of the Soviet Trade Delegation. Since I had occasion to speak to you about F.D. Kudashkin, two new cases, one of them particularly serious, have been brought to my attention. And I am told that a visa application had recently been submitted for A.P. Safronov, whom we know to have engaged in inadmissible activities when he worked at the Soviet Trade Delegation between 1962 and 1966.[6]

The competent Soviet authorities will be able to give you full information about the various kinds of inadmissible activities which have been conducted from the Soviet Trade Delegation. They have included the running of agents, instruction in the use of clandestine techniques, the offer and payment of considerable sums of money to persons resident in this country either to suborn them or to secure their help in obtaining classified information (both official and commercial) or commodities subject to embargo or other restrictions.[7]

[5] Cf. No. 49, note 7.

[6] Mr. Safronov had been involved in the case for which Mr. Drozhdov was expelled in February 1968: see No. 5, note 4.

[7] It is clear from related papers that an extra paragraph was included at this point—as it was in the draft letter sent to Sir D. Wilson by telegram on 28 November (see note 1). In the draft this paragraph ran: 'To round off my comments on the use made of the Soviet Trade Delegation, I would add that Mr. V.M. Ivanov, who has been selected to replace Mr. B.S. Gordeev as the head of the Soviet Trade Delegation, has come to our attention in the past as having been engaged in certain intelligence activities earlier in his career. Nothwithstanding this, we are not refusing to accept him. I trust that his future responsibilities will keep him busy in legitimate activities from which both our countries stand to benefit: but I assure you that we shall keep an

You will be aware that Her Majesty's previous Government felt compelled to place a limit on the growth of the staff of the Soviet Embassy in 1968.[8] Even so, since last August we have had to request the withdrawal of L.Y. Tyukhin: and the attempt to appoint F.D. Kudashkin to the Embassy has re-awakened old suspicions.

When you were in London, you said that Anglo-Soviet relations could not be described as bad, but that more could be done for their development and improvement.[9] In this letter I have indicated a field which is becoming an increasing obstacle to the development of our relations, and with regard to which the kind of improvement of which you spoke would be most welcome. The representations which Sir D. Greenhill made on this subject to Vice-Minister Kozyrev earlier this year[10] appear, from subsequent developments to have been ignored. I hope that this personal letter to you will be handled in the spirit of your opening remarks to the Prime Minister and myself during your visit to London.

ALEC DOUGLAS-HOME

eye on him.' This paragraph was omitted from the text of the letter published in the press in September 1971 when a large number of Soviet diplomatic and STD staff were expelled from the UK: see No. 76, note 10 below.

[8] See No. 19.   [9] See No. 53.   [10] See No. 45.

A number of important meetings had been held in the first week of December 1970. On 1 December the European Defence Ministers (except for the French) met in Brussels to discuss a proposed European Defence Improvement Programme based on the findings of a major report on 'Allied Defence in the Seventies' (AD 70), which had revealed many gaps in NATO's military disposition and had concluded that in view of the already formidable Warsaw Pact military strength, NATO needed not only to maintain but substantially to improve its own defensive capability. The decision to implement a special and wide-ranging programme for improving Alliance capability in specific fields was taken on the basis that the US would maintain its forces in Europe at substantially current levels. Work would also be accelerated on the NATO Integrated Communications System to improve Alliance consultation and control in times of tension, and on aircraft survival measures to improve NATO's ability to survive enemy strikes on their bases.

This meeting was followed by the NATO Ministerial meeting 3-5 December, and a statement on 'Alliance defence for the seventies' was annexed to the NATO Communiqué.[1] NATO Foreign Ministers noted developments in East-West relations since the last meeting in Rome (see pp. 238-9) and affirmed the readiness of the Governments 'as soon as the talks on Berlin have reached a satisfactory conclusion and in so far as the other on-going talks are proceeding favourably', to enter multilateral contacts with a view to exploring when it would be possible to convene a conference or series of conferences on security and cooperation in Europe. Meanwhile, a meeting of the Political

[1] Both documents are printed in Watt and Mayall, 1970, pp. 690-99.

Consultative Committee of the Warsaw Pact states held in East Berlin 2-3 December—
the timing considered in NATO circles to be related to that of the Brussels meeting,
though also chosen to put pressure on the inner-German talks—issued a communiqué and
a series of separate documents dealing with European security, Indo-China, the Middle
East and Africa, all of which were seen in NATO as representing a shift away from the
seemingly forthcoming pattern established in the Prague and Budapest documents (see
pp. 196-7 and 239), and a return to the approach of emphasizing points of difference in
East-West relations.

Sir A. Douglas-Home's view of the Brussels meeting was favourable: 'The outcome
reflects satisfactorily my thinking on East-West relations.' The Council had had little
difficulty in reaching agreement on East-West issues, and the result was a communiqué
which 'holds NATO's position and does not move forward for the time being. The
arguments put forward at Rome remain valid, but are now well balanced by a cautious
attitude towards Soviet intentions in Europe, the Mediterranean and indeed outside the
NATO area. Internal studies on the substantive matters for East-West negotiation and
on MBFR will continue. Meanwhile, we await further development of the situation in
Berlin, and on the Federal Government's Ostpolitik.'[2] Document No. 59 shows that this
cautious approach, approved by the Secretary of State, found little favour with the Soviet
Government.

[2] UKDEL NATO telegram No. 686 of 4 December, WDN 21/4.

No. 59

Sir A. Douglas-Home to Sir D. Wilson (Moscow)
No. 1068 Telegraphic [ENS 3/548/8]

Confidential   FCO, 23 December 1970, 4.15 p.m.
Repeated for information Saving to UKDEL NATO, Washington, Bonn, Paris.

Following from Permanent Under-Secretary.

The Soviet Ambassador asked to call on me this morning to discuss
'subjects of current interest'.[1] He stayed for about forty minutes, leaving me
with the impression that he might have wished to get across the idea that
business was as usual despite the events in Poland[2] (which was mentioned by
neither of us).

[1] On 22 December Mr. Walden had suggested to Mr. T. Daunt, Private Secretary to Sir D.
Greenhill, that 'the formula "matters of current interest" may disguise an intention to deliver a
reply to the Secretary of State's recent letter to Mr. Gromyko' (No. 58), but the subject does not
appear to have been raised on either side.

[2] The announcement by the Polish Government on 13 December of substantial rises in the
price of food, fuel and clothing provoked demonstrations and strikes from 14-18 December in a
number of Polish cities, in particular Gdansk and Szczecin, which led to violent clashes with the
authorities. On 20 December Mr. Gomulka resigned as First Party Secretary and was replaced
by Mr. Gierek.

2. The Ambassador said that he wanted us to know that the recent NATO *Communiqué*[3] 'made not everyone happy' in Moscow. He had found that people considered in Moscow that NATO Ministers had moved backwards rather than forwards. The Russians themselves were trying to make progress over Berlin and had put forward some suggestions which took account of Western points.[4] But they could not see why progress towards a conference on European security should necessarily be connected with Berlin. Why did we not get on with the preparations for a conference, for example by accepting the Finnish proposal?[5] Not only was Berlin made the pretext for holding things up but there were references, for example to 'on-going talks' by the Secretary of State recently in the House,[6] which, the Ambassador implied, indicated that other preconditions were being held in reserve. He also had the impression that, instead of talking about mutual and balanced force reductions, the NATO Allies were now suggesting that reductions by the Soviet Union alone, or disproportionately, were called for. The increases envisaged in Western defence preparations[3] were not a good response to opportunities for reducing tension.

3. I told the Ambassador that we regarded the NATO *Communiqué* as a plain and realistic statement of the situation. I underlined the importance of Berlin and the underlying determination of the NATO Allies to pursue *détente*. We remained especially interested in the discussion of concrete problems. It was the case that discussions in any important area of East-West relations, e.g. the SALT, were relevant to the prospects for a conference on European security. As regards NATO's defence arrangements, these, to use a Soviet phrase 'corresponded with the realities of the situation'. It was no good pretending things were not as they were.

4. We discussed the Middle East briefly on established lines. I told the Ambassador that the recent discussions in Washington had encouraged me to believe that the Israelis would agree to start talking soon. Our own emphasis remained on the need to get talks going. The Ambassador suggested that the Israelis' attitude was being allowed to be the deciding factor. I repeated that they must be drawn into negotiations.

[3] See pp. 294-5.

[4] At the most recent session of the Quadripartite talks on Berlin on 10 December, Mr. Abrasimov 'was at pains to appear positive, and give the impression that considerable progress had been made since the Four Power talks began. He took a non-polemical line . . . For the first time Abrasimov had advanced detailed proposals for access improvements, without making these dependent upon new Allied points on Federal activities' (Bonn telegram No. 1529 of 14 December, WRL 2/10). The next Ambassadors' meeting was scheduled for 19 January 1971.

[5] On 2 November the Finnish Government had issued a memorandum inviting the diplomatic representatives in Helsinki of all European countries plus the USA and Canada to concert preliminary arrangements for the holding of a European security conference.

[6] An extract from Sir A. Douglas-Home's speech in the House of Commons on 9 December relating to preconditions for a European security conference is printed in Cmnd. 6932, No. 31 (see also *Parl. Debs.*, 5th ser., *H. of C.*, vol. 808, cols. 442-5).

5. On bilateral affairs, the Ambassador, speaking without instructions on this point, said that he hoped it would be possible to discuss the timing of certain visits before long. I mentioned Ministers' heavy engagements in the early part of the New Year.

6. The Ambassador mentioned the forthcoming meeting of the Anglo-Soviet Joint Commission.[7]

7. Finally, he said that he hoped that something could be done to prevent the continuation of window-breaking and such like attacks on the Aeroflot office here, about which his Embassy had complained to the Department. These attacks cost the Soviet Government about £1000 a time and it ought to be possible to prevent them. He was assured that the police did everything possible to this end.[8]

[7] See No. 57, note 7.

[8] In a letter to Sir D. Greenhill of 28 December Sir D. Wilson said that he was glad that Mr. Smirnovsky had 'conveyed indirectly the idea that the barometer marks "business as usual", and noted that he had 'not had a serious discussion at the Ministry for Foreign Affairs here since delivering the Secretary of State's message on the activities of the STD [No. 58], but in casual contacts have found them in reasonably good mood' (ENS 3/548/12). Mr. Smirnovsky called on Sir D. Greenhill again on 29 December to express Soviet views on European security, but made 'no new points of significance' (EN 2/1, 1971).

CHAPTER IV

1971

The exchange of despatches between Sir D. Wilson and Sir A. Douglas-Home (see No. 57) led to a flurry of minuting and correspondence over the New Year, as FCO officials and HM Embassy staff in Moscow debated the best approach to relations with the Soviet Union and the assumptions on which this approach should be based. The first document in this chapter continues this dialogue. Meanwhile, however, a number of issues remained unresolved which had an important effect upon the bilateral relationship: plans for a European Security Conference and discussions on Mutual and Balanced Force Reductions; negotiations for a Quadripartite agreement on Berlin; the apparent stalemate in attempts to formulate a peace plan for the Middle East; and the Soviet Government's resolute silence in the face of high-level British protests about unacceptable intelligence activities in the UK (see No. 58).

No. 60

Sir D. Wilson (Moscow) to Sir A. Douglas-Home

No. 2/28 [*ENS 2/2*]

Confidential   MOSCOW, *8 February 1971*

Summary . . . [1]

Sir,

Soviet Foreign Policy

1. I have the honour to thank you for your despatch of the 1st of December on Soviet policy.[2] I have also read with interest Mr. Millard's letter of the 22nd of December 1970 to Sir Thomas Brimelow commenting on my despatch of the 16th of November.[3] I have further had the chance on a

---

[1] Not here printed.

[2] No. 57.

[3] *V. ibid.*, note 1. In his letter setting out 'what we believe to be American views on Soviet foreign policy', Mr. Millard said he did 'not think the Americans would quarrel with the general identification of the factors underlying Soviet foreign policy' in Sir D. Wilson's despatch, but thought that 'A factor to which they would ascribe greater importance than any of these is what they see as a Soviet assertiveness and desire for acceptance as a global power on terms of equality with the US in all fields of activity' (ENS 2/4 of 1970).

recent visit to London,[4] to discuss with your advisers some of the issues raised in these two despatches. As a result a number of misconceptions on my side at least have been cleared away, and I am encouraged to say something more on a subject which is bound to be of very great importance to the national interest.

2. I should say immediately that the remaining differences of analysis between your advisers on the one hand and myself and the senior political and economic staff of this Embassy on the other need not, and should not, affect the main lines of Her Majesty's Government's present policy towards the Soviet Union. I fully agree that it is important not to forget the Communist background of Soviet society (it is in any case not easy to do so in Moscow during the run-up to a Party Congress),[5] nor to exaggerate the significance against this background of the new trends which seem to me to be developing. If I am right in thinking that the present leaders are primarily concerned with strengthening the position of the Soviet Union as the world's second superpower, I would not see—and nor, I feel sure, would they— incompatibility between this concern and any long-term requirements of doctrine to work for the 'defeat of world imperialism' and the victory of world revolution. And if we are confronted over the long term with hostile acts by an expansionist great power, the cause or ultimate object of its hostility may seem to be of secondary importance. I believe that, for the immediate purposes of our own policy formation, this is so. I should therefore make it quite clear that I am far from suggesting, in Mr. Millard's phrase, that we should 'let a desire to be on good terms with the Soviet Union override the interests of Western cohesion', and that I support from deep conviction HMG's policies towards the EEC and NATO and their present tactics on the specific issue of Berlin and its relation to the proposals for a European Security Conference.[6]

3. Having said this, however, I must also say that the differences of analysis that remain between your advisers in London and this Embassy are large and important. They concern both the effective determinants of the Soviet leaders' actions and the present trend of development of Soviet society; and my own analysis leads me to recommend, not a change in policy, but certain changes in the style of our dealings with the Soviet leaders and the Soviet Government as a whole. I submit that these changes in style would be very much in HMG's political and commercial interests.

The determinants of Soviet policy

4. This is an important and difficult subject. When faced with positive pronouncements on it, I am put in mind of Lord Melbourne's exclamation: 'I wish that I was as sure of anything as Tom Macaulay is of everything'—or as a shrewd colleague of mine here often puts it—'For a foreigner in the Soviet

[4] Sir D. Wilson was in London in January for the first meeting of the Anglo-Soviet Joint Commission: see note 12 below.

[5] See No. 55, note 5.

[6] Cf. pp. 294-5.

Union, there are no degrees of knowledge, only degrees of ignorance'. With this general proviso, I should say that I stand in no need of being convinced that the Communist Party, the Politburo and Brezhnev himself are dominant: a fact which is of course reflected in the close interrelationship between the top echelons of Party and Government. I do not doubt either that Brezhnev and the other Party leaders of his generation have been brought up on the full range of Marxist mythology, including the doctrine of the class struggle magnified to a world-wide scale, and that they continue in some sense to believe in it. But beliefs can be held with varying intensities and at different levels of the mind, and can be more or less closely related to actions. I personally find it hard to think that the CPSU does not by now include its fair share of pious agnostics; or that even Brezhnev and men of his generation believe very intensely in the sort of text quoted in paragraph 2 of your despatch; or that they find the concept of the class struggle the most helpful guide to most of their current decisions on foreign policy. (The concept could indeed be of some hindrance to their advisers at Soviet Embassies abroad; I wonder whether Mr. Smirnovsky, for example, has felt bound duly to report the fact that the annual conference of one of the two main political parties in the United Kingdom traditionally ends with the singing of the words 'Wider still and wider shall thy bounds be set', and that of the other party with 'Though cowards flinch and traitors sneer, we'll keep the Red Flag flying here'.)

5. I believe myself, consciously and firmly, that it suits the Soviet leaders very well for various purposes, internal and external, to present the traditional Marxist picture of the forces of progress and reaction perpetually struggling and clashing throughout the world. (It can also be very useful to us to reflect their own picture back at them in argument, as I have recently heard Sir Thomas Brimelow do, with great effect.) I am sure that the basic ideology will be preached as long as the present generation of leaders exist and until all those associated in any way with Stalin's rule have faded from the scene. These are in a sense guilty men, guilty towards their own peoples and towards the world outside, who can best maintain their position by positing a Manichean world-struggle between good and evil.[7] Even when they have gone, one must assume that much at least of Communist ideology and ritual will die hard. I would recall to you some apt words of de Tocqueville which I cited to your predecessor, when I first assumed charge of this Embassy. 'The last thing that a party will give up is its language ... It is the tragedy of great passions in decline that the traces of them can be found on the lips of men long after they have lost their hold on the heart'.[8] Already however the effect

[7] In conversation with Sir D. Wilson on 8 January (see note 4), Sir D. Greenhill 'said that his impression of the Soviet leaders was that the present generation still had to some extent the mentality of persons who had committed a crime'.

[8] Sir D. Wilson had quoted this passage more fully in his despatch of 28 November 1968 entitled 'First Impressions of the Soviet Union' (ENS 1/6 of 1968, not printed). The summary of this despatch noted the 'empty rhetoric of the press and propaganda machine' which was 'a reflection of the profoundly conservative mentality of the Soviet leaders. The régime propagates

of Soviet ideology, as opposed to Soviet power, has decreased in the world outside the Soviet Union. The effect of a decrease in faith in the Soviet Union itself is harder to predict. I would personally expect the habit of compromising with the realities (I hope the hard realities) of the world outside to have some beneficial long-term effect on at least the younger generation of Soviet leaders. Such compromises were represented by Lenin as single steps backward which would facilitate in due course two steps forward in a revolutionary sense. One can reasonably hope that the habit of the step backward will obscure the vision of the two steps forward. More hopefully— and I recognise this to be a long-term hope—it seems at least possible that as Communist ideology is pushed further into the background of their minds, some radical questions will begin to emerge both about the validity of the concept that the world is divided into imperialist 'baddies' and popular democratic 'goodies', and even about its usefulness for the national interest of the Soviet Union. How quickly such questions will emerge depends to a large extent on the future development of the Chinese schism—a dark glass through which I shall not attempt to peer in this despatch.

6. However this may be, I would suggest that we have already reached a stage in which it is misleading to concentrate on Marxist doctrine as the main key to our assessment of Soviet policy in general and of Soviet foreign policy in particular. I must admit that successive British Ambassadors to Moscow have been reaching this conclusion for a long time, and it has been the subject of a debate conducted at intervals, often between this Embassy and the Department, since the Soviet state began: I would respectfully suggest that you might derive enjoyment, as I have done, from reading a despatch of my predecessor Sir R. Hodgson to Sir Austen Chamberlain, dated the 6th of May 1926 and published in *Documents on British Foreign Policy* (Series IA, Volume I), in which he said: 'The Soviet Government has been continually in conflict with the conceptions to which it owes its being—to cope with practical exigencies it has had to recede little by little from the ideas which inspired the Revolution and one of the difficulties which confront it today is so to camouflage its continued retreat as to allow a trusting proletariat to cherish the illusion that it, and not a very ordinary bureaucracy governs Russia . . . Moscow, however much nonsense is exhibited on red banners, stuffed into youthful brains, or poured out through loud speakers to the populace, has to deal with precisely the same problems as any of its neighbours—and is dealing with them in very much the same way'.[9]

7. There have no doubt been many occasions since then when the ideological motivation has seemed to be uppermost, though never I think at the expense of national interest; but it seems to me that in recent years the Soviet leaders, faced with many difficult decisions affecting their relations with foreign countries, both Communist and non-Communist, have increasingly

a Marxist Utopian mythology which, together with the imperialist bogey, justifies its authoritarian internal policy.'

[9] *DBFP*, Series IA, Volume I, No. 504.

tended to take such decisions on the merits of the case, calculated in terms of national interest; and that while there are many cases in which the claims of ideology and national interest coincide (as in Czechoslovakia in 1968), there are others in which the coincidence of interest is much less clear-cut and in which the objective of consolidating the position of the Soviet Union as a world power has seemed to be paramount, even at the expense of ideological considerations, at least in the short term. However conventionally orthodox the public pronouncements of the Soviet leaders continue to be, they have, I suggest, been obliged to regard the relationship of the Soviet Union, as a superpower, with the outside world in a manner totally different from Stalin's view of the world in the 1950s; and while the Politburo remains the arbiter on all political questions, including external issues, it is much less inhibited by ideology than earlier generations of party leaders in the pursuit of the interests of the Soviet state. I will not weary you by citing examples, which I have mentioned in previous correspondence, nor by restating the formidable problems of choice which now face and will continue to face the Soviet leadership (I attempted to analyse some of these in my despatch of the 16th of November 1970 and no doubt more will be apparent from the proceedings of the XXIVth Congress of the CPSU). I can only repeat that, if we examine the deeds of the Soviet leaders, it is possible to find very considerable evidence of a pragmatic approach to the solution of their problems, and of a tendency to act as a superpower rather than as a standard-bearer for revolution. 'If so', as Mr. Thomas Wolfe put it in a thoughtful article in a recent issue of *Problems of Communism*, 'the world may find that the problems of getting along with a Soviet Union dedicated to revolutionary Communist goals have been replaced by those of coping with a Soviet Union disposed to throw its weight around in furtherance of its great power interests'. I need hardly say that this is not a particularly cheerful prospect in itself, even if it may appear so in comparison with the idea of a Soviet leadership pursuing what is really a consistent course, despite apparent twists and tactical retreats, towards world revolution.

The future development of Soviet society

8. Will the Soviet economic base remain sufficiently strong to support both the needs of the policy of a superpower and the growing aspirations of the Soviet people? The answer to this crucial question is the second main point of analysis on which my own view, and that of many shrewd observers on the spot, seems to differ from that of your advisers. 1970 has, I think, been a very important year in the evolution of Soviet economic policy as well as of Soviet foreign policy (the two phases of evolution are closely connected as aspects of Soviet policy as a whole). In this field the basic fact seems to me the increased realisation by Soviet leaders that the pace of technological advance has enormously accelerated in the world at large, but not in the Soviet Union, and their public recognition of this fact. It is important, as you say, to attend to all the words of the song, and the following verse, so to speak, is culled from among Brezhnev's (it dates in fact from 1968) pronouncements: 'One can say without exaggeration that it is precisely in this sphere, the sphere of scientific

and technological progress, that one of the main fronts of the historic competition of the two systems lies today. For our Party this makes the further intensive development of science and technology and the broad implementation in production of the latest scientific and technological achievements not only a central economic, but an important political task. At the present stage questions of scientific and technological progress are acquiring, it can be directly stated, a decisive significance.' There are few more significant statistics today than the fact that Soviet computer technology lags behind that in the West by five years or more. This means that, if the Soviet economy is not to lose further ground to the West, and if the Soviet Union is to avoid a condition of national constipation, to which Krasin predicted in 1917 Soviet communism would inevitably lead, quantitative growth is not enough. Qualitative improvements in the economy are required, which cannot any longer be obtained by big investments of capital and manpower. I am sure that the present Soviet leaders will try, up to and perhaps beyond the eleventh hour, to contain such improvements within the old centralised system, and that they will be most unwilling to admit any large-scale economic reform. (The so-called economic reform of 1965 is a pale shadow of what the needs of the 1970s seem likely sooner or later to impose.) But even to attain this limited objective, they have, I believe, no choice but to rely both on increased foreign help and on increased efforts by the Soviet technocrats. And so, I think, the views of the industrial managers and technocrats are increasingly assuming more importance in the eyes of the Soviet leadership. Although the natural instinct of the old style party leader will be to keep such men 'on tap but not on top' as Mr. Bertram Wolfe expressed it, the task is not as easy now as it was when Mr. Wolfe was writing in 1957, and will, I believe, become increasingly harder.[10]

9. This trend is not likely to have any immediate effect on the social structure of the Soviet Union. I certainly do not expect the new men to be good Western-style liberals any more than standard-bearers for the world revolution of Communism. I would expect them however to demand and to obtain the possibility of rather more foreign travel and contacts in the technical sphere (this was what I meant when I talked in my despatch of the 16th of November about a policy of 'increased contacts'). I entirely agree

[10] Cf. No. 57, note 6. In a minute of 31 December Mr. J.E. Killick (an Assistant Under Secretary superintending Defence and Research Departments and PUSD, who was to succeed Sir D. Wilson as HM Ambassador at Moscow in September 1971) commented that 'The really fundamental point which the Moscow despatch [*ibid.*, note 1] overlooks, however, and the real Soviet dilemma, is that the crucially important aspect of achieving industrial efficiency is not just technology but management. Even if the Soviet Union could acquire from the West all the technology it needed it would still not have solved its problems so long as Marxist/Leninist thought continued to distort the Soviet approach to management. The Japanese are demonstrating the validity of this thesis—they buy technology but this would avail them little if they did not go on to apply it most efficiently through good management techniques. I see no reason to believe that the Soviet Union is capable of doing the same without such a change in its approach to economic management as would totally undermine the very foundations of Marxism/Leninism. Technology alone does not of itself create economic efficiency.'

with what was said in your despatch about the Soviet leaders' determination to restrict contacts; indeed I have often reported on this myself, not least in my despatch of the 16th of November, and have personally had much evidence of restrictions placed on my friends here. I do not think however that it will be entirely simple for the leaders to seal off new ideas neatly into scientific (and thus permissible) and other compartments: Yevtushenko's recent quotation from Plekhanov, cited in my Annual Review, is very relevant.[11] Finally it seems likely that in ten years or so the younger party leaders, many of whom will be technocrats by education, will see the need further to modify in practice a whole range of doctrines if party and state are not to petrify.

10. All this is of course speculative, and I agree that it is important neither to forget the Communist background of Soviet society, nor to exaggerate the significance of new trends. My own position, and in Moscow terms it is not very eccentric, is that it is equally important not to neglect the existence of trends because they are long-term and operate gradually; and that, since all thought about the future of Soviet policy is bound to be speculative, it is better to speculate on the basis of current trends as well of historical background, important as the latter is both in itself and in determining the trends themselves.

Anglo-Soviet relations

11. As I have said, these trends in the development of Soviet foreign policy and of Soviet society are unlikely to make this country any less hostile to British and Western interests, in the short and medium term, though they may make it somewhat easier to live with. I would therefore repeat that I see no reason to suggest any fundamental change in HMG's policies towards the Soviet Union. Nor have I ever thought that HMG's policies can in themselves have 'critical importance . . . in the determination of how and by whom the Soviet Union shall be ruled'. But I must admit that in my despatch of the 16th of November, I used the word 'we' in the two senses of 'Britain' and 'the Western allies', and did not always make it explicitly clear in which sense I was using it. I believe, as I meant to say in that despatch, that the Western Powers can do something, at least indirectly, to hasten or facilitate the tendencies towards pragmatism in the Soviet leadership which I have described; and that *faute de mieux* it is in the Western interest to do so. The Western allies, not excluding the United States, seem already to be set on a sensible course of increasing trade and contact, wherever possible, while keeping their guard up. HMG can well claim, as you say, to have been the pioneers of this policy, and I recognise with satisfaction that we are still

[11] Sir D. Wilson's Annual Review of the Soviet Union in 1970 was despatched on 1 January 1971. The quotation, cited by the distinguished Soviet poet E.A. Yevtushenko, ran: 'It is time, finally, for Russian scientists to understand that science can develop unimpeded only where its study is free and that such freedom is conceivable only in a free state. On the basis of this axiom it can be said that our political martyrs are doing more for the future development of Russian science than the scientific Philistines who do not see the needs of our contemporary reality from behind their retorts, papers or crystals' (ENS 1/1).

committed to it. From Moscow however it looks at times as if there were now some division of labour in Western Europe, HMG playing the main part in advertising the necessary defensive posture, and our allies concentrating more on the policy of contact. This is no doubt an exaggerated picture. We are more widely vulnerable to threats to sea communications than our allies and we have to concentrate more attention on them (though we do not hear France speaking from the housetops about the greatly increased Soviet presence in the Mediterranean, despite their preoccupation with this threat and the measures they have felt obliged to take to counter it). So far as contacts are concerned, I did not mean to suggest in my previous despatch that it was anything more than a theoretical alternative to let the Soviet Union stew in its own juice; and we have indeed worked hard in the last year to secure the establishment of the Anglo/Soviet Consultative Committee and Joint Commission.[12] The fact remains, however, that compared with the French, German and even American efforts in the field of political, parliamentary and official relations, we have been and remain inactive. I attach as an Annex to this despatch[13] a list of some recent bilateral activities by these countries which illustrate this point; this does not include planned exchanges for this year, which include considerable activity on the parliamentary front notably by the Germans.

12. I do not think that such a low posture is forced on us by lack of interest on the Soviet side. The Germans have indeed more goods to deliver; the French must be encouraged to keep their distance from the Americans; and the American-Soviet relationship is in a class by itself. But just because we have maintained closer ties than others with the United States and have at times been more vocal in our opposition to Soviet policies, and because our interests as opposed to our power are still world-wide, the Soviet leaders seem convinced that they have something to gain by cultivating closer relations with us. This is a process which I believe involves some concrete advantages for us too (a point to which I shall return at the end of this despatch) and some more general and less tangible ones, in that it helps, however little to remove barriers of ignorance and prejudice on the Soviet side. On the basis of one index at least the Soviet leaders could be thought to have shown more interest in contacts than ourselves. Over the last year there have been separate official visits to the United Kingdom by Mr. Gromyko and two of his senior official advisers;[14] whereas since I have been at this post

[12] See Nos. 45, note 3 and 57, note 7. The first meeting of the Joint Commission had been held in London from 12-15 January 1971. Mr. Kirillin, leader of the Soviet delegation, found the meeting satisfactory with 'positive results' but the British assessment was less optimistic: although the meeting went smoothly, 'little new ground was broken, and the Russians showed unwillingness to commit themselves. But they had clearly been briefed to maintain our interest . . . The Russians were left in no doubt about our concern over static British exports to the USSR. It was also made clear to them that we expected the Joint Commission to produce concrete results'. It was agreed that a second meeting should be held in Moscow later in the year (PW 1/303/1).

[13] Not printed.

[14] See Nos. 45 and 53-4.

(for nearly two and a half years now, though this period includes the freeze following the invasion of Czechoslovakia) there has been only one touchdown by a Foreign and Commonwealth Office Minister at Moscow Airport, and one brief visit by a senior official on his way back from the Far East.

Recommendation

13. I submit that, in our dealings with the Soviet Union, we should adopt not new policies but rather a new style in executing old and agreed ones. The new style would involve a greater readiness to involve the Russians in a dialogue through Ministerial and official visits in both directions, some modification in our attitude towards other forms of political contact, and—in due time—a more *nuancé* public attitude towards the Soviet threat.

i. *Visits.* I am well aware of the pressure of urgent work to which the Prime Minister and yourself are subject, and realise that you are unlikely to be able to accept in the near future the invitations conveyed by Mr. Gromyko in London last October. Nor do I think that at present there are likely to be important issues, with the single possible exception of the Middle East, which either of you could usefully discuss in person. But, with an eye on the future, I believe that it is important before long to convey an interim answer to the Soviet Government, even if it has to be negative, simply in order to observe the courtesies and indicate your personal interest in our relations with the second superpower. For the latter purpose, I also hope that Sir Denis Greenhill may be authorised before long to accept an often-repeated invitation to return the visit made to the UK last April by Vice-Minister Kozyrev;[15] and that the possibility may be borne in mind of official visits to and from Moscow at a lower level, e.g. in connection with the Middle East (I am glad to note that there is the possibility of a visit, however brief, from the Head of your Planning Staff).[16] Our European Allies, not to mention the Americans, manage a good deal of this sort of thing, without harm if without conspicuous benefit to our common cause, and we have, I believe, long reached the point where our apparent lack of interest is conspicuous.

ii. *Other contacts.* I am well aware that HMG cannot control Parliamentary exchanges, and visits by prominent journalists, representatives of research institutions, etc. and that financial support, which might indirectly promote

[15] Cf. No. 49. Sir D. Greenhill had in fact informed Mr. Smirnovsky on 4 February that he had been authorised to visit Moscow during May in response to the Soviet invitation. The visit was subsequently arranged for 22-27 June: see Nos. 67 and 68 below.

[16] Mr. Cradock, accompanied by Mr. C. Powell of Planning Staff, visited Moscow from 29-30 March for talks with officials from the Soviet Foreign Ministry, led by Mr. Makeev, and with members of the staff of the Institute of World Economics and International Relations, led by Dr. Kulish. Mr. Cradock described talks with the former as 'not particularly rewarding though they allowed us to establish with a fair degree of certainty that there is nothing corresponding to our Planning Staff in the Soviet Ministry of Foreign Affairs'. Talks with the Institute, however, were 'very interesting . . . They indicate that sophisticated forward-looking work is done in at least this Institute and is one element in Soviet planning. Another and decisive element presumably comes from the Party apparatus' (RS 10/2).

them, is hard to provide in the present climate. I can only repeat that here too we are well behind the field—again the Americans as well as our Western European allies do a good deal more than us—and state my conviction that our lack of activity has become conspicuous.

iii. *Public attitude to the Soviet threat.* As I have said, I fully realise that we shall have to deal with the Soviet Union as a hostile power for many years to come, whatever differences of interpretation there may be as to the causes and ultimate objects of this hostility; Soviet naval power has increased and we must pay a suitable premium by way of defence expenditure against risks of the Soviet leaders misusing their increasing power (the exact nature of the risks and of the suitable premium is of course a matter for debate);[17] further, in a society such as ours in Britain it is necessary for Ministers to explain clearly in public the reasons for paying such a premium. I also realise that in practice so long as the issue of South African arms is in the forefront of public debate, references to the Soviet threat to our interests will continue to recur frequently in public statements. But once this issue has been decided, and unless thereafter some completely new circumstances emerge, I submit that, in the interests not only of Anglo/Soviet relations but of East/West relations in general, our public posture in the 1970s should be to avoid more public emphasis than is absolutely necessary on the Soviet threat. What is said publicly on this subject by HM Ministers may increase our readiness to recognise and meet the threat, but is not otherwise, I believe, likely to diminish it—in fact the reverse. To judge by Soviet reactions to the Singapore conference,[18] they are trying hard to discredit HMG by exploiting our attitude in their propaganda for the 'third world' as a deliberate effort to inspire an anti-Soviet political campaign, to influence Asians and Africans against the Soviet Union, and thereby to inflame 'cold-war attitudes'. I have no means of judging how successful they have so far been in their attempt, but I would not under-estimate their ability to make mischief on this score. Furthermore, I believe that there is a direct relationship between what we say publicly about the Russians and the intensity of their own hostile propaganda against us; and, while this need not worry us too much in itself, there is also a direct relationship between the climate of propaganda and the readiness of the Soviet Government to do business with us, literally as well as metaphorically. We may perhaps have something to learn in all this from the way in which the French have reacted (or failed to react) publicly to the Soviet naval build-up in the Mediterranean—a problem which after all concerns their national interest very closely indeed and at a vital point.

[17] The Prime Minister drew attention to the preceding passage beginning 'Soviet naval power', and asked that the Embassy should elaborate their view of these risks (letter from Mr. Moon to Mr. Graham, 22 March). Sir D. Wilson's response is printed as No. 63 below.

[18] The reference is to the Commonwealth Heads of Government Meeting held in Singapore from 14-22 January 1971: see p. 321 below.

14. The thoughts on changes of style in sections i. and ii. at least of the preceding paragraph may appear as mouse-like and, theoretically at least, uncontroversial conclusions in comparison with the rather mountainous analysis preceding them. I am however convinced that some change of style towards the Soviet Union would be consistent with and indeed useful in furthering some concrete, immediate and important British interests:

i. *British Trade.* I find it ironic that a member of our trade-oriented Diplomatic Service should have to recommend old-fashioned political diplomacy as a means of ensuring commercial success. I remain however firmly of the opinion that rather easier political relations with the Russians would have some beneficial effect on our trade. At least they would give us a fair chance of obtaining equality of opportunity in relation to our Western allies, whereas at present the dice are sometimes weighted against us. Easier political relations might also facilitate the eventual conclusion of one or more contracts in respect of the large-scale joint ventures now under discussion between the Russians and ourselves. These could in turn lead to a significant change in the level, and indeed to some extent in the nature of Anglo-Soviet trade. We are still in the exploratory stages and much groundwork remains to be done. Thus some change in political style would have time to take effect, and at the crucial stage demonstration of interest by the Prime Minister might prove to be the catalyst which would precipitate success.

ii. *Europeanism.* I think that it is in our national interest, particularly at the present time, to bring our *Ostpolitik* more closely into line with that of our main future partners in Western Europe. We have backed Herr Brandt's *Ostpolitik* without reserve. His own powerfully stated justification of this policy is essentially that, in the long term, it will assist peaceful evolution in Eastern Europe (including the Soviet Union). This has also long been one of the aims of French policy. Whatever we may think of the means by which President de Gaulle earned his 'special position', President Pompidou's visit to the Soviet Union[19] has shown that France has found a way both to promote her own national interests and to further East-West cooperation, without any further sacrifice of Western interests. The kind of policy which I believe Britain should follow in the 1970s should, I believe, be as near as possible in our particular circumstances to that already being pursued by Germany and France. If it is not, we may find ourselves out of line with them at a time and in a field crucial for inter-Western relations. In short, I find it hard to see that there is any antithesis (as seems to be suggested in paragraph 10 of your despatch of the 1st of December) between developing our relations with Western Europe and developing them with the USSR. On the contrary, I submit that the two policies go logically hand in hand.

iii. *Realism.* I believe that a change of style could have ultimately useful effects for our relationship with the Soviet Union on extra-European

[19] See No. 52, note 8.

problems. As a major European power with world-wide interests, there are areas outside Europe in which we, more than Germany and perhaps more than France, come up against the Soviet Union as the major power in Europe and the second superpower of the world. In some of these areas, Soviet interests are obviously in direct conflict with our own, or with American interests in such degree that as a loyal ally we cannot but oppose them. But there are other, intermediate areas, one of which—the Middle East—is of vital importance to British interests. Here, if anywhere, we must admit the implications of the possibility that what suits the Soviet Government is not necessarily undesirable to ourselves, be ready for bilateral discussion with them, and work for an atmosphere in which this can most usefully take place. An important step towards this state of affairs has been implicit in the way in which Her Majesty's present Ministers have somewhat distanced themselves from their predecessors' close identification with American policy in the Arab/Israel dispute.[20]

15. I can see that, small as the changes of style recommended may appear, it may not be easy to give full effect to them, particularly during the period when—as I clearly realise—the main thrust of Britain's foreign policy must be directed towards a single aim: the success of the Brussels negotiations. I do not, I hope, underestimate the difficulties involved. I recognise that Soviet responsibility for the present bad state of Anglo/Soviet relations is very heavy—I need only mention the extra-curricular activities of the Soviet Trade Delegation in London[21]—and I know that an inordinate amount of time and energy is thus already spent (and believe that even more may have to be spent) in purely negative activities, such as the phrasing and timing of those routine and more than routine protests which will no doubt continue to flow between London and Moscow. But if major British interests are not to suffer, we must not concentrate entirely on this aspect of our relations with the second superpower. More needs to be done, I believe, both to analyse the state of the Soviet Union and future trends, and to get ourselves into a position where more meaningful dialogue is possible with the Soviet authorities. On both points I hope that this Embassy may make its full contribution.[22]

---

[20] See No. 54, note 13. In his memoirs (*op. cit.*, p. 258) Sir Alec Douglas-Home expressed his conviction that 'the Conservatives must proclaim a policy more definite than that which the Socialists had felt able to pursue'.

[21] Cf. No. 58.

[22] On 19 February Sir T. Brimelow wrote to thank Sir D. Wilson for his 'well pondered and beautifully written' despatch: 'a major contribution to that discussion of assumptions which I regard as essential for the proper formulation of policy. We shall wish to consider it very carefully before we reply.' Sir A. Douglas-Home's formal reply of 6 April was closely based on a discussion held between Sir T. Brimelow, EESD officials and Sir D. Wilson on 12 March when the latter was home on leave. The Secretary of State wrote that he was 'attracted by your suggestion that we should adopt something of a new style in our dealings with the Soviet Union, while maintaining the substance of our present policies . . . I see no advantage in causing annoyance gratuitously to any foreign country, least of all a super-power. A forthcoming style,

16. I am sending a copy of this despatch to Her Majesty's Representatives in Washington, Paris, Bonn, Warsaw, Prague, Budapest, Bucharest, Sofia, Belgrade, Berlin, the UK Delegation to NATO and the UK Mission to the United Nations in New York.

I have, etc.,

DUNCAN WILSON

accompanied by strict attention to our own self-interest on matters of substance, is a dictate of common sense. But I confess I do not expect great positive advantages to result . . . If a change of style is unlikely to achieve much, one might ask whether we should go further and change the substance of our policies. There are overwhelming reasons against it, which are the reasons why our present policies are what they are. There is nothing we can give the Russians which is comparable in value to them to the French partial withdrawal from NATO and the West German acceptance of the European *status quo*. Nor is Britain a super-power like the USA. As regards our taking the lead in East/West relations, these relations at present consist essentially of the German question . . . And on German questions we cannot go faster than the Federal German Republic . . . Moreover, even if it were in our power and were our wish to purchase the kind of relationship with the Soviet Union which General de Gaulle established, the Russians would be likely to use that relationship as a lever for persuading us against greater political and defence cooperation in Europe after the enlargement of the EEC . . . This suggests that, apart from all the other considerations, the coming period may not be a suitable one for establishing or maintaining any new kind of relationship with the Soviet Union . . . We must be very careful to ensure that our change of style is never used, whether or not it produces benefits, as an argument for less firmness where firmness is necessary.'

While debate continued between Moscow and London on the future course and conduct of Anglo-Soviet relations in the broader sense, the next document illustrates the difficulties encountered by HM Embassy in Moscow in maintaining viable day-to-day relations and building up satisfactory contacts with the Soviet Foreign Ministry. It also shows, as Mr. Scott points out in Document No. 61, that however bad bilateral relations may have been the Russians made it their business to preserve a 'normal and workmanlike, sometimes cordial and even civilised relationship'.

No. 61

Letter from Mr. K.B.A. Scott (Moscow) to Mr. J.L. Bullard[1]
[*ENS 3/548/10*]

Confidential   MOSCOW, 26 *February 1971*

Dear Bullard,
Contacts with the Soviet Foreign Ministry
Our respective predecessors had some correspondence in 1969, resting with Sydney Giffard's letter of 25 November 1969 to Tom Bridges,[2] about this Embassy's contacts with the Soviet Foreign Ministry. Since then, on the Ambassador's instructions, we have been doing what we can to extend our range of contacts in the Foreign Ministry and have found this on the whole to be a useful and sometimes rewarding exercise. Certainly I myself, on returning to Moscow after 12 years,[3] have been very agreeably surprised by the degree to which this Embassy now finds it possible to do business with Departments other than the Second European Department and to establish, in some cases, something approaching the sort of relationship with the Foreign Ministry which might be expected in a normally not particularly friendly country. You may find it useful to have on record the following general review of our present state of relations.

2. At Ambassadorial level, the Ambassador has had little contact with Gromyko himself—no less than the general run of Ambassadors, but definitely less than his French, German and US colleagues (the two latter have of course had special business with him in the last year). He had hoped for more contact after Gromyko's visit to London,[4] but the STD question has been an inhibition.[5] He has been able to pay fairly regular calls on most of the Deputy Foreign Ministers to discuss a wide range of subjects, though he has not been able to establish any very satisfactory relationship with 'our' Vice-Minister Kozyrev: this has meant that calls have had to be on specific items of business rather than for *tours d'horizon* and that there has been little free exchange of views on more informal occasions. The most fruitful dialogue has undoubtedly

[1] Mr. Scott had been First Secretary in HM Embassy in Moscow since September 1970: Mr. Bullard had succeeded Mr. Giffard as Head of EESD in February 1971.

[2] Cf. No. 37, note 9.

[3] Mr. Scott had been Third, later Second Secretary in Moscow 1956-8.

[4] See Nos. 53 and 54. The *communiqué* issued at the end of Mr. Gromyko's visit (see p. 267) recorded agreement to 'intensify contacts and hold consultations on matters of common concern', but Mr. Giffard wrote to Lord Bridges on 20 November 1970 that 'for the moment there is insufficient material for a worthwhile exchange of views between the Ambassador and Gromyko'. In reply on 27 November Lord Bridges reported that Sir D. Wilson thought 'he should seek an interview before too long . . . the fact that we have nothing of urgent importance to impart does not mean that we should be precluded from a general *tour d'horizon*' (ENS 3/548/12, 1970).

[5] Cf. No. 58.

been that which he conducted last year with Deputy Minister Vinogradov (now Soviet Ambassador in Cairo) on the Middle East crisis.[6] The Ambassador has also from time to time called on Heads of Departments other than Makeev, e.g. Kapitsa (formerly Head of South East Asian Department now transferred to First Far Eastern Department to look after China); Falin, the outgoing Head of Third European Department (Germany) who is now going as Ambassador to Bonn; and Sytenko, Head of the Near Eastern Department; and has regularly entertained Makeev or members of his department at lunches or dinners involving other Soviet Ministries; but on the whole contact below the level of Deputy Minister has been maintained by Robin Edmonds and the Chancery, and in this we are in line with the practice of the American and French Embassies.

3. As regards the Second European Department itself, we have marked our special relationship by instituting a fairly regular series of lunches, held roughly at 6-weekly intervals, with either the Minister or Head of Chancery as host, three-a-side. Every now and again either Makeev or Vasev, his Deputy, has responded by giving us a lunch in a Soviet restaurant—perhaps about 3 times a year. The most recent of these was Vasev's farewell lunch for Tom Bridges, on which I reported in my letter 10/10 to you of 1 February.[7] Some of these lunches are more useful than others, but there are two conclusions to be drawn from our experience of them over the past 15 months. First, the Russians seem to distinguish between the kind of conversation which is appropriate over or after a meal and that which should take place during a formal call at the Foreign Ministry, presumably because at the latter they always provide a note-taker. Secondly, at certain of these meals we have been able to do some important business: for example elucidation of Soviet proposals for the holding of a European Security Conference, and the genesis of Gromyko's visit to London last October, which might very well not have happened when it did had it not been for a discussion which Robin Edmonds and Tom Bridges had with Vasev last August at a lunch in a Moscow restaurant. We have tried to do a certain amount of entertaining of Second European Department at desk level also; last summer Nick Livingston, Roy Reeve and Chris Meyer[8] had three members of the Department to lunch, and shortly after my arrival I got two of them with their wives to come to dinner with other members of the Chancery (a third, who was invited, was genuinely ill at the last moment). Roland Smith gave a cocktail party in the autumn to introduce Michael Robinson,[9] to which four members of the Second European Department and a couple of members of Protocol Department came, some with their wives. We hope to develop the

[6] Sir D. Wilson had held discussions on the Middle East with Mr. Vinogradov on 17 March and 27 May 1970.

[7] Not printed.

[8] Mr. Livingston and Mr. Meyer were Second Secretaries, and Mr. Reeve a Research Officer at HM Embassy in Moscow.

[9] Mr. Smith and Mr. Robinson were respectively Second and Third Secretaries at HM Embassy in Moscow.

habit of rather more frequent entertaining of this kind (it used to happen quite a lot in earlier days, as I remember), even though we must recognise that there will be little opportunity for our Soviet contacts to reciprocate.

4. As regards other Departments, we have begun to develop a series of lunches with two senior members of Near Eastern Department (the most recent of these was referred to in Moscow telegram No. 213[10]) though our ability to do this successfully may turn out simply to be a consequence of the present state of the Arab/Israeli dispute and of the new look which the Russians have taken at our Middle Eastern policy since the Secretary of State's speech at Harrogate.[11] There is a move afoot to institute a series of monthly lunches among the 'four power' desk officers on the Middle East, but although all concerned are in favour, nothing has as yet taken place. As occasion arises, we shall try to institute similar lunches with other Departments.

5. We have in any case had fairly regular contacts one way or another not only with the Near Eastern Department but also with International Organisations Department (mainly on disarmament on which you will have seen the encouraging letter—DS2/303/1/ of 12 February—which David Summerhayes was good enough to send to Robin Edmonds the other day),[12] South East Asian Department, Third European Department (mainly on Berlin), Third African Department (on Nigeria) and to a lesser extent First Far Eastern Department (on China). We have also exchanged the odd word with the Legal Department on the proposed Law of the Sea Conference;[13] and we hope to use Percy Cradock's visit to establish links with the Planning Department, if it turns out to exist.[14]

[10] Of 12 February, not printed (NEM 2/5).

[11] Cf. Nos. 54, note 13 and 60, note 20. Dr Jarring had resumed his mission with a visit to Jerusalem in January, but talks appeared deadlocked on procedural questions until President Sadat, in response to an appeal from U Thant, agreed on 4 February to an extension of the cease-fire for one month, linked to proposals for Israeli withdrawal from the East Bank of the Suez Canal and Egyptian agreement to open the Canal to international navigation. The Egyptian Government made a positive response to proposals of 8 February from Dr. Jarring for Israeli withdrawal and an Egyptian commitment to peace, but despite pressure from the US and UK the Israeli Government replied on 21 February refusing to withdraw to the armistice lines of 4 June 1967. On 1 March Mr. Smirnovsky delivered a message to the Prime Minister from Mr. Kosygin denouncing the Israeli position and accusing the US of supporting it: on 10 March Sir D. Wilson passed on Mr. Heath's reply, stating that it was wrong to conclude that the Israeli reply was their last word and expressing the hope that the Soviet Union would continue to work for a peaceful settlement of the conflict (NEM 3/303/1).

[12] In this letter of 12 February Mr. Summerhayes, Head of Disarmament Department, thanked Mr. Edmonds for his account in a letter of 18 January of a discussion with Mr. Timerbayev of the Soviet Foreign Ministry on 15 January concerning Soviet attitudes to disarmament, in particular chemical and biological warfare (cf. No. 45, note 16), a comprehensive test ban treaty and the NPT. Mr. Summerhayes thanked Mr. Edmonds 'for having gone over the ground so thoroughly with Timerbayev. Your conversation should have served to establish a useful channel for exchanges with the Russians on disarmament questions.'

[13] Cf. No. 51, note 10.

[14] Cf. No. 60, note 16.

6. There are still a number of obvious gaps in this pattern—for example, we have yet to penetrate the Chief Administration for General International Questions, which is said to deal *inter alia* with European security; we ought to see more of the two Far Eastern Departments; and it might be rewarding to try to cultivate the Latin American Department. What is interesting is that, on the basis of recent experience the only barriers to developing contacts of some interest in most parts of the Foreign Ministry seem to be those set by the time and energy available on our side. I hope you will agree that there is much to be said for continuing to extend our range as opportunity offers. Meanwhile, there is also of course the steady stream of bilateral business, ranging from the jejune to the mutually offensive, which we conduct with the Second European Department (which incidentally is also responsible for such questions as Cyprus, South Africa and Rhodesia).[15]

7. On re-reading the above, it seems to me a little extraordinary that I should have felt these very normal activities to be worth reporting in detail. But the fact remains that most of these contacts are of comparatively recent date, and in view of the misgivings which were obviously felt at one time in London about our establishing them, I think you may find it of interest to know the results. Two points are particularly worthy of note. First, that however bad our bilateral relations may be on the surface, and in particular however nasty the Soviet press comment on Britain, the members of Second European Department seem to make it their business to preserve a normal and workmanlike, sometimes cordial and even civilised relationship with the Embassy. Secondly, there have been several quite striking cases in which our contacts with other Departments have yielded useful insights into Foreign Ministry thinking on current issues of wider interest. Taken together, these experiences—if they serve no other purpose—at least help us here to remember that it may be misleading to construe Soviet policy exclusively from our daily drudgery of reading *Pravda* (although we are not in danger of forgetting that this represents the Party line) and thereby, I hope, reinforce the case for maintaining a strong, capable and well-informed political staff in Moscow.

Yours ever,

KEN SCOTT

[15] Replying to this letter on 16 March, Mr. Bullard told Mr. Scott that 'We have consulted the departments responsible for the areas which you have mentioned as subjects for discussion. The general view is that there is a strong case for discussion of subjects such as Indochina, the Middle East, disarmament and East-West questions, where there are problems to be solved and with which we and the Russians are both directly concerned . . . Our only proviso in this field of questions must be the obvious one, of which you are well aware, that we must avoid giving the Russians opportunities for driving wedges between us and the Americans and our other allies.'

In response to a request from Mr. Graham for his views on whether attention should be drawn to the unfavourable contrast between his own continuing difficulties in getting to see Mr. Gromyko and the fact that Mr. Smirnovsky had probably seen Sir A. Douglas-Home 'more than any other Ambassador in London', Sir D. Wilson replied on 5 April that he 'would not find it very easy or very suitable to go in for a general chat with Gromyko, while a reply is pending [to No. 58] without making some reference to the subject' (ENS 3/548/10).

The next document was written as part of the UK's contribution to ongoing work in NATO preparatory to a European security conference, and its standpoint is that of HMG in NATO, rather than HMG alone. It is, however, an important statement of the basis of British policy towards the Soviet Union: whatever efforts might be under way to foster practical and productive bilateral relations, the underlying threat posed to the West by the Soviet Union was never forgotten. It also reflects the central position in policy planning which the prospect of a European security conference continued to occupy.

The Communiqué issued after the NATO Council meeting in December 1970 (see pp. 294-5) defined the circumstances in which NATO members would be ready to embark on multilateral exploratory contacts to prepare a Conference on European Security, and renewed the invitation to interested States to take part in the discussion of mutual and balanced force reductions. It produced a certain amount of probing by Warsaw Pact representatives, which was probably intended both to expose differences among NATO countries about the precise interpretation of the circumstances required before taking the next step towards a Conference, and also to support their propaganda thesis that the position of NATO had hardened. This propaganda was carried a bit further by the short and insubstantial communiqué issued by the Warsaw Pact foreign ministers after their meeting in Bucharest from 18-19 February 1971,[1] though there was no response to the invitation for discussions on mutual and balanced force reductions.

Meanwhile there had been a perceptible shift in FCO views on a possible European Security Conference, encapsulated in a letter of 25 January to Sir E. Peck from Mr. Cable: 'Whereas we once came near to sharing the American attitude that a Conference should be resisted and delayed by every possible device, we have for some time been moving towards the position that, although unlikely to do any good, a Conference is probably inevitable and if properly managed need not be particularly harmful . . . This shift in our attitude has, somewhat paradoxically, coincided with a hardening in our position on mutual and balanced force reductions (MBFR). The more these have been studied, the more convinced we have become that any reductions that could be negotiated would be damaging to the security of Western Europe.' He envisaged a further shift in HMG's position: 'Ministers have long said publicly that a European Security Conference would be no good unless it discussed issues of substance. But many major issues of substance are being discussed in the "on-going" talks, and once an agreement has been reached on Berlin, we may find that the value of a Conference lies not in achieving further progress on matters of substance, but in improving the political atmosphere and in consolidating an agreement or agreements negotiated elsewhere.'

[1] The *Communiqué* is printed in Cmnd. 6932, No. 32. The Warsaw Pact Ministers reaffirmed their support for the idea of early preparatory talks in Helsinki, but drew attention to the fact 'that those circles which are not interested in the deepening of the *détente* in Europe are intensifying the opposition to the convocation of the all-European conference . . . The decisions of the recent NATO Council session in Brussels are directed towards the pursuit of this line and the intensification of the arms race in Europe.' They also stressed the importance of establishing 'equal relations' between the GDR and other States, including the FRG, and that the ending of opposition to the GDR's admission to the UN and other international organisations would 'serve the interests of *détente*'.

Mr. Cable wrote on similar lines on 5 February to Mr. Henderson, copied to other representatives in Eastern Europe. The Ambassador in Warsaw thought that the letter 'exposes some pretty terrific volte-faces', while Mr. Laskey, in Bucharest, found it striking that 'we seem to have moved through 180 degrees in relation to the position we held only a few months ago'. Both pointed to recent statements by Ministers and officials in contradiction to the line set out by Mr. Cable, and Mr. Henderson asked 'What, then is our public stance going to be?', while Mr. Laskey pointed out that the shift in the British position had 'narrowed the gap between ourselves and the Romanians'. Mr. Cable's reply of 23 March, however, insisted that 'the analysis on which our current line is based has changed little since the autumn, though it may have been somewhat refined', although he conceded that the 'evolution in our private thinking . . . can indeed be described, not without justification, as a volte-face compared with our original attitude to the Warsaw Pact proposals of March 1969.' The range of East-West negotiations which had been taking place since then were responsible for the change in HMG's attitude. He stressed that it would not in any case be practical politics for HMG to take in public a line which rejected the idea of an eventual Conference or of discussions about force reductions: 'We want in private to persuade our Allies of the need for caution and clarity, especially in our approach to MBFRs. In public we want to advocate common sense and realism, while not exposing surface unnecessarily and avoiding inconsistencies.'

No. 62

The Brezhnev Doctrine and a European Security Conference[1]

[*WDW 1/1*]

Confidential   UKDEL NATO, BRUSSELS, [*16*] *March 1971*

Purposes of the paper
1. After describing the Brezhnev doctrine, this paper suggests how the Alliance might deal with it during discussions about the principles of international relations at a European security conference.

The nature of the doctrine
2. The Brezhnev doctrine claims in effect that the 'socialist' countries have the right and obligation to intervene, by force if necessary, in a 'socialist' country in order to maintain or restore what they deem to be the achievements of 'socialism'. The doctrine was formally enunciated in 1968 by Brezhnev and others as a justification for the invasion of Czechoslovakia, but the germ of it has already existed in Marxist/Leninist theory for a long time.

---

[1] This paper had been prepared in Western Organisations Department as a contribution to the forthcoming report of NATO's Senior Political Committee (SPC) on East-West negotiations: cf. pp. 294-5. An earlier draft had been sent on 11 February to Sir E. Peck, who suggested a slight amendment and proposed to show the draft to his Belgian colleague and to announce at the next SPC meeting on 25 February that a UK paper on this subject was in preparation. The text of the memorandum printed here is the one circulated to the SPC by UKDEL NATO, apparently on 16 March.

A selection of relevant quotations is attached at Annex A.[2] Some statements of the doctrine have seemed to apply it only within the Warsaw Pact. But Brezhnev's speech in Warsaw on 12 November 1968[3] seemed to apply the doctrine to any 'socialist' state.

3. The use of force under the doctrine outside the Warsaw Pact area could be a major threat to European security. If it happened in Yugoslavia or Albania, it would place Soviet troops on the southern flank of NATO. If it happened in a European country not at present under communist rule, NATO could be faced with a choice of either war or a serious shift in the balance of power, resulting from the deployment of Soviet troops in the NATO area. These dangers are examined further in Annex B.[4]

4. In the West the Brezhnev doctrine has been interpreted as limiting the sovereignty of socialist states in that it is designed to prevent them from reverting to a non-socialist form of government. The Russians have been at pains to deny that limited sovereignty is part of their policy and to pretend that the Brezhnev doctrine is an invention of Western propaganda. Though the phrases 'Brezhnev doctrine' and 'limited sovereignty' are not used by the Soviet authorities, the Soviet statements of the doctrine are nevertheless there for all to see and the Soviet complaints about Western propaganda show that the Russians realise that the doctrine puts them at a disadvantage.

5. The doctrine is an important tenet in the Soviet policy of maintaining hegemony in Eastern Europe. It must be assumed that the Soviet Union will not explicitly retract it nor do anything to weaken its validity. The doctrine will presumably remain on the record after any conference or conferences on European security, whatever the outcome of these. Even if in time the Russians stop re-affirming the doctrine, they will no doubt later resuscitate it if ever they judge it useful in relation to developments in any communist country. One illustration of its intended permanence was its inclusion in the

---

[2] Not printed.

[3] See No. 22, note 2.

[4] Not printed. Para. 4 of Annex B stated: 'If a western European country, whether a member of NATO or a neutral, came under communist rule, there would be a risk of subsequent Soviet intervention, either in order to prevent the ruling Communist Party from adopting a brand of communism unacceptable to Moscow or in order to forestall or reverse the replacement of the communist government by another. NATO could then be faced with a very critical situation. For example, the Russians might try to send troops through a neutral country or over-fly a NATO country without permission. If they sent troops through a neutral country, that country might appeal to members of the Alliance for military support. Important elements, perhaps a majority, within the country threatened by intervention might also appeal to the Alliance. If the Alliance responded to such appeals, war might result. If the Alliance did not respond, its credibility and security would be seriously weakened. If the Soviet intervention was successfully carried out, the Soviet Union would have advanced its forces into western Europe, thus increasing seriously the threat to the Alliance and achieving a major shift in the balance of power. The prospects for successful resistance to future communist threats would have been seriously reduced.'

20-year Treaty of Friendship concluded between the Soviet Union and Czechoslovakia in May 1970[5] (see Annex A).

6. On the other hand, the Russians have often made statements, even since the invasion of Czechoslovakia, which have supported the principle of national sovereignty. The contention is of course based on the unspoken premise that the defence of 'socialist' sovereignty is compatible with, or even superior to, the defence of sovereignty *tout court*. Some statements of this kind are given in Annex C.[2] The Russians have also subscribed to, and put forward, international declarations and other documents which on any normal reading would seem to contradict any notion of limited sovereignty. A notable recent example was the 'Declaration on the Strengthening of International Security' adopted by the UN General Assembly in December 1970.[6] The Russians initiated the idea of such a declaration and voted in favour of the text adopted. Annex D shows how the Russians might seek to reconcile this Declaration with the Brezhnev doctrine.[7]

7. The Soviet position is *prima facie* self-contradictory in that they proclaim a principle contrary to international law but also proclaim their adherence to the principles of international law. They have not attempted seriously to reconcile the two. But in 1970 they revived the theory that the principles of 'socialist internationalism', including the Brezhnev doctrine, are a higher development of inter-state law than the accepted international law governing international relations as a whole. In essence the Soviet position implies that there is a special type of international law among 'socialist' countries and a general type which applies between 'socialist' countries and other countries as well as among those other countries. This is consistent with the Soviet interpretation of 'peaceful co-existence' as applying only between states with differing social systems.

Western treatment of the doctrine in any European security negotiations

8. NATO and the Warsaw Pact have proposed that different aspects of the question of the principles governing relations between states should be discussed at any European security conference. The subject is therefore very likely to be raised in discussion at any conference. In view of the threat posed by the Brezhnev doctrine to the security of any European state which has come under communist rule and of the justified dislike of the doctrine in the

[5] Article V of this Treaty, signed on 6 May 1970, contracted the Soviet Union and Czechoslovakia to 'undertake the necessary measures to protect the socialist achievements of the people'.

[6] See No. 37, note 8, and cf. No. 51.

[7] Annex D argued that 'on any normal reading' the UN Declaration should 'leave no room for the Brezhnev doctrine. Paragraph 1 of the UN Declaration excludes all exceptions from the validity of principles of the UN Charter, which include the principle of sovereignty. The phrase "irrespective of their political, economic and social systems" should mean that the principles of the Charter apply between any two states, whether or not they have the same political, economic and social system . . . This would not, however, deter the Russians from arguing if necessary that the Brezhnev doctrine was compatible with the UN Declaration, still less from applying the doctrine in practice.'

West, some at least of the NATO countries are likely to criticize the doctrine and try to make its future application more difficult and embarrassing for the Russians. The neutral countries, Yugoslavia and Romania may be expected to sympathize at least tacitly with the West on this issue. Some of the other smaller members of the Warsaw Pact, although they will be unable to say so, are likely to welcome the Alliance's efforts against the Brezhnev doctrine.

9. There are broadly four ways in which the Alliance could in theory try to handle the Brezhnev doctrine at a European security conference:

(*a*) to challenge it directly and insist upon its renunciation;

(*b*) to challenge it unmistakably but indirectly, e.g. by stressing that we observe the sovereignty of *all* states whether or not their social system is the same as ours;

(*c*) to put forward a document, as a basis for agreement on principles of international relations, which would specify and emphasize 'the application in practice of the principles' between all states whether or not their social systems are similar. This could be marginally more embarrassing for the Russians in relation to the Brezhnev doctrine than a document referring in the usual way to *respect* for the international principles;

(*d*) to challenge the doctrine only by implication, by insisting that any agreed document on respect for the principles of international relations should refer to the sovereignty of all states.

10. Paragraph 5 above shows that (*a*), despite its attractions, is not a realistic course. The Russians would not renounce the doctrine. Any attempt to make them do so would demonstrate Western inability to influence them on this. It could also poison the negotiations, and thus increase rather than decrease East/West tension in the short term.

11. Option (*d*) is also unsatisfactory. Since the Russians are known to be ready to subscribe to documents such as the UN 'Declaration on the Strengthening of International Security', which seem to go against the doctrine (paragraph 6 above and Annex D), Western adoption of this tactic could be regarded as acquiescence by default in the doctrine. It would be difficult for Western Ministers to defend themselves against public or parliamentary criticism on these lines.

12. This leaves options (*b*) and (*c*), which, pursued together, are likely to provide NATO's best tactics. The Alliance could put forward a draft declaration, emphasising the *application* of the principles of international relations between all states, whether or not their social systems are similar. This could incorporate some language from the Yugoslav documents on European security[8] and other material designed to appeal to European

[8] The reference is to two documents communicated to HMG by the Yugoslav Government on 7 April 1970, described by the Yugoslav Chargé d'Affaires as 'working papers', the first setting out Yugoslav views regarding the problems of European cooperation and security, the second a memorandum on European cooperation. They stressed the desirability of strengthening contacts in Europe and that the non-use of force should be observed between all states, and welcomed the current talks on Germany and Berlin. FCO telegram No. 123 to Belgrade of 13 April 1970

neutral countries and to the smaller members of the Warsaw Pact. It could also include a passage about the freer movement of persons and information between European countries. By putting forward a draft declaration the Allied position would be strengthened in three ways:

(a) the efforts of the Alliance would be shown to be sincere;
(b) the Allied negotiating position on the basis of our own ideas would be reinforced;
(c) our opposition to the Brezhnev doctrine would be made apparent to our public opinion, whatever the result of the negotiations.

13. If the Soviet Union refused to agree to a document on the application of the principles of international relations (option (c)), the Alliance would have little alternative to proceeding with negotiations on the basis of a document which spoke only of respect for principles. It could then reply to any criticism in the West by drawing attention to the statements made in the negotiations by NATO countries under (b). Publicity for such statements would also serve the purpose of drawing world attention to the existence of the doctrine and thus embarrassing the Russians.

14. Western statements of this kind in the negotiations could make good use of the United Nations Charter and other suitable United Nations documents, which stress the sovereign equality of all member states. Articles 2(1) and 2(4) of the Charter, taken with Article 103, leave no room for any doctrine of 'socialist' or other limited sovereignty.[9] Western statements could also make use of the UN 'Declaration on the Strengthening of International Security' (Annex D) and could quote from some of the statements about sovereignty and independence by Soviet and other Warsaw Pact representatives, which on any normal reading are incompatible with limited sovereignty such as the Soviet Yugoslav Declaration of 2 June 1955[10] (see Annex C).

Western tactics during the preparatory period before a conference

15. There are arguments against frequent public references to the Brezhnev doctrine by NATO Ministers before any conference. The principal argument is that Western public opinion might gain the impression that the Alliance expected to be able to use a Conference to kill the doctrine. As is shown by paragraph 5 above, there is no prospect of achieving this. To awaken such hopes might be to cause subsequent disappointment, as well as criticism of NATO's handling of the doctrine at the conference.

16. As a first step the Alliance should perhaps work out guide-lines for handling the doctrine at a conference. It will also be advisable to prepare a

stated that the Yugoslav ideas 'if not dramatic or very constructive, are interesting, and . . . distinctly different from those of the Warsaw Pact' (EN 2/33, 1970).

[9] The Charter is printed in *BFSP*, vol. 145, pp. 805-32.

[10] In this Declaration the two Governments listed the principles upon which their relations would be based, including 'The indivisibility of peace, on which collective security can alone be based', and 'Mutual respect and non-interference in internal affairs for any reason': *BFSP*, vol. 163, pp. 535-39.

draft Declaration on the principles of international relations, on the lines suggested in paragraph 9(c) above, with a view to tabling it during eventual multilateral exploratory talks.

17. During and before such talks, members of the Alliance could point out to European neutral governments (and to the Yugoslav Government, whose dislike of the Brezhnev doctrine is as great as anyone's) that a declaration on the *application* of international principles might make action on the basis of the Brezhnev doctrine marginally more embarrassing to the Russians for a time. NATO's draft of such a declaration could be shown to these neutrals. Consideration should also be given at the time to showing the draft Declaration to members of the Warsaw Pact, with explanations which might vary according to the interests and attitudes of each Pact country. But this might run the risk that information about NATO's approaches would emerge during Warsaw Pact consultations, thus prejudicing NATO's position.

18. If Warsaw Pact representatives should warn members of the Alliance, during or before multilateral exploratory talks, against attempts to undermine the 'special nature' of relations between socialist states, members of the Alliance could deflect this by drawing attention to the purposes and principles of the United Nations, which are valid between all members of the UN and which prevail if they conflict with any other international agreements.[11]

[11] Mr. P.H. Grattan of UKDEL NATO wrote to Mr. Braithwaite on 19 March that the SPC had showed 'warm appreciation' of the UK paper at their meeting on 18 March, the US representative stating that it was 'the best bit of substantial work on the issues involved at a conference which we had seen for some time'. The memorandum was discussed again on 25 March, when it was proposed that NATO's report on relations between states should contain an agreed definition of the Brezhnev doctrine, and the SPC Secretariat undertook to prepare a list of reference documents concerning the principles governing relations between States and the Brezhnev doctrine. The memorandum and its annexes eventually formed the basis for papers drawn up by WOD and EESD on the strategy and tactics which HMG should adopt during the preparation for a European security conference, and at the conference itself: see Volume II, No. 1.

The next document reflects the increasing concern of the British, and other governments about the growing Soviet naval presence in the Indian Ocean. Although the Anglo-American agreement on the Diego Garcia communications centre (see p. 263) had been severely criticised at the Commonwealth Heads of Government Meeting held in Singapore from 14-22 January 1971, when a number of Commonwealth leaders had expressed concern as to what use the base might be put in future—the Indian Minister of State for Home Affairs, Mr. Mirdha, had asked 'why Britain now wished to start on a policy of confrontation and cold war in the Indian Ocean'—it was clear that a number of countries were worried by the introduction of Great Power naval rivalry into the area, especially in view of the conflicts in South-East Asia, the Middle East and southern Africa. Mrs. Bandaranaike, Prime Minister of Ceylon, had proposed that the Indian Ocean should be both a peace zone and a nuclear free zone. Sir A. Douglas-Home defended British policy, pointing out that while British forces and bases in the area had been reduced, and the number of US bases remained static, Soviet strength was increasing: and reminded the meeting that the Soviet Chief of Naval Staff had said that the 'next war with the imperialists would not occur in warm coastal waters, but in oceans far from the Soviet Union'. In February it was announced that an additional British frigate would be deployed East of Suez after 1971.

Tension in the region was increased by an insurrection of left-wing rebels in Ceylon beginning on 6 March, which led Mrs. Bandaranaike to appeal for help to India, the UK and US, and then, under pressure from Communist members of her Cabinet, to the Soviet Union. The UK supplied helicopters, arms and ammunition: the Soviet Union MiG fighters, pilots and ground personnel. The FCO were concerned at the possible extension of Soviet influence and believed that the defeat of the insurgent movement would be slow, the economic cost heavy and the long-term political repercussions profound.

Mr. Heath expressed publicly his concern over the Soviet presence in the Indian Ocean on a number of occasions, including in the House of Commons on 2 March when he said that the Soviet Union was 'playing cat and mouse with the Americans in the Caribbean at this moment. They can at any time use the same tactics to menace or threaten traffic in the Indian Ocean.' Sir D. Wilson's assessment of the Soviet threat, printed as No. 63 below, was made in response to the Prime Minister's request noted in No. 60, note 17.

No. 63

Minute by Sir D. Wilson on the Soviet Naval Threat[1]

[*ENS 2/2*]

Confidential   MOSCOW, *29 March 1971*

This minute attempts to assess the significance of the recent increase in Soviet naval power in the Mediterranean and the Indian Ocean; the degree to which this development represents an actual or potential threat to British interests: and the courses open to Her Majesty's Government, as seen from Moscow, to deal with this threat.

Significance of increased Soviet naval power

2. The increased Soviet naval presence in the Mediterranean and the Indian Ocean is a recent development, but it must have been planned and

---

[1] Sir D. Wilson sent this minute to Sir D. Greenhill on 29 March, commenting: 'I am conscious that there are many in London who are better equipped and qualified than I to assess almost any single aspect of this complex subject; and that my own view from Moscow of the general nature of the risks involved is as arguable as anyone else's . . . My main concern is that, by reacting publicly to the Soviet threat in the way that we have [cf. p. 263], we may be in danger of increasing the political risk rather than diminishing it.' He also noted that he had received advice on the minute from Mr. Cradock, who was then in Moscow: see No. 60, note 16.

budgeted for several years ago.[2] Two conclusions can be drawn from this assumption:

(*a*) The motives behind this development are long-term and strategic ones, even if the Middle Eastern crises of the last four years have facilitated and hastened it;

(*b*) Resources currently available for naval expansion and the maintenance of naval deployments are not necessarily commensurate with the plans originally made.

3. The programme of increased Soviet naval deployment is presumably part of a general policy of enhancing Soviet capability to act as a superpower on the world stage by being able, and being seen to be able, to influence events, or to counter US influence on events, in every part of the world in accordance with Soviet interests. In particular the Soviet naval programme should be seen as part of the general Soviet strategic programme, and as a response to the presence of the American Sixth Fleet in the Mediterranean and of American nuclear submarines in the Indian Ocean;[3] the Soviet authorities must regard the former in particular, which is comparatively near to their Black Sea frontier, as a threat to Soviet interests. The Soviet naval programme will thus have a high priority in claims on Soviet resources, but there must also be many other high-priority military claims (Chinese border, Middle East and Europe).

[2] Cf. No. 22, note 7, No. 31 and pp. 206-7. On 24 March Mr. Barrington had sent to Mr. Moon, as an initial response to Prime Minister's expressed interest in this subject, a Planning Staff paper of February 1971 on the *Political Aims and Implications of Soviet Global Naval and Maritime Expansion*, which stated that in 1970 the Soviet naval presence in the Mediterranean had peaked at 30 combatant ships and 10 submarines and posed a continuing strategic and political threat to Western interests. Soviet naval units had begun to appear in significant numbers in the Indian Ocean in 1967, and had reached a level in 1970 of 11 combatant ships (including 4 submarines), which constituted 'the most effective naval force in the area'.

The paper noted that there were good military reasons for Soviet naval expansion, as until the mid-1960s US had far outweighed Soviet naval power, but the Soviet Union also sought political gains: 'They cannot be defined with any great certainty or precision, but it seems probable that they include the intention to undermine Western influence in the Persian Gulf and the Southern parts of the Arab world; to gain a greater influence over Indian policy and actions; to check Chinese influence in Africa; to encourage the formation of friendly governments in strategically situated countries such as Mauritius and Somalia; to acquire naval and air facilities in the Indian Ocean area; and possibly to undermine the credibility of Five Power defence arrangements in South-East Asia. While the deployment of naval forces will not in itself provide the means of achieving these ends, they will make an important contribution to the Soviet's overall political capabilities in the area.'

[3] The immediately preceding phrase was deleted from the version of this minute sent to Mr. Heath on the recommendation of Mr. Mallaby, who pointed out on 6 April that 'it could be misleading since no US submarines are stationed in the Indian Ocean'. Mr. R.M. Tesh (Defence Department) agreed: 'it is neither necessary nor easy for American nuclear missile submarines to deploy in the Indian Ocean given that they can perform most of their tasks against the USSR from other and less distant seas' (6 April).

4. Soviet naval policy is also inspired to some extent simply by the desire to show the flag. In an article on the subject of the Ark Royal collision in November 1970[4] the Soviet army newspaper *Red Star* wrote: 'Soviet ships have sailed and will continue to sail in the international waters of the world's oceans: and no one dares hinder them in this.' This exemplifies the mood in which many Russians view Western protests about their increased naval presence. They argue that their ships, including warships, have as much right as the Americans' or our own to sail the Mediterranean or Indian Ocean, if only for the benefit of their growing merchant fleet.

The threat to British interests

5. We are faced with the special combined effect of increased Soviet naval strength (for whatever purpose this is designed), the particular vulnerability of our sea-routes, and general Soviet hostility. Given the nature of Soviet policies for the foreseeable future, even a limited Soviet naval presence in the Indian Ocean and the Mediterranean clearly represents a potential direct threat to British interests. In time of war or in conditions of major East/West tension this threat could be formidable, but on the assumption that the Soviet Union will continue to seek to avoid a major confrontation with the West it is difficult to believe that British merchant shipping, naval and port facilities or commercial interests will be, so to speak, at separate and particular risk: and even in times of crisis the vulnerability of the Soviet fleet will place limits on its directly hostile activities.

6. The very presence of the Soviet fleet, however, as distinct from any use to which the Russians may put it, can in itself be potentially damaging to British interests in two ways. It advertises the increasing power of the Soviet Union and the Russians may thereby hope to influence the policies of non-aligned countries in a direction unfavourable to the West. They may also hope that it will provoke reactions by the British Government which will in turn have an adverse effect on our relations with those countries and thus provide opportunities for further increase of Soviet influence.

7. In normal peacetime conditions therefore, or even in cases of local conflicts, the threat from the Soviet fleet seems likely to be political or politico-military rather than purely military. It therefore seems likely to be counter-productive if our efforts to counter it seriously increase our political difficulties and the possibilities of effective arrangements for regional defence cooperation in the areas concerned.

Conclusion

8. The Western response to the Soviet naval threat must, like the threat itself, have both military and political aspects. In taking such military countermeasures as we (the Western alliance) can, and (so far as Britain is concerned) in explaining and justifying these measures in public statements, we should seek to ensure that we do not thereby increase the political threat. This is not so much a matter of refraining from actions or statements which might harm Anglo-Soviet relations, though it would of course be desirable to

[4] See No. 56.

do this if possible. It is more important that our military and political efforts to counter the threat should be coordinated in such a way as to minimise certain alternative risks. These are that by advertising the Soviet naval presence, we may magnify Soviet power in Afro-Asian eyes, and so increase Soviet influence. Alternatively, there is the danger that, if the Soviet naval presence is not over-visible, Western defence responses will be misrepresented as contributing to a cold-war atmosphere and will thus again bring about an increase in Soviet influence and a reduction in British influence in the countries of the area. We cannot make the threat go away; we can certainly take steps to counter it militarily, though the degree to which we can do so is clearly limited by the resources available; but it may be open to us, by careful planning of our public responses, to do much to neutralise its political effects.[5]

[5] Mr. Barrington sent a copy of this minute to Mr. Moon on 8 April, commenting: 'we should like to make the obvious point that, apart from the factors mentioned in the Ambassador's conclusion, there are others to be borne in mind, such as the need to bring home to regional countries the dangers of a Soviet presence in their areas and to explain our defence expenditure to British public opinion.'

The Communist Party of the Soviet Union had been consolidating its own position during the 24th Party Congress held from 30 March to 9 April. According to a note by the Joint Intelligence Committee, the tone of the Congress was sober, moderate and confident: there were no grandiose promises about the early achievement of full communism in the USSR or overtaking the USA economically or the quick spread of communism to new countries. Mr. Brezhnev's Central Committee report, which opened the Congress, stated the aims of Soviet foreign policy, featuring 'peaceful co-existence', in established terms. He frequently referred to the threat of imperialism and the Soviet Union's military strength, made the usual assertion that 'the total triumph of socialism all over the world is inevitable', and gave the usual warning that others should not try to deal with the Soviet Union from positions of strength'. However, he gave these themes, and also ideology in general, less emphasis than might have been expected on a major Party occasion, while he repeatedly dwelt on the theme of peace. On the other hand, the speech contained no indication that Soviet foreign policy would alter in any way.

Mr. Brezhnev paid most attention to the world communist movement, clearly implying the continuing validity of the doctrine of limited sovereignty (cf. No. 62): in contrast with previous speeches, he did not pay lip service, in his passage on bloc affairs, to the principles of sovereignty and non-interference. His speech also contained sections on China, disarmament, the Middle East, Indo-China, European security and East-West relations, with customary references to the constant readiness and first-class equipment of the Soviet armed forces, but no speaker at the Congress mentioned Anglo-Soviet relations. Mr. Brezhnev made two brief and critical remarks about Northern Ireland and industrial unrest in Britain, and complained about the 'imperialist myth of a Soviet threat' with reference to the Indian Ocean (No. 63). Mr. Kosygin's speech, too, was by implication slighting towards the UK by failing to mention Britain in a list of countries with which there was a tendency for the Soviet Union to conclude long-term agreements covering various aspects of economic relations.

Mr. Smirnovsky had attended the Congress, and on his return asked to see the Secretary of State, who was interested to hear from him Mr. Gromyko's views on a range of topics, particularly the Berlin negotiations (see No. 64, note 3 below). The record of their conversation on 4 May, though containing no new or startling insights, is a useful tour d'horizon of the respective British and Soviet views on international questions of mutual interest.

No. 64

Record of conversation between Sir A. Douglas-Home and the Soviet Ambassador in the Foreign & Commonwealth Office on Tuesday, 4 May 1971 at 4.45 p.m.

[*ENS 3/548/1*]

Confidential

Present:

The Rt. Hon Sir A. Douglas-Home, MP   HE Mr. M.N. Smirnovsky
Mr. J.A.N. Graham   Mr. A.M. Vavilov
Mr. J.L. Bullard

Soviet Party Congress

1. *Mr. Smirnovsky* said that the main topic had been internal affairs, particularly the Five Year Plan, but a great deal of attention had been devoted to foreign policy also. He wished to draw attention to the tasks of Soviet foreign policy which had been announced for the next five years. These included:

(*a*) the elimination of conflicts in South East Asia and the Middle East on the basis of respect for the rights of all nations living in the area.

(*b*) Renunciation of the use of force in the settlement of various questions; the Soviet Union was prepared to negotiate bilaterally or multilaterally with other countries which shared this approach.

(*c*) The final recognition of territorial changes resulting from the Second World War.

(*d*) The promotion of peace and *détente* on the continent of Europe, in which connection the Soviet Government attached great importance to the holding of a European Security Conference.

(*e*) Measures for disarmament, e.g. steps towards banning nuclear, bacteriological and chemical weapons; a conference of the five nuclear

powers to ban nuclear weapons; reduction of armed forces and armaments in areas where armed conflict would be of special danger, above all
in central Europe; measures to prevent surprise attack; and negotiated
agreements on reducing military expenditure, first of all by the major
powers.

2. In general, Mr. Smirnovsky said, the Soviet Government was prepared
to expand and deepen its relations with every state willing to reciprocate.
They would cooperate in work on conservation, the environment, the use of
power and natural resources, transport and communications, diseases and
outer space. He looked forward to an exchange of views on some of the
points which he had mentioned.

The Middle East

3. Mr. Smirnovsky said the Soviet side thought that the official talks on 2
April had been helpful.[1] He understood this was also the British view. He
asked what were the latest British impressions in the light of Mr. Rogers's
visit.[2]

4. *Sir Alec Douglas-Home* confirmed that the official talks had been useful.
From time to time we should consider exchanging views further. There was
much more interest on both the Arab and Israeli sides in the idea of an
interim arrangement between Israel and Egypt than he had expected. He
could not say more on this until we saw how Mr. Rogers's tour of the Middle
East went. How far would Egypt press her insistence that an interim
arrangement must be part of a total solution? On the other hand, could

[1] On 19 March Mr. Smirnovsky had told Sir A. Douglas-Home that the latter's Harrogate
speech (see No. 54, note 13) had been appreciated in Moscow and that the Soviet authorities
agreed with the remarks in Mr. Heath's reply to Mr. Kosygin (No. 61, note 11) about the need to
coordinate more closely efforts for a settlement. The Ambassador suggested that Mr. Sytenko
should visit London for discussions on the Middle East. Mr. A.D. Parsons, Assistant Under
Secretary superintending Near Eastern and North African Departments, held talks with Mr.
Sytenko on 2 April, when they agreed that a limited arrangement based on the Suez Canal
offered the best means of reaching a package deal for an eventual comprehensive settlement. Mr.
Parsons pressed Mr. Sytenko on what guarantees the Four Powers could offer Israel, but Mr.
Sytenko refused to discuss guarantees and reiterated Soviet complaints about Israeli aggression
and American obstructionism, stressing the need to take active steps towards peace: 'We could
not let the Americans and the Israelis boil the eggs by themselves.' Reporting the talks to Sir D.
Wilson on 8 April, Mr. Parsons commented that 'A combination of genuine concern at the
possible future development of the situation in ways which could damage their position in the
area and a desire to get back in on the peace-making act, from which the Americans have so
unceremoniously excluded them, seem to provide the most plausible explanation of current Soviet
attitudes' (NEM 2/23).

[2] The US Secretary of State had visited London from 26-28 April for the SEATO
Ministerial Council meeting. On 27 April he had two conversations with Sir A. Douglas-Home
during which they discussed the Arab-Israeli conflict, the Persian Gulf, EEC negotiations,
Ceylon, Pakistan and China. Mr. Rogers said that the US was embarrassed by the failure of
Israel to respond positively to Dr. Jarring's approach (see No. 61, note 11), while the Egyptians
'had said yes to questions to which they had never responded affirmatively before'. He had
appealed to the Israelis 'not to say just "no"'; the present state of affairs could 'lead to a major
confrontation between Israel and the United States'.

Israel ever accept this? The Four Powers should continue to keep themselves at Jarring's disposal, but not much could happen in this forum so long as the interim arrangement was being discussed. If this was agreed by the two sides, presumably nobody else would object. But this was far from certain. What was the Soviet view of an interim arrangement on the Canal? *Mr. Smirnovsky* replied that the Soviet Government supported the Egyptian view. Meanwhile it seemed that nothing had changed in Israel's position. *Sir A. Douglas-Home* said that there had been one change: Israel was now contemplating the possibility of some withdrawal from her very strong tactical position along the Canal to a line to be agreed further back.

Berlin[3]

5. *Mr. Smirnovsky* said that Mr. Gromyko's statements in London in October[4] were still valid. We should work within the framework of allied agreements and decisions and nobody should seek unilateral advantages. The sovereign rights of all states should be respected, including those of the GDR. He thought that in their latest proposals the Soviet Government had taken account of all the West's wishes. They had made a substantial step and had met these wishes half-way. In the Soviet proposals nobody's rights or interests were infringed. All conditions were provided for civilian travel without restriction, and for travel by West Berlin citizens to the GDR. The Soviet Government had made a big step forward in agreeing that the FRG could assume some consular representation of the interests of West Berlin citizens, provided they did not become citizens of the FRG.[5] The Soviet proposals were very reasonable. What was now holding things up?

6. *Sir A. Douglas-Home* said the Soviet insistence that the GDR must originate the thinking on access and the Allies merely endorse it seemed to us to push the claims of East Germany too far and to diminish the position of the Allies. It should be the Four Powers who agreed on improvements to

---

[3] Cf. No. 59, note 4. Quadripartite Ambassadorial meetings had been held on 19 January, 8 and 18 February, 9 and 26 March and 16 April, but the atmosphere at the first three meetings had been soured by recent harassment of civilian and Allied military traffic on the *Autobahn* to West Berlin, and little progress had been made. On 5 February France, the UK and US had put forward a draft Agreement which Mr. Abrasimov said he regarded as 'something of a maximal demand made for tactical reasons', and by the meeting on 9 March the Russians had 'showed no readiness to move on any point of substance (Berlin telegrams 41 and 68, WRL 2 / 1). A Soviet counter-draft was tabled on 26 March which was described in the brief prepared for Sir A. Douglas-Home for his meeting with Mr. Smirnovsky as 'a deliberate attempt to erode the Western position. It seeks to limit the scope of the agreement to the western sectors of Berlin. And it pushes the claims of East Germany. We are prepared to negotiate patiently for as long as is necessary to get an agreement; but we want the agreement to be a good one' (WRL 2 / 13). The next Ambassadors' meeting was scheduled for 7 May.

[4] See No. 53.

[5] A note on 'Some Objectionable Elements in Soviet Draft Berlin Agreement' attached to the brief for Sir A. Douglas-Home (see note 3) described the formulation concerning representation abroad by the FRG as 'severely circumscribed', and pointed out that the Soviet draft contained 'undertakings about Soviet interests in the Western sectors [of Berlin], and in particular the establishment of a Soviet Consulate-General and Soviet foreign trade and similar offices'.

give the Berliners a more normal and relaxed life. We did not wish to alter the status and authority of the Allies. We could certainly find out what the East and West Germans respectively wanted, but we should take the initiative and keep the Four Power machinery in being. Was it the Soviet intention to increase the power of the GDR?

7. *Mr. Smirnovsky* denied this, but said that the GDR was there. It had been dealing with such matters for many years. During Mr. Gromyko's visit it had been understood that there should be two agreements, a four power agreement in principle, and an intra-German agreement on practical matters. The Soviet Government had given the East Germans the right to control civilian access as long ago as 1955. It would be enough if the Four Powers agreed on a document in which the Soviet Government declared to the other three governments that they had obtained the agreement of the GDR to such and such measures.

8. *Sir A. Douglas-Home* said that unless the Allies were to be put in a position of simply waiting for the East Germans the Four Powers must agree not only in principle but largely in fact also. We must agree on the broad lines of what improved access should mean. The Four Powers must retain the right to say no. Would the Soviet Government agree if we said that we must accept whatever the FRG asked for by way of a Federal German presence in West Berlin?

9. *Mr. Smirnovsky* replied that the cases were different. West Berlin was on the territory of the GDR and access to it had been controlled by the GDR since 1955. The Federal Republic had no rights in West Berlin.

10. *Sir A. Douglas-Home* said that the Federal Republic had been active in West Berlin for many years. We would rather make up our own minds on these matters.

11. *Mr. Smirnovsky* said that the Soviet Government was asking the GDR to make things easier, not harder. Probably the East Germans were not anxious to do all these things, but the Soviet Government was asking them to cooperate. This was not an attempt to infringe anybody's interests. We were dealing with a very unusual situation and we must operate within the framework of realities.

12. *Sir A. Douglas-Home* said he would like to think over what Mr. Smirnovsky had said.

Hess[6]

13. Sir A. Douglas-Home said that there was quite a lot of parliamentary interest accumulating in this case.[7] It was reasonable that Hess should be

[6] Rudolf Hess, Reich Minister without Portfolio and Deputy to Hitler 1933-41, had been sentenced in 1946 by the Nuremberg War Crimes Tribunal to life imprisonment in Spandau Prison, Berlin: cf. *DBPO*, Series I, Volume V, Nos. 8 and 88. Four Power agreement was required to change his place of imprisonment or release him. HMG had made an unsuccessful appeal to the Soviet Government in February 1970 on behalf of the three Western Governments for his release on humanitarian grounds.

[7] Mr. Airey Neave, MP had met Mr. Royle on 15 January 1971 and impressed upon him parliamentary concern at Hess's continuing imprisonment. Mr. Royle, and subsequently Sir A.

allowed to live the last few years of his life with his family. He had been in various prisons for 30 years, longer than was normal under Soviet or most other laws. Humanity required that he should now be released. He asked the Ambassador to convey to Mr. Gromyko that these were his feelings.

European Security Conference

14. Mr. *Smirnovsky* said that in the Soviet view it was time to begin preparation of this conference. Sir A. *Douglas-Home* replied that everything depended on Berlin.[8] If an arrangement could be arrived at on Berlin, Chancellor Brandt could ratify the two treaties[9] and we could then start preparing a meeting on other things. Some of the points which the Ambassador had mentioned were very interesting. But if we could not settle the problem of access to Berlin we should not be able to settle anything else. It would be no use simply to set up another piece of machinery.

South East Asia

15. Sir A. Douglas-Home asked whether there had been any progress on the Soviet side towards reconvening the Geneva Conference. Mr. *Smirnovsky* replied that the Soviet approach was still the same. What news had Mr. Rogers brought? Sir A. *Douglas-Home* said that the US withdrawal was going ahead.[10] The Americans thought that South Vietnam was now strong enough to stand on her own feet, with some US support in arms.

16. Mr. *Smirnovsky* asked why Washington did not name a date for final withdrawal. This would change the whole picture. Sir A. *Douglas-Home* asked whether North Vietnam would name a date for withdrawal from Laos and Cambodia. Why should not negotiations be started to fix dates for the withdrawal of all foreign forces from all three countries? Clearly neither side

Douglas-Home, agreed that Mr. Smirnovsky should be approached about the matter at a suitable opportunity, although the reply was almost certain to be negative (WRL 14/ 2).

[8] In a minute of 26 April to Mr. Wiggin (appointed Assistant Under Secretary in March 1971,) Lord Bridges, who had now returned from Moscow to succeed Mr. Wiggin as Head of WOD, noted that according to Sir E. Peck 'some members of the Alliance may want to abandon the "Berlin pre-condition" in NATO's December *Communiqué* if it seems that breakdown in the Berlin talks might endanger the holding of a European Security Conference . . . our general line on the European Security Conference is that we should not take the lead in promoting or opposing it at present, and that we should take full account of the views of our most important Allies, and particularly the Germans, whose national interests are most directly involved . . . the main thing would seem to be to avoid being too categorical in our attitudes, so that we could modify them if events or a change in the opinion of our Allies make this seem desirable' (WDW 1/ 1). Mr. Wiggin agreed that guidance on these lines should be sent to the posts concerned.

[9] i.e. the Soviet-FRG and Polish-FRG treaties: see Nos. 50, note 3 and 52, note 5.

[10] On 8 February South Vietnamese forces, supported by US air strikes, had crossed into Laos to try and cut the North Vietnamese supply lines, the 'Ho Chi Minh' trail. These troops withdrew in March after limited success. On 7 April President Nixon announced a withdrawal of 100,000 US troops, leaving a ceiling of 184,000 by 1 December (*Public Papers: Nixon, 1971*, pp. 522-7). Commenting on the President's speech Mr. J.O. Moreton, HM Ambassador in Saigon, said in a despatch of 12 July: 'President Nixon declared "tonight I can report that Vietnamisation has succeeded". If he had used the present tense I would not disagree. Vietnamisation *is* succeeding; but it has not yet done so' (FAV 10/ 6).

would be willing to give a final date unless the other did so. *Mr. Smirnovsky* said that the whole problem was one of US involvement. *Sir A. Douglas-Home* asked why the Soviet Government did not help to get the Americans out by means of a conference. But Washington would want to know that the North Vietnamese were going to leave also. He thought the Geneva conception was right. This had been the object in 1954 and again in 1962. On the second occasion the peace review procedure had been insufficient; it did not get the North Vietnamese or the Americans out. But everybody was now fed up with this war. Why should we not work out a programme of withdrawal at a conference?

17. *Mr. Smirnovsky* said that if and when the US would name a date for their own final withdrawal, this could be discussed. He recalled that it had been agreed in 1956 to hold free elections throughout Vietnam, but these had been prevented by the US. The Vietnamese had been fighting for almost two generations. *Sir A. Douglas-Home* said that they could end it so easily. He believed the US would undertake a phased and dated withdrawal, but only if the North Vietnamese agreed to do the same. He knew that Mr. Gromyko thought otherwise, but he could not understand why. He personally saw no other way. He was not wedded to the Geneva pattern but the machinery of co-chairmanship existed. He asked the Ambassador to inform Mr. Gromyko that these were his views.

The next document is included as a revealing snapshot of the Anglo-Soviet relationship in the cultural sphere at a time when Soviet artists, writers and musicians felt harshly treated by their native bureaucracy. The formal expression of the cultural relationship had been confirmed with the signature on 2 March 1971 of a new Cultural Agreement for 1971-73, following a very short period of negotiation (3 days) which reflected the comparatively few changes made to the existing Agreement (see No. 29). Lord Lothian, Parliamentary Under Secretary of State, led the British delegation, referring in his opening speech to HMG's interest in an 'open door' policy on cultural and information matters, and their wish to see more Russian tourists in Britain, more British papers on sale and more British cultural manifestations in the Soviet Union. He referred in particular to the forthcoming 'Days of British Music', described in detail below by Sir D. Wilson.

No. 65

Sir D. Wilson (Moscow) to Sir A. Douglas-Home

CU 66/2 [PW 7/303/2]

Confidential   MOSCOW, *7 May 1971*

Summary . . . [1]

Sir,

'Days of British Music' in the Soviet Union

This was the first major British cultural event in the Soviet Union since 1967, and took place from the 14th to the 23rd of April. The main participants were the London Symphony Orchestra (on their way to Japan), conducted by André Previn and Benjamin Britten, the Allegri Quartet, John Lill, Noel Rawsthorne and Peter Pears. The orchestral concerts were confined to Leningrad and Moscow, but the soloists went as far afield as Tashkent, Dagestan and the Baltic Republics. A full account of their programmes and movements, compiled by the Cultural Section of this Embassy, is attached.[2]

2. The 'Days of British Music', first discussed between the Soviet Minister of Culture, Madame Furtseva, and myself on the 15th of June 1970,[3] fell into a pattern familiar to the Soviet authorities. Similar French and Italian 'Days' have taken place in the course of last winter. In effect however the British 'Days' have been on a larger scale and have made a more considerable impact for many reasons—the presence of a full-scale and first-class orchestra, and of such notable composers as Sir William Walton and Benjamin Britten, the active participation of Benjamin Britten and Peter Pears, and not least the performance of Britten's works at 'British' concerts by Sviatoslav Richter and Mstislav Rostropovich.

3. So far as I myself and my staff were able to witness and hear them, the performances in Leningrad and Moscow were a triumphant success although the opening concert by the London Symphony Orchestra in Leningrad was received with some reserve because of the unfamiliarity of the music. For the concerts of Britten's works performed by Richter and Rostropovich and

---

[1] Not here printed.

[2] Not printed.

[3] A proposal by the British Council and the impresario Victor Hochhauser for a festival of British music in the Soviet Union, to which the Russians agreed to give official support provided they were given reciprocity in London, received FCO Ministerial approval in April 1970. Sir D. Wilson called on Madame Furtseva on 15 June to enlist her official support for the proposal: she made it clear that 'there were certain "customs" regarding the presentation of the arts in the Soviet Union and she hoped, therefore, that we would only send worthy examples of British music'. When the Ambassador assured her that Benjamin Britten would figure prominently in the programme and that there would be 'no problems in this case about "extremism"', she remarked that 'it was not by chance that the great composers Britten and Shostakovich had such close personal links' and indicated that she 'foresaw no difficulties in arranging the "Festival" as far as the Ministry of Culture was concerned' (PWS 4/4 of 1970).

conducted by himself, the halls were desperately over-crowded and the police cordons outside suggested the Beatles at the height of their popularity rather than a concert largely devoted to 20th century music. An expert estimate given to me in Leningrad suggested that there were four thousand people packed into a hall that is not meant to accommodate more than two thousand. This may well be an exaggeration, but both in Leningrad and Moscow the concerts were being observed (listening could hardly have been possible) from a height by students who had climbed on to the roof of the hall. We were particularly happy to see in Leningrad that Walton, who was in some danger of being overshadowed by Britten (to the latter's own evident distress) was given a tremendous ovation after the performance of his First Symphony. A similar success attended his concert in Moscow, the last of the series, where he was in danger of being mobbed by well-wishers and autograph-seekers. It was a moving tribute both to his music and to the splendid and spirited playing of the orchestra.

4. As far as the other concerts were concerned Noel Rawsthorne's two organ recitals were well received and the Allegri's playing was very favourably commented on in the Leningrad press. John Lill, who gave two solo recitals in Moscow and one in Leningrad, was desperately tired and rather nervous on his first appearance in Moscow since winning the Tchaikovsky competition last year. Some tension was thus apparent in his opening recital. His second performance, however, was rewarded with prolonged applause and he was equally successful in Leningrad.

5. In general it must be said that the Soviet authorities, as well as Soviet musicians and the Soviet public, received our musicians warmly and did all that could have been required of them, with the exception of certain incidents noted below. In Leningrad, the Mayor, after first refusing the tickets which we had offered him for Britten's concert, in the end turned up with his daughters and paid a lot of attention to us. In Moscow the first orchestral concert (again Britten's) was attended by Madame Furtseva together with a large retinue from the Ministry of Culture, and the Vice-Minister of Foreign Affairs, Kozyrev, and his wife. I gave a reception after this for the whole orchestra and other members of the British party. This was well attended by Soviet officials and musicians, including Richter and Rostropovich. Madame Furtseva attended a large formal lunch at this Embassy on the 23rd of April and gave a buffet lunch herself on the 24th of April for larger numbers in the Palace of Congresses (this must have been the first case in the Soviet Union when the guests were still hungry when they left). In both cases she made eloquent speeches, was at pains to be pleasant all round, and was profuse in full frontal kisses to Benjamin Britten. The 'Days' were rounded off by a notable event outside the regular programme—a house concert in this Embassy by Pears and Britten, given at their own suggestion on the 24th of April to a select audience, including virtually no Soviet cultural officials (though a decent minimum had been asked), a few Ambassadors, members of this Embassy, a large number of young Soviet musicians, and such established stars as Shostakovich, Richter, Barshai, Plisetskaya, Timofeeva and

Liepa. Even the representatives of the French Embassy, who are more accustomed than ourselves to such manifestations, could hardly forbear a cheer at the quality of the attendance. This was a tribute to Britten and Pears who responded by making it into a musically unforgettable occasion.

6. The whole event can thus be reckoned as a success from the point of view of artistic and general prestige. Even though press coverage was disappointingly small, particularly in Moscow, the concerts, and especially those of the London Symphony Orchestra, made a big general impact. One had only to see the rows of cars outside the Moscow Conservatory on the 20th of April and the jewels inside (in both cases Soviet) to realise that the event was not simply one of musical importance. The most important effect of the 'Days of British Music' was however to contribute to the wider appreciation in the Soviet Union of contemporary British music and musical standards.

7. On the administrative side there was that large amount of tedious preparatory work which is usual in any dealings with Goskoncert, the Soviet official agency concerned with musical exchanges. There were also the usual number of administrative headaches and crises on the spot, once the tour had started. On the whole, the Soviet authorities were helpful in solving these (as well as being responsible for causing many of them) and I am particularly grateful to Mr. Field and Mr. Jackson, who constitute the Cultural Section of this Embassy, for their hard work in sorting out the various problems both before and during the LSO's tour.

8. The 'Days of British Music' involved another and political dimension, which added to the problems, but also, I think, to the success. This dimension resulted from the prominent part played by Benjamin Britten in the concerts, from his very special relationship with the great cellist Mstislav Rostropovich and (to a much lesser extent) from our own relationship with both. From the beginning of negotiations last summer it was fairly clear that Britten would only come to the USSR if Rostropovich and Richter were allowed to perform at his concerts, and that, in view of Rostropovich's protection of Solzhenitsyn, this would be unwelcome to the Ministry of Culture (though the Minister did not commit herself against the possibility when I first raised it with her in general terms). In the course of the summer and early autumn the official climate in relation to Rostropovich became colder, and Britten cancelled a separate visit with the English Chamber Orchestra, owing to the need for a minor operation. The musical world in Moscow regarded this as a political gesture—minor operations, it was felt, can usually be postponed if other factors are favourable. At the end of October, on the eve of a visit abroad, Rostropovich addressed his famous letter to *Pravda* about the Soviet authorities' attitude to the award of a Nobel prize to Solzhenitsyn.[4] From that point on it seemed likely that, at anything but the highest level, every

---

[4] The letter, criticising the Soviet authorities for their attitude to Solzhenitsyn and other Soviet writers and musicians, was not published in the Soviet press. Rostropovich was banned from performing outside the Soviet Union for six months from January 1971 as a punishment for assuming the role of Solzhenitsyn's protector.

possible obstacle would be put in the way of participation by Rostropovich (and of any other Soviet artists) in any British musical event here, and that Britten might therefore not feel able to participate himself.

9. For some time it appeared to us here, after consultation with Mr. and Mrs. Hochhauser, that the best hope of arranging a programme to include the Soviet stars was to go ahead quietly without mentioning any awkward names on the assumption that Britten would come, to hope that the Soviet official attitude to Rostropovich would soften with the passage of time, and to leave scope and time for him himself to exercise his remarkable powers of persuasion on Madame Furtseva. I obtained Britten's own agreement to these tactics last January. In the event however it proved unnecessary to employ such a devious approach. To our surprise, at their round of talks with Mr. Hochhauser in early February, Goskoncert were in comparatively forthcoming mood and showed that their main object was to bargain for a Festival of Soviet Music in Britain in the fairly near future. In this new climate we thought it best to negotiate immediately and specifically for participation by Richter and Rostropovich in our own 'Days of British Music' and came up against no veto. So (though this is by no means the end of the story of preliminary negotiations) concerts went ahead according to the programme originally envisaged.

10. This is not to say however that the political dimension of Britten's concert with Richter and Rostropovich playing the solo parts in his early piano concerto and late cello Symphony was not made very apparent on the spot. In Leningrad the concert marked the end of a long boycott by Rostropovich himself, who had quarrelled bitterly with Mravinsky, Chief Conductor of the Leningrad Philharmonic Orchestra about the latter's attitude to Shostakovich, and for over five years had made no 'official' solo appearance in Leningrad. Britten told me that, on this occasion of Rostropovich's eventual re-appearance the tension in his performance was remarkable and disturbing, but it earned him a tremendous ovation. In Moscow the corresponding concert ended with a similar ovation, deserved on purely musical grounds, but no doubt accorded with Rostropovich's political record also in mind. The occasion however did not pass off without unpleasantness. It was marked, as I have already mentioned, by the presence of Madame Furtseva and a considerable retinue. Furtseva went backstage to greet Britten before the concert and did her best to see him in the interval, when she had to content herself with making much of Richter and his wife, who received her attentions with apparent enthusiasm. Her behaviour towards my wife and myself in the meantime had been just correct but no more. During Rostropovich's performance of the Britten cello symphony she put on a conspicuous display of boredom, conversing with her staff in the row behind her and with her neighbour on her right (an unpleasant lady-spy from Goskoncert). At the end of the performance, she left without waiting for the applause to reach its climax and took Vice-Minister Kozyrev and his reluctant wife with her (Kozyrev had been pleasant enough throughout, though the music clearly gave him no joy).

11. This was the low point of the Soviet official performance. The Ministry of Culture were represented at my reception after the concert (which included Rostropovich and his wife) by a Vice-Minister who was actually interested in music. It remained however for them to organise the non-delivery to the Richters and Rostropoviches of invitations to lunch with me on April 22. It was in these circumstances a pleasure for my wife and myself to keep Madame Furtseva waiting for half-an-hour, while an elaborate comedy was played of trying to find out what had happened to the invitations and their addressees, and to observe her marked displeasure with her own officials for not organising things better. Once the food was on the table, she was at her most charming (and there is no irony in my use of this word). She was also a very good hostess at her own return buffet lunch on Friday the 23rd of April, which was attended by the Richters and a large number of young Soviet musicians. Rostropovich himself refused on genuine grounds of business. Under the new policy of keeping him active within the Soviet Union (he had recently been sent on tour among the music-loving Eskimos of Kamchatka), he had to leave on the night of the 23rd of April (after conducting an opera) for another tour, in and around Tashkent. Britten himself in the meantime had been engaged in a sort of private duel with his 'escort' from Goskoncert, Miss Sokolova, who felt cheated of her prey by reason of him and Peter Pears staying with me at this Embassy. This involved some nerve-storms and comedy which are better recorded elsewhere.

12. Britten thus looks back on this visit to Moscow with very mixed feelings. Perhaps there is some advantage in him having seen with his own eyes the sort of petty persecution to which his great friends, Rostropovich and Vishnevskaya, are subject; but the sight has caused him acute pain. I hope and think that Rostropovich himself will have gained something from the visit (this was Britten's main object in coming). The Soviet authorities have been able to see for themselves how close the link remains between Rostropovich and a composer who is an international figure and *persona grata* to themselves. I hope too that Britten has enjoyed some aspects at least of his visit. There was plenty of visible and audible proof for him of Rostropovich's own enormous popularity with the Soviet public in spite of the winter of official discontent. Again, even a man of Britten's own extreme modesty could hardly doubt the extent of the respect and affection in which he himself is held in the Soviet Union, not only by the established artists who know him. I saw myself a small triumph which he enjoyed at the Bolshoi Theatre after the performance of *War and Peace* on April 23 when Rostropovich introduced him backstage. His progress along any corridor of the theatre was halted regularly by autograph-hunting boys and girls, and members of the cast, orchestra and 'collective' of the stage-hands, etc., greeted him and Rostropovich with heart-warming enthusiasm. The whole incident contrasted most happily with an official attempt to arrange some public greeting for him in the Bolshoi Theatre on the morning before he left (April 25), in an interval of a performance of his own *Midsummer Night's Dream*. The effort was genuine, but Goskoncert inefficiency prevailed, and all it produced was a

conventional speech by the Director of the Theatre before an audience of five or six visitors. Even Britten, whose good manners are well known, could hardly reply civilly—his patience had already been sorely tried by the performance, and he is thinking how to devise a 'Bolshoi-proof' opera. The implicit contrast between a sensitive warm-hearted artistic public and the narrow-minded prigs and knaves of the ruling bureaucracy was manifest and poignant. But it is of some comfort to know that the warm hearts are still there, and that visits like that which has just been concluded do something to cheer them.

I have, etc.,

Duncan Wilson[5]

[5] On 13 May the Prime Minister sent a formal letter of thanks to Madame Furtseva for making the festival possible, and expressed the hope 'that I may have the pleasure of seeing you next year when we have the Soviet musical days here'. Submitting Sir D. Wilson's despatch on 14 May, Mr. Walden commented that it 'serves to remind us that co-operation with the Russians is often only satisfactory on the most abstract and uncontroversial plane—though even here, as Sir Duncan Wilson demonstrates, Soviet cultural bureaucrats have a long reach'. Mr. Bullard agreed: 'I found this event symbolic of Anglo-Soviet relations as a whole. There is great interest on each side in what the other has to offer in non-controversial fields, but the hand of the Party simply cannot be circumvented and its interventions are clumsy and spiteful.' The despatch was sent to the Prime Minister's office on 27 May, and in a letter of thanks to Sir D. Wilson of 25 May Sir D. Greenhill commented that 'Many of those who read it including the Prime Minister and Sir Alec will be aware of the very special personal role which you yourself played in the arrangements.'

The next document concerns the question of reducing the scale of Soviet intelligence activities in the UK—a problem which was to dominate Anglo-Soviet relations for the rest of 1971 and beyond. There had been no reply to Sir A. Douglas-Home's letter of 3 December to Mr. Gromyko (No. 58), and Soviet intelligence activities had continued unabated. Further instances of inadmissible activities by Soviet Embassy staff had been drawn to the FCO's attention by the Security Service, and expulsions of Soviet spies had led to retaliatory action against members of HM Embassy in Moscow: one member of staff had been told of his expulsion during the 'Days of British Music'. The 'ceiling' on the number of Soviet Embassy staff (cf. No. 19) was circumvented by increasing the number of 'working wives', and there had been a steep rise in the number of 'representatives' of Soviet firms in the UK. Of a total of just under 500 Soviet officials in Britain, 120 had been identified as intelligence officers. These issues had been discussed on a number of occasions in the early months of 1971 by EESD, PUSD and Security Service representatives, who agreed that continuation of the present scale of hostile intelligence activity presented a serious threat to national security, and that no significant impact could be made on this threat simply by dealing with individual cases as they occurred.

The case for radical action grew stronger as the Russians extended their intelligence network and it became harder to find convincing answers to press and public criticism of official inaction. What form this action might take had been the subject of long debate in the FCO, the Security Service and elsewhere. HM Embassy in Moscow had suggested engaging the Russians in a negotiation designed to arrive at an agreed ceiling for all Soviet personnel in Britain, combined with some improvements in the position of British businessmen in Moscow: the view in London, however, was that the Russians had no inducement to agree to this kind of negotiation, and that it would be more effective to impose a ceiling on STD and ancillary organisations next time one of their members was caught in 'impermissible activities', and to reduce the ceiling by one every time such an incident occurred.

The debate moved into a new gear in March 1971 when the Prime Minister, following representations to him by several MPs, expressed his concern about Soviet intelligence activities to Sir Burke Trend and a meeting was arranged between the Cabinet Secretary, Sir D. Greenhill and Sir P. Allen to discuss the issue. Inter-departmental consideration of possible courses of action led to the preparation of a draft memorandum from the Secretary of State to the Prime Minister, which was discussed at a meeting with the PUS on 5 May: circulating the draft on 3 May, Mr. Bullard noted that the codeword 'FOOT' had been allocated to this subject and should be used in future on all papers referring to it. The memorandum proposed that the Secretary of State should hand the Soviet Ambassador an aide-mémoire stating that 6 weeks later the total Soviet diplomatic, commercial and press establishment in Britain would be limited to 400 persons, and listing a substantial number of known intelligence officers who were to be removed at this date.

Sir D. Wilson, present at the 5 May meeting, expressed strong reservations on his return to Moscow, asking 'how far our principal future EEC partners would welcome a first-class row between us and the Russians at the present juncture', and arguing instead that a time limit, such as the end of 1972, should be set for the reduction of the Soviet Embassy to parity for diplomatic staff, to be accomplished by quarterly reductions the first of which would include the most objectionable persons on the Security authorities' list. He also prepared a paper detailing possible Soviet counter-measures to FOOT, ranging from a rupture in diplomatic relations to 'business not as usual'. Although Sir D. Greenhill agreed that an alternative memorandum should be prepared incorporating the Ambassador's proposals and that both would be considered, he made it clear that he preferred more immediate action: 'The drawback to this idea of action taken in stages over a period is that it would give ample time for the Russians not only to re-deploy their espionage effort but also to mobilise all available means of causing us trouble . . . if the various stages in the contraction of their staff were not completed until the end of 1972, we could be sure that relations between our two countries would be at rock bottom until then. Under our (more rapid) scheme, we should hope to get the worst over within a few months and to see some recovery in our relations within a year or 18 months.'

Copies of the draft memoranda were sent for comment to Permanent Secretaries in Ministries affected by this issue, who were asked to attend a meeting in Sir D. Greenhill's office on 25 May.

No. 66

Record of a meeting in the Permanent Under-Secretary's Office on Tuesday, 25 May 1971, at 3.30 p.m.

[*PUSD*]

Top Secret

Soviet Intelligence Activities in the United Kingdom

Present:

Sir Denis Greenhill

Sir Stewart Crawford

Sir Thomas Brimelow

Mr. J. Killick

Mr. J.L. Bullard

Mr. G.G.H. Walden

Sir Burke Trend

Sir Philip Allen

Sir Antony Part

Sir James Dunnett

Sir Martin Furnival Jones

'C'[1]

Sir Denis Greenhill said that the question of Soviet intelligence activities in the United Kingdom was a serious matter. The Soviet establishment here was proportionately much larger than in other western countries. It was clear that at least 25% indulged in undiplomatic activities. Everything pointed to the desirability of cutting down these numbers. The real problem was how to do so. Was it agreed in principle that the Russians must be cut down to size?

2. *Sir Antony Part* said that he would like to know more about the threat. Soviet reprisals against our exports were likely to be fairly severe. How much damage did the Russian intelligence effort do?[2] *Sir Martin Furnival Jones* emphasised the weight of the Soviet attack. In the last fifteen years there had been evidence of penetration of the Foreign and Commonwealth Office, the Ministry of Defence, the Army, Navy and Air Force, the Labour Party, Transport House and the Board of Trade. It was difficult to say exactly how much damage was being done. But it was equally difficult to believe that the Russians maintained such a large establishment for no profit. At least thirty or forty Soviet intelligence officers in this country were actually running secret

---

[1] Sir S. Crawford was a Deputy Under-Secretary in the FCO superintending (with Mr. Killick) PUSD. Sir P. Allen, Sir A. Part and Sir J. Dunnett were respectively Permanent Secretaries at the Home Office, DTI and Ministry of Defence. Sir M. Furnival Jones was Director General of the Security Service (MI5), and 'C' was Sir J. Rennie, Head of the Secret Intelligence Service (MI6).

[2] In a minute to Sir T. Brimelow of 27 May Mr. Bullard expressed surprise that a number of those present at the PUS's meeting seemed to be largely unaware of the threat to British interests posed by the scale of Soviet intelligence activities: 'If we are to overcome the resistance of the Department of Trade and Industry to 'FOOT', it is important that Sir Antony Part should have clear evidence of the scale and nature of the Soviet intelligence attack.' A letter was sent to Sir A. Part on 1 June summarising the information which Soviet intelligence officers were seeking to obtain by clandestine means and enclosing some reports received from the Security Service about Soviet intelligence officers who were subsequently expelled from the UK: 'nearly all of them operated under the aegis of the Soviet Trade Delegation.'

agents in government or in industry. 'C' agreed. It was pointed out that the Russians attached high priority to acquiring scientific and technical secrets, and to commercial information with military overtones.

3. *Sir Denis Greenhill* said that he did not think we could achieve a sensible relationship with the Russians until we removed to a large extent those elements which prevented the growth of mutual confidence. *Sir Thomas Brimelow* said that the cases he had seen in the last two years were different from those of Blake and Philby[3] and involved the cultivation of commercial or defence officials. But we must infer that the best Soviet agents were well-protected. He agreed with Sir Antony Part that radical action would cause major trouble in Anglo-Soviet relations. But he was sceptical about the possibility of achieving a satisfactory relationship with the Russians in present circumstances. We were continually conscious of Soviet operations against this country. The Russians often spoke of European security, but paid no regard to the security of this country. This situation falsified our relations as a whole. It would be difficult for the Russians to resume operations on their present scale if we had it out with them now. HM Ambassador in Moscow doubted whether the game was worth the candle, and had suggested that our future partners in the European Economic Community might react badly. Sir Thomas Brimelow did not find these views convincing. We were open to public criticism for tolerating Soviet activities on their present scale for so long. It would be better to achieve a reduction without a major row, but this would probably be impossible.

4. *Sir Burke Trend* asked whether the Russians would not increase their 'illegal' operations if we cut down their 'legal' residency, and consequently create greater problems for us. *Sir Martin Furnival Jones* said that this would be difficult, as 'illegals' were much more difficult to run, and could not themselves actively recruit.

5. *Sir Denis Greenhill* again drew attention to the disproportionate size of the Soviet establishment in this country compared with our major allies.[4] We could not allow things to go on in this way. The number of trade officials bore no relation to the actual scale of trade. In his view, the most defensible basis of action was to go for parity between our embassies. This would be easier to present to the public. On the commercial side, we should limit the Russians to a figure which would be related to the actual and intended business to be done in this country. We would keep our list of 100 identified agents in reserve as evidence of their misbehaviour.

[3] Members of SIS and Soviet agents: George Blake had been sentenced to 42 years' imprisonment in 1961 (from which he escaped in 1966), and Harold (Kim) Philby defected to Moscow in 1963.

[4] On 24 May Mr. Bullard submitted to Sir T. Brimelow and Sir D. Greenhill a table showing the number of Soviet officials in major Western countries and Japan, and listing the restrictions imposed by those countries on Soviet establishments: 'By comparison with the other countries mentioned, British practice is indulgent . . . The Soviet official strength in Britain is larger than that in any other country mentioned, including the United States, if the Soviet Delegation to the UN is excepted.'

6. *Sir Martin Furnival Jones* said that this method of procedure was very much less attractive from the security point of view. The aim should be to get rid of the people we knew to be spies. However we went about reducing the Soviet establishment, the Russians would react badly. The British public would understand the ejection of identified spies more readily than the principle of parity and negotiations about the size of the Soviet Trade Delegation. *Sir Philip Allen* suggested that the public might ask why 100 spies had been allowed to operate in the first place.

7. *Sir Thomas Brimelow* pointed out the advantages of requiring the Russians to remove the 100 or so intelligence officers on the list. If the Russians ejected our people from Moscow, we could take counter reprisals against their remaining people here on the principle of parity. *Sir Denis Greenhill* said that there was a case for not giving the Russians the list but keeping it as evidence of their inadmissible activities. *Mr. Killick* suggested that the principle of parity was difficult to justify in the abstract. *Sir Martin Furnival Jones* pointed out that, numerically, the principle of parity would not be upset if we required the Russians to remove the 100. *Sir Burke Trend* said that if we were going to have a row anyway, it was better to get what we wanted out of it. We should tell the Russians that the 100 known spies must go, but offer to help them by presenting this to the public as an attempt to achieve parity between our diplomatic embassies. *Sir Martin Furnival Jones* agreed.

8. There was then some discussion about proposals made by HM Embassy in Moscow for dealing with the Soviet Trade Delegation, and about the numbers involved. It was pointed out that there would be considerable administrative difficulty in requiring the Russians to justify the presence of commercial officials by reference to the amount of trade done in the fields for which they were appointed. There would also be wide scope for circumvention. This would involve us in a perpetual wrangle with the Russians. To the suggestion that the Security Service could keep an eye on Soviet officials to guard against circumvention, *Sir Martin Furnival Jones* replied that this would be impossible in view of the numbers involved. He would like to see these reduced to manageable proportions. *Sir Antony Part* expressed his preference for a reduction in the overall total of trade officials. His department did not want a continual wrangle with the Russians. *Mr. Bullard* suggested that both the Embassy and the Soviet Trade Delegation should be restricted to the number remaining when the 100 had been removed. *Sir Thomas Brimelow* agreed, and added that we should tell the Russians that this ceiling would be reduced by one each time we were obliged to expel an official detected in espionage. *Sir Burke Trend* agreed.

9. *Sir Denis Greenhill* proposed that a minute to the Prime Minister should now be prepared covering a draft *Aide-Mémoire*. This would:

(a) assert the principle of parity between our two embassies;
(b) limit the number of non-embassy officials to a specific figure (275 was suggested);

(*c*) warn the Russians that this ceiling would be reduced by one each time an intelligence officer was caught;

(*d*) inform the Russians that those removed must include the 100 on the list.

10. *Sir Burke Trend* said that we still had to consider whether the game was worth the candle. *Sir Denis Greenhill* agreed that we were particularly vulnerable to commercial reprisals and to general beastliness. But he did not think that the Russians would go so far as to break off relations. *Sir Antony Part* expressed concern at the possible commercial consequences. A machine tool exhibition was due to be held in Moscow in July. This was marginal, but many millions of pounds were involved in British exports to the Soviet Union as a whole. The security threat to this country would have to be shown to be severe to justify the possible damage to our trade. We would also have to ensure that the operation was conducted in such a way as to prevent the Russians rebuilding their intelligence machine in the near future. *Sir Martin Furnival Jones* said that, if we removed the 100 identified intelligence officers, it would take the Russians a very long time to repair the damage. He also pointed out that HM Commercial Counsellor in Moscow had expressed the view that our commercial position might be rebuilt within eighteen months to two years.

11. 'C' said that our allies in Western Europe, far from viewing our action badly, would probably welcome it. It was clear that the French were concerned about the numbers of Russians in their country. They might emulate our action. This would make it difficult for the Russians to switch their trade. *Sir Denis Greenhill* agreed, and said that other countries had generally taken a tougher line than the United Kingdom. *Sir Burke Trend* said that the commercial stakes involved appeared very high and he was not sure which way Ministers would jump. They might ask how the situation had been allowed to develop to this point. It was suggested that provided action was taken soon there would be little difficulty in explaining that the present situation was to some extent a legacy of the last Government.

12. *Sir Burke Trend* said that we should point out in the memorandum to the Prime Minister that the Americans were more firm in these matters than we are.

13. It was generally agreed that action on the lines of Scheme 'A' in the paper[5] would be preferable. Permanent Secretaries should see the minute and *Aide-Mémoire* in draft before it went forward to the Secretary of State for Foreign and Commonwealth Affairs.

14. On timing, *Sir Burke Trend* said that it would be better to carry out the operation during the summer recess. *Sir Thomas Brimelow* added that a further advantage of this period was that it would fall in the interim between Sir Duncan Wilson's departure in August and the arrival of Mr. Killick in

[5] i.e. the scheme in the version of the memorandum originally drafted (see pp. 337-8) as opposed to that suggested by Sir D. Wilson.

September.[6] *Sir Burke Trend* suggested that the Ambassador's presence might be desirable to lead his team.[7]

[6] Cf. No. 60, note 10.

[7] Following this meeting a shorter redraft was prepared of the proposed memorandum from the Secretary of State to the Prime Minister, together with a draft *aide-mémoire* to the Soviet Ambassador. Sending these drafts on 11 June to those who had attended the meeting, Sir D. Greenhill said that 'We have given further thought to the question whether we should or should not proceed at once to impose parity of establishment. We have come to the conclusion that we should keep the principle of parity in reserve as a weapon to be used if Soviet retaliation forces us into a second round of action. We calculate that after the first round of expulsions, the Soviet Embassy in London would still outnumber ours in Moscow by about half a dozen, and we think that their desire not to see their establishment further reduced may perhaps inhibit their urge to retaliate on a scale comparable to the action we are now recommending.'

Sir D. Greenhill also sent the drafts to Sir D. Wilson, commenting 'that you will find these disappointingly far from your own ideas', but that those present at the meeting on 25 May felt that 'it would be better to go for the expulsion of the majority of known Soviet spies in this country rather than leave it to the Russians to decide whom to withdraw and allow them ample time in which to minimise their losses'. He told the Ambassador that it was planned to submit the papers to the Secretary of State 'as soon as possible after my return from my visit' (to Moscow: see below).

As agreed in February (see No. 60, note 15), Sir Denis Greenhill was to visit the Soviet Union from 22-27 June. Among the subjects for discussion were the Berlin negotiations, the link between these and future talks on European Security, and Mutual and Balanced Force Reductions. When the North Atlantic Council met in Ministerial session in Lisbon on 3 and 4 June, the main task had been to reach a common line on East-West political questions, in the context of a general agreement that the Lisbon communiqué would have to add something to the previous two communiqués (see pp. 238-9 and 294-5), although on all issues of substance the Alliance should 'not only stand firm but be seen to be standing firm'. The Communiqué issued on 4 June took an optimistic line on the Berlin negotiations, expressing the hope that they would be concluded by the time of the next Ministerial meeting, but maintaining the position that there should be no move to multilateral contacts on European Security until a Berlin agreement was concluded. On MBFRs, in response to recent Soviet statements expressing willingness to discuss reductions of both foreign and national troops in a 'non-CES forum', Ministers agreed to a special NATO meeting of Deputy Foreign Ministers to review exploratory contacts, and to the appointment of a NATO representative charged with conducting further exploratory talks with the Soviet and other interested governments. The Communiqué also welcomed the agreement between the US and Soviet Governments, announced on 20 May, to concentrate in the 1971 SALT talks on working out an agreement on the limitation of deployment of ABMs and offensive strategic weapons: a breakthrough that seemed significant in the context of earlier deadlock on the issue of which weapons would be discussed.[1]

[1] For the announcement of this agreement, which President Nixon called a 'major step in breaking the stalemate on nuclear arms talks', see *Public Papers: Nixon, 1971*, No. 175. Extracts from the Lisbon *Communiqué* are printed in Cmnd. 6932, No. 34.

Writing to Sir D. Greenhill on 7 June, Sir D. Wilson stated: 'I feel very strongly that the timing of your visit may well coincidentally make it an ideal occasion to do two things: first to explain to the Russians that they need not be worried about the consequences of our membership of the EEC (which will, we hope, look imminent by the time of your visit, domestic British complications apart) for Anglo-Soviet and East-West relations, and to illustrate the general point by your readiness to engage in bilateral discussions on a broad front; and second, to make the points (unless for some reason you think them premature), that the present activities of large numbers of the Soviet representatives in the UK are intolerable to us; that the continuation of these activities may well lead to a serious crisis in Anglo-Soviet relations which we are anxious to avoid; and that conversely a much more fruitful period of bilateral relations could lie ahead if this cancer can be removed.'

The PUS's programme included talks with Mr. Kozyrev on 23 June, with Mr. Gordeev and Mr. Makeev on 24 June, a call on Mr. Gromyko on 25 June and talks about Indo-China and the political and humanitarian problems arising from current disturbances in East Pakistan with Mr. Firyubin, the responsible Vice-Minister at the Soviet Foreign Ministry. The visit concluded with a trip to Leningrad on 26-27 June. Documents 67 and 68 below report the Permanent Under-Secretary's talks with Mr. Kozyrev and Mr. Gromyko respectively. His conversation with Mr. Kozyrev was clouded by the request a few days earlier to withdraw two members of HM Embassy in Moscow, in retaliation for the withdrawal earlier that month of two members of the Soviet Embassy in London detected in espionage activities; and by the granting of permission to stay in Britain to the Soviet scientist Anatoly Fedoseev, who defected while in Paris as a member of the Soviet delegation to the air show.

No. 67

Sir D. Wilson (Moscow) to Sir A. Douglas-Home

No. 895 Telegraphic [ENS 3/548/8]

Priority. Confidential MOSCOW, *24 June 1971, 7.16 a.m.*

Repeated for information Routine to Washington, Paris, UKDEL EEC, UKDEL NATO, Bonn and UKMIS New York.

Following from PUS.

I had a total of five hours' discussions with Vice-Minister Kozyrev yesterday in which we covered Anglo-Soviet relations, European questions, disarmament and the Middle East. Apart from the question of Soviet intelligence activities, defections etc. (which Kozyrev raised and on which I have telegraphed separately)[1] the atmosphere was friendly and businesslike.

[1] In Moscow telegram No. 894 of 23 June Sir D. Greenhill reported that in their conversation that morning Mr. Kozyrev had 'referred to "hostile and provocative activities of the British special services" against the Soviet Union and its citizens and Soviet agencies in Britain, saying that these could not help towards the creation of a favourable atmosphere for the development of Anglo-Soviet relations . . . Kozyrev said he had mentioned these questions not with the object of

Kozyrev was backed by an array of heads of departments[2] who seemed to welcome the opportunity of questioning me on various aspects of our policy and for the most part concentrated on current questions of substance. I hope the result will have been to strengthen Soviet willingness to do business with us at official level without excessive atmospherics.

2. Except on MBFR[3] and the question of the UN Secretary-Generalship[4] (on which I am telegraphing separately) we covered little new ground. On Anglo-Soviet relations there were the usual reciprocal complaints about the development of trade[5] and the need to do better on scientific and cultural exchanges,[6] and mutual assurances of desire for improved political relations. Kozyrev said that your speech to the Muscovite Society[7] and your state-

entering into polemics but in order to emphasise the need to get rid of obstacles to the development of good bilateral relations'. In reply Sir D. Greenhill recalled that he had raised the problem of 'the continuous inadmissible activities of some members of the Soviet Embassy in London' with Mr. Kozyrev during the latter's visit to London in April 1970 (cf. No. 45), that Sir A. Douglas-Home had done the same with Mr. Gromyko in October (see pp. 267-8) and had subsequently written to him on the subject (No. 58), but that these approaches and the letter had been 'unanswered and in effect ignored'.

[2] In addition to Mr. Makeev and other members of Second European Department, the talks were attended by Mr. Gorinovich, Mr. Sytenko, Mr. Novikov and Mr. Nesterenko, respectively heads of the Soviet Foreign Ministry's Third European (responsible for relations with Germany), Near Eastern, International Organisations and Economic Organisations Departments.

[3] Cf. p. 343. In Moscow telegram No. 896 of 24 June Sir D. Greenhill reported Mr. Kozyrev as saying that MBFR talks could be held before or after, but not at, an 'all-European Conference'. The NATO proposal to appoint a representative for preliminary talks 'implied that the talks would be between the two military blocs' which the Soviet Government did not think 'need necessarily be the basis'; Mr. Kozyrev was vague when questioned about the scope of discussions, but confirmed that 'the need for equal security meant what it said (equal equals equal) and applied to troop reductions in Europe as well as to limitations on fleets'. Mr. Novikov pressed the PUS to define what NATO meant by 'balanced' and was not convinced that 'equal security could be achieved by unequal reductions' (WDN 27/1).

[4] In Moscow telegram No. 897 of 24 June Sir D. Greenhill reported that he told Mr. Kozyrev that HMG took at face value a statement of 18 January by U Thant that he did not wish to stand for re-election as UN Secretary-General, and thought it desirable to 'start moving towards a consensus on a candidate to succeed him'. Mr. Novikov, however, said that 'the Russians were not convinced that this was [U Thant's] last word', and that 'the time was not ripe' to begin discussion of a successor (UL 2/3).

[5] Mr. Kozyrev had said: 'Further increases in trade would be helped by the removal of obstacles on the British side both for Soviet exports . . . and for British exports to the Soviet Union of so-called strategic goods'; Sir D. Greenhill had responded that 'British exports to Russia had not risen at anything like the rate of increase world-wide . . . and said that he hoped steps could be taken to remove the imbalance in trade'.

[6] Mr. Kozyrev had complained that some of the important recommendations of the first meeting of the Anglo-Soviet Consultative Committee (see No. 45, note 3) had not been carried out: 'Soviet concern at this fact had been expressed in a letter he had just written to Lord Trevelyan.'

[7] Sir A. Douglas-Home had used the occasion of a dinner held by the Muscovite Society on 16 March commemorating the fiftieth anniversary of the first Anglo-Soviet trade agreement to make 'a serious speech on Anglo-Soviet relations . . . which would be realistic and at the same

ments to Gromyko during his visit last October[8] had not gone unnoticed and had been welcomed, but contrasted them with statements about the Soviet threat.[9] I confirmed that we wanted discussions of substance on concrete problems, and general improvement in relations, but pointed to hostile statements of the Communist Party. I am seeing the Deputy Minister of Foreign Trade and possibly Gvishiani today and hope to call on Gromyko tomorrow.

3. On European security and Berlin nothing new was said but the Russians gave the clear impression of wanting an early agreement on Berlin.[10] They rehearsed the recent range of Soviet proposals in the field of disarmament but added no new points.[11] On the five-power nuclear conference they did

time make it more difficult for the Russians to go on saying that we are deliberately worsening our relations' (minute by Sir D. Greenhill, 19 February). The Secretary of State spoke of the benefits which would come from increased Anglo-Soviet understanding, cooperation to solve practical problems and acceptance of the principle of non-interference in the affairs of others; Sir T. Brimelow, reporting the delivery of the speech to Sir D. Wilson on 18 March, noted that Sir Alec had followed his usual habit 'to revise drafts and transform them into his own language'. Mr. Smirnovsky had been cautious in reply and spoken of 'the duty of an Ambassador, when hearing a speech by a Foreign Minister, to listen, to study and to report to his government' (ENS 6/548/13).

[8] See Nos. 53 and 54.

[9] Cf. p. 322. Mr. Kozyrev said that 'these statements were not believed by many people, but they could not contribute to a favourable atmosphere for the development of Anglo-Soviet relations'.

[10] Cf. No. 64, note 3. Significant progress had been made at Ambassadorial meetings on 7 and 25 May, with agreement on common language for more than half a draft working paper, and on 7 June both sides gave a substantial measure of endorsement to a draft Berlin Agreement covering access, inner Berlin communications and the relationship between the FRG and Western sectors of Berlin. However, in Berlin telegram No. 1 to Moscow of 23 June Sir R. Jackling had told the PUS that in Counsellors' meetings on 9 and 22-23 June 'The Russians had become much more hesitant to move. In general they have been reluctant to discuss compromise language, and have in some cases introduced proposals very close to their original draft of 26 March on a take-it-or-leave-it basis. Under strong Western pressure they have agreed to a few elements of a common text on the outstanding subjects, but without making any moves on substance, so that many unresolved points of difficulty still remain.' Sir R. Jackling suggested that Sir D. Greenhill make the point in Moscow that 'it is necessary to restore the impetus of the talks if the West is not to suspect that the Soviet movement in May was purely a tactical gambit' (WRL 2/1). The next Quadripartite Ambassadorial meeting was to take place on 25 June.

In discussion with Mr. Kozyrev on 23 June Sir D. Greenhill said that 'there was not much hope of success at a European Security Conference until Berlin was settled; conversely a Berlin settlement would indicate that it was possible to make a success of the Conference'. In response, Mr. Kozyrev 'welcomed the indications of a favourable British attitude to a European Conference, but repeated that British insistence on prior agreement on Berlin was unacceptable'. In reply to a request from Mr. Gorinovich for an estimate of the time needed to reach agreement, Sir D. Greenhill said 'that the earlier agreement could be reached the better, but the essential point was that the agreement should be satisfactory, unambiguous and complete, and should not be such as to create new problems for the future'.

[11] In his speech to the 24th CPSU Congress (see p. 326) Mr. Brezhnev had referred to long-standing Soviet proposals for nuclear-free zones, the liquidation of foreign bases, reductions in military expenditure and the abolition of NATO and the Warsaw Pact. He had made two new suggestions for a conference of the five nuclear powers and for a world disarmament conference.

not answer my question about Chinese attitude.[12] They confirmed that Brezhnev's proposal for discussions on limitations of naval deployment applied to all parts of the world.

4. I was questioned on consequences of British entry into the EEC for Anglo-Soviet trade, sterling, the Commonwealth and EFTA, but there was no reference to the political aspects of expansion of the communities.[13] Officials coming here next month for the trade talks[14] should be briefed on these points.

5. On the Middle East, Sytenko delivered a familiar lecture on the iniquities of Israel and the United States but was able to produce no concrete answers to our questions on guarantees.[15] He took the line that negotiation of a possible interim agreement as part of a package settlement should be in the hands of Jarring. It was wrong for three of the four powers to be expected to sit with folded arms while the Americans pretended to make the running. I told him I saw no point in their being jealous about seeking a settlement and rejected his suggestion that we were not as active as we should be. He did not rise to my suggestion that it would help if the Soviet Union could establish direct contact with Israel. He and Kozyrev welcomed my suggestion of further bilateral official talks at an appropriate time.

6. Full record by bag.[16]

In an election speech on 11 June he had spoken of the reduction of 'armed forces and armaments in Europe' as applying to national as well as foreign forces. He said that the Soviet economy could develop much faster without the burden of arms spending and proposed to solve 'on the basis of equality' the problems caused by the naval presences of Great Powers in distant waters (cf. No. 63).

[12] Sir D. Greenhill told Mr. Kozyrev that HMG would wish to take part in a five-power conference but much depended on the Chinese attitude, and he 'would be grateful for any indications which the Soviet Government had had on this point'.

[13] A meeting in Paris between President Pompidou and Mr. Heath on 20-21 May had achieved a breakthrough in the negotiations on Britain's entry into the EEC: Sir Con O'Neill later called it 'by far the most significant meeting that took place in the whole course of the negotiations'. When agreement on the important questions of New Zealand dairy products and Community finance was reached at a Ministerial meeting at Luxembourg on 21-23 June the terms of British entry were virtually settled, and a White Paper was published on 7 July on *The UK and the European Communities* (Cmnd. 8715 of 1971). Drafting of the Accession Treaty began in September, and the vote in favour of British entry was carried in the House of Commons on 28 October.

[14] Mr. Bellamy and Mr. Woolmer of the DTI visited Moscow from 7-9 July for the annual review of Anglo-Soviet trade provided for in the 1969 agreement: see No. 33.

[15] See No. 64, note 1. HMG continued to support American diplomatic efforts for an interim solution based on the re-opening of the Suez Canal, but the Egyptian and Israeli positions remained widely divergent and there was little confidence in the FCO that agreement would be reached. Meanwhile the signature on 28 May of a USSR/Egyptian Treaty of Friendship. although emphasising cooperation in the political, economic, scientific, technical and cultural spheres rather than the military, was considered in the FCO to give the Soviet Union 'everything it could possibly desire to facilitate their ambitions in the UAR and, by extension, in the Middle East' (brief by Mr. R.C. Hope-Jones of North Africa Department, 1 June, NEM 3/548/1).

[16] Not printed.

No. 68

Sir D. Wilson (Moscow) to Sir A. Douglas-Home
No. 910 Telegraphic [*ENS 3/548/8*]

Immediate. Confidential   MOSCOW, *25 June 1971, 3.09 p.m.*

Repeated for information routine to Washington, Paris, Bonn and UKDEL NATO.

Following from Permanent Under-Secretary.

I saw Gromyko today for about forty minutes, accompanied by HM Ambassador. He was personally cordial and warmly reciprocated your good wishes.

2. I open[e]d by referring to your agreement with him last October that there should be more contacts on the official as well as on the ministerial level,[1] and said that my own visit was taking place in this context. There were four main points in HMG's policy towards the Soviet Union—agreement not to interfere in each other's affairs, to expand trade, to increase technical, scientific and cultural contacts, and to establish an effective political dialogue on concrete subjects.[2] I emphasised in particular your own concern with the key question of a Berlin settlement.[3] Here was negotiation on which we were actively engaged. It should be finished constructively, and could lead to further and wider negotiations. In the meantime the various Soviet statements on disarmament[4] would be examined.

3. In reply Gromyko welcomed my visit in the context which I had already described. He thought that it came at a specially useful time considering the present state of Anglo-Soviet relations. He felt that progress had been made in some fields, and mentioned in this category the Berlin talks, which he hoped would develop favourably. He was however concerned with two particular points on which there had been difficulties, or bottle-necks, to use his own expression. One of these, he said, lay in the various declarations

[1] Cf. No. 54.

[2] Sir D. Greenhill had also outlined these points on 23 June to Mr. Kozyrev, who agreed with these 'four basic directions for improving relations'.

[3] See No. 67, note 10. The main features of the Ambassadors' meeting on 25 June were a review of progress made by Counsellors, the opening up of discussion on Soviet interests in West Berlin (hitherto blocked by the Americans) and the setting of guide lines for further work by Counsellors before the next Ambassadorial meeting on 8 July. In Bonn telegram No. 817 of 25 June Sir R. Jackling noted that although the proceedings had been 'of a somewhat general character, they were marked by an increased sense of urgency all round'. The review of Counsellors' work 'revealed a convergence of opinion between the Allied and Soviet Ambassadors . . . the number of outstanding points of difference, though large, was continuing to diminish: and . . . the work already done had resulted in the structure of the proposed agreement being pretty clear'. Sir R. Jackling hoped that the Counsellors could now attempt a second reading of the complete agreement 'to reduce to the minimum the existing points of difference, and so bring us to a stage when it would be possible for the Ambassadors themselves to attempt a settlement of those hard-core issues which remained' (WRL 2/1).

[4] Cf. No. 67, note 11.

made over roughly the last year by various high British personalities about the 'threat' constituted by the Soviet Navy.[5] It seemed that objection was being made even to the presence of Soviet ships in certain waters. The Soviet Government were bound to take note of such statements and to ask themselves what was the object of making them. He hoped that it was not a deliberate attempt to worsen our relations. It would be very easy for the Soviet Government to retort in kind and what had been built up over ten years or so could thus be destroyed in two or three days; but he did not think that such exchanges would serve the best interests of the UK, the Soviet Union or the world in general.

4. Gromyko's second point was the activities of the 'British special services' in creating difficult conditions for Soviet offices and personnel in London. Such activities, he said, had intensified recently—perhaps over the last year. He would not go into detail o[r] indulge in guesswork about them. Evidence had reached the Soviet Government that some sort of statement was being prepared about further steps to be tak[e]n in London, perhaps against socialist countries in general or perhaps against the Soviet Union. This was an area in which it was easy to take ill-considered action which would have an undesirable impact on Anglo-Soviet relations as a whole.[6] He hoped that the artificial problems created by the British 'special services' would disappear, and that we could then concentrate on areas where we could make concrete progress together.

5. In reply to Gromyko's first point I said that your speech to the Muscovite Society last March[7] gave a full and fair picture of British policy towards the Soviet Union. Your responses to Tsarapkin[8] similarly showed our

---

[5] Cf. *ibid.*, note 9.

[6] Mr. Simons commented on 28 June in a minute addressed to Mr. Bullard, Sir T. Brimelow and Sir S. Crawford: 'It is clear from Gromyko's and Kozyrev's statements that the Russians have no intention of mending their ways. On the contrary, if we continue to deal with Soviet espionage on a case-by-case basis [cf. pp. 337-8], they will find increasingly painful means of retaliation. They must already be redeploying their intelligence effort in anticipation of a more forthright defensive policy by us. But this is an additional reason for speedily implementing plans outlined elsewhere [cf. No. 66] for a comprehensive attempt to right the present unsatisfactory position.' A brief prepared for a meeting between the Secretary of State and Home Secretary on 30 June (see No. 70, note 1 below) noted: 'There are security risks in further postponement. After the Prime Minister's remark in the House on 17 June that in due course the Foreign and Commonwealth Secretary would make a statement about measures to reduce espionage in this country [*Parl. Debs.*, 5th ser., H. of C., vol. 819, cols. 642-3] the Russians must realise that our patience is wearing thin, and they are probably asking themselves what form our action might take. Further delay will probably result in leaks, which in turn will prompt the Russians to take measures to minimise any damage to their intelligence machine.'

[7] See No. 67, note 7.

[8] Mr. S. Tsarapkin, Soviet Ambassador at Large, had arrived unexpectedly in London on 5 June and asked to see Sir A. Douglas-Home. He held discussions with Sir D. Greenhill on 7 June, the Secretary of State on 8 June and Mr. Godber, Minister of State in the FCO, on 9 June, covering a wide range of topics. Sir A. Douglas-Home reiterated his desire to further *détente* in Europe, and to see peaceful solutions in the Middle East and Indo-China (ENS 2/2).

intention to work for cooperation. No-one on the British side contested the right of Soviet ships to go where they wanted, but we had seen a number of official statements on the Soviet side which gave us cause to question Soviet intentions and we were entitled to draw our own conclusions. On Gromyko's second point, I mentioned your unanswered letter to him,[9] and said that I had already discussed the subject in some detail with Vice-Minister Kozyrev.[10] The main trouble was that the staff of the Soviet Embassy and other institutions had been indulging for some years in entirely irregular activities towards members of official and commercial organisations within the UK. I undertook however to report to you fully, as Gromyko has requested, about his remarks under both headings.

6. Gromyko ended by repeating that the attention of both governments should be concentrated on the complex and serious international problems of the world, not least but not only in Europe. If we worked in this direction we could do much together.

7. At the end of our conversation the question of your visit arose. I told Gromyko that you would probably feel unable to consider a visit until the parliamentary business connected with our entry into the EEC had been completed; but round about the beginning of next year you might wish to accept the invitation extended to you by Gromyko last October.[11] He said that, so far as he could at present foresee, this might be a suitable time. He would confirm later this year. The question of a visit by the Prime Minister was not raised.[12]

[9] No. 58.

[10] See No. 67, note 1.

[11] Before leaving for Moscow Sir D. Greenhill had discussed the outstanding Soviet invitations to the Prime Minister and Secretary of State with Mr. Heath, who agreed that the PUS should maintain the line 'that we are grateful for the invitations conveyed by Mr. Gromyko but that we are still not yet able to suggest dates'. FCO telegram No. 833 of 5 August, referring to the present telegram, instructed Sir D. Wilson to tell Mr. Gromyko that Sir A. Douglas-Home would like to take up the outstanding invitation to visit the Soviet Union in February 1972 (ENS 3/548/19).

[12] In his despatch of 5 July reporting on the PUS's visit, Sir D. Wilson drew attention to the opportunity it had provided for discussion of European questions and welcomed the 'useful spin-off effect for this Embassy, by confirming contact between us and a number of senior members of the Foreign Ministry whom we do not often see'. The timing of the visit had been less fortunate with regard to bilateral relations, falling under the shadow of recent reciprocal expulsions and the defection of Mr. Fedoseev (see p. 344): Sir D. Wilson considered that 'The burden of Mr. Gromyko's message, and no doubt this was reflected in the attitudes of junior officials, was that there was plenty of room for substantial discussion and even cooperation between HMG and the Soviet Government on important international issues; don't let us complicate this by polemics and "inadmissible activities" . . . Mr. Gromyko's remarks could be designed to convey the suggestion that we have much to gain by taking any counter-action on the KGB front with the minimum of advertisement and publicity. Whether or not this was Mr. Gromyko's intended message, it should, I think, be our conclusion. But of course it is easier said than done.'

Mr. Bullard minuted on 13 July that this despatch was 'in my opinion too ready to put the best construction on Soviet behaviour. This applies particularly to the paragraphs about espionage and expulsions.' Sir D. Greenhill's reply of 14 July to Sir D. Wilson, drafted by Mr.

Bullard and Sir T. Brimelow, was mainly concerned with 'the problem of the best machinery for doing business with the Russians', and suggested that the latter 'may have been spoiled by the number of high-level visits to Moscow in recent years and have drifted into the habit of regarding Western Ambassadors as men with whom it is neither necessary nor advantageous to transact serious business'; Sir D. Wilson was asked to consider the possibility of inviting members of the Politburo to the UK. 'All this however is contingent on our avoiding serious trouble over Soviet intelligence activities . . . The audacity of Kozyrev and later Gromyko when speaking on this subject is breath taking. Gromyko's message seemed to me to be simply that it would be the worse for us if we did not leave the spies alone, and so long as this is his attitude there is a limit to what we can do to improve relations.'

No. 69

Submission from Mr. Bullard to Sir T. Brimelow on Anglo-Soviet relations[1]

[*ENS 3/548/10*]

Confidential   FCO, *12 July 1971*

Problem

1. The PUS visited Moscow last month and the Secretary of State hopes to go there early next year.[2] We should consider what ought to be the direction of Anglo-Soviet relations during the interval, in order to secure the best results from the Secretary of State's visit when this takes place. Paras. 2 to 17 examine various possibilities which are then summed up in para. 18. I have taken account of the comments you made on an earlier draft.

Background and argument

2. The Russians claim to be disappointed with British attitudes towards the Soviet Union. Both Smirnovsky in London and Dobrynin in Washington have recently complained that Britain is 'more difficult' than other countries of Western Europe. Gromyko, in his talks with the PUS, reduced this general complaint to two specific ones: British Ministerial statements about the Soviet threat, and British counter-measures against Soviet intelligence-gathering.

3. The PUS replied to Gromyko on both points and there is little to add to what he said. The clear implication of the Soviet attitude is that if HMG want good relations with the Soviet Government, they should abstain from public criticism of Soviet policies and make no fuss about Soviet intelligence activities in the United Kingdom. This is roughly the policy followed by the French Foreign Ministry, which has no illusions about Soviet policy, but which keeps its comments confidential.

[1] According to a minute of 7 July by Mr. Bullard, this submission incorporated comments by Mr. J.A. Dobbs, HM Minister at Moscow since April 1971, and had the general agreement of Sir J. Killick (Mr. Killick had been created KCMG in the Queen's Birthday honours in June).

[2] See Nos. 67-8, and No. 68, note 11.

4. It is against this background that we have to consider whether, over the next six months, we could introduce some more positive elements, so that the Secretary of State's visit may take place against a reasonably propitious background.

5. A convenient framework is the list of four points which the PUS suggested to Kozyrev as the components of a satisfactory relationship between London and Moscow, and which Kozyrev too accepted.[3] These were as follows:

(*a*) non-interference in each other's social and political system;
(*b*) expanding and mutually beneficial trade;
(*c*) a network of technological and cultural exchanges;
(*d*) an effective and continuing political dialogue on matters of common interest.

(A) *Non-Interference*

6. The Russians wish others to observe the principle of non-intervention, and for this purpose are always willing to endorse the principle. But they do not practice it themselves. This is not the place to survey once again the current situation on espionage. As to defectors, we make no special effort to seek out and recruit defectors, but we allow them to stay when they turn up. The Fedoseev case will blow over,[4] but not before he has published further articles about his experiences, which the Russians will dislike. In other fields we have been careful not to antagonise the Soviet Union unnecessarily. On two recent occasions (the Katyn debate in the House of Lords[5] and the incident at the Soviet Consulate in May)[6] our attitude was criticised in some circles as too soft towards the Soviet Union. The Russians gave us no thanks for this. The other point raised with the PUS by Makeev was that of the BBC

[3] See No. 68, note 2.

[4] Cf. p. 344.

[5] Responsibility for the Katyn massacre had been disputed since the German authorities first announced in 1943 the discovery of a mass grave of Polish officers in Katyn Forest near Smolensk, and accused the Soviet Government, who maintained it was a German crime. HMG had always maintained that there was no conclusive proof of responsibility. In 1971 there was a revival of concern with Katyn in connection with the publication of Mr. L. Fitzgibbon's *Katyn: A Crime without Parallel* and a BBC documentary accusing the Soviet Union of the crime. Lord Barnby asked the House of Lords 'to secure pronouncement establishing beyond contention the authorship of the mass murder', but Lord Aberdare, for the Government, stated that 'Her Majesty's Government have absolutely no standing in this matter' and could not force either the Polish or Soviet Governments to support an official enquiry (*Parl. Debs.*, 5th ser., *H. of L.*, vol. 320, cols. 738-75, 17 June). See further *The Katyn Massacre: an SOE Perspective* (FCO History Note No. 10, February 1996).

[6] On 13 May a group of Jewish protesters seeking visas to attend the trials of Jews in Leningrad had staged a violent demonstration at the Consular Department of the Soviet Embassy. Sir T. Brimelow had telephoned an apology to the Soviet Embassy, and assured Mr. Ippolitov that HMG deprecated all attempts to disrupt the normal activity of foreign missions.

Russian Service.[7] On this the PUS offered to study a representative selection of broadcasts over a two week period on condition that Makeev did the same for Radio Moscow. This is being arranged, but the result is a foregone conclusion: there is far more spite and bias in Soviet broadcasts than in ours. We should take a suitable opportunity of pointing this out to the Russians, either here or in Moscow. This may not lead to any moderation in the tone of Radio Moscow but it will show the Russians that we have taken the trouble to explore their complaint.

(B) *Trade*

7. The answers given to the PUS's questions in Moscow bring us no nearer to solving the puzzle of why British exports to the Soviet Union have stood still since 1968, while British exports elsewhere (not to mention Soviet exports to Britain) have expanded. Gordeev denied that there was any political reason for this and implied that it was the fault of British firms. He cited high prices, late delivery, unaggressive marketing, etc. This is familiar ground, and it was gone over again when Mr. Bellamy of the DTI conducted the annual Anglo-Soviet trade talks last week.[8] Mr. Bellamy also did his best to satisfy the Russians on the four points where they say that they fear adverse consequences of Britain's entry into the EEC.[9] (Incidentally, one of the results of the PUS's visit was to secure the most explicit statement so far of Soviet apprehensions on this score.) The Russians gave Mr. Bellamy to understand that the final figures for British exports to the Soviet Union in 1971 would be better than the present trade suggests.[10]

8. Most British businessmen, and the DTI too, think it likely that the pattern of Anglo-Soviet trade will remain broadly as it has been, since the time of Queen Elizabeth I: primary products shipped from the Soviet Union in exchange for manufactured items from Britain. There are theoretical possibilities in what the Russians call 'industrial cooperation', but these will take time to identify and develop, and the practical difficulties resulting from the differences of the two systems will not be easy to overcome. Another new element, and potentially a very important one, is the group of 'large projects' about which the Russians have been talking for the last two or three years. I

---

[7] During their meeting on 24 June Mr. Makeev had complained to Sir D. Greenhill about BBC Russian Service broadcasts making critical comments about Soviet leaders, and using material originating from Soviet defectors (ENS 3/548/8).

[8] Cf. No. 67, note 14.

[9] At a meeting between Sir D. Greenhill and Mr. Kozyrev (see No. 67), Mr. Nesterenko said that British entry into the EEC would affect the Soviet Union directly, and asked four questions: what would happen to the most-favoured-nation status of the Soviet Union; what would happen to sterling, which the Soviet Union used for trade with many countries; what would be the future of the sterling area and Commonwealth trading arrangements and how would this affect Soviet trade with the Commonwealth; and what would happen to EFTA? Sir D. Greenhill had replied that there would be long-term benefits to the Soviet Union from British entry.

[10] Sir D. Greenhill here noted in the margin: 'They told me the same.'

attach a note showing the present state of affairs on each of these.[11] I do not think it can be said that the British side has shown too little energy or imagination here. Rather, the Russians themselves seem not to have made up their mind what kind of foreign participation they want. They appear to have launched the discussion of these projects long before most of them are likely to receive a final 'go-ahead'.

9. In the annual trade talks, the Five-Year Trade Agreement,[12] the East European Trade Council and the Anglo-Soviet Joint Commission we have the machinery to develop trade far beyond its present level if both sides are willing and able. The obstacles have not been political on our side, though if Anglo-Soviet political relations became very bad we might well see this reflected in a reluctance by British businessmen to undertake the risks of large-scale, long-term credit sales to the Russians, as well as in a Soviet switch from British to other suppliers. What chiefly stands in the way of increased trade at the moment are the humdrum facts that the Russians are short of foreign currency; that at the moment they seem to be giving some preference to French and West German suppliers; and that in the field of manufactured goods they have little to offer that British firms feel inclined to buy.[13]

10. As regards the next six months,

(*a*) the annual trade talks have just taken place in Moscow;

(*b*) The Chairman (Sir John Stevens) and Secretary of the EETC are to go there in September;[14]

(*c*) The Joint Commission is to hold its second meeting, also in Moscow, either in November 1971 or in January 1972.[15]

If the Secretary of State's visit can be timed to follow the Joint Commission, this will be as favourable a moment from the commercial point of view as any that could be devised. The only action needed is to ensure that these three meetings are as fruitful as possible.

(C) *Culture and technology*

11. Here again the machinery exists already:[16] what matters is how it is used or misused. It is not encouraging to know that out of 316 British students

[11] Not printed. The note summarised Soviet proposals to develop six 'large projects' in the fields of mineral extraction, containerisation, engineering and lorry manufacture, and the current state of interest in them by British firms.

[12] See No. 33.

[13] At a meeting between Mr. Bullard, Sir J. Killick and Mr. N. Cox (Commercial Counsellor, Moscow) with Mr. Bellamy and Mr. Hughes of the DTI on 27 July it was noted that 'it is becoming hard to resist the conclusion that the Russians are discriminating against British exports for political reasons. Perhaps they are not so much penalising us as favouring our competitors. This would not matter if British firms were not always in the technological vanguard' (MX 303/1).

[14] Sir J. Stevens, Mr. J.B. Scott (Deputy Chairman) and Mr. A.R.B. Hore (Executive Secretary) of the EETC visited Moscow from 5-11 September for talks with Mr. Manzhulo, Mr. Gvishiani and Mr. Misnik.

[15] Cf. No. 60, note 12. It was later confirmed that the second meeting of the Joint Commission was to be held in Moscow during the week beginning 3 January 1972.

[16] See p. 331.

sent to Soviet universities during the last 11 years under the Cultural Exchange Programme, at least 70 have been involved in incidents of some kind, apparently organised by the KGB: or that two Soviet academics admitted to the Public Record Office under the same Programme went straight back to lecture in Moscow on how the British Government connived with Hitler in 1939. We have prepared a leaflet to warn our students about the dangers awaiting them in Russia, and we are considering whether to refuse future Soviet applications to work at the PRO. These will no doubt be interpreted as anti-Soviet actions by HMG. The Cultural Exchange Programme has only recently been renewed and will continue. The main obstacles to exchanges are not on the British side. They are either objective factors such as the rival temptations of the USA and elsewhere for British students, or difficulties arising from the Soviet system such as the heavy-handed control of the Ministry of Culture. Theatrical and musical manifestations could certainly be more frequent in both directions, but our general view is that a first-class artist does not need governmental auspices and a second-class artist does not merit them.

12. We have however agreed with HM Embassy in Moscow on one new initiative in the Cultural field. This is to sound out British historians with a view to reviving the Anglo-Soviet Historical Protocol from which they withdrew in 1968 in protest against the invasion of Czechoslovakia. If Dr. Bolsover and others agree, the British Historical Exhibition scheduled for 1968 could be mounted in 1972 or 1973, and the other projects foreseen in the Protocol could also go forward, e.g. the joint publication of early documents on Anglo-Soviet economic relations. It should however be mentioned that many British historians have been reluctant to renew the relations with the Soviet Union which they interrupted in 1968.[17]

13. If other possibilities for intensified non-political exchanges exist, they are likely to emerge at the second meeting of the Anglo-Soviet Consultative Committee in Moscow in December.[18] Lord Trevelyan and his team have worked hard to make this body successful, and Kozyrev's complaints to the PUS are to some extent bluster calculated to conceal Soviet inefficiency and

[17] Cf. No. 14, note 7. Sir T. Brimelow had written on 1 June asking whether Sir D. Wilson had any objection to British historians being approached about reviving the Protocol, and the Ambassador replied in the negative. Dr. George Bolsover, Director of the School of Slavonic and East European Studies, confirmed that his relations with Soviet historians were good but expressed misgivings about the re-activation of all points of the Protocol, especially the joint publication of documents. Mr. Rohan Butler, Historical Adviser to the Secretary of State, suggested that as a beginning the idea of a historical exhibition in Moscow might be revisited, and Mr. Walden wrote in this sense to Mr. Scott in Moscow on 30 November: 'I think you will agree that the atmosphere has still not improved sufficiently [cf. Nos. 76-7 below] to approach the Russians about this. But we are clearing the tactics on our side in order to be ready to launch the idea at the Russians at the most effective moment' (PW 6/303/9).

[18] Cf. No. 60, note 12. Mr. Kozyrev had given a letter to Sir D. Greenhill for Lord Trevelyan suggesting that a meeting of the Anglo-Soviet Consultative Committee be held in Moscow in December 1971. Committee members agreed, but no date had been finalised.

delay.[19] Lord Trevelyan's brief for the meeting in December is to discharge his obligations to the full but not to commit himself to a programme of future work. After two years of not very productive activity the *raison d'être* of the Consultative Committee will need to be re-examined. So far the response from private British organisations to the idea of closer contacts with their Soviet equivalents has not been enthusiastic, but this could gradually change as the invasion of Czechoslovakia recedes. We have no wish either to kill the Committee off if it is doing good work, or to prolong its life if it is not. Should an extension be agreed upon, Lord Trevelyan has indicated that he would be happy to step down in favour of Sir D. Wilson, who will be available after his retirement in August[20] and may bring some new ideas, as well as greater optimism.

14. Technology is covered by the Joint Commission, referred to in para. 10 above. This too will need to review its own usefulness after its next meeting at the end of this year or the beginning of next. The Working Groups have admirably served the Soviet purpose of familiarising them with British technology without their having to pay for it, but the hoped-for commercial spin-off for us has not been obvious. It may be that the Groups need a centralised secretariat provided by the DTI or the CBI.

(D) *Political dialogue*

15. This is potentially important, but in practice it has not yet proved rewarding. The PUS's visit to Moscow was the most recent of a number of contacts at various official levels. These should continue. Among the events of this kind in prospect are:

(a) a second round on the Middle East,[21] this time in Moscow;

(b) a visit to London by Firyubin, the Soviet Deputy Foreign Minister responsible for South and South-East Asia, or by Nemchina, Head of the South East Asia Department of the Soviet MFA.

(c) a second meeting between Mr. Wright, Head of the Economists Department, and Soviet economists.[22]

16. This year's meeting of the UN General Assembly offers the usual possibilities. The Secretary of State will presumably meet Mr. Gromyko in New York, and may then be able to be a little more precise about dates and

[19] See No. 67, note 6.

[20] Sir D. Wilson had been elected Warden of Corpus Christi College, Cambridge. He had written to Lord Trevelyan in March 1970 expressing his willingness to serve on the Consultative Committee after retirement, but was surprised by the suggestion that he might become Chairman. He wrote to Mr. Bullard on 31 July 1971 that he would 'have to think twice' about taking it on, especially if Mr. Kozyrev continued as Soviet Chairman. Mr. Walden replied on 4 August that the Committee's future was doubtful and the question of a new Chairman was unlikely to arise.

[21] Cf. No. 64, note 1.

[22] Mr. J. Wright visited Moscow from 13-18 April for talks with Gosplan advisers on planning aspects of foreign trade. Mr. Lebedinsky of Gosplan was invited to London but declined the invitation on 22 November (MM 10/ 1).

nature of his visit to Moscow. I have also suggested to Mr. Stratton[23] that the Secretary of State's speech this year should include a passage on relations with Eastern Europe and especially the USSR.

17. Finally we should bear in mind that Sir J. Killick will reach Moscow on 9 September. The coincidence of his arrival with the resumption of international activity after the summer lull, and the interest created by the appointment itself, will make this something of an event. To make the most of it we shall need to think carefully about the language to be used when Sir J. Killick presents his credentials, and about the note to be struck at his first meetings with the Soviet leaders. There may be a case for a personal message from the Secretary of State.

Conclusions

18. Anglo-Soviet relations are likely to remain adversely affected by the problem of Soviet espionage and the counter-measures which it necessitates. Provided this can be either solved or kept within reasonable proportions, the following events should ensure a more positive tone in our relations during the next six months and provide a suitable build-up to the visit of the Secretary of State to the Soviet Union early in 1972:

(A) *Non-interference*
(i) Comparison of texts of sample broadcasts by BBC Russian Service and Radio Moscow, leading perhaps to a more moderate tone in the latter.

(B) *Trade*
(ii) A possible upturn in British exports to the Soviet Union, as predicted by the Soviet side at the annual trade talks.
(iii) Visit to Moscow by the Chairman and Secretary of the East European Trade Council (6-9 September), leading perhaps to some progress on some of the 'large projects'.
(iv) Second meeting of the Anglo-Soviet Joint Commission (November 1971 or January 1972), leading perhaps to establishment of a centralised Secretariat for Working Groups.
(v) Meetings of Working Groups (as necessary).

(C) *Culture and Technology*
(vi) 'Days of Music of the Soviet Union' (1972)
(vii) If British historians agree, revival of the Anglo-Soviet Historical Protocol.
(ix) [*sic*] Second meeting of the Anglo-Soviet Consultative Committee in December, leading (if so decided) to a programme of further work and possibly to the replacement of Lord Trevelyan by Sir D. Wilson as British Chairman.

[23] Mr. R.J. Stratton had been Head of UN (Political) Department in the FCO since February 1971.

(D) *Political dialogue*

(x) Further meetings between officials, e.g. a second round on the Middle East and a visit to London by Firyubin or Nemchina.

(xi) Meeting between the Secretary of State and Gromyko in New York (October).

(xii) Secretary of State's speech to the General Assembly (October).

(xiii) Sir J. Killick's arrival in Moscow (9 September).

19. The Soviet Foreign Ministry would no doubt hold that any good which these activities may do for Anglo-Soviet relations will be vitiated if HMG continue to talk publicly about the Soviet Union or if they take steps to limit Soviet intelligence-gathering operations in the United Kingdom.

J.L. Bullard[24]

[24] Sir D. Greenhill minuted on 14 July: 'I think this is about right. We are bound to have a further row over the spies [cf. No. 66] and in the event it may be convenient to have this problem out with Gromyko in N.Y. in October but we must see what sort of reception the Sec[retar]y of State's second letter (now being drafted) [see No. 70 below] receives. For the rest I think the four points (para. 5 above) which I gave the Russians is [*sic*] a good basis for relations and we should go on saying this publicly. We can lower our voice a little on the Communist threat since we have already had the benefit of calling attention to the Indian Ocean situation [cf. No. 63]. The Americans have woken up and some impression has been made on the Africans.

'On trade I wish we could make progress on the large projects (para. 8 above). I have spoken to Sir Val Duncan [Chairman of RTZ Ltd] who is much respected in the Soviet Union and he will try again on Copper. The Russians themselves told me the "containerisation" project was the "ripest" from their point of view. I hope the Sec[retar]y of State will encourage Mr. Davies to go for the Joint Commission in Nov. rather than Jan.

'I was particularly struck by the common ground between us on India/Pakistan and I hope we can draw some benefit from this.'

Sir A. Douglas-Home minuted on this submission on 19 July: 'I think trade is on the whole the best hope. Sir John Stevens and Sir Val Duncan may well have ideas. I will write to Mr. Davies about the Trade [*sic*] Commission.' Sir D. Greenhill had enclosed a copy of the submission in his letter of 14 July to Sir D. Wilson (see No. 68, note 12), who replied on 31 July that it was 'a very helpful review of the field as a whole'.

Mr. Bullard's detailed proposals for improving Anglo-Soviet relations were overtaken by events. Interdepartmental plans for dealing with the Soviet espionage threat were maturing (cf. No. 66) and by the end of July were ready for presentation to the Prime Minister.

No. 70

Memorandum from Mr. Maudling and Sir A. Douglas-Home to the Prime Minister[1]

[*PUSD*]

'FOOT'. Top Secret   *30 July 1971*

Soviet Intelligence Activity in Britain

1. Officials of our two departments and of the Security Service have been examining for many months the problem of Soviet espionage in this country. We think this is a suitable moment to make you aware of the facts and seek your agreement to the method we propose for handling the problem.

2. Identified Soviet intelligence officers in Britain number at least 120; the total may be some 200. This is more than the Security Service can be expected to contain. If the cases of which we have knowledge are typical, the total damage done by these Soviet intelligence gatherers must be considerable. Known targets during the last few years have included the Foreign Office and Ministry of Defence; and on the commercial side, the Concorde, the Bristol 'Olympus 593' aero-engine, nuclear energy projects and computer electronics.

3. Soviet intelligence officers operate under cover of the various Soviet establishments in this country. Apart from the Soviet Embassy (189), there are the Soviet Trade Delegation (121), contract inspectors (73) and other organisations such as TASS, Aeroflot and the Moscow Narodny Bank (134). The total of 517 is much higher than the Soviet establishment in any other country of Western Europe (see table attached).[2] It is higher even than that

---

[1] This memorandum was submitted to Mr. Heath under cover of a minute from Mr. Maudling which stated that a copy had been sent to Sir B. Trend.

The Home Secretary had been consulted about the revised draft memorandum on Soviet intelligence activities from Sir A. Douglas-Home to the Prime Minister (see No. 66, note 7), and had asked Sir P. Allen to inform Sir D. Greenhill that 'in view of his Ministerial concern for security in this country and his responsibilities for the Security Service, and having regard to the domestic and political problems which this issue raises, he thinks that any submission to the Prime Minister . . . should be a joint submission by the Foreign Secretary and himself'. The Secretary of State welcomed this idea, and the Home Secretary's proposal for a meeting to discuss the memorandum, though he told Mr. Maudling on 22 June that he was anxious 'not to lose momentum in moving towards action', in view of Mr. Heath's statement in the House (see No. 68, note 6) and the danger of leakage. The Ministers, together with their Permanent Secretaries and Sir M. Furnival-Jones, met on 30 June, and agreed to Mr. Maudling's suggestion that Sir A. Douglas-Home should 'write again to Mr. Gromyko, following up his earlier approaches and Sir Denis Greenhill's discussions in Moscow, in rather sharper terms than before'; if there was no response, the Soviet Government should be approached again 'and told both that the numbers must be reduced and the individuals who should go'. Meanwhile the Prime Minister was to be consulted about the course to be pursued by a paper to be submitted jointly by the Home Secretary and the Secretary of State.

[2] Not printed: cf. No. 66, note 4.

in the United States, if the Soviet delegation to the United Nations is subtracted.

4. In November 1968, the previous Government limited the Soviet Embassy to the size which it had then reached,[3] i.e. 86 diplomats and 62 non-diplomats, not counting working wives (this is about double the size of our own Embassy in Moscow). No limit was placed on the Trade Delegations or other organisations, and their staffs have grown by about 60 people in the intervening period. In this respect British practice is more tolerant than that of other comparable countries, as the attached table[4] shows.

5. Soviet intelligence-gathering activities are not merely harmful in themselves. Our failure to stop them lays us open to public and parliamentary criticism. Moreover, our constant consciousness of the scale of their activities, our occasional expulsions of Soviet officials, our refusal of visas to known Soviet intelligence officers and the occasional Soviet acts of retaliation together constitute a recurring irritant in our relations with the Soviet Union.

6. Hitherto we have dealt with each new case ad hoc, expelling spies caught red-handed and refusing visas (with certain exceptions when the balance of advantage at the time demanded departures from the general rule) to known intelligence officers. This may have slowed down the growth of Soviet espionage but it has not prevented it.

7. The Foreign and Commonwealth Secretary raised this question with Gromyko during his visit to London last October.[5] At his suggestion, the Foreign and Commonwealth Secretary subsequently wrote him a letter asking him to give his personal attention to the problem.[6] He has received neither a reply nor even an acknowledgement. Meanwhile Soviet espionage activity has continued. Since Gromyko's visit, expulsions of Soviet officials and refusals of visas to known intelligence agents have continued; and in retaliation the Soviet Ministry of Foreign Affairs have expelled three perfectly innocent members of HM Embassy in Moscow. This tit-for-tat game is one in which we stand to lose.

8. After careful consideration we have been able to devise two alternative schemes designed to bring about a reduction in Soviet intelligence activities.

9. The first would be the drastic one of telling the Russians that a specified list of some 100 intelligence officers must be removed by an early date; that their numbers both inside and outside the Embassy would thereafter be limited to the reduced establishments thus created; and that this new ceiling would thereafter be reduced by one every time an official was caught in intelligence activities and required to leave the country.

10. The second would be to impose parity between our Embassies and enter into negotiations over the size of the Soviet official community outside the Embassy; and this would be made more effective if we asked the Russians

[3] See No. 19.
[5] See pp. 267-8.

[4] Not printed.
[6] No. 58.

at the same time to remove the 100 specified intelligence officers but presented it to them in a way which would avoid putting their prestige at issue—by offering to keep this list of 100 names confidential and dealing with the matter publicly on the basis of a straightforward reduction in numbers, provided that they undertook to cooperate in arranging that the people who left were those named in the list.

11. The advantage of the first course is that it would be the one most certainly effective from the security point of view. The disadvantages are that it could lead to retaliation of various kinds, including a hurtful cutting down of trade; and the Home Secretary feels that there could be difficulty with public opinion in this country when we had to say that spying had been going on for a long time on this scale—and that some of the intelligence officers had been allowed in since we took office.

12. The second scheme, with the refinement suggested, would have considerable advantages as regards presentation. But the negotiations could be protracted by the Russians and, if the Russians declined to cooperate, we would then in effect be forced to go to the first course, whatever the disadvantages.

13. But, overriding all this, is the fact that either of these approaches would cause a major disturbance in Anglo-Soviet relations. We are of the opinion that it would be wrong to provoke this disturbance now, when both the Soviet Union and we are engaged in extremely delicate and important negotiations on Berlin.[7] Although logically there is no connection between the two subjects, an Anglo-Soviet row of the likely dimensions could not fail to damage the atmosphere for the Berlin talks.[8] It could also give the Russians a pretext for breaking them off or causing them to fail, if they should decide

[7] Cf. No. 68, note 3. At the Ambassadors' meeting on 8 July broad agreement had been reached on a more intensive programme of work at ambassadorial and counsellor level. There were signs that the Soviet Government were 'ready to move', and this, combined with the risk of leaks, the political situation in the FRG and the danger that the atmosphere might be 'disturbed by some extraneous and unforeseen factor if we take longer than necessary', led Sir R. Jackling to express the view on 17 July that 'there is a reasonable hope of signing a first stage quadripartite agreement, and initialling a final quadripartite protocol, during the first half of August' (Bonn telegram No. 917). The FCO were sceptical of this forecast, and considered that it would be a good idea for the negotiations to pause for a while, but Sir R. Jackling and the other Western Ambassadors were concerned at the likely effect of a pause on public opinion in the FRG and West Berlin; in addition, Dr. Kissinger told Lord Cromer in Washington that 'the President and he were of the opinion that it was better to go ahead on the basis that one final heave might bring the negotiations to a conclusion' (Washington telegram No. 2582, 30 July). It was clear to WED that 'we have now reached the crunch', and following a visit to London by Sir R. Jackling for consultations on 4 and 5 August extended Ambassadorial talks began in Berlin on 10 August in an attempt to conclude a first stage agreement in a prolonged negotiating session (WRL 2/1).

[8] On a submission of 22 June by Mr. Bullard concerning the recent expulsion of two members of HM Embassy in Moscow (cf. p. 337), recommending that no action should be taken which would risk 'escalating the situation in advance of FOOT', the Secretary of State had minuted: 'I agree with all this. My only anxiety is over Berlin. If these talks are going well it seems a pity to have a major row at this point of time.'

that this was what they wanted. We should then be exposed to the charge of having frustrated not only an agreement on Berlin but the wider negotiations which are expected to follow.

14. We therefore propose, if you agree, to defer any radical action until the situation on Berlin is clarified. This should happen in the autumn, or at least before the end of the year. We should then wish to revert to the problem and to consider the choice between the two alternatives described above.

15. Meanwhile the Foreign and Commonwealth Secretary proposes, if you agree, to send a letter to Gromyko in somewhat sharper terms than before, setting out the present situation and latest developments in a manner suitable for publication in case this should turn out to be desirable at some later stage. This would help later on to satisfy public and parliamentary interest by enabling us to take the line that we have had the problem under constant review and have on a number of occasions been in touch with the Government concerned. But this is a line which cannot be held indefinitely, and, whatever happens over Berlin, we propose to look at the situation again in the autumn.[9]

[9] Mr. Heath replied to Mr. Maudling on 3 August: 'Thank you very much for your Memorandum of 30 July on Soviet espionage in this country. I agree that this must be firmly and speedily settled. When we take action we must do everything required at one blow. I personally doubt whether this action would affect Soviet intentions over Berlin, but it could be used as a cover by them if required. But even that I doubt. Nevertheless, the Foreign and Commonwealth Secretary's excellent letter should go at once, and we can then review at the end of October, to consider both the position on Berlin and the Soviet reply, if any. By then they will have got away with it all for a year since Gromyko's London visit. I am sending copies of this minute to the Foreign and Commonwealth Secretary and Sir Burke Trend. E.H.'

No. 71

Sir A. Douglas-Home to Sir D. Wilson (Moscow)

No. 823 Telegraphic [PUSD]

Immediate. Secret   FCO, *4 August 1971, 3.55 p.m.*

Following for Ambassador. My telegram No. 820: Soviet espionage.[1]

[1] This telegram of 3 August informed Sir D. Wilson that Sir A. Douglas-Home had summoned the Soviet Ambassador at 11.30 on 4 August to receive a second letter to Mr. Gromyko about Soviet espionage in the UK. Sir D. Greenhill had suggested that the letter should be delivered in London rather than in Moscow, in view of Sir D. Wilson's impending departure on 11 August, and that the Secretary of State might consider handing it over personally. Sir S. Crawford endorsed this suggestion on 3 August: 'It would particularly mark the importance of this second letter if the Secretary of State would summon the Ambassador to receive it. This is I think to be recommend[ed], since other action in this field may be somewhat delayed, and we do not want the situation to deteriorate meanwhile.' Mr. Heath approved this procedure, and the Secretary of State minuted on 4 August: 'I look forward to the interview.'

1. When the Soviet Ambassador called this morning, I gave him another letter to Gromyko on this subject.[2] I said that Gromyko and I had already talked privately about the number of people in the Soviet Embassy and the Soviet Trade Delegation who ought not to be here and the proposal that others, whom we knew to have engaged in undesirable activities, should join them. I still hoped we could settle this matter privately, but I had had no answer to my two earlier approaches and Gromyko continued to allow these people to be sent here. The Soviet Ambassador having read my letter, I repeated that the present situation was impossible, and referred to the case of Glushchenko.[3] How could we carry on the kind of relations both the Soviet Ambassador and we ourselves wanted when this kind of thing went on? I was asking Gromyko to put a stop to it.

2. After a considerable pause for thought, Smirnovsky expressed regret that we could not deal with the important questions concerning our relations rather than reverting once again to this subject. He too had a lot of complaints. He did not think we were going in the right direction. It would be better to take a more positive attitude to our relations.

3. I asked Smirnovsky how we could be expected to allow this sort of thing to continue? The proposal that Glushchenko should join the Embassy was an insult. Nor was it the only case. It was inconceivable that Gromyko did not know about these matters. I hoped he would deal with them. When I had approached him privately, Gromyko had undertaken to look into it. But there had been no answer. Sir Denis Greenhill had later spoken about this question too. I asked Smirnovsky to tell Gromyko that I wished to make progress on important matters, but that this problem made such progress more difficult.

4. Smirnovsky said that there were many harmful aspects of our relations. His Embassy had been unable to meet Fedoseev[4] and had no knowledge of his position. They had learned from Nadeinsky[5] what really happened in these cases. I said that we had heard these complaints before, for example in the case of the ballerina, Makarova.[6] She had made her own decision not to return to the Soviet Union and we had no control over her whatsoever. She was now travelling round the world and was free to go back to the USSR if she wished. I hoped she would. I did not know whether Fedoseev would return home. It was up to him.

5. Smirnovsky repeated that the Soviet Embassy had a right to see these people and again referred to the Nadeinsky case, which had given them

[2] The text of this letter, as transmitted to Moscow in telegram No. 821 of 4 August, is printed as the Enclosure to this document.

[3] See Enclosure below.

[4] Cf. p. 344.

[5] A senior official at the International Maritime Consultative Organisation in London, who had sought permission to stay in Britain but returned home after considerable Russian pressure.

[6] Cf. No. 51.

reason to doubt our word. But there were more important things for us to discuss.

6. I agreed but repeated that Gromyko must deal with the matter I had raised. How could the Soviet Government seriously propose that Glush-chenko should return to this country? Smirnovsky denied knowledge of this case, and said that his staff had clear instructions not to take part in activities of the kind I had mentioned. He undertook however to deliver my letter.

ENCLOSURE IN NO. 71

Letter from Sir A. Douglas-Home to Mr. Gromyko, dated 4 August 1971

I have received with interest Sir Denis Greenhill's reports of his conversations with Mr. Kozyrev and yourself,[7] in which you both referred to the allegedly hostile and provocative activities of the 'British special services' against the Soviet Union and its citizens and against Soviet agencies in the United Kingdom, and in which you argued that these alleged activities did not contribute to the creation of a favourable atmosphere for the development of Anglo-Soviet relations.

Since you have raised this matter, I think it right to tell you that I see the situation in a very different light.

The Soviet Union conducts espionage against Great Britain on a large scale. Even if I were to mention only those cases which have become public knowledge during the last few years, the list would be a long one. Many more cases, some of them very serious, are known to me and doubtless to you also. Governments which engage in intelligence activities on such a scale as this must expect that the authorities in the countries attacked will take such precautions and counter-measures as may be open to them.

I do not accept your contention that, in the interests of Anglo-Soviet relations, Her Majesty's Government should abstain from taking measures to prevent, limit or inhibit the espionage conducted by Soviet officials and other Soviet citizens in this country on such an extensive scale. It is this which places a strain upon our relations.

I take it that you yourself are fully informed of the scale of Soviet intelligence activities in this country. You are no doubt aware that the total number of Soviet officials on the staff of Soviet diplomatic, commercial and other organisations has now risen to more than 500, and you are presumably able to ascertain what proportion of these are intelligence officers. I would ask you to consider how the situation must appear to me, the Foreign Minister of the country against which all this activity is directed. I would add that the number of Soviet officials in the United Kingdom exceeds the number of Soviet officials in any comparable country and indeed even in the United States (excluding the United Nations).

With the information at my disposal I find it hard to interpret the remarks made by Mr. Kozyrev and yourself as other than a suggestion that Her

[7] See Nos. 67 and 68.

Majesty's Government should allow these intelligence agents of yours to conduct their activities in the United Kingdom unhampered lest Anglo-Soviet relations should suffer. I consider this a proposition which it is unreasonable for any government to make to another, whatever the state of their relations.

As an example of the present situation I will mention one particular case. It is in no way exceptional, but it happens to be the most recent. Last month Her Majesty's Embassy in Moscow received an application for a visa from a man named B.G. Glushchenko, together with the statement that he had been nominated to the post of First Secretary at the Soviet Embassy in London. This man was in Britain from 1964 to 1968. At that time he was described as the representative of *Aviaexport* at the Soviet Trade Delegation. Mr. Glushchenko's activities however had little to do with the sale of aircraft. He came to our notice on various occasions: for example he offered a large sum of money to a British businessman if he would obtain details of certain British military equipment. This is the man whom some Soviet organisation has nominated to serve as First Secretary at your Embassy in London. You will hardly be surprised to learn that I am not prepared to permit such a person to return to this country.

This is not the first time that I have had occasion to bring such matters to your attention. I spoke to you on the subject during your visit to London in October 1970.[8] I did so in a manner which would have permitted the question to be pursued in a non-polemical way. You suggested that I should write you a letter, and on 3 December, 1970, I did so.[9] To this date to my surprise I have received no reply, nor even an acknowledgement. Meanwhile inadmissible Soviet activities in this country continue unabated.

I ask you to reflect upon this and to consider the extent to which these activities are obstructing the development of Anglo-Soviet relations.

I note that Mr. Kozyrev tried to obscure the central issue, namely the scale and nature of your government's intelligence activities in this country, by dragging in the irrelevant question of the few Soviet citizens who, at various times, have sought and received permission to stay in this country, and by repeating a number of unwarranted accusations against the behaviour of the British authorities. The accusations, which referred to past incidents, were dealt with at the time in separate exchanges. As for the Soviet citizens, I again assure you that any Soviet citizen in this country who decides to return to the USSR is free to do so.

I trust that you will now feel able to reply to my original letter and to this one, which I send in the hope that you will say that you are ready immediately to terminate such activities.[10]

[8] See pp. 267-8.

[9] No. 58.

[10] FCO telegram No. 829 to Moscow of 5 August informed Sir D. Wilson that although News Department had told the press that the subject of Mr. Smirnovsky's call on Sir A. Douglas-Home was 'matters of mutual interest', the popular press had 'drawn the correct inference from our reticence', and speculation centred around the possibility of further expulsions

of Soviet intelligence officers. 'Some papers also suggest that the Soviet Ambassador was given a "last warning". There is no repeat no mention of a personal message to Gromyko.' Mr. Walden minuted to Sir S. Crawford and Private Office on 5 August that it was 'regrettable' that the press should have guessed the subject of the call, but 'perhaps not very surprising'. He thought that any attempt to put the record straight would 'compound confusion, besides giving the Russians an opening to complain'. Mr. Graham agreed, but added (5 August): 'My worry is that the leak serves to confirm what would be a natural Russian suspicion that we are engaged in a public relations exercise and do not really mean business; thus the possibly small chance that they might actually act on the letter is further reduced.'

No. 72

Sir D. Wilson (Moscow) to Sir A. Douglas-Home

No. 93/1 [ENS 3/548/10]

Confidential   MOSCOW, *10 August 1971*

Sir,

1. I have the honour to submit, in accordance with tradition, some 'valedictory' observations on the occasion of my departure from Moscow and retirement from the Diplomatic Service. This occurs at a time when Anglo-Soviet relations, political and economic, are in poor shape and may well get worse before they can get better. I have just re-read with nostalgic interest my predecessor's despatch of the 21st November 1966 to Mr. (now Lord) George Brown.[1] 'The fact', he wrote 'that we represent what the Russians might call the sensible wing of the Western camp, but are quite definitely of it, makes us of more interest to them—in the positive field of co-existence, if not in propaganda haymaking—than, for instance, the France of General de Gaulle. This is, I believe, our image in the minds of the Soviet leaders. I am sure it is an image which it is to our advantage to preserve and develop.' I am afraid that our image in the eyes of the Soviet leaders is very different today, and I cannot congratulate myself on the results of my own mission here.[2]

2. At the same time in the general field of East-West relations, much has begun to change quickly after twenty years or so of comparative stability,

[1] Not printed (NS 1022/69 of 1966: FO 371/188906).

[2] Submitting this despatch to Sir T. Brimelow on 19 August, Mr. Walden commented: 'I am not sure Sir Duncan Wilson is right to deprecate the results of his own mission . . . it is more important that our policy should be sensible in our own eyes than in the eyes of the Russians. In Soviet usage "sensible" can be a euphemism for "malleable" . . . I do not therefore think that we should take the change in our image too badly.' In his reply of 6 September to Sir D. Wilson, Sir T. Brimelow wrote: 'I think you did well in circumstances which any Ambassador must have found discouraging. I question whether any British Ambassador in Moscow has exercised a decisive influence on Anglo-Soviet relations. The forces at play are not accessible to his influence. He can advise, encourage and discourage: but on both the Soviet and British sides his advice is offset by considerations other than those which he would wish to prevail.'

stagnation or recurrent and predictable crises. From the sidelines I shall observe with the keenest interest the emergence of China on to the international stage, the progress towards integration of Western Europe, and Soviet attempts to influence or freeze the European situation by means of 'all-European' negotiations or conferences. I have done my best in recent despatches or telegrams to describe or forecast Soviet actions and reactions on these subjects, and I may perhaps be excused any further attempt to prophesy about what may well be a rapidly changing scene.[3]

3. The internal Soviet scene is likely, alas, to be much less affected by external circumstances than Soviet foreign policy, and perhaps the most useful contribution which I can make at this stage is to offer a few last remarks upon it. As a prelude to doing so, I have re-read my own 'First Impressions', dated November 1968.[4] It is depressing to find how many of these first impressions remain valid for myself today, but I would not admit to having learned and forgotten precisely nothing. In particular my wife and I have travelled a certain amount within the Soviet Union over the past three years. We have also, by a series of chances, had access to a number of contacts (some of them inherited, so to speak, from our daughter and her five years at the Moscow *Conservatoire*) which are not normally within range of Ambassadors. These have enabled us to see something in detail of odd areas of Soviet life, not extensive nor entirely typical, but of some interest in a field where first-hand observation is inevitably rare.[5]

4. So far as travel is concerned, one can state as a rough general law that the further you go away from Moscow the more sympathetic will be your

[3] In a despatch of 30 July Sir D. Wilson had argued that Soviet *Westpolitik* was at present as much defensive as offensive, insofar as immediate Soviet aims were, to a considerable extent, determined by fears of a united Western Europe, exercising an attraction for the Eastern European countries and dominated by the FRG. He concluded that 'There is every reason for Western self-confidence in proceeding to the strengthening of Western European unity and in conducting negotiations with the East, despite the obvious need for caution especially over force reductions.' Mr. C. Hulse of EESD minuted on 6 August that Sir D. Wilson's main thesis was that 'Soviet policy towards Europe is in many areas defensive and represents a reaction to events over which Moscow has no control. This is true insofar as the EEC is concerned, but I think that the Russians have certainly not been on the defensive in the Berlin talks and they need not have taken up the force reduction issue had they not seen advantage for themselves in doing so.' He considered the Ambassador over-optimistic in his analysis of where the balance of advantage lay in a European security conference, and that he underestimated the difficulties for the West in discussing force reductions (ENS 2/2).

[4] See No. 60, note 8.

[5] Sir T. Brimelow commented: 'I have no doubt that in the peculiarly frustrating circumstances of your mission, the wisest and most profitable course was for you to develop those personal and private contacts which your wife and yourself found so illuminating. It was precisely this kind of contact which Stalin was determined to make difficult and dangerous. We have always assumed that most members of the Soviet intelligentsia had interests broader than those officially approved by the Party, and that many of them would welcome contacts with their opposite numbers in the non-Communist world . . . This assumption has underlain our whole policy of contacts and exchanges and in this field your own contribution has been outstanding.'

impression of the Soviet régime.[6] More precisely, in some of the more 'backward' parts of the Soviet Union which I have visited (and I cannot claim to have made anything but the most obvious journeys) there is a sense of purpose and of pride in achievement which is not always easy to find among the Ministries in Moscow. The basic jobs of government and party at the edges have been to make something of a quite long period of comparative stability, to provide such basic services as housing and irrigation, and to interest people in education and new methods of agriculture and industry. In general the local leaders have something to show for their efforts and display a considerable sense of pride in what they have achieved.

5. The most important element in the background has been twenty-five years of peace and at least since the death of Stalin an absence of wild experiment. The resulting stability may not have been conducive to efficiency (in the strict sense of producing the maximum of results from the minimum of effort). But stability has perhaps been the first essential for the Soviet Union as a whole. One could go further and say that economic efficiency may do much to disturb social stability and is therefore something to be introduced quite cautiously. I have been impressed by the amount of concealed unemployment—perhaps ill-concealed under-employment would be a better phrase—which is observable in practically every Russian institution open to our inspection. At one extreme is the big ZIL diesel engine factory at Yaroslavl, which we recently visited. This gave the impression more of a way of life than of a factory. The Director, exuding what now seems to be the typical confidence of a big Soviet provincial boss, claimed to employ a work force of 30,000 and to provide nearly all of them with housing on the spot. We were taken to visit not only the workshops, but also the sports centre which the workers had built for themselves, and finally attended a concert at their 'House of Culture'. No doubt as good economic results could have been achieved by a lesser number of people; perhaps it was not very efficient that they should have built their own sports centre themselves; probably some of the highly skilled entertainers whom we heard in the evening had not been hired primarily as engineers or electricians. But the factory turns out a product which is very widely used, and it does a considerable social service by looking after the very large number of workers 'ascribed' to it. At the other extreme, the deaf and dumb son of a musician friend of ours was taken on by a small factory of 'Father Frost' toys in his local village (he is a most individual artist, and has produced some delightful impressions of factory life from the floor). When he left work after about two years, they managed to

---

[6] In a minute of 18 August Mr. Murrell expressed the view that the overall impression the despatch gave of the Soviet internal scene was 'perhaps rather too charitable. I would not for example subscribe to the general law propounded in para. 4 . . . This very much depends on where you go and how carefully your steps are guided by Protocol Department or Intourist. Even in the very limited number of places the Western visitor is allowed to see it is not difficult to get some idea of the squalor and brutality which still pervades provincial Soviet life especially in the smaller Russian towns.'

provide him with a small pension. Perhaps Western standards of efficiency should not be the main criterion in such cases.[7]

6. Another and strong general impression is of the Soviet people's deep feeling for 'togetherness'. To start at the top again, I can personally imagine nothing more ghastly than the sort of 'sanatorium' holiday enjoyed yearly by high Soviet officials, who congregate together in what amount to large private hotels, with a certain amount of medical attention laid on (the Soviet Russian seems to be a hopeless hypochondriac, particularly with regard to possible ailments of the heart). The whole routine seems to be incredibly drab and discouraging to individual tastes and enterprise. On the other hand at a lower level, I can see the attraction of Pioneer camps or joint archaeological digs for school children. And somewhere in between there is a thoroughly cheerful and collective atmosphere about the picnic and camping parties which one sees along the banks of rivers near Moscow, or the sailing clubs which we saw on a recent progress down the Moscow/Volga Canal. Even at a completely private level, something persists of the old Russian feeling of togetherness, so much missed by emigrés from the Soviet Union. In the apartment of one of my former Soviet diplomatic colleagues (now ambassador to Bulgaria), we never know on our occasional visits which of the numerous relations we shall find engaged on which domestic chore. And we have seen, in the 'dacha country' around Moscow, that while unannounced guests no longer drop in to stay for two or three weeks, the main meal of the day will be served to almost any number who happen by.

7. In any case there is plenty of variety within the Soviet Union on a local or national basis. Leningrad patriotism is notorious and very easy to feel even by the casual visitor. Georgia and Armenia, perhaps the two most extreme cases, seem to have profited by the period of stability since the war to revive a frank nationalism, which often seems to be directly subversive of Moscow authority. Certainly the average Muscovite, including our senior chauffeur and the Embassy barber, make no secret of their dislike and envy for Georgians, lazy folk for whom the southern earth produces such an abundance (many of them in fact make a pile by flying to Moscow to sell fruit and flowers). The Secretary-General of the Georgian Foreign Ministry during my first visit to Georgia over two years ago frankly expressed his preference for the French as opposed to the Russian language. The Armenians seem to me rather more cautious (the popular Moscow doctrine is that all the really clever ones left Armenia many years ago). But it is a

[7] Mr. Walden commented that this paragraph contained 'The most important (and perhaps the most debatable) point in the despatch . . . I suspect that the comfortable provincial inefficiency described so graphically by the Ambassador in paragraphs 4-5 is probably a source of extreme exasperation to the Soviet leaders'. Sir T. Brimelow expressed agreement in his reply: 'I have never been convinced that instability within the Soviet empire would necessarily work out to the advantage of the West: and I have never thought that attempts actively to promote instability added up to a prudent long-term policy for the West. I fear, however, that within the USSR some factors, not least demographic, may work over the longer term in favour of an instability which could have important consequences.'

pleasantly ironic thought that most of the foreign exchange that reaches Armenia comes from the faithful Christians abroad, in response to appeals by the *Katholikos*. Some of it may go to the party coffers, but a lot is certainly spent in restoring churches. Georgians and Armenians alike display an open and almost pathetic desire for foreign contacts, and in these areas I would recommend as much 'town twinning' and other formal devices for legalising foreign travel as may be practicable.[8]

8. The local patriotism and pieties of these outlying nations is best illustrated by the care with which they preserve their cultural monuments—the Armenian National Library at Yerevan is a particularly fine example. There are also strong local pieties within Russia itself. We have made pilgrimages to the shrines of Tolstoy, Chekov and Pushkin, which have some slightly depressing implications. The extreme care with which the original houses are reconstructed and converted into museums suggests the attitude that culture is simply an inheritance to be treasured, and not a pattern to be lived daily. But the reverence shown by the keepers of the shrines is none the less impressive and respectable, and we have found them to be among the most attractive Soviet citizens whom we have met. Moreover their devotion to the great authors of the past raises the important question whether anyone can seriously study Pushkin, Tolstoy and Chekov, without seeing through much of the pretentiousness and nonsense of the present régime.

9. This is unfortunately everywhere visible. It reached its height during the Lenin centenary celebrations, which were incredibly unimaginative and dull, and were reminiscent of the worst stock pieties of Puritan New England or Victorian England. But at least the man in the street reacted to a prolonged special occasion with a large crop of more or less irreverent jokes. It is the routine everyday slogans, posters, etc., that are more depressing, since they seem to be regarded just as part of the landscape, which is unthinkable without those inspiring slogans 'Glory to our Party', 'Glory to Work', or 'Visit the cinemas of our capital and see documentary, scientific-artistic, and entertainment films!' It is hard to judge how much of official Soviet propaganda sticks. I would guess that by and large more people here are better informed about a larger number of subjects than before—but that is not saying much. The dangers seem to me firstly for the general public that, while they may not actively believe much official propaganda, it keeps a lot of better stuff from reaching their eyes and ears; and secondly for the more educated public, that the modes of Marxist-Leninist language make 'straight' and concrete thought increasingly difficult. Herzen[9] noted the effect of

---

[8] Mr. Walden noted that both EESD and Central European Department had 'always had reservations about "town-twinning" arrangements. The Ambassador may under-estimate the Soviet ability to use such contacts for their own purposes and to minimise the danger of contagion. We should also remember that the most active British participants in schemes of this kind are often unrepresentative figures.'

[9] Alexander Herzen (1812-70), of mixed Russian-German parentage, author and advocate of political and social reform.

Hegelian modes of thought on the young Russian intellectuals of his time in words which apply all too well today: 'Our young philosophers distorted not only phrases, but also the powers of thought. Their relation to life and reality became scholastic and artificial—an over-learned way of grasping simple things . . . Every really immediate effect, every simple feeling, had to be filtered through abstract categories and reappeared only as a pale algebraical shadow without a drop of live blood. In all this process there was a certain naiveté, because it was all so completely sincere. A man who went to Sokolniki for a walk would go in order to enjoy the pantheistic feeling of individuality, in the universe. If on the way he happened to fall in with some soldier or old woman and start talking with them, this would not be just a conversation for our philosopher, but a determination of the popular essence in its immediate and occasional form.' The Germans have indeed caused great suffering in Russia.

10. I have no more means than I had when I wrote my 'First Impressions' of judging how much these categories of thought and this type of verbiage really mean to the inner circles of the Party. I shall never, I suppose, have a cosy chat with Suslov or any of his fellow-ideologues. Through former diplomatic contacts, however, and work undertaken by my wife at or around the English Linguistics Faculty of Moscow University, we have met privately a few of the orthodox up to and including Central Committee level, and have occasionally been in their houses, to pass some agreeable but intellectually not very exacting hours. I find it hard to think that there are many among them or their bosses who could sustain a philosophic disputation about the tenets of Marxism. I imagine that they have a general loyalty to Party ancestors and a general desire to preserve the system, a feeling that they are well fitted to run it, and considerable faith in the capitalist devil:

> The things we must believe are few and plain,
> But since men will believe more than they need
> And ev'ry man invents himself a creed;
> In doubtful questions t'is the safest way
> To learn what unsuspected Ancients say,
> For t'is not likely we should higher soar
> In search of heav'n than all the Church before.

> T'is some Relief that points not clearly known
> Without much hazard may be let alone:
> for points obscure t'is little use to learn
> But Common Quiet is ManKind's concern.

The title is *Religio Laici*, the date 1682, the author Dryden, the wit unlike anything Soviet; but I suspect that many good Party leaders, with the

Chinese, Romanians and Yugoslavs in mind, would heartily sympathise with the attitude both to dogma and to dissent.[10]

11. My guesses about the extent of Party faith lead me to speculation about the extent of Party and KGB influence on the life of Soviet individuals. Here we have something more definite to go on, in the experiences of our personal friends in the musical and university worlds. Rostropovich is of course an outsize example, since he has courageously advertised his own connexion with Solzhenitsyn.[11] He has behaved with an extraordinary and very clever mixture of impudence, cunning and sincerity. He likes openly to advertise his connexions with the outside world, thus reminding the bosses what a row there will be abroad if they act too openly against him. Thus he will arrange by telephone (no doubt monitored) to have his Land Rover or Mercedes serviced at this or the Federal German Embassy, and will spend a family evening with us, or attend a diplomatic meal with the Germans, on such occasions. At the opposite extreme, I have watched him exert to the full his enormous gaiety and charm on Madame Furtseva. But he is by now subject to a strict limitation on visits abroad, and to other types of petty persecution. The last time we saw him at his flat in the 'Composers' House', we were followed blatantly into the lift outside his door and into the street by what we have agreed to call a 'promising young composer'. And the great man has to earn what freedom he has with monster concert-tours within the Soviet Union, including to the music-loving Eskimoes of Kamchatka.

12. We have many less conspicuous friends in the same profession, who are subject in even greater degree (just because they are less eminent) to petty persecution by the cultural authorities. It is the now stricter travel restrictions and customs procedure that they resent most, but even more humiliating perhaps are the arguments with authority about their concert programmes—'no late Beethoven without Tchaikovsky' or 'no Shostakovich without Khachaturian'. Such people meet us regularly and without concealment as friends, and again with some idea of proving to authority that they have foreign friends. They are careful how and where they talk, are generally suspicious, and in some cases one feels have acquired a sort of protective habit of lying on indifferent matters even among themselves. The depth of typical suspicions was illustrated for me lately by the family mentioned in paragraph 5. We were visiting the deaf and dumb son's studio, at the father's dacha. I was particularly delighted by one of the son's humorous pictorial comments on local manners and personalities. Much as

[10] In his reply Sir T. Brimelow stated that the main point on which he differed from Sir D. Wilson was 'the extent to which ideology has been eroded among the Soviet leaders. I agree that there are probably few of them who could sustain a philosophic disputation about the tenets of Marxism. But most members of the Central Committee were brought up under Stalin, i.e. at a time when people had to know the line, lest every slip cost them their career and perhaps their freedom and their life. Their outlook, I think, is very far from that expressed in *Religio Laici*. If they really did subscribe to the doctrine that 'Common Quiet is Mankind's concern', I think that by now our relations with them would be other than what they are.'

[11] Cf. No. 65, note 4.

the family enjoyed showing it off in the studio, they would not let me photograph it outside in the garden, since 'there are eyes everywhere'. The general atmosphere among the artists that we know is in fact of petty persecution more reminiscent perhaps of the Tsarist police as described by Herzen[12] than of Stalinist times, as pictured for example by Nadezhda Mandelshtam in her memoirs[13] (though one recognises plainly in this remarkable book some of the informer-types who now operate so to speak in miniature).

13. Artists and musicians are *ex hypothesi* prone to individualism and thus suspect to a totalitarian régime. The University world, as seen by my wife in her work at Professor Akhmanova's Department of English Linguistics, is much more orthodox, and the problems of the academics are very different. There is no question for any but the very eminent few of an ivory tower, or remote island, where politics and ideology simply do not intrude on professional interests. Our picture is rather of a community which includes plenty of 'politics', and would be politically suspect if it did not. Some of these are no doubt just concerned to further their own careers by obeisance to the Party and by giving information as necessary against their fellows. Some of them are engaged on a much more complicated process. The most interesting and complicated example is probably the formidable Professor Akhmanova herself, known to generations of British Ambassadors in Moscow and their staffs. I have little doubt that she is a loyal Communist, within the limits of faith described in paragraph 10 above, i.e. she thinks that there is little choice for the Soviet Union and does quite well out of the present régime. I do not doubt either that it is part of her job to get acquainted with the British Embassy and to report on personalities there to Party channels. But equally I do not doubt that she is a very competent professional, devoted to preserving the highest possible academic standards in her Department, and to protecting the Department against too much incompetence and political intervention. I suspect that this mixture of political and professional loyalties is very typical of the Soviet scientific and academic world, and would be happy to think that the normal proportions of the mixture were those which we have had the chance of observing ourselves.

14. I am conscious that a number of questions may be raised by the preceding paragraphs, and will try to anticipate one or two of them. First of all, while we have been fortunate personally in inheriting many private contacts, we have made many others ourselves, even at a time when Her Majesty's Government is high on the Soviet list of officially hostile foreign governments. I do not exclude, of course, that things might get worse from the social point of view, possibly as the result of what might be roughly

[12] Mr. Walden pointed out that 'Herzen, it will be recalled, found little difficulty in exchanging his far from intolerable exile in Siberia for that of an emigré agitator in the West. It is hard to imagine the same thing happening today. The essential difference between the KGB and their Tsarist analogues lies in the blanket efficiency of the former.'

[13] *Hope Against Hope* (Harvill, 1961).

described as the 'Romanian formula'—the more flexibility towards the West in foreign policy, the tighter the controls at home. But under present conditions a certain (not necessarily advanced) knowledge of the Russian language, some persistence, and a modicum of tact can earn a number of private contacts for the foreign diplomat—perhaps most easily for Ambassadors, who are no doubt regarded as too stupid to be spies. The more fundamental question may be raised: Is it all worth while? The sort of contacts one can make are not likely to be typical and have at best only a remote influence on Soviet Governmental or Party policies. Do they not distract our energy and attention from the 'ruling few', to whom one of my predecessors devoted so much trouble? I can only give very brief and subjective answers here to these questions. We should certainly not exaggerate the value of private contacts in terms of political influence (probably nil) or of sociological importance. But a little—even a very little—value is better than none. Nor is there any problem yet about having one's attention distracted from men of real power. In the present state of relations between HMG and the Soviet Government, it is out of the question to have contact with the Party bosses, and even Ministers and Vice-Ministers, including Vice-Ministers of Foreign Affairs, are hard to come by without a special excuse. There remains a quite important circle of senior journalists and men from e.g. the Institute of International Politics and Economics. We have been in touch with some of them, and much more may yet be done in this field, if inter-Governmental relations improve. At present it is the Soviet side which is inclined to hold back. There remains also a sort of *demi-monde* of licensed contact-men, perhaps attached to newspapers or institutes, who like cultivating Ambassadors and give them to understand that they have special links with e.g the Central Committee. Here too more may be done. It is however worth bearing in mind the advice of my long-experienced and wise Canadian colleague, who at present enjoys all the official and semi-official contacts that he wants, as well as many private ones in virtue of his talents as a poet and translator of modern Soviet poetry. He regards some of the main '*demi-mondains*' as not only not worth while, but even as positively dangerous. In any case, I would answer my own original question by saying that, with all the private contacts that we can acquire, we are still likely to have time and energy for what official or semi-official ones are available.

15. So much for the opportunities and dangers of Moscow. I would like to record my thanks for the privilege of serving in this post, which can never have less than a sombre fascination, even at a time when a 'low profile' has been *de rigueur* officially. I would like also to thank the staff who have served with me here with such enthusiasm and good judgment, particularly those who have formed my own 'Politburo'. Owing to a system which I think counter-productive (but that is another story), there have been three generations of them during my rather less than three years *en poste*. But they, as well as many others, have contributed much to the running of what has been for me an essentially happy Embassy.

16. Finally, I would use the license of a 'Valedictory' despatch to record a few personal reflections on my twenty-five years in the Diplomatic Service. I remember that at my original 'viva' for the Foreign Service in 1935, Major (subsequently Mr., subsequently Earl) Attlee asked me why I wanted to join the Diplomatic Service. I cannot remember what I replied at the time. Probably the most accurate answer would have been 'lack of imagination—my family always wanted me to'. Their and my own desires were frustrated at the time by a series of official doctors, who declared me unfit at first for the rigours of diplomatic life, and then successively for any responsible position in any branch of Government Service. Thus, eleven years later, when I did join the Service, the correct answer to that original question would probably have been: 'Obstinacy, and a desire to prove wrong the medical authorities of 1935.' If someone were now to ask me why a young man should wish to join the Diplomatic Service (and perhaps some of my future charges at Cambridge[14] will put the question), I should find it hard to give answers as short and accurate. I recognise that it is, compared e.g. with medicine or architecture, a secondary profession, not concerned with the first things of life; nor, if one is thinking in terms of power or influence, are the top posts of a diplomatic career likely to bring with them so much as those in politics or in the Home Civil Service. None the less, it is not so small a thing to represent one's country in various parts of a fastly [sic]changing and increasingly accessible world, or to advise the political authorities in London from various angles on the world framework within which they can shape one's country's future. There may be professional deformations peculiar to the diplomatic life, but these should not include ossification of the mind or the tyranny of an unchanging habit of life. At a less exalted level, the Diplomatic Service seems to me an excellent one for the 'fox' (in Archilochus' and Sir Isaiah Berlin's sense of the word),[15] the man of many sympathies, or, more simply and in no derogatory sense, the amateur. Here is a profession in which, apart from the fulfilment of the basic calls of duty, to do what you will and what you have the talent to do is not only permissible but can be positively important. It brings with it (and here I connect with the themes of my previous paragraphs) the possibility of getting to know like-minded people of the country in which one is stationed, and thus the possibility of an understanding, otherwise hardly to be attained, of the inner life of that country and the deeper background of its Government's policy.

17. If I have learned anything of general import in the course of my own years as an Ambassador, it is that in the process of diplomacy (which is increasingly likely to begin at home) the question of tone is all important. It is of course wrong to be anyhow but deliberately imprecise, but one can be too direct as well as too clever by half. 'Diplomatic phraseology' is in bad repute, but there is much to be said for it, and this has never been better put than in the words of that great persuader, Benjamin Franklin. 'This habit' (of

[14] Cf. No. 69, note 20.

[15] Isaiah Berlin, *Hedgehog and the Fox: Essay on Tolstoy's View of History* (London, 1967).

expressing himself without any unduly positive air) 'I believe has been of great advantage to me when I have had occasion to inculcate my opinions, and persuade men into measures which I have been from time to time engaged in promoting; and as the chief ends of conversation are to *inform* or to be *informed*, to *please* or to *persuade*, I wish well-meaning sensible men would not lessen their power of doing good by a positive, assuming manner, that seldom fails to disgust, tends to create opposition and to defeat every one of those purposes for which speech was given to us, to wit, giving or receiving information or pleasure.' I am profoundly conscious that I have not lived consistently up to this admirable precept, and I would like to take this last opportunity of saying, without any of the modest diffidence prescribed by Franklin for matters of possible dispute, that

> I have the honour to be,
> Sir,
> Your obedient servant
> DUNCAN WILSON

By the beginning of September 1971 the FCO had come to the view that the timing of Operation 'FOOT' should be advanced: cf. No. 70. Mr. Gromyko had not replied to Sir A. Douglas-Home's letter (No. 71), and the tone of Soviet press and radio comment had grown increasingly sharp, culminating in a long and ferocious attack in Pravda on 26 August on HMG's foreign and domestic foreign policy, with strong personal criticism of the Prime Minister: the Secretary of State commented on 1 September 'I think that the publicity on the intelligence-gathering in which they indulge has got under their skin'. Soviet espionage in the UK continued, with the refusal of visas to known Soviet intelligence officers leading to an intensification of the 'visa war' between London and Moscow which caused great inconvenience to HM Embassy: on 3 September Mr. Dobbs wrote to Sir T. Brimelow recommending that 'the sooner the action which has to be taken is taken the better'.

Another reason for advancing Operation FOOT was the signature of the Quadripartite Agreement on Berlin on 3 September. In the continuous Ambassadorial sessions which began on 10 August (see No. 70, note 7) both Mr. Abrasimov and Mr. Rush (US Ambassador) were clearly under instructions, for reasons which were unclear to the FCO, to press forward urgently to conclude an agreement. The Soviet Ambassador was prepared for genuine negotiation at the table, while the US Ambassador, abetted by the French Ambassador, was determined to force the pace. Following a meeting on 18 August lasting over 12 hours a draft text was agreed, and a First Stage Quadripartite Agreement on Berlin was signed on 3 September, accompanied by texts of a draft Final Quadripartite Protocol, to be signed after completion of the inner-German talks (cf. No. 64), correspondence between the Western Ambassadors, the Soviet Ambassador and the Federal Chancellor concerning Federal links, and agreed minutes on the establishment of a Soviet Consulate-General in West Berlin and the use of Federal passports by West

Berliners.[1] FCO officials considered that the Agreement met the essential requirements of HMG and their Western Allies, who had obtained a Soviet undertaking that civilian traffic between the Western Sectors of Berlin and the FRG would be unimpeded, recognition that non-political ties between the FRG and Western Sectors of Berlin were to be maintained and developed, Soviet acceptance of Federal responsibility for the representation of Western Sectors abroad, and the promise of improvements in inner-Berlin communications. In return, the Russians had obtained a reduction of the Federal political presence in Berlin, appreciable enhancement of the status of the GDR, and tacit acceptance that the Berlin Wall was here to stay and that Allied interests would in future be confined to the Western Sectors rather than to Berlin as a whole.

Summarising the talks for the Prime Minister, who had taken a close interest in them, Sir A. Douglas-Home stated that 'although the Agreement is not perfect, it is rather better than we hoped for when we embarked upon the talks in March 1970 and certainly better than I had come to expect as the talks progressed. There are, inevitably, advantages in it for the Russians and there will, equally inevitably, continue to be occasional crises in Berlin as long as the underlying anomalies in the City's situation persist. We must also recognise that the very fact of an agreement (incomplete as it is) will encourage Western complacency and increase the pressure for hasty movement in East/West relations in particular towards a Security Conference and force reductions, with the dangers that these might entail. Finally, the inner-German talks on the implementation of the principles set out in the Agreement may well prove difficult . . . But taken all in all I believe that the draft Agreement with its ancillary documents represents a fair bargain for the three Powers and the Federal Government.' Mr. Heath, however, replied: 'I do not accept that the Agreement with its ancillary documents in any way represents a fair bargain for the Three Powers and the Federal Government. What has happened is that the Soviet Union, having de facto removed the rights to which we and our allies are entitled de jure has now succeeded in securing considerable benefits for itself and the GDR by promising to restore them in part—but only in part . . . The signature of this Agreement may well be right on the basis that we are prepared to recognise realities now that the Federal German Government has decided to do so itself. But I feel that it should be done on this basis rather than for us to claim that nothing fundamental has been changed. In other words the most that we can say is that we have made the best of a bad bargain, not that we have got a fair deal.'[2]

With the risk of jeopardising agreement on Berlin removed, Sir A. Douglas-Home agreed that FOOT should be brought forward, and put the argument to the Home Secretary on 11 September.

[1] The Quadripartite Agreement signed at Berlin on 3 September, together with related agreed minutes and inter-governmental correspondence, is printed in Cmnd. 6201, Nos. 136-144.

[2] Minute of 1 September to Sir A. Douglas-Home, WRL 2/5.

No. 73

Minute from Sir A. Douglas-Home to Mr. Maudling
FCS/71/69 [PUSD]

'FOOT'. *Top Secret*   FCO, *11 September 1971*

FOOT

You will remember that in his minute of 3 August the Prime Minister agreed with our joint recommendation that the question of Soviet espionage in this country should be reviewed at the end of October.[1]

2. For various reasons I am now wondering whether this timing should not be advanced. Gromyko has not replied to my letter, and there has been no reduction in the numbers of Soviet intelligence officers seeking admission to this country in various official guises. The signature of the first stage of the Four Power Agreement on Berlin has made it harder for the Russians either to accuse us of sabotaging a settlement on Berlin or to sabotage it themselves using FOOT as a pretext. The cases of Sub-Lieutenant Bingham and of the recent defector from the Soviet Trade Delegation, as details become known, will tend both to revive pressure upon us to deal with this whole problem, and also to reassure critics that we are acting on the basis of sound and up-to-date information.[2] Finally the Russians themselves, who have already been alerted to the possibility of our taking action, will now be planning the redisposition of their intelligence effort. We do not want to allow them any longer for this than can be avoided.

3. I therefore suggest that we should seek the Prime Minister's agreement to putting FOOT into effect as soon as the necessary preparations can be made. If possible, I should like to act before I see Gromyko in New York on 27 September, but otherwise early in October.

4. In paragraphs 9-10 of our joint memorandum we offered the Prime Minister a choice of two possible courses of action. In his minute of 3 August he said that when we take action we must do everything required at one blow. I take this to mean that he prefers the first course of action. He may wish to discuss this further but it is the course that I now recommend.[3]

5. I am copying this minute to the Defence Secretary and the Secretary of State for Trade and Industry, whose departments were concerned in the

[1] See No. 70, note 9.

[2] Details of the cases of Sub-Lieutenant David Bingham, who was to be tried for espionage, and of the Soviet defector Oleg Lyalin of the STD, who had communicated information regarding Soviet intelligence techniques and sabotage plans, are given in Andrew and Gordievsky, *op. cit.*, pp. 431-6.

[3] Sir A. Douglas-Home flew to Cairo on 12 September for talks with Egyptian leaders on the Arab-Israeli dispute. In Cairo telegram No. 1160 of 13 September he informed Sir D. Greenhill: 'I think that it is right that we should carry out FOOT and I have so recommended to the Home Secretary. I trust that in the event we shall do it really thoroughly and make a clean sweep of all we know to be implicated.'

earlier discussion of this problem, and also to the Secretary of the Cabinet and the Prime Minister's Private Secretary.[4]

ALEC DOUGLAS-HOME

[4] Mr. Moon wrote to Mr. Barrington on 15 September that the Prime Minister had agreed that subject to the Home Secretary's concurrence the proposed action should be taken 'at once'. Mr. Barrington replied on 16 September that the Home Secretary, Defence Secretary and Secretary for Trade and Industry had now all agreed with the proposals in the minute, and that planning was going ahead with a view to taking action before Sir A. Douglas-Home left for New York to attend the UN General Assembly.

In a submission of 16 September to Mr. C. Rose, Assistant Under-Secretary superintending PUSD, and Sir T. Brimelow, Mr. Bullard suggested that in view of Mr. Heath's and Sir A. Douglas-Home's comments in No. 70, note 9 and in note 3 above 'we should now forget about the second alternative scheme (the negotiated settlement) and *a fortiori* the still more cautious variants suggested earlier by Sir Duncan Wilson', and prepare plans on the basis of the scheme set out in para. 9 of No. 70. He submitted drafts of an *aide-mémoire* to be presented to the Soviet Ambassador, speaking notes for use at the interview, the list of names of those to be expelled and publicity material (stating that Ministers must decide how much publicity should be given to the operation), a warning telegram to Sir J. Killick in Moscow, and a list of further measures to be taken if required. Sir D. Greenhill minuted on 17 September: 'These are difficult decisions and the Secy. of State will wish to discuss with Mr. Maudling, Mr. Davies (who is greatly concerned about Anglo-Soviet trade) and probably the PM. On publicity, I think it is right to take command of the situation *at the start*. It would theoretically be better if we could, by avoiding publicity, spare the Russians such direct challenge to their prestige. But with an operation on this scale it is, in my view, impossible to avoid publicity—therefore such an option does not exist in reality. The Russian response will certainly be ugly and they may be tempted to hurt people rather than things e.g. arrest UK citizens unprotected by diplomatic immunity e.g. press, technicians etc. etc. I think therefore we should ask the Home Office to keep back from the expulsion at least one Russian non-diplomat against whom charges could be brought' (Mr. Bullard noted that this was not necessary as there were STD officials not on the list 'against whom charges could be brought at any time').

In these inauspicious circumstances Sir J. Killick had arrived in Moscow on 9 September to take up his appointment as HM Ambassador. He informed the Secretary of State on 16 September that he had been summoned to call on Mr. Gromyko the following morning and asked 'whether there is anything particular you wish me to say'. Sir A. Douglas-Home replied that he should tell Mr. Gromyko 'that I am looking forward to our meeting in New York. There is no reason for us to appear negative about a properly prepared C[onference on] E[uropean] S[ecurity] or to give the Russians a pretext for accusing us of dragging our feet. In welcoming the first stage of the Berlin agreement [see pp. 376-7] you might say that we look forward to working together towards a CES when the agreement as a whole has been duly signed. If Gromyko raises the subject of espionage, defectors, etc. you should take note of his remarks but not repeat not offer any comment.'[1]

[1] Telegram No. 1032 to Moscow, 16 September (ENS 3/548/10).

No. 74

Sir J. Killick (Moscow) to Sir A. Douglas-Home

No. 1358 Telegraphic [ENS 3/548/10]

Immediate. Confidential   MOSCOW, *17 September 1971, 1.36 p.m.*

Thank you for your telegram No. 1032.[1]

2. My call on Gromyko this morning was supposed to be of a formal courtesy nature but he raised no objection when I made a few general observations on the grounds that this might be my only chance of talking to him for some while.

3. I passed on your message about the New York meeting and asked whether Gromyko would have any special points. I added that I expected you would wish to express your concern, which was widely shared in London, at the evident misunderstanding on the Soviet side of HMG's approach to international relations. I was conscious of representing a government which believed more in deeds and practical action than words. This was no less true in its conduct of foreign policy, and I reminded Gromyko of what the Prime Minister had said in his address to the UN General Assembly in October last year (see m[y] i[mmediately] f[ollowing] t[elegram]).[2]

4. It was also true that HMG gave very high priority to joining an enlarged EEC but not just as a matter of self-interest. They believed that it would strengthen stability and peace in Europe, an aim which was fully shared by the Soviet Government.

5. Nor were our European interests limited to the EEC. We were no less interested in other proposals serving the same ends. In particular I knew that you welcomed the recent successful conclusion of the most important first stage of agreement on Berlin[3] and looked forward to working together with the Soviet Government and others concerned in the thorough preparation of a CES when the Berlin agreement had been duly completed.

6. On more general questions such as disarmament for instance HMG were likewise concerned to make progress and would cooperate in the search for concrete and practical further steps.

7. These were all multilateral questions in which HMG were playing and would continue to play an active and positive role. The fact that they did not

---

[1] See p. 379.

[2] Not printed. Sir J. Killick had quoted the following passage from Mr. Heath's speech of 23 October 1970 to the UNGA (printed in Watt & Mayall, 1970, pp. 546-52): 'I speak today for a newly-elected British Government committed to vigorous policies in the interests of the security and prosperity of the British people . . . the policies which we propose are fully in accord with our commitments under the Charter and our record as a member of this Organisation. We are determined to work for peace and for harmony between peoples because it is only in these conditions that Britain, as part of the international community, can prosper.'

[3] See pp. 376-7.

advertise this all the time in public statements did not detract from the realities.

8. Bilateral relations were no less important and trade was the most significant field in which to pursue them. I looked forward to the meeting of the Joint Commission in January which I hoped would enable us to identify progress on this front. I hoped that your own visit in February[4] could soon be firmly agreed.

9. Gromyko said he looked forward to his meeting with you. He hoped to discuss bilateral relations not only in general but also in concrete terms. The Soviet Government had observed, as we too must have done, that a certain amount (he would not attempt to quantify it) of coolness had entered into our relations since HM present Government assumed office. There had been a certain set-back which should not be exaggerated but the two governments should find positive means of restoring relations to their old level and even of improving them.

10. He expected also to discuss European questions, including the all-European conference. The Middle East problem was acute because although there was no actual fighting it was not yet solved and we could not be sure that the present situation would last.[5] We had a common interest in promoting a settlement with all the other major powers.

11. Finally Gromyko drew my attention to his proposal for a world disarmament conference.[6] The Soviet Government sought no special advantage from this. We were all in an equal position. The proposal did not involve substance or solutions but was a question of the form of further discussion. The proposed conference had been tried between the two world

[4] See No. 68, note 11. On 18 August Mr. Dobbs had delivered the message to the Soviet Foreign Ministry about Sir A. Douglas-Home's possible visit to the Soviet Union in February 1972; Mr. Lunkov, who had succeeded Mr. Makeev as Head of Second European Department, replied on 9 September that there should be no difficulty with this date (ENS 3/548/19).

[5] Cf. No. 67, note 15. While British policy towards a Middle East settlement 'remained in neutral gear', supporting US efforts 'as being the only horse at present running', there was a growing feeling in the FCO, with which the Prime Minister concurred, that 'there is much to be said for stating our own position, even if this may mean cutting adrift from the Americans'. Mr. C.M. Le Quesne, Deputy Under-Secretary superintending NED, expressed 'no enthusiasm at all for the idea that we should strike out a line independent of the Americans', but thought that before the UNGA debate on the Middle East scheduled for the second half of November HMG should consider 'the extent to which our interests and those of the Americans might at some stage diverge', particularly with respect to oil: if Egypt were to organise a boycott of oil supplies to European powers in order to exert pressure on the Israelis through the Americans 'it could place us in an extremely uncomfortable position' (minute of 20 September). In a minute of 22 September to Mr. Parsons after Sir A. Douglas-Home's visit to Cairo (cf. No. 73, note 3), Mr. Graham said he did not believe 'that the American method of negotiating will make progress fast enough and the risk must be that there will be an explosion before they have achieved anything. My impression after the talks in Cairo is that the difficulty is not now so much the wide gap between the parties as total lack of trust.' (NEM 3/548/1).

[6] See No. 67, note 11.

wars in a somewhat different form.[7] Why not try it again? He repeated that it was not made with any hope of gaining one-sided advantage, we were all in an equal position.

12. He would of course be ready to discuss any other questions you wished to raise.

13. In reply I said that HMG would certainly share Gromyko's general approach to disarmament. Agreements of this sort must be based on mutual advantage. As regards the world conference, you might wish to discuss practical problems, such as for example how it could in fact avoid prejudicing the C[onference of the] C[ommittee on] D[isarmament]. As for Anglo-Soviet relations, I would certainly agree with him that there had been a change in character since the present Government took office but I continued to believe that this was because the Soviet Government were mistaking a change in style for a change of substance. Gromyko said it was up to HMG to improve their style.

14. No other subject was mentioned on either side. The atmosphere was relaxed and friendly and although I gather Gromyko has not yet had a holiday this year he seemed in good form. Whether his rather general outline of an agenda for this talk with you indicates that he has no other more practical points in mind, I cannot judge. Obviously however the Middle East would be high on his list.

15. I leave it to you to decide whether it is worth repeating this telegram to other posts.[8]

[7] i.e. the Disarmament Conference held in Geneva from February 1932-October 1933: see *DBFP*, Second Series, Volumes III-V.

[8] The FCO repeated this telegram Saving to Bonn, Paris, Washington, UKDEL NATO and UKMIS New York.

The next group of documents concerns the implementation of Operation FOOT. When Sir A. Douglas-Home returned from his North African visit he reviewed the papers prepared in EESD (cf. No. 73, note 4) and agreed that 'the action must be taken and that we must make it public'. On 21 September the Prime Minister held a meeting attended by the Home Secretary, Foreign & Commonwealth Secretary, Lord President, Defence Secretary, Secretary of State for Trade and Industry, Sir B. Trend, Sir P. Allen and Sir D. Greenhill; Mr. Moon reported its conclusions to Mr. Graham later that afternoon. Sir A. Douglas-Home said that it was desirable to act quickly before he saw Mr. Gromyko in New York and in case 'the Russians might get wind of our decision and try to stop us by one means of another'. The possibility of a statement in the House was discussed (Parliament having been reconvened to discuss the situation in Northern Ireland), but the Lord President stressed the difficulties that this would present: 'There would be strong left-wing criticism in Parliament of what we were doing.' There was also some discussion of the extent of the real threat represented by Soviet espionage, but it was agreed that 'in addition to the risks involved in the Russians acquiring secret information in this way, there were strong political grounds for putting an end to this obstacle to a fundamental improvement in British/Soviet relations'. Summing up, Mr. Heath said that the Secretary of State should see the Soviet Chargé, Mr. Ippolitov, on Friday, 24 September, to inform him of HMG's decision, followed by an announcement made through an on-the-record FCO statement.

Preparations for the démarche continued, but on 22 September the Prime Minister sought further reassurance that the FCO had thought through all the implications of the proposed action. As Mr. Moon wrote to Mr. Graham that day, Mr. Heath 'would be grateful to know that the Foreign and Commonwealth Secretary is satisfied that our case is fully prepared to defend the steps we are taking against those who will criticise them on political grounds and to show that there was no satisfactory alternative way of handling the situation'; he wished the Secretary of State to ensure 'that all likely forms of Soviet retaliation are considered and that, so far as possible, we are ready to deal with them . . . The Prime Minister would be grateful if the Foreign and Commonwealth Secretary could consider these, and any other matters on which advance planning is possible, before the action is taken on Friday.' Mr. Graham asked Mr. Bullard to submit a draft, and to 'examine your conscience once again that all possible has been done'. Mr. Wiggin, Sir S. Crawford and Sir D. Greenhill all amended and then approved the draft reply, which the Secretary of State signed on 23 September.

No. 75

Minute from Sir A. Douglas-Home to Mr. Heath
PM/71/79 [PUSD]

'FOOT'. Top Secret   FCO, *23 September 1971*

Prime Minister
   FOOT
   I see from your Private Secretary's letter of 22 September that you are still concerned about certain aspects of this operation.[1]
   2. I am completely satisfied that we shall be able to show that the problem is very serious and that it could not have been solved in any other way. The alternative of a negotiated reduction of Soviet Missions is not in my view a practical proposition. This will be clear, I think, to anyone who reads my letters to Gromyko[2] (which we propose to publish) and studies the information now made available about the nature and scale of Soviet espionage, even if for tactical or security reasons we do not release the whole of this at the outset. The Security Service are the experts at assessing the threat and know the full extent of what the Russians have attempted here. These activities put an excessive strain on our resources and the Security Service are firmly of the opinion that the punishment fits the crime.
   3. There is another point. As things are at present the development of our relations with the Soviet Union is continually being checked by some incident

[1] See above.   [2] See Nos. 58 and 71.

arising out of their espionage activities, be it the expulsion of a diplomat caught red-handed, the refusal of a visa to a known intelligence officer, or a prosecution against one of their agents. The way they have played these incidents in the past has caused disproportionate damage to our relations. This operation will give a new and much healthier basis for good relations.

4. We have of course looked very carefully at the possible forms of Soviet retaliation. I have always recognised that these might well be severe. I regard this as inevitable, given that our purpose is to improve the security of this country by inflicting serious damage on what is at the moment a very successful Soviet intelligence operation. I consider that this is an objective for which it would be worthwhile to pay a price. I am also convinced that to take half-hearted measures would provoke much the same reprisals without securing corresponding benefit.

5. We have planned FOOT in such a way as to confront the Russians with a *fait accompli* and leave them no chance of deflecting us from our purpose by bringing pressure to bear. As you know, our intention is to point out to the Soviet Chargé d'Affaires that we have not by any means taken all the steps open to us and to state specifically that if they retaliate in a manner we consider unreasonable we shall not hesitate to impose further measures. By putting the situation to them in this way and by showing firmness and determination in the subsequent phase, we stand the best chance of keeping Soviet reprisals within bounds. But the risk to British subjects will undoubtedly be there. And we cannot reduce it by showing our hand in advance without ruining the operation.

6. I enclose a note prepared here about possible Soviet reprisals, and also a list of further measures which we might take.[3] To the former list must be added cancellation of my visit to Moscow for which the Russians in a message to me from Gromyko delivered yesterday, have now proposed 31 January to 4 February next year.[4] I have always reckoned that that might be a casualty but as things have turned out the onus of cancellation is now on the Russians.

7. I am copying this Minute to the Home Secretary, the Lord President, the Secretary of State for Trade and Industry, the Secretary of State for Defence, and the Secretary to the Cabinet.

A. D.-H.[5]

[3] See Enclosures I and II to this document.

[4] See No. 74, note 4. On 17 September Mr. Ippolitov had asked if he might call on Sir A. Douglas-Home on 22 September to deliver a message about the latter's visit to Moscow. Consideration was given to putting off the call in view of the impending implementation of Operation FOOT (see pp. 382-3) but EESD's opinion was that 'if we were to try to put the call off the Soviet Embassy would smell a rat', and that it should stand if the Secretary of State were not embarrassed. Sir A. Douglas-Home minuted: 'I don't think one need feel embarrassed with the Russians although with others one might.' He also asked if there were a danger that 'he is really coming with some message on spies', but it appears that Mr. Ippolitov made his call unsuspecting.

[5] The Prime Minister held a further meeting on the afternoon of 23 September, when the Secretary of State said that he 'remained firmly of the view that the operation had to take place and the question was one of timing'. It was decided to take action on Saturday, 25 September

Enclosure I in No. 75

Possible Soviet reprisals

1. It is to be expected that the Russians will reply to our *Aide-Mémoire* in strong terms, denying the accusations against the persons named and threatening serious consequences if we persist. They might also refuse to withdraw the officials in question, thus forcing us to declare the diplomats *personas non gratas* [*sic*] and to cancel the visas of the rest. We must reckon with the likelihood of Soviet propaganda on the theme that HMG are suffering from spy mania and embracing McCarthyism. At the same time there would probably be pressure on HMG through British businessmen and commercial organisations to suspend action against the Soviet Trade Delegation. All these Soviet reactions are more or less inevitable and can be accepted.

2. It must be assumed also that the Russians will seek ways of hitting back, in order to give themselves the pleasure of wounding us and in the hope of forcing us to back down, at least partially. How would they do this? It seems unlikely that they would choose some multilateral forum such as the UN or the quadripartite talks on the Middle East. More probably they would look for possibilities in bilateral fields.

3. Two main areas suggest themselves for Soviet retaliation. The first is the presence of British citizens visiting the Soviet Union or resident there. It would be very easy for the Soviet authorities to make life uncomfortable for these people, using either overt official measures or so-called 'private citizens' in the same way as American journalists have been harassed as a reprisal for Zionist activities in the United States. It is possible that they might 'frame' British subjects who are not protected by diplomatic immunity, in an effort to bring the pressure of public opinion to bear on HMG in favour of a less tough line. The Russians have it in their power to cut down the numbers of HM Embassy in Moscow, either by expulsions or by refusing visas, or both. Our Embassy is not over-staffed, and action of this kind would curtail useful work. We should have to make up our mind to accept this risk. The best counter to it might be to reduce the size of the Soviet Embassy in London to the size of our reduced Embassy in Moscow. A series of expulsions or reductions could nevertheless be very unpleasant, and would involve much personal inconvenience.

4. The other likely area for retaliation is Anglo-Soviet trade. Here the Russians probably regard us as particularly vulnerable. It is true that in general the Russians trade with Britain not because they like us but because

rather than on 24 September, to ease the 'Parliamentary difficulty' (cf. pp. 382-3) but this decision was reversed when an article appeared in the morning edition of the *Evening News* on 24 September headlined 'Top Russian flees to London', leaking details of the recent Soviet defector. Sir A. Douglas-Home had left for New York, but on his instructions Sir D. Greenhill asked the Soviet Chargé to call at 3.15 p.m. that afternoon. A telegram was drafted warning Sir J. Killick of what was to happen, and telegrams were despatched later that day to UKDEL NATO, Washington, Paris, Bonn, Ottawa, Canberra and other Posts.

it is in their interest to do so. But there are certainly many contracts which they could place just as easily in France or Western Germany or Italy, as in Britain. To give a specific example, the Soviet Union buys a large number of pairs of shoes every year from Western suppliers, and it would be a simple matter for her to distribute the usual British share amongst other countries of Western Europe. Machine-tools are another field where the Russians could damage our export trade by switching orders. Such switches could be highly damaging to individual British firms and could greatly reduce Anglo-Soviet trade, at least in the short term. This in itself would not be too serious, since British exports to the USSR have virtually stood still since 1968 and amount to only 1.2 per cent of British exports as a whole. But there would undoubtedly be bitter complaints from some of the British firms and commercial organisations trading with the Soviet Union, some of which command political support.

5. In the light of these considerations, the following list of possible Soviet actions has been prepared. So far as it is possible to estimate likely Soviet reactions, the list is in roughly descending order of probability. We think that the Russians would select items at least as far down as No. 10.

1. Restrict or stop travel by Service Attachés and/or other members of the staff of HM Embassy in Moscow.
2. Begin administrative harassment of HM Embassy in other ways, e.g. refusal to renew leases for accommodation, refusal to provide servants, refusal to authorise imports of necessary supplies.
3. Refuse visas to persons nominated to the staff of HM Embassy in Moscow.
4. Refuse visas to selected British businessmen and journalists.
5. Expel selected members of the staff of HM Embassy, possibly even including HM Ambassador.
6. Expel selected British businessmen and journalists.
7. Break off commercial discussions with selected British firms; place selected contracts with other suppliers in preference to Britain; make difficulties for the firms engaged in construction projects in the Soviet Union and then subject them to penalty clauses for non-fulfilment of contractual obligations.
8. Close the offices of one or both of the two British firms in Moscow (Golodetz and ICL).
9. Postpone or cancel the meeting of the Anglo-Soviet Consultative Committee fixed for November-December 1971.
10. Postpone or cancel the second meeting of the Anglo-Soviet Joint Commission fixed for January 1972.
11. Threaten to terminate the leases of properties in Moscow used by HM Embassy (the Dacha, the Commercial Office and possibly the Embassy Residence/Chancery itself).

12. Sell Soviet diamonds through Amsterdam or elsewhere instead of going through London (diamonds to the value of over £90 million were sold through London in 1970).

13. Physically molest members of HM Embassy and/or British businessmen, journalists and tourists in the Soviet Union.

14. Arrest one or more British subjects (e.g. a British student at Moscow University) on a trumped up charge.

ENCLOSURE II IN NO. 75

Further measures we might take (roughly in ascending order of severity)

1. Initiate publicity, if this was not done at the outset.

2. Release names of those expelled, if this was not done at the outset.

3. Reject Soviet travel notifications, using the standard Moscow formula: 'This journey cannot be registered, for reasons of a temporary nature.'

4. Expel further members of the staff of the Soviet Embassy (diplomatic, non-diplomatic or both) in order to reach parity of numbers with HM Embassy in Moscow. Those selected for expulsion could either be from categories involved in intelligence work but deliberately spared in the 'first strike' (e.g. Service Attachés), or ordinary members of the Soviet diplomatic service, depending on the nature of Soviet measures. The size of the Soviet Embassy would then be limited to this new and lower ceiling.

5. Expel further members of the Staff of the Soviet Trade Delegation and/or other organisations. Here too the new and lower ceiling would then be maintained.

6. Reduce from 35 to 25 miles the radius within which Soviet officials are allowed to travel. (The radius in Moscow is 40 kms.)

7. Make difficulties over the building plans for the new Soviet Embassy.

8. State that we shall not be willing to extend leases of Soviet Embassy properties when these expire.

9. Suspend or abrogate the Anglo-Soviet Cultural Agreement leading to withdrawal of students on both sides and suspension of visits in both directions.

10. Announce that we regard the 1934 Anglo-Soviet Trade Agreement as null and void by reason of Soviet misuse of the Trade Delegation's premises for intelligence work. This would have the effect of withdrawing immunity from those premises.

11. Arrest one or more Soviet officials (not enjoying diplomatic immunity) on charges of espionage.

12. Break off diplomatic relations.

No. 76

FCO to Sir J. Killick (Moscow)

No. 1075 Telegraphic [*PUSD*]

Flash. Confidential   FCO, *24 September 1971, 1.45 p.m.*

1. The PUS asked the Soviet Chargé d'Affaires to call at 1515 BST today.[1] He spoke from the notes in m[y] i[mmediately] f[ollowing] t[elegram][2] and handed over the *aide-mémoire* which is being telegraphed to you separately,[3] together with two lists containing respectively 90 and 15 names.[4] He also handed over a copy of your speech on the presentation of your credentials.[5]

2. Ippolitov said that Soviet policy towards Britain corresponded to what you had said in Moscow about British policy towards the Soviet Union. His country had taken a number of initiatives in this field, and no-one could doubt their sincerity. As for allegations about Soviet intelligence activities these had been rejected many times. They had only been made in the interests of certain persons who were working to damage our relations. The *aide-mémoire* contained very serious and drastic measures. He would report it at once to Moscow. But he could not accept the statements which it contained. Soviet officials had instructions not to engage in any activities incompatible with their status, nor did any of them conduct such activities.

3. The PUS said he understood why Ippolitov had to say this, but it was not the view or the experience of HMG, as Ippolitov himself well knew. It gave us no pleasure to take this step, but we felt it had been forced upon us by the refusal of the Soviet Government to take any account or any notice of the approaches made to them at a high level and in a manner which could have produced a discreet solution if the Soviet Union had been willing to respond. We had made repeated efforts in this direction, but they had been entirely ignored. HMG therefore felt that the only remedy open to them was to take the action described in the *aide-mémoire*.

---

[1] See No. 75, note 5. Telegram No. 1073 to Moscow of even date had set out a line to take by Sir J. Killick if the subject of the British *démarche* were raised by the Soviet leaders. He was instructed to point out that HMG's decisions were communicated to Mr. Ippolitov by Sir D. Greenhill rather than by Sir A. Douglas-Home: the Secretary of State had written personally to Mr. Gromyko because he was conscious that comprehensive action to terminate Soviet intelligence activities in the UK would 'subject our relations to serious strain', but 'once action has to be taken on grounds of security, the details are handled by officials'; the responsibility of foreign ministers was 'to think about the future of our political relations'.

[2] Not printed: the PUS's speaking notes are reproduced in Enclosure I below.

[3] See Enclosure II below.

[4] Not printed. The names were of 90 Soviet officials who were to leave the country within 2 weeks and 15 others holding valid re-entry visas who would not be permitted to re-enter the country.

[5] Not printed. Sir J. Killick had presented his credentials to President Podgorny on 20 September (see Watt and Mayall, 1971, p. 830).

4. Ippolitov repeated that he would report at once to Moscow, and added that the consequences for Anglo-Soviet relations would rest upon our shoulders.

5. The PUS repeated that it was the failure of the Soviet Government to respond to our approaches which had driven us to take this action.[6]

ENCLOSURE I IN NO. 76

Notes used by the PUS in speaking to the Soviet Chargé d'Affaires

You will have heard about Sir John Killick's opening call on Mr. Gromyko[7] and of his presentation of credentials to Mr. Podgorny. We are very pleased that he has been so well received at the start of his mission. You may like to have a copy of his speech on the presentation of his credentials. It sets out HMG's policy towards the Soviet Union in some detail, and of course it carries the authority of the Secretary of State. You will see that we attach much importance to our relations with your country.

Unfortunately there is another side to the picture. I mean the intelligence activities of Soviet officials in this country. This has prevented our relations from being put on a sound basis. The problem has been the subject of many conversations here and in Moscow, and of correspondence between our respective foreign ministers.

I am instructed to give you this *aide-mémoire*, together with the two lists of names attached. When you have read it, I have an oral statement to make, of which I should like you to take very careful note.

The *aide-mémoire* explains itself. The situation is as well known to you as it is to us, and you are, I hope, equally disturbed by it.

This action is as distasteful to us as it is to you. But we have been patient long enough. The present situation cannot be allowed to continue.

I am instructed to make it absolutely clear to the Soviet Government that there can be no question of reconsidering our decision. Any efforts to persuade us to do so will merely damage our relations further.

In this connection I am instructed to say that we have taken into account the possibility of reprisals against HM Embassy in Moscow or against other British interests in the Soviet Union.[8] Such reprisals would not be justified, because there is no parallel in the Soviet Union to the situation in Britain as described in the *aide-mémoire*. But I must ask you to make it clear to your Government that in the event of such reprisals, HMG will have to consider

---

[6] According to Sir D. Greenhill's memoirs (*More by Accident, op. cit.*, pp. 158-9), Mr. Ippolitov 'conducted himself well' during the interview and left quietly: 'Our security people who were watching the Embassy reported his arrival back in Kensington Palace Gardens. He disappeared into his office building and within a minute or two a figure was seen running at high speed across from the KGB office which was on the other side of the road. The Russians were, of course, furious . . .' According to Andrew and Gordievsky, *KGB: The Inside Story, op. cit.*, 'Moscow Centre was stunned. The expulsions marked a major turning-point in the history of KGB operations in the United Kingdom . . . The London residency never recovered' (p. 436).

[7] See No. 74.   [8] Cf. Enclosure I in No. 75.

other aspects of the Soviet presence in the United Kingdom with a view to bringing conditions here more closely into line with those existing in the Soviet Union.[9] You will be able to think for yourself what measures of this kind are open to us, but examples are:

(*a*) the imposition of strict parity between our respective Embassy establishments;

(*b*) the correction of the anomaly whereby the Soviet Trade Delegation premises enjoy immunity, although only three of its members have diplomatic status;

(*c*) movement of Soviet personnel in this country.

We hope that when the Soviet Government have considered the matter as carefully as we have, they will agree that once this cancer of large-scale and expanding intelligence activities has been eradicated we shall be able to build a mutual relationship of a much sounder and healthier kind.

As you are aware, there has been widespread anxiety on this subject in Parliament and amongst the British people in general. We have no wish to engage in a propaganda battle with the Soviet Government on this issue but we must make known the main facts, without disclosing the names of the individuals involved. News Department will therefore be making a statement on the record at 4.00 p.m. today, indicating what action has been taken and the course of events which led up to it.

At the same time we shall release the text of the *aide-mémoire* which I have just given you (without the names), and also of the Secretary of State's letters to Mr. Gromyko, dated 3 December 1970 (omitting the paragraph mentioning the name of the Soviet Trade delegate Mr. Ivanov) and 4 August 1971.[10]

ENCLOSURE II IN NO. 76

Text of aide-mémoire handed to the Soviet Chargé d'Affaires by the PUS

When Mr. Gromyko visited London in October 1970, he spoke of the desirability of improving Anglo-Soviet relations.

It is the sincere wish of Her Majesty's Government to bring about such an improvement.

There is however one matter of importance which has repeatedly caused friction in Anglo-Soviet relations. This is the scale of intelligence-gathering activities by Soviet officials in this country. This subject was raised with Mr. Gromyko by Sir Alec Douglas-Home, first in conversation in London and

---

[9] Cf. Enclosure II in No. 75.

[10] Telegrams No. 1078 and 1079 to Moscow transmitted the texts of the on-the-record statement issued by News Department at 4 p.m. on 24 September, and of material released for unattributable use. The statement, *aide-mémoire* and the texts of Sir A. Douglas-Home's two letters to Mr. Gromyko were published in *The Times* on 25 September 1971 and elsewhere amid extensive press coverage. The paragraph concerning Mr. Ivanov was omitted from the 3 December 1970 letter (cf. No. 58, note 7) as it had been decided not to expel him from the UK.

subsequently in a letter dated 3 December 1970, written at Mr. Gromyko's suggestion, and in a further letter dated 4 August 1971.

These letters have not been answered, nor even acknowledged.

Meanwhile inadmissible activities by Soviet officials in Britain have continued. During the last 12 months a number of Soviet officials have been required to leave the country after being detected in such activities. During the same period it has been decided not to issue visas to a number of officials nominated to Soviet establishments in the United Kingdom on account of their previous activities.

The staffs of the Soviet Embassy and the Soviet Trade Delegation, which form the two largest elements in the Soviet official establishment in Britain, far outnumber the British officials working in the Soviet Union. Her Majesty's Government have tolerated the growth of these establishments. They have not sought to bargain increases in the Soviet establishment in this country against increases in the British establishment in the USSR, nor have they sought to establish any fixed relationship between the Soviet commercial establishment in this country and the growth of British exports to the Soviet Union. Evidence has however been accumulating that this tolerance has been systematically abused.

This abuse is a matter of serious concern to Her Majesty's Government as a direct threat to the security of this country. Moreover the recurring need to request the withdrawal of Soviet officials from this country, or to refuse visas to certain officials selected for service in this country, imposes strains on Anglo-Soviet relations. So do unjustified acts of Soviet retaliation such as the recent expulsions of Mr. Miller, Mr. Nicholson and Mr. Jackson.[11]

The Soviet Government can hardly fail to be conscious of the contradiction between their advocacy of a conference on European Security and the scale of the o[p]erations against the security of this country which Soviet officials and agents controlled by them have conducted. Her Majesty's Government would like to see this contradiction resolved before the preparation of a conference on European Security begins.

The Soviet Embassy is therefore requested to arrange for the persons named on the attached list, all of whom have been concerned in intelligence activities, to leave Britain within two weeks from the date of this *aide-mémoire*.

Henceforth:

(*a*) The numbers of officials in (i) the Soviet Embassy, (ii) the Soviet Trade Delegation, and (iii) all other Soviet organisations in Great Britain will not be permitted to rise above the levels at which they will stand after the withdrawal of the persons named in the attached list;

(*b*) if a Soviet official is required to leave the country as a result of his having been detected in intelligence activities, the permitted level in that category will be reduced by one.

[11] Members of HM Embassy in Moscow expelled in 1971 in retaliation for expulsions of Soviet officials in London: cf. p. 344 and No. 70.

The Soviet Embassy is also asked to take note that the Soviet citizens named on the second list attached, who are believed to have left the country but still hold valid re-entry visas, will not be permitted to return to Britain, on account of their participation in intelligence activities.

The first official Soviet reaction to the British démarche came on Sunday, 26 September, when Sir J. Killick was summoned by Mr. Kozyrev to receive an aide-mémoire registering a strong protest at HMG's 'absurd action' and denouncing the British accusations as 'an unfounded fabrication whose aims are clearly provocative and hostile to the Soviet Union'. The Soviet communication asserted that in the light of the British aide-mémoire HMG's assurances of their desire to develop and improve Anglo-Soviet relations 'look nothing less than hypocritical', and Mr. Kozyrev stressed that he 'expected an answer': if the British Government did not revoke the measures announced against Soviet officials in the UK, the Soviet side would 'have no alternative but to take corresponding reciprocal measures'.

The tone, if not the substance of Mr. Kozyrev's representations was polite and calm: he apologised to Sir J. Killick for calling him in on a Sunday. The Ambassador reported 'so far so good', and it is clear that the FCO considered the Soviet reaction mild in the circumstances, leaving open the possibility of constructive discussion: according to a brief for the Cabinet, dated 28 September, HMG's firm action had been well received in the British press and in the country at large, and there had been widespread favourable comment in the press of Allied countries; 'we have injected a note of realism which will counteract a tendency to see Soviet actions only through rose-coloured spectacles in some Allied capitals'. The Home Secretary also congratulated Sir D. Greenhill warmly on 26 September 'on the way in which the Department had handled the FOOT operation . . . he had been very sceptical about the whole thing but he saw now that he had been completely wrong. He greatly admired the way the operation had been mounted.'

Mr. Gromyko took a hard line with Sir A. Douglas-Home in New York on 27 September, as reported to London in No. 77 below. The Secretary of State, however, gave the Soviet Foreign Minister no grounds for thinking that there was any chance of the British Government's changing their minds.

No. 77

Sir C. Crowe¹ (UKMIS New York) to FCO

No. 1172 Telegraphic [PUSD]

Immediate. Confidential   UKMIS NEW YORK, *28 September 1971, 3 a.m.*

Following from Secretary of State.

Moscow telegram No. 1420 to FCO: expulsions.²

I called on Mr. Gromyko this evening [27 September] at 5.30 in the Soviet Mission. He opened by asking me if I had anything new to say. I replied that I had not.³ A situation had arisen between us which had to be dealt with. I hoped it was over. HMG wished to make a fresh start on a new and sound basis.

2. Mr. Gromyko then launched into a vigorous protest against what he called the provocation engineered against the Soviet Union. He referred to the *aide-mémoire* handed to Sir J. Killick in Moscow which set out the Soviet Government's attitude. The British Government was aware of the full extent of the provocation for which they must bear full responsibility. I replied that I could not accept the word 'provocation'. As Mr. Gromyko knew, he had had every opportunity to deal with the matter privately and he had returned no reply to my personal approach and my two letters.

¹ UK Permanent Representative at the United Nations, New York since September 1970.

² This telegram of 27 September commented on an exchange of telegrams between UKMIS New York and the FCO on 26 September concerning the line Sir A. Douglas-Home should take with Mr. Gromyko at their meeting the following day. Sir J. Killick agreed that the principal aims should be to minimise retaliation and to persuade Mr. Gromyko that British policy was neither anti-Soviet nor designed to prejudice the prospect of progress on European security. He suggested that the Secretary of State 'need not and should not waste many words on further justification of what we have done', but should try to adduce arguments supporting HMG's wish to deal with the matter as quietly as possible: 'we need arguments which might carry weight with Brezhnev who is the only person in a position to over[r]ule Comrade Andropov [KGB Chairman]. It is presumably in the latter's interest to argue that if we are allowed to get away with it, other governments will be encouraged to follow our example. Although chances of success may therefore be small, we must obviously do everything we can.' The Secretary of State should point to the opportunity for the Soviet Union to establish a positive image for itself in the world: Soviet intelligence activities in the UK had been a 'serious setback' to this image, and retaliation would 'only damage Soviet standing still further'; but there was 'an enormous fund of goodwill towards the Soviet Union in Britain which would very soon make itself felt if these blatantly anti-British activities . . . were abandoned.'

³ FCO telegram No. 693 to UKMIS New York of 28 September pointed out that the Soviet Foreign Ministry might still be expecting a reply to their *aide-mémoire*, and suggested that Sir J. Killick should inform them that Sir A. Douglas-Home's conversation with Mr. Gromyko should be regarded as the reply. Sir J. Killick, however, expressed the view in Moscow telegram No. 1448 of 29 September that 'this uncertainty in the situation is no disadvantage to us. I would prefer not to force the pace by taking an immediate further initiative . . . If the Soviet side still feel they want an answer, they can always send for me and ask for one.'

3. Mr. Gromyko said that however much I might protest a provocation remained a provocation. The grounds for our action were a complete fabrication, a mirage of our own making. The British police authorities had not ceased for a single day their sallies against the Soviet Union so that every Soviet engineer or diplomatist had come to be regarded as an intelligence agent and the 'hooligan-like' acts of the British police had disorganised the proper activities of Soviet Embassies and other institutions. Did Britain not recognise the normal rules of international relations? By their action the British Government had brought relations between the two states to a state of great tension. He had not replied to my letters because he had dealt with the matter personally when he had told me in London last October that the allegations against the Soviet Union were fabrications.[4] One reply given personally was quite enough.

4. I said that the recent defector had confirmed what we had known for a long time of the numbers and scale of the Soviet intelligence operation in Britain.[5] It was deplorable that the KGB should be allowed to act in this sort of way as the casualty was the diplomatic service. Mr. Gromyko replied by asking how it was possible to speak of better relations between our two states if one *agent provocateur* was sufficient to cause us to take a long step back in our relations. This was an 'inadmissible' approach to relations with the Soviet Union. He said that he noted that we paid well for these special services but what surprised the Soviet Government was not these special services themselves but that the British Government should appear to sanction them. Presumably the British Government had taken this step to distract attention from the bottle necks, the rents and tatters of their own policies. The Soviet Union would not descend to such depths but would certainly retaliate.

5. I suggested that it was profitless to exchange these sort of words and that it would be better to move on to real problems and made the point that if we talked about security as the Soviet Government had proposed, it was necessary first to establish confidence between our countries. Mr. Gromyko replied that it appeared that the United Kingdom was afraid of some of the proposals put forward by the Soviet Union and rather than come out openly against them had found pretexts to 'bring out these darker things' in an attempt to intimidate the Soviet Union. The Soviet Union had a lot of experience and knew how to deal with such approaches which should be sent to another address.

6. I said that I was very willing to be judged on our actions. The Berlin agreement was a useful step forward and Britain had played a helpful part in the negotiations. Britain and the Soviet Union were close in their views on the Middle East. In our approach to the Conference on European Security we were not far apart I thought in practical terms. In fact it seemed to me that Britain and the Soviet Union were closer on many things than they had been for some time past. Mr. Gromyko agreed that there had been positive

[4] See p. 268. [5] Cf. No. 73, note 2.

steps and that Britain had shared in them. He had hoped that we would want to build on that progress but Britain seemed to find it too boring. The Soviet position was set out in their *aide-mémoire*. Relations between states were a two way strait and if we wanted to play it in this way the Soviet Union would reciprocate.

7. I replied that I should like nothing better than to build on the progress that had been made on Berlin and to discuss important problems such as those of the Middle East and disarmament, particularly naval disarmament. We had deplored the necessity of acting as we had done but we hoped to get our relations on to a constructive basis of trust. I could understand the shock that our action must have been to the Soviet Government.

8. The discussion then moved on to the Middle East and disarmament. Mr. Gromyko adopted the standard Soviet position on the Middle East in a markedly belligerent manner, accusing Britain of refusing to call for Israeli withdrawal in an outright and clear fashion and suggesting that there was a watershed between our two approaches, one in favour of settlement and the other of connivance in expansion. I said that Britain was firmly on the side of settlement. The British position was clearly explained, in much greater detail, I thought, than anything I had read in the Soviet side in my speech at Harrogate.[6] I would send Mr. Gromyko a copy, since he evidently had not read it.

9. On disarmament Mr. Gromyko refused to be drawn on any details of Brezhnev's proposal for naval disarmament or on the proposals for a general conference on disarmament,[7] instead he demanded that I should say whether I accepted them in principle, or not, arguing that questions were merely a device cloaking opposition. I said that I had an open mind on a general conference. It might be argued that it would be better to start with particular fields of disarmament such as MBFRs and naval disarmament rather than to tackle the whole field in a large conference, but I was open to persuasion. We needed to be practical, NATO had done a good deal of work on MBFRs and would shortly be in a position to explore the matter further with the Russians.[8] There would be sense therefore in starting with them. But I agreed with Mr. Gromyko that there was no reason in principle, if there were practical advantages in doing otherwise, why we should be confined to the CCD.

10. In leaving I told Mr. Gromyko that I would tell the press if asked that he had delivered a vigorous protest and that I had replied and would say no more. He said that that was my business.[9]

[6] See No. 54, note 13.

[7] See No. 67, note 11.

[8] Cf. pp. 343-4.

[9] In FCO telegram No. 697 of 28 September Sir D. Greenhill told Sir A. Douglas-Home that Mr. Gromyko's reactions were 'very much as expected and I am sorry you had to put up with the bluster'.

The FCO had expected a sharp reaction to their expulsion of the Soviet officials, but there was no news from Moscow of reprisals and press coverage in the UK continued to be satisfactory. Mr. Heath reported to the Cabinet on 29 September that Mr. Gromyko's reaction suggested 'that the Soviet Government had not been entirely surprised that we should have required the removal of the intelligence officers but that the scale of the operation had taken them aback'. In the FCO hopes remained high that the episode might actually improve, rather than damage bilateral relations. While they waited to see what the considered Soviet reaction might be to recent events, Sir J. Killick and his staff turned their attention to analysis of Soviet policy and the major influences upon it, with a view to stimulating a discussion which might inform HMG's own policies towards the Soviet Union when the situation had returned to some form of normality.

No. 78

Letter from Mr. Dobbs (Moscow) to Mr. Bullard

[*ENS 2/2*]

Confidential   MOSCOW, *30 September 1971*

Soviet policy in Europe[1]

In this letter I should like to try to set down one or two reflections on current Soviet policies, particularly European policy.

2. It seems to me that many Western observers are now making wrong appreciations of Soviet motives and aims by seeking unnecessarily sweeping explanations and trying to bring into one coherent overall picture events or developments which are in fact widely separated whether by geography or their own nature. For example, the speed-up on the Soviet side over the Berlin agreement[2] has been linked with Soviet apprehensions on account of the impending Nixon visit to Peking[3] and the appeal of China's new diplomacy. The Soviet Union, it is argued, is traditionally afraid of commitments on two fronts, and this is why she is anxious now to get things settled in Europe. We have ourselves partially subscribed to this theory (Moscow telegram No. 1201),[4] and it may have a certain general validity.

[1] The opening salutation was omitted from the filed copy of this letter.

[2] See pp. 376-7.

[3] The US President had announced on 15 July that he had accepted an invitation to visit China some time before May 1972: on 29 November the date of the visit was confirmed as 21 February 1972. He announced on 12 October that he would visit Moscow in May 1972, after his visit to China.

[4] In this telegram of 27 August speculating on the reasons behind Soviet agreement to the acceleration of the last stage of the Berlin talks, Mr. Dobbs expressed the view that the announcement of President Nixon's visit to Peking had 'clearly increased Soviet anxieties about China (which are of course generally considered to be one of the factors underlying the whole *Westpolitik*), and this could in turn have made the Russians decide to intensify efforts for a degree of *rapprochement* with the West' (WRL 2/13).

3. Reflecting on recent events I wonder if we would not get nearer the truth if we accepted that as a general rule Soviet policies in particular parts of the world or in particular situations are conceived mainly in terms of immediate Soviet requirements or opportunities in that particular situation; and that more remote events usually play no role at all, or only a subsidiary or fortuitous one. In their European policy the Russians are concerned with the situation in Europe now and only in the vaguest way with, say, a potentially threatening situation in the Far East or with the consequences of changes in Chinese diplomatic methods. Whatever happens, it is inconceivable that the Chinese could now acquire a foreign policy role in Western Europe; and even Chinese interest in the Balkans[5] seems to us to have been blown up out of all proportion by some observers, that is as a factor in Soviet European policy.

4. Commentators on the Berlin agreement, on the Brezhnev/Brandt meeting[6] and on Soviet hopes for a European conference etc. have surely not put enough emphasis on the essence of the question, as the Russians must see it, which is the problem of Germany itself. There may have been a time when the Russians envisaged the possibility of an all-communist Germany, but it is now long past. Their best hope now for a solution of the German problem is a permanently divided Germany; and that is now at last within their grasp, and with full international endorsement to boot. I recently re-read Gromyko's speech to the Supreme Soviet of 27 June 1968.[7] It is full of apprehension, which one must assume was not altogether feigned, about the rise of neo-nazism, about the use that could be made of the 'emergency laws', about revanchism and the Kiesinger Government's refusal to recognise Germany's post-war frontiers or to 'give up the demand for a return to the

[5] During 1971 there had been increased contact between China and Eastern European countries, including the visit of a Chinese military delegation to Roumania and of a number of Chinese 'tourists' to Yugoslavia.

[6] Herr Brandt had met Mr. Brezhnev at Oreanda in the Crimea from 16-17 September. According to the account given to Sir R. Jackling by Herr Brandt on 20 September, the main issues discussed were the likely timescales for ratification of the FRG's Treaties with the USSR and Poland (see Nos. 50, note 3 and 52, note 5), prospects for both German states to enter the UN, subjects for consideration at a European Security Conference, the scope of MBFRs and bilateral issues such as the development of economic cooperation. Herr Brandt reported that Mr. Brezhnev had opposed the use of the word 'balanced' in relation to force reductions, saying it was 'NATO slang', and had preferred instead 'without disadvantage for the participants'.

Herr Brandt had gained three main impressions from the meeting: Mr. Brezhnev's desire to appear genuinely interested, in the eyes of the US and Europe, in reducing tensions; Soviet acceptance that ratification of the FRG Treaty with the Soviet Union would take time (although a failure to ratify would represent 'a very serious setback'); and Soviet interest in whether any special German problems would arise in connection with European security or whether the FRG position was common to their NATO allies. Herr Brandt added that Mr. Brezhnev had appeared 'very definitely as No. 1' in the Soviet hierarchy, in contrast to their meeting for the signature of the Soviet-German Treaty in August 1970 when 'he would have described him as "No. 1a"' (Bonn telegram No. 1192, WRG 3/303/2).

[7] See *The Times*, 28 June 1968, p. 1 for a report of this speech.

frontiers of the German *Reich* of 1937'. The German 'threat' perhaps looks different today, but the old fears are not dead, and on top of them there is the prospect of growing German economic strength making its weight increasingly felt, politically as well, through an enlarged EEC. In this situation, Brandt is the best Chancellor they could hope for. But the Russians must be extremely conscious of the weakness of his position, and the possibility of his defeat at the next election; and to judge by the Soviet press they probably exaggerate the degree of revanchism in the attitudes of Strauss and other West German right-wing politicians. The favourable circumstance of the Brandt Government must therefore be seized in order to settle the German question before the chance disappears. Hence the Soviet hurry to press ahead with the Berlin Agreement, the ratification of the treaties and the international recognition of the GDR, implying as these things do the virtually permanent division of Germany, with Eastern Germany securely locked in the Warsaw Pact zone and covered by the Brezhnev Doctrine.[8]

5. The urgency with which the Russians have been pressing for progress in the Berlin talks is fully understandable in these terms. Admittedly it is tempting on grounds of timing to connect the sudden speed-up in August with the announcement of Nixon's visit to Peking and developments concerning China generally. But I do not think this connexion is at all proved.[9] It may have been that it was just the natural moment for a speed-up to occur in the circumstances of the Berlin negotiations on its merits.

6. We have in the past put forward from this Embassy the thesis that the Russians may wish to delay the final signature of the complete Berlin agreement until they feel that they are sure of getting the kind of European conference they want. Our suspicion was that the Russians would make their own *junktim*[10] and try to get the best *quid pro quo* they could for their final signature to a Berlin agreement. To judge, however, by Washington telegram No. 3235[11] we got the first part of the proposition right but the choice

[8] Cf. No. 62.

[9] In a letter of 12 October, replying to Nos. 78 and 79, Mr. Bullard commented: 'It seems clear that President Nixon decided upon his visit to Peking in the belief that the announcement would have the effect of making the Russians more rather than less anxious to do business with the West, and with the United States in particular . . . The most I would claim is that the news of President Nixon's visit must have sent a *frisson* through the Soviet leadership, causing them at least to pause and think whether any change in their *Westpolitik* was required, before deciding that it was definitely not . . . But one should perhaps not conclude from this that China is not an important factor at least in the background of Soviet thinking about Europe.'

[10] i.e. link, making 'x' dependent on 'y'.

[11] This telegram of 29 September reported information from Mr. Hillenbrand, Assistant Secretary of State in the State Department, that in conversation at the UN in New York the previous day Mr. Gromyko had told Herr Scheel 'that the Russians would not agree that signature of the Berlin protocol should take place before the ratification of the Moscow Treaty by the *Bundestag* . . . Hillenbrand commented that if Gromyko was now saying that ratification had to come first, this was the *junktim* in reverse and would be a serious development'. Mr. Gladstone of WED played down the likelihood that the Russians had changed their minds about the timing of future East-West developments 'not least because I cannot believe that if Soviet

of *quid pro quo* wrong: it is the ratification of the Moscow Treaty that the Russians want to make sure of first of all. But this surely confirms rather than goes against the thesis set out in paragraph 4 above that the basic Soviet interest is the permanent division of Germany with formal recognition of the new frontiers of the two German states. At the same time, a European conference, as soon as it can be organised, would reinforce the international endorsement of the German settlement as well as serving other purposes, particularly the organisation of an 'all-European' counterweight to Western European integration (political and military) through the enlargement of the EEC. A settlement of the Munich agreement question is also of course on the agenda, with probably a lower degree of priority.

7. I have so far not mentioned the problem of reduction of armed forces and armaments. This comes into a rather different category since it affects the USSR/US relationship so closely. If we accept the importance to the Russians of the permanent division of Germany we may perhaps question whether there is still a strong Soviet interest, as a further stage in their European policy, in getting American forces out of Europe. I am not at all sure that this objective now has much if any priority. Because of the American domestic situation, quite a lot of American troops may leave anyway. The existing situation, in which the presence of American troops in West Germany implies a sort of American guarantee of the division of Germany, may well suit the Russians better than a Europe totally deprived of American troops and led, as the Russians might fear it could be, by revanchist West Germans and, as they seem to think, basically anti-Soviet British Conservatives. The Russians might fear that a withdrawal of American troops would be compensated by further political and military integration in Western Europe, which they might dislike even more. In any case, the Russians are now used to living with the fact of American troops in Europe; a Europe without them might be less stable and less comfortable. If there is to be a reduction of American forces in Europe the Russians might prefer it to be by agreement (even if it involves a reduction on their own side) rather than by a unilateral American decision. For an agreement can be chalked up as another Brezhnev foreign policy success and fits into the picture, which must be important to the Russians, of a European situation generally under control and not subject to sudden change.[12]

8. Politically then, it looks to me as if the Soviet interest, as they would see it, lies at present in a continuing American military presence in Europe. This leads to the question: what, then, is the degree of Soviet military interest in

aims had changed Brezhnev would not have dropped some hint of the change to Brandt' (minute of 30 September, WRL 2 / 13).

[12] In his reply Mr. Bullard agreed that 'we should look to Europe for the motives behind Soviet policy', and accepted that in the short term that policy was directed at the FRG, although he questioned Mr. Dobbs's analysis of Soviet thinking about American troop withdrawals from Europe and offered his own 'less subtle' guess: 'I really wonder whether the Russians would see much need for American troops in Europe if both Germanies were in the United Nations and if they and the rest of Europe were engaged in the pursuit of "all-European cooperation".'

MBFRs[?] The US nuclear capacity must be a major factor in Soviet minds, and the threat of its use cannot be sep[a]rated from the continued presence of US forces in Europe, insofar as the latter (as Field Marshal Montgomery always used to say so bluntly) are an additional trigger to the former. The main advantage to the Russians now of the removal of American forces from Europe would be to remove this additional trigger. But the Russians can hardly expect the total withdrawal of all US forces from Europe in the foreseeable future. The trigger therefore will remain, more or less irrespective of the size of the trigger forces (indeed the smaller they become, the less valid the possibility of graduated response, and the more we move back towards 'massive retaliation', if we assume that the European members of NATO do not make compensating increases). The Russian interest therefore in MBFRs, at least so far as they affect North American forces, would seem fairly limited. A *truly balanced* agreement on reductions would introduce an element of stability and at least prevent any increase in the future; it could save the Russians a bit of expenditure or free some forces for the Far East; and it might encourage a less cautious American approach to fundamental agreements in SALT.[13] Apart from these advantages in the American connexion, an agreement on reductions of forces and armaments would presumably set a ceiling on the West European contribution to the NATO shield. With talk of an enlarged EEC leading to greater political and military integration in Western Europe this could be an important Soviet objective. And even if an agreement on MBFRs were not reached the Russians would probably calculate that the fact of negotiations being held would tend to check further tendencies to greater military integration in the West.

9. All this would of course redound to Soviet advantage *vis-à-vis* China, but this could well be a bonus rather than a prime objective.

10. The Ambassador has seen this letter and generally endorses it. We are not copying it elsewhere as it is meant for discussion in the Office rather than anything else. The same applies to a companion piece which will reach you by the same bag on the connexion between present trends in Soviet foreign policy and Brezhnev's evidently increased authority.[14]

Yours ever,
J.A. Dobbs

[13] Cf. p. 343. US-Soviet talks in Helsinki from 8 July to 24 September had apparently made little progress. The sixth round of SALT talks opened in Vienna on 16 November, and adjourned on 22 December with both sides refusing to disclose how far agreement had been reached.

[14] No. 79 below.

No. 79

Letter from Mr. Dobbs (Moscow) to Mr. Bullard
[*ENS 2/2*]

Confidential   MOSCOW, *30 September 1971*

Dear Julian,

Brezhnev and Soviet Foreign Policy

1. In this letter I should like to consider the connexion between current moves in Soviet foreign policy and internal developments. It is obvious to all that Brezhnev is now taking personal charge of the more important questions of foreign policy to a degree that did not apply up to a fairly short time ago. It first became clear at the Party Congress in April[1] that the other leaders were now leaving it to Brezhnev to be the principal spokesman on foreign affairs and it seems probable that his new authority in this field is based on the confirmation of his general position which the Party Congress provided. We seem to be witnessing what we would call in the West a trend towards presidential government. In Brezhnev's personal secretariat (see our telegram No. 1388)[2] there seems to be developing something of the equivalent of a White House or Elysée staff, providing advice on foreign affairs more or less independently of the Foreign Ministry. As things are now developing it will hardly be necessary for Brezhnev to follow Khruschev's example and assume the post of Chairman of the Council of Ministers in addition to his present post (which would be contrary to a Central Committee resolution of October 1964). With his visit to Paris[3] he is on his way to getting his position as General Secretary accepted in the world as the equivalent of that of executive President. It will be interesting to see whether his personal secretariat play the same role in Paris as they did at Orianda [*sic*][4] and may have done in Belgrade,[5] to the further down-grading of the Ministry of Foreign Affairs. Brezhnev, incidentally, did not leave the talks with Mrs. Gandhi to Kosygin, her official host, but took the chair himself.[6]

---

[1] See pp. 325-6.

[2] Not printed.

[3] Mr. Brezhnev was to visit France, on his first visit to the West, from 25-30 October: see pp. 417-18 below.

[4] See No. 78, note 6.

[5] Mr. Brezhnev visited Yugoslavia from 22-25 September.

[6] Following the signature of an Indo-Soviet Treaty of Peace, Friendship and Cooperation on 8 August 1971 in Delhi, the Indian Prime Minister Mrs. Indira Gandhi visited Moscow from 27-29 September: the talks were deferred until 28 September so that Mr. Brezhnev could be present at them. The Joint *Communiqué* issued at the end of the visit emphasised the importance of the Treaty as a basis for cooperation for economic and social progress, and noted that Mrs. Gandhi reaffirmed that the Indian Ocean should be a peace zone.

2. The French Ambassador claims to have some evidence, albeit inconclusive, that the other leaders accept as normal and necessary that Brezhnev should be identified as the spokesman of the Soviet Union on the world stage on a par with other leaders; indeed that there may well have been pressure in the Party generally that the Soviet Union's principal leader should be seen to be playing this role. (At the same time, Seydoux says he has been privately advised that while Brezhnev wants suitable publicity in Paris, he does not want his public exposure overplayed, on the grounds that there are still some people who would exploit this against him.) We just don't know; but the effect can only be to reduce the importance of Kosygin. It may be that these changes reflect a changing balance of power and personalities, the importance of which lies not so much in the relationship between Brezhnev and Kosygin personally (Kosygin never seems to have been cast as a rival to Brezhnev) as in the manoeuvring between groups of young men in the Party who will have tended to form up behind these two leaders. The emphasis by the Soviet press on the success of Brezhnev's initiatives (e.g. readers' letters welcoming the discussions with Brandt) may help this Brezhnev group to consolidate their position in the higher Party organs. It will not be surprising if Brezhnev gives a report on foreign policy to the next Central Committee Plenum; and it is conceivable that a Brezhnev faction could use the general approval of it to advance their own cause. Politics is politics everywhere, and it is hard not to believe, especially in the light of past internal conflicts, that some such political manoeuvring is not going on. Brezhnev is of course also being built up by the Soviet press and television as the great protagonist of rising living standards for the people.

3. The immediate point, though, is the effect of Brezhnev's personality on the conduct of Soviet policy. A special interest in the European situation, perhaps even an obsession with it, seems to be one feature; and this may go far to explain recent Soviet activity in European affairs. Since he succeeded Khruschev, Brezhnev's main foreign policy interest, to judge particularly by his journeys abroad, has been the consolidation of the Soviet position in Eastern Europe. On top of that it was Brezhnev who had to take the final decision over the invasion of Czechoslovakia, and the whole of that episode must have been a traumatic experience for him. He may well now consider that his decision turned out well for the Soviet Union. There seems to be a certain line of consistency between the decision over Czechoslovakia and present Soviet policies for Central Europe. What interested the Russians in the invasion of Czechoslovakia was the permanence of that country as a reliable piece in the security zone around the Soviet Union; and one must think of 'security' in both political and military senses. What Brezhnev is trying to make certain now is the permanence of the other Warsaw Pact countries, and particularly of East Germany, in the same role.

4. *Détente* with the West may well have several attractions for Brezhnev. The most solid of them could be that it implies recognition of the Soviet Union's security zone in Eastern Europe, and makes less likely any Western intervention in Soviet insistence on maintaining their own proletarian

internationalist order based on the Brezhnev doctrine throughout the Warsaw Pact countries. In Yugoslavia Brezhnev has just denied the Brezhnev doctrine.[7] This does not mean that he has ceased to believe in it. It is just that the Russians have never gone so far as to apply it to Yugoslavia; and as far as the Warsaw Pact countries, to which it does apply, are concerned, Brezhnev would obviously prefer to have it accepted implicitly without any need to talk about it explicitly.

5. Brezhnev taking personal charge of European policy has another implication which is worth noting. It should make a forward, active policy in Europe more easily realised. More than ever, since Stalin perhaps, the decisions are clearly in the competence of one man, and by all the evidence a fairly decisive man at that. In the present active phase of Soviet diplomacy, especially in Europe, we are probably already seeing the first fruits of this situation. The *immobilisme* of the previous period could have been due to differing approaches by different leaders. The new concentration of authority is already bringing a new decisiveness into Soviet foreign policy. It will be interesting to see if there is any kind of confirmation of Brezhnev's authority in this field at the next Central Committee Plenum.

6. If this is the way things are, a problem for us (or the very considerable intensification of an existing one) will be how to establish any sort of day-to-day working relationship with the main centre of policy-making power in the Soviet Union. It seems possible that Aleksandrov-Agentov[8] will become, if he is not already, more influential in foreign policy in some ways than V.V. Kuznetsov or Gromyko himself. In the last resort I expect the only way to affect Brezhnev's policy will be top-level contact with Brezhnev himself. But that, so far as the UK is concerned, is to look a long way ahead.

7. Finally, there is the connexion between all this and the expulsions.[9] Quite apart from the havoc these will have played with the KGB's operations in the UK they must be very unwelcome to the Soviet leaders and Brezhnev through the fact that the revelations of the dark side of the Soviet moon spoil the Soviet image at the very moment when Brezhnev and the other Soviet leaders are making such an active effort to improve it, with their peace proposals and programme of high level visits. As the Russians would see it, the effect of the British action will have been to undermine their efforts to improve their own image. From there it is a short way to the argument

[7] See note 5. During his visit Mr. Brezhnev reaffirmed the Belgrade Declaration of 1955 and the Moscow Declaration of 1956 (cf. No. 62, note 10), and in a speech on 23 September spoke of 'separate roads to socialism', stating that 'the choice of concrete forms of the organisation of social life is an internal affair and differences in form should be no cause for alienation or mistrust in relations amongst socialist states. We are against the practices of socialist construction in different countries being set off against one another, let alone somebody imposing his concrete methods of development on others' (Belgrade telegram No. 275 of 24 September, WDW 1/1).

[8] Mr. A.M. Alexsandrov-Agentov, formerly of the Soviet Ministry for Foreign Affairs, had been Mr. Brezhnev's assistant and an adviser on foreign affairs since 1966.

[9] See Nos. 76 and 77.

that the British intention was to sabotage these Soviet initiatives. Whether the Russians believe this argument or not is questionable, but they could easily half-believe it. It is a fairly common human experience to identify the effect of other people's actions with their purpose.[10]

Yours ever,

J.A. DOBBS

[10] In his reply (see No. 78, notes 9 and 12) Mr. Bullard wrote in regard to Mr. Brezhnev's impact on foreign policy that he hesitated to 'ascribe to his personal influence any change in direction . . . There are dangers, but I think also opportunities, in having someone apparently very much in charge of Soviet foreign policy who seems to want to get things done. We obviously wish to guard against the one without letting slip the other . . . I hope that you will continue to keep us informed of developments in the Brezhnev style, and especially of the extent to which he or his secretariat are willing to have dealings with Western diplomats and visitors. But I recognise that for the time being Britain is at the back of the queue.'

No. 80

Sir J. Killick (Moscow) to Sir A. Douglas-Home

No. 1527 Telegraphic [PUSD]

Flash. Confidential   MOSCOW, *8 October 1971, 8.50 p.m.*

Soviet retaliation

Following is a summary of my conversation this evening with Kuznetsov, First Deputy Foreign Minister.[1] Lunkov (Head of Second European Department, MFA) and an interpreter were also present on the Soviet side. I was accompanied by acting Head of Chancery.

2. After Kuznetsov had read the text of the Soviet statement (my telegram No. 1524),[2] I asked for details of the Soviet allegations about the

[1] Earlier on 8 October Sir J. Killick had reported in telegram No. 1521 that he had been summoned to the Soviet Foreign Ministry. Telegram No. 1522 summarised the Soviet reprisals set out in a statement handed to him by Mr. Kuznetsov: cancellation of Sir A. Douglas-Home's proposed visit to Moscow, that of Mr. Julian Amery (Minister for Housing and Construction), and Mr. Patolichev's visit to the UK; cancellation of the forthcoming meetings of the Joint Commission on Science and Technology, the Anglo-Soviet Consultative Committee and the Anglo-Soviet Shipping Committee; expulsions of Embassy staff in the Russian Secretariat, the Assistant Naval Attaché and the Archivist, and of a number of British businessmen; and no readmission to the Soviet Union of a number of former Embassy staff and businessmen. However, no present Embassy staff on leave or absent from the Soviet Union were affected, no ceiling was imposed, it was specifically accepted that those expelled could be replaced, and there was no statement that outstanding visas would not be granted.

[2] Not printed. The statement set out the proposed reprisals (note 1) which it stated had been forced on the Soviet Government by a continuing 'provocative campaign centred around absurd accusations against Soviet representatives in Britain, and the whipping up of an atmosphere of spy-mania and hostility to the Soviet Union . . . The Ministry again states that it depends only on the British side whether Soviet/British relations will continue to be strained or whether such

activities of the eighteen persons listed which had been described as incompatible with their official status, pointing out that the businessmen concerned had no such status. Kuznetsov said he did not wish to go into details. The persons concerned had engaged in activities incompatible with the functions which they should carry out in accordance with existing international practice. I said that there was no foundation whatever for such charges in regard to members of my own staff. In respect of the members of the British community, I could not accept these charges in default of any evidence to support them. Kuznetsov declined to add to what he had said.

3. I asked whether it would be in order for replacements to be sent for the members of the Embassy and businessmen affected, given that the Soviet allegations appeared to be directed against the personal activities of those named. Kuznetsov replied that the Soviet Government were basing themselves on the fact that, on the basis of reciprocity, they would not leave vacant those posts which could be filled. I interpreted this as confirmation that replacements would be permitted and thanked Kuznetsov for this clarification. (My private immediate assumption is that there is no par[allelis]m on the Soviet side in imposing a ceiling on staff here at the nett level following the expulsions.)

4. I confirmed that I would report the Soviet statement to my government. I knew that you, your colleagues and British public opinion would be greatly disappointed over the Soviet decisions regarding your visit, those of Mr. Amery and Patolichev, and the cancellation of the meetings of the various commissions. I reminded Kuznetsov that HMG, and you personally, had been concerned to make clear that the action which you had been forced to take should not be thought to be aimed at worsening Anglo-Soviet relations, or at placing obstacles in the way of the settlement of European problems. Our object had been to remove a major obstacle in Anglo-Soviet relations. HMG's action had corrected a one-sided situation: reprisals were therefore not justified. I recalled that the PUS had told Ippolitov that if the Soviet Government retaliated against HMG, then HMG would have to consider what further measures they might take.[3] I would not forecast what your reaction might be. I affirmed that the British Embassy in Moscow did not pose any threat to Soviet security, and rejected the charges made against its personnel. HMG had found the activities of certain Soviet officials in London to be inadmissible. There was no reciprocity here—quite the contrary. The same situation was reflected in the activities of certain Soviet officials in Moscow directed against members of my staff. One of my commercial officers had recently been approached by members of the Soviet Special Services while engaged on legitimate Embassy business. I regarded such action by the Soviet Special Services as comparable with the activities of Soviet officials in Britain against which HMG had been obliged to act.

an undesirable development will be terminated and normal relations re-established between the USSR and Britain.'

[3] See No. 76.

5. Kuznetsov said he could not agree with my remarks. He was astonished at statements by UK officials that HMG's actions which led to a worsening of Anglo-Soviet relations should be regarded as a means for developing those relations. 'This is ridiculous. You can't call white black.'

6. I pointed out that HMG and public opinion in Britain would not fail to note that a major topic proposed by the Soviet Union for discussion at a European Conference on Security and Cooperation was economic cooperation, including trade. They would observe who was worsening the conditions for trade by these measures against British businessmen who were working for an improvement in Anglo-Soviet trade relations. Kuznetsov replied at length to the effect that certain circles in Britain, whom he later identified with the government, were not interested in normalisation of relations or cooperation in Europe. Such circles were now taking actions amounting to an ultimatum. The British Government was against the evident tendency in Europe towards preserving peace. Despite mounting support for the idea of a CES, British officials, as I had just confirmed, were in practice against it and trying to impose an ultimatum on it. Britain had already taken detrimental steps and perhaps intended to take more.

7. I answered that the proof of the pudding would be in the eating. HMG stood by what they had said, and their future actions would demonstrate that they meant what they said. They had expressed the view that since the signature of the first stage of the Berlin agreement, there were now opportunities for agreement on other problems confronting us. There was no statement on record by any British Minister nor by HMG which justified Kuznetsov's remarks.

8. I finally asked for confirmation that the Soviet Government would be responsible for informing those on their list of names other than British officials. I made it clear that I could only accept responsibility for my own staff. It might in practice be difficult or impossible for me to contact some of the non-officials on the list. It was only reasonable that the fourteen days' notice to leave the USSR should begin from the time when the individuals were located and notified. In the case of non-officials I could no[t] accept any responsibility for ensuring that the persons concerned had left the Soviet Union within fourteen days from now. Kuznetsov replied that they left it to the British Embassy to find and inform all those listed. I reserved my position on this, but said that I would nevertheless do my best to contact those concerned.

9. Kuznetsov's manner was courteous and calm. He (and I also) expressed regret that our first meeting should be concerned with these matters, although Kuznetsov asserted that it was in no way the fault of the Soviet Union. I finally expressed the hope that despite this exchange, it would still prove possible to establish before long a sound working relationship.

10. See m[y] i[mmediately] f[ollowing] t[elegram].[4]

---

[4] This telegram stated that Sir J. Killick wished to reflect further on the possibility of counter-measures to the Soviet reprisals, and on 9 October in telegrams Nos. 1530 and 1531 he

advised that there was 'a strong case for calling it quits so far as concerns expulsions of personnel'. HM Embassy had 'got off very lightly indeed', and 'while the reasoning behind the choice of names is incomprehensible, the Russians have evidently wanted to combine the minimum provocation to us to take further counter-reprisals with the appearance of moderate, though adequate, retaliation on their side . . . If I read the Soviet message correctly it is that Brezhnev is so keen for Western cooperation in his present diplomatic offensive that if we keep at least on a level with our allies in moves towards *détente* it will be possible to get our relations back to something like normal fairly quickly.' The FCO agreed that no further action should be taken against the Soviet Embassy in London, and on 11 October Sir A. Douglas-Home minuted to Mr. Heath in this sense: 'It would not be in our interest now to appear to be carrying on a vendetta against the Soviet Union. This would lead to accusations that we were trying to sabotage *détente* and obstruct the Conference on European Security . . . We expected that there would be reprisals: having assessed these and having considered the situation as a whole we see no need to take further measures now' (ENS 3/548/26). Mr. Heath had already expressed the view that 'steps should be taken to cool things off', and on 12 October Sir J. Killick was informed in telegram No. 1176 that no counter-reprisals would be taken and that he should pursue the matter of outstanding visa applications with Second European Department of the Soviet Foreign Ministry: 'Our immediate aim should therefore be to restore normal diplomatic relations, especially in Moscow between you and the MFA.'

No. 81

Sir J. Killick (Moscow) to Sir A. Douglas-Home
No. 1576 Telegraphic [PUSD]

Immediate. Confidential   MOSCOW, *15 October 1971, 1.45 p.m.*

My telegram No. 1565: Anglo-Soviet relations.[1]

Minister accompanied by Consul called this morning on Deputy Head of Second European Department.

2. Vasev was extremely, even unnaturally, cold and reserved. He was obviously under instructions to listen to what Dobbs had to say and to give the minimum himself in reply. He brought the interview to an end as soon as possible, saying he would report to his authorities.

3. Dobbs said that after the regrettable events which had led to our action of 24 September and the measures announced by the Soviet Government on 8 October we needed to restore a normal working relationship. We interpreted positively the statement at the end of the Soviet note of 8 October to the effect that it depended only on the British side whether Soviet-British relations would continue to be strained or whether normal relations could be re-established.[2] We took this to mean that on the Soviet side no difficulties would be raised. You hoped and believed that we had now turned this difficult corner in Anglo-Soviet relations.

---

[1] Not printed.
[2] See No. 80, note 2.

4. There being no response from Vasev, Dobbs then went on to the practical problems of the staffing of our two Embassies. He went over the figures for the ceilings for Embassy diplomats, Embassy non-diplomats, the Soviet Trade Delegation and other organisations as communicated to Mr. Ippolitov by Sir T. Brimelow (your telegram No. 1125).[3] It would help if the Ministry could let us know which visa applications they wished to maintain in the light of the new ceilings. We understood that the diplomatic staff in the Soviet Embassy was now below the limit of 44. We were therefore prepared to grant visas to applicants assigned to the diplomatic staff of the Embassy up to this limit, provided we had no reason to object on individual grounds. We could grant visas forthwith to Gventsadze, Gribanov and Galitsky. Our information was that the non-diplomatic staff of the Embassy and the staffs of the Soviet Trade Delegation and other Soviet organisations were up to the new limits. Visas under these ceilings could be granted as soon as there were vacancies, or if they wished to expedite matters as soon as we were notified

(a) who would be leaving to make room for the new applicant,
(b) when this person would leave,
(c) what handover period, if any, was requested.

5. As regards our own staff, Dobbs mentioned that there were now twelve outstanding visa applications and told Vasev which ones were most urgent (Miss Molyneux, Miss Bird, Richards, Beel, Payne, Greetham and Webber).

6. Vasev said that the Soviet position had been clearly set out in the two statements given to HM Ambassador and he did not wish to add anything or to engage in polemics. Extremely grave damage had been done to Anglo-Soviet relations by our action of 24 September. It would take a long time and much effort on the British side to repair that damage. Whether or not a friendly relationship could be restored would depend to a great extent on whether there were any further unfriendly actions by the British side.

7. Dobbs then said that HMG were not proposing any specific actions in reply to the measures announced in the Soviet note of 8 October. If of course the Soviet Government themselves created further difficulties for us in addition to the measures announced in that note a new situation would arise. Also, if there were further activities in London of the kind which had led to our original action of 24 September, HMG would inevitably be forced to react. Vasev here objected to 'allegations' that Soviet officials had engaged in any form of improper activities. A difficult period would be ahead if the British side persisted in such allegations. After a reference to the great inconvenience for the Embassy which our expulsions had involved (he mentioned particularly the lack of experienced staff for the Consular

[3] This telegram of 1 October reported a call by Mr. Ippolitov, to whom Sir T. Brimelow explained the new 'ceilings' for Soviet officials in the UK: 44 Embassy diplomats, 49 Embassy non-diplomats, 97 STD staff and 179 for other organisations. He told Mr. Ippolitov that the ceilings for the Embassy were 'not subject to argument, but that there might be room for discussion of our starting figures for the STD and other organisations, since there was a time lag between arrivals and departures and our being informed of them' (ENS 3/548/25).

Department and the clearing out of political counsellors) he then brought the interview to a close.[4]

[4] Mr. Dobbs's and Sir T. Brimelow's representations were reinforced in London on 26 October, when Mr. P.N. Filatov, First Secretary at the Soviet Embassy, was asked to call at the FCO. Mr. Bullard repeated that it was not HMG's intention to 'disturb any legitimate activities', and gave Mr. Filatov a list of recent events 'which could be interpreted as suggesting that the Soviet intention was the exact opposite of ours', including the cancellation of tours by the musicians Oistrakh and Richter, the non-arrival of invitations to FCO Ministers to attend the 7 November reception at the Soviet Embassy, and a statement by the Soviet Ministry of Agriculture that they were under instructions not to receive British visitors for the next month or so. The list also detailed outstanding visas for prospective members of the British Embassy. Mr. Filatov maintained 'that the British side was responsible for the present situation and should not be surprised if it included disagreeable elements . . . It was impossible to maintain Anglo-Soviet technical contacts at the same level as before the expulsions, since there were now not enough people in the Soviet Embassy and Trade Delegation to handle them.' Mr. Bullard replied that 'we on the contrary regarded the Soviet side as entirely to blame for the situation . . . What we wanted to know was whether these events of the last 10 days meant that the Soviet Government were deliberately prolonging and widening the dispute. If that was the case, as Dobbs had told Vasev, we would want to consider the situation very carefully' (ENS 3/548/25).

The next document reflects the period of analysis of Anglo-Soviet relations, and of East-West relations generally, which followed the shock to normal diplomatic intercourse administered by the expulsion of the Soviet spies. The efforts of Sir J. Killick and his staff to restore 'a normal working relationship' with the Soviet Government received little reward. Soviet authorities kept HM Embassy at arms length, requests for the Ambassador to pay his first calls on important officials were denied or simply ignored, and official contacts generally reflected an attitude of deliberate coolness on the Soviet part. British commercial interests reported that business was more or less 'as usual', but conditions were more difficult, and some concern was expressed that American firms might step into the breach and make a serious attack on the Soviet market.

British Embassy staff in Moscow and officials in London devoted much time to considering how relations with the Soviet Union might be restored to at least their pre-expulsion state. On 15 October Mr. B.L. Barder, First Secretary in Moscow, sent Mr. Bullard a list of 'Indicators of Temperature' drawn up by Sir J. Killick for measuring changes in the Anglo-Soviet relationship: these included the resumption of social contacts with Embassy staff, the trend of Soviet press comment on the UK, the pattern of approval for trips outside Moscow and the level of shadowing and harassment of Embassy staff, as well as the state of working relations with the Foreign Ministry and Ministry of Foreign Trade. The FCO were also asked to comment on 'London indicators' such as news of the return of Mr. Smirnovsky to his post, information on the granting of visas for Embassy staff and businessmen and the state of commercial relations. Reports on the state of these 'Indicators' were passed between London and Moscow for the rest of the year, but their chief message was 'little change'.

No. 82

Letter from Sir J. Killick (Moscow) to Mr. Bullard

[*ENS 3/548/10*]

Confidential   MOSCOW, *28 October 1971*

Dear Julian,

Anglo-Soviet relations

1. Many thanks for your stimulating letter of 19 October about the way ahead.[1] As I said in my brief acknowledgement, I entirely agree that we should not just sit back and let things take their course.[2] This is not a matter of form, but of policy. This said, it is not so easy to work out a very clear plan of action.

2. Before I comment on the various specific ideas and suggestions in your letter, it might perhaps help if I try to set out the main parameters within which, it seems to me, we shall have to try to operate. The chief of these are:

(*a*) We must start from the basic objective of giving the lie to the Soviet assertion, in the last paragraph of their statement of 8 October in which they notified us of their retaliatory measures (my telegram No. 1524),[3] that the restoration of normal relations depends on Britain rather than on the Soviet Union. This means that we should seek to make it clear that we ourselves are ready and willing to resume business and that if this does not happen, the responsibility is exclusively that of the Soviet side. And we should not hesitate to publicise the evidence of our readiness as appropriate (nor of Soviet unwillingness).

(*b*) We cannot afford to leave it to the Russians to take the initiative in those areas and on those questions which are of interest to them, while

---

[1] In this letter Mr. Bullard set out 'some preliminary thoughts on the way ahead' for Anglo-Soviet relations, starting from the assumption that neither Mr. Heath nor Sir A. Douglas-Home would be visiting Moscow before President Nixon's visit in May 1972. He suggested that the reinstatement in January 1972 of the postponed meeting of the Joint Commission might be 'the best we may be able to hope for . . . Technically, there is no doubt that all the balls are in the Russian court, but you may think it would not be wise for us to stand upon form in this way. If we do nothing, we shall encourage those in Moscow who may be happy to see the force of lethargy working on the side of a continuing freeze, whereas our aim should be to encourage those who may be concerned to bring our relations back to something near normal as soon as possible. This can perhaps best be done, once we get out of the period when any proposal from our side would risk almost certain rebuff, by offering the Russians a series of carefully graduated proposals which would lead us in the direction we want without it seeming that we were being brought in from the cold too quickly . . . We must clearly insert the thin end of the wedge first, but we must also try to choose the fly which the Russians are likely to find most attractive.'

[2] In a letter of 22 October Sir J. Killick expressed agreement 'that we do not just want to leave the ball in the Russian court and have already had in mind the possibility of sending in ferrets repeatedly to see what reaction they produce. We have already started this here in a small way but must certainly now think further ahead.'

[3] See No. 80, note 2.

maintaining the freeze on questions which we ourselves are anxious to discuss. Similarly, I hope that we can avoid a situation in which the Russians contrive to resume normal business of their own choosing through their Embassy in London while maintaining the freeze in dealings between this Embassy and Soviet ministries and other official bodies in Moscow. (I state this as an objective, while acknowledging that it may be difficult to attain it.)

(c) At the same time, I assume that Ministers would not wish to give the impression that we are in any way running after the Russians or begging them to forgive us and resume normal relations. Apart from being morally unjustified and repugnant, it seems to me wrong from the policy point of view that we should appear to be doing this. If we make premature attempts at an unduly high level to re-establish contacts, visits and exchanges, we run the risk of a Soviet rebuff on the record which may prove more difficult to undo later. This can only be avoided by acting at a lower level and a more deliberate speed. Moreover, if we appear too eager to re-establish dealings with the Soviet side, we may encourage them to try to resume KGB activities in Britain in the expectation that our eagerness for good relations will deter us from further measures against them. More broadly, I would like to hope that the Russians will come to realise that they need us over Europe, even though some of our allies, by their 'bicycle race' activities, are not doing much to help the process.[4]

3. If we consider the various suggestions in your letter with these broad parameters in mind, it becomes apparent, I think, that there can be no question for some time of raising the possibility of a visit by the Prime Minister or a re-instated visit by the Secretary of State—as you yourself make clear. Indeed I have always assumed that a visit by the Prime Minister would only be considered in the light of the results of a visit by the Secretary of State. Certainly there could be no question whatever of a visit by Mr. Heath before President Nixon comes to Moscow in May. Similarly, I am not enthusiastic about the suggestion for concentrating on re-instating the meeting of the Joint Commission. I take it that your reference to the possibility of a visit for the Joint Commission by Mr. Davies in the first week of January applied to the time-table as it stood before the Soviet statement of 8 October, and that

---

[4] Mr. Barder's report on 'Indicators' for the period ending 14 October (see p. 409) commenting on No. 9, 'Views of friendly Embassies', stated that 'When the Ambassador called on his Finnish colleague on 11 October, he was struck by the fact that the latter volunteered (in non-secure surroundings) that HMG had in his view acted rightly and successfully. In the present state of Soviet European policy the Russians needed us.' The Canadian Ambassador had 'expressed a basic worry that the Russians might continue their propaganda campaign against HMG over European questions to try to drive a wedge between HMG on the one hand and other European Governments, especially the French and Germans, on the other'. The French Press Attaché had told his British opposite number that the 'timing of HMG's action was especially embarrassing for Paris in view of the forthcoming Brezhnev visit' (see No. 79, note 3), but 'friendly and admiring reactions' had been received from 'American, German, Japanese, Chinese (!), Belgian, Italian, Canadian and, to a somewhat lesser degree, Indian colleagues'.

you were not meaning to imply any possibility of reinstating the meeting of the Joint Commission at that time. The Soviet statement was explicit in rejecting a meeting in January of the Joint Commission, and we must take it that there is no question of their retracting this decision, as far as timing is concerned. In any case, our own inclination at this stage is to 'hasten slowly' so far as concerns the Joint Commission. The Soviet interest in the Commission is greater than ours, and on this issue if no other we shall be in a stronger position if we let the Russians come to us than if we go to them. I feel pretty sure in any case that Mr. Davies will have no particular interest in haste, and one would have to find quite strong arguments to overpersuade him, in terms of practical results (other than the holding of a meeting for the meeting's sake). One would have to be pretty disingenuous to invent any in the foreseeable future!

4. As regards the various other possible visits enumerated in your letter (including the suggestion of a visit by yourself to Moscow),[5] there seems to me to be no practical alternative to deferring any approach to the Russians until after we have surmounted two basic preliminary hurdles: first the resumption of my own programme of initial calls on ministers and senior officials; and, secondly, the granting of at any rate some of the outstanding visas for members of the Embassy waiting to join us in Moscow. We are writing separately about the visa question,[6] and it may be that we could contemplate some approaches on other visits and exchanges in the absence of a solution to this thorny problem, if there was some evidence of a thaw in other fields. But this would imply our being satisfied that the Soviet attitude on visas did not amount to a second round of additional retaliation, and in any case, I think it would be a mistake to take any initiative on other visits and exchanges before my programme of calls has started up again. If the Russians are not prepared to do me the elementary courtesy of arranging my formal first calls on those with whom I expect to do business in my official capacity, we can certainly take it that they will not agree to other contacts which are inherently of 'second stage' character (not so much in their own importance as in their symbolic significance as indicators of a return to normal). One would be in effect trying to lay them on 'by post' as it were, with the risk referred to in paragraph 2(c) above.

5. My conclusion, therefore, is that our first priority should be the resumption of my first calls. However, when these calls are eventually resumed, they will very probably (depending on how the temperature feels at the time) provide a suitable occasion for raising with the Russians the possibilities of reinstating or initiating some of the visits and meetings which you have

[5] In his letter of 19 October (see note 1) Mr. Bullard had offered to go to Moscow 'on a visit which would require neither publicity nor very much in the way of recognition by the Soviet authorities' and which might provide a suitable opportunity to discuss with the Russians the resumption of visits and a political dialogue between officials.

[6] Cf. No. 81. Mr. Dobbs wrote to Mr. Bullard on 29 October pointing out the problems caused for the Embassy by delays in granting visas for replacement staff, and welcoming Mr. Bullard's representations to Mr. Filatov on 26 October (*ibid.*, note 4).

suggested. Thus, if and when I am able to pay a call on Firyubin (or indeed on Fomin and Nemchina), it would be helpful if I might have the authority to raise with any one of them the proposal that all three should visit Britain for talks on South and South East Asia, with special emphasis on India and Pakistan (Gordon's letter of 15 September to Ken Scott, Barder's letter of 30 September to Gordon, and FCO telegram No. 1153 of 7 October).[7] I should be grateful for confirmation that I may do this if and when the opportunity offers. It would also be helpful if you could give me some indication of possible dates which I could put to Firyubin or either of the other two as being convenient from the FCO point of view for a visit of the kind we envisage. I would, however, try to avoid the impression of a definite invitation for specific dates, to which an immediate 'yes or no' reply is required: I would merely put the suggestion of a visit and talks to them, making it clear that we would quite understand if they preferred not to let us have any very early reaction, and implying perhaps that we would not object, should the Soviet side so prefer, if they left the idea on the table for a few weeks until the general atmosphere in Anglo-Soviet relations had improved.

6. Similarly, I envisage that I might use my initial call on Madame Furtseva or Sofinsky, the Head of the Cultural Relations Department at the Foreign Ministry, to raise the possibilities of visits to the Soviet Union by Lord Eccles (preferably with the former) and to Britain by Yevtushenko (with the latter).[8] I doubt in fact if my call on Furtseva will be very promising in this respect, but it might be worth a try, assuming that Lord Eccles still wants to come.

7. My first call on Patolichev would provide the obvious opportunity to re-confirm the invitation to him to visit London. If Alkhimov carries out his intended visit to London before I see Patolichev, it might be useful for Con Seward also to take soundings on the invitation to Patolichev (especially since it was to Seward that Patolichev first mentioned his wish to go to London).[9] But apart from a possible contact on this between Seward and Alkhimov, I should prefer not to make any further approach to Patolichev in advance of my own initial call on him. I should add that I have had a very useful talk in company with Norman Cox with Land and the local ICL people about Alkhimov, and about a further possible ploy involving Sir John Wall coming out to open the new ICL office.[10] I will leave Norman to deal with this in greater detail.

[7] Not printed. Sir J. Killick was instructed in telegram No. 1277 of 3 November that invitations for Messrs. Firyubin, Yevtushenko or Patolichev (see paras. 6 and 7 below) to visit the UK would 'have to be fed in gradually and with circumspection'.

[8] An invitation from Madame Furtseva to Lord Eccles, Paymaster-General with responsibility for the Arts, to visit the Soviet Union in 1972, and a proposed visit by Mr. Yevtushenko had been cancelled in retaliation for the expulsions of Soviet spies.

[9] Mr. Alkhimov was Deputy Minister of Foreign Trade. Mr. Patolichev had been officially invited to visit the UK by Mr. Davies on 7 September, but no reply had been received.

[10] Sir J. Wall was Chairman, and Mr. R. Land Manager, Eastern Europe, of International Computers Ltd.

8. I entirely agree that a visit by yourself could play a very useful part in the process of fence-mending—indeed I nearly listed it as an 'indicator'—and I am grateful for your offer to come for this purpose. The question here is again one of timing. I do not think that it would be appropriate or even possible for you to come here with the object of paying calls on officials at the Foreign Ministry and meeting them socially in advance of the resumption of my own initial calls. As I have already said, this would seem to me to be getting the priorities wrong, not just in terms of protocol but, more important, as an index of Soviet willingness to do business through normal channels before we turn to more exceptional types of contact. I therefore suggest that we keep this one up our sleeves until we see how we get on with my initial calls. But it would have high priority on my list (especially if it involved a performance by you at the Embassy Christmas Party, which will be on 17 December!)

9. I am grateful for the suggestion that we might put forward the idea of another round of talks between Parsons and Sytenko on the Middle East,[11] in London or Moscow. However, since as you say the object of this would be purely to assist in breaking the ice, rather than because we have anything of substance to discuss on the Middle East, my instinct is not to play this card for the moment. We have a fair number of genuine topics and initiatives which can be used for ice-breaking purposes when the time is ripe; I doubt if it is necessary to invent others.

10. I agree with what you say about the Consultative Committee, and I would not wish to ask you to reconsider this (paragraph 5 of your letter).[12]

11. If you accept that the timetable and procedure should be on the lines I have suggested, the next point which arises is whether there is anything to be done to accelerate the resumption of my initial calls, on which the other initiatives depend. One possibility which we have considered is a message, or even a letter, from the Secretary of State to Gromyko, which I could be instructed to deliver, if possible in person. Such a message could be hung on the peg of the last paragraph of the Soviet statement of 8 October, quote the Secretary of State's speech to the Foreign Affairs Club,[13] and assure Gromyko that HMG's attitude both to current European questions and to the resumption of normal relations with the Soviet Union is far from being negative. [I] could also put it to Gromyko that if there is a corresponding desire on the Soviet side to resume business with us, we look to them to provide the evidence of it by themselves resuming dealings with this Embassy in general and myself in particular. Such a message has the attraction of

[11] Cf. No. 64, note 1.

[12] Mr. Bullard had not included the Anglo-Soviet Consultative Committee in his suggested subjects for approaching the Russians as 'I do not want to attract publicity at this stage for a meeting which might well lead to the conclusion that the Committee should be wound up or at least put on ice for a while'.

[13] Sir A. Douglas-Home's speech at the Foreign Affairs Club on 19 October, in which he spoke of a new exploratory and possibly hopeful phase in East-West relations, was reported in *The Times*, 20 October 1971, p. 1.

being publishable later as part of the indictment against the Soviet Government. However, I think there are sound reasons for not recommending such a course. A message of this kind would entail the risk of a rebuff or total lack of response at a high level; and it would, I fear, be extremely difficult to draft it in such a way as to avoid in some degree the impression that we are going cap in hand to the Russians for forgiveness.

12. However, there is an alternative possibility which I hope might be considered. I see no reason why we should not adopt the practice of repeating or elaborating in Moscow the replies which have been given in London to representations or messages delivered by the Soviet Embassy to the FCO. The obvious example is the PUS's response to Ippolitov's message on 18 October about a European conference on security and cooperation (FCO telegram No. 1208).[14] I would see considerable advantage in your instructing me to seek an interview with Lunkov in order to speak to him on the subject of a CES and to confirm the PUS's reply to the Soviet message of 18 October. My instructions might include the transmission to Lunkov of the text of the Secretary of State's speech to the Foreign Affairs Club, perhaps with certain passages in the speech singled out for special note. If this gambit were to succeed, it would have the dual advantage of stressing HMG's positive attitude to European questions, while simultaneously giving me an opportunity to raise with the official who is probably the most flexible and receptive of all those with whom we deal in the MFA the question of the resumption of my initial calls on ministers and officials. I should be grateful to hear fairly soon what you think of this possibility.[15] If it is to be done, there would be some advantage in doing it quickly, since the peg of the Soviet message of 18 October will begin to look rather implausible if too long a period elapses before I ask to discuss it with Lunkov. He himself will soon be back from the Canada/Cuba trip.[16]

13. Instructions to me to call on Lunkov would not of course preclude other ice-breaking initiatives, if we could think of any which are compatible with the general parameters which I have suggested earlier. For example, it would be convenient if matters could be so arranged as to enable me to take some action with the Russians on behalf of NATO if the circumstances for

[14] This telegram of 18 October reported that Mr. Ippolitov had called on Sir D. Greenhill to urge that multilateral consultations in preparation for a Conference on European Security should begin in Helsinki as soon as possible, to agree a date, agenda and procedures. Sir D. Greenhill replied emphasising HMG's positive attitude to the conference: 'we would have points to make on the substance of the agenda but did not foresee any particular problem. As far as the timing of the multilateral preparations was concerned our view was that of our Allies. The Berlin Agreement as a whole should be completed first.' Mr. Ippolitov rejoined that 'the Russians wanted both the Berlin Agreement and the ratifications as soon as possible and did not think that either should be linked to the CES'. Similar Soviet *démarches* were made in other NATO capitals (WDW 1/1).

[15] FCO telegram No. 1277 of 3 November authorised Sir J. Killick to approach Mr. Lunkov on these lines: cf. No. 83 below.

[16] Mr. Lunkov accompanied Mr. Kosygin, who visited Canada from 17-26 October, travelling on to Cuba from 26-31 October.

such a message should arise at the right moment (on the analogy of the Belgian mandate to lay on Brosio's visit).[17] Presumably this could only be done if Britain happened to be the Chairman for the month of the NATO Permanent Representatives at a time when some communication required delivery: and I doubt whether all our NATO allies would be enthusiastic about selecting the UK as their spokesman for the special purpose of helping us mend our fences with Moscow! The possibility might be worth considering with WOD, but I imagine the right combination of circumstances is unlikely to arise.

14. Finally, a word of warm appreciation for your and the Secretary of State's efforts to put on record in a public forum HMG's positive stance in regard to European problems and East-West relations generally. The speech at the Foreign Affairs Club was, if I may say so, exceedingly useful from our point of view, and I hope that we shall be able to make full use of the text. You will have seen from our telegrams Nos. 1632 and 1633 of 26 October[18] that Matveyev, in his *Izvestiya* article, was unable to find anything in the speech to quote against the Secretary of State or HMG: he was forced back on the assertion that the irrefutable principles enunciated by the Secretary of State were inconsistent with HMG's actions. But in doing so he gave quite a favourable account of those principles, with a clear endorsement (however grudging) of the general thesis put forward by Sir Alec. This in itself is quite an advance.

15. To sum up, I recommend that we should aim:

(*a*) To get my initial calls started up;
(*b*) To press for the outstanding visas;
(*c*) To use my initial calls, when they are permitted, to float or revise the invitations to Firyubin, Patolichev, Evtushenko [*sic*] and Lord Eccles;
(*d*) To consider at once the possibility of instructing me to call on Lunkov to repeat the reply on CES and to press him on my initial calls (and visas).

This may not look very forward; but I think that to attempt more would run the risks of casting ourselves in the role of suitors, and of inviting a rebuff.

---

[17] A meeting on 4-5 October of NATO Deputy Foreign Ministers (at which Mr. Godber represented the UK) had nominated Signor M. Brosio, outgoing Secretary-General of NATO, as an 'explorer' to visit various countries, beginning with the Soviet Union, to discuss some of the basic issues raised by the possibility of MBFR negotiations (cf. p. 343).

[18] Not printed.

And in any case I think we have to test the ground underfoot at each step before venturing the next one.[19]

Yours ever,

JOHN KILLICK

[19] Sir A. Douglas-Home gave his agreement in FCO telegram No. 1277 of 3 November to the guidelines suggested in para. 2 of Sir J. Killick's letter, and stated: 'It is not our intention to court rebuffs. But we propose, as occasion offers, to make further representations about the undesirability of interfering with legitimate relations, both in order to make it clear which side is seeking a return to normal conditions and also to provide a choice of openings which the Russians can take up as soon as they feel able to do so. We agree that it is important that we should not appear to be running after them . . . we should like you to pursue the four aims in your paragraph 15 in parallel, making progress in whatever directions you can.'

As the next document shows, the Soviet Government remained determinedly unreceptive to British attempts to improve relations—in contrast with the boost to Franco-Soviet relations bestowed by the visit of Mr. Brezhnev to Paris, 25-30 October. As Mr. Christopher Soames, HM Ambassador in Paris, pointed out in his report on the visit, it could not have come at a more interesting juncture: 'while Mr. Brezhnev was paying his first visit to a Western country, the British Parliament voted to turn the Six into the Ten [see No. 67, note 13], the United Nations voted to turn the Big Four into the Big Five [with the recognition by the USA of the People's Republic of China and her admission to a permanent seat on the Security Council], the American Senate threw out the Foreign Aid Bill [rejecting on 29 October the President's request for $3,600m], and Mr. Nixon decided the date of his visit to China [see No. 78, note 3]. With these greater events Mr. Brezhnev competed, not altogether successfully, for the headlines. They also set the context for what he was trying to do. They each reflected developments that give added incentive to Soviet policy to consolidate Eastern Europe and to divide Western Europe.'[1]

Mr. Brezhnev arrived in Paris accompanied by Mr. Kirillin, Mr. Gromyko and Mr. Patolichev, and had four meetings with President Pompidou during a visit where he was treated with considerable pomp as a head of state. At the end of their final plenary meeting President Pompidou and Mr. Brezhnev signed a 'Franco-Soviet Declaration'— the equivalent of a communiqué—welcoming the development of Franco-Soviet cooperation in all fields, and a statement ('énoncé') setting out thirteen principles as the basis for Franco-Soviet cooperation, including the inviolability of existing frontiers, non-interference in the internal affairs of other states and non-use of force or threats. A ten-year economic agreement was also signed. Although, as Sir J. Killick commented, the outstanding feature of the visit was the contrast between the enormous publicity build-up and the relatively thin content of its outcome, 'for the Soviet leaders the appearance is probably at least as important as the substance'. The visit had fulfilled a 'psychological need' for the CPSU: Mr. Brezhnev was now seen to occupy 'the chair at the world's council table, left empty or only intermittently filled after the removal of Khruschev', and would figure honourably in Russian history books; 'The entente with France provides

[1] Paris despatch of 8 November, WRF 3/303/1.

"instant history" where real history is taboo.' Sir T. Brimelow's verdict was more prosaically phrased: 'we feared that the French might be tempted to make to the Russians during the Brezhnev visit a number of concessions which might create difficulties for us and the other members of the Alliance . . . However, [Mr. Soames's analysis] bears out our belief that the French have not given much away . . . One would have wished for a less effusive and euphoric tone. But there is nothing new about the French representing themselves as being in the vanguard of progress towards détente (MBFR apart).'[2]

[2] Letter of 9 November to Sir J. Killick, WDW 1/1.

No. 83

Sir J. Killick (Moscow) to Sir A. Douglas-Home

No. 1771 Telegraphic [ENS 3/548/10]

Priority. Confidential   MOSCOW, *16 November 1971, 8.40 a.m.*

My telegram No. 1769: call on Lunkov.[1]

1. I told Lunkov that I had been instructed to see him primarily in order to follow up the conversation between the PUS and Ippolitov on 18 October[2] and to supplement what the PUS had said about European security in the light of subsequent developments. What I had to say related also to Anglo-Soviet relations, in particular to the last paragraph of the note handed to me by Kuznetsov on 8 October.[3] I had not had the opportunity of elu[c]idating the latter, but assumed that it called for a positive attitude on HMG's part towards Soviet initiatives in Europe. I then drew his attention to the Queen's message to Podgorny on 6 November,[4] the passages about Anglo-Soviet relations in the Queen's speech at the opening of Parliament[5] and the Prime Minister's speech in Zurich on 17 September,[6] and your own speeches to the Foreign Affairs Club on 19 October[7] and to the House of Commons on 4

[1] In this telegram of 15 November Sir J. Killick reported that Mr. Lunkov had received him that afternoon.

[2] See No. 82, note 14.

[3] See No. 80, note 2.

[4] i.e. on the anniversary of the Soviet Revolution.

[5] HM The Queen's speech of 2 November, in which she stated that her Ministers would work for good relations with the Soviet Union and the countries of Eastern Europe, is printed in *Parl. Debs.*, 5th ser., H. of C., vol. 825, cols. 4-6.

[6] Speaking at a ceremony to mark the 25th anniversary of Mr. Churchill's plea for a United States of Europe on 19 September 1946, Mr. Heath said that 'our aim must be to develop peaceful cooperation with the countries of Eastern Europe and with the Soviet Union wherever the policies of those countries permit'. The speech is printed in Watt and Mayall, 1971, pp. 806-10.

[7] See No. 82, note 13.

November.[8] I handed over copies of lengthy extracts from the two latter speeches and expressed the hope that the Soviet Government would study them in the positive spirit in which they had been delivered. I then referred to M. Schumann's recent visit to London and to the statement in the joint declaration that the French and British Governments had found a close identity of views on all questions discussed,[9] pointing out that these questions included all the ones which had been discussed between the Soviet and French Governments during Br[e]zhnev's visit to Paris.[10] Speaking personally, I said that if the French Foreign Minister found himself in close agreement both with the Soviet and British Governments i[t] was surely difficult to maintain that HMG was adopting a negative attitude to European questions. I hoped that the Soviet Government would conclude from this evidence that HMG were making serious efforts to play their full part in European developments, and would reciprocate.

2. Lunkov said that the Soviet Government was already familiar with the public statements to which I had referred. He did not wish to go into the substance of the matter, but would only point out that public statements by HMG of readiness to cooperate with the Soviet Government were contradicted by the actions of the British Government, and in particular the measures which it had taken against Soviet representatives in London,[11] and he did not see how the two could be reconciled.

3. I said that I had hoped that in this conversation we could look forwards rather than backwards, but I assured him that there was no contradiction between our statements and our actions. I quoted your remarks that, if we had not taken the action which we took on 24 September it would not have been possible to find a basis for fruitful Anglo-Soviet relations in future, and that it was difficult for the British and Soviet Governments to work together for European security at a time when representatives of the Soviet Government were working against the security of the United Kingdom. Lunkov's reply to this was merely that he could not add to what Gromyko himself had said to you in New York on 27 September,[12] which still represented the position of the Soviet Government.

4. I suggested that the right course was for us now to work towards resuming working relations between the two governments for the following reasons:

[8] During the debate on the Address on 4 November Sir A. Douglas-Home referred to the 'recent spy incident' and stated that 'As far as I am concerned, the incident is closed. I share Mr. Kosygin's opinion which he recently expressed that there is no reason why this episode need affect the security conference negotiations or progress towards them or other proposals for *détente*. It was a necessary clearing of the air if relations are to be conducted on a basis of trust' (*Parl. Debs., 5th ser., H. of C.*, vol. 825, cols. 344-48).

[9] M. Schumann had visited London for talks from 11-12 November. The Joint Declaration issued at the end of his visit is printed in Watt and Mayall, *op. cit.*, pp. 1001-3.

[10] See pp. 418-19.

[11] See No. 76.

[12] See No. 77.

(*a*) The Soviet Government, however serious its reaction to what we had done, had not broken off diplomatic relations, I concluded from this that it was their view that the diplomatic machinery should be kept in being, and should be used.

(*b*) If the Soviet Government thought that HMG was adopting a negative attitude, it would be logical for them to discuss the relevant questions with us and to seek to bring about a better understanding.

Lunkov said that he would report what I had said. He admitted that the public statements to which I had referred contained positive elements, but repeated that they were incompatible with our actions. I said that we were content to be judged by our actions, and the Soviet Government would find that we were making a positive contribution to the discussion of European questions. As an example, I said that HMG had fully supported the attitude of a number of countries to talks on force reductions in Europe, and had joined with them in the proposal that Brosio should visit Moscow to discuss these questions.[13] I hoped that the Soviet Government would respond positively to this proposal.

5. Lunkov said that he noted my remarks about the positive attitude of HMG towards European security and reduction of forces and armaments in Europe, questions on which the Soviet Government had taken a positive and active position. But the actions we had taken in complicating and worsening bilateral relations with the Soviet Government went in the opposite direction.

6. I then referred back to my remarks about the use of diplomatic channel and said that I had so far been unable to make my customary first calls on senior members of the Foreign Ministry and other ministers and officials. My government hoped that it would soon be possible for me to begin to discharge my functions in this way. I quoted your statement in Parliament on 4 November that, so far as you were concerned, the 'incident' was closed, and said that you had made this statement on the assumption that the Soviet Government's note of 8 October had represented the full extent of Soviet counter action. I did not wish to be misunderstood as issuing any threat, but if I were not enabled to resume my normal functions my government might have to conclude that this was an additional measure of retaliation on the part of the Soviet Government. There were plenty of current international problems which you might wish to instruct me to discuss with the Soviet Government. I hoped that the Protocol Department of the Foreign Ministry would soon be able to resume organisation of my initial calls. Lunkov said that he would pass this on to Protocol Department, but that the essence of the problem was well known to me and was indeed implicit in what I had said.[14]

[13] Cf. No. 82, note 17.

[14] In telegram No. 1885 of 3 December Sir J. Killick reported that he had called on the Acting Head of Protocol Department, Mr. Borunkov, who seemed 'totally unprepared' for the Ambassador's visit and 'could only reply that the list of calls which we had given Protocol Department some time ago been distributed to the various ministries and organisations

7. I referred to my meeting with Smirnovsky at the 7 November reception[15] and said that I would have liked to return the hospitality he had given me in London, but that I did not wish to embarrass him in present circumstances. I knew that HMG would be interested to know when Smirnovsky was likely to return to his post. Lunkov said that Smirnovsky and I were both experienced Ambassadors and would know how best to handle the question of hospitality. He had nothing to say at the moment about Smirnovsk[y]'s return to London.

8. I then took my leave. It was plain that Lunkov did not feel able immediately to respond in any way to what I had said, other than by playing the gramophone record. But he played it in a distinctly mellower tone, and clearly did not wish to embark on a detailed post-mortem. I would not exclude the possibility that there will now be some response from Protocol Department to my representations about initial calls. I do not propose to pursue the question of Smirnovsky for the moment.

9. I think it may be useful for my Head of Chancery, who was present, to follow up this conversation by calling on Vasev in about a week's time. This would be appropriate given Scott's recent return from leave. You may wish to consider whether there is any further message (e.g. about the Schumann talks) which could be fed in on that occasion.

concerned'. In telegram No. 1886 of even date Sir J. Killick said that the call had served 'to establish that I have been batted from Second European Department to Protocol Department and now from the latter to nowhere in particular. I think it would be wrong and undignified for me to subject myself to further similar treatment.' He suggested that Sir A. Douglas-Home should register 'dissatisfaction and displeasure' with the Soviet Chargé in London, but Mr. Walden submitted to Sir T. Brimelow that it would be more appropriate for the matter to be raised in the course of an interview on other matters, and the latter incorporated the point in his representations to Mr. Voshchankin, First Secretary at the Soviet Embassy on 14 December: see No. 86, note 2 below.

[15] In telegram No. 1714 of 8 November Sir J. Killick reported that at a Kremlin reception the previous day 'we ran into a pair of very glum Smirnovskys. He said "I don't know" to all questions about his return to London. We had a sterile exchange about what had occurred. He said it had done "enormous damage". I said not so enormous that the Soviet Government had broken off relations, so we ought both to get on with our jobs.'

No. 84

Letter from Sir J. Killick (Moscow) to Sir S. Crawford
[*PUSD*]

Secret   MOSCOW, *25 November 1971*

Dear Stewart,

Expulsions

1. I hesitate to bother you with a letter when you must be up to the ears in Ireland,[1] over which you have my deep sympathy. No doubt however you will be able to pass this on to an appropriate quarter.

2. I do not know whether you in London have done any sort of 'wash-up' exercise following the expulsions and counter-expulsions.[2] If you had, I imagine that your main conclusion might have been the same as mine—that we came out of it very well but that things must never again be allowed to develop in such a way as to necessitate a similar operation on such a major scale at any time in the future. What this means in practical terms is of course that in reconstructing their staffs in London, the Soviet Government must not be allowed to get away with reinserting intelligence operators. It is disturbing to see from the latest telegrams that they appear to be trying to do so.[3] At a time when my job is to try to reconstruct Anglo-Soviet working relations, it is obviously worrying to have to contemplate possible setbacks to the process which may result from our having to tell the Russians that they must withdraw certain applications for visas which have no chance of being granted for reasons of which they must surely themselves be aware. But there is no doubt in my mind that we cannot afford to let the Russians start to insert the thin end of a wedge. If they are at the very outset of their reconstruction operation given the slightest encouragement to believe that they can get away with this, we shall only be storing up that much more trouble for ourselves later on. If this does further damage to my working relations here, it simply cannot be helped and I for my part will bear the resulting situation with fortitude. My only suggestion is the purely tactical one which I hope you will not think pusillanimous, that it would probably help me marginally if the bad news (from the Soviet point of view) on these applications were given by the FCO to the Soviet Embassy in London.

[1] Since the introduction of internment without trial on 9 August the security situation in Northern Ireland had deteriorated, with border clashes and increasing terrorist activity, and further British troops had been sent to Ulster.

[2] See Nos. 76 and 80.

[3] Evidence received by the FCO that the Russians were again attempting to insert intelligence officers into the STD included the submission of urgent visa applications for STD posts on behalf of identified intelligence officers, evasion of the requirement for a detailed job description on application forms for STD personnel, and a 'disingenuous pretence' that there were vacancies under the STD ceiling.

3. Despite natural curiosity, I have no wish to ask for information derived from the whole operation (and notably from Lyalin)[4] which I do not need to know. I should however be grateful for any views or relevant information you may have on the following few points which are closely relevant to my job here.

4. The first is whether the KGB, for all their resources and efficiency, are out of their minds? I pose this question because I have the strong feeling that they must be extremely angry and frustrated that the Soviet Government did not retaliate against us to anything like the extent they must have wanted. It would not surprise me at all, and there are some shreds of evidence, if the KGB were to have as a high priority the aim of still fixing us somehow. Short of the actual Soviet counter-measures in effect, they must clearly have a lot of freedom of action locally and they seem disposed to use it. The sort of evidence I have in mind is their move against Counihan of the BBC, but even more some distinctly ambiguous activities involving members of this Embassy staff and even of planting on us phoney seekers for political asylum. All of this would seem to indicate a desire to manufacture new evidence to support a case for further retaliation. Although I do not believe that the Armenians were phoney, I do believe that the KGB at once seized on the possible opening this gave them to catch us putting a foot wrong (my telegram No.).[5] Details of all these activities have of course all been reported separately and you need not bother with them.

5. In this situation we are of course doing our best to exercise extreme care and caution but how far may we expect the KGB here to go? If they think they can get away with re-stocking the Soviet staffs in London with their people and if they were before the expulsions sending the people they then had there such incredible material as the sabotage plans sound to be, one begins to wonder how rational they are and consequently how far they might go in mounting attacks on us here in Moscow. If there is anything you can say of a general nature which would enable one to make a firmer assessment of this, I would find it helpful.[6]

6. A second point which puzzles me somewhat here is the true role of the State Committee for Science and Technology. They are proving themselves to be just about the toughest and most obdurate of all Soviet agencies over the resumption of normal contact here. It is becoming increasingly clear that the Soviet Ministry for Foreign Trade are at least extremely jealous of them,

---

[4] Cf. No. 73, note 2.

[5] Reference omitted in the original.

[6] In his reply of 23 December (cf. note 7 below) Sir S. Crawford said that he did not 'think we need assume that [the KGB] are out of their minds . . . It is accepted that the KGB, having been publicly humiliated, must now be aiming to get their own back . . . But the relative mildness of the Soviet official response to the expulsions suggests that there must have been a high-level political decision, confirmed if not instigated by Brezhnev, in favour of moderation. Presumably Brezhnev's *Westpolitik* was an important factor in this decision. If this is right, it follows that the KGB will stop short of provoking a major political row between the Soviet Union and ourselves.'

if not worse, at any rate in so far as Soviet external economic and trading activities are concerned. Yet Kirillin is the Chairman of the Soviet side of the Anglo-Soviet Joint Committee and we have in the past had little alternative as regards major economic projects to dealing with him, at any rate in parallel with the Ministry of Foreign Trade. I shall expect to have to establish contact with him and with Gvishiani as and when it proves possible.

7. Yet you have expelled so far as I know the State Committee's principal representative in London, Akimov, their Atomic Energy representative and possibly others. Akimov was, I believe, identified as GRU. Furthermore, I recollect that at least one of the State Committee representatives in the Soviet delegation which came to London last January was positively identified as KGB. He continues to be very active at the Moscow end in the State Committee's international activities.

8. It is hard to believe that people like Kirillin and Gvishiani themselves do not play a genuine and important role in the legitimate scientific and technological policies and activities of the Soviet Government. The question is how far the State Committee organisation as a whole is similarly occupied or how far it is not really under their control but is used as nothing more than a cover and tool by the KGB and the GRU. Here again I wonder whether there is any information in London which would throw any light on this.

9. I hope this letter will not cause anybody a lot of work and I emphasise that I am only concerned to be sure that I have anything useful on a 'need to know' basis and that not necessarily in detail but in the form of summary conclusions and assessments. There may of course be things within this general definition of which I have not thought and have not therefore specifically referred to above.

Yours ever,

J.E. Killick

P.S. I drafted this without having discussed the problem with various colleagues here. Having now done so it is clear that my proposition about the thin end of the wedge in paragraph 2 above is really an over-simplification. A case can be made out for the supposition that quite a lot of KGB and perhaps even GRU characters have become in some areas so involved in legitimate work as part of their cover that the Russians cannot do without them even on more legitimate business. What I say about the State Committee for Science and Technology is a good illustration. There is no doubt that people like Lopatin and Akimov were doing a real job on the legitimate side. It could be extremely difficult for the Russians to unscramble this sort of situation. This leads to the question whether it is our objective that our 'detergent' operation should indeed wash 'whiter than white'. As I understand the situation, even following the expulsions, there are a few residual intelligence operators still left in London. We have made it clear to the Russians that if further cases arise involving inadmissible activities, the consequent expulsions will reduce the new permitted ceilings. But these people will, I take it, not be expelled simply because they are identified as having an intelligence past so long as we do not catch them out. The residual people in London cannot stay there for ever. Can we realistically expect the Russians to accept without counter-action that they cannot replace them or even perhaps to top up their numbers a bit? Would it be tolerable, within manageable limits, to have a small number of known intelligence operators rather than people under such deep cover that we do not identify them? I raise these questions because although I still think that the principle in my paragraph 2 is broadly valid, we may have to face the fact that if we let in no new KGB representatives at all, we may find the present trickle of visas for our own staff here drying up altogether. Of course, HMG would no doubt in such a situation wish to consider further action against Soviet staffs in London but it would surely be much more difficult to take and justify the necessary decisions and above all it would seem unlikely to help us much if we wish to go on maintaining a viable Embassy. The question in short is must we not contemplate, as most other countries have to do, tolerating a certain level of Soviet intelligence activity in our country, albeit carefully controlled and limited, if we are to continue to have any relations with this country at all?

I am sorry to put in this very fundamental and difficult question as an afterthought but it seems to me not only a very real one but one which we may need to face pretty soon. This is not to say that I am suggesting that we ought to let in the four current Soviet applicants to [*sic*] whom two are already identified as bad eggs and the third is likely to be. I do not pretend to know the answer but it might perhaps lie in some sort of proposition that if it became clear that we were suffering serious retaliation because of our refusal to grant visas we could let in a small number of people with a known intelligence background if their records did not show that they had been caught out in the UK or elsewhere in active intelligence operations. We would still of course throw them out if they subsequently became involved. We are in any case, as I see it, stuck with a situation in which we shall probably from time to time admit known bad hats for meetings and conference (e.g. Lopatin) although I appreciate of course that this is a very different proposition from admitting them to residence. I confess that I do not at all like to contemplate anything short of 'whiter than white', but I don't really see how we can hope to achieve it, even if we had agreed on equal ceilings for our respective staffs in London and Moscow. J.K.[7]

[7] Sir J. Killick's letter, and in particular his postscript, led to considerable discussion in London. At an interdepartmental meeting on 3 December it was decided that there should be a double reply: a letter from Sir T. Brimelow, answering the main policy questions (No. 86 below), and a personal letter from Sir S. Crawford regarding Operation FOOT and intelligence matters. The meeting also discussed the visa situation in the light of Sir J. Killick's letter, and Mr. Walden minuted to Sir T. Brimelow later that day that 'All participants in the meeting disagreed with the views expressed in the postscript to the Ambassador's letter, and agreed to recommend that you ask the Soviet Chargé d'Affaires to withdraw unacceptable visa applications'; see No. 86, note 2 below.

The NATO Ministerial meeting held in Brussels on 9-10 December took place against a background of uncertainty whether Stage Two of the Berlin agreement would be rapidly completed, and whether Ministers should declare their readiness to move immediately thereafter to multilateral preparations for a European Security Conference. France took the view that they should, but the Americans were more cautious and in the week preceding the meeting had made approaches in NATO capitals calling for endorsement of their view that multilateral preparations should only begin after signature of the final Quadripartite Protocol. The West Germans had after some hesitation adopted the US view, fearing that premature movement might prejudice the ratification of the Moscow and Warsaw treaties and hence the Berlin agreement. A compromise form of words reached in quadripartite talks immediately before the NATO meeting barely concealed division on this point, but as Sir A. Douglas-Home pointed out, 'since multilateral preparations cannot effectively start until all (or at least all the main) powers are in agreement, the Berlin precondition on the approach to the Security Conference has not been eroded in practice. In the future (as in the recent past) it will be the position of the German Government which counts most on timing.'[1]

In the Communiqué Ministers took note with satisfaction of the Berlin agreement, noted that the German arrangements to implement and supplement the agreement (i.e. the inner-German talks) were nearing completion, and affirmed their readiness to undertake multilateral conversations intended to lead to a Conference on Security and Cooperation as soon as the negotiations on Berlin had reached a successful conclusion: in the meantime they proposed to intensify bilateral contacts with other interested parties and to consult with the Finnish Government on the latter's suggestion that heads of mission in Helsinki should undertake multilateral conversations. On MBFR Ministers reaffirmed the decisions taken at the Deputy Foreign Ministers meeting (see No. 82, note 17), and 'noted with regret' that the Soviet Government had so far failed to respond to this initiative. They also emphasised the importance of measures which would 'reduce the dangers of military confrontation and thus enhance security in Europe', and noted that a CSCE should deal with these 'in a suitable manner'.[2]

On 17 and 20 December the FRG/GDR Traffic Agreement and Senat/GDR Arrangements—the results of the inner-German talks, and a vital link in the stages of the Berlin agreement—were signed, thus opening the way to the signature of the Final Quadripartite Protocol foreshadowed in the 3 September agreement (see pp. 376-7) The next document indicates the Soviet reaction to these events in the light of their refusal to sign the Protocol until the FRG/Soviet Treaty had been ratified. Documentation on preparations for a Conference on Security and Cooperation in Europe in 1972 is printed in Volume II of this Series.

[1] UKDEL NATO telegram No. 643 of 10 December, WDN 21/4.

[2] Extracts from the *Communiqué* are printed in Cmnd. 6932, No. 39.

No. 85

Sir J. Killick (Moscow) to Sir A. Douglas-Home

No. 1991 Telegraphic [*WDW 1/1*]

Routine. Confidential   MOSCOW, *23 December 1971, 3.05 p.m.*

Repeated Routine for information to Bonn, Washington, Paris, UKDEL NATO, Berlin, Helsinki and Ottawa, and Saving to Rome, Brussels, The Hague, Copenhagen, Oslo, Warsaw, Bucharest, Budapest, Sofia, Prague and Belgrade.

M[y] i[mmediately] p[receding] t[elegram]: ratification and CESC.[1]

Grigoriev's article is the clearest account to appear so far in the Soviet press of the time-scale of the ratification process in Bonn. Although the Soviet reverse *junktim* is not spelled out, the references to the Berlin agreement imply some connection between its implementation and ratification.

2. There has also been a noticeable falling off in Soviet press commentaries and speeches pressing for immediate preparations for a CESC. This may be a temporary lull, but it now looks as if the Soviet leadership accept that CESC multilateral preparations are unlikely to begin until the second half of 1972 and that accordingly the conference itself might well not take place before 1973. G[r]igoriev's article may even be intended to start the process of accustoming Soviet opinion to this. Although the Russians will no doubt seek to blame 'opponents of *détente*' in the West, and especially HMG, for these delays, they must be aware that their own refusal to sign the final protocol on Berlin until ratification of the treaty lays them open to the charge that it is they rather than the West who are holding up the preparations for a CESC. They will no doubt keep up a background noise of propaganda for *détente* and a conference, but there is no sign yet of the campaign to get on with multilateral preparations which we rather expected following the completion of stage two of the Berlin agreement. For the moment the real steam seems to have gone out of Soviet *Westpolitik*, partly because they accept that they have to wait for ratification before the next steps can be taken and partly, perhaps, because so much of their European policy, in view of this slippage in the timetable, might best now await the outcome of President Nixon's visit in May.[2]

---

[1] Moscow telegram No. 1990 of 23 December reported an article that day in *Pravda* by its Bonn correspondent, Mr. Grigoriev, in which the FRG parliamentary timetable for ratification of the FRG-Soviet Treaty was explained, and the signature of the GDR-FRG Transit Agreement was described as 'a useful contribution to the cause of *détente* and evidence for the West Germans of the correctness of a realistic foreign policy'. Herr Brandt was quoted as saying at a press conference that 'both intensive multilateral preparations for a CESC and the Conference itself could take place next year'.

[2] See No. 78, note 3.

No. 86

Letter from Sir T. Brimelow to Sir J. Killick (Moscow)

[*PUSD*]

Secret   FCO, *23 December 1971*

Dear John,

This is the reply to those parts of your letter to Stewart Crawford of 25 November[1] which deal with our general visa policy and its effect on establishments. The rest of your letter is being answered by him.

2. We agree with paragraph 2 of your letter rather than with your postscript. We are sorry that the Soviet attempts to replace a few of the expelled Intelligence Officers should have the effect of delaying visas for certain junior members of your staff. It seems to be Soviet policy to slow down the pace of the normalisation of our relations. It may well be their calculation that our own wish to get back to normal will sooner or later induce us to give visas to their applicants even when we know them to [be] Intelligence Agents. To do so would be incompatible with the decisions that led to 'FOOT'. We do not feel contrite about 'FOOT', and are certainly not inclined to let the Russians reconstitute their network of spies and planners of sabotage.[2]

3. Your question about the degree to which the State Committee for Science and Technology is a front for intelligence activities will be answered by Stewart Crawford.[3] Thus I will only say that there is every reason to believe that many employees of the Committee who have intelligence-

[1] No. 84.

[2] As agreed (cf. *ibid.*, note 7) Sir T. Brimelow had asked Mr. Voshchankin to call on 14 December and read out to him a list of complaints about KGB activities, the credentials of recent applicants for visas to take up posts in the STD, the Soviet MFA's failure to arrange calls requested by Sir J. Killick (cf. No. 83, note 14), undue delay in granting visas to UK officials assigned to HM Embassy in Moscow, the proposed opening of a branch office of the Anglo-Soviet Shipping Co. Ltd in Liverpool and the Soviet Embassy's failure to comment on the provisional figures given to Mr. Ippolitov regarding the ceilings for the STD and other Soviet organisations (see No. 81, note 3). Mr. Voshchankin replied that it was 'his duty' to reject allegations that the KGB were sending officials to the UK or engaging in 'inadmissible activities' either in London or Moscow. 'He said that the British allegations seemed to be an attempt to continue the atmosphere created by the expulsions . . . the Soviet Union wanted cooperation with the UK in solving existing conflicts and the British attitude was making this impossible. What mattered was action and not words, which often differed.' Reporting this conversation to Sir J. Killick in telegram No. 1454 of 15 December, Sir T. Brimelow commented that Voshchankin was 'obviously expecting complaints of some kind and had apparently prepared in advance his piece about the KGB. He was ill at ease in making it and seemed anxious to avoid any unpleasantness' (ENS 3/548/10).

[3] See No. 84, note 7. Sir S. Crawford told Sir J. Killick that while there was no reason to doubt that the State Committee had a 'very important genuine function . . . we also know that it is extensively used for intelligence purposes'. Recent information confirmed that the KGB Scientific and Technical Department had cover places available to it in the Committee.

gathering responsibilities do also carry out perfectly legitimate tasks. This is their 'cover', which masks their more sinister assignments. Their cover enables them to make extensive contacts. I believe that Lyalin transacted bona fide business in woollen goods in Leicester. But that did not make him any more welcome from the point of view of this country's security. The point is that we do not wish to have in this country large numbers of people who have been trained in the techniques of collecting intelligence by clandestine means.

4. As regards the suggestion in the postscript to your letter that we may have to allow replacements for intelligence personnel already here, or even 'top them up', I think we should bear in mind that we left behind a rump of about forty known or suspected intelligence officers in September. Most of these are accounted for by Service Attachés and journalists: two categories which we deliberately excluded from the list of expellees. We shall continue to allow replacement Service Attachés provided that the intelligence background of any applicant is not too obtrusive (e.g. provided he has not been detected and exposed in clandestine operations). The same will be broadly true of correspondents, though our policy may become more restrictive here if the Russians continue to victimise British correspondents assigned to temporary or permanent work in Moscow. As for the remainder of the estimated present strength of the Soviet intelligence organisation in the UK, we should remember that there are still approximately 350 Soviet officials in the country. We shall no doubt allow some intelligence officers to enter the country because we are not aware of their background. We can therefore assume that the Russians will retain a sizeable number of intelligence personnel here however stringent our visa policy. They will need no further help from us to achieve this end. I find it difficult to imagine in what terms we could recommend to Ministers (and possibly if necessary to No. 10) that we should grant visas to 'a small number of people with a known intelligence background' or that we should allow the Russians to 'top up their numbers a bit'. I find it less difficult to imagine the terms in which Ministers would reject such a recommendation.[4]

5. I realise that our policy is causing staff problems in Moscow. But the balance of advantage is important. I could not reasonably recommend to Ministers that, for example, we should allow a suspected Soviet Intelligence Officer into the UK in order that a bona fide junior official appointed to HM Embassy in Moscow should obtain a visa. If Ministers were to ask whether the benefits obtained by the presence of the junior official in Moscow would

[4] In Moscow telegram No. 1988 of 23 December Sir J. Killick expressed the view that 'we have now reached the point where we cannot avoid informing the Russians squarely that a number of their visa applications cannot be granted', and asked that urgent consideration be given to informing the Soviet Embassy in London of this. However, in the light of reports that Mr. Smirnovsky had unexpectedly returned to London on 29 December, Sir J. Killick was informed on that day that it was proposed to wait and raise the subject with the Soviet Ambassador in the context of a more general talk expressing the hope that his return meant that a move to normal relations would be accelerated (ENS 3/548/25).

outweigh the risks to national security of strengthening the Soviet espionage effort against us, I should have to answer that in my opinion they did not.

6. We are not aiming at absolute security, or 'whiter than white'. We have achieved a paler shade of grey; and we wish to obstruct darkening with age.[5]

Yours ever,

TOM [BRIMELOW]

[5] In reply on 7 January 1972 Sir J. Killick told Sir T. Brimelow that 'I fully accept the general line of policy set out in your letter.'

CHAPTER V

1972

    The British Government entered 1972 willing to re-establish businesslike relations with the Soviet Union but unrepentant over their action of September 1971 and wary of Soviet attempts to wear down opposition, through a protracted 'visa war', to suspect Russian nominees to diplomatic and other posts in the UK. The Soviet Union was, however, hardly HMG's chief preoccupation at the turn of the year. The Prime Minister's signature in Brussels on 22 January of the Treaty of Accession to the European Communities heralded a new phase of the UK's external relations with potentially far-reaching implications for East-West relations. This achievement was celebrated against a troubling backdrop of industrial unrest: the official unemployment figure topped 1 million for the first time in 25 years on 20 January, and a bitter miners' strike beginning on 9 January plunged the country into power cuts, a three-day working week and a State of Emergency on 9 February. In Northern Ireland, mounting tension and an escalated bombing campaign led to the death of 13 people during a demonstration on 30 January, 'Bloody Sunday', the burning of HM Embassy in Dublin on 2 February and eventually to the imposition of Direct Rule over the province on 24 March.

    On the international scene, peace in the Middle East seemed as unattainable as ever in the light of President Nixon's announcement on 1 January that the US was resuming the supply of Phantom jets to Israel; perceptions of the negotiations to end the Vietnam conflict were shaded by the President's revelation on 25 January that Dr. Kissinger had been engaged in secret negotiations with the North Vietnamese for the past two and a half years; and Pakistan prepared to leave the Commonwealth over HMG's recognition of Bangladesh following the Indo-Pakistan war. When the Soviet Ambassador asked to pay his first call on the PUS since the expulsions of September 1971 FCO officials held out little hope that he could be persuaded into constructive discussion of pressing international events of mutual interest. Nevertheless, Sir D. Greenhill approached the interview in a positive spirit, welcoming Mr. Smirnovsky's avowal that he wished for a 'general discussion'.

No. 87

Sir A. Douglas-Home to Sir J. Killick (Moscow)
No. 56 Telegraphic [ENS 3/548/5]

Immediate. Confidential   FCO, *14 January 1972, 2.55 p.m.*

Repeated for information Saving to Washington, Paris, Bonn, UKDEL NATO, Warsaw, Prague, Budapest, Bucharest, Sofia, Belgrade.

Your telegram No. 62 (not repeated).[1]

1. The Soviet Ambassador called on the PUS this morning at his own request. This was his first contact with the FCO since he returned to London on 29 December.[2]

2. Smirnovsky arrived wearing a grave expression, which he put on again as he left. He also refused to let News Department describe the conversation as friendly. But he was perfectly amiable.

3. Smirnovsky said he had called for a general discussion. What were we going to do now? It would be unrealistic to pretend that nothing had happened. You had assured the Soviet MFA that Britain wanted good relations.[3] The Soviet Union was prepared to develop and improve relations on a basis of reciprocity. What specifically did we propose?

4. The PUS replied that it had been a consistent part of HMG's policy to seek good relations with the Soviet Union for both bilateral and international reasons. Our action in September[4] had been justified. We had tried to keep it separate from our general relationship and so far as we were concerned the matter was closed. All doors open to the Soviet Ambassador before were still open to him and we hoped that when you returned from leave[5] this would be reflected in Moscow. The lack of contact during the last 4 months had been detrimental to both sides. We should like to resume the kind of discussions that we had before. The PUS then made a proposal on visas (see my immediately following telegram, not to all).[6]

[1] In this telegram of 13 January Sir J. Killick reported a 'bland but totally unproductive' conversation with Mr. Lunkov the previous day (ENS 3/548/3).

[2] Cf. No. 86, note 4.

[3] See Nos. 74, 81 and 83.

[4] See No. 76.

[5] Sir J. Killick left Moscow on 19 January for several days' talks at the FCO, including discussions with the Secretary of State and Sir D. Greenhill, before taking five weeks' leave.

[6] Not printed. Sir D. Greenhill suggested that 'a way out of the present situation [cf. No. 88 below] was for the Soviet side to propose a date such as 1 February for a mutual granting of outstanding visas', subject to HMG's refusal to grant visas to people with known intelligence backgrounds, information as to which branch of the STD applicants were appointed to, and the maintenance of the ceilings imposed after the expulsions: cf. No. 81, note 3. On 1 February Mr. Ippolitov told Sir T. Brimelow that this suggestion was acceptable, but then handed over a list of applicants which infringed HMG's conditions. Sir A. Douglas-Home minuted on 4 February on telegram No. 110 to Moscow of 2 February reporting Mr. Ippolitov's call, 'We must not be driven off our position' (ENS 3/548/1).

5. Smirnovsky said it had not been his intention to go back to the September events but he must confirm the statements made by his government at the time. The British action was not consistent with a desire for good relations. We could not have expected any other reaction from Moscow. When presenting your credentials on 20 September[7] you had said that Britain wanted better relations but we knew what had happened 4 days later in London. The atmosphere now was different. If we wanted good relations we should have much to do to repair them.[8] Bilateral relations had been damaged in various fields, because the competent officials in the Soviet organisations concerned were no longer in London.

6. The PUS said we made no apology for what had happened. The Ambassador seemed to underestimate the effect upon British opinion of the situation which led up to our action in September. As to the change of atmosphere, this must be balanced against the fact that Soviet actions in the preceding period were much resented in Britain. Nevertheless, we were prepared to put that episode aside. The Ambassador would find this reflected in his official dealings and in the Embassy's unofficial contacts also. It was our sincere desire to do constructive business with the Soviet Union. We were ready for positive discussions on a variety of international issues. Our approach to bilateral questions was also positive. Excellent contacts had been made between the Soviet Union and Britain in the fields of science, culture, etc. These were valued here, and we did not wish to see this improvement wasted.

7. Smirnovsky said he could not accept the PUS's reference to the responsibility of the Soviet side. They regarded the British measures as a political act.[9] (This was said with great emphasis.) As to British public opinion, we ourselves had created this. He was sorry to say that the unfriendly propaganda was still continuing. He would have to mention it in his reports.

8. The PUS retorted that this was mutual. For example Soviet comment on the situation in Northern Ireland went far beyond the limits of decency. Nevertheless we were ready to take a positive attitude. At the Ambassador's

---

[7] See No. 76, note 5.

[8] In a minute of 15 January Mr. Walden commented on Mr. Smirnovsky's insistence that 'we must take the initiative in restoring Anglo-Soviet political relations. The fact that the Ambassador has returned suggests that the Russians might respond to the right approach. My hunch is that they want us to solicit new dates for the Joint Commission and/or the Secretary of State's visit.' At Mr. Bullard's suggestion Sir D. Greenhill mentioned the Joint Commission on 28 January to Mr. Smirnovsky, who 'rose quickly to a fly cast on the subject . . . and expressed the personal view that a meeting might be arranged for September or October'. Meanwhile other indications were being received in the FCO that the Russians were looking to HMG to make the first move in normalising relations: on 19 January, for example, Sir J. Killick reported that Mr. Zhukov of *Pravda* had told M. Seydoux that 'a "gesture" from the British side' was needed (ENS 6/548/10, ENS 3/548/3).

[9] On 17 January Sir A. Douglas-Home minuted on another copy of this telegram: 'I hope the "political act" won't have to be repeated' (cf. Nos. 84 and 86).

convenience we should like to talk to him about India and Pakistan,[10] the Middle East,[11] and Europe. As to the latter, it was quite untrue that Britain or NATO as a whole was showing hesitation. The delay in starting multilateral preparations for the CSCE had arisen from the Soviet Government's attitude (which the PUS found understandable) about the relationship between the Berlin agreement and the treaties. This was how things had worked out. Six months ago it has seemed probable that the CSCE would take place in 1972: now it looked doubtful.[12] But Britain was ready and would play an appropriate role whenever discussions began.

[10] On 3 December 1971 Pakistan attacked India in retaliation for continuing Indian support for the *Mukti Bahini* who were fighting for an independent state, Bangladesh, in East Pakistan. With the surrender of Pakistani forces on 16 December the People's Republic of Bangladesh was established, and India declared a ceasefire the next day. On 8 January Sheik Mujibur Rahman arrived in Dacca to be named as President of Bangladesh, and formed a government based on the results of municipal elections. On 4 February Sir A. Douglas-Home announced HMG's formal recognition of Bangladesh in the House of Commons (*Parl. Debs., 5th ser., H. of C.,* vol. 829, cols. 823-32).

[11] President Nixon's announcement (see p. 431) that the US had agreed to supply Israel with more Phantom jets in order to restore the military balance in the region was followed by an Israeli statement on 2 February of her willingness to enter into 'proximity talks' with Egypt for an interim agreement with the US as a 'passive intermediary'. In Egypt, however, the US move had led to student riots and calls for an end to US involvement and President Sadat's government reshuffle on 13 January emphasised his rejection of a US-brokered solution. Following his visit to Moscow from 2-4 February, however, he gave a positive reception to Dr. Jarring who arrived in Cairo on 18 February.

[12] Cf. No. 85. Mr. Smirnovsky called on the PUS and Sir T. Brimelow on 28 January to talk about Europe. Discussion centred on the *communiqué* issued in Prague on 26 January by the Political Consultative Committee of the Warsaw Pact (printed in Cmnd. 6932, No. 40) which proposed that the CSCE be convened in 1972. Sir D. Greenhill told Mr. Smirnovsky that 'practical considerations, including the links with the Berlin agreement and the ratification of the FRG treaties, and the US elections, meant that the Conference was in practice likely to slip into 1973. This was not a matter of British choice nor a reflection of unwillingness on our part.' He went on to draw the Soviet Ambassador's attention to the speech made by Mr. Heath in Brussels on 22 January at the ceremony following the signature of the Treaty providing for Britain's accession to the EEC (printed in Watt and Mayall, 1972, p. 38): 'We in Britain have every reason to wish for better relations with the states of Eastern Europe. And we do sincerely want them.' Mr. Smirnovsky 'required reassuring that the reference to better relations with the states of Eastern Europe was not meant to exclude the Soviet Union. He was left in no doubt that our intentions were quite the opposite and welcomed this assurance.'

No. 88

Mr. Dobbs (Moscow) to Sir A. Douglas-Home

No. 220 Telegraphic [ENS 3/548/1]

Priority. Confidential   MOSCOW, *15 February 1972, 3 p.m.*

My telegrams Nos. 214 and 215: Visas and Anglo-Soviet relations.[1]

I think it may well turn out that the recent spate of signals from the Russians (including those reported in your telegrams Nos. 141 and 144)[2] about the extent to which the visa situation is holding up the development of Anglo-Soviet political and commercial relations represent a last effort to induce us to cave in before the Russians do so themselves. But I doubt if they will cave in completely without being able to show some *quid pro quo* (Scott's letter of 11 February to Walden).[3] The Russians may also still be genuinely not quite clear about the position with respect to temporary visitors on three-month renewable visas, inspectors, etc.

2. It may be worth considering whether we should not now attempt to get back to the concept of a two-stage approach (your telegram No. 16).[4] It is too late to attempt such an approach in the form originally envisaged: the fact that the clarification of the new ceilings (your tel[egram] No. 81)[5] took

[1] These telegrams of even date are not printed. Moscow telegram No. 214 reported that Mr. Shevchenko of Second European Department had told Mr. Dobbs the previous day that 'the visa question was holding up a general improvement in our relations'.

[2] These telegrams of 11 February reported that Sir Con Seward (Russo-British Chamber of Commerce) and Mr. Godber had been told recently by Mr. Ivanov and Mr. Smirnovsky respectively that restrictions on the STD would lead to a reduction in Anglo-Soviet trade. Mr. Smirnovsky had added that he could not square the British attitude on visas with statements about seeking better relations with the Soviet Union (ENS 3/548/1, ENS 6/548/5).

[3] In this letter Mr. Scott said: 'It is quite clear that, before we can get anywhere, the Russians will have to accept the ceilings; and once they have done so I should imagine that some kind of deal to exchange visas will be possible. What chiefly worries us is that, as always in dealing with this oriental régime, we may find ourselves up against a prolonged deadlock unless the Russians can find some way of saving a little bit of face.' He admitted that 'it is not at all easy to see where such minor concessions might be made' but suggested that one possibility might be to raise the ceiling for the STD if the Russians could show that it failed to take into account the vacancies the STD was carrying in September 1971.

[4] This telegram of 6 January had suggested breaking the present deadlock through (a) the proposal subsequently made to Mr. Smirnovsky on 14 January (see No. 87, note 6) and (b) the re-establishment of the procedure which had existed before the expulsions whereby each side agreed to give early decisions on visa applications.

[5] This telegram of 20 January reported that when Mr. Filatov had called on Mr. Bullard that day they had agreed that the number of Soviet officials remaining at the STD was 47 (plus Mr. Ivanov and two deputies), with 106 at other organisations. Mr. Filatov contrasted these figures, which were to be the ceilings, with those mentioned by Sir T. Brimelow to Mr. Ippolitov on 1 October 1971: respectively 97 and 179; see No. 81, note 3. Telegram No. 81 also stated that the figures quoted by Sir T. Brimelow included temporary STD staff and other officials who had now been identified as belonging to commercial organisations and whom it had been decided to deal with separately.

place before the Russians had had a chance of replying to our proposal for an exchange of visas (your tel[egram] No. 57)[6] has led inevitably to the situation envisaged in para. 1 of the Ambassador's telegram No. 34.[7]

3. One possible way of resolving the deadlock might be to speak to the Russians on the following lines.

(*a*) As we have said, the ceilings for the STD and for other organisations are the result of a Cabinet decision and cannot be changed. The Russians will simply have to learn to live with them and organise their representation in London accordingly.

(*b*) However, as we have made clear, representatives of foreign trade corporations, technical experts and industrial inspectors on short term visits for specific purposes are not repeat not subject to these ceilings. Visas for these will be issued initially for three months, and will be renewed if we are satisfied that the visitor in question has a particular job to finish and if there are no other objections to his presence.

(*c*) We are prepared, subject to the maintenance of the ceilings, to help the Russians to ensure that their various trading organisations are adequately represented in London. We see no reason why such representation need in every case take the form of a permanent post in the STD which enjoys the unique privilege of immunity for its premises, and which even under the new ceiling is large compared with similar representations in other capitalist countries.

(*d*) The Russians have not been generous in permitting representatives of British firms to be registered as resident in Moscow for business purposes. There may well be a number of other British firms who would be interested in establishing permanent representation in Moscow, and thus could help the development of Anglo–Soviet trade.

(*e*) We therefore propose that the two sides should discuss the whole question of trade representation in each other's countries, the procedure for registration of permanent representatives, for the granting and renewal of temporary visas, and the conditions applicable to trade representatives in London and Moscow. Such discussions could lead to the establishment of a broader base on both sides for the development of trade.

(*f*) These are however complicated questions. They can be solved with goodwill on both sides and we are ready to adopt a reasonable attitude. But let us first clear the ground by carrying through the exchange of visas which we have proposed and then start new discussions from there.

4. Negotiations for some kind of new trade representation agreement or understanding are likely to be complicated and long drawn-out, and we

[6] See No. 87, note 6.

[7] In this telegram of 7 January Sir J. Killick advised separating the two stages of the approach suggested in note 4 above: 'I fear that once we broach discussion of future policy this may involve us in considerable further delay . . . This would hurt us more than them.' Sir D. Greenhill had followed this advice in making the proposal in No. 87, note 6.

would have to work out our own position very carefully in advance of them. We do not, for example, know how many British firms would be interested in permanent representation here if suitable facilities were made available (as you know only two firms, ICL and Golodets, at present have permanent representation in Moscow, the total of representatives being five). In any case our objective would be more to seek an agreement on the principles governing representation than to obtain specific concessions for individual cases.

5. The Russians may well be reluctant to enter into negotiations of this kind, particularly since they will realise that the present situation is much in their favour. But even so the proposal could be worth making. If it is turned down, the Russians would be put on the defensive and perhaps deterred from further complaints about the ceilings. If on the other hand they agree to negotiations we may be able to secure better facilities for British representation here in exchange for spelling out the facilities we are already prepared to grant for temporary visitors to Britain (even 'registered' commercial representatives in Moscow hold only annual visas and have to justify their activities each year). In either case, the fact that we have made a constructive proposal may be sufficient of a gesture on our part to get the visa deal through.[8]

6. The approach suggested is also calculated to appeal to British business opinion, which may be increasingly inclined to view the dispute over the size of the STD as sterile. Efforts to improve UK business representation in the Soviet Union would presumably attract wide support at home.[9]

[8] In a minute of 16 February Mr. Bullard objected to the course suggested by Mr. Dobbs in para. 3 above: '(a) We are not in a position to decide what would be our objectives in any negotiations of the type proposed . . . neither we nor the DTI know for certain what British firms would like to have permanent representation in Moscow (which is extremely expensive) and we have no authority to speak for them. (b) The Russians have no interest in negotiating, so long as the basis of their own commercial representation in London remains the 1934 Trade Agreement, which has been interpreted as giving diplomatic immunity to the entire premises of the STD.'

[9] On 18 February Mr. Godber decided at a meeting with Sir T. Brimelow, Mr. Goodall and Mr. Bullard that during his forthcoming absence in Latin America the matter should be handled on present lines, without offering the Russians the appearance of a concession, and that during his absence a paper should be prepared on the possibility of adopting the approach suggested by Mr. Dobbs in the present telegram.

The next document formed part of a wide-ranging reassessment of HMG's overseas policy in the light of British entry to the EEC (see p. 431). The paper printed in No. 89, drafted largely by Sir T. Brimelow for the approval of Sir D. Greenhill and the Secretary of State, is the final version of a memorandum originating in EESD in the summer of 1971, in response to a suggestion by Mr. Bullard that a more active policy towards the Soviet Union and Eastern Europe might follow British accession.

No. 89

Memorandum by Sir A. Douglas-Home on policy towards the Soviet Union and Eastern Europe

DOP (72)6 [EN 2/7]

Confidential   FCO, *29 February 1972*

1. Relations with Moscow are beginning to recover after the shock of last year's expulsions. But by comparison with our continental partners, the British relationship with the Soviet Union and Eastern Europe as a whole seems cool and politically negative. High-level political exchanges in particular have been lacking since 1968.

2. Now that the important decisions on entry into the EEC are behind us,[1] HM Ambassadors in the posts concerned agree that there are good commercial and political reasons for adopting a more active policy towards the East than has been possible in recent years.

3. *Commercially*, we may face a diminution of our total exports. Japan and the US are taking a growing interest in the possibilities of a market that is already sharply competitive. Entry into the EEC will reduce our capacity to absorb agricultural imports from non-EEC countries, and insofar as the COMECON countries like to balance their trade bilaterally (except when the balance is in their favour), they are likely to adjust their purchases from us to their export earnings. In this situation the extra handicap of a cool political relationship may be reflected adversely in our balance of payments.

4. *Politically*, we have a continuing responsibility to make British views known to the Governments of the countries concerned in the most effective manner, and to keep abreast of their thinking in return. We want also, as part of a long term policy of working against the whole concept of the Iron Curtain, to promote better contacts with those countries at all levels and in all fields. In the absence of a comprehensive and positive policy of contacts, our relations tend to be overshadowed by negative events which capture the headlines, e.g. expulsions and defectors. Lastly, we need in 1972-3 to play an active and conspicuous part in East-West relations, in order to be in a position to influence the preparations for the Conference on Security and Cooperation in Europe (CSCE), the Conference itself and the developments which could follow.

5. The Prime Minister's references to our wish for good relations with the Soviet Union and Eastern Europe in his speech in Brussels on 22 January[2] have been noted, both in those countries and at home. We should now take

---

[1] Although HMG had signed the Treaty of Accession, considerable parliamentary time and Government attention had still to be devoted to the passage of a European Communities Bill, which received its 3rd reading on 13 July after more than 100 parliamentary votes, was passed in the House of Lords on 20 September and received the Royal Assent on 17 October. British entry into the European Communities took effect on 1 January 1973.

[2] See No. 87, note 12.

advantage of this by initiating a policy of closer and more frequent contacts with these countries.

6. A more active policy towards the East will be largely a matter of style, but to be effective it *should include an intensification of contacts at Ministerial level and their extension from the technical to the political field.*

7. The paper attached at Annex sets out the case for such a policy in greater detail. It recommends the following programme of Ministerial visits to the Soviet Union and Eastern Europe in 1972:

(*a*) The Prime Minister should give priority to a visit to Yugoslavia, possibly in the summer of this year;

(*b*) If the Prime Minister thinks he can, in addition, visit a Warsaw Pact capital in 1972, the choice lies between Moscow, Warsaw or Bucharest. Moscow will probably not be possible. Given the intrinsic importance of Poland, Warsaw should rank before Bucharest.

(*c*) If the Prime Minister does not visit Warsaw, the Foreign and Commonwealth Secretary should do so.

(*d*) If the Prime Minister is able to visit both Yugoslavia and Poland, the Foreign and Commonwealth Secretary should go to Romania.

(*e*) Other visits to Eastern Europe by FCO Ministers, and visits to London by Ministers or Vice Ministers of Foreign Affairs from Eastern Europe, should be fitted into this programme.

(*f*) *Visits to the Soviet Union should be arranged when the Soviet Government shows itself ready for this.*

(*g*) Departments other than the FCO should be encouraged to make visits in 1972 to the Warsaw Pact countries of Eastern Europe and to Yugoslavia.

(*h*) Ministerial exchanges with East Germany must await recognition and the establishment of diplomatic relations.

(*i*) Our present policy towards Albania excludes ministerial exchanges.

A. D.-H.

ANNEX TO No. 89

Policy Towards the Soviet Union and Eastern Europe

1. In the early and middle 1960s, the United Kingdom was among the pioneers of a policy of fairly frequent exchanges of Ministerial visits with the Soviet Union and the East European members of the Warsaw Pact. The thinking behind this policy was roughly as follows:

(*a*) HMG have a responsibility to make foreign governments (including Communist governments) aware of current British views, and to seek to keep abreast of their thinking, which is likely to evolve as the Conference on Security and Cooperation in Europe draws nearer.

(*b*) We wish to promote all forms of contact between Eastern and Western Europe, as part of a long-term policy of working against the whole concept of the Iron Curtain.

On their side, the Communist leaders have made it clear that they too (no doubt for somewhat different reasons) regard personal contacts as a useful element in inter-state relations.

2. The invasion of Czechoslovakia in 1968 was followed by an interruption of British Ministerial visits to the Soviet Union and Eastern Europe (except Romania).[3] After about a year they were cautiously resumed, with Departments other than the Foreign and Commonwealth Office taking the lead. As the table in Appendix A[4] shows, our non-political contacts have developed quite well in these two or three years. Other West European countries have been less reticent in renewing exchanges with the Foreign Ministers, Prime Ministers and First Secretaries of Warsaw Pact countries, and the UK is now conspicuously lagging behind in this 'bicycle race' (a term coined by President Pompidou to indicate the way in which Ministerial exchanges with the East should not be regarded, but sometimes are). With the prospect of an early visit by President Nixon to Moscow[5] and possibly elsewhere in Eastern Europe, with the visit of his Secretary of Commerce to Moscow and Warsaw,[6] and with the rapid growth of Japanese commercial competition, HM Ambassadors in the Warsaw Pact countries think that United Kingdom interests have begun to suffer and that we could with advantage revert to a more active policy, for both political and commercial reasons.

3. In the 'bicycle race' we are handicapped as compared with some of our competitors. We are not in the same political league as the USA, and our trade with the Warsaw Pact states would suffer at once if the US were to enter this market in strength. The French exploit to the full their position as mavericks within the Western alliance, and are reaping a certain commercial reward in their trade with the Warsaw Pact countries. The Federal Germans have several advantages—their nearness to Eastern Europe, the fact that German engineering standards and practices are those which the engineers of the Warsaw Pact countries know best, the diligence of German exporters, and the fact that the Warsaw Pact Governments regard Herr Brandt as the best Federal Chancellor in sight and would like to see him re-elected. Italy has a large Communist Party, and in addition imports large quantities of Soviet sources of energy (as do West Germany and, increasingly, France). These factors have probably favoured the growth of Italian sales to the Warsaw Pact countries. The United Kingdom, lacking the status of the USA, geographically more remote than the other countries mentioned above,

---

[3] See Nos. 13-15.   [4] Not printed.   [5] See No. 78, note 3.

[6] Mr. P. Peterson was to visit Moscow from 21 July to 1 August to continue economic discussions begun during President Nixon's visit to Moscow (see No. 97 below); he visited Warsaw from 2-3 August.

cold-shouldered at present by the USSR on account of the expulsion of Soviet spies, a source of growing anxiety to East European sellers of agricultural produce as admission to the Common Market comes nearer, a sober and steady member of the North Atlantic Alliance, a sceptical commentator on MBFR and the proposed Conference on Security and Cooperation in Europe, neither courts the Warsaw Pact Governments nor is courted by them. During the preparations for entry into the European communities, United Kingdom ministers have made it plain by word and act that our priorities lie elsewhere.

4. Our exports to Eastern Europe have been doing less well in recent years than those of our main competitors within the EEC. To some extent the buoyancy of the EEC markets and the stagnation of the United Kingdom economy have accounted for this, but political factors too have probably played a part. The figures for the past five years are given in Appendix B.[4] The DTI believe that the political coolness between London and Moscow which followed the invasion of Czechoslovakia must have contributed to the cessation of growth in British exports to the Soviet Union in the years 1968-71, when British exports to the rest of the world were expanding steadily. It does not follow that a decision on our part to develop closer political contacts with the Warsaw Pact Governments would be quickly followed by an increase in our exports to these countries. It is easier to lose trade than to recover it, and the Warsaw Pact Foreign Trade Ministries, uncertain about the level of their exports to the United Kingdom after our accession to the European Communities, may be unwilling to expand their commitments to buy from the United Kingdom in the medium and longer term. But even if the increase in our exports to the enlarged Common Market is likely far to exceed any absolute or relative decline in our exports to the countries of the Warsaw Pact, we still have an interest in maintaining the highest possible level of exports to these countries. And to that a less chilly political climate than that of the past three and a half years might contribute.

5. Now that the Conference on Security and Cooperation in Europe is drawing nearer,[7] there may be political disadvantages in our holding aloof from bilateral contacts. We shall need the best and most up to date information we can get about the evolution of thinking in the various Warsaw Pact capitals, and visits from the United Kingdom will help in this. We shall want to exercise as much influence as possible on the preparations for the Conference, on its course, and on the developments which may flow from it. Our voice will be more attentively listened to in Warsaw Pact capitals and in NATO if we are seen to be active participants in everything that is going on. As regards the Soviet Union, we want to bring to an end as soon as possible (without of course compromising our principles on the question of espionage) the situation in which Britain has so little political contact with one of the two superpowers. All this will require effort at various levels, including that of Ministers. It is true that for the foreseeable future we shall wish to give

[7] See Volume II, No. 1.

Western Europe, i.e. the construction of Europe and relations between Europe and America, priority in our efforts. But it does not follow that we should be less active than our future EEC partners in the Warsaw Pact capitals. Indeed there is every reason to bring British policies, as far as may suit our interests, into line with those of the Six, on East/West relations as in other fields. This might incidentally help to reassure those in this country who dislike British entry into Europe because they think it will work against East-West *détente*. Whether the Communist rulers of the Warsaw Pact countries regard *détente* as anything more than a tactical phase in their political strategy remains an open question. But in general Western Governments have found it inexpedient to refuse to explore the possibilities of *détente*; and such exploration is one of the publicly declared intentions of NATO.

6. The suggestion that we should work for better political relations with the Warsaw Pact Governments gives rise to questions of timing and content. As to timing, the Prime Minister said of his own visit to Poland (proposed for early 1972 but now unfortunately postponed) that an early visit would 'demonstrate that the British Government's firm policies are not incompatible with cordial relations with the East and show that our 'Europeanism' goes wider than Western Europe and our commitments to better East-West relations'.[8] Unfortunately the Parliamentary programme is such that senior Ministers will hardly have time for travel to Eastern Europe, or to receive Ministerial visitors from Eastern Europe, except in fulfilment of commitments already made, until the second half of 1972.

7. As regards content, by about mid-1972 the multilateral preparations for the proposed Conference on Security and Cooperation in Europe will presumably have begun or will be about to begin. The United Kingdom has already begun to participate in the process of political consultation under the 'Davignon rules'.[9] These circumstances suggest clearly enough the general content of discussions with Ministers of Warsaw Pact countries—our views on the preparation, holding and consequences of a Conference on Security and Cooperation in Europe; our views on East-West political and economic relations in Europe; our views on the political and economic consequences of the enlargement of the Communities; our views on MBFR and associated questions. On all these issues our views are somewhat more astringent than those of some of our partners in NATO. But the events which led to the invasion of Czechoslovakia left a corresponding astringency in the minds of the rulers of the Warsaw Pact countries about the potential dangers of *détente*

[8] Mr. Heath had accepted in principle an invitation in September 1971 to visit Poland early in 1972.

[9] i.e. the procedural proposals for political cooperation in foreign policy drawn up by a committee of heads of political departments of EEC member states, under the chairmanship of Belgian Foreign Minister Vicomte Davignon, as instructed by The Hague summit in December 1969. The system evolved under the Davignon 'Rules' or 'Procedure', which provided for foreign ministers to meet at least twice a year with prior preparation by a committee of political directors empowered to set up working parties, was called European Political Cooperation (EPC).

and the risks of loss of control. Once the multilateral preparations for a Conference on Security and Cooperation in Europe begin, the Warsaw Pact leaders will have to face up to the problems which such a Conference may create for them. Some realistic talk might be welcome in Eastern Europe.

Yugoslavia

8. The discussion so far has turned on the question of our relations with the Warsaw Pact countries. Yet if we are to resume Ministerial political discussions with members of the Warsaw Pact, there is a strong case for beginning with a high level Ministerial visit to Yugoslavia, where such a visit would be particularly welcome, given the troubles through which Yugoslavia has recently been passing.[10] A public speech in Yugoslavia in the summer of 1972 outlining a British philosophy of East-West relations, and emphasising in particular that respect for existing frontiers and renunciation of the use of force should apply to the frontiers of Yugoslavia as well as to those of any other state, should attract attention in all the Warsaw Pact capitals. If such a visit and such a speech could be made by the Prime Minister, who has a long-standing invitation to visit Yugoslavia, so much the better. But it should be accompanied or quickly followed by the resumption of high-level political contact with members of the Warsaw Pact itself: otherwise the initiative towards Yugoslavia would look like no more than a continuation of the present British hard line towards the Warsaw Pact and especially the Soviet Union.

USSR

9. The Soviet Government is still sulking about the expulsion of its spies and planners of sabotage. The Russians made it plain that they did not wish the Foreign and Commonwealth Secretary to visit Moscow in January 1972, as he had proposed; and they had postponed the meeting of the Anglo-Soviet Joint Commission on Trade, Science and Technology, also proposed for January 1972. The Minister of Agriculture, Fisheries and Food has since had a good visit to Moscow, although this was in the context of an international conference.[11] Visits by Ministers from other Departments will be arranged as appropriate occasions occur. Discreet efforts will be made to induce the Russians to reinstate the Foreign and Commonwealth Secretary's visit and the postponed meeting of the Joint Commission.[12] They may find it awkward to maintain a complete freeze in Anglo-Soviet Ministerial relations as the Security Conference approaches. At other levels there are already slight signs of an incipient thaw. It does not seem that the East European countries will feel inhibited by the Soviet attitude from responding to any proposals that we are able to offer them for Ministerial contacts later this year.

[10] In 1971 Yugoslavia had twice devalued the dinar and experienced political unrest, particularly in Croatia, linked to economic problems and growing nationalist sentiment in the individual republics.

[11] Mr. J. Prior had visited Moscow 14-16 December 1971 to attend a conference on the depletion of herring stocks.

[12] Cf. No. 87, note 8.

Poland

10. The Polish Government fear that our entry into the Common Market will lead to a fall in Polish bacon exports to the United Kingdom. This is probable. Increasing consumption of pigmeat other than bacon inside Poland may prove to be a factor pulling in the same direction. While Poland's sterling earnings are likely to fall, Poland's need for foreign credits, including sterling, is likely to increase. Our exports to Poland could be threatened by a reduction of Polish earnings of sterling, by a switch of Polish orders from the UK to other suppliers, or by a lack of adequate sterling credits. We cannot hold out the prospect of an undiminished market for Polish agricultural produce once we join the EEC, nor should we go beyond the limits of commercial prudence in financing British exports to Poland by the expansion of credit, (though at the moment our problem is in getting the contracts, not in financing them). It follows that economic talks with the Poles are likely to be difficult. On the other hand, once the Treaty between the Federal Republic of Germany and Poland is ratified, the issue of the Oder-Neisse line will have been resolved. A visit by the Prime Minister or the Foreign and Commonwealth Secretary to Poland thereafter, welcoming the acceptance of the present frontiers of Poland and emphasising the good-will felt in this country towards Poland, could do nothing but good. Mr. Gierek might wish any such visit to come after his visit to Paris, the date of which has been twice postponed, and which is not at present definitely known. This in itself should ensure an adequate gap between the date of a visit by President Nixon, should he decide to visit Warsaw, on his way to or from Moscow in May, and the date of any visit by the Prime Minister. If the Prime Minister were to decide not to go to Warsaw there would be much to be said for a visit by the Foreign and Commonwealth Secretary, emphasising political rather than economic relations. It should take place after the ratification of the FRG/Polish Treaty, but well before the 30th anniversary in April 1973 of the discovery of the Katyn Massacre, which may be marked by controversy with the Polish Government over a proposal by Polish émigrés in the United Kingdom to unveil a monument to the Katyn victims.[13] In the summer of 1972, discussion with the Poles of the whole complex of questions associated with European security should be easy and might, to a limited extent, be fruitful.

Czechoslovakia

11. Mr. Marko, the then Foreign Minister, was invited to come to London on an official visit in mid-November 1971. Shortly before the date agreed for his visit the Netherlands police intercepted a cargo of Czechoslovak arms

---

[13] See No. 69, note 5. Mr. Airey Neave informed Sir A. Douglas-Home on 23 February 1972 that a Memorial Fund, of which he and Lord Barnby were Vice-Chairman and Chairman, had been set up to raise funds for a memorial to the victims of the Katyn Massacre to be erected in London, possibly in a Royal Park. Replying on 3 March, the Secretary of State said that he understood the motives behind the Fund, but 'the erection of a monument to the victims of Katyn in one of the Royal Parks in London would be an act of political significance. I am bound to say that as things stand I should be strongly opposed to it' (ENP 10/1).

destined for the IRA, and Mr. Marko deemed it wise to 'postpone' his visit. Since then he has been replaced as Foreign Minister by Mr. Chnoupek, who has now indicated that he might be willing to visit the United Kingdom in the second half of 1972. We should see advantage in his doing so, and he is being offered a choice of dates in October or November. Meanwhile, visits by other Ministers can take place. The Czechoslovak Minister of Agriculture has been invited to come to Britain in the spring.

Hungary

12. Prince Philip's visit to Hungary in 1971 in his capacity as President of the *Fédération Equestre Internationale* gave great satisfaction and lessens the need for a visit by an FCO Minister. For 1972, we may have to be content with visits to Hungary by Ministers from Ministries other than the FCO, two or three of which are in prospect. The First Deputy Foreign Minister of Hungary, Mr. Puja, has already been invited to London for talks in return for Mr. Royle's visit last year,[14] and has agreed to come in May 1972.

Romania

13. The Romanians would dearly like Mr. Heath to repay the visit which Mr. Maurer paid to this country in 1970. The Foreign and Commonwealth Secretary has received a pressing invitation also. If Mr. Heath is unable to go to Warsaw, the case for a visit by him to Bucharest will be strengthened.

Bulgaria

14. A Deputy Foreign Minister from Bulgaria has been invited to visit London to return the visit paid to Bulgaria by Mr. Royle. He may come in the second half of 1972, unless recent events connected with the expulsion of a Bulgarian official for espionage make it impossible.

East Germany

15. Ministerial exchanges cannot be organised until after recognition and the establishment of diplomatic relations: but short of this, no reasonable steps should be overlooked which could serve to promote trade and build up a strong British position for the future.

Albania

16. Unlike East Germany, Albania is recognised by Britain as a state and its régime as a government. We lack only diplomatic relations, broken off when Albania refused to pay the £834,947 awarded to Britain by the International Court in the Corfu Channel case of 1946.[15] For 25 years our position has been to refuse to discuss the establishment of relations until Albania made at least some move towards payment. Neither the political nor the commercial rewards at present seem great enough to justify modifying

[14] Mr. Royle visited Hungary and Bulgaria in March 1971.

[15] On 22 October 1946 two British destroyers were damaged by mines in international waters between Corfu and the Albanian mainland. On 10 December the British Government delivered a Note to the Albanian Government demanding payment for damage and compensation, but the Albanian Government denied responsibility and refused. On 9 April 1949 the International Court of Justice ruled that Albania was liable and awarded damages to HMG on 15 December; the matter was not finally settled until 1996.

this position. Ministerial exchanges are therefore impossible at the moment, and the trade possibilities do not justify any special efforts of other kinds.

Summary

17. The pattern of visits suggested by the foregoing considerations is as follows:

(*a*) The Prime Minister should give priority to a visit to Yugoslavia, possibly in the summer of this year;

(*b*) If the Prime Minister thinks he can, in addition, visit a Warsaw Pact capital in 1972, the choice lies between Moscow, Warsaw or Bucharest. Moscow will probably not be possible. Given the intrinsic importance of Poland, Warsaw should rank before Bucharest.

(*c*) If the Prime Minister does not visit Warsaw, the Foreign and Common-wealth Secretary should do so.

(*d*) If the Prime Minister is able to visit both Yugoslavia and Poland, the Foreign and Commonwealth Secretary should go to Romania.

(*e*) Other visits to Eastern Europe by FCO Ministers, and visits to London by Ministers or Vice-Ministers of Foreign Affairs from Eastern Europe, should be fitted into this programme.

(*f*) Visits to the Soviet Union should be arranged when the Soviet Government shows itself ready for this.

(*g*) Departments other than the FCO should be encouraged to make visits to the Warsaw Pact countries of Eastern Europe and to Yugoslavia in 1972.

(*h*) Ministerial exchanges with East Germany must await recognition and the establishment of diplomatic relations.

(*i*) Our present policy towards Albania excludes Ministerial exchanges.[16]

[16] Mr. Bullard informed HM Ambassadors in the Soviet Union and Eastern Europe on 16 March that the DOP Committee had approved the above recommendations on 15 March: 'I gather that Ministers saw no contradiction between these decisions and a policy of frankness in public statements about the risks as well as the rewards of *détente* in Europe.'

The next two documents record conversations in London and Moscow between British and Soviet officials. Though the talks touched on a range of subjects of mutual interest, Sir D. Greenhill, Sir J. Killick and their colleagues found it very difficult to progress to general discussion beyond the barrier erected by their Soviet interlocuteurs, who returned constantly to their twin themes of the damage inflicted on Anglo-Soviet relations by the expulsion of Soviet intelligence officers in September 1971, and the impossibility of the Soviet Trade Delegation's work with the ceiling imposed on the number of its staff.

A subject barely touched upon, but of pressing interest to both governments at this time, was President Nixon's visit to Peking from 21 to 28 February. The FCO considered that the major importance of the visit was that it took place at all. Although little of substance emerged, and the gap between the two countries on major issues, such as relations with Japan, remained as wide as the juxtaposition of opposing views in the Communiqué suggested,[1] *the FCO's assessment was that the effect of the visit on American attitudes towards China had been profound: 'in particular, it has strengthened American understanding of Chinese fears of the Soviet Union and of Chinese policies towards Indo-China'; the Chinese had revealed serious concern about the increase of Soviet influence in the sub-continent. There was little or no mention of the Middle East, Latin America, Africa and Europe, and Hong Kong and the United Kingdom were apparently not brought up. The Americans were now convinced that the fundamental reason for the Chinese decision to agree to the President's visit was fear of the Russians: 'The Chinese must have had some difficulty in explaining their decision to Communist governments and parties which had regarded China's hostility to the United States as something to be taken for granted.'[2]*

[1] The text of the joint *communiqué* issued at the end of the visit is printed in *The Times*, 28 February 1972, p. 4.

[2] Memorandum by Far Eastern Department, 16 May, AMU 3/548/6.

No. 90

Record of conversation held during lunch at the Soviet Embassy on 7 March 1972

[ENS 3/548/5]

Confidential

On 7 March, the PUS and Sir J. Killick lunched at the Soviet Embassy with the Soviet Ambassador and Mr. Ippolitov.[1]

2. *Sir J. Killick* said he looked forward to getting down to business on his return.[2] He had found it most unfortunate that there had been no exchanges of view in Moscow on current questions where the two Governments had common interests, e.g. the Bangla Desh problem.[3] In particular, with the London Chamber of Commerce Trade Mission only two weeks off,[4] his immediate intention would be to call on Mr. Patolichev. He would also of course be giving full practical support to the mission and assumed that there would be full attendance from the Soviet side at social functions at the Embassy. *Mr. Smirnovsky* expressed regret that a number of important

[1] Mr. Bullard had told Sir J. Killick on 24 February that this lunch had been 'arranged at a surprisingly relaxed reception at the Soviet Embassy yesterday (to mark the Soviet Armed Forces day)' (ENS 3/548/4).

[2] Cf. No. 87, note 5. Sir J. Killick was returning to Moscow on 9 March.

[3] *V. ibid.*, note 10. Both the UK and Soviet Governments were concerned with the estimated 10 million refugees in India who had fled East Pakistan during 1971 and were now returning to the new state of Bangladesh. The British Government had given £14.75m in aid for refugees in India, and a further £3m for relief work in Bangladesh. Sheik Mujibur visited Moscow from 29 February to 5 March seeking Soviet aid and received a pledge of £18m.

[4] A delegation from the London Chamber of Commerce, led by Lord Erroll, a former President of the Board of Trade, was to visit Moscow from 19-25 March: for an assessment of the visit see No. 91, note 5 below.

members of the mission seemed to be dropping out, and it was explained to him that it was out of the question to expect all leading interested businessmen to be able to visit the Soviet Union at the same time.

3. Mr. Smirnovsky asked what effect the Nixon visit to Peking would have on Anglo-Chinese agreement on the exchange of Ambassadors.[5] *Sir D. Greenhill* said that it had admittedly delayed things somewhat, but he was confident that agreement would soon be reached without too much difficulty. He would not be drawn further on details despite further questions.

4. *Mr. Smirnovsky* asked about the situation in Bonn on ratification of the Eastern Treaties. In particular, were HMG pleased at the turn of events?[6] *Sir D. Greenhill* said that Herr Scheel at a recent meeting in Brussels had been quite relaxed and confident about the prospects for ratification. HMG of course wished to see ratification go through. *Sir J. Killick* added that HMG supported Herr Brandt's policies and had no wish to see them fail. Personally he would be very concerned by the possibility of adverse Soviet reactions if ratification did not take place. He was bound to observe, although he understood the Soviet position, that as a matter of fact the process of ratification would have been much easier if the Berlin Agreement had first been signed.

5. *Mr. Smirnovsky* said it was a pity that the German opposition, most of which supported ratification, were opposing it for domestic political reasons. This would hold up progress towards a CESC. As regards the CESC, why were HMG not making any approaches to the Finnish Government as other Governments were and as the NATO *communiqué* envisaged?[7]

6. *Sir D. Greenhill* said that HMG's attitude to the CESC remained positive. They were getting on with their preparations on the substantive issues which would arise. It remained for NATO to discuss and agree on

[5] See pp. 448-9. Long-running negotiations between the British and Chinese Governments for an exchange of Ambassadors had increased in impetus since late 1971, the remaining point of difficulty being the wording of a statement to be used by HMG in answer to questions about their position on Taiwan, which the Chinese Government insisted should be referred to as 'China's internal affair'. Notification of HMG's acceptance of a compromise based on the Chinese text with a modified English translation was delayed until 4 March, after President Nixon's visit from 21-28 February. Formal agreement was signed in Peking on 13 March and Mr. J. Addis, HM Chargé d'Affaires since 26 January 1972, was appointed Ambassador (FEC 3/548/1).

[6] The Eastern Treaties had been debated for the first time in the Federal Republic's Parliament on 9 February when the *Bundesrat*, the Upper Chamber, had passed a twelve point resolution criticising the Treaties. They were given their first reading in the *Bundestag*, the Lower Chamber, on 22-25 February, in a debate which concluded without a vote and referred the Treaties to committees, in preparation for their second and third readings in May. The *Bundesrat* resolution and the terms of the *Bundestag* debate confirmed the strong objections to the Treaties amongst the CDU/CSU Opposition to Herr Brandt's governing coalition which, after the defection of an SPD Deputy on 29 February, had a majority of only four. Sir R. Jackling reported on 3 March that 'a possible failure to obtain ratification cannot now be excluded' (WRG 1/4, WRG 3/513/1).

[7] Cf. p. 426.

many of these. Meanwhile approaches to the Finnish Government could only be on procedural questions.

Mr. Smirnovsky said the Soviet Government continued to hear from various sources that HMG were negative to the idea of a CESC.

7. *Sir D. Greenhill* said bluntly that the fact was that various Governments expressed superficial enthusiasm about the CESC while in fact holding ideas no different from those of HMG. It was easy for them to say that they were willing to move ahead rapidly but that their partners were holding them back. *Sir J. Killick* added that HMG were a businesslike Government which believed in coming to grips with the realities rather than making speeches. He had tried to explain this to Mr. Gromyko.[8] He was willing to bet that when it came to a CESC, the Soviet Government would find HMG not only positive but better prepared than any other participant.

8. *Sir D. Greenhill* recalled his recent remark to Mr. Smirnovsky that the Soviet Government always seemed to misinterpret HMG's aims and motives.[9] If the Soviet Government believed what they said about HMG, then there was serious misunderstanding. He did not hold Mr. Smirnovsky personally responsible for this. *Sir J. Killick* added that he could not understand why the Soviet Government went on condemning HMG's attitude on various issues like CESC without ever discussing them with HMG. *Mr. Smirnovsky* said that he had discussed CESC with Sir D. Greenhill.

9. *Sir D. Greenhill* said the Soviet Government still apparently professed to believe that the expulsion of the 105 Soviet personnel[10] had had the political purpose of wrecking progress in East-West relations in Europe. This was frankly absurd. It had related solely to the protection of the security of the United Kingdom. *Sir J. Killick* said that the Soviet Government of all governments surely ought to understand this. Its preoccupation with the security of the Soviet Union often overrode political considerations. *Sir D. Greenhill* rehearsed the whole history of HMG's approaches to the Soviet Government on the question of illegitimate activities, to none of which there had been any response. HMG's action had ultimately been inevitable. But he wanted to look to the future and not to the past. If HMG's aim had been to sabotage progress in Europe, obviously they would have made further efforts in this direction. But having cleared up the security question, they had adopted a positive attitude on questions such as CESC and had done nothing else whatever in a negative sense.

10. *Mr. Smirnovsky,* after a half-hearted attempt for the record to assert that HMG had been misinformed about Soviet activity in the United Kingdom, and misled by one defector, agreed that it was right to look to the future. This raised the practical problem of the visa question. The fact was that the ceiling imposed on the Soviet Trade Delegation made it impossible for the

[8] See No. 74.

[9] Sir D. Greenhill had made this remark to Mr. Smirnovsky on 28 January when reassuring him about Mr. Heath's speech of 22 January: see No. 87, note 12.

[10] See No. 76.

STD to do its work. There had been 3,000 British business men in the Soviet Union last year, as compared with the British ceiling for STD of 47. HMG were not even prepared to grant visas for four teachers of English who were intended to join STD for a period in order to improve their knowledge of the language. It was clear that HMG's intention was to cut down trade.

11. *Sir D. Greenhill* said that he must leave shortly for another appointment and could not pursue this discussion at length and in detail. He pointed out that other countries conducted trade perfectly satisfactorily with Soviet trade representation of comparable size and quoted the case of Japan. Mr. Smirnovsky was presumably informed of the British position as explained that morning to Mr. Ippolitov by Sir T. Brimelow.[11] This position was firm, and offered a perfectly reasonable basis for moving forward. He urged earnestly that the Soviet Government should accept this and then see for themselves over the months ahead that the re-establishment of normal working relations would prove that HMG's attitude in all fields was positive. It was apparently impossible to convince the Soviet side of this at present so why not let events speak for themselves. After say a year we could take stock and see where we stood.

12. *Mr. Smirnovsky* rehearsed the Soviet proposal as put by Mr. Ippolitov and said this surely offered a better basis. What were HMG's objections to it?

13. *Sir D. Greenhill* repeated that it was unacceptable and that the British position was firm. On the way out, *Sir J. Killick* remarked to Mr. Smirnovsky that the Soviet side surely knew why their proposal was unacceptable. The answer lay in the names of the people on the Soviet list suggested for putting on one side by Mr. Ippolitov.[12]

[11] In an attempt to overcome objections to the list of visa applicants handed over on 1 February (see No. 87, note 6), Mr. Ippolitov proposed on 1 March that each side remove certain names from their list of applicants and issue visas to the remainder. Sir T. Brimelow said that HMG would consider the proposal, although he was 'doubtful about the principle . . . which seemed essentially negative . . . the Russians were asking us to remove straightforward applicants from our list because we were not prepared to give visas to suspicious Soviet applicants' (telegram No. 196 to Moscow, 2 March). Sir J. Killick agreed in Moscow telegram No. 312 of 3 March that 'these proposals should be rejected and that we should hold out for a straight exchange of visas . . . It seems to me quite possible that this is a final Soviet effort to get most of the visas they need, while still retaining some leverage for a second round. If we continue to stand firm and reject this almost wholly unattractive compromise, they might possibly conclude that we really mean what we say and give way wholly or in part' (ENS 3/548/1). On 7 March Sir T. Brimelow rejected the proposal in a telephone conversation with Mr. Ippolitov.

[12] On 8 March Mr. Smirnovsky called on Sir A. Douglas-Home officially for the first time since August 1971. Their discussion centred on prospects for a CSCE (cf. Volume II, No. 4, note 5), but when the Soviet Ambassador mentioned visas the Secretary of State said he 'should understand that the ceilings were fixed. We could not accept people from the KGB, but it should be possible to agree on two lists of visas to be issued now'. Mr. Bullard commented on 15 March to Sir J. Killick that he was 'present at the meeting, and did not find the Ambassador's remarks any more convincing than the line we have heard so often from Ippolitov . . . You will note that the Secretary of State did not give any undertaking to look into . . . the problem as a whole. We are not inclined to recommend making any further concessions on this issue at the moment' (ENS 3/548/1).

No. 91

Letter from Sir J. Killick (Moscow) to Mr. Bullard

[*ENS 3/548/3*]

Confidential   MOSCOW, *17 March 1972*

Dear Julian,

Anglo-Soviet relations

1. I apologise for reporting in such detail in my telegrams 361 to 363 on my first contact with Lunkov since returning,[1] but it seemed to me that at this stage you might welcome a full account as a means of assessing how things are going.

2. On the visa front we can only wait and see; I am glad that you have been good enough to make the position clear once again to Ippolitov.[2] At this end, I am satisfied that we can soldier on despite present staff shortages, for as long as may be necessary for the Soviet side to make up its mind. I only wish I could be certain that the Soviet Embassy and the Ministry of Foreign Affairs here will leave the KGB in no doubt that there is no more juice to be squeezed out of the British lemon (or would you rather be an orange?). So long as the Soviet Embassy go on reporting that they have ended conversations with the Foreign Office with the assertion that it is up to us to take action and with requests, like Smirnovsky's to the Secretary of State, that we should reconsider the position,[3] there is always I suppose a danger that the KGB will think they have not yet reached the end of the road. At all events, we at this end are doing everything we can to make sure that they get the message.

3. On the more general front, things are distinctly brighter and I have a real feeling of returning to something approaching normal in business relations both in connexion with the trade mission visit[4] and more broadly. But if there is no development on the visa front in say the next fourteen days we must face the fact that the Russians are moving back to 'business as usual' in areas where it suits them to do so while still leaving a major and essential

---

[1] Sir J. Killick called on Mr. Lunkov on 14 March. Moscow telegram No. 362 of 15 March reporting a discussion of attitudes towards the CSCE is printed in Volume II, No. 4. In telegrams Nos. 361 and 363 of even date Sir J. Killick reported his discussion with Mr. Lunkov of a number of bilateral issues, principally trade, his calls on Soviet Ministers and visas (ENS 3/548/6, 1).

[2] Cf. No. 90, note 11. Telegram No. 249 to Moscow of 15 March informed Sir J. Killick that Mr. Bullard had telephoned Mr. Ippolitov that afternoon to repeat Sir T. Brimelow's message of 7 March rejecting the Soviet proposal for a solution based on mutual deletions from the visa application lists. A minute of 13 March also recorded that when during lunch that day Mr. Ippolitov reverted to his proposal of 1 March, Mr. Bullard responded that 'to balance identified intelligence officers against innocent diplomats was unacceptable in principle and in practice' (ENS 3/548/1).

[3] Cf. No. 90, note 12.

[4] *V. ibid.*, note 4.

element unresolved. If this proves to be the case, we shall need to consider the need to make it clear to them—probably best in another talk between the Secretary of State and Smirnovsky—that they cannot play things this way. I think it ought to be possible to do this without practical prejudice on the trade front in terms of following up the London Chamber of Commerce Mission. It is conceivable of course, though I think it unlikely, that the Mission's visit will itself prove negative and give us grounds for somewhat similar action. We and they will of course be giving you our assessment at the end of the visit.[5]

4. Against this background I went to see Lunkov undecided whether or not to ask firmly for an appointment with Gromyko himself, despite the opening for this offered by Smirnovsky's remark to the Secretary of State that I would no doubt be talking in similar terms to Gromyko following my return. Lunkov's response on the general question of my starting my proper programme of calls, while by no means negative, was at the same time not sufficiently encouraging to bring me to the point of asking for a definite appointment with Gromyko. In any case, on this particular front I think we need for the moment to preserve a balance between our short-term interest in using current issues like CSCE in order to bring about such a meeting as a demonstration of a return to normal relationships; and on the other hand the longer-term consideration whether we really wish at the moment to become involved in any substantial exchanges with the Russians on current issues, particularly those relating to the CSCE. I hope it will not be felt in the Office that I went too far in referring to the general desirability of this.[6] I was careful not to commit us to anything and I would now certainly not wish to make a further move towards a meeting with Gromyko without instructions. In particular, I think I would like either to be able to tell him that HMG are responding positively to the suggestion of establishing a bilateral contact with the Finnish Government (and as I see it from here, although this might not achieve much, it could do no harm) or alternatively to be armed with some good reasons why we had not the intention to do so. More generally, would you wish me to pursue further and in more detail with Gromyko the sort of discussion which the Secretary of State had with Smirnovsky on either the

---

[5] Sir J. Killick reported in Moscow telegram No. 469 of 30 March that Lord Erroll's mission had been 'a distinct success'. The Delegation from the London Chamber of Commerce had held meetings with the Ministry of Foreign Trade, Gosplan and the State Committee for Science and Technology, as well as the Chamber of Commerce and Industry of the USSR. The Ambassador reported that he had 'profited greatly from the fact of the Mission in making first contact, or renewing former contacts, with a wide range of senior Russians . . . Although some potentially difficult discussions with the SCST lie ahead, the Embassy is now back in working relations with what has hitherto been the most obdurate Soviet agency since last September' (ENS 6/548/7).

[6] Sir J. Killick told Mr. Lunkov in relation to bilateral contacts in preparation for the CSCE that 'no contact was more important than with the Soviet Government. Though I had no instructions to see Gromyko, it was possible that I might receive them: I was in any case at his disposal any time' (cf. Volume II, No. 4).

security or the cooperation aspects of the agenda?[7] I fully appreciate that we may not be ready on our side to do this; on the other hand, I think the possibility of getting much out of Gromyko on this subject is small unless I have something to contribute and can consequently make him see some value in further meetings. Meanwhile there is the separate issue of the ratification situation in Bonn (about which I am writing separately).[8] There is I think a case for giving Gromyko reassurances on our continued support for Brandt's policies and in particular for the Moscow and Warsaw Treaties, underlining our hopes that they will be ratified.

5. I shall of course continue with such other calls as may be offered to me and if Gromyko should summon me and if there is time I will let you know in advance so that you can send me instructions if you wish.

6. Finally, until the situation both on visas, on trade prospects and on my programme of calls is clearer I cannot see any other useful possibilities of action and certainly no cause for messages to Gromyko from the Secretary of State or anything of that sort.

7. In sum, much though we would all welcome outward manifestations of a return to normal, we still ought to avoid the appearance of running after the Russians or of lending ourselves to attempts on their part to soften our position on either the timing or the substance of CSCE on which, generally speaking, we have a perfectly solid and defensible position. The only issue raised by this letter is the extent to which we want to put into effect the reference in the NATO *communiqué* to the establishment of exploratory bilateral contacts with 'other interested parties'.

[8.] I am sending a copy of this letter to Rodric Braithwaite and will leave it to you and him to decide who should reply.

Yours ever,

JOHN KILLICK [9]

---

[7] Cf. Volume II, No. 4, note 4.

[8] In a letter of 17 March to Mr. Bullard Sir J. Killick considered the impact on Soviet foreign and domestic policy of a rejection by the *Bundestag* of the FRG-Soviet Treaty (cf. No. 90, note 6). In addition to the setback to Mr. Brezhnev's *Westpolitik*, HM Ambassador and some of his colleagues in Moscow thought it likely that non-ratification would affect Mr. Brezhnev's personal standing (WRG 3/513/1).

[9] Replying on 22 March, Mr. Bullard wrote that 'So far from objecting to the length of your telegrams about your talks with Lunkov, I was very glad of them . . . I am not sure that I follow the thinking behind the second sentence of your paragraph 3, which appears to link visas with political exchanges. We had it in mind to pursue our objectives in these two fields separately, though of course in parallel. On visas, we would continue to insist firmly but quietly that our own reasonable offer remains upon the table . . . It follows that we should be as active as suits our interests in pursuing our political dialogue. If we are to ensure that this is to our mutual advantage, it is important that we should seek to restore and maintain reciprocity in access to Ministers, insofar as our differing practice and the realities of the power game allow. This approach argues in favour of an attempt by you to call on Gromyko after you have completed your long delayed courtesy calls . . . I do not think that after Lord Erroll's mission this would give the appearance of running after the Russians. It would be more a question of keeping abreast with them in the level of our political exchanges.'

P.S. Patolichev asked me to call to-day and I saw Borisov yesterday. Nemchina on Monday. Distinct progress. Meanwhile, I have your letter on a possible alternative approach on visas.[10] My initial reaction is that it amounts to tacit acceptance of the Ivanov [*sic*] proposal, but I will send a considered comment.[11]

[10] In this letter of 15 March Mr. Bullard referred to his letter of even date (see No. 90, note 12) 'stating our official point of view, which is that we should continue to stand firm and wait for the Russians to make a move', and suggested 'a new tack that we might try at a slightly later stage if the deadlock continues'. This was for each side to request visas only for names known to be acceptable to the other side: outstanding visas would then be left until the initial exchange had taken place. 'By representing the proposal as a new start, we might possibly be able to get away from the notion of rejecting visas or deleting names from lists. This might help to save Soviet face.'

[11] On 24 March Sir J. Killick wrote to Mr. Bullard that he saw little difference between the suggestion in note 10 and Mr. Ippolitov's proposal of 1 March (No. 90, note 11) (ENS 3/548/1).

During March preparations were in hand in the FCO for the biennial Conference of Ambassadors from the Soviet Union and Eastern Europe, to be held from 24-28 April 1972: see Nos. 10 and 46 for the Conferences of 1968 and 1970. On 2 March Mr. Bullard had sent the Ambassadors a provisional programme, and it was decided that to concentrate their minds on the issues for discussion at the Conference a list of questions covering a variety of subject areas should be prepared, and circulated in advance. Despite Sir T. Brimelow's assertion that he wished to concentrate discussion at the Conference 'on the future at the expense of the past and even the present', the questions addressed to the Ambassadors in the Enclosure to No. 92 clearly reflect international developments during the last two years, as well as the awareness, on which the memorandum in No. 89 was based, that Britain's entry into the EEC changed the European scene in a way that was bound to impact on East-West relations.

No. 92

Letter from Sir T. Brimelow to Sir J. Killick (Moscow)

[*EN 2/1*]

Confidential   FCO, *22 March 1972*

Dear John,

  Conference of Ambassadors from Soviet Union and Eastern Europe, 24-28 April 1972
  1. You and the other participants have already received the programme and I gather that it has been found generally satisfactory. I have to be in Brussels myself on 24 April. This means that your free day will be the 24th (when the Commercial Counsellors will meet at the DTI), and that the political talks will start on the 25th. Apart from this I shall hope to make myself available throughout the week and I will take the chair at all meetings except when Ministers attend and wish to do so.

2. The starting point of our discussions will be the fairly large volume of paper about East-West relations that either has already been circulated or will be issued before the conference starts. HM Representatives can assume that we shall have read and digested all their reports and they in turn will by then have seen the following:

(*a*) draft Position Paper on European Security (already issued);[1]
(*b*) UK paper for the NATO Soviet and East European experts' meeting in May (not yet circulated);[2]
(*c*) revised drafts of country assessment sheets (in preparation);[3]
(*d*) UK paper on the External Relations and Responsibilities of the EEC (FCO telegram No. 206 to Brussels, copy enclosed);[4]
(*e*) UK paper for the Ad Hoc Working Group on East-West Contacts (to be circulated by Eric Vines);[5]
(*f*) paper by IRD on publicity aspects of European Security (to be circulated);[6]
(*g*) paper on East European attitudes to the CSCE (about to be circulated).[7]

3. I should like to concentrate the discussion as far as possible on the future at the expense of the past and even the present. As a focus for your thoughts during the next month I enclose some sheets of questions[8] under the following headings:

A. General Western policy on Security in Europe;
B. Developments within the Warsaw Pact and CMEA;
C. Warsaw Pact policy towards the West;
D. Western policy towards the Soviet Union and Eastern Europe;
E. Cultural Relations;
F. Administration and Security;
G. Information.

The questions are by no means exhaustive of the subjects, and if participants have other questions of general interest that they would like to see on

[1] Volume II, No. 1.

[2] This paper on *Trends in the Soviet Union and Eastern Europe and their Policy Implications* was not finalised in time to be seen by Ambassadors before the Conference (EN 2 / 20).

[3] Not printed: the drafts were circulated to Ambassadors at the beginning of the Conference (EN 2 / 17).

[4] Not printed.

[5] Mr. Vines of CED informed Sir J. Killick and his colleagues in Eastern Europe on 11 April that the proposed meeting of the Ad Hoc Working Group had fallen through, and he had therefore not prepared this paper. Instead, he enclosed a note on developments in cultural work since the 1970 Ambassadors' Conference which recorded that 'The last two years have been a period of consolidation rather than of expansion or rapid change'.

[6] Not printed: circulated to the Ambassadors in draft (EN 2 / 1).

[7] Volume II, No. 5.

[8] See Enclosure to this document.

the agenda we will gladly add them. The time-scale should be assumed to be the next two years unless the contrary is stated.

4. As regards the economic day, the DTI tell us they think that if a list of questions is required it can be compiled by the Commercial Counsellors during their separate talks on the Monday. I understand that Peter Preston[9] proposes to attend on the Wednesday, and in my absence I think he should take the chair.

5. EESD will as usual function as a kind of conference secretariat, and they will have ready a folder for each participant containing invitations and any late additions to the agenda or papers for discussion. They will also have copies of reference papers available, in case they are needed, but it would be helpful to them if you could send on ahead through the bag your own copies of any papers which you expect to want to make use of.

6. I look forward very much to seeing you all in a month's time. It looks to me as if this year's Conference might be of particular interest.

7. I am sending copies of this letter to HM Ambassadors at Belgrade, Budapest, Bucharest, Prague, Sofia, Bonn, Helsinki, Warsaw, and to Bushell in Berlin, Thomson at UKDEL NATO, Hannay at UKDEL EEC and Brenchley at Oslo.[10]

Yours ever,
TOM BRIMELOW

ENCLOSURE IN No. 92
A. General Western Policy on Security in Europe
What is the validity of the following assumptions?

(*a*) Despite developments in ABM technology, there is still no prospect of security for either the US or the Soviet Union against strategic nuclear attack by the other;

(*b*) At present the balance of conventional forces in the West favours the Warsaw Pact;

(*c*) What Europe has is not security, but an absence of military operations in Europe between the Warsaw Pact and NATO;

(*d*) This absence is likely to continue so long as the estimated rewards of military operations in Europe are well below the potential cost. At present the margin of safety is high;

(*e*) This depends first on the deterrence provided by NATO but ultimately on the credibility of the US strategic deterrent;

(*f*) If the credibility of the US deterrent were to decline, there might be a need to strengthen the conventional armed forces in Western Europe to satisfy the condition at (*d*), given (*b*), this is said without prejudice to the question of the strengthening of European nuclear forces;

[9] Deputy Secretary at the DTI.

[10] Mr. J.A. Thomson was HM Minister at UKDEL NATO, Mr. D. Hannay a First Secretary at UKDEL to the EEC and Mr. T Brenchley HM Ambassador at Oslo and Ambassador designate to Warsaw, in succession to Mr. Henderson.

(*g*) A reduction in the credibility of the US deterrent, together with a relative worsening *vis-à-vis* the Warsaw Pact of the conventional forces in Western Europe, would cause a reduction in the margin of safety at (*d*);

(*h*) The Warsaw Pact Powers are trying to change the military balance of power in Europe in their favour. Any successes they may have will reduce margin of safety at (*d*).

(*i*) The US Government still regard the security of Western Europe as essential to the security of the United States. So long as this holds good, the Americans will maintain sufficient troops in Europe to ensure the credibility of the commitment of the US nuclear deterrent to the protection of Western Europe;

(*j*) The margin of safety is high enough to permit some reduction in American forces in Europe, some reduction in the relative strength of other NATO conventional forces in Europe, and some further change in the military balance in favour of the Warsaw Pact;

(*k*) But if, for internal American reasons, the American commitment to the protection of Western Europe were to be withdrawn, or if, for any other reason, the US deterrent were to lose its credibility in the context of Europe, the Soviet Government would then work to transform Western Europe into their sphere of influence. If ever they were to succeed in this, the principles governing the use of armed force by the Soviet Government would be those which have hitherto applied within the Warsaw Pact area;

(*l*) The Soviet Government regard the Conference on Security and Cooperation in Europe as a step towards this eventuality, but they do not regard this eventuality as likely to be achieved in the foreseeable future.

B. *Developments within the Warsaw Pact and CMEA*

1. Are we right in believing that the leaders of every East European country (with the possible exception of Bulgaria) desire the maximum degree of independence from Moscow that is compatible with preserving their own régime and the security and integrity of the country? Is the strength of this motive likely to grow or to diminish?

2. Are we right in thinking that the Soviet leaders will want, in all foreseeable circumstances, to retain a high degree of control over the policies of the East European countries in defence, foreign affairs, foreign trade, economics and ideology?

3. Is the conflict in questions 4 and 5 [*sic*] above likely to be resolved, and if [so] how? In particular, is the CSCE likely, or not, to increase the freedom of movement enjoyed by the East European countries, as some of them hope?

4. If some or all of the East European countries do succeed in extending the boundaries of their independence from Moscow, as a result of the CSCE or of other developments, is there a risk that this process may threaten to develop beyond the control of the local leaders, or of Moscow? If so, what kind of Soviet reaction should we envisage?

5. Short of developments which lead to Soviet military intervention, what prospects are there of political liberalisation within the next two years in the

various countries of Eastern Europe? To what extent might differences of pace in the development of political liberalisation lead to tensions between the various countries of Eastern Europe (e.g. of the kind brought to public attention by Bilak in his criticism of the attitude of certain other Communist Parties towards Czechoslovakia)?[11]

6. To what extent is the enlargement of the EEC likely to lead to demands for consolidation in COMECON? To what extent may this be expected to inhibit diversification in the development of economic reform into various COMECON countries? Is it to be expected that COMECON will be reorganised to form a single negotiating body for foreign trade *vis-à-vis* the enlarged EEC? To what extent is the Soviet reaction to the enlargement of the EEC likely to be followed by an increase in the economic dependence of the Eastern European countries on the USSR?[12]

7. Is the degree of military integration and interdependence already attained in the Warsaw Pact such that no useful purpose would be served by strengthening it as a demonstrative counter-move to any enhancement of military cooperation in Western Europe?

8. What is the most likely course of events in Yugoslavia during the next two years, and how will the Warsaw countries react to it, both collectively and individually?

9. What are the prospects for the growth of Chinese influence in Eastern Europe?

C. *Warsaw Pact policy towards the West*

1. Is it true that the Warsaw Pact Governments, in their approach to the proposed Conference on Security and Cooperation in Europe, now place less emphasis on security and more on cooperation? If so, is this due to the fact that the essential negotiations on European security (SALT, the Berlin Agreement, Inner German talks, the admission of the two German States to the United Nations, MBFR), are being conducted in form [*sic*]other than that of the Conference? If this is so, and if the Federal Republic's Treaties with Moscow and Warsaw are not ratified,[13] is there likely to be a Warsaw

[11] On 12 February 1972 *Le Monde* had published extracts from a speech delivered on 21 October 1971 by Mr. Vasil Bilak, a member of the Czech Praesidium and Party Secretary responsible for foreign affairs, who had criticised Romanian and Yugoslav international attitudes, Hungarian economic policy and Polish policy towards the Church. He also attacked Western Communist parties for maintaining their criticism of the invasion of Czechoslovakia in 1968.

[12] In a major speech to the 15th Congress of the USSR Trade Unions in the Kremlin on 20 March Mr. Brezhnev had indicated Soviet willingness to accept an expanded EEC—the first time a Soviet leader had expressed any but a hostile view of enlargement. He stated that 'Our relations with the participants in this grouping, naturally, will depend on the extent to which they, on their part, recognize the realities existing in the socialist part of Europe, specifically the interests of the member countries of the Council for Mutual Economic Assistance. We are for equality in economic relations and against discrimination' (see *The Times*, 21 March 1972, p. 1).

[13] The latest FCO assessment was that 'the Treaties will in the event be ratified though it may be very close run' (FCO telegram No. 271 to Moscow of 20 March, WRG 3/513/1).

Pact campaign for the abandonment of NATO's 'Berlin precondition' for the holding of a Conference, a concerted Warsaw Pact agreement that the non-ratification of the Treaties increases the need for and the urgency of a Conference, and a recrudescence of Warsaw Pact interest in the security aspects of the Conference?

2. Is it likely that differences of motive as between the various countries of the Warsaw Pact will lead to serious divergences before, during or after the CSCE?

3. How much importance do the Warsaw Pact countries attach to the CSCE as a vehicle for the development of their policies towards the West? Do they feel they can conduct their policies better through multilateral than bilateral channels?

D. *Western policy towards the Soviet Union and Eastern Europe*
1. *Chancellor Brandt's Ostpolitik*

HMG have supported the *Ostpolitik*, including signature of the Federal Republic's Treaties with Moscow and Warsaw. If the Treaties are not ratified, presumably the Berlin agreement will not be signed and the NATO precondition for the holding of a Conference on European Security will not be fulfilled. Presumably the Warsaw Pact Governments will continue to press for the Conference. What considerations relevant to the Soviet Union and Eastern Europe should influence the line taken by HMG in NATO Ministerial meetings?

2. What benefits have the French derived from their continuation of de Gaulle's policy of trying to maintain a special relationship with the Soviet Union?[14] To what extent would it be open to us to seek similar benefits, given our reluctance to admit Soviet spies to this country?

3. Which of the measures listed below, or what other measures, can contribute most to the policy towards the Soviet Union and Eastern Europe adopted by Ministers on 15 March in DOP(72)6?[15] (This paper cannot be circulated but will be available in EESD.)

High level visits in both directions
Machinery for regular political consultations
Favourable references in speeches by British Ministers
Support for moves by the countries concerned towards international organisations such as GATT, OECD, EEC
Concessions in import quotas
Military exchanges
Initiatives towards visa abolition agreements (security considerations permitting)
Improvements in ECGD's terms of credit

[14] During the third meeting of the Conference on 26 April Sir J. Killick said that 'it remained to be seen how far the French got. Political gestures could avoid some prejudice but would not of themselves produce benefits.'
[15] No. 89.

Cultural manifestations in both directions
Participation in trade fairs
Establishment of joint commissions for technology, trade etc.
Establishment of non-official consultative committees on the Anglo-Soviet model
Talks between planning staffs in the Foreign Ministries
Meetings between the Secretary of State and other Foreign Ministers during the UN General Assembly
Extradition treaties
Technical assistance for infrastructure projects
Improvements in youth exchanges (especially with Yugoslavia)
Parliamentary talks
Visits to Britain by high level party figures (how to organise these?)
Visits by members of the Royal Family
Visits to Britain by political commentators
Meetings between the PUS and Deputy Foreign Ministers
Meetings between Sir Thomas Brimelow and political directors
Magazines like *Anglia*[16]

4. What kind of common political policy towards the Soviet Union and Eastern Europe should be adopted by the EEC, and what should be the British contribution to this?

5. By what means should we 'work for the development of a coherent commercial policy towards Eastern Europe on a basis that is fair to all the members'? (Planning Committee paper enclosed with the PUS' circular 0.40/72 of 29 February).[17]

6. Does the need of the Soviet Union and Eastern Europe for access to Western technology and credits offer a lever which the West could use for its own commercial or political advantage?

7. What opportunities could the CSCE be made to yield?

E. *Cultural relations*

1. Should we negotiate more frequently or less frequently than we do? Is the current form of our negotiations the one which best furthers our interests?

2. Is any change of priorities in our cultural effort called for if new openings arise, e.g. increased demand for English language teaching, requests for more specialists exchanges? To what extent has the British Council's success

---

[16] In a letter to Mr. Walden of 21 April Mr. Scott enclosed a minute he had written on 4 April to Sir J. Killick, setting out an order of priorities for the measures listed above. In his letter he concluded that 'our objective should be to begin to move forward in the field of political consultations, beginning perhaps with a visit by Julian Bullard, leading on to Mr. Godber's visit and at the same time preparing some kind of offer which we could put to the Russians . . . for a piece of paper establishing a regular programme of political consultations at various levels. In parallel with this process, which should try to move ahead where we can on exchanges of visits of a less official nature, such as Parliamentary exchanges . . . Activities of less political interest, such as cultural and military exchanges, can really only flourish once the political climate has been established' (ENS 3/548/3).

[17] Not printed.

in developing the teaching of English in Eastern Europe been favoured by our low political posture?

3. Are the Great Britain/USSR Association and the Great Britain/East Europe Centre fulfilling their functions? Is there more that they could do?

4. How 'avant-garde' should our cultural manifestations be?

5. Do Film Weeks continue to perform a useful function, given the problems arising from increasing loss of interest on the part of film distributors and the type of films now being produced?

6. Should we continue to work on the basis that any money we have to spend is best allocated to bilateral exchanges? What advantages might there be in a multilateral approach?

F. *Administration and Security*
1. Should the FCO seek to persuade the MOD to accept a reduction in the establishments of Service Attachés at some or all posts?

2. Should we take the position that an official of a Warsaw Pact country who has been positively identified as an intelligence officer in the past should never be permitted to join the staff of his Embassy in London?[18]

G. *Information*
1. What repercussions would the closure of Radio Free Europe and/or Radio Liberty have in Eastern Europe?[19] What repercussions would there be for our information effort? Should the BBC be expected to take over the roles of RFE and/or RL? Would we need to replace RFE's research papers?

2. Is there anything we can do to persuade British journalists to take a more realistic and less sensational line on Anglo-Soviet and Anglo-East European relations?

3. Is there anything we can do to promote a more favourable tone in articles about Britain in the Soviet and East European press?

[18] In a letter to Mr. Bullard of 14 April about the visa war, Sir J. Killick said: 'I think we must return an unqualified "Yes", so far as the Soviet Union is concerned.' If an identified intelligence officer wished to visit Britain, he suggested that 'the guidelines should be that known KGB men coming on Soviet delegations in which there is a definite positive British interest . . . should be admitted; but that those coming on a Soviet initiative which brings no great benefit to HMG . . . should be firmly kept out' (ENS 3/548/1).

[19] Radio Free Europe and Radio Liberty, based in West Germany, were funded by the CIA until 1971 when public criticism led to Congressional funding approved annually. On 14 March 1972 Senator W. Fulbright, Chairman of the Senate Foreign Relations committee, secured a Congressional decision not to renew funding after 30 June 1972, but the US Secretary of State subsequently successfully laid a Bill before Congress providing $38.5m to finance the two Radio networks until 30 June 1973, and on 10 August President Nixon announced the establishment of a Commission to recommend legislation for further US Government financing after that date.

No. 93

Sir J. Killick (Moscow) to Sir A. Douglas-Home

No. 584 Telegraphic [ENS 3/548/3]

Immediate. Confidential   MOSCOW, *20 April 1972, 3.55 p.m.*

Repeated for information Routine to Washington, Paris, Bonn, UKDEL NATO, UKDEL EEC, Warsaw, Prague, Sofia, Belgrade, Budapest and Bucharest.

Anglo-Soviet relations

I was summoned to Gromyko at short notice at 15.30hrs local time today.

2. I reminded Gromyko that I was about to leave for London[1] and that HMG would want my assessment of the present state of Anglo-Soviet relations. He would recall your message through Smirnovsky of 8 March,[2] emphasising the need to revert to normal relations and get down to business. Though nobody could erase what had happened from the book, I hoped I was right in construing the success of Lord Erroll's London Chamber of Commerce Mission[3] as 'turning the page': we must now consider what to write on the new page.

3. Gromyko replied that recently British policy on questions regarding relations with the Soviet Union had been 'as changeable as the British weather'. When talking to the British about Anglo-Soviet relations, everything seemed good: but as soon as any talks were over, the actions of the British Government had in fact turned in quite another direction. 'The page was turned but it does not lie down properly.' The events of last year were not so distant: they were still fresh in the consciousness of the Soviet Government and not easy to erase.

4. As regards economic and commercial relations, Lord Erroll's visit had led to some useful results. The group's approach had been positive: this had been appreciated and would be a help. But we were still at an early stage and it was hard to see how things would turn out. He went on 'tell your government that we are not convinced of its serious desire to improve relations. Facts lead us to conclude the contrary.' He cited as an illustration Britain's approach to the ratification of the German treaties (see m[y] i[mmediately] f[ollowing] t[elegram]).[4]

---

[1] To attend the Conference of Ambassadors from the Soviet Union and Eastern Europe: see No. 92.

[2] Cf. No. 90, note 12.

[3] See No. 91, note 5.

[4] In telegram No. 585 Sir J. Killick reported that Mr. Gromyko had said: 'Rumours sometimes reached the Soviet Government that HMG would not like to see treaties ratified. They did not take these rumours for truth—but still, "HMG had not said a word".' In telegram No. 589 of 21 April Sir J. Killick expressed the view that 'Whatever Gromyko may really believe, it seems to me important to demonstrate that you take him seriously on this question and to return an authoritative and early answer. You might consider it worth while to send him a personal message on this particular point.' Sir A. Douglas-Home minuted 'Shall I send him a message?' on his copy of the telegram, but Mr. Unwin of WED noted on 24 April the 'general

5. He continued 'if one wants to talk of improving relations and if both sides are serious, improvement is possible, though it is hard to forget what has happened. We do not consider improvement impossible, but it is very difficult if one side approaches the matter seriously and the other says it is serious but engages in gymnastics.'

6. Having replied to his point about ratification, I said that the trouble with the English weather was that it was not under the control of HMG: as regards the events of last year it had been under the control of some outside agency, and HMG had been forced to act as they did. I appreciated what he had said about the possibility of better relations, and so would you. Neither you nor I were expecting to be able to write a lovely poem at once on the new page that had been turned. I looked forward to engaging in normal business with the various ministries, but you felt there was a need to establish some focal points in relations between our countries. Perhaps the Soviet Government would think it premature to reestablish your visit or the Joint Commission meeting. You would now like to propose one such focal point: I was instructed to propose that Mr. Godber, who now had responsibility within the Foreign Office for East-West relations, should visit the Soviet Union during the coming autumn, perhaps in October.

7. There were other things that could be done to improve relations. Following a suggestion from the Soviet Embassy we were looking into ways to resume Anglo-Soviet parliamentary exchanges, which had not taken place since 1968. On the cultural front, there was the project for 'Days of Soviet Music', which I looked forward to discussing with Furtseva on my return.[5] I was bound to say personally that cancellations of performances by Soviet artists in London had not helped improve the Soviet image in this field. On the proposal for a visit by Mr. Godber I could not of course expect any immediate reaction, but I hoped he would give it due consideration. He replied that he would, but offered no comment. (I later underlined the value of Mr. Godber's visit in the context of the last sentence of m[y] i[mmediately] f[ollowing] t[elegram].)[6]

8. See m[y] i[mmediately] f[ollowing] t[elegram].[7]

view in the Office is that a message is probably undesirable. It might give an impression of undue sensitivity to Soviet views and of running after the Russians. Instead, it is proposed that the PUS should summon the Soviet Ambassador in London and take Mr. Gromyko's remarks . . . as an occasion for urging him to ensure that HMG's statements and attitudes on the Eastern Treaties as on other matters are fully reflected in reporting to Moscow'. The Secretary of State agreed this course of action on 25 April: see No. 94 below (WRG 3/513/1).

[5] Cf. No. 65, and see No. 99 below.

[6] See note 4. The last sentence reported Sir J. Killick's remark, in answer to Mr. Gromyko's accusation that HMG were taking a '50-50' approach to the ratification of the German treaties, that 'whatever he might think of HMG's attitude, we were working on the assumption that ratification would come about, and would open the way for further developments in Europe'.

[7] See notes 4 and 6.

No. 94

Sir A. Douglas-Home to Mr. Dobbs[1] (Moscow)

No. 393 Telegraphic [ENS 3/548/3]

Priority. Confidential   FCO, *27 April 1972, 1.40 p.m.*

Repeated for information to Washington, Paris, Bonn, Berlin, UKDEL NATO, UKDEL EEC, Warsaw, Prague, Sofia, Belgrade, Budapest, Bucharest.

Moscow telegram[s] Nos. 584, 585 and 589: Anglo-Soviet relations.[2]

1. The PUS asked the Soviet Ambassador to call on 26 April. Smirnovsky appeared anxious to please and expressed himself as keen to develop a dialogue.

2. The PUS opened by referring to Sir J. Killick's telegrams under reference which had been read with interest by the Prime Minister and Secretary of State.[3] The lesson we had drawn from this exchange was that the lack of a proper dialogue was a grave mutual disadvantage. It clearly led the Soviet Government to interpret British policies not on the basis of what HMG said but on other evidence. He quoted remarks by Gromyko as reported in telegram No. 584 to demonstrate that the Soviet Government appeared to be attaching undue importance to rumours, unofficial articles etc.

3. Turning to the German treaties, the PUS said there were two separate questions: whether HMG supported Herr Brandt's *Ostpolitik* in general, and what were their views on the specific situation in the *Bundestag* as regards ratification. HMG's attitude to the *Ostpolitik* was not in doubt. Since 1970 British ministers had made dozens of statements in support of *Ostpolitik*. During Herr Brandt's visit the previous week the Prime Minister had repeated this support.[4]

4. The PUS said that the ratification issue was the guts of the *Ostpolitik* and we therefore supported the treaties as well. However, the situation in the *Bundestag* was comparable to the situation in the British parliament on the European Bill.[5] We would not expect the Federal Government to instruct us

[1] Sir J. Killick was in London: see No. 93, note 1.

[2] See No. 93, and *ibid.*, notes 4 and 6.

[3] Cf. *ibid.* In a letter of 25 April to Mr. M. Alexander (APS to Sir A. Douglas-Home), Lord Bridges (now Private Secretary to Mr. Heath) wrote that 'The Prime Minister was interested to read the remarks by Mr. Gromyko concerning the British attitude to the ratification of the Moscow and Warsaw Treaties' (WRG 3/513/1).

[4] Herr Brandt visited London from 20-22 April. During his meeting with Mr. Heath on 20 April the Prime Minister stated that the British position 'was that we had always supported Herr Brandt's Eastern policy. We had been pleased when the Berlin Agreements had been reached, and were anxious to bring them into effect' (WDW 1/13).

[5] Cf. No. 89, note 1.

on how our parliament should proceed. In return we did not interfere in theirs.[6]

5. As to Soviet doubts about the consistency of our desire to improve East-West relations, the PUS drew attention to numerous British statements which should remove all doubts on this score. He quoted from the Prime Minister's statement in Brussels at the Accession Treaty ceremony[7] and his address to the Foreign Press Association.[8] The Soviet Government had clearly taken note of the latter address since it had been the subject of a commentary in *Pravda*. But no effort had been made by the Soviet Government to seek an official explanation of the address from our Embassy in Moscow.

6. Smirnovsky said that *Ostpolitik* was one thing: the specific issue of the treaties was another. The British Government had said not a word in support of ratification. Sir D. Greenhill had described the treaties as the guts of the *Ostpolitik* but they were still not the same thing. He asked if he could be shown a British statement in support of ratification.

7. The PUS quoted a number of ministerial statements, particularly the Prime Minister's interview with Second German Television on 12 April 1972[9] and Mr. Godber's statement in the House of Commons on 24 April.[10] He stressed that we could not openly express our support for ratification of the treaties without thereby putting pressure on the *Bundestag* and interfering in German domestic affairs. Contrary to Gromyko's statements about oscillations in British policy we had been wholly consistent. Nevertheless, if the Russians were in doubt about our policies or disagreed with them, they should come and discuss them.

8. Smirnovsky said that HMG had welcomed the treaties when they were signed.[11] He could not understand why we could not still support them or at least say that they were important. This was all that the Soviet Government

[6] Cf. No. 90, note 6. Opposition parties failed to carry a vote of no confidence on 27 April but the following day Herr Brandt failed to secure a majority for the Federal budget and began negotiations with Opposition leaders to secure a postponement of the proposed second reading in the *Bundestag* on 3-4 May of the bill on the Eastern treaties. The debate was postponed until 17 May in order to reach Parliamentary agreement on an all-party joint resolution whose purpose was 'clearly to place the Eastern Treaties in the most favourable domestic context' (Bonn telegram No. 619 of 8 May, WRG 3/513/1).

[7] See No. 87, note 12.

[8] For Mr. Heath's speech of 16 March see Watt and Mayall, 1972, p. 195; cf. also Volume II, No. 6.

[9] In his letter of 25 April (see note 3 above) Lord Bridges said that 'Mr. Heath has suggested that it might be appropriate . . . to draw the Russians' attention to his remarks to the [S]econd German television programme', in which he said that 'We obviously want to see the Berlin Agreements carried through. We, of course, are quite ready to sign the last stage. We want to see this brought about. But the relationships between the Eastern Treaties and Berlin are very clear. We have always appreciated them.'

[10] Mr. Godber said that 'we have always supported the *Ostpolitik*, and, if the *Bundestag* should ratify, we should welcome it' (*Parl. Debs.*, 5th ser., H. of C., vol. 835, col. 1047).

[11] See No. 53, note 5.

themselves were saying. They were not asking HMG to satisfy just the Soviet Union on this issue: but it was in the interest of *détente* in Europe.

9. Turning to Anglo-Soviet relations, Smirnovsky said that his government appreciated British statements to the effect that they wanted improvements in relations. However, the two sides must work together on practical problems. A number of minor matters remained unsettled. He had raised one such problem during his previous call but had had no reply.[12]

10. The PUS said he did not wish to discuss with him the question of visas. But he stressed again that HMG could not accept people whose intelligence history was well known to them. It would of course create a new situation if the Soviet side could remove from their list those known to be unacceptable to us. He said that Sir T. Brimelow would restate our position to Ippolitov.

11. For discussion of Vietnam, see my tel[egram] No. 114 to Saigon (not to all).[13]

[12] Cf. No. 90, note 12.

[13] Not printed. In Moscow telegram No. 586 of 20 April Sir J. Killick reported that as instructed he had renewed with Mr. Gromyko HMG's proposal to re-convene the Geneva Conference in the light of the serious situation in Vietnam (an incursion into South Vietnam by North Vietnamese forces had prompted renewed US bombing on 16 and 17 April of Hanoi and of the port of Haiphong, where four Soviet ships were damaged). Mr. Gromyko had replied: 'We do not think this proposal is realistic. It was not practicable one, two or three years ago [cf. Nos. 9, 45, note 15, 46, note 5, 55, note 7 and 66], and it is not practicable at present (he stressed "at present")' (FAV 3/303/1).

The Conference of HM Representatives which convened in London on 24 April (see No. 92) concentrated its discussions on future developments in the Soviet Union and Eastern Europe with special reference to policies towards the West. As Sir J. Killick emphasised in his opening statement, however, 'the Soviet Union was a global power with global concerns', and the Conference opened against a backdrop not just of President Nixon's forthcoming visit to Moscow (see No. 97 below), but of disturbing international developments. In the wake of Egypt's rejection in March of a Middle East peace plan put forward by King Hussein of Jordan, Mr. Kosygin's visit to Iraq and the signature of a 15-year Soviet-Iraqi Treaty of Friendship and Cooperation on 9 April was clearly significant. The conflict in Vietnam had continued to escalate with a major North Vietnamese invasion of Quang Tri province at the end of March and their attack on the US 7th Fleet in the Gulf of Tonkin on 19 April. On a more positive note, the UK, USA, USSR and 46 other countries had signed a convention outlawing biological weapons on 10 April. The Ambassadors spoke, however, in the knowledge that while Soviet policy was not currently centred on Europe it nevertheless had a considerable impact on the European powers.

No. 95

Record of the Seventh Meeting of the Conference of HM Representatives from the Soviet Union and Eastern Europe, held on Friday, 28 April 1972, at 12 noon[1]

[*EN 2/1*]

Confidential

Present:

HM Representatives	Foreign & Commonwealth Office
Sir R. Jackling (Bonn)	Sir A. Douglas-Home
Sir J.E. Killick (Moscow)	Sir T. Brimelow
Mr. D.L.L. Stewart (Belgrade)	Mr. J.A.N. Graham
Mr. D.R. Ashe (Bucharest)	Mr. J.L. Bullard
Mr. D.S.L. Dodson (Budapest)	Mr. M.O'D.B. Alexander
Mr. R.S. Scrivener (Prague)	Mr. C. Hulse
Mr. D.A. Logan (Sofia)	
Mr. J.N. Henderson (Warsaw)	
Mr. T.F. Brenchley (Warsaw designate)	
Mr. J.C.W. Bushell (Berlin)	
Mr. W.B.J. Ledwidge (Helsinki)	

Presentation of the Conclusions to the Secretary of State[2]

1. *Sir T. Brimelow* began by referring to Sir J. Killick's view that Soviet policy was not at present centred on Europe. The Russians were worried by the present Chinese policies and they wanted stability at home and in Eastern Europe. They wished to consolidate this by means of the CSCE. However they would use the Conference to work against a consolidation of an enlarged EEC, since they did not want the latter to become a political or defence unity. Sir J. Killick had stressed that the West must not succumb to any Soviet blandishments; the Russians were not interested in East-West trade, they wished to consolidate CMEA and achieve autarky themselves.

[1] Cf. No. 92. After the free day on Monday 24 April for individual appointments with EESD and OGDs, the First and Second Meetings on 25 April concerned political developments, and the Third Meeting on 26 April economic affairs and commercial work. The Fourth Meeting on 27 April began with a discussion of the political situation in the FRG, where a CDU/CSU motion of no-confidence had been proposed against Chancellor Brandt, and then considered practical suggestions for improving bilateral relations with the Soviet Union and Eastern European countries. The Fifth Meeting that afternoon concerned information work and cultural relations, and the Sixth Meeting on the morning of 28 April discussed the preliminary conclusions. The meeting recorded here was succeeded by a final session on security and administrative questions.

[2] On 27 April Mr. Bullard had submitted a summary note for the Secretary of State of the Conference's conclusions on likely developments in the Soviet Union and Eastern Europe, economic relations and future Western policy in the region: 'I assume that, as happened two years ago [cf. No. 46, note 15], Sir T. Brimelow will present the conclusions of the Conference and invite the Secretary of State to comment.'

2. Within this framework the picture of Eastern Europe was more complex than it had been two years ago. The Ambassadors had stressed that it was necessary to distinguish between régimes and populations. But even the régimes wished to maintain a degree of independence. In certain fields they were anxious for closer relations with the West, they were becoming increasingly dependent on the West for technology and also raw materials. The Soviet Union was unable to meet the Eastern Europeans' increasing demands for supplies and this should be a factor in the commercial policies of the EEC. Attitudes to contact with the West varied greatly. Some countries, such as Hungary, Czechoslovakia and the GDR, were exposed to Western television, and some were experiencing a great flow of tourists. Knowledge of the West was increasing. The BBC was listened to, although there were problems of signal strength. In no country, with the possible exception of Bulgaria, could one say that the people supported the régime. They felt a strong need to be able to travel abroad.

3. The Ambassadors had stressed the importance of ministerial visits, although the treatment of visitors tended to be stereotyped. The degree of importance attached to them varied from one country to another. Romania and Yugoslavia believed that it was beneficial to multiply contacts with the outside world since this might help to inhibit Soviet interference. In the case of Yugoslavia a target of one ministerial visit per year by a British Minister of State had been agreed with Mr. Godber.[3] If a Royal visit to Yugoslavia could be arranged so much the better.

4. Apart from day to day tactics, it had been suggested that we should try to formulate a more strategic long-term policy towards the East. Mr. Henderson had suggested that the elements of instability latent in all the countries of Eastern Europe would lead to periodic intervention by the Soviet Union. This presented Western Governments with a dilemma: they did not wish to stimulate a spirit of independence to the point where the Russians intervened, yet did they wish to appear to be conniving at the perpetuation of Soviet domination[?] There might be a case for attempting to write a paper on this question.

5. The Conference had shown that the Ambassadors did not seem to be familiar with the difficulty of maintaining an adequate defence for Western Europe. The latter could be aggravated by the CSCE. The problem was that progressive American troop reductions in Europe seemed inevitable, and that Western European Governments were showing a marked reluctance to face up to the problems this would present. In the atmosphere of a Conference the Russians would argue strongly against the need for improved defence. This might result in a shift in the balance of power in Europe. Perhaps we had not hitherto done enough to explain the problems of defence to HM Representatives in Warsaw Pact countries.[4] Finally, Sir T.

---

[3] Cf. No. 89.

[4] In a minute of 20 June to Sir T. Brimelow submitting a draft despatch covering the conclusions of the Conference (see note 14 below), Mr. Bullard speculated as to the need for

Brimelow said that the conclusions of the Conference could be more precisely formulated, and a revised version would be produced.[5]

6. *The Secretary of State* said that this seemed to be the right way to proceed. He had difficulty in believing that the Russians were as worried about the US/Chinese relationship as they confessed. The Russians were doing well in the Middle East and the Indian Ocean.[6] Their behaviour in these areas looked like old-fashioned imperialism, and their activities in Iraq and the Gulf looked as though they might be interested in getting a stranglehold on Western oil supplies. *Sir J. Killick* agreed that the Russian fears about the Chinese were probably exaggerated. Their real worry was that the Americans now had a pivoted position between Moscow and Peking. The Russians were certainly taking greater risks and playing for higher stakes in Bangladesh and India, for example. He had for some time been worried about Russian oil policy. It was a subject which the JIC should examine.[7] He did not think they were capable of getting a stranglehold but they could nevertheless be a considerable nuisance.

7. *The Secretary of State* asked whether the Russians' preoccupation with China was encouraging them to mend their fences in Western Europe. *Sir T. Brimelow* said they would like to stabilise Eastern Europe, but had not renounced the hope of changing the balance of power in Western Europe in their favour. If they succeeded, this would give them a better basis for dealing with China. *The Secretary of State* said that this would be a victory for them. The present balance of power seemed to suit the West fairly well. One did not want premature revolutions in Eastern Europe.

8. The Secretary of State asked what effect our membership of the EEC would have on trade with Eastern Europe. How could one compensate for the losses which some East Europeans would certainly suffer[?] *Mr. Bullard* replied that trade with the UK might suffer in some cases, but since overall trade with the EEC would probably grow the Eastern Europeans would stand to benefit.

9. *The Secretary of State* then asked why the Russians wanted a CSCE. It presented certain risks *vis-à-vis* Eastern Europe. *Sir J. Killick* said that it was an old idea; Soviet motives had evolved since it was originally put forward. The Russians were now stressing the importance of economic cooperation as a way of sabotaging the enlarged EEC. In a reply to a question from the

shorter and more frequent conferences: 'There is no doubt that HM Ambassadors in Communist countries do become out of touch with FCO thinking, notwithstanding the provision for annual leave. On politico-military subjects, in particular, security rules make it difficult to keep Sir J. Killick and others in Eastern Europe abreast of events.'

[5] A revised version was circulated to HM Representatives for comment on 11 May, and the agreed conclusions sent out on 28 June under cover of a despatch drawing together the Conference as a whole: see note 14 below.

[6] Cf. the Appendix to this Volume, pp. 523-26.

[7] The consequences of Soviet involvement in the Middle Eastern oil question were examined in a note produced by the JIC on 14 August 1972 (JIC(A)(72)(N)77). This note was drawn upon for para. 22 of the JIC paper printed as the Appendix to this Volume: see p. 525 below.

Secretary of State about the Polish attitude *Mr. Henderson* said that we tended to underestimate the influence of the Eastern Europeans on the campaign for a conference. They had played a major part in launching it,[8] and the Russians had been obliged to listen to them. The Russians had probably decided that it was safer for them to let the East Europeans talk to the West in a collective form such as a security conference than to let them go it alone.

10. *Sir T. Brimelow* explained that in 1969 the Eastern Europeans had wanted to get out of the post-1968 freeze. The situation was then changed by the Berlin and SAL talks which were talks on genuine and important issues affecting European security. The FRG's two treaties[9] had confirmed the European status quo. The Russians now wanted to see what they could get out of a CSCE in order to minimize the possibly adverse consequences to them of the enlargement of the EEC.[10] *Sir J. Killick* remarked that he doubted whether there would be scope for the Eastern Europeans to express independent views. *Sir T. Brimelow* observed there was already a precautionary turning of the screws in Eastern Europe. *Mr. Stewart* pointed out that the Yugoslavs were much involved in a CSCE. They knew that the Warsaw Pact was their enemy and NATO was their first line of defence, although they were officially against bloc to bloc policies. In short, their attitude was very confused. *The Secretary of State* said that ministerial visits were incurably dull. He did not feel they had much impact unless they were televised; *Mr. Henderson* observed that President Nixon's visit to Warsaw[11] would have more effect than a comparable visit by a Soviet leader; *Mr. Logan* mentioned the successful visits to Bulgaria by Mr. Royle and Mrs Thatcher.[12]

11. *Mr. Ledwidge* referred to the unpopularity of communism in Eastern Europe. To the Finns the Russians looked very strong militarily, but had growing political problems in their relations with Eastern Europe. Brezhnev was so deeply engaged in the Soviet *Westpolitik* that its failure would be a considerable blow to his prestige, although it would not result in his downfall. Finland had a certain attraction for the Eastern European countries, because it showed them something to which they might aspire. *Sir J. Killick* hoped that the time would come when the Russians would be inhibited from intervening in Eastern Europe, although this was a long way off. Referring to the Polish riots of 1969 [*sic*][13] the *Permanent Under-Secretary* pointed out that in spite of

[8] Cf. No. 26, note 2.

[9] See No. 50, note 3 and No. 52, note 5.

[10] At the 4th session of the Conference on 27 April Sir T. Brimelow had said: 'The Russians might hope to create a climate of over-optimism in Europe at a CSCE, to secure a withdrawal of US forces and to reduce Western Europe's will to maintain its defensive capability.'

[11] President Nixon was to visit Warsaw from 31 May to 1 June 1972.

[12] Cf. No. 89. Mrs. Margaret Thatcher, Secretary of State for Education and Science, visited Bulgaria from 20-26 September 1971.

[13] See No. 59, note 2.

high hopes the new Government had been similar to the old. *Sir T. Brimelow* said that in his view the changes amounted only to a decision within the Party that it must shuffle its top people. The *Permanent Under-Secretary* observed that the timing had however been dictated by the people. *Mr. Henderson* said he thought that the UK counted more in Eastern Europe than was realised. The French, Germans and Italians pursued a more forward policy than the UK did. *The Secretary of State* asked how this was done. *Mr. Henderson* replied that the French offered a relationship. The Polish Party leader, Mr. Gierek was to visit Paris in the autumn. The British attitude should change; more governmental interest should be shown. *Mr. Stewart* added that HMG was now showing much less interest in Yugoslavia than it did ten or twelve years ago. The Italians, Germans and French were now more active. *The Secretary of State* asked whether the difficulties were financial ones. *Mr. Bullard* said that the Yugoslavs had asked for a financial loan but it was difficult to persuade the Treasury to agree. *The Secretary of State* said that the time could be spared for ministerial visits. *Mr. Stewart* said that a realistic plan of visits to Yugoslavia had been agreed with Mr. Godber. *Sir T. Brimelow* pointed out that Eastern Europe did not do too badly on the whole for ministerial visits, as compared with the rest of the world.[14]

[14] In his despatch of 28 June transmitting the agreed conclusions (see note 5), Sir A. Douglas-Home repeated his agreement to 'pursue the policy, recently accepted by my colleagues, of active contacts with the Soviet Union and Eastern Europe, including the political field and including the ministerial level. I have only one qualification . . . Governmental activity must reflect a genuine mutual interest and, on our side at least, it must enjoy a certain level of public support. No amount of ministerial effort will make an unimportant country important, or an unpopular one popular . . . There is a certain tradition of plain speaking in British public life which I should be unwilling to forego. What we can do, however, is to take suitable opportunities for statements in a different sense, emphasising Britain's interest in Eastern Europe . . . and hoping eventually to get across the message that plain talk about what Communist governments are actually doing is perfectly compatible with a sincere desire for better relations with Communist countries.'

No. 96

Minute from Mr. Goodall to Mr. Rose

[ENS 3/548/1]

Secret   FCO, *15 May 1972*

Anglo-Soviet Visa War

1. I have read with interest the reports of Mr. Bullard's two recent conversations with Mr. Ippolitov contained in FCO telegrams Nos. 429 and 432 to Moscow and Sir John Killick's comments thereon in his telegram No. 686.[1] I note Mr. Bullard's impression (paragraph 7 of FCO telegram No.

[1] These telegrams of 10, 11 and 12 May respectively are not printed. Mr. Bullard had given Mr. Ippolitov updated lists of those to whom visas would be issued if the Soviet Government

432) that the Russians may now think that we are anxious for a solution to the visa problem and ready to make further concessions.[2]

2. The fact is that since Operation FOOT[3] it has consistently been the British side which has taken the initiative in trying to resolve the visa problem. Whereas the Russians have stood pat on their position that our measures are unjustified and unreasonable, and have sought to insist that all their demands (and particularly those in respect of the STD) should be met, we have volunteered various alternative ways of tackling the difficulties and have offered at least one significant though small concession (consent to short overlaps of Soviet staff in London on the understanding that those replaced would leave within two weeks).[4] Our latest clarification amounts to the reduction of our own list of applications by two and, taken in conjunction with our decision (for quite separate reasons, which I do not question) not to retaliate for Mr. Bonavia's expulsion,[5] is almost bound to have suggested to the Russians that our front may be beginning to crack and that they have only to keep up the pressure in order to achieve some major concession. If this is right, we must expect them over the next few weeks to try both blandishments and aggressive tactics in an attempt to shift us.

3. It looks as if their immediate objective is the amalgamation of the ceilings for the STD and the 'other organisations'. As Mr. Walden has pointed out in a recent submission,[6] this would provide them with a secure base, protected by diplomatic immunity, for expanding their intelligence operations against us under STD cover. In the light of what the Russians know we know from Lyalin[7] about their abuse of the STD for intelligence purposes, they would also interpret such a concession as tacit acknowledgement on our part that their abuse of STD cover would be allowed to continue. The position established as a result of FOOT would thus be significantly eroded.

4. Nor is it likely that this or any other single concession would in fact solve the problem. Although it might temporarily break the log jam to the extent

accepted the proposal made by Sir D. Greenhill on 14 January: see No. 87, note 6. Sir J. Killick commented that he was 'a little disturbed by the effect of this new initiative on our future staffing position . . . even if the Russians accept our latest offer, we shall almost immediately wish to submit a further series of visa applications . . . [which] will then be balanced by further applications from their side for candidates who are unacceptable either on security grounds or because of the ceilings. We would then be faced with a black-for-white exchange and a further impasse.'

[2] Mr. Bullard had also expressed the view that there were 'signs that the Russians may have resigned themselves to the immutability of the ceilings . . . To this extent therefore the gap has been somewhat narrowed, and the Russians should be under no illusion that the next move must come from them.'

[3] See No. 76.

[4] Mr. Walden had made this offer to Mr. Filatov on 23 February.

[5] Mr. David Bonavia, *The Times* correspondent in Moscow, had been expelled on 5 May.

[6] Of 10 May, not printed.

[7] See No. 73, note 2.

of enabling us to top up the staff of HM Embassy at Moscow, everything we know about Russian tactics suggests that before very long they would resume pressure on us for some further concession, and so on until all the restrictions imposed by FOOT had effectively been circumvented.

5. As we have all along recognised, we are engaged with the Russians in a battle of wills. Because, unlike the Russians, we are vulnerable to a wide range of domestic pressures, it is a battle in which we are inevitably at a disadvantage. We have, nevertheless, succeeded in making some impression on the Russians, as is shown by their recent tendency to concentrate on securing an amalgamation of the two ceilings rather than (as at first) their abolition. Provided we continue to stand our ground and stick to the position that the terms of our *Aide-Mémoire* of last September[8] are not negotiable, I believe that we stand a reasonable chance of getting the Russians eventually to accept those terms as facts of life with which they will have to live.

6. The main limiting factor on us is of course the viability of HM Embassy at Moscow, which is being progressively reduced. (The Russians no doubt face similar growing difficulties here, but for a variety of reasons are better placed to withstand them.) It may be that we shall in the end be faced with an unpalatable choice between allowing HM Embassy (or sections of it) to become unviable and making some concession to the Russians. If so, it will be no more than we bargained for when we decided on FOOT: at that time we were braced for much more drastic and immediate retaliation than in fact materialised.[9] But this choice (if indeed the Russians force it on us) is still some way off. Sir John Killick's assessment is that the Embassy can continue to discharge its essential tasks at least until September. Although the implications of what happens thereafter will have to be considered before then, this gives us at least four months in which to seek to convince the Russians that there is no further give in our position. I believe (and the Security Service, whom I have consulted, strongly agree) that our only hope of achieving this lies in making no further concession, and taking no fresh initiative, during this four month period. Mr. Bullard has already left Mr. Ippolitov under no illusion that the next move must come from the Soviet side; and I very much hope that we shall continue to maintain this stand.

A.D.S. GOODALL[10]

---

[8] No. 76.

[9] Cf. No. 75.

[10] Further approaches by Mr. Ippolitov to Mr. Bullard (on 18 and 23 May) and by Mr. Smirnovsky to Mr. Godber (on 18 and 25 May) left the Minister of State with 'the very firm impression . . . that an early exchange of visas was still both possible and very desirable. There is no doubt that we could have such an exchange at once if we accepted the latest Soviet proposals [for the removal of 5 names from the Soviet and 3 from the British list], but we see no reason to do this. It would look weak and would encourage the Russians to believe that a tough policy on their part will pay off in future. It would also give the Russians much the better of the initial bargain' (telegram No. 498 to Moscow, 26 May). Sir J. Killick agreed in Moscow telegram No. 805 of 31 May, adding: 'I hope you will agree that we need not be in too much of a hurry to reply to the latest Soviet proposal, since we do not wish to give the impression that we are as anxious as they appear to be to reach a quick settlement.'

The next document concerns President Nixon's visit to the Soviet Union, 22-30 May 1972. While it may not have been what Dr. Kissinger, according to the President, called 'one of the greatest diplomatic coups of all times',[1] it was undoubtedly a visit of considerable international significance. Careful and little-publicised preparations for the visit since the original announcement (see No. 78, note 3)—including a secret and private visit to Moscow by Dr. Kissinger in April—seemed likely to be derailed at the eleventh hour by the North Vietnamese attack on Quang Tri and on the US 7th Fleet (see p. 466): on 8 May President Nixon announced that in addition to bombing Hanoi and other targets in North Vietnam, US forces would mine Haiphong and other North Vietnamese ports; a number of Soviet ships were trapped. However, a visit by the President to the Soviet Union, in any case desirable, was essential to both sides following his visit to Peking (see pp. 446-7) and important enough to the Soviet leadership to make them face criticism from within the Party and elsewhere by going ahead with the visit just after the mining of Haiphong. President Nixon, telling his advisers that 'The summit isn't worth a damn if the price for it is losing in Vietnam', nevertheless felt that 'to cancel the summit . . . would inevitably be criticized as an impulsive action that dashed the hopes for progress towards a more peaceful world'.[2]

Sir J. Killick reported that the President's welcome in the Soviet Union was elaborate and correct, but not warm: 'a major political event but not a Soviet-American love-feast'.[3] The results of the visit were embodied in a Communiqué and a joint declaration of 'Basic Principles of Relations between the USA and USSR'.[4] The importance of the Basic Principles, which affirmed the two Governments' intentions to conduct their mutual relations on a basis of peaceful co-existence (cf. No. 104 below) and to do their utmost to avoid military confrontation and prevent the outbreak of nuclear war, was mainly psychological: the Americans were under no illusions about their ability to inhibit the Russians' pursuit of traditional aims by traditional methods; and to the Russians, détente did not mean an ideological ceasefire. Sir J. Killick considered the main significance of the Principles to be their reflection of better understanding between the two superpowers.

In addition to two important agreements on arms limitation (see No. 97, note 5 below) agreement was reached on a variety of exchanges in the scientific and technical fields, but despite considerable progress on commercial and economic questions, no immediate agreement proved possible there. There appeared to be no unforeseen results of discussion of international affairs: both countries were running the risk of being accused of discussing the affairs of third countries behind their backs and of carving up the world into spheres of influence, and both had an interest in seeing that such accusations were as little substantiated as possible. Dr. Kissinger's belief that bilateral agreements could serve as a basis for the creation of vested interests in a better Soviet-American under-

[1] *The Memoirs of Richard Nixon, op. cit.,* p. 609.

[2] *Ibid.,* pp. 601-2.

[3] Moscow despatch No. 3/12 of 15 June, ENS 3/304/2.

[4] Printed in *Public Papers: Nixon, 1972,* pp. 632-42.

standing appeared to the FCO a reasonable one, as expressed by Sir J. Killick: 'On this score alone the visit was a success, but mutual acceptance by the United States and the USSR that neither can dominate or destroy the other by the application of material power is of far greater significance, perhaps justifying description of the visit as historic.'

No. 97

Minute by Mr. B.J. Fall on President Nixon's visit to Moscow[1]

[ENS 3/304/2]

ECLIPSE.[2] Confidential   FCO, 30 May 1972

1. I attach the texts of the *Communiqué* and joint declaration issued on 29 May at the end of President Nixon's visit to Moscow, together with a Note on some of the points of interest.[3]

2. From the point of view of this department the most significant thing about the visit is that the Russians not only agreed that it should take place in the light of events in Vietnam, but that they participated to all intents and purposes as if these events had not occurred. Agreements were signed on matters of relatively minor importance which could easily have been postponed; the atmosphere was businesslike but by no means unfriendly; the emphasis on bilateral relations (including the agreement to a joint declaration of principles) went far beyond the minimum required by the circumstances; and only on Indo-China was the device of separate statements used to cover points of disagreement in the foreign affairs section of the *Communiqué*.[4]

3. The results of the visit have confirmed the importance which the Soviet leaders attach to their super-power relationship with the United States. This is most directly reflected in the SALT agreement;[5] but it receives added

[1] This minute by Mr. Fall (EESD) was addressed to Mr. Bullard and Sir T. Brimelow.

[2] A code word for documents containing information not to be communicated to the US or to other countries except, on a need to know basis, Canada, Australia and New Zealand.

[3] Not printed.

[4] The *Communiqué* stated that 'Each side set forth its respective standpoint with regard to the continuing war in Vietnam and the situation in the area of Indochina as a whole.' The US side emphasised the need to end the military conflict as soon as possible through an internationally supervised Indochina-wide ceasefire and the subsequent withdrawal of all American forces stationed within Vietnam within four months. The Soviet side stressed its solidarity with 'the just struggle of the peoples of Vietnam, Laos and Cambodia for their freedom, independence and social progress' and called for a cessation of US bombing of the DRV and 'a complete and unequivocal withdrawal of the troops of the USA and its allies from South Vietnam'.

[5] The Treaty of Limitation of Anti-Ballistic Missile Systems and an accompanying interim agreement on the Limitation of Strategic Offensive Weapons were signed on 26 May: the texts are printed in Cmnd. 6932, Nos. 44 and 45. The Treaty limited both sides to 200 ABMs each at two sites in each country, and the agreement stabilised at roughly the current level the numbers of land and sea based strategic missiles, Soviet superiority in numbers being set against US qualitative superiority and a greater number of nuclear warheads. During the five year period of

emphasis from passages in the *Communiqué* and declaration which (despite occasional protestation to the contrary) underline the special responsibility which the two powers regard as theirs. The Russians will see in the agreed texts an American acceptance of their claim to equal status; and they will welcome this particularly in the light of President Nixon's visit to China.[6] They have succeeded in what for them must have been the important aim of contrasting the substance of the Soviet/American relationship with the hollowness of the Sino/American *Communiqué*.

4. On the costs side, the Russians may well have lost ground in Hanoi and elsewhere by receiving President Nixon in these circumstances. Their agreement to a joint passage on the *Communiqué* on the Middle East may give them some explaining to do.[7] And the references in the declaration to avoiding military confrontations and 'efforts to obtain unilateral advantage at the expense of the other', expose a considerable amount of left flank. It is a sign of confidence in the Soviet leaders that they feel that they can get away with this, both internally and *vis-à-vis* their clients and rivals abroad. They seem to feel that they can safely await a more suitable occasion to give due emphasis to the class struggle and wars of national liberation.

5. Brezhnev must take the primary responsibility for the visit, whatever balance of cost and benefit is drawn on the Russian side. He had a number of private sessions with President Nixon; and he alone signed the SALT agreement and the joint declaration for the Soviet Union. But a considerable effort was made to emphasise the collective involvement of the leadership. Podgorny and Kosygin made the two public speeches, took an active part in the talks, and are listed in the *communiqué* as principals on the Soviet side. Other members of the Politburo were in attendance at various stages of the visit.

6. I must leave it to the American and NATO experts to assess the balance from President Nixon's point of view and from that of the Alliance.[8]

the interim agreement further negotiations were to be held to agree a permanent treaty limiting offensive strategic weapons.

[6] See pp. 446-7.

[7] The *Communiqué* stated that both sides reaffirmed their support for a peaceful settlement in the Middle East in accordance with Resolution 242, and for the success of Dr. Jarring's mission. In his note on points of interest (see para. 1 above) Mr. Fall commented that the fact that the Russians agreed to this joint passage 'with no explicit unilateral statements of position, is of considerable interest'.

[8] In a minute to Mr. Graham of 1 June Mr. E.T. Davies, Assistant in North America Department, commented that 'From President Nixon's point of view, the visit must rank as a considerable triumph. Although he did not carry off all the prizes . . . he has secured enough by way of concrete achievement to demonstrate the success of his policy of peace through negotiation.' He added with regard to SALT that 'we have no reason to think the Americans were not successful in honouring their latest undertakings to us and in NATO with regard to those aspects which particularly affect us'. In a personal message to the President on 1 June Mr. Heath, who had been briefed by the Secretary of State on the basis of Mr. Rogers' report to the NATO Council (see p. 478 below), sent his 'warmest congratulations on the successful conclusion

On the whole, I think we can welcome the outcome of the visit. But it is striking how much of concern to us all is treated as essentially a bilateral matter between the two super-powers.

7. The drafting of the two final texts—especially the declaration—shows signs either of undue Soviet influence or of too great an impatience on the American side with 'bureaucratic' points (such as the acceptance of peaceful coexistence as a basis for relations, and the reference to the quadripartite agreements relating to the Western sectors of Berlin).[9] I hope that the references in the declaration to a 'juridical basis' for mutual relations, and to 'the establishment of an effective system of international security in accordance with the purposes and principles of the United Nations' are not quoted against us at the CSCE. And I very much regret that the American 'hard line' on freer movement is apparently confined to NATO. The relevant principle in the joint declaration[10] gives away the ground won by the French, and makes the Danes and Norwegians look robust.

BRIAN FALL[11]

of this visit' and noted that he was 'especially pleased to hear how carefully you took account of the interests of the North Atlantic Alliance'.

[9] The *Communiqué* stated that both sides viewed the Quadripartite Agreement of 3 September 1971 relating to the Western Sectors of Berlin (see pp. 376-7) as 'a good example of fruitful cooperation between the states concerned' and that its implementation in the near future would 'further improve the European situation and contribute to the necessary trust among states'. Mr. Fall commented: 'This seems to be an unnecessary concession to the Soviet thesis.'

[10] Principle 9 of the Joint Declaration reaffirmed the two sides' intention to 'deepen cultural ties with one another and to encourage fuller familiarization with each other's cultural values'. Mr. Fall commented that the omission of any reference to the freer exchange of peoples, ideas and information was 'a considerable step backward from the corresponding Franco-Soviet principle, and must be very welcome to the Russians in the CSCE context'; cf. Volume II, No. 5, paras. 19-23.

[11] This minute was incorporated by Mr. Davies into his minute of 1 June and also formed the basis of a JIC assessment of 5 June on President Nixon's visit. Sir A. Douglas-Home informed the Cabinet on 6 June that the visit 'had been completed to the general satisfaction of both the United States and the Soviet Governments. The former were entitled to claim credit for the conclusion of the agreement on strategic arms limitation, in which they had had due regard to our interests; while the Soviet Government, for their part, were gratified by the attention paid to them by the President, which they regarded as confirming their own estimation of themselves as no less influential a world Power than the United States. It was unlikely that any significant changes in the foreign policies of the two Governments would result from the meeting, although the Soviet Government appeared to be more inclined to regard the war in Vietnam as a relatively minor obstacle to the development of better relations with the United States' (CM(72)29th meeting).

President Nixon's visit to the Soviet Union was followed immediately by the NATO Ministerial meeting held in Bonn, 30-31 May. Preparations for the meeting had been overshadowed both by the President's visit and by the controversy over the ratification of the FRG's Eastern Treaties: see No. 94, note 6. At the meeting itself, however, business was briskly done and decisions taken. Mr. Rogers made a statement on President

Nixon's visit which was heard in attentive silence. The main points of the Communiqué[1] were the statement that the Alliance was now committed to entering multilateral preparatory talks for a CSCE in Helsinki, following signature of the Berlin Protocol, although Mr. Rogers said that the Americans would not in practice be ready for these until after the Presidential election in November; a formula was found, to which the French could subscribe, to distinguish military measures to be examined at the Conference, and it was agreed that multilateral explorations on MBFR should be undertaken either before or in parallel with the CSCE. Sir A. Douglas-Home reported that the atmosphere at the meeting was good, with everyone inclined to minimise differences: 'there was a general feeling that the Alliance should move reasonably united into the territory ahead'.[2]

There was little discussion at the meeting of other international issues, apart from Germany and Berlin. The FRG's Eastern Treaties had been approved by the Bundestag on 17 May and by the Bundesrat on 19 May, and the Ratification Law signed by the Federal President on 23 May. The exchange of instruments of ratification in Bonn on 3 June made possible the simultaneous signature in Berlin by Sir A. Douglas-Home, Mr. Gromyko, Mr. Rogers and M. Schumann of the Final Quadripartite Protocol, bringing into force the entire Berlin Agreement.[3] Sir Alec and Mr. Gromyko took advantage of the occasion for a conversation on Anglo-Soviet relations.

[1] Extracts are printed in Cmnd. 6932, No. 43.

[2] Bonn telegram No. 741 of 31 May, WDN 27/1.

[3] See Cmnd. 6201, No. 153.

No. 98

Record of conversation between Sir A. Douglas-Home and Mr. Gromyko in Berlin on Saturday, 3 June 1972

[ENS 3/548/3]

Confidential

Present:

The Rt. Hon. Sir Alec Douglas-Home	Mr. Gromyko
Sir Thomas Brimelow	Mr. Efremov
Mr. J.H.G. Leahy[1]	Mr. Bondarenko
Mr. M.O'D.B. Alexander	Mr. Khlestov
Mr. K.A. Bishop	Mr. Makarov
	Mr. Smirnov[2]

Sir Alec Douglas-Home opened the conversation by saying that he wanted to assure Mr. Gromyko that HMG's policy was not in any sense anti-Soviet. He

[1] Head of FCO News Department.

[2] Mr. Efremov, Mr. Bondarenko, Mr. Khlestov and Mr. Makarov were respectively Soviet Ambassador in East Berlin, Heads of 3rd European and Treaty and Legal Departments in the Soviet Ministry of Foreign Affairs, and Head of Mr. Gromyko's Chancellery. Mr. Smirnov was an Interpreter.

recognised that relations were not as easy as they might be. It was our policy to have the best possible relations with the Soviet Union and we hoped that it would be possible to re-establish something closer to normality as soon as possible. In particular it should be possible to make greater use of the Embassies in Moscow and London.

2. *Mr. Gromyko* said that it went without saying that the present state of affairs was not satisfactory, but it was another matter to decide how things could be put right. HMG's actions had been responsible for the deterioration of relations and therefore it was our responsibility to produce ideas for improving them. He would be willing to listen to any proposals which HMG wished to put forward. An increase in diplomatic contacts would represent an improvement in the form of relations but what about the substance?

3. *Sir Alec Douglas-Home* repeated that there should be more contacts. He would be willing to have such contacts with Mr. Smirnovsky if Mr. Gromyko would do the same with Sir John Killick. We were bound to have differences. The Soviet Government had their alliances. We were members of a defensive alliance. We wished to work towards *détente. Mr. Gromyko* said that he would like to see bilateral relations improved. The Soviet Government were willing to cooperate. They had been waiting for progress on the Conference on European Security, about which they were especially concerned.

4. *Sir Alec Douglas-Home* suggested that in the short term bilateral discussions might focus on matters relating to the Conference. *Mr. Gromyko* agreed that this was a useful idea. He was prepared to use all channels and he accepted the suggestion that greater use should be made of the Embassies in London and Moscow. His Government had not overlooked the statements made by the Prime Minister and by Sir Alec Douglas-Home in support of the ratification of the Treaties.[3] He pressed for further information about our ideas, both on the improvement of bilateral relations and regarding the Conference. *Sir Alec Douglas-Home* said that HMG saw no difficulties here. They had an open mind about Soviet proposals for the Conference. He assumed that it would take place early next year and multilateral preparatory talks would begin in the autumn.[4] *Mr. Gromyko*, who said that the sooner the Conference began the better, asked twice precisely when HMG thought the multilateral preparations could begin. *Sir Alec Douglas-Home* said that he did not think it mattered much in which month they began. They might begin in earnest when the United States elections were over.[5] As regards the agenda itself, HMG wanted one which allowed everyone to express their views on the subjects to which they attached importance.

5. *Mr. Gromyko* suggested that it was not enough to agree on the items of the agenda. There remained the question of the substance. *Sir Alec Douglas-Home* asked whether Mr. Gromyko wished to tackle the substance before the agenda. *Mr. Gromyko* replied that he was not talking about the preparations

[3] Cf. No. 94.

[4] Cf. Volume II, No. 13.

[5] The US Presidential Election was to be held on 7 November 1972.

for the Conference. *Sir Alec Douglas-Home* said that we should first have to identify certain themes. The Conference would need to set up committees to consider in more detail those matters which it appeared profitable to pursue. They could perhaps report back to the Conference, at a later stage. He did not see this Conference as the only one. *Mr. Gromyko* said that the shorter the Conference was the better. It was the final result which mattered. On substance it would be very good if representatives of the two Governments met for an exchange of views. *Sir Alec Douglas-Home* said that he would welcome this.

6. *Mr. Gromyko* noted that several representatives of HMG, whom he declined to specify, had spoken in a very unfriendly way about the Soviet Union and its foreign policy. The Soviet Government paid attention to this phenomenon. He asked why HMG continually impugned Soviet motives. A comparison between a number of articles on certain themes in the British press and in the Soviet press would be highly unfavourable to us.

7. *Sir Alec Douglas-Home* said that HMG was bound to recognise the facts of life. As our calm reaction to the Soviet treaty with India showed,[6] we did not criticise simply for the sake of criticism. But we were bound to react to Soviet policy in for instance the Eastern Mediterranean and Iraq.[7] The Soviet/Iraq Treaty had been followed by the nationalisation of our oil companies.[8] HMG's attitude was not unfriendly: it was simply that we saw the possibility of a clash of interests and felt it necessary to consider and interpret Soviet intentions as best we could. *Mr. Gromyko* said that if we did not understand Soviet intentions, why did we not go to the Soviet Government? If we had objections to what they were doing, we were at liberty to raise with them any questions we might wish to discuss. We were ascribing motives to the Soviet Government in the Mediterranean and the Middle East. Was this a good approach to relations?

8. *Sir Alec Douglas-Home* replied that Soviet policy was expansionist. As for public statements, not all the guilt was on one side. Soviet statements on Northern Ireland had been quite unacceptable (Mr. Gromyko claimed that there has been no Soviet official statement criticising HMG's policy in Northern Ireland). There was constant criticism of British imperialism, although the British Empire had long been a thing of the past.

9. *Mr. Gromyko* remarked that neither side was likely to change the other's philosophy. *Sir Alec Douglas-Home* repeated that he hoped that both sides would renew their efforts to improve bilateral relations using normal diplomatic channels. He stood by the 1970 Anglo-Soviet *communiqué*, agreed with Mr. Gromyko on his last visit to London, as a statement of objectives for Anglo-Soviet relations.[9] The practical problems of the approaching Conf-

[6] See No. 79, note 6.

[7] Cf. Appendix to this Volume, pp. 523-4.

[8] See p. 466. The Western-owned northern oilfields of the Iraq Petroleum Company were nationalised on 1 June 1972.

[9] See p. 267.

erence on European Security would provide the best subject on which to re-open bilateral consultations. *Mr. Gromyko* agreed.

10. *Sir Alec Douglas-Home* asked Mr. Gromyko why the Soviet Government had not responded to British proposals for the reactivation of the Geneva machinery.[10] *Mr. Gromyko* said that they had not favoured the proposal because it was unrealistic. HMG knew the reasons for this. It was no good pursuing the proposal unless everyone was prepared to accept it.

11. *Sir Alec Douglas-Home* referred to the Hess case[11] but Mr. Gromyko did not respond.[12]

[10] Cf. No. 94, note 13.

[11] See No. 64, note 6.

[12] Sir A. Douglas-Home commented in Berlin telegram No. 83 of 3 June that although Mr. Gromyko 'maintained the standard Soviet view that the responsibility for the current coolness in Anglo-Soviet relations rests entirely with HMG, his general attitude suggested a willingness to see our relations return to something nearer normality'. Sir J. Killick reported in Moscow telegrams Nos. 874 and 875 of 14 June a conversation the previous day with Mr. Lunkov, with whom he had discussed his impressions of the meeting in Berlin, drawing attention to Mr. Gromyko's remark 'that if we did not understand Soviet intentions in other areas we should go to the Soviet Government . . . How could we do this if I were not given interviews with e.g. Kuznetsov and Firyubin?' In telegram No. 359 to Moscow of 16 June the Secretary of State said that he, too, had been reflecting on Mr. Gromyko's remark, and instructed Sir J. Killick to seek an interview with Mr. Gromyko 'for a general discussion of our bilateral relations and of certain questions arising from our respective relations with third countries': see No. 100 below.

No. 99

Brief for Lord Eccles on Cultural Relations with the Soviet Union[1]

[ENS 9/2]

Restricted FCO, *16 June 1972*

General

1. Our cultural relations with the Soviet Union are defined by the agreement on relations in the 'scientific, educational and cultural fields', negotiated every two years and due for re-negotiation in Moscow in February 1973.[2] The British Council, which is HMG's agent in implementing the exchange programme, is not directly represented in the Soviet Union, as the Cultural Attaché is a Foreign Service appointment and the Assistant Cultural Attaché post, normally filled by the Council, has been vacant since their officer was expelled last year in retaliation for our own expulsion of the 105 Soviet officials.[3]

[1] This brief by Mr. Vines was prepared for the Paymaster-General with responsibility for the Arts, who was to attend a UNESCO conference from 19-28 June in Helsinki, at which Madame Furtseva would represent the Soviet Union.

[2] See p. 331, and Nos. 12, note 3 and 29.

[3] See Nos. 76 and 80, note 1.

Specialist cultural exchanges

2. In the educational and scientific fields, our relations with the Soviet Union were less affected than they might have been by the expulsion of the 105. Nevertheless, many Soviet organisations obviously received instructions to suspend action on proposals not already implemented and this inevitably led to delays in a variety of exchanges. However, outside the programme, things became more difficult for many individuals and organisations seeking exchanges outside those specifically covered by the agreement. For example, Bradford and Salford Universities whose efforts at direct exchanges seemed to be meeting with some slight success, have now been rebuffed.

Cultural manifestations

3. The most noticeable effect of Soviet displeasure towards HMG's policies has been in the cultural field, particularly the refusal of the Russians to allow their better musicians and dance companies to fulfil their contracts to appear in this country. They also cancelled the proposed Soviet design exhibition in London and showed complete disinterest in the proposed visit this autumn of Peter Brook's *Midsummer Night's Dream*. However, the Soviet Embassy has just confirmed the Soviet intention to go ahead with the festival of Russian music (*Days of Soviet Music*), planned for 7 to 30 November in London and various British cities and Mr. Hochhauser has received similar advice from Madame Furtseva. This is the return leg of a similar British event in Moscow last year.[4] The Cultural Agreement invites both Governments to encourage these events. In correspondence with Madame Furtseva about the successful days of British music in Moscow, the Prime Minister last year indicated his hope that he might see her in Britain for the Soviet musical days.[5]

4. Exchanges of film weeks do not figure so prominently in our official cultural programme with the Soviet Union as in those with other countries in Eastern Europe, primarily because the Russian industry is strong enough to make its own impact here. Our film producers are reluctant to cooperate with us in sending films to Moscow, where they are known to be copied illegally. Through its own resources, the National Film Theatre put on a week of Soviet films last year, and we are again in touch with the NFT and the Film Producers Association to see whether they are interested in seasons supported by FCO under the Exchange Agreement.

Talking Points

5. Lord Eccles will wish to express to Madame Furtseva our pleasure at the news that the Festival of Russian Music will go ahead this autumn and to remind Madame Furtseva that, as the Prime Minister said in his letter to her last year, we should be very pleased to see her in London for the event. He will also wish to suggest (as requested by the Prime Minister) that

---

[4] See No. 65. Mr. Vines minuted on 9 August that the decision to go ahead with the concerts was 'a significant indication that they are ready to return to more normal relations' (PW 7/303/5).

[5] *V. ibid.*, note 5.

Rostropovich should be allowed to perform at the Aldeburgh Festival.[6] The inability of Soviet artists to fulfil their contracts here has been difficult for our public to understand and made an unfortunate impression on them and our artists who do not see why cultural contacts should suffer just because governments cannot agree. The breaking of contracts only attracts adverse publicity and comment which is in no one's interest and has not helped to improve the Soviet cultural image.

6. Lord Eccles may also wish to express our disappointment that the Soviet authorities were unable to respond to our proposal to send to Moscow this autumn the Royal Shakespeare Company's production of *Midsummer Night's Dream*. He may also wish to refer to our wish to send a Turner exhibition to the Soviet Union next year and to invite Madame Furtseva's cooperation in making this possible.[7]

E.V. Vines

[6] This request had been passed on to Lord Eccles' office in a letter of 14 June 1972 from Mr. C.W. Roberts of Mr. Heath's Private Office, noting that 'the Soviet authorities have refused Rostropovich permission to come to England for this purpose'.

[7] In Helsinki telegram No. 323 of 21 June Mr. Ledwidge reported that Madame Furtseva had told Lord Eccles that she would 'use her best endeavours' to settle Rostropovich's appearance at the Aldeburgh Festival and that 'If her programme permits she will accept the Prime Minister's invitation to attend the Festival of Russian Music in November'. She had also invited Lord Eccles to Leningrad after the UNESCO conference but pressure of work meant that he had to decline.

No. 100

Sir J. Killick (Moscow) to FCO[1]

No. 980 Telegraphic [ENS 3/548/3]

Immediate. Confidential   MOSCOW, *30 June 1972, 9.15 a.m.*

Repeated Priority for information to UKDEL NATO, Washington and Paris.

Your telegrams Nos. 581 and 582: call on Gromyko.[2]

Gromyko received me for one and a half hours yesterday afternoon. His general attitude was friendly and constructive, and the conversation was very businesslike and without rancour. We talked mainly about the CESC (see m[y] i[mmediately] f[ollowing] t[elegram])[3] and MBFRs (my second

[1] Sir A. Douglas-Home was on an official visit to Bangladesh, Australia, New Zealand, Indonesia and Afghanistan from 22 June to 6 July.

[2] These telegrams of 22 June instructed Sir J. Killick on the line to take in his forthcoming interview with Mr. Gromyko: see No. 98, note 12.

[3] Not printed. Sir J. Killick and Mr. Gromyko discussed Soviet proposals for the CSCE to issue declarations on the inviolability of frontiers and the non-use of force, and Mr. Gromyko asked about HMG's attitudes towards the timing of the 'preparatory conference', prospects for an eventual second CSCE and the procedure to be adopted at the conference, including the possibility of a concluding 'meeting of statesmen at the highest level'.

i[mmediately] f[ollowing] t[elegram])[4], with a question on the world disarmament conference (my 3rd i[mmediately] f[ollowing] t[elegram])[5] and a
final exchange on wider problems including the meaning of 'peaceful
coexistence' and Soviet policy in Asia (my fourth i[mmediately] f[ollowing]
t[elegram]).[6] No specific problems on Anglo-Soviet relations were discussed,
and there was no mention of visas.

2. I began by referring to your conversation with Gromyko in Berlin[7] and
your exchanges with the Soviet Ambassador in London,[8] who, I pointed out,
had constant access to British Ministers (I made no other reference to the
problem of my calls here). I then referred to our proposal that Mr. Godber
should visit the Soviet Union,[9] and said that we did not regard this as a
substitute for a visit which you yourself still hoped to make to the Soviet
Union at some stage. You hoped in any case to see him in New York this
autumn. HMG would be glad to welcome leading members of the Soviet
Government or Party leadership to Britain whenever we received an
indication that such an invitation would be welcome.

3. Gromyko said that his conversation with you in Berlin had been very
brief, because of other commitments on both sides, but he had regarded it as
useful. It had been possible only to touch briefly on questions of substance, but
he thought that both sides had understood each other very well. It was
necessary now for both sides to take practical steps, both bilaterally and
multilaterally, including consultations on European questions. It remained to

[4] Not printed. Mr. Gromyko said the question of MBFRs 'should not be mixed up with the
CSCE . . . It required much time, attention and energy and was a very large scale problem in
itself. It would overload the CSCE.' Sir J. Killick agreed it was a complex subject but 'all
European countries were interested in the question and could presumably not be prevented from
raising it at CSCE'. Cf. Volume II, No. 9.

[5] Not printed. In reply to a question from Mr. Gromyko about HMG's attitude to a world
disarmament conference (see No. 67, note 11), which he noted had been referred to in the
communiqué issued after President Nixon's visit (see p. 474), Sir J. Killick replied that 'we were
very ready to consider this proposal if it looked like producing fruitful results, but that the
attitude at present of certain govts. whose participation would be essential did not seem to be
sufficiently positive to give hope of real progress'.

[6] Not printed: cf. No. 104 below. Sir J. Killick told Mr. Gromyko that 'Britain wanted peace
and stability in which her interests, and the interests of others, could prosper . . . We were
worried about Soviet purposes and intentions in the Indian Ocean area . . . Britain looked at
the world as a whole, and could not separate Europe from developments elsewhere . . . It would
be of advantage if our two governments could work together, in areas where this seemed
possible, with a view to creating the basis of mutual confidence which was still lacking.' Mr.
Gromyko replied that the Soviet Union 'had vital interests in Europe but was also an Asian
power . . . The concept that Britain had special rights and privileges in certain oceans and areas
still seemed, for some reason, to play a part in British thinking . . . it would be more useful to
concentrate on bringing our points of view together where we could, and not dwelling on points
of difference.' Sir J. Killick commented that the 'restrained tone of Gromyko's response was
quite striking, but should not encourage us to pile on the pressure on this front.'

[7] See No. 98.

[8] See No. 90, note 12.

[9] See No. 93.

be seen what steps the British side was prepared to take in practice. On the question of ministerial visits, he thought it was hardly appropriate to talk in concrete terms at this stage: time would put these specific matters into their proper place.[10] It would not be contrary to his wishes to meet with you in New York during the General Assembly.

4. Gromyko went on to say that you had told him in Berlin that you thought consultations on European problems, including a CESC, would reveal closer coincidence of views between our two positions than in other areas, and had suggested bilateral consultations on these questions. He had replied positively to this suggestion, and said that he regarded my visit as a development of the Berlin meeting as a beginning of concrete consultations. We then embarked on a discussion of European questions.

5. At the conclusion of our meeting, I mentioned with specific reference to his remark about bringing our points of view together, Parsons' wish to visit Moscow for a talk with Sytenko on Middle Eastern questions,[11] and said that we would be happy to invite Firyubin to visit London.[12] Gromyko said he sa[w] no obstacle in principle to these proposals, and we would be informed about a convenient time for such meetings.

6. Apart from our exchange on the Indian Ocean etc. (my fourth i[mmediately] f[ollowing] t[elegram])[13] Gromyko indulged in no real criticism of British attitudes and the tone of the conversation encouraged me to believe that he is now ready to continue a dialogue with us in the spirit of your talk with him in Berlin. There was no further reference to the need for 'proposals' from the British side. In other words, this is an important step forward in the return to normal, though the pace is still very much under Soviet control. I did not have time to pursue all the questions raised in my instructions, and there is plenty of scope for a further round, which might take place at Deputy Foreign Minister level. I will seek an opportunity of discussing future steps with Lunkov, who was present at today's conversation.[14]

[10] Sir J. Killick commented in Moscow telegram No. 985 of 30 June that he regarded these remarks 'as covering a Joint Commission meeting as well'.

[11] There had been little progress on either an interim or comprehensive Middle Eastern settlement since the beginning of 1972: cf. No. 87, note 11 and p. 466. On 27 April Mr. A.J.M. Craig, head of Near East and North Africa Department, minuted: 'we view the Arab/Israel situation with some gloom: the Israelis are tougher and more intransigent than ever. Sadat is weak and embittered, the Four Power talks are dead, Jarring is getting nowhere, the interim solution has come to a halt, the proximity talks have not g[o]t off the ground' (NE 3/304/1).

[12] Cf. No. 69.

[13] See note 6 above.

[14] In telegram No. 1 of 2 July sent to Moscow from Wellington, Sir A. Douglas-Home congratulated Sir J. Killick on his conduct of 'this very useful talk with Gromyko. I am studying it carefully and it could provide the basis for a more fruitful relationship. I am grateful for the way in which you handled this delicate affair.'

No. 101

Memorandum by Mr. Bullard on Anglo-Soviet Relations[1]
[ENS 3/548/3]

Confidential   FCO, [5] *July 1972*

Political

1. The Secretary of State has congratulated Sir J. Killick on his handling of the conversation with Mr. Gromyko on 29 June.[2] The exchange on the CSCE[3] did not add significantly to our knowledge of Soviet views, but the Russians showed themselves as forthcoming as they have with other Western interlocutors. The effect therefore was to put us back in the game. This will be particularly welcome to Sir J. Killick, after almost nine months during which he has had to rely mainly on his NATO colleagues for first-hand and up-to-date statements of the Soviet position. The conversation with Gromyko did not exhaust the 'European questions' which the Secretary of State and Mr. Gromyko agreed should be explored between us.[4] We shall be sending Sir J. Killick instructions on points arising from this conversation and there may subsequently be scope for a further exchange of views.[5] Disarmament Department are preparing separate instructions on the question of the World Disarmament Conference, which Gromyko also raised.[6]

2. Gromyko's remarks about non-European subjects were a good deal less encouraging. On the Indian Ocean, for example, he came fairly near to telling Sir J. Killick to mind his own business.[7] He certainly made it clear that the Soviet Union would continue to follow whatever policy it saw fit, there or in any part of the world. By implication, he reproached British Ministers for the tone of their public statements about the Soviet threat. I do not think we have anything to be ashamed of here, least of all since President Nixon's strong line at his press conference on 29 June. President Nixon said for example that you get something from Communist leaders only when you have something they want to get from you; and also that the Communist nations respect strength.[8] As we have said in the despatch on the Conference

---

[1] Mr. Bullard submitted this undated memorandum to Mr. Wiggin on 5 July, commenting that 'This may be a suitable moment to take stock of Anglo-Soviet relations, in the light of Sir J. Killick's talk with Mr. Gromyko [No. 100] and the break in the log-jam on visas' (see note 14 below).

[2] See No. 100, note 14.

[3] *Ibid.*, note 3.

[4] See No. 98.

[5] FCO telegram No. 646 to Moscow of 5 July commented on the questions regarding CSCE which Mr. Gromyko put to Sir J. Killick on 29 June. On 9 August the Ambassador had a further exchange on this subject with Mr. Lunkov.

[6] See No. 100, note 5.

[7] *Ibid.*, note 6.

[8] For President Nixon's remarks see *Public Papers: Nixon 1972*, pp. 705-18.

of Ambassadors, which is about to issue, there is no contradiction between plain talk about what Communist governments are actually doing and a sincere desire for better relations with Communist countries.[9]

3. Gromyko indicated that he had no objection to our proposals for official Anglo-Soviet conversations on the Middle East and South Asia.[10] It was left that 'we would be informed about a convenient time for such meetings'. If necessary, the Embassy will be able to check on progress.

4. In general it seems better to concentrate our talks with the Russians on fields where we have something to offer them, or at least something to contribute to the discussion. Talks about the world at large, in the light of Sir J. Killick's telegram No. 984,[11] seem destined to lead only to an agreement to disagree.

5. As regards bilateral relations, I think we should pursue these in whatever fields appear to hold possibilities, without trying to take the temperature too often. In particular, we should not press too eagerly the proposals which we have made for resumption of contact at Ministerial level, e.g. Mr. Godber's suggested visit in October[12] and a meeting of the Joint Commission under Mr. Davies.[13] Gromyko told Sir J. Killick that time would put these matters into their appropriate place. I take this to mean that the Russians are aware of our proposals and will respond to them when they think the moment is appropriate. Meanwhile we do not wish to appear in the attitude of supplicants or *demandeurs*. Paragraphs 12 to 15 below contain some suggestions about lines to pursue.

Visas

6. The long awaited exchange of visas took place on 4 July as agreed.[14] We gave the Russians 40 visas and they gave us 20. (The round figures are

[9] See No. 95, note 14.

[10] See No. 100.

[11] *V. ibid.*, note 6.

[12] See No. 93. On 10 July Mr. Godber directed that 'There should be no further mention of a visit by me unless and until the Russians raise the matter themselves.' Sir A. Douglas-Home agreed on 12 July that 'This posture is right.'

[13] See Nos. 87, note 8 and 93.

[14] On 8 June Mr. Bullard had minuted that the Secretary of State, following his meeting with Mr. Gromyko (see No. 100), wished 'to settle the visa problem without delay'. Mr. Bullard accordingly told Mr. Ippolitov later that day that the latter's proposals of 18 May (see No. 96, note 10) were acceptable, subject to a number of amendments to the list of FCO officials who required visas for the Soviet Union. On 27 June Mr. Filatov told Mr. Bullard that 'the Soviet side had considered the British proposals of 8 June, and was prepared to come some way to meet us', although two British visas were refused. In Moscow telegram No. 974 of 30 June Sir J. Killick commented that he did 'not see how we can hope to improve on the present deal in practical terms'; rejection 'would involve us in a further prolonged battle, in which the Russians would use every opportunity to turn British business and Parliamentary opinion against us, and it is difficult to see how such a course would bring a more satisfactory result than we may still hope for by accepting the present deal and returning to more normal visa procedures'. The Secretary of State agreed with this analysis, and on 30 June Mr. Bullard told Mr. Filatov that HMG accepted the Soviet proposals, and agreed to an exchange of visas on 4 July (ENS 3/548/1).

accidental, but it was recognised many months ago that the balance of numbers would be in the Soviet favour, owing to the greater size of the Soviet establishment in the UK, even since the expulsions.) The press naturally got hold of the story, and News Department have confirmed that the majority of outstanding visa applications on both sides have now been granted.

7. We now have to feel our way cautiously back to a normal state of affairs, i.e., one in which we ask for visas when we need them and the Russians do the same, and in which applications are treated as matters of routine and not of high policy. We have 19 Soviet applications already on our books, of which 11 have been processed and are ready for issue. The Russians have seven applications of ours, all of them more recent. We are proposing to issue three or four visas this week or next, as a signal to the Russians that we want to get back to normal procedures as soon as possible, and then to wait a little and see if they respond by issuing some of ours.[15]

8. The key question is whether we are going to be able to continue to keep out Soviet intelligence officers. As you know, the Russians nominated 14 such persons between December 1970 and May 1972. The tacit withdrawal of these 14 names was one of the two chief rewards of our patience during the last nine months, the other being Soviet acceptance of the fact and level of the ceilings imposed in September.[16] We assume that the Russians will in due course resume nominating intelligence officers for posts in London, but there is no clear evidence of this yet.

9. In the longer term, we have to recognise that we can be sure of keeping individual Russians out of Britain, but not of getting individual British officials into Moscow. The only way to keep Soviet intelligence officers out is to refuse visas and accept the risk that the Russians will refuse visas to our people in retaliation. Here it should be an advantage to have agreed with the Soviet Embassy that decisions on visa applications will in future be given within a month. It might in some cases be possible to apply for visas as soon as an officer is warned for a post in Moscow, in order to ensure that, if the Soviet decision is negative, he can be reposted before embarking on language and other training courses. The worst element in the present situation is the disturbingly long list of British officials trained in Soviet affairs and/or the Russian language who have now been effectively banned from serving in Moscow.[17] The implications in this are being examined with Research Department and P[ersonnel] O[perations] D[epartment].

[15] In a letter of 6 July Sir J. Killick sent Mr. Bullard 'our warm congratulations and thanks for the successful negotiation of Round One' of the visa war, and speculated that this, together with 'Gromyko's marked change of approach when I saw him on 28 [*sic*] June' (No. 100) and 'small signs of loosening on the cultural front' (see No. 99) was 'evidence that there really has been a fundamental change of policy on the Soviet side' (ENS 3/548/1).

[16] See No. 76.

[17] Mr. Wiggin minuted on 5 July that 'The one thing we cannot compromise on is the question of known Soviet intelligence agents. We may well therefore face prolonged difficulties on this. But it is safe to assume that the KGB are working flat out to introduce unidentified

Commercial

10. Lord Limerick flies to Moscow on 10 July to visit a large international industrial exhibition called Elektro '72 (at which more than 40 British firms are represented) and also to have talks with Soviet trade Ministers and officials.[18] The visit has been well prepared. Lord Erroll's group spied out the land in March and wrote an excellent and realistic report about the prospects (copy attached).[19] More recently ECGD have come very near agreement with the Russians on an exchange of letters by which we would offer a line of credit amounting to £150 million on terms equal to any available in Western Europe.[20]

11. Even if the ECGD agreement goes through, it does not follow that Soviet orders will result. There is no magic recipe for success in the Soviet market, which can only come through persistence and competitiveness in quality, delivery, price, etc. All that HMG can do is to ensure that British firms are not burdened with the handicap of a chilly political climate. Lord Limerick's visit should make an important contribution. He is intending to renew the invitation to Mr. Patolichev, the Soviet Minister of Foreign Trade, to visit London in the autumn. (This was one of the events cancelled by the Russians last year.) The hope is that the Russians will agree, and that the second meeting of the Anglo-Soviet Joint Commission may then take place in Moscow early in January 1973, i.e., exactly a year late.[21]

Cultural

12. Although the Russians seem to have now decided to proceed with the 'Days of Soviet Music' due to take place in Britain during the last three weeks of November,[22] they have still not got down to discussing detailed requirements with Victor Hochhauser, the impresario who is arranging this event. Nor are there any signs yet that eminent Soviet musical performers will be allowed to appear again in this country. Lord Eccles reminded Mme

agents into the Russian establishment here. To the extent that they succeed we may find the Russians relaxing their policy somewhat towards our experts!'

[18] Lord Limerick was Parliamentary Under Secretary for Trade: see No. 102 below for an account of his visit to Moscow.

[19] See No. 91, note 5.

[20] Following Lord Erroll's visit ECGD officials had held discussions in London and Moscow with STD and Ministry of Foreign Trade officials about the conclusion of a credit agreement covering trade worth £15om over a period of two years. On 5 July Mr. Godber wrote to the Chancellor of the Exchequer supporting a request from Mr. Davies to fix the rate of interest at 6% for the term of the agreement: 'from the political point of view I would certainly urge that we ought not to refuse a concession on interest rates which the French and Italians have already made. As you will perhaps have heard, we have recently turned a difficult corner in our political dealings with the Soviet Union, and these now seem set on a somewhat more favourable course than for some time past. It would be most unfortunate if this were followed almost immediately by a negative reply on the question of the interest rate, leading possibly to the collapse of the negotiations which ECGD have been conducting with the Russians over many weeks' (ENS 6/548/9).

[21] Cf. No. 80, note 1.

[22] See No. 99.

Furtseva, during the UNESCO conference in Helsinki, that Sir J. Killick was still awaiting an opportunity to call on her, and asked if she intended responding to the Prime Minister's letter of a year ago, in which he said he would be pleased to see her if she came to London for the 'Days of Soviet Music'. Lord Eccles received an encouraging reply on both counts.[23]

13. I think it would be worthwhile doing what we can to bring about a visit by Mme Furtseva. Although, on the whole, our relations with the Soviet Union in the educational and scientific fields have not been unduly affected by the events of last September, on the cultural front it has been a different story. If a visit by Mme Furtseva were to take place, I think that this would be a good indication that the Russians were prepared to let the flow of cultural events in both directions get back to normal. But we shall have to face the problem of anti-Soviet demonstrations, especially by Jewish organisations.

Other events

14. Now that Anglo-Soviet relations in general are on the up grade, it is possible to consider a variety of other events cancelled, postponed or put on ice since last September. I attach a check list of these.[24] You will note that the Russians have agreed to a meeting of the Maritime Commission in November: this is the first of the events cancelled last autumn to be reinstated.[25]

15. I suggest that we should now give a general green light on all these events, while accepting that the pace will be dictated by the Russians and that progress in some directions will be more rapid than in others.[26]

[23] *V. ibid.*, note 7.

[24] Not printed.

[25] A Soviet Delegation led by Mr. I.M. Averin, Head of the Foreign Relations Department of the Ministry of the Merchant Marine, visited London for the 4th session of the Joint British Soviet Maritime Commission, 13-14 November 1972 (ENS 21/4).

[26] Mr. Wiggin endorsed Mr. Bullard's recommendations in a minute of 5 July: 'I believe that barring untoward developments we can expect to see a distinct change in the Russian attitude towards major Ministerial visits before all that long. My own guess is that this could happen early next year. (I am sure that the Russians attach considerable political significance to our membership of the Community.)' Sir D. Greenhill minuted on 7 July: 'We are now in a reasonably satisfactory position provided Tsy and DTI agree on the credits.'

In a letter of 12 July Mr. Bullard informed Sir J. Killick that the Secretary of State approved the memorandum and 'you may therefore take this as a general guide'. In response to the Ambassador's speculation that a fundamental change in Soviet policy had occurred (see note 15), Mr. Bullard said: 'I think I should wish to examine Soviet motives more carefully before concluding that there has been anything beyond a tactical readjustment to reality on the Soviet side. One thing we can be certain of is that there has been no change of heart . . . It must have become increasingly apparent to the Soviet leadership that their resentful posture was becoming undignified and difficult to maintain . . . It is in this context that we are inclined to place Gromyko's major gesture towards you in responding so quickly to the understanding reached with the Secretary of State in Berlin . . . The important point is that the Russians stopped sulking and talked business to us before the visa settlement was reached' (PUSD).

No. 102

Sir J. Killick (Moscow) to Sir A. Douglas-Home

No. 1090 Telegraphic [ENS 6/548/8]

Immediate. Confidential   MOSCOW, *14 July 1972, 12 noon*

Repeated for information Routine to DTI (CREDA distribution), Mr. Gill, ECGD and Mr. Cotterell, ECGD.

Lord Limerick's visit[1]

1. Lord Limerick's visit to Moscow, as I had hoped, proved a useful further move forward in the restoration of Anglo-Soviet working relations.

2. The time which he devoted to Elektro-72,[2] particularly to visiting the stands of all the UK firms, the close and helpful interest which he took in their affairs and the special problems presented by the Soviet market, were greatly appreciated and will have given great encouragement to the British exhibitors. This alone which was the official purpose of the visit, fully justified it.

3. His official talks with the Russians were however also fruitful and revealing. It was clear from the outset that the Russians had taken a deliberate decision that a visiting Minister should not return to London simply with the impression that, following the visa settlement,[3] all was now set fair for a quick return to normal. Manzhulo[4] took the lead at a lunch at the Embassy on 11 July when, in conversation with Lord Limerick, he accused HMG of creating obstacles to good trading relations between the United Kingdom and the Soviet Union by cutting down Soviet trade representation in London, imposing anti-dumping duties or alternatively obliging the Soviet Union to price some of its products out of the UK market, going slow over liberalisation and being unhelpful over quotas, etc. He also implied that if we wished to grant credit it was only because it was in our interest to do so, that Anglo-Soviet trade was a matter of indifference to the Soviet authorities, and that we might accordingly reach what determinations we chose. This was very much the polemical Manzhulo who occasionally surfaces. In addition to the presumed general intention of his remarks suggested above, he may have considered that they would also help as part of a 'softening-up' process in relation to the annual Anglo-Soviet trade talks which start next week.[5]

[1] See No. 101: Lord Limerick visited Moscow from 10-13 July.

[2] *V. ibid.,* para. 10.

[3] *V. ibid.,* note 14.

[4] Deputy Minister in the Ministry of Foreign Trade since 1971.

[5] The Annual Anglo-Soviet Trade Review was held in the DTI from 18-20 July. Mr. F.W. Willis of EESD noted on 9 August that 'The Russians confined themselves to a repertoire of familiar themes—the expulsions, the staffing problems of the STD, quantitative restrictions, anti-dumping measures and the uncompetitiveness of British firms. They made no constructive suggestions for improvement in Anglo-Soviet trade (neither, to be fair, did the UK side), and their general approach suggested a desire to mark time defensively' (ENS 6/548/14).

4. The same theme, in a minor key, was taken up by Borisov[6] at the Chamber of Commerce and Industry, but he was inhibited by a poor brief and his position as official host. He spoke with no great conviction and it was not difficult to refute his arguments. Antonov, Minister for the electro-technical industry also touched on the general theme of Anglo-Soviet relations but spent more time on the alleged lack of interest displayed by UK firms in the possibilities of the Soviet market (blatantly contradicted, of course, by the size of our participation in Elektro-72). He asserted that contacts with UK firms were a matter of indifference to his ministry. The Soviet electrical industry was, he said, powerful and to a large extent self-sufficient, and there were in any case plenty of other foreign partners from which to choose.

5. I should add that the tone in which all these points were made was never sharp, and that they did not monopolise the discussions, the tenor of which was generally friendly. Borisov went out of his way to be personally amiable and Lord Limerick was both met and seen off at Moscow Airport by Prikhdodov, his senior deputy, and a party from the Chamber. Antonov readily agreed to discussions between his ministry's experts and UK exhibitors.

6. The two meetings with Alkhimov were in a category of their own in so far as they focussed on the credit issue.[7] At the first meeting, on 11 July, which he took over at short notice from Manzhulo, he gave the impression of being a rather harassed man and there can be little doubt that the US credit issue is weighing heavily on him.[8] Lord Limerick's willingness to get down to concrete detail appeared to take him, moreover, completely by surprise and this led him to react, presumably for defensive reasons, somewhat negatively.[9] At the second meeting, on 12 July, held at very short notice at his own request, he had fully regained his composure and was commendably brief and businesslike. It was soon apparent that a decision had been taken that he should visit London next week, first to tackle the bankers on their sundry commissions and charges, and secondly to sign an agreement. For the text of the letter which Lord Limerick handed to him see my CREDA 89.[10] He

[6] Chairman of the Chamber of Commerce and Industry.

[7] See No. 101, note 20.

[8] Mr. Alkhimov was involved in US-Soviet negotiations for a trade agreement, foreshadowed in the *Communiqué* of 29 May issued after President Nixon's visit (cf. pp. 474-5): agreement on Russian repayment of Lease-Lend debts was central to the negotiations.

[9] Telegram No. 666 to Moscow of 10 July informed Lord Limerick that the Chancellor of the Exchequer had agreed to a credit agreement with an interest rate fixed for two years (cf. No. 101, note 20). Lord Limerick proposed to Mr. Alkhimov on 11 July that an immediate agreement be concluded on this basis, subject to a minimum of £50m worth of orders being placed in the first year of the agreement. Mr. Alkhimov, who appeared 'increasingly ill at ease', asked whether Lord Limerick would be available for a further meeting: the latter replied that he 'would be happy to give Mr. Alkhimov time to reflect and to meet with him again' (notes for the record of Lord Limerick's visit, 25 July).

[10] Not printed. On 12 July Mr. Alkhimov indicated that the principle of a target for the amount of business to be transacted in the first year of the agreement was acceptable. He subsequently visited London from 19-20 July for discussions about bank charges on the credit and

made no more than a token attempt to resist the inclusion of the sum of £50m worth of contracts (which, after discussion[,] Lord Limerick suggested as an opening bid) as the qualifying figure for leaving the interest rate pegged for the second year. At this meeting he was careful to observe the usual courtesies by stressing that the M[inistry] of F[oreign] T[rade] was very much at Lord Limerick's disposal if there was anything which they could arrange to make his stay in Moscow more pleasant.

7. The State Committee for Science and Technology were represented at my lunch by a very affable Pronsky. I deliberately sought no interview for Lord Limerick with the SCST but invited Gvishiani to lunch, leaving the initiative for a business talk with them. They did not take it. Lord Limerick spoke to Pronsky along the lines of points A, B and C of paragraph 5 of my letter to Julian Bullard of 7 July.[11] The following day unheralded, Pronsky led a delegation of four, including Chuev, on a detailed tour of the UK Pavilion, which ended with drinks with Lord Limerick at the bar. The intention was, no doubt, to underline the role of the SCST in all technological questions. But in a long conversation with Cox, he seemed very pleased that the green light had been given for his visit to London and said he looked forward to a normalisation of relations. He did not mention the Joint Commission, but, in a separate conversation, Chuev tried hard to convince Quentin Davies[12] that it was up to the UK side to reinstate the second meeting, or at least to indicate a desire to meet. (For my money, this is a desirable situation which should be allowed to continue to have its effect.) Pronsky agreed that discussions with both HMG and the CBI would be useful and said that he hoped it would be possible to call on a number of UK firms. He added that Gvishiani also hoped to visit Lord Zuckermann in London in September and that their visits might coincide.

8. Lord Limerick's final engagement was with Pavlienko, the Director of Moscow's proposed new permanent exhibition and trade centre which is to be built over the next few years at Krasnaya Presnaya. It was very much a sales pitch for the building of a UK pavilion, qualified, of course, by the statement that we were not being pressed to participate. (Despite this, he pressed me generally on the subject at a reception last night and was concerned to regard my expression of non-committal interest as 'positive'.) The project has implications for our commercial representation in Moscow. Details and comment will follow by bag.[13]

signed the agreement on 19 July with Lord Limerick, who announced its conclusion in a speech to the Russo-British Chamber of Commerce on 20 July: see Watt and Mayall, 1972, pp. 519-23.

[11] In para. 5 of this letter on future relations with the SCST, Sir J. Killick drew attention to the tendency of the SCST to try and keep HMG out of Anglo-Soviet technological discussions by involving e.g. the CBI. It was important to 'stress that it is <u>HMG</u> who have reached the determination to allow the Agreement on Technological Cooperation to run on for another five years, indicate that <u>HMG</u> would welcome a visit by Pronsky to London . . . ensure that <u>HMG</u> are closely involved, alongside the CBI, in arrangements for the visit' (ENS 6/548/6).

[12] Second Secretary at HM Embassy in Moscow.

[13] Not printed.

9. Overall there was a noticeable mellowing in the Soviet attitude during the course of Lord Limerick's visit as practical considerations asserted themselves over the set pieces which his contacts had been instructed to rehearse. They will be content, I suspect, to report that they carried out their instructions. Having done so, they in fact got down to 'business as usual'. Alkhimov's proposed visit to London is a positive achievement, made possible by the Chancellor of the Exchequer's timely agreement to the pegging of the interest rate, for which we were all most grateful. It has opened the way to yet another step in the restoration of Anglo-Soviet relations. I think it is important that Alkhimov should be entertained at as high a level as possible, and it could prove useful to have a more general discussion of credit problems with him. As I understand it, the Soviet Government is now committed to spend on foodstuffs alone in the next twelve months $250 million under the US grain deal,[14] $330m cash on Canadian grain and $250m on sugar from Brazil.

10. I was not able to clear foregoing with Lord Limerick before his departure. You may wish to seek his comments.

11. Please pass advance copy to Lord Limerick and also ensure that Cox is given a copy first thing Monday.[15]

[14] The Soviet and US Governments signed an agreement in Washington on 8 July for the Soviet Union to purchase at least $750 million worth of US grains between 1 August 1972 and 31 July 1975, with a commitment to spend at least $200 million in the first year of the deal. The FCO showed some surprise that the Russians had made an agreement of such size on commercial terms apparently favourable to the Nixon Administration in an election year, but in a letter to Mr. Fall of 20 July Mr. Crowe reported information from the CIA Office of Economic Research which indicated 'that the answer is less of a mystery to the Americans (and with less in the way of political implications) than I had thought . . . in the American view the short fall in Soviet grain production both this year and in coming years will be of sizeable proportions . . . The Americans have no doubt that the Russians need the grain badly and this is borne out by the as yet unconfirmed but no doubt accurate report . . . that the Russians have bought for delivery within the next few months . . . four million tons of wheat and five million tons of maize worth $500 million. This is already two-thirds of the $750 million the Russians are committed to buying under the Grain Agreement over 3 years, and represents the total amount of credit outstanding which they are allowed' (ENS 6/304/1).

[15] Mr. Cox was returning to London for the annual trade talks (see note 5 above).

No. 103

Letter from Sir J. Killick (Moscow) to Mr. Walden

[*ENS 3/548/6*]

Restricted   MOSCOW, *3 August 1972*

Dear George,

Call on Promyslov

1. I called on 31 July on Promyslov, Chairman of Mossoviet.[1] Though *Tass* subsequently reported that the call was made at my own request, I had in fact made no specific request beyond including Promyslov's name in a list of still unsatisfied applications for first calls which I recently left with the MFA. However, Mossoviet gave a mammoth reception on 13 July for the participants in Elektro-72,[2] and I made a point of introducing myself to Promyslov and saying I looked forward to calling on him some time. We had a very friendly talk, and his office took the initiative in offering the appointment.

2. I had expressed interest at the reception in urban problems, the human environment etc. At my call, Promyslov did not draw breath for 40 minutes after my arrival, treating me to a wide-ranging dissertation on the City Plan, transport, water supply, environmental problems and the creeping menace of hippyism. I was interested that he repeatedly emphasised that the City Plan did not envisage the indefinite expansion of Moscow's population; the existing shortfall in labour supply was to be met in the short run by better use of the existing labour reserves (including women and old-age pensioners) and in the long term by increased automation; industry and housing in Moscow were both to remain at roughly their present level while being wholly reconstructed and greatly improved in terms of quality. This was all in strong contrast with the attitudes which I encountered during my calls on senior city officials in Tashkent and Samarkand last week,[3] where the standard response to my enquiry whether the towns intended to set any limit to their own expansion was blank incomprehension accompanied by a stream of statistics demonstrating the unbounded fertility of Uzbek women. Promyslov was at pains also to emphasise the relevance of the experience of the great capitalist cities to Moscow, saying several times that the problems of London and Tokyo today would be the problems of Moscow in five years' time unless suitable action was taken. He illustrated his plans for limitation of the car population in the city centre and the development of public transport. He was fully alive to the problem of water supply and water pollution. He had

[1] Mossoviet was the authority responsible for the administration of the city of Moscow.

[2] See Nos. 101 and 102.

[3] Sir J. Killick toured Uzbekistan from 21-29 July to acquaint himself with 'the conditions of life in a non-Russian part of the Soviet Union'. During his trip, reported to London in a letter to Mr. Walden of 19 October (ENS 25/3), he held meetings with the Uzbek Vice Foreign Minister, Mr. Mirzamukhamedov, and officials from the *Gorispolkom* in Samarkand and Tashkent.

personally flown in a helicopter through a several hundred kilometre radius round the city to locate sources of expanded water supply. He seemed markedly less sure that he could cope with hippies, beyond the provision of more restaurants and cafés.

3. I finally took the opportunity of a momentary pause in the flow of Promyslov's rhetoric to raise, before making my escape, questions connected with the GLC's intended invitation to a Mossoviet delegation to visit London in the near future. I have written separately on this subject to Vines in Cultural Exchange Department and have copied the letter to you.[4]

4. Promyslov is an impressive chap—genuinely proud of his achievements and concerned to emphasise the magnitude of his—and Mossoviet's—task. Not to mention his—and its—importance, the size of the budget, and so on. He is still much wedded to the idea of joint meetings of the Mayors of Moscow, London, Paris, New York and Tokyo—put into his mind during the last GLC visit to Moscow in 1971,[5] and mentioned by him during my predecessor's farewell call on him in August last year.

5. I think it right to regard the fact of this call, and the atmosphere and substance of it, as a not insignificant indicator in the process of returning to normal working relations.

Yours ever,
JOHN KILLICK

[4] Not printed. On 4 July Mr. A. Peterson, Director General and Clerk to the GLC, wrote to Sir D. Greenhill to ask if he saw any difficulties in an invitation to Mr. Promyslov. Sir D. Greenhill replied positively, but although Mr. Peterson spoke to Mr. Filatov on the subject no dates were fixed and it was agreed that the invitation would be renewed after the GLC elections in April 1973 (PW 9/303/3).

[5] Mr. D. Plummer, Leader of the GLC, had made this suggestion to Mr. Promyslov during the visit by a delegation from the GLC to Moscow from 9-16 April 1971 (PW 9/303/6 of 1971).

The next document, on 'Peaceful Co-existence', seeks, rather like the analysis of the Brezhnev Doctrine printed as No. 62, to probe the inner meaning of phraseology employed regularly and confidently by Soviet spokesmen but regarded as potentially threatening or at best as deliberately misleading by FCO officials and Ministers. 'Peaceful co-existence' was considered especially pernicious, as it had positive connotations which appealed to public perception, but carried with it the unavoidable sub-text of 'ideological struggle'. Both the Brezhnev Doctrine and 'Peaceful Co-existence' seemed to the FCO to be different ways of saying that the Soviet Government reserved the right to interfere in other countries' internal affairs.

No. 104

Letter from Sir J. Killick (Moscow) to Mr. Tickell[1]
[WDW 1/1]

Confidential   MOSCOW, *4 August 1972*

My dear Crispin,

Peaceful Co-existence

1. I have been following with interest the argument in the NATO Political Committee about the inclusion of the phrase 'peaceful co-existence' in the Nixon/Brezhnev Declaration of Principles,[2] which was the subject of Justin Staples's letter 2/1 of 7 July to Rodric Braithwaite.[3] I fully share the concern of various NATO Governments (including our own) that this phrase should be treated with great caution; but I am a little worried that we may be in danger of putting ourselves in a disadvantageous tactical and public position unless we are equally careful about the manner in which we express our opposition in the CSCE context to the concept of 'peaceful co-existence' as the basis for relations between European states. I have in mind in particular the formulation in paragraph 5 of FCO tel[egram] No. 581 of 22 June to Moscow (not repeated to all).[4] The points in this paragraph are entirely valid in themselves, and suitable for use in bilateral debate with the Russians which of course was the context of the telegram under reference, in which I have already used them. But I think there may be a risk that, if we use this sort of argument publicly in an effort to discredit the concept, we shall unnecessarily provoke accusations of 'out-dated cold war attitudes' from British and European public opinion as well as from Soviet propaganda. This is liable to be counter-productive.

2. As I have said, I fully agree that the phrase 'peaceful co-existence' as used by the Russians is a fraud and should be exposed as such. The fact that the phrase itself was coined by the Russians (unlike 'democracy', 'cold war', 'arms race', 'positions of strength' etc. which are Western concepts distorted by the Russians for their own use) does not make this task any easier; and we

---

[1] Mr. C.C.C. Tickell was Head of Western Organisations Department (WOD).

[2] See p. 474.

[3] In this letter of 7 July Mr. Staples (Counsellor and Head of Chancery at UKDEL NATO) reported that in meetings of the Council and Political Committee on 14 June and 4 July respectively there had been criticisms of the inclusion of the term 'peaceful co-existence' in the Declaration of Principles and *Communiqué* issued after Mr. Nixon's visit to Moscow, on the grounds that it would complicate NATO's task in drawing up a proposed Declaration of Principles to be tabled at the CSCE.

[4] See No. 100, note 2. Sir J. Killick had been instructed that in his forthcoming conversation with Mr. Gromyko he 'should be careful not to imply blanket endorsement of the principles in the US-Soviet Declaration, which contain a number of points which may cause difficulty to us and to the Alliance. The most important of these is the reference to peaceful coexistence . . . Both in the bilateral and the multilateral context, I wish to see substituted for ideas based on ideological conflict the principle of mutually advantageous co-operation' (ENS 3/548/3).

must face the fact that, in the public mind in Western countries, 'peaceful co-existence' is a Good Thing because it is simplistically contrasted with war or the threat of war, and with the policies of bullying, bluster and open pressure which have characterized Soviet European policies in the past. To oppose 'peaceful co-existence' *tout court* can therefore very easily appear to the man in the street (or on the back benches of the House of Commons) as equivalent to being opposed to *détente*. What is needed is to try to capture the concept for ourselves by endorsing it in our own definition and illustrating its practical application in to-day's world (not yesterday's) by the Russians. I would like to hope that HMG would not need to undertake this task alone and unaided, nor even as the principal spokesman of NATO.

3. The root of the trouble, of course, is that the Russians define peaceful co-existence in different ways for different purposes, while at the same time defining 'aggression' 'imperialism' etc. in similar fashion so as to justify their own breaches of the principle. A great deal has been written on the subject in the Soviet press in recent months, and I enclose an anthology (by no means exhaustive) of some of the more striking recent statements.[5] The Arbatov article of 21 June (No. 11 in the enclosure) is unique, and ought to provide a good basis for demonstrating that the Russians do not practise what they preach. Three points of interest emerge from this anthology:

(*a*) While the standard formulation is 'peaceful co-existence between states with different social systems', there are variations from this norm; for example, the Soviet/Yugoslav communiqué of 11 June (No. 20 in the enclosure)[6] refers to 'peaceful co-existence of states *regardless* of their social systems', a formula which has appeared from time to time and to which the Yugoslavs in particular clearly attach importance; and an article by Matveyev on 5 July (No. 14 in the enclosure) takes a somewhat defensive line in refuting bourgeois allegations that peaceful co-existence is 'selective', and implies that it applies to 'all countries and peoples, big and small'. It is clearly important, that we should do our best to exploit this discrepancy and argue that 'peaceful co-existence' in our definition should apply, e.g. to Soviet-Czech as well as Soviet-British relations; but we cannot do this if we reject the concept altogether. This seems to be the essence of the American defence of its inclusion in the Principles.

(*b*) In their constant repetition of the view that peaceful co-existence should be accompanied by 'ideological struggle', it is striking that the Russians tend to adopt a defensive rather than an offensive tone; they seem at times much more concerned about the risk of contamination by 'Western bourgeois ideology' than with the opportunities for Communist subversion of the West which might be offered by a general atmosphere of *détente* (see items 6, 10, 13 and 15-18 of the enclosure). Since we are ourselves (I hope) confident that the consequence of genuinely free exchanges of ideas and persons between East and West would be the

[5] Not printed. The article by Mr. Arbatov appeared in *Izvestiya*.

[6] Issued following an official five-day visit to Moscow by President Tito of Yugoslavia.

infinitely greater attractive force of our own social system and way of life, it is not entirely consistent for us simply to complain that 'peaceful co-existence' involves 'ideological struggle'; the latter will of course go on whether we accept the concept of peaceful co-existence or not, and what concerns us is that competition (rather than 'struggle') between the ideologies and social systems should take place on a fair and equal basis. We can argue this, I should have thought, more effectively within the concept of peaceful co-existence than from outside it.

(*c*) While we can, of course, legitimately complain among ourselves that Soviet support for 'national liberation struggles' (see items 1-8 and 18 in the enclosure) ought to be incompatible with 'peaceful co-existence', this again is an argument which we must deploy with care if we are not to be accused of opposing 'national liberation struggles' as such. Here again, Soviet 'anti-colonialist' and subversive activity can be expected to continue to give us trouble whether we accept the concept of 'peaceful co-existence' or not, and we ought to put ourselves in the position of being able to argue that peaceful co-existence is Good but that interference in internal affairs and subversion are not only Bad, but incompatible with the concept. We are then much better placed to expose and counter Soviet exploitation of their distortion of the term 'national liberation struggles' to camouflage subversion.

4. What this adds up to, I think, is a suggestion that we should take a leaf out of the Russians' book. The Russians do not say that they are opposed to 'democracy', 'freedom', 'self-determination of peoples' or even 'free exchanges of ideas'. They simply accept these concepts and re-define them for their own purposes. We ought perhaps to consider ways in which we can do the same to them with their phrase 'peaceful co-existence', so that it may return to plague the inventor. Instead of marshalling arguments for its exclusion from CSCE documents we might rather be working out tactics designed to put the Russians on the defensive by evolving more satisfactory formulae based on the use of the term, and by demonstrating that they themselves are not practising it. In other words, instead of being defensive and running scared, let us mount a counter-offensive.

J.E. KILLICK

P.S. It seems to me that one ought not to make the suggestion I have put forward above without offering some idea of how to put it into effect. The sort of formula I have in mind would be:

'Peaceful coexistence, based on the principles of sovereignty, equality, mutual advantage, non-interference in internal affairs, respect for the legitimate rights and interests of all states, and self-determination for all peoples; and universally applicable to all states regardless of their social systems.'[7]

J.E.K.

[7] Mr. Braithwaite noted at this point: 'I would like to add "or political affiliations".' This letter provoked some debate in the FCO, leading Sir T. Brimelow to ask on 23 September: 'Should it not be our line that the time has come to re-define the concept of "peaceful

coexistence?'" Mr. Bullard, however, in an undated minute, said that 'there can be no doubt that acceptance by the West of a declaration including the phrase "peaceful coexistence" . . . would be seized upon by the Russians as proof that everybody in the West has accepted the philosophy of "peaceful coexistence" as Soviet spokesmen have never ceased to define it, i.e. the dogma that there are two systems in the world and that the relationship between them is and must always be one of struggle.' Nevertheless, in a letter of 2 November to Mr. Tickell, Mr. Graham, Counsellor at HM Embassy in Washington since October 1972, said that the White House and State Department had made it clear that if the question of referring to "peaceful coexistence" arose in future they 'would see no difficulty in accepting the phrase provided it was satisfactorily defined'.

No. 105

Minute from Mr. Walden to Mr. Daunt[1]

[ENS 3/548/3]

Confidential   FCO, *25 August 1972*

Anglo-Soviet relations

1. The upturn in Anglo-Soviet relations has become more marked. We are talking to the Russians more frequently and at a higher level. Sir J. Killick has had another exchange of views, this time with the Acting Soviet Foreign Minister, Kuznetsov, on foreign policy questions including the CSCE.[2] The Russians have proposed that Lunkov, the Head of the Western European Department in the Soviet MFA, should visit London to discuss the CSCE. We are trying to arrange a date when we can get together a full team.[3] There has still however been no invitation to Mr. Godber, although he dined

[1] This minute was evidently prepared for Sir D. Greenhill's return from leave: a copy was also sent to Mr. Bullard.

[2] Mr. Gromyko was on leave. Mr. Kuznetsov received Sir J. Killick on 16 August for a general discussion of CSCE (cf. Volume II, No. 13, note 6), the Middle East, South Asia, Indochina and Anglo-Soviet relations: they agreed on the desirability of further exchanges of view on areas of common interest. The Ambassador reported in Moscow telegram No. 1253 of 16 August that the 'atmosphere was friendly and relaxed, and we had a business-like conversation which lasted some 45 minutes'.

[3] In a letter to Sir D. Greenhill of 25 August Sir J. Killick commented that he was 'a little surprised at the suggestion that Lunkov should come to London but he is, after all, only a senior official so probably no loss of face is involved on the Soviet side . . . Lunkov's visit . . . may also be designed to establish that British attitudes on certain matters of substance (not only related to CSCE) are satisfactory before moving on to the next stage. What these matters of substance may be I can only guess . . . the Soviet Foreign Ministry may not appreciate that they are creating a bad impression by playing things this way. However, while we are fully agreed, both in London and Moscow, that we ought not to be running after the Russians, I think it would no less be wrong to let them see that their way of doing things is getting under our skin. If things are, as they seem to be, moving in the right direction, it is the end result which matters, and not the means by which we get there (provided no sacrifice of principle or policy on our part is involved).' Mr. Lunkov's visit was subsequently arranged for 15-20 September: see Volume II, No. 14.

with the Soviet Ambassador again on 14 August.[4] The Duke of Edinburgh's visit to Moscow may take place in 1973, and has been mentioned by the Ambassador to the Russians.[5]

2. Some progress has also been made in other fields: a Parliamentary exchange is likely to take place later this year;[6] the Russians have agreed to discuss the next Joint Commission meeting;[7] and an important Soviet technical Delegation is to visit Farnborough at the invitation of the Electrical Engineering Association.[8]

3. Visits to Moscow by Messrs. Callaghan, Thorpe and four Labour MPs were unspectacular.[9] Mr. Callaghan showed signs of succumbing to Russian pressure on spies and the size of the STD, and we are recommending that, in debriefing him, the Secretary of State should consider showing him some convincing material in his capacity as a Privy Councillor.[10] Mr. Callaghan is also likely to press for institutionalised and officially financed Parliamentary exchanges with the Russians.

4. Meanwhile however we continue to be dogged by problems on the Security/Intelligence front. Both sides have been gradually clearing up the backlog of visas, but we are now faced with one clearly objectionable application, and are considering recommending counter-retaliation against Soviet MFA officials, if, as we fear, the Russians refuse a visa to a British expert on Soviet affairs in reply to our refusal of a visa to the Soviet official in question.[11] Two Soviet Intelligence Officers were also detected *in flagrante* in

[4] Cf. No. 101, note 12.

[5] The Duke of Edinburgh was considering accepting an invitation extended on 30 April 1972 by the National Equestrian Federation of the USSR.

[6] See No. 93. On 18 August Mr. Zhukov had suggested to Sir Fitzroy Maclean, President of the GB/USSR Association, that the Anglo-Soviet Parliamentary Group should invite a group of Soviet parliamentarians to visit the UK.

[7] The possibility of holding a meeting of the Joint Commission in the first half of 1973 was due to be discussed during Mr. Pronsky's visit to London, subsequently arranged for 8-17 October (cf. No. 102, note 11).

[8] The Farnborough Air Show was held from 4-10 September.

[9] Mr. Callaghan, Opposition Spokesman on Foreign Affairs and Mr. T. McNally, head of the Labour Party's International Department, visited Moscow and Leningrad from 7-13 August; Mr. J. Thorpe, Leader of the Liberal Party, visited Moscow and Leningrad from 27 July to 2 August; MPs Mr. C. Morris, Mr. E. Deakins, Mr. N. Kinnock and Mr. G. Strang visited Moscow and a number of provincial cities from 8-16 August (ENS 3/548/12).

[10] Sir J. Killick reported in a letter to Sir T. Brimelow of 11 August that Mr. Callaghan had told Mr. Vasev on 9 August that he 'would be willing to advocate an increase in the staff of the STD in return for an assurance from the Soviet Government that the STD would not engage in espionage' (ENS 3/548/12). It appears that the Secretary of State was not able to arrange a meeting to discuss this question with Mr. Callaghan (PUSD records).

[11] In Moscow telegram No. 1319 of 29 August, addressed to Sir T. Brimelow, Sir J. Killick agreed that 'we must now soon make it clear to the Russians that refusal of visas to qualified staff for this Embassy, in retaliation for our exclusion of KGB officers, is intolerable and will in future lead to retaliation on our side against genuine Soviet MFA officials . . . Our objective, as I see it, must be to provide those elements in the Soviet Foreign Ministry (and hopefully elsewhere) who are interested in developing relations with us with the best possible case for

Hong Kong, and we agreed with the Acting Governor's request to leak the story to the press to relieve pressure on the Hong Kong Government to allow easier entry to Soviet and East European citizens. We ourselves protested at desk level, but have sought to leave Hong Kong to make the running.[12]

G.G.H. WALDEN

overriding the arguments of the KGB. From this point of view I agree that Lunkov's visit to London provides an excellent opportunity for putting across the message . . .' (ENS 3/548/1).

[12] Mr. Daunt minuted on 29 August: 'Thank you: the PUS has seen this minute . . .'

The next document reflects ongoing Soviet sensitivity in regard to the Katyn Massacre (see No. 69, note 5)—an issue which was to remain a point of contention in bilateral relations between Britain and the Soviet Union until the latter finally admitted responsibility for the massacre in 1990.

No. 106

Sir J. Killick (Moscow) to Sir A. Douglas-Home

No. 1438 Telegraphic [ENP 10/1]

Priority. Confidential   MOSCOW, *13 September 1972, 2.55 p.m.*

Repeated Saving to Warsaw.

Katyn Massacre

1. I was summoned at short notice by Kozyrev, Deputy Foreign Minister, this afternoon to receive an oral communication (text in m[y] i[mmediately] f[ollowing] t[elegram])[1] expressing the hope that HMG would take all appropriate measures to prevent the erection of a memorial in London to the victims of the Katyn Massacre.[2]

2. I undertook to forward this to you, but said that it was implicit in the wording of Kozyrev's statement that he understood that this was not a

[1] Not printed.

[2] See No. 89, note 13. On 6 June Mr. Neave and Lord Barnby told Sir A. Douglas-Home that they hoped to gain the permission of the Royal Borough of Kensington and Chelsea to erect the memorial, for which £2000 had so far been raised, in the Borough. In a submission of 11 July Mr. Bullard said 'I see no reason why HMG should authorise a monument to the victims of Katyn rather than to those of any other atrocity which occurred in a foreign country during the War, or indeed at any other time. In fact I see it simply as a question whether or not we wish to create a gratuitous irritant in our relations with both Poland and the Soviet Union, with effects that could well last for a long time.' Sir D. Greenhill minuted on the submission on 14 July that 'I would hope that the D[epartment] O[f the] E[nvironment] could block the Kensington scheme and the sponsors could be persuaded to go for a Polish church or cemetery . . . perhaps the site of the Polish Air Force memorial at Northolt could be used'. Mr. Royle, however, thought it unwise to intervene with the local authority: 'we will be involved in a major political row when our action is inevitably leaked to the press' (note on minute of 17 September by Mr. Bullard).

matter within the direct responsibility of HMG, and it was therefore impossible for me to say whether the Soviet Government's hope could be fulfilled. I was not informed of the details, but my personal impression was that the authors of the proposal to erect a memorial were concerned not to pursue aims hostile to the Soviet Union but to establish the true facts of an historical event. Kozyrev said that unfortunately this was not so: certain people had fanned up specifically anti-Soviet propaganda with the aim of fixing the blame for this Nazi crime on the Soviet Union. If HMG wished to take appropriate steps to prevent this, they could of course do so. They were well aware of the true facts of the case: Mr. Eden had made a statement about it in the House of Commons at the time.[3] As an experienced Ambassador I could surely imagine the reaction of the British public if someone in a foreign country tried to pretend that British airmen killed in the war were the victims of their own government and not of the Germans. The Soviet public might be expected to react very strongly against the proposed memorial, and it could not but damage Anglo-Soviet relations.

3. I said that Mr. Smirnovsky, as an experienced Ambassador in London, was no doubt as concerned as I was to avoid damage to bilateral relations, and would be aware of the reaction of the British public to the presentation of events in Northern Ireland by the Soviet Press, which were a travesty of the true facts. I recalled that an ugly cartoon about Ulster had been published in *Izvestiya* on the very day on which I presented my credentials.[4] (Mr. Kozyrev intervened to say that it was quite inappropriate to connect the two things: the events in Northern Ireland attracted the attention of the world press, and he knew from his reading of the latter that Soviet press reports added nothing to what was really happening in Northern Ireland, and were entirely objective.) I continued that we had never made official representations on this subject, because we had assumed that the Soviet Government would maintain that this was something outside their competence. If I were to express the hope that the Soviet Government would take appropriate measures to avoid damage to our relations by such press reports, I would no doubt get the same answer as I had just given to Kozyrev.

4. Kozyrev said that the question he had raised was not one of mere press stories, but of actions and decisions by local authorities in London. If we were really anxious to improve relations, we must be careful not to poison the

[3] In the House of Commons on 4 May 1943 Mr. A. Eden, Secretary of State for Foreign Affairs, referred to 'the cynicism which permits the Nazi murderers of hundreds of thousands of innocent Poles and Russians to make use of a story of mass murder, in an attempt to disturb the unity of the Allies . . . His Majesty's Government have no wish to attribute blame for these events to anyone except the common enemy' (*Parl. Debs.*, 5th ser., H. of C., vol. 389, cols. 30-31). Cf. also FCO History Note No. 10, *The Katyn Massacre: an SOE Perspective*, p. 6.

[4] Cf. No. 76, note 5.

atmosphere. Better relations involved efforts on both sides. At this I took my leave to go to another appointment.[5]

[5] It was agreed that Sir T. Brimelow should give an oral reply to this *démarche* to Mr. Lunkov on 19 September (cf. No. 105, note 3), but telegram No. 993 to Moscow of 27 September reported that Sir T. Brimelow had been able to mention the matter only briefly and informally. Sir A. Douglas-Home instructed Sir J. Killick to inform the Soviet Government orally that 'HMG have certain powers in relation to the erection of monuments in public place[s], but these do not extend to land owned by private individuals, institutions or local authorities': the message was delivered to Mr. Vasev on 29 September. The Katyn Memorial, inscribed with the date 1940, was unveiled on 18 September 1976 in Kensington Cemetery.

No. 107

Record of conversation between Sir A. Douglas-Home and Mr. Gromyko at the Russian Permanent Mission to the United Nations, New York, on Monday, 25 September 1972[1]

[ENS 3/548/3]

Confidential

Present:

Sir Alec Douglas-Home, KT, MP	Mr. Gromyko
Mr. A.D. Parsons	Mr. Malik
Mr. M.L. Hudson	Mr. Sukhodrev
Mr. A.A. Acland[2]	
Mr. J.H.G. Leahy	

Sir Alec Douglas-Home asked Mr. Gromyko how things were going. *Mr. Gromyko* said that different matters were going in different ways. He would be addressing the General Assembly on the following day and would be touching on Europe, the Middle East, disarmament, some general matters and would be saying something about the Soviet ideas on the non use of force and the prohibition of nuclear weapons.[3] It remained to be seen whether this General Assembly would make any progress.

[1] Sir A. Douglas-Home and Mr. Gromyko were in New York to address the 27th Session of the UN General Assembly, which opened on 19 September.

[2] Mr. Hudson and Mr. Acland were respectively Political Secretary and Principal Private Secretary to the Secretary of State.

[3] In his speech on 26 September Mr. Gromyko said: 'our Country believes that it is possible to eliminate or, at least, to reduce drastically the danger of a conflict between States provoking a nuclear catastrophe. That can be done if renunciation of the use of force in international relations is elevated to the level of international law and if at the same time . . . the use of nuclear weapons is prohibited.' The Soviet Union introduced an item to the Plenary Session on 'Non-use of force in international relations and permanent prohibition of the use of nuclear weapons', which was adopted as Resolution 2936 (XXVII) on 29 November.

European Security matters

2. *Sir Alec Douglas-Home* said he would like to begin with Europe. His views on the CSCE were not far from Mr. Gromyko's. He thought that the right course was to agree on the agenda for the Security Conference and then see what would be worth pursuing in Commissions or Committees. *Mr. Gromyko* said that he thought there had been some movement forward in European matters recently. He was not sure whether Britain had made a formal pronouncement about the proposed date of 22 November for the preparatory conference in Helsinki.[4] Was it acceptable?

Sir Alec Douglas-Home said that we agreed to 22 November or the earliest date thereafter acceptable to all concerned. It would be wrong to spend too long on fixing the agenda. We must, however, expect a long substantive meeting if thirty Foreign Ministers were going to speak. *Mr. Gromyko* said that he envisaged three stages for the conference—first, at Foreign Minister level, second, at Committee or Commission level and a final stage, probably at a level higher than Foreign Ministers, perhaps Heads of Government or State. *Sir Alec Douglas-Home* said he was not prepared to commit himself to a Summit meeting until he could see what was likely to come out of the Conference. *Mr. Gromyko* said that he assumed however that the three stages were agreed. *Sir Alec Douglas-Home* said he thought there must be some link with the MBFR discussion. *Mr. Gromyko* said he was going to use harsh words against any link.[5] *Sir Alec Douglas-Home* said perhaps there should be some link in time, or perhaps some parallelism as suggested by the Americans. *Mr. Gromyko* said there must be no formal link or parallelism. It was better to think in concrete terms. The preliminary meeting for the Security Conference could take place in Helsinki in November. In January there could be a procedural conference or preliminary conference on MBFRs. The Security Conference might take place in June 1973 and after it had finished a multilateral conference on MBFRs. *Sir Alec Douglas-Home* said that this seemed a sensible programme on the whole. As for the Security Conference, the Russians had proposed it but general declarations did not get very far. Had Mr. Gromyko got any ideas about practical steps? *Mr. Gromyko* said he would answer in two parts. First, the substance and, second, the form that decisions should take. As for substance, cultural and economic questions should be discussed as well as political. Questions of territorial integrity and inviolability of frontiers, together with non-use or threat of force should be included, as well as economic and cultural cooperation. As for the form of decisions, the stronger the better, either a Treaty or an Agreement. They should have juridical force. *Sir Alec Douglas-Home* said that this seemed good

---

[4] See Volume II, No. 13.

[5] Cf. No. 100, note 4. During a visit to Paris from 12-15 June Mr. Gromyko had also asserted that there should be no link between the CSCE and MBFR negotiations. At the Moscow Summit, however (see No. 97), President Nixon gained the impression that the Soviet Union agreed that negotiations should proceed in parallel, an idea also embodied in the *Communiqué* issued after the NATO Ministerial meeting in Bonn (see pp. 477-8). Cf. also Volume II, No. 13, note 4.

sense on the whole and in general he could go along with Mr. Gromyko's ideas. What about including discussion on greater freedom of movement and ideas[?] *Mr. Gromyko* commented that this seemed a reasonable proposition, but what was the reason for it? *Sir Alec Douglas-Home* said that shortly we would be a member of the expanded Community which, among other things, envisaged free movement of labour. The greater the area of freedom the better. There had been improvements in the arrangements in Berlin for example.[6] The Russians seemed also prepared to talk about increased cultural exchanges. *Mr. Gromyko*, reverting to Russian and speaking with some emphasis, said that he would like it agreed from the very beginning that this should be free from all propaganda aspects. Sir Alec Douglas-Home knew in fact that there could be no absolute freedom of movement and if the Russians suggested this the United Kingdom would not agree. Furthermore, on occasions when there was no justification for limiting movement, the British Government invented reasons. Each State had its own concept of freedom of movement and there must be a reasonable and businesslike approach. *Sir Alec Douglas-Home* said that we certainly did not want propaganda. We would be realistic, but we genuinely wanted increased movement, exchanges and culture. *Mr. Gromyko* said that there could be an item on the agenda on economic and cultural ties between the countries of Europe. Each side could then propose what they wanted which could include scientific cooperation. If agreement could be reached, there would be a decision. *Sir Alec Douglas-Home* said that he had a similar approach. On MBFRs he thought the substance very difficult and it would take a lot of time. *Mr. Gromyko* agreed.

Middle East

3. *Sir Alec Douglas-Home* asked whether Mr. Gromyko had any ideas for arms limitation. Would he make any new proposals in his speech[?] *Mr. Gromyko* said that he must draw attention to an old standpoint of the Soviet Union. They were ready to discuss arms limitation in the context of a final settlement, but it could not be discussed with one side occupying the territory of the other. *Sir Alec Douglas-Home* said that present situation was very difficult.[7] The trouble was that no one could get the two sides talking. How could the pace of the dialogue be increased[?] *Mr. Gromyko* said that the crucial point was not the absence of machinery, but the difference in policies. The Soviet Union still supported Jarring, but the wisest man in the world

[6] See p. 478.

[7] See No. 100, note 11. On 18 July President Sadat had announced that all Soviet advisers and experts would be asked to leave Egypt, and all Soviet military equipment and military installations would be placed under Egyptian control. Commenting in telegram No. 1128 of 20 July, Sir J. Killick thought that the Soviet Government were 'worried about the danger of a super-power confrontation' in the area, and had decided that 'whatever the Egyptian retaliation might be, the need to avoid a confrontation with the United States and the risk of being involved in a repetition of the 1967 *débacle* made it imperative for them to reject Egyptian demands for equipping and unleashing of Egyptian forces' (NAU 10/11). On 2 August Egypt and Libya signed an agreement forming a union of the two countries.

would not succeed because of the position of Israel. *Sir Alec Douglas-Home* asked Mr. Gromyko what proposals he would make to solve the problem. Mrs. Meir had told him that if she announced that she had no desire to annexe territory there would be nothing more to negotiate about.[8] Israel had to have her security ensured before playing her last card. Was there any chance of a peace conference being set up in such a way that the Egyptians did not have to negotiate alone with Israel? *Mr. Gromyko* asked a number of questions about the composition and form and whether Britain had approached the Egyptians with the idea. *Sir Alec Douglas-Home* said that he thought that the Egyptians would not necessarily reject the idea of a Conference. *Mr. Gromyko* said that this was not enough. Withdrawal by Israel was essential. It was for the Arabs to make up their own minds on what basis there might be a conference while Israel was still in occupation. The core of the whole problem was withdrawal. *Mr. Malik* asked whether any proposals had been made to Dr. Zayyat when he was in London.[9] *Sir Alec Douglas-Home* said that he had tried to tell the Israelis that Egypt and Jordan really did want to live at peace. The real sticking point was over Israeli withdrawal and Sharm-al-Shaikh was crucial for Israel. It should however be possible to concede Egyptian sovereignty and make arrangements for Israeli occupation or leasing. *Mr. Gromyko* said that all this must be left to the Arabs. Four or five months ago, he thought that someone had talked to them on these lines, but they had not taken a positive attitude. Basically, it was up to the United States and in part to the United Kingdom to ensure Israeli withdrawal.[10]

[8] Sir A. Douglas-Home had visited Israel from 21-24 March and held discussions on 22 March with Mrs. Golda Meir, who repeated that the Israeli Government would not accept the concept of total withdrawal or return to the June 1967 borders. When pressed by the Secretary of State she agreed that Israel wanted the annexation of territory, particularly Sharm al Shaikh, a cove on the Sinai Peninsula which controlled access to the Straits of Tiran, and land linking the cove to the Mediterranean (NER 3/548/2).

[9] The Egyptian Foreign Minister, Dr. Mohamed Hassan al Zayyat, had visited London from 17-19 September, asking for British help to provide a deterrent against Israeli attacks against Lebanon and Syria (Israel launched airstrikes against bases in Syria and Lebanon on 8 September following the killing of 9 Israeli athletes at the Munich Olympics on 5 September by members of the 'Black September' group). He told Sir A. Douglas-Home on 18 September that Egypt was prepared to recognise Israel, would undertake not to attack her from Egyptian soil and 'was no longer asking for unconditional withdrawal'. On the question of Sharm al Shaikh he said that Egypt accepted that security arrangements must be found for Israel and that a UN force would be stationed at the cove. Dr. Zayyat added that Egypt would accept a peace conference, an interim agreement and proximity talks provided they were all linked to a final settlement (NAV 2/3).

[10] Despite the Egyptian willingness to negotiate indicated in note 9, the stalemate in the search for either an interim or comprehensive solution to the crisis in the region persisted, with all sides waiting for the USA to resume their efforts after the Presidential election. On 8 December the UNGA adopted Resolution 2949 (amended by the UK), criticising Israeli activities on the West Bank, declaring the acquisition of territories by force to be inadmissible and inviting Israel to declare publicly her adherence to the principle of non-annexation.

Disarmament

4. *Sir Alec Douglas-Home* asked Mr. Gromyko whether the main reason for the Russians wanting a world disarmament conference was to bring in the Chinese. *Mr. Gromyko* asked why he should put it in such a way. The main purpose was to get decisions on disarmament. *Sir Alec Douglas-Home* said there would be no point in a world disarmament conference without the Chinese. *Mr. Malik* commented that the first speaker in the General Assembly for the Third World had emphasised the importance of the disarmament conference.[11] *Sir Alec Douglas-Home* said that the Third World did not have significant weapons. Those who had were the ones who must discuss disarmament. The United States and the USSR had already made a start in the SALT talks.[12] Britain would not object to a world disarmament conference, provided the main powers participated, but it should not be instead of those disarmament activities which were already going on. *Mr. Gromyko* said that the Russians were flexible about the timing of a world disarmament conference. It should be possible not to specify a concrete time, but nevertheless to take some steps to start things moving. He was flexible on this. He agreed that a world disarmament conference should not be a substitute for other existing disarmament activities.

The Middle East

4. [*sic*] *Sir Alec Douglas-Home* said he would like to revert to the Middle East for a moment and to the question of arms limitation. *Mr. Gromyko* said firmly it could only be dealt with in the context of a general settlement and it was an old question which had been raised by successive British Governments.

· *Security Conference*

5. Reverting to the Security Conference, *Mr. Gromyko* suggested that Britain and Russia should consult together about the character of the decisions to be taken, both for the preliminary and substantive conferences. *Sir Alec Douglas-Home* said that Britain did not want to spend too much time on the preparations, provided the agenda could be agreed. *Mr. Gromyko* said he agreed with this.

German Talks and Quadripartite Rights

6. *Sir Alec Douglas-Home* asked what Mr. Gromyko knew about the prospects for a General Relations treaty.[13] *Mr. Gromyko* said that some

---

[11] See Nos. 67, note 11 and 77, note 7. Secretary-General Waldheim reported to the General Assembly that nearly all delegations favoured a world disarmament conference if adequately prepared. During the debate, China restated its pre-conditions that all nuclear weapon countries should renounce first use and that they should withdraw all their overseas armed forces and military bases. The Assembly adopted on 29 November a Resolution (2930) providing for the establishment of a committee of 35 members 'to examine all the views and suggestions expressed by governments on the convening of a world disarmament conference' (Cmnd. 5236 of 1973, UN Report on proceedings of the 27th General Assembly).

[12] See No. 97, note 5.

[13] At the initialling ceremony in Bonn on 12 May of the General Transport Treaty (GTT) regulating all traffic between and across the FRG and GDR, Herr Bahr and Herr Kohl said

progress had been made but on certain matters the sides were still far apart. As regards quadripartite rights and responsibilities, he thought that it should be agreed that if and when the two Germanies joined the United Nations, the question of quadripartite rights should not be touched.[14] The situation would remain exactly as it was at present and it need not become a subject for discussion. If discussions started and the parties began to dig deeper, all sorts of problems would be unearthed. There was no need to create any impression that there was a problem. *Sir Alec Douglas-Home* asked whether he should assume that if the Four Powers were asked a question about their rights they should say that the position remained as before. *Mr. Gromyko* repeated that the question of the Four Powers' rights need not be touched as a result of a general relations treaty or the entry of the two Germanies into the United Nations. *Mr. Parsons* asked how it would be possible to be sure that the two Germanies themselves would still consider the rights as continuing. *Mr. Gromyko* said that they would neither be asked nor would they be required to answer. The fact was that nothing would be changed. The best position for the Four Powers was not to raise the question of rights. *Sir Alec Douglas-Home* said that he would be prepared to say that the question of quadripartite rights was not involved and that they therefore remained as they were before. *Mr. Gromyko* said that that would make it a subject for discussions and that was not necessary. *Sir Alec Douglas-Home* said that he would like to think about what Mr. Gromyko had said and how the matter should be expressed. *Mr. Gromyko* said that what he was suggesting was the best possible thing for the British, although Sir Alec still seemed to have doubts. There was no reason to give grounds for developing discussions on the subject. *Sir Alec Douglas-Home* said that he could not give any commitments and would like to think more about Mr. Gromyko's proposal.[15]

they intended to go on to discuss the general relationship between the two Germanies. Talks began on 15 June and a Treaty on the Basis of Relations between the FRG and the GDR (known as the General Relations or Basic Treaty) was initialled on 8 November and signed on 21 December 1972. The Treaty, which paved the way for general international recognition of the GDR and for both German States to apply to join the UN, is printed in Cmnd. 6201, No. 154.

[14] In Berlin on 3 June (cf. p. 478) the US Secretary of State, Mr. Rogers, had proposed to Mr. Gromyko that an understanding should be reached on a Quadripartite Declaration reaffirming Quadripartite Rights and Responsibilities (QRR) in parallel with the negotiation of the GRT. Mr. Gromyko had not yet replied to this proposal. In a minute of 9 August to Mr. Heath and the DOP Committee Sir A. Douglas-Home noted that 'Four Power rights and responsibilities symbolise the fact that the German question remains unresolved and reunification an option' (WRE 3/309/1).

[15] Mr. Gromyko's remarks on QRR were reported to the FCO in UKMIS telegram No. 1304 of 26 September. When Mr. Gromyko saw Mr. Rogers at Camp David on 2 October, however, he agreed to the opening of Four Power talks on QRR and discussions opened in Berlin on 23 October (WRL 2/11). An agreed Quadripartite Declaration was issued in London, Moscow, Paris and Washington on 9 November: see Cmnd. 6201, No. 156.

The final document in this collection contains a brief analysis of the bilateral relationship at a time when both the domestic scene in the UK and the international context were troubled and uncertain. In Britain, a prolonged period of industrial unrest—a state of emergency was declared twice in 1972, during miners' and dockers' strikes—led to a change in government policies and the imposition on 6 November of a 90-day wage, price and rent freeze. The conflicts in the Middle East and Vietnam seemed little nearer solution than they had been at the beginning of the year, and Sino-Soviet tensions and expansionist policies in the Third World were cause for concern to HMG and her Western partners. The imminent opening of the preparatory talks for a CSCE seemed promising, but it was clear that many intractable issues would need to be tackled. Britain's relations with the Soviet Union, though operating on a 'business as usual' basis, had still not recovered from the shock of the expulsion of the Soviet intelligence officers in 1971. The view expressed by Mr. Acland, that 'If there is to be a new and major step forward in our relations with the Russians . . . it is for them to take the initiative', was a restatement of HMG's position ever since the invasion of Czechoslovakia; meanwhile, the FCO continued as ever to think of ways in which to improve bilateral relations and to give the lie to the recurring Soviet accusation that Britain took by far the hardest line in the West.

No. 108

Letter from Mr. Acland to Lord Bridges (10 Downing St.)[1]
[ENS 3/548/3]

Confidential   FCO, *20 November 1972*

Anglo-Soviet relations

In his letter to Sir Burke Trend of 2 October,[2] Sir Denis Greenhill mentioned that our Ambassador in Moscow had learned in confidence from Mr. Callaghan during his visit from 7 to 13 August that the Russians had told him that they would prefer to leave some Anglo-Soviet problems on one side for discussion with a Labour Government rather than seeking solutions with the present Government.[3] You may wish to be aware of some recent events

---

[1] In a submission of 10 November Mr. Bullard had drawn Sir T. Brimelow's attention to continuing indications that the Soviet leaders 'appear a little reluctant to be seen doing business with the present Conservative administration', and Sir D. Greenhill had minuted that the Private Secretary and No. 10 should be informed about this (EN 2/30). The present letter was drafted by Mr. Bullard and approved by Sir A. Douglas-Home on 20 November: opening and concluding salutations were omitted from the filed copy.

[2] Not printed.

[3] See No. 105, note 9. Sir D. Greenhill told Sir B. Trend that according to Sir J. Killick Mr. Ponomarev, Secretary of the CPSU's Central Committee, had told Mr. Callaghan that 'if a Labour Government came to power, the Soviet Government would seek to improve relations with it and this might lead to "a broad-based treaty with Britain"'. Writing to the Ambassador on 19 September, Mr. Bullard commented that this 'explains a good deal about the current Soviet attitude to Britain' (ENS 3/548/12).

which tend to confirm that this is indeed the attitude of the Russians at present.

Although our contacts with Moscow are picking up again, particularly in the field of political exchanges about the forthcoming Conference on Security and Cooperation in Europe,[4] the Soviet leaders still appear a little reluctant to be seen to be doing business with the Conservative Administration. There has still been no positive response, for example, to the proposal we made in April that a Minister of State at the FCO should visit Moscow in October this year.[5] This apparent disinclination to resume Ministerial visits has not of course prevented the Russians from criticising, both publicly and in private, Sir Alec Douglas-Home's trip to China.[6]

At the same time, there are signs that the Russians are increasingly keen to develop their non-Governmental contacts in this country. The visits to Moscow by Mr. Callaghan and various Labour and Liberal MPs[7] have been followed by a flurry of Soviet activity in the Trade Union field. British visitors to Russia in recent months have included Mr. Joe Gormley and a group from the NUM.[8] Averyanov, the Head of the Foreign Relations Department of Soviet Trade Unions, persuaded the head of the TUC's International Department, Mr. Alan Hargreaves, to invite him to London for three days of talks from 16 to 18 November. Another sign of Soviet interest in the TUC is the Russians' lightning response to a casual indication by Mr. Victor Feather[9] that he would welcome the re-establishment of contact with Russian Trade Unionists. Within twenty-four hours of Mr. Feather giving this hint to a Polish comrade, he was telephoned in London by the powerful Head of the Soviet Trade Union Organisation, Shelepin, who invited him to Moscow for a talk. Mr. Feather intends to make this visit on 6/7 December.

The Russians have for some time been trying to heal the breach with the TUC which resulted from the invasion of Czechoslovakia. They have no doubt been encouraged to renew their approaches by the TUC's recent decision to abolish the ban on Communists holding office on its General Council. But the Russians may also have two specific political purposes in mind: to persuade the TUC to support a European Trade Union Conference in advance of the CSCE, and to bring what influence they can to bear on the British Trade Union movement in favour of militant confrontation with the Government, e.g. over pay and prices. It should however be emphasised that we have seen no evidence whatever to suggest that the Russians have been directly involved, organisationally or financially, in recent

[4] See No. 107, and Volume II, No. 14.

[5] See No. 93.

[6] The Secretary of State visited China from 25 October to 2 November 1972.

[7] See No. 105, note 9.

[8] Mr. Gormley, Chairman of the Labour Party International Committee and President of the National Union of Mineworkers (NUM), visited Moscow with two NUM officials from 16-26 August.

[9] General Secretary of the TUC.

industrial disputes in the UK or in the political decisions of British Trade Union leaders. Any influence they are able to bring to bear will, we suspect, be mainly exhortatory. The *Morning Star* openly preaches the simple Communist doctrine 'The worse—the better'.

I expect you will see confirmation in all this, as we do, that in dealing with Moscow our present policy of cautious pragmatism based squarely on our national interests is the right one. If there is to be a new and major step forward in our relations with the Russians, we believe that it is for them to take the initiative. At the same time we think it right to handle our contacts with Peking in such a way as to reassure the Russians that we are not entering into some kind of anti-Soviet conspiracy, and to avoid appearing to apply different standards to China from those which we have learned by bitter experience to apply to the Soviet Union.[10] The sentences which the Prime Minister included in his speech at the Guildhall on 13 November should have been useful in this regard.[11]

A.A. ACLAND

[10] Sir A. Douglas-Home minuted on 20 November (see note 1): 'It does them [the Russians] no harm if we have a gentle flirtation with the Chinese and keep them guessing how far it will go.'

[11] The Prime Minister's speech at the Lord Mayor's banquet was reported in *The Times*, 14 November 1972, p. 1. Mr. Heath declared that Britain and her European partners were committed to a policy of *détente* and peace with the nations of Eastern Europe, and insisted that this included the Soviet Union.

APPENDIX

Report by Joint Intelligence Committee (A) on the Soviet Threat[1]

JIC(A)(72)34

Secret. UK Eyes Only   CABINET OFFICE, *14 September 1972*

A. *Summary*

1. This paper considers the principal threats posed by the Soviet Union to the United Kingdom and Western Europe over the next five years. It falls into two parts. Part I considers likely Soviet policies in the fields of principal interest to us and Soviet chances of achieving their aims. Part II identifies the Soviet threat in the light of the foregoing and of our assessment of British interests.

PART I. SOVIET POLICIES

2. Soviet external policy seeks certain general objectives: to maintain the security of Soviet and Warsaw Pact territory; to consolidate the Soviet position as a super Power; to extend Soviet influence and reduce Western and Chinese influence; and to promote Soviet leadership of the world Communist movement. It partakes of the cautious quality of the Soviet leadership but reflects their confidence in Soviet military and industrial strength.

3. The principal Soviet foreign policy preoccupation is the relationship with the United States. This is a relationship of underlying antagonism, but qualified or masked by Soviet strategic caution, by tactical choices, e.g. promoting *détente*, and more recently by the development of Soviet/United States bilateralism, i.e. the habit of dealing *à deux* on certain issues, in particular those relating to strategic weapons. This habit has been greatly encouraged by the Moscow Summit[2] and has profound implications for United States allies and the rest of the world. It offers the Soviet Union a number of advantages, notably reasserting the primacy of United States/Soviet relations, promoting an atmosphere of *détente* suitable for the prosecution of Soviet policies in Western Europe, and giving opportunities for wedge-driving between the United States and its allies. It may, however, raise doubts among Soviet clients of their patron's

---

[1] This report originated in a request from Sir A. Douglas-Home, passed on to Mr. Goodall by Mr. Graham on 12 June, for 'a considered assessment of the Soviet threat to our security and supplies, particularly related to oil'. It was subsequently agreed with the Cabinet Office that 'the assessment would concentrate on politico/economic aspects of the threat and would pay attention to Soviet capabilities as well as intentions', with the oil question to be considered separately and in detail: see No. 95, notes 6 and 7. The paper was drafted by Mr. Cradock in consultation with, among others, Sir D. Greenhill and Sir T. Brimelow, and approved by the JIC out of Committee following a preliminary discussion at their meeting on 7 September. Copies were sent to Mr. Heath, Sir A. Douglas-Home, Lord Carrington (Secretary of State for Defence) and Mr. Robert Carr, Home Secretary since July 1972 (PUSD records).

[2] See pp. 474-5.

reliability, as has already occurred in Egypt. We consider that the extent of United States/Soviet communication and even agreement is likely to grow, but that, under President Nixon at least, the United States will probably remain robust over temptations to neglect NATO interests. We also see participation in this bilateral dealing as essentially tactical on the part of the Russians and as not affecting their basic philosophy or longer term objectives.

4. In Europe, the Russians seek to consolidate their position in the East while leaving themselves maximum opportunity to influence events in the West and, if possible, obstruct the development of the European Community in the political and defence fields. At the strategic level, the Russians will hope that their attainment of nuclear parity with the United States will erode the credibility of the United States guarantee to Europe. In conventional arms the steady improvement of the Soviet military position of strength as against NATO continues unabated and NATO's Northern and Southern flanks are particularly vulnerable. The Soviet long-term objective is a Western Europe from which United States defence cover has been largely withdrawn, which remains divided, and which like Finland, exists under the shadow of Soviet military strength and is increasingly compelled to adjust its policies accordingly.

5. The Russians will derive encouragement from a number of recent and prospective developments in Western Europe. In the atmosphere of *détente* associated with a European Security Conference a lowering of Western vigilance is likely. Domestic United States pressures for United States troop withdrawals from Europe are likely to grow. At the same time, the enlarged Community has not so far developed any great momentum towards unity or towards development in the political and defence fields. Western Europe has considerable assets, but they are in the longer term, and require the preservation of political confidence and a convincing defence posture by the West over what may be a long intervening period. It is during this period, with United States defence support in greater question and Western Europe still in disarray, that Soviet policy will have its major opportunities.

6. In the Far East, the Soviet Union has over the last year been passive rather than an initiator of policy. The great developments over this period, the movements of Sino/United States and now Sino/Japanese rapprochement, threaten to leave them isolated. They are unlikely to be able to exert a great influence upon Japan. China is likely to remain a profound anxiety for them; and China's emergence on the world scene and her improved relations with the United States only serve to intensify that anxiety. The Russians have resisted the temptation to seek a military solution while China is still weak in modern weapons. They follow a 'long haul' policy, exerting their superior resources to contain China and reduce her influence as far as possible, while waiting for the day, after Mao's death, when it may be possible to improve Sino/Soviet relations on terms satisfactory to the Soviet Union. Soviet preoccupation with China affects Soviet policies throughout the world and is on the whole to the advantage of the West.

7. In the Third World, the Russians pursue an opportunist policy availing themselves of the openings provided by the era of decolonisation, their own willingness to supply economic aid and sophisticated military equipment, and the political influence accruing from their increasing naval deployment. They have sought to formalise their relations

with selected Third World States by means of treaties, probably in the hope of deriving thereby a more lasting foundation for their presence by building up local political influence.

8. Their most spectacular encroachments have been in the Middle East, where, even after the recent Egyptian reverse,[3] there is a formidable Soviet effort and stake. At the same time, the last year has brought out serious weaknesses in the Soviet Middle East position, deriving *inter alia* from Arab nationalism, the inherent instability of the area and Soviet strategic caution. The Soviet setback in Egypt is serious and will compel Soviet re-examination of their Middle East and Third World policies. But the Middle East retains its strategic importance for the Russians; they retain important levers there; and, while Soviet tactics may be modified, Soviet long-term aims are unlikely to change.

9. Soviet involvement in the oil industries of Middle East oil-producing countries and recent purchases of small quantities of oil raise the question whether they intend to interfere in some way with oil supplies to the West. We think their ability to engineer a substantial interruption is limited. The Soviet Union does not need Middle East oil and is reluctant to pay the hard currency the Arab States require. The Russians will wish to encourage Arab oil producers to restrict the role of Western oil companies and to strike harder bargains with the West; but their capacity for mischief is limited, and is more a threat to the interests of Western oil companies and possibly the cost of oil to Western consumers than a threat to the continued availability of oil.

10. In the Sub-Continent, the last year has been a good one for the Russians and a bad one for the Americans and Chinese. The Russians will, however, find it hard to translate their enhanced prestige in India into practical benefits and, given time, United States and even Chinese influence is likely to make some recovery. Nevertheless, Soviet influence will remain strong. In South-East Asia the Russians seek to increase their influence in the context of the Sino/Soviet dispute and also to benefit from any Western withdrawals; but they are unlikely to become more than one element in any balance of power in the area.

PART II. THE NATURE OF THE SOVIET THREAT

11. The threat posed by the Soviet Union must be analysed by reference to the account above and also by reference to our assessment of British interests, which, though widely spread, centre on the West European and Atlantic area. In the most basic sense, the threat arises from the Soviet leaders' commitment to struggle by all means short of war and their sense of historical mission as convinced Communists, supported by the national ambitions and strength of the Soviet State.

12. On the military side, we do not see the Soviet Union launching a military attack on the West in the period under review. Nor do we foresee Soviet physical interference with our supplies and shipping, except in circumstances in which they were ready to face a full-scale confrontation with the United States. Nevertheless, Soviet military power will threaten our security in a variety of ways. In an era of nuclear parity and of United States reduction of a number of its overseas commitments, Soviet superiority in

---

[3] See No. 107, note 7.

conventional arms is likely to have serious political implications in Western Europe and to give the Soviet Union added opportunities for acquiring influence outside Europe.

13. On the economic side, the Soviet Union is less well placed: the Russians face the greater flexibility of capitalist economies and their own deficiencies in various areas of applied technology and in the consumer sector. But they are able to mobilise their efforts for priority goals and to maintain a rate of growth which compares favourably with that of most advanced Western countries. They could gain from economic quarrels in the free world, and will wish to encourage raw material producers, particularly those producing oil, to drive as hard a bargain as possible with the West. Their own considerable supplies of raw materials may give them some long-term advantage.

14. A further aspect of the struggle is that of Soviet subversion. In the period under review we expect the Soviet Union to intensify its world-wide campaign of subversion, espionage and propaganda.

15. The real Soviet threat, however, derives not from these individual factors in isolation but from their combination in the area of struggle short of hostilities. Essentially the threat is that the Soviet Union, by using military, political and economic means of influence and relying on its own consistency of purpose and any infirmities on the part of the West, may acquire such a position of dominance in vital areas that it will be able to achieve many of its objectives without resort to hostilities. We identify two danger areas: Western Europe; and that part of the Third World lying to the south of the Soviet Union, i.e. the Mediterranean, Middle East and Indian Sub-Continent.

16. Of these, the threat in Western Europe is unquestionably the more serious. In the conditions of *détente* fostered by the Soviet Union, Western Europe may be gradually deprived of credible United States support without providing a substitute of its own and may fail to attain the unity in the political and defence fields which will be necessary if Soviet influence and pressures on Western Europe are to be repelled. The threat derives as much from Western inaction as from Soviet design; therefore the remedy lies largely in Western hands. Nevertheless, we foresee a period of danger in the immediate future and fear that the Soviet Union may significantly improve its position in Europe in the period under review.

17. Specifically we expect the Soviet Union to strengthen its persuasions that efforts to improve West European political or military integration are provocative or even fruitless and its efforts to detach the weaker members from NATO. At the same time, pressures within NATO countries for a reduction in defence spending are likely to grow and there is a danger that West European countries may come to attach greater importance to good bilateral relations with the Soviet Union than to building up Western Europe in political and defence terms.

18. The second area, the Third World will remain one of steady Soviet effort, but the dangers are less acute and some corrective forces operate. There may well be striking Soviet successes in particular countries. Nevertheless, we expect this to be a patchy performance, in which success will be interspersed with setbacks, and we doubt whether it by itself will give the Soviet Union the lasting influence that will be needed fundamentally to improve its world position.

HAROLD MAGUIRE
Acting Chairman on behalf of Joint
Intelligence Committee (A)

B. *Main Report*

The Soviet Threat

1. What are the principal external threats the Soviet Union poses to the United Kingdom and Western Europe? What are the Soviet leaders trying to do in those areas of their external policy that most affect us and how successful are they likely to be in pursuit of their policies? This paper tries to answer these questions, necessarily in very general terms. It looks ahead over the next five years. It also looks back over the last year and seeks to assess future Soviet policy and performance with particular reference to the major events that have occurred over this period.

2. The paper falls into two parts. In the first we examine some of the main areas of Soviet foreign policy activity as they now are and as they are likely to evolve. In the second part, in the light of the foregoing and our assessment of British interests, we analyse the nature of the Soviet threat.

PART I. SOVIET POLICY

The Basic Factors

3. The principal factors determining Soviet foreign policy have been fully rehearsed in other papers and we shall only note them briefly here. The Russians seek first security for the Soviet homeland and the Warsaw Pact area; secondly, the consolidation of the Soviet Union's super Power status; thirdly, the growth of Soviet influence overseas, which involves the weakening of Western, in particular United States influence and the containment and reduction of Chinese influence; fourthly, the promotion of Soviet leadership in the world Communist movement, which means in particular struggle against the Chinese heresy. Their policy is governed by considerations both of national interest and of ideology; for the most part these are complementary, but where conflict occurs, ideology takes second place. Their policy is also affected by the quality of the leadership. It is still a collective leadership, though Brezhnev has increasingly asserted his primacy. It is grey, cautious, suspicious, nationalist to the point of chauvinism, but it is also persistent and, within a given framework, opportunist and capable of tactical switches that may take the West by surprise. It is keenly aware of the sources of Soviet strength: in particular Soviet military power, both the achievement of nuclear parity with the United States and an increasing capacity to project Soviet power in conventional military terms; and Soviet industrial strength (though progress in agriculture has been unsatisfactory and civil industry lags in the application of advanced technology and in the consumer sector, GNP is increasing at about 5 per cent per annum). They are conscious of an increasingly recognised Soviet role in virtually all world situations, as Gromyko boasted at the 24th Party Congress.[4] Underlying all are the historical assurances of Marxism-Leninism. Though the world for the Russians has numerous puzzling or threatening features, they have considerable grounds for confidence.

[4] See pp. 325-6.

Soviet/United States relations

4. In practice the Soviet Union's principal preoccupation in the field of external affairs is its relationship with the United States. The Russians see the United States as their main antagonist. In their long-term aims to shift the balance of world power in their favour it provides their principal, though by no means their only, obstacle. They wish to consolidate their position as a world Power on a par with the United States; but in the longer term they aspire beyond that to a condition in which the relationship will become one not of uneasy equality but of manifest Soviet superiority in a number of important fields. In the meantime, they seek to build up their power, military, political and economic, to meet the needs of this struggle by all means short of war, which is their reading of peaceful co-existence.

5. This basic antagonism is, however, qualified or masked in a number of important respects. In the first place, the Russians are anxious to avoid any direct military confrontation with the United States. They may also seek tactical advantage in promoting periods of *détente*. They are aware of a number of deficiencies in their own economy, in particular in the wider application of advanced technology, which may be remedied by closer dealings with the United States and the West generally. Another important qualification is that the position of the United States and the Soviet Union as the two military super Powers, in a class of their own and involved in all world issues, has tended to encourage bilateral communication and even recognition of a certain community of interest. There is a tendency to deal *à deux* on certain issues, in particular those relating to strategic weapons. This bilateralism has been greatly encouraged by President Nixon's Moscow visit and by the successful outcome of the SALT negotiations resulting in the signature of the Treaty on ABMs and the Interim Agreement on Offensive Missiles.[5] The importance the Soviet Government attaches to its global business with the United States was demonstrated by its willingness to hold the Moscow summit despite United States action in mining North Viet-Namese ports.

6. The Soviet Government have good reasons for encouraging this bilateral dealing. It reasserts the importance of United States/Soviet relations in a world which to the Soviet leaders has become disturbingly multi-polar and, in particular, it brings out the relative thinness of Sino/United States relations. By encouraging an atmosphere of *détente* between the United States and the Soviet Union, it facilitates the prosecution of Soviet policy towards Western Europe. It fosters the useful impression that the Soviet Union is simply a great Power, protecting its national interests, like any other. At the same time, it offers openings for wedge-driving between the United States and its allies. Finally, Soviet/United States trade, in which the Russians could acquire American technology and grain in return for Soviet fuels and raw and semi-processed materials, offers considerable attractions to both sides. On the other hand, this bilateralism could work to Soviet disadvantage by arousing doubts among Soviet clients of their patron's reliability as a loyal ally. The Moscow summit has further reduced Soviet influence in Hanoi; and by strengthening Egyptian suspicions of Soviet trustworthiness has contributed to the recent severe Soviet setback in Egypt.

7. In assessing future Soviet relations with the United States we therefore face a difficulty: on the one hand, there is the basic antagonism; on the other, there is a

[5] See No. 97, note 5.

tendency to engage in communication on and possibly common management of some world problems. A major question for the future is the way in which this second tendency will develop; in their politico/military and in their trade aspects United States/Soviet bilateral relations have immense implications for the rest of the world, in particular for America's allies. Despite its enunciation of basic principles endorsed by both parties, the Moscow summit suggested that United States/Soviet agreement would probably be confined to certain specific areas and that over Third World questions it would be harder to obtain. It was also clear from the proceedings at the summit that the Americans remained robust in the face of Soviet inducements to neglect NATO interests. On the whole we think that this will remain true, at least under President Nixon, though we consider that the extent of United States/Soviet communication and even agreement is likely to grow. In any event we see such agreement as essentially tactical on the part of the Russians and as not affecting their basic philosophy or their determination to pursue traditional ends by traditional means.

SALT

8. Negotiations to limit strategic arms are likely to remain a particularly important aspect of the United States/Soviet relationship. In recognition of the need to reduce military risk and future economic burdens, the Russians and the Americans have agreed to stabilise certain aspects of United States/Soviet strategic relations. But many aspects remain untouched: research and development, improvement of the quality of existing weapons and development of new weapons will remain areas of continued intense Soviet (and United States) effort. Both sides will see advantage in continuing the dialogue in pursuit of rather more comprehensive agreements. In the first stage of SALT both United Kingdom and NATO interests were adequately protected; but the second stage will give the Russians special opportunities to raise questions bearing on nuclear relations between the United States and the United Kingdom and relations between the United States and NATO generally.

Western Europe

9. In Europe the Russians seek to consolidate their position in the East, while leaving themselves maximum opportunity to influence events in the West. Soviet hegemony in Eastern Europe has already been implicitly recognised by the West; the frontiers in key areas have now been explicitly recognised by Federal Germany in the Soviet/German and Polish/German treaties;[6] and the Russians seek a final general endorsement of these frontiers and of the post-war political settlement in Eastern Europe from a Conference on European Security and Co-operation, which we must now expect will be held in the next 18 months.[7] They will also hope at the same time to ensure international recognition of East Germany.[8] The fact that the *status quo* in the East is recognised will not preclude the Soviet Union from questioning it in the West. They no doubt calculate that the atmosphere of relaxation or euphoria engendered by a European Security Conference will facilitate their work of easing American troops out of Western Europe and will make it harder for West European Governments to adopt sensible defence policies. The Russians have had to accept the

---

[6] See Nos. 50, note 3 and 52, note 5 .   [7] Cf. No. 107.   [8] *V. ibid.*, note 13.

enlargement of the European Community,[9] but they will do their best to obstruct its development in the political and defence fields and will offer the mirage of 'all European co-operation' as an alternative to the more exclusive Western grouping. They will hope by cultivating bilateral relations with individual West European countries, in particular France, and perhaps the Federal German Republic, to play on European differences. They will also continue to tempt the United States to come to a bilateral deal with them on the question of European security. At the same time, they will seek to use their improved contacts with Western countries in order to remedy the deficiencies of their system in technology.

10. In the military field, while they may see the negotiations on Mutual and Balanced Force reductions as a useful element in creating the general impression of *détente*, they are unlikely to make substantial reductions in their forces stationed in Europe. The steady improvement of their military position of strength as against NATO continues unabated. At the same time, they will hope that their attainment of strategic nuclear parity with the United States and increasing United States introversion will erode the credibility of the United States nuclear guarantee to Europe. Their long-term objective is a Western Europe from which United States defence cover has been largely withdrawn, which remains divided, which, like Finland, exists under the shadow of Soviet military strength and is increasingly compelled to adjust its policies accordingly.

11. The current Russian policy is one of *détente* but it is also in the proper sense of the word an attacking policy, making use of natural advantages enjoyed by the Soviet Union and probing serious weaknesses in the Western position. It is a policy to which the Soviet leaders attach special importance and with which, as with policy towards the United States, Brezhnev himself is personally associated. At the moment it has good chances of progress. The events of the last year (President Nixon's Moscow visit, the SAL talks, the Eastern treaties, the Berlin Agreement,[10] the movement towards a Security Conference and towards Mutual and Balanced Force Reductions) are likely to encourage a lowering of Western vigilance. Political developments in the United States are likely to increase pressures for United States troop withdrawals and to pose serious questions for NATO's strategy. At the same time, the enlarged Community has not so far developed any great momentum towards unity or towards development in the political and defence fields.

12. This is not to overlook factors in the situation to the Soviet disadvantage. They will face recurrent trouble, for economic and nationalist reasons, with their East European empire, though until the remoter future they will retain the means and the will to suppress these discontents. Any freer communication between East and West Europe flowing from *détente* should be to the West's benefit. The greater political and economic dynamism of Western Europe should eventually assert itself and bring the Warsaw Pact countries increasingly under the attraction of the West. But these are only long-term assets for the West; if they are to be drawn on they require the preservation of political confidence and a convincing defence posture by the West over what may be a long intervening period. It is during this period, with United States

[9] Cf. No. 92, note 12.   [10] See pp. 376-7 and 478.

defence support in greater question and Western Europe still in disarray, that Soviet policy will have its major opportunities.

13. Before leaving Western Europe, we draw particular attention to the position on the flanks of NATO. The Soviet setback in Egypt has weakened the Soviet strategic position in the Eastern Mediterranean but we must expect the Soviet naval presence throughout this sea to be maintained and no doubt in time strengthened. Any force reductions and withdrawal of NATO troops on the central front are bound to arouse concern on the part of the countries on NATO's southern flank. Tito's death, which may occur in this period, could well give the Russians the occasion to seek to restore their position in Yugoslavia; if they were to succeed in this the repercussions on the self-confidence and solidarity of NATO, particularly its members on the southern flank, would be grave. At the same time, we note the strengthening of the Soviet military capability on the northern flank and the increasing Soviet ability to dominate the sea area to the north of the Iceland/Faroes gap, linked as this may be with Soviet hopes of an end to Iceland's defence arrangements with the United States. An end to such arrangements would reinforce the argument of Soviet propaganda that Norway and Denmark would be safer outside NATO.

The Far East

14. In the Far East the Soviet Union faces intractable problems and has as neighbours two major Powers, China and Japan, upon whom it can exercise only limited influence. Relations with China are a subject of profound concern to the Soviet leaders. They watch with apprehension the development of a strong, populous, hostile and heretical power on their long eastern frontier. The events of the last year, China's emergence on the world stage, President Nixon's Peking visit[11] and the American use of Peking as an essential lever in 'triangular politics', Chairman Mao's 'revolutionary line in foreign policy', which means in effect *rapprochement* with the United States and unabated hostility to the Soviet Union, and the fall of Lin Piao,[12] who may have advocated an opening to the Soviet Union, as well as to America, all these must have deepened Soviet fear and suspicion. The Russians have resisted the temptation to use their superior military strength against China while the latter is still weak in modern weapons. They have adopted a policy which might be called the long haul, applying their strength to contain China and to reduce Chinese influence as far as possible, while waiting for the day, after Chairman Mao's death, when Sino/Soviet relations may be improved on terms satisfactory to the Soviet Union. But even when Mao has gone and, despite the inducement given by United States 'triangular politics' to both Moscow and Peking to improve relations, the difficulties in making substantial improvements in Sino/Soviet relations will remain very great. We expect the Russians to remain obsessed with China, and to some degree, in political and diplomatic terms vulnerable on account of China. Their military containment of China, even though they have built up 40 divisions, near the frontier, has been done without weakening their military strength in the West; but their wish to avoid simultaneous trouble on two

[11] See p. 446-7.

[12] Marshal Lin Piao, Chinese Minister of Defence, Vice-Chairman of the Communist Party and Mao Tse-Tung's designated successor, died in a plane crash in September 1971 after being forced to flee the country accused of plotting to assassinate Mao.

fronts, their preoccupation with China and sensitivity on the subject and their compulsion to combat Chinese influence wherever it appears in the world are bound to affect the whole conduct of their external policy.

15. In the Far East over the last year the Russians have been passive and reactive rather than initiators of policy. The great developments over this period, the movements of Sino/United States and now Sino/Japanese *rapprochement*, threaten to leave them isolated in the area. They will wish to improve their relations with Japan, in order to reduce this isolation, to obstruct closer Sino/Japanese links and as a step towards their long-term aim of a neutralist Japan under Soviet influence. But, though they have certain bargaining counters, possible concessions over the Northern Islands[13] and the bait of Siberian raw material resources, they are unlikely to be able to divert Japan from her current major objective, that of normalising relations with Peking or, of themselves, to detach Japan from her alliance with the United States. The Soviet Union will continue to form an essential member of the Asian Quadrilateral, i.e. the four Great Powers principally involved in North-East Asia, but its capacity to mould events there is likely to be limited.

The Third World

16. In the West the Russians currently pursue their aims in an atmosphere of *détente*; in the Third World their policy is essentially opportunist, seizing on such openings as are available. They wish to exploit the opportunities which the era of decolonisation has opened up for them, generally to demonstrate their position as a world Power and to secure newly independent countries as clients, allies or at least as 'non-aligned' sympathisers. Within the framework of this broad strategy, they seek to counter Chinese activities, which are directed to similar ends. There are obvious openings for them in the existence of new and unsophisticated régimes often involved in local disputes or still suffering from anti-colonialist resentments. The Russians have been able to exploit these openings by giving political and diplomatic support, by providing economic aid, by supplying large quantities of military equipment, by promoting expanded trade and cultural relations and by using the political influence accruing to them from their increasing naval deployment.[14] They have worked mainly by State contacts, regarding local Communist parties as secondary and in the last resort expendable, though they have not excluded subversion and have been prepared to give covert aid to guerilla movements, e.g. in Portuguese African territories.

17. They have also sought to formalise their relations with selected Third World States by means of treaties; three have been signed over the past 18 months, with Egypt, India and Iraq,[15] and others have been canvassed, e.g. with Syria. The Russians may legalistically see in these treaties a means of binding their clients to their cause. In the case of South and Eastern Asia a particular impulse may be a wish to create a network of bilateral treaties, with the object of containing China. But the basic impulse is probably to be found in the Russian wish to find a more lasting foundation for their presence in the Third World and their probable view that this can only be found by political influence with the ruling élite and the encouragement of domestic political

[13] See No. 31, and *ibid.*, note 6.

[14] See No. 63.

[15] See Nos. 67, note 15, 79, note 6 and p. 466.

groupings, hopefully groupings including Communists. The role of a treaty would be to provide a cover and entry for such penetration. In other words, they may calculate that influence by economic and military aid needs buttressing by building an internal political base. Whether the treaties will fulfil these purposes remains to be seen, the Egyptian treaty did not prevent the recent serious setback in Egypt, though it may facilitate a return to better relations.

18. Soviet activities in the Third World as a whole are too large a subject to be dealt with adequately in a paper of this scope. We shall therefore neglect Latin America and much of Africa and concentrate on two areas, the Middle East and South and South-East Asia. This is not to say that threats to Western interests could not arise in sub-Saharan Africa or in Latin America. Latin American crises could in particular be of major concern to the United States and divert its attention from problems elsewhere.

Middle East

19. It is in the Middle East that the Russians have made their most spectacular encroachments, exploiting their role as supporters of the Arab cause against Israel and their willingness to provide sophisticated military equipment as well as economic aid. They have built up close relations with radical Arab régimes, Iraq, Syria, the People's Democratic Republic of Yemen and, to a lesser extent, Algeria, and have begun to develop relations with Libya. In Syria, in addition to economic aid, they provide sophisticated military equipment and military advisers and over the last year have developed machinery for closer political consultation. In Iraq they provide economic aid, assistance to the oil industry, sophisticated military equipment and large numbers of military advisers. They have helped construct large military airfields which might be intended for use by Soviet units. Article 9 of the Soviet/Iraq treaty provides a general cover for military cooperation. Until July they had a great military as well as economic stake in Egypt: they provided some 7,000 advisers and experts for the Egyptian Armed Forces and had stationed in Egypt independent Soviet units giving a capability against NATO in the Mediterranean and against any Western vessels in the Red Sea. Almost all of this military presence is now being removed at Egyptian request; but the Egyptian forces will remain dependent on Soviet supplies of spares; Soviet economic aid is apparently unaffected and Soviet economic advisers remain. Soviet activity in the Middle East has not been confined to the Mediterranean and NATO's southern flank; it has also extended to the People's Democratic Republic of Yemen and Somalia, probably with the aim of improving Soviet strategic facilities in the Indian Ocean area. The Russians will seek to exploit the opportunities given by British withdrawal from the Gulf. At the same time they seek to build up their influence in the Western-aligned States on their immediate southern border: both Turkey and Iran are in receipt of substantial Soviet economic assistance.

20. This has been and remains a formidable effort and challenge to the West. At the same time, certain serious weaknesses in the Soviet/Middle East position have grown more apparent over the last year. Their strategic caution referred to in paragraph 5 above has always imposed limitations to their support for the Arab cause and Arab suspicions on this score were reinforced by the Moscow summit. Essentially the contradiction inherent in Soviet/Egyptian relations was that the Egyptians wanted more offensive weapons and rapid recovery of territory and the Russians wanted to

avoid hostilities and to extend their independent facilities. Such a situation always contained the makings of a clash. Soviet influence in Iraq (and to a lesser degree Syria) gives some alternative to the positions lost in Egypt and one less closely involved in the Arab/Israel conflict, on which Soviet caution is always likely to be displeasing to the Arabs. At the same time, it is questionable how far the Russians can have an effective Middle East policy without good relations with Egypt; and a situation based on Iraq presents problems in terms of Soviet/Iranian relations, which the Russians cannot afford to neglect. In addition to these problems, the Russians, merely as a result of their involvement in the area, face recurrent trouble with Arab nationalism and inter-Arab rivalries. They risk being led into the essentially conservative role of upholders of particular situations and régimes, as well as simply protecting their own considerable stake. Finally, they lack a reliable local political base. Their setback in Egypt and the setback in 1971 in the Sudan following the abortive Communist plot there are reminders that their encroachment involves them in an inherently unstable area, and one that is basically unsympathetic or hostile ideologically, and that any privileges they obtain are likely to be expensive and precarious.

21. Soviet policy towards the Middle East must now be under examination following the military withdrawal from Egypt. Questions must be raised in Soviet minds of the reliability of facilities they may acquire not only in the Middle East but in the Third World generally. There may be doubts of the value of large-scale military involvement, in the shape of independent Soviet units, in the Third World. Greater weight may be given to the need to build up local political influence. The precise Soviet response cannot be predicted at this point. But certain general observations can be made: that the Middle East retains its strategic importance to the Russians; that they retain important levers there as supporters within certain limits of the Arab cause, as a major source of economic and military aid, and as a State with a strong position in a number of Middle East countries outside Egypt. While Soviet influence in the Middle East may suffer a temporary setback and Soviet tactics may be modified, Soviet long-term aims are unlikely to change. In the shorter term we may expect strenuous Soviet diplomatic efforts to retain as much as possible of their position in Egypt, no doubt invoking the Treaty. They are likely to reinsure in their remaining areas of influence; their military need will be for an airbase providing some substitute for the facilities lost in Egypt and Syria may therefore come to acquire a greater importance in their eyes. While seeking to consolidate in Iraq, they will also continue to hedge their bets by giving attention and reassurance to Iran. We may see a more cautious approach to the area in future, with a greater emphasis on the build-up of local political influence; but there are limits to the possible changes in style; supplies of sophisticated military equipment will remain an essential prerequisite for influence in the Middle East.[16]

[16] Writing to Sir S. Crawford on 20 October Sir J. Killick commented on paras. 19-21 above: 'I would take it as almost axiomatic that the Soviet Government's policy on the Arab-Israel dispute and its relations with the Arab Governments, the PLO and Israel, will for the foreseeable future be conducted in such a way as to further long-term Soviet aims only to the extent that this can be done without serious damage to the Moscow-Washington relationship, provided of course that even more vital Soviet interests . . . are safeguarded . . . other long-term Soviet objectives are less important, in present circumstances, than the super-power relationship. This balance, if my assessment is right, imposes major limitations on Soviet freedom of

Oil

22. The Russians and other Warsaw Pact countries have long been involved in the oil industries of leading Middle East producing countries, mainly through technical assistance programmes, but in the last few years this assistance has deepened. In particular, they have become associated with the new national oil companies in the radical Arab States. They have begun to buy small amounts of oil from the area. This raises the question whether they intend to interfere in some way with oil supplies to the West. We see serious limitations on Soviet ability to engineer a substantial or sustained interruption of supplies to the West. The Soviet Union does not need Middle East oil; she is not only self-sufficient in oil but is a large exporter. She is reluctant to pay for oil in the hard currency the Arab States require and her policy is to earn as much hard currency as possible from her own exports. We do not think that the Soviet Union could attain sufficient influence in Middle East oil-producing countries to induce them to do substantial harm to their own interests by depriving Western countries, their natural market, of significant quantities of oil. Nor do we think that the Russians will be willing or able to conserve their own oil and buy large quantities of Middle East oil in replacement, thereby disrupting supplies in the West. One overriding difficulty will be their lack of the means to pay for the very large quantities of Middle East oil involved. The Russians may none the less urge producing countries to demand the maximum revenues from their oil, hoping thereby to put at disadvantage the Western importers and to assist themselves as net exporters of oil. They will also encourage Arab Governments to restrict the role of Western oil companies by expanding the operations of national oil companies and may offer encouragement by purchasing small quantities of such oil. They will also continue to offer technical assistance for oil-producing operations largely as a means of retaining or increasing a political influence in the countries concerned. The Russians therefore have some capacity for mischief in this field, which will increase as United States dependence on Middle East oil increases. But we think it is limited and that it constitutes rather a threat to the interests of Western oil companies and possibly the cost of oil to Western consumers than a threat to the continued availability of the oil.

South and South-East Asia

23. In the sub-continent the last year has been a good one for the Russians. The Indo-Soviet Treaty, the Indo-Pakistan war[17] and the Soviet vetoes in the United Nations in the course of that war gave the Russians the opportunity to strengthen their standing in India, now unquestionably the dominant Power in the sub-continent. The Soviet Union was also able to start off on a good footing in Bangladesh and to avoid any break with Pakistan. The war demonstrated Chinese inability to save her ally, Pakistan, and was the occasion for certain self-inflicted wounds by the United States

manoeuvre in addition to those inherent in dealings with Arab countries (paragraph 20 of the JIC paper) . . . I think the JIC paper describes very adequately what the Russians have actually been doing in the Middle East in recent times. I would not really blame the authors for saying so little about Soviet aims; I sometimes think we perhaps try to be more precise about them than the Russians are themselves.' Mr. Parsons minuted on 23 October: 'This seems to me to be an absolutely first rate letter' (NE 3/303/2).

[17] See No. 87, note 10.

which left United States influence in Delhi at a low ebb. The overall result was good from both an anti-Chinese and an anti-Western point of view.

24. The Soviet objective will be to use their improved standing as far as they can to increase their influence in India, now their principal ally in the Third World, which is an essential element in their policy of containing China and which they may see as a useful ally in expanding pro-Soviet and anti-Chinese influence in South-East Asia. Their recent setback in Egypt may cause them to attach enhanced importance to India and to make greater efforts to translate their improved prestige into practical benefits. There will, however, be severe constraints on what they can achieve. Indian self-confidence, increased as a result of the war, will make her less amenable; and the size of India and of her needs will provide some degree of immunity. In time the position of the United States, and even of China, in India is likely to be repaired. In Bangladesh, again, the Russians will in time have to face the competition of the Americans and Chinese. There are therefore grounds for the view that Soviet influence in the sub-continent is at an artificially high level and that it is likely to suffer some reduction in time as other major Powers restore their position. In any event, however, it is likely to remain strong. In the sense that the Soviet Union has an interest in the stability of the sub-continent, whereas the Chinese may see advantage in greater fragmentation, Soviet influence will not be entirely malign.

25. In South-East Asia the Russians have sought by expanding trade .and diplomatic relations and by increasing naval deployment to increase their influence, mainly in the context of the Sino-Soviet dispute, but also in order to benefit from any Western withdrawals. Despite recent gains in the sub-continent, they are not, however, operating from a position of great strength, since this is an area where, apart from Western influence, Chinese, Japanese and, in certain areas, North Vietnamese influence, is likely to be strong. The Soviet Union will be one essential element in any balance of power in the area, but is unlikely to achieve more than that.

PART II. THE NATURE OF THE SOVIET THREAT

26. Against this background, how do we identify and analyse the Soviet threat? We do so, not only in the light of Soviet policy as outlined above, but also in the light of British interests, which, though widely spread, centre on Western Europe and on British and European links with the United States. Soviet activity outside this priority zone will certainly constitute a threat to us, both because it may threaten British interests in the area in question and because of its impact on the global power balance, but will be less alarming than activity directly affecting Western Europe and NATO.

27. In the most basic sense, the threat arises from the fact that the Soviet Union is a State committed to world change of a particular kind. In many aspects it appears as a great conservative State, concerned to maintain the status quo, cautious in its leadership, pursuing national interests more or less as any other great Power. Its present leaders, however, and any leaders likely to emerge in the foreseeable future, have a view of the world which is dogmatic, dynamic and confident. They see the course of history as charted, the world as divided into two camps and the relationship between those two camps as one of struggle. They consider that history is on their side but that they have a duty to assist the course of history. It is this philosophy and sense of mission which, reinforcing Soviet national ambitions and supported by Soviet military

and industrial strength, give an underlying consistency and menace to Soviet external policy.

28. What is the nature of the military threat? We do not see the Soviet Union launching a military attack on the West in the period under review. As between the United States and the Soviet Union, the deterrent balance has been reinforced by the conclusion of the recent ABM Treaty. As regards the possibility of a Soviet attack confined to Western Europe, the attainment of nuclear parity and United States introversion and retrenchment have eroded the credibility of the United States nuclear guarantee for Western Europe, but there remain sufficient doubts of United States reactions and sufficient Soviet caution to obviate this risk in present circumstances. Nor do we foresee any Soviet physical interference with our supplies and shipping except in circumstances in which they were ready to face a full-scale confrontation with the United States. The more blatant military threats may therefore be absent; nevertheless Soviet military power will be relevant to our security in a variety of ways. Although the recent ABM Treaty, limiting Soviet ABM deployments, is to the benefit of smaller nuclear Powers like the United Kingdom, continuing Soviet improvement in their weapons could undermine the effectiveness of our nuclear deterrent. Moreover, United States/Soviet negotiations in the next phase of SALT[18] are likely to touch on vital issues for the United Kingdom and for NATO, with recurrent opportunities for Soviet inducements to the United States to neglect the interests of its allies. In an era of nuclear parity and of United States withdrawal from a number of its overseas commitments, Soviet superiority in conventional arms is likely to have serious political implications in Western Europe and to give the Soviet Union added opportunities for acquiring influence outside Europe.

29. In the economic struggle the Soviet Union is less well placed: capitalist economies have much greater flexibility and the Russians cannot match the West in various areas of applied technology or in the consumer sector. Nevertheless these drawbacks have in the past been balanced by Soviet ability to concentrate resources on priority goals and the Soviet economy has hitherto maintained an overall growth rate higher than that of most of the advanced Western countries. The Russians may gain from any lack of unity between the financial and trading centres of the free world and the consequent political strains, e.g. the current trade quarrels between the United States, the European Economic Community and Japan; but they do not have an active role. They will wish to gain as much as possible from trade with advanced Western countries and at the same time to encourage raw material producers,. particularly those producing oil, to drive as hard a bargain as possible with the West. In the long term they may find that their own considerable supplies of raw material and their autarchic economy give them advantages at a time of shortage of raw materials or Western anxiety on this score.

30. Another aspect of the struggle requires separate mention. In seeking to erode Western influence and to encourage complacency and divisions in Western Europe, we expect the Soviet Union to intensify its world-wide campaign of propaganda, espionage and subversion. The scale of Soviet external propaganda is vast and increases yearly. The main impact of this 'open' propaganda machine is felt in the less sophisticated

[18] See No. 97, note 5.

countries of the Third World, but it is not without its effect in the West. The Soviet Union will also make full use of its extensive machinery for espionage and clandestine means of influence. At present there are, in Europe alone (excluding the United Kingdom), more than 800 identified or suspected Soviet intelligence officers with official cover, the greatest number being in France. Outside Europe, the greatest concentrations of Soviet intelligence officers are in the United States and in the Indian Sub-Continent. It has been observed that the number of Soviet intelligence officers appears to increase at periods and in areas in which the Soviet Union is striving hardest to promote *détente*. In addition to conducting espionage to discover the intentions and capabilities of the West, therefore, it is likely that, in the period under review, the Soviet Union will increase the number of agents of influence and sympathisers, e.g. in politics, government service and the mass media, whom they already have in Western Europe, in order to influence Western policies and undermine Western resistance to Soviet aims. The Soviet Union will be assisted in this process by the indigenous European Communist parties, notably those in France and Italy. Although these are no longer the pliable instruments of Moscow as they were in the Stalin era, a basic loyalty and readiness to cooperate with Moscow remain.

31. Strictly, however, the above are only facets of a general threat. Properly defined, the threat lies in the area of struggle short of hostilities and involves all the individual factors discussed above. Essentially it is that the Soviet Union, by using military, political and economic means of influence and relying on its own consistency of purpose and on any infirmities on the part of the West, may acquire such a position of dominance in vital areas that it will be able to achieve many of its objectives without resort to hostilities. We identify two danger areas: Western Europe; and that part of the Third World lying to the South of the Soviet Union, i.e. the Mediterranean, the Middle East and the Indian Sub-Continent.

32. Of these, the threat in Western Europe is unquestionably the more serious. Its circumstances are outlined in paragraph 15 [*sic* ?9] above. In essence it is that, in the conditions of *détente* fostered by the Soviet Union, Western Europe may be gradually deprived of credible United States support; indeed Soviet policy is likely to be actively to undermine West European confidence in the credibility of United States support. While this happens Western Europe may fail to provide a substitute of its own and may fail to attain the unity in the political and defence fields which will be necessary if Soviet influence and pressures on Western Europe are to be repelled. A development of this threat will not require any dramatic exertions on the part of the Soviet Union; dramatic action by the Russians or dramatic withdrawals of United States troops could shock Western Europe into remedial action. What is required by the Russians is rather consolidation of the Soviet position in Eastern Europe while creating a situation favourable to a steady erosion of NATO's strength in the West. In this situation the difference in the rates of change in the two societies is likely to work to the Soviet advantage: their own system, much more conservative and resistant to change, will allow them to pursue consistent political and military policies involving large conventional forces and heavy defence expenditure at a time when Western Governments are increasingly subject to the stresses of what has been called post-industrial society. At the same time, since the threat is derived as much from Western inaction as from Soviet design, the remedy lies largely in Western hands. Western

Europe has the resources to maintain credible conventional defences and perhaps in the longer term will be in a position to apply these resources. Nevertheless, we foresee a period of danger in the immediate future and fear that the Soviet Union may significantly improve its position in Europe in the period under review.

33. The forms this improvement may take cannot be predicted with any precision; but the following developments seem most likely. We expect the Soviet Government to seek by all means to promote the belief that efforts to improve political or military integration in Western Europe, or even to preserve the cohesion of the Western Alliance, are provocative to the Soviet Union and thus likely to increase the risk of war. A parallel theme, as Soviet military strength develops, will be that the effective defence of Western Europe is no longer possible, so that safety should be sought in accommodation rather than collective resistance. The Russians may exploit these arguments in the hope of detaching the weaker members of NATO (Belgium, Denmark, Italy and even Norway) as a preliminary to making the Federal German Republic feel more acutely their isolated and exposed position. These arguments will be persuasive, since at the same time on the Western side the cohesion and strength of NATO will be under strain. Strong pressures already exist in some of the smaller NATO countries, e.g. Denmark and Belgium, for a reduction in defence effort, and these pressures are likely to grow. There is a distinct danger that West European States may come to attach greater importance to good bilateral relations with the Soviet Union than to efforts to build up Western Europe in political and defence terms. If this happens, the Russians may reasonably conclude that they are well on the way to achievement of their aims.

34. The second area, the Third World, for reasons explained above is likely to be an area of steady Soviet effort. But we do not rate the danger so highly here as in Europe. In the first place, this is not so vitally important an area to us. Secondly, there are a number of natural checks operating. There is a strong commercial nexus between the producers and the Western importers of raw materials. There are other actors on the scene: the Russians have to contend with the Chinese as well as with the West; they also have to contend with the nationalism and the inherent instability of the countries concerned. Experience to date, whether in Egypt in 1972 or Indonesia in 1965, suggests that any lodgement the Russians may make is likely to be precarious and expensive. In the Middle East their unwillingness to give all-out support for the Arab cause and their inability to provide a market for more than tiny quantities of Middle East oil will further restrict their capabilities. We may be sure that there will be further Soviet effort in this area and there may well be striking Soviet successes in particular countries. Nevertheless, we expect this to be a patchy performance in which success will be interspersed with setbacks and we doubt whether it will give the Soviet Union the lasting influence that will be needed fundamentally to improve its world position.[19]

[19] At a meeting of the JIC on 21 September the report was commended as 'a cogent statement of the thesis that although Soviet activity in the Third World should not be underestimated, much the more serious threat was to Western Europe. It threw into focus the dangers that could face the area over the next five years; the Russians had no need to make a new effort, but stood ready to catch a tide that was running their way.' The nature of the Soviet maritime threat should also be reconsidered in the light of the report's conclusions. Sir A. Douglas-Home minuted on 5 October: 'I think that all the information which I could require is in this excellent analysis. The

question is are any of us willing to increase our armaments?' Sir S. Crawford noted on 4 October that the paper would serve as part of the preparation for a Ministerial Review of Defence Policy, and that it was to be discussed during a meeting of Ministers at Chequers on the weekend of 11-12 November.

Index of Main Subjects and Persons

Since most documents in the volume refer to aspects of Anglo-Soviet relations, relevant index entries normally come under the main subjects and not under the countries. Entries for the main persons have been limited to items of special interest not otherwise mentioned in the main subject entries or Chapter Summaries. In a departure from previous *DBPO* practice, references in this Index are to page, rather than document numbers.